With Anza to California, 1775–1776

The Journal of Pedro Font, O.F.M.

With Anza to California, 1775–1776

The Journal of Pedro Font, O.F.M.

Translated and edited by
ALAN K. BROWN

UNIVERSITY OF OKLAHOMA PRESS
Norman

ALSO BY ALAN K. BROWN
A Description of Distant Roads: Original Journals of the First Expedition into California, 1769–1770, by Juan Crespí (San Diego, 2001)

This book is published with the generous assistance of the Program for Cultural Cooperation between Spain's Ministry of Culture and United States Universities.

Library of Congress Cataloguing-in-Publication Data
Font, Pedro, d. 1781. With Anza to California, 1775–1776 : the journal of Pedro Font, O.F.M. / translated and edited by Alan K. Brown.
    p. cm. Includes bibliographical references and index.
ISBN 978-0-87062-375-2 (hardcover) ISBN 978-0-8061-9093-8 (paper)
1. Font, Pedro, d. 1781—Diaries. 2. Anza, Juan Bautista de, 1735–1788. 3. Franciscans—California—Diaries. 4. Chaplains—California—Diaries. 5. Geographers—California—Diaries. 6. California—Discovery and exploration—Spanish. 7. Southwest, New—Discovery and exploration—Spanish. 8. California—Description and travel. 9. Southwest, New—Description and travel. 10. Indians of North America—Southwest, New—History—18th century. I. Brown, Alan K. II. Title.
F864.F59 2011
917.9404'2—dc22
                    2010026867

Copyright © 2011 by the University of Oklahoma Press, Norman, Publishing Division of the University. Originally published in hardcover as Volume 1 in the Early California Commentaries series by the Arthur H. Clark Company, Spokane, Washington. Paperback published 2022 by the University of Oklahoma Press, Norman, Publishing Division of the University. Manufactured in the U.S.A.

The paper in this book meets the guidelines for permanence and durability of the Committee on Production Guidelines for Book Longevity of the Council on Library Resources, Inc. ∞

All rights reserved. No part of this publication may be reproduced, stored in a retrieval system, or transmitted, in any form or by any means, electronic, mechanical, photocopying, recording, or otherwise—except as permitted under Section 107 or 108 of the United States Copyright Act—without the prior permission of the University of Oklahoma Press.

Contents

Illustrations	7
Preface	9
A Note from the Series Editors	13
Introduction	15
1. From Sonora to the Gila	73
2. Yuma and the Desert	115
3. Alta California and the San Diego Diversion	167
4. Northward to Monterey	215
5. The San Francisco Reconnaissance	257
6. The Two Commanders	331
7. The Return to Sonora	375
Appendix. The Days' Marches: Distances and Bearings in the Three Texts and in Anza's Journal	407
Bibliography	435
Index	445

Illustrations

1. Title page of the calligraphic copy of the shortened version of the journal 18
2. Map of San Francisco Bay and River, 1770 29
3. Solar observations being made at Mexico City 34
4. The church at Pitiquito 61
5. Map corresponding to Pedro Font's journal 64
6. Geographical map of the coast and part of the peninsula of California 67
7. San Miguel Arcángel 74
8. Font's general map (redrawn), southeast section 77
9. San Xavier del Bac marriage register 88
10. La Casa Grande de Moctezuma 93
11. Ichnographic plan of the Casa Grande of the Gila River . . . 97
12. Font's general map (redrawn), south-central section 120
13. A view of the Colorado River 127
14. A train of explorers, mules, and horses 148
15. A native *kish*, San Jacinto 171
16. The Canaleño town at Santa Bárbara 218
17. Font's general map, northwest section 225
18. Font's general map (redrawn), northwest section 226
19. Sea fennel 231
20. Map of the journey from Monterey to the port of San Francisco . 258
21. Reconstructed map of the San Francisco vicinity 271
22. Plan of the mouth of the port of San Francisco 273
23. South Farallon 275

24. North Farallon	275
25. Angel Island	276
26. Topographic plan of Fort Point and vicinity	278
27. San Bruno Mountain	283
28. The *palo alto* a century after Font	287
29. Coyote Hills	288
30. Alameda Peninsula	295
31. Richmond Peninsula	297
32. Mare Island	300
33. Tule-reed boat on San Francisco Bay	302
34. Reconstructed sketch of view from hills near Willow Pass	308
35. Plaza del Presidio de Monte-Rey	329
36. California mission boy	360
37. Santa Cruz Island	364
38. Raft crossing the Colorado River	385
39. San Miguel de Horcasitas	400

Preface

The need for a new edition of Pedro Font's classic work of western travel has become obvious in recent years. As geographer and chaplain, the Franciscan missionary Font accompanied Juan Bautista de Anza's colonizing expedition from Sonora through present-day Arizona to California, helping to bring settlers to what he referred to as the new Promised Land, and scouting out the territory that they were to occupy. All along the thousand-mile way, Font noted rivers and mountain ranges and devoted special attention to the native groups he encountered, notably the Quechán nation and its neighbors near the lower Colorado and Gila Rivers. He visited and described the natives and settlements of the newly explored Alta California districts, from San Diego, where he recorded eyewitness accounts of an uprising that destroyed a Spanish mission, to San Francisco, where he and Commander Anza determined the site for the new settlement and destroyed a geographical myth that had helped to inspire Anza's expedition—in Font's opinion, his most important accomplishment. After becoming briefly but deeply involved in local politics concerning the settling of San Francisco, Font returned with Anza on an epically swift overland ride back to Sonora. Four months later, an Apache attack nearly destroyed both him and the day-by-day account of his travels that he had composed.

In 1998 the Spanish Franciscan historian José Luis Soto Pérez, who worked for many years in Mexico, published a previously unknown text of the Font journal. Overturning previously accepted ideas about the work's composition and preservation, Father Soto Pérez pointed out that the new manuscript was the actual draft journal that Font wrote during the course of his travels. As such, it proves to contain details that were omitted in Font's two later versions, as well as descriptions and opinions that the author later saw fit to correct. Although Font's purpose in making such changes is usually clear once the relationship of the texts is understood, the modern reader's interest lies rather in being given access to all details and in having the author's serious afterthoughts marked, while still respecting his intention of giving a connected account. This new translation presents a combined text by including the significant information found in all three versions of the Font journal, versions which, where necessary, are distinguished by the use of typographical devices and footnotes. Unlike the rediscovered Juan Crespí journals, which I edited and translated in 2001, the separate Font texts in their original language are now found in printed editions, so that a Spanish companion text is not immediately necessary. At the same time, any lack of similarity between other publications and the compiled texts upon which I have based my translation are intentional on my part.

My interest was directed to Anza expedition records by Meredith Kaplan, then of the Juan Bautista de Anza Historic Trail Program of the National Park Service. I first came to realize the importance of the then newly published Rome text (which I have called the "field" manuscript) while pursuing related historical work on specific areas of northern and southern California; and having once lived in southern Arizona, I had an immediate interest in the Font journal's description of that part of the trail as well. After that, it was a pleasant surprise to find that recently, so many others had developed both parallel and complementary interests in the Anza expedition and were working and publishing upon its many aspects.

The Anza expedition has been much studied. Particularly at a time when access to some research collections is less easy than it was formerly, a lone scholar has the thankful job of acknowledging help from many other directions, especially help in obtaining information to enrich the annotation and understanding of the texts. I have to record special gratitude to Phil Valdez, Jr., and Greg P. Smestad, both of them descendants of members of the Anza expedition, for giving me access to the Anza–Rivera correspondence in advance of its publication, a timing which allowed it to be fully used in the introduction and notes. During the later stages of the work, Dr. Smestad provided enormous aid and critique. He always tactfully kept me from making a number of mistakes. His *Trail Guide to the Expedition* (Smestad 2005) is the indispensable source of accessible information about the march and should be used alongside the present book, which I hope corresponds to his interest and involvement. Collectively, other Anza expedition descendants, in the form of the association "Los Californianos," bestowed a highly valued honor by designating me an adjunct historian, an affiliation which had a practical value in approaching certain research institutions.

Both Fernando Boneu Companys and Joseph Carotenuti performed individual researches which, for one reason or another, I was unable to pursue at the time myself. David Challe gave excellent references and advice on matters relating to Font's recordings of the language and mythology of the O'odham Nation. Cecilia Mushenheim provided wonderful research and documents from the resources of the Marian Library, University of Dayton. For still other essential help, I am indebted to Robert M. Senkewicz (Santa Clara University) for an immensely valuable reading and criticism of the final manuscript; to Harry Crosby, for some items of information; to Marianne Hinckle (Hinckle and Sons Printing) for a necessary inquiry; and to Pam Meeds (Moraga Historical Society) for access to records. There were useful conversations and sometimes correspondence with Glen Farris, Don Garate, Alice Hudson, Keith Paulson-Thorp, Dean McLeod, and Paula Rebert, and, in much earlier times, with Jacob Bowman, Richard Dillon, Kieran McCarty, Thomas Workman Temple II, and Theodore Treutlein. Assistance has been received from the Juan Bautista de Anza Historic Trail project of the National Park Service.

To the John Carter Brown Library, Providence (Susan Danforth) and the Franciscan Historical Archive, Rome, and its archivist (Pedro Gil Muñoz, O.F.M.), I owe access to the texts and maps that provide the essentials of this book. The Bancroft Library, Berkeley (Susan Snyder) allowed access to a Font manuscript and furnished a number of the illustrations. For special assistance with illustrations I also owe thanks to the conservator-general of manuscripts of the National Library (Bibliothèque Nationale) of France, Monique Cohen, and to the staff of the libraries of Denison University, the University of Arizona Library (Olivia Olivárez, Verónica Reyes), the State Library of Ohio (Audrey Hall), and to Ohio Wesleyan University and the College of Wooster. The Huntington Library, San Marino, and the Newberry Library, Chicago, have willingly produced previously unutilized documentary treasures for my references. The Ohio State University Library Interlibrary Loan service and the Special Collections division have, as always, been indispensable.

Despite these splendid professional services, it is an unfortunate fact that administrators of some research collections tend to believe that public-service aspects of librarianship can be reduced because Internet resources for research are so easily available. But this opinion, which is not true now, may never be true, and to administer such collections, with various excuses, as limited-access archives or closed warehouses will always be disastrous for cutting-edge research. A medievalist such as me can detect a long-range but disturbing parallel to the ideological confusions that led to the defunding of the Library at Alexandria.

Of course, information collected on websites has also been valuable for this book, especially the diplomatic transcript of Commander Anza's 1775–1776 journal accessible at http://anza.uoregon.edu/ and the "Mission 2000" database accessible at http://home.nps.gov/applications/tuma/. Both of these are the work of Don Garate of the National Park Service. Other accessed sites are given in the bibliography.

Columbus, Ohio
June 2009

A Note from the Series Editors

Alan Brown's untimely death in September 2009, as he was approaching the conclusion of years of labor in preparing this edition of the Pedro Font diary, was a great loss to all students of early California, the American Southwest, and Northern Mexico. Alan's meticulous research in archives and repositories on three continents resulted in a series of invaluable publications over many decades that have enriched the scholarly understanding of the interactions between the indigenous peoples of the regions and the Spanish missionaries and soldiers who entered their territories in the seventeenth and eighteenth centuries. In particular, Alan's discovery of the "field notes" kept by two of the most important Franciscan diarists of the Portolá and Anza expeditions, Juan Crespí and Pedro Font, have enormously deepened our appreciation of indigenous life and of the first encounters between the native peoples and the Spanish newcomers.

We were privileged and humbled when Alan agreed to have his translation and edition of the Font diary become the first volume in this series, *Early California Commentaries*. We were fortunate to be able to discuss this project with Alan at conferences in 2008 and 2009, and we were delighted when he began to send us sections of what we all expected would be the next-to-last draft of his work in spring 2009. We spent a good part of the summer of 2009 in correspondence with Alan on a variety of theological, linguistic, and historiographical questions that clustered around the Anza expedition, the history of the indigenous peoples of Sonora, Arizona, and California, and the California missions and presidios. We will always remember that summer as a time of invigorating intellectual exchanges from which we both learned a great deal. We talked about anthropological and ethnohistorical research, late medieval Catholic devotional practices, early modern Spanish literature, and many other topics. Alan proved himself quite adept at e-mail, but he never lost his basic love for letters delivered by the U.S. Postal Service!

These exchanges were tragically cut short by Alan's death. His wife, Isabel, and his son, Stephen, graciously sent us as many of his notes on this project as they could find. In addition, Dr. Greg Bernal-Mendoza Smestad and Phil Valdez, who had worked with Alan for many years on this and other ventures relating to the Anza expedition, allowed us to consult the extensive correspondence between Alan and themselves. These materials helped us to complete this volume. We had to make a series of choices on issues that had been left unresolved. We have tried to present this volume as we think it would have been presented if our exchanges and collaboration had been able to run their natural course. We were always aware that we were editing Alan Brown's final work and we took that responsibility seriously. We hope that readers will learn as much from Alan as they read this volume as we learned from him as we prepared it. Alan always told us that this project was not about him, but rather about Pedro Font. He wanted to make Font's writings, through all of the various texts he had discovered, come alive in a way they never had before. We think he succeeded magnificently. This volume is his final gift to all of us.

Finally, Alan created an inclusive color-coded Spanish text showing the variants found in all of the versions of the Font diary that he used in preparing this volume. This valuable primary source has been posted on the website of the Santa Bárbara Mission Archive-Library, at www.sbmal.org.

ROSE MARIE BEEBE
ROBERT M. SENKEWICZ
April 2010

Introduction

November 16, 1776, at Magdalena de Kino, Sonora

Arrows flying through the burning building drove the Spanish missionary, along with the Christian O'odham women and children and their few defending bowmen, back into the fifth chamber of the long, narrow building. The settlement of Santa María Magdalena, with its church, chapel, and the mission house where the few escapees were huddled, was under attack by dissident O'odham and Seri Indians. They were joined from beyond the frontier by Apaches, some of whom were mounted and accoutered with lances, shields, and protective leather jackets like those used by the local Spanish soldiers who protected the settlements. On the building's thatched roof the leader of the native assailants, a renegade O'odham known as *Juan Cocinero*[1] was spreading flames in the direction of the trapped group. In the seventh and last room, behind them, along with "some books and utensils" there was a pile of dry wheat stalks, yet to be threshed and ready to explode like gunpowder when the fire reached it.

As the warriors, yelling in the smoke, started to break through the door of their room, the refugees' three remaining defenders used up their last arrows. Pedro Font, the missionary, called upon God to the best of his ability and resigned himself to death. That may have been the first moment when his fear was focused entirely on himself rather than on the manuscripts of the book which he was writing, which was stored among other papers alongside the dry tinder in the last room.

The louder sound of the fire swelled to fill a sudden silence outside the door. The attackers had withdrawn. The smoke from the burning and pillaged little Indian town of Santa María Magdalena had been seen from the main mission station five miles down the road. A mounted rescue party had arrived just in time to aid those trapped in the house. But when Font came out into the courtyard of their building with the other weeping survivors, he found a pregnant woman,

---

[1] John the Cook.

one of his parishioners, pinned to the ground by lances and dying at his feet. Another young child of hers was already dead and lay eviscerated beside her. The living all worked to put out the fire. Shortly after that, another friar came to escort the survivors to the main settlement at Mission San José de Imuris.[2] Although Font was still traumatized and panicking at any unexpected noise or movement—as he would continue to do for months to come—during the next two weeks he returned several times to the burned-out building at Magdalena, first to bury the dead woman, whose Christian name was Josefa María, and then to gather up the papers in the back room.[3] Meanwhile, danger remained from raiding parties in the vicinity, but when the missionaries appealed to the nearest frontier military garrison for protection, their request was denied. They were told that nothing could be done without orders from the higher command.

Pedro Font

Font's North American career, which included the triumph of authoring the Anza expedition book manuscript and the disaster of the near destruction of book and author at Magdalena, began thirteen years earlier without any particular fanfare. In November 1763, the twenty-four-year-old friar arrived on the shores of the New World carrying papers of embarkation that described him as middling in height, stout-bodied, round-faced, and with a blanched (pale) complexion. He was described as having black hair with a receding hairline and a thick beard—which he kept shaved, of course, since it was a clean-shaven century. His place of birth was listed as Gerona in northeastern Catalonia. And his most recent religious affiliation had been with the Franciscan Province but apparently not with any particular convent.[4] Eleven other aspiring missionaries were aboard his smallish vessel during the stormy crossing of the Atlantic Ocean which lasted nine weeks. Included in this group was Francisco Garcés, Font's future and more famous companion on the northern frontier.[5] Font and Garcés

---

[2] The account of the attack and rescue at Magdalena de Kino is in the letter which Font wrote to his superiors two weeks later, preserved in the Franciscan Historical Archive, Rome, Curia Generalizia dei Frati Minori, Marcellino da Civezza Collection, 201.78; image in University of Arizona Library Film 305; translated in Matson 1975: 273–75, Brown 2006: 96–105.

[3] Font's returns to Magdalena are witnessed by the church register, into which he copied some loose documents that had been found (Alphonse Pinart Papers, The Bancroft Library, as extracted in Garate 2000—: Event IDs 2449, 2450, 2456). In the twentieth century, Font's description of the mission house perhaps proved useful in the discovery of the remains of the famous early Jesuit missionary Kino (so claimed by Valenzuela 2007 although not mentioned in Olvera 1998). It seems possible that the seven-chambered "shotgun" house described by Font extended southwestward from the original church in the line later occupied by a nineteenth-century school building.

[4] Borges 1982: 840. Mostly quoted by Gómez Canedo 1971: 50 in note, from a different copy.

[5] The voyage of the *Júpiter*, carrying Francisco Garcés, Pedro Font, and their group of fellow friars, is described in excellent detail in Kessel 1970: 188–89.

managed to avoid the experience of ten or eleven companion friars who were traveling on a sister ship. Those friars had been shipwrecked and left marooned for months on a desolate portion of the Mexican shore.[6]

Font was either preceded or followed to Mexico by a cousin, presumably a paternal one, named Pablo Font. The two men became affiliated with two different Franciscan missionary *colegios*. Pablo served at the *Colegio de San Fernando* in Mexico City, while Pedro joined the *Colegio de la Santa Cruz* in the city of Querétaro.[7] Both cousins were artists skilled with pen and brush.[8] Pedro Font's education obviously was quite good although nothing else at present can be said of his family background.[9] Catalán he certainly was, since in describing the unfamiliar flora of the Pacific Coast in his Anza expedition journal, he takes, or rather makes, every opportunity to introduce terms from his native tongue. A remark such as "a very dense wood of what they call *bruc* in Catalonia and I believe is called *abrojo* in Castile" may even express a certain snobbism, since it is hard to believe that Font was not well acquainted with the standard Spanish word *abrojo*. On the other hand, one well-known vulgar term seems to have been unfamiliar to him.[10]

The stone buildings of the Colegio de la Santa Cruz in Querétaro, now commonly referred to simply as *El Templo*, overlook the old municipal center and provide the official designation of *La Cruz* for a part of the city. Querétaro lies one hundred miles north of the old viceregal capital of Mexico City and nine hundred miles south of the mission stations that the colegio staffed, supplied, and, at least in theory, administered across an enormous distance of indirect roads, mountain paths, and desert. In 1776, even farther off on the Colorado River, the missionary Tomás Eixarch impressed the Quechán chief known as Palma by descriptions of the physical splendor, ceremonies, and personnel of his mother house.[11] The prestige of the foundation, directed by a Guardian and a council or *discretorio*, was very great, especially locally. The local municipality's pride in the colegio's accomplishments extended to commissioning expensive professional

---

[6] Sphar circa 2006: [biography of] Juan Crisóstomo Gil de Bernabé.

[7] The relationship is mentioned in his journal entry for March 20, 1776, in this book.

[8] See figure 7 in chapter 1 for an example of Pablo Font's artistic lettering. His redrawn version of the 1772 Juan Crespí sketch of San Francisco Bay and the "River of San Francisco" is preserved in Spanish governmental archives in two original drawings, one more elaborate than the other and frequently reproduced. The less elaborate is reproduced in [Spain,] Servicio Geográfico del Ejército 1948–1957 carpeta 2: no. 129.

[9] Having had to look up the word "ichnographic" in a dictionary, I cannot criticize Font's failed first attempt to spell the corresponding Spanish term correctly in his journal entry for October 31, 1775. (Note by the present translator-editor.)

[10] See the footnote to December 7 on the word *amaricados*. One repeated minor peculiarity—minor in terms of eighteenth-century spelling standards—is Font's spelling of the month name *Diciembre* as *Deziembre* (*Deciembre*).

[11] Eixarch is pronounced "Ay-SHARK." Eixarch was from Valencia; the old Valencian language is essentially identical with Catalán, but even Font, in the field text of his journal, uses a slightly more Castilian spelling. The present book does not include Eixarch's journal, which Font copied into a part of his own work.

DIARIO QUE

forma el P.F. Pedro Font, Predicador Apostolico de la Santa Cruz de Queretaro, sacado del Borrador que escrivió en el Camino, del Viage que hizo à Monterrey, y Puerto de S. Francisco, en compañia del Señor Ten.te Coronel de Caballeria, Capitan del Presidio de Tubac, y Comandante de la Expedicion de conducion de Familias, y Soldados para el nuebo establecimiento de aquel Puerto, D. Juan Bauptista de Anfa, por orden, y disposicion del Exc.mo Señor Baylio Fr. D. Antonio Maria Bucareli, y Ursua, Ten.te Gen.l Uirrey, Governador, y Capitan General de esta Nueva España, comunicada al R.do P.e Guardian del Colegio de la S.ta Cruz de Queretaro Fr. Romualdo Cartagena por carta que le escrivió, dada à 2 de Enero de 1775, è intimada à mi por dicho R.do P. Guardian por carta, su fecha de 20 de Enero del mismo año, con encargo de acompañar à dicho S.r Comandante en todo el Viage, y de observar las alturas del camino.

Acompaña à este diario un Mapa de todo el Viage, en el qual se señala con puntos el camino, se expresan por numeros las Jornadas, y se distinguen por Abecedario los Lugares, ò Parages particulares, de que se hace mencion en este Diario. Todo hecho, y trabajado de buelta del Viage, en esta Mission de Ures, por el mes de Junio del presente año de

1776.

ADUERTENCIAS

Advierto, que en las Observaciones que pude hacer en el Quadrante Astronomico de la Expedicion que trajo el S.r Comandante Calculè las Alturas por unas Tablas de D.n Jorge Juan, que casualmente pude adquirir, las quales por estar hechas para el Meridiano de Cadiz, y para los años de 1756, 1757, 1758, y 1759, necesitan de dos correcciones. I aunque las Alturas que apunto estàn segun las Observaciones que, y procurando emplear en las Tablas las dos correcciones necesarias para el Calculo: Expreso la altura meridiana del bordo inferior del Sol, que apuntò dicho Quadrante en todas las Observaciones para maior satisfaccion de los inteligentes.

Advierto tambien, que en quanto à los Rumbos del Camino puedo haber tenido alguna equibocacion, por quanto no pude adquirir una Brujula buena, y solo en S.te Jabier

FIGURE 1. Title page of the calligraphic copy of the shortened version of the journal, 1776. By Antonio Martínez Velasco. *Courtesy of The Bancroft Library, University of California, Berkeley.*

calligraphic copies of Font's official (shortened) journal of the 1775–1776 expedition and of Francisco Garcés's preliminary report of his explorations.[12]

The later chronicler of the colegio tells us that while at Querétaro, Font labored in the institution's library. There he arranged and copied the collection of music for the choir, in which he sang well and which he left thoroughly supplied with musical texts.[13] It seems likely that the inventory and arrangement of the colegio's archive, completed in 1772 and qualified by a modern scholar as "excellent," was also Font's doing.[14] During his tenure as a librarian, he seems to have improved on his knowledge, since in his journal there are a number of references to religious and legal works that deal with New World affairs and problems. It is worth noting, however, that some quite good professional libraries were found even in the frontier missions at which he later served.

Such information, thin though it may be, calls attention to some of Font's talents. His singing led off the beginning of each day's march (October 22). His voice led those of other friars in the Mass of thanksgiving for the Anza expedition's arrival at Monterey (March 11). On one occasion, his morning chants got him into a friendly vocal contest with natives (April 2). At Mission San Carlos Borromeo (March 19), he accompanied a service by playing the mission's organ. This was not too surprising, since he was also able to perform upon Mission San Diego's spinet, which was a primitive keyboard instrument. In addition, Font played his own psaltery, which was a small, roughly triangular stringed instrument that would be played flat upon the lap or on a table. Font brought the psaltery along on the journey at Anza's urging and he found occasional uses for it in California. As a draftsman and copyist, his work is superb, particularly the maps that he drew during the expedition under the most unfavorable conditions, as well as the maps that he produced afterward. These maps had a great influence on later cartography. One of Font's letters holds a characteristic complaint that while he was at Querétaro, a Guardian of the colegio ordered him to stop his work at copying music texts, and also insulted him by telling him he was given to "writing superfluities."[15] That he was a compulsive writer is the truth, and the present book is the result.

By 1773 Font had spent ten years in supposedly preparing to become a missionary in New Spain. It was a half dozen years since the Querétaro Franciscans had taken over the enormous mission field which previously had been staffed and administered by the Jesuits. Font's original shipboard companion, Garcés, had been out in the Sonora field for six years where he very successfully ran

---

[12]Garcés, "Relación."
[13]Arricivita 1792: 560.
[14]Gómez Canedo 1982: 21.
[15]Brown 2006: 97.

the northernmost mission and gained fame by his explorations beyond. Another missionary candidate who had come from Spain with the Font and Garcés contingent as a mere subdeacon—not yet a priest—now had three years of field work to his credit.[16] The beginning of Font's long-delayed achievement of his ambition is hard to pinpoint precisely. He might have set out from the colegio for Sonora accompanied by another friar who left in August 1773.[17] However, early in 1775 it was said that Font had not yet had a full year in the missions.[18] Whatever the case, it was only a relatively short time before he departed again upon the expedition to California. When he returned from there, the mission which had been in his charge had already been permanently handed over to other clergy.

This mission, San José de Pimas, isolated in the midst of dusty plains and heights, was a small settlement that long ago had lost its resident priest and was just now regaining one, in the person of Pedro Font. The records of a visitation (inspection) of the Pimería Baja missions provide a window into the conditions at the mission in 1774, not long after his arrival. Font's report, supposedly summarized by the *visitador* but clearly composed by Font, mentions the "utmost difficulty and great toil" that he has undergone merely in providing for his own sustenance. The report also claimed that Font's industriousness produced some advances. Cultivation has been promoted to the point where "this year, his parishioners had wherewith to remedy their bodily needs, which had never been achievable at any other time before now." As for religion, "by all particular accounts" the inhabitants now are much better instructed in the catechism than they had been under the Jesuits, and have been removed from their old vices and ancient customs although—here the tone of the report begins to turn negative—not entirely so. Some of them are given to constant wandering about and others have stayed in a state of rebellion against God and the king for many years. Although their inconstancy and flightiness "does not allow any degree of assurance of their continued good conduct and they have given sufficient cause to doubt of it, still, there are reasons also to suppose that they will remain in the faithful state that they now present."[19] Here, Font's characteristically critical or even morbid tone, which was going to be given free rein in his expedition journal, contrasts with the upbeat way in which his colleagues at the other missions showcased their achievements.

The papacy in Rome had very recently decreed that all missionaries should learn to speak the language of the people they worked among. The noteworthy

---

[16]Juan Bautista de Velderrain. Cf. Kessel 1976: 137.
[17]Soto Pérez 1998 2: 1191, note.
[18]Juan Bautista de Anza to the viceroy, January 17, 1775, Garate 1995: 33, 35, 216.
[19]Marcellino da Civezza Collection, 201.5. Visitation by Father President Fray Juan Díaz, April 25, 1775.

lament found in Font's California journal concerning the hardship of being stranded among strangers speaking a different language (March 7) suggests, however, that he had not had the opportunity or the time to learn to talk directly to his Sonora parishioners. Among the missionaries in Sonora at the time, apparently only his colleagues Francisco Garcés and Juan Díaz knew enough of the O'odham language to comfortably preach and converse in it.[20] Font's journal shows only that he was able to recognize a common phrase used by the converts, if perhaps not to translate it completely accurately.[21] Nonetheless, his interest in linguistic matters appears throughout.

Looking Beyond the Frontier:
Juan Bautista de Anza and Francisco Garcés

Hundreds of miles northwestward beyond the last Franciscan mission, the junction of the Gila and Colorado Rivers had been visited earlier by far-traveling missionaries of the Society of Jesus, who lobbied for the placing of a presidio there.[22] After the Franciscan takeover in 1767, the newly active viceregal government received a plan for new exploration in that direction and beyond from the presidio captain, Juan Bautista de Anza. According to the historical notes compiled later by Franciscan Father Francisco Antonio Barbastro, long talks with the missionary Garcés convinced Anza that this was the route to gaining promotions in rank.[23] Certainly, Anza never hid the fact that he regarded his ambitiousness as a virtue. But Anza's father, the presidio captain of the same name, had also wanted to explore northward. As early as 1760 his son was implicitly recommended in a Jesuit pamphlet to be the "prudent and zealous conquistador" who would lead a Spanish expansion to the Colorado.[24] It was also certainly true that the missionaries who arrived in Sonora between 1767 and 1768 were already looking northward. Font's old shipboard companion, Garcés, was in the lead both physically and metaphorically.

The farthest-out agricultural settlements of the Pimería Alta were those of the non-Christian River O'odham, referred to in Font's journal as the "Gila Pimas." These villages were located sixty or seventy miles north of the existing mission

---

[20] McCarty 1981: 73–76.
[21] See the note to November 1.
[22] See especially Chapman 1916: 29–44; Donohue 1957: 257 etc.
[23] Barbastro, "Compendio."
[24] Anonymous, "Convite evangélico," folio 38r. Cf. Brown 2001: 38–39, where I erroneously identified the mention of Anza as applying to his father. There is no cause to doubt the sincerity (as is done by Guerrero 2006, for instance on p. 58), of Anza's repeated, if frequently frustrated, attempts to explore new routes across the unknown.

of San Xavier del Bac. Ever since the beginning of the eighteenth century, these people had been receptive to the idea of having missionaries sent to them. From the bare beginning of his famous travels which Font helped to chronicle, Garcés wasted no time before visiting the Gila. Four years later, he threw himself into the Papaguería, the wasteland inhabited by the Desert O'odham. He crossed not only the desert but also the great river which the O'odham called Red (that is, the Colorado) although because of the faulty geographical information available at the time, he thought it was the Gila.[25] Garcés bestowed a thick sprinkling of religious place names as he traveled. Although Font mentioned these names in portions of his journal, they were mostly ignored by later travelers.

In 1774 Captain Anza's expedition to the Colorado and beyond, which was co-led by Garcés, seemed to clear the way for a quick expansion to the Gila, especially when the civil-military governor of the Spanish province personally made a follow-up visit. Garcés, however, came to doubt Anza's actual intentions for the project. At the end of the 1775–1776 expedition, he expressed a fear that his colleague Pedro Font's journal, when completed, would support Anza's plans for the Colorado at the expense of missions on the Gila.[26] Actually, there is little or no trace of such a bias in Font's journal.

In the journal, Font provides his famous depiction of Garcés as a being divinely appointed for missionary work, practically an Indian himself, capable of sharing with relish their diet of lizards and mice, and sitting around a fire with them for hours, hardly talking (December 9). The description gives only one side of a complex and vastly influential personality. On leaving Spain at a very young age, Garcés was described in his embarkation papers as a "theologian"—not just a theological student—and this is all the more remarkable because his autograph writings prove that he suffered from extreme dyslexia.[27] According to his own admission, Garcés was unable to compose even a private letter without someone standing at his elbow.[28] A committee of his fellow missionaries that sometimes included Font would put together Garcés's so-called journals after his travels, using his illegible notes and relying on his memory.[29] However, many of the descriptions are perceptive beyond the level that Garcés's collaborators could have achieved by themselves. A good example is the depiction of the

---

[25] Garcés's spotty recording left this fact undetected until it was deduced independently by Charles Chapman and Herbert Bolton early in the twentieth century.

[26] Garcés in a letter to his Guardian, January 12, 1775 ("Cartas" K/.24), and in his "Relación." The charge against Anza was echoed afterward by Father Barbastro in his manuscript notes.

[27] Borges 1982: 840.

[28] In a letter from Ures, [no day date] March 1775, Civezza Collection 201.22. Apparently Garcés is using the word *amanuense* in its original Latin sense (*a-manu-ensis*) of one who stands at hand, rather than as meaning just a copyist.

[29] Kessell 1976: 98.

entertainment staged by the "*danzantes*" in California (see the quotation in the note to Font's December 24 entry).

What Garcés, as well as Anza, was looking forward to was no less than the extension of the Spanish empire throughout the unknown interior of western North America. The means to this end would be the presidio and mission. In those years it was a project that seemed possible—a newly activist viceregal government at Mexico City was sending sea explorations far up the Pacific Coast to perform acts of territorial possession and Garcés's travel accounts were being read with fascination at the colonial capital and in Madrid. In 1774, the presidio captain and the missionary had come to very favorable terms with the large Quechán (Yuma) nation at the Gila–Colorado junction. They succeeded in laying a foundation for peace treaties between the tribes which promised to open up all of the country beyond. As part of creeping hispanization, Spanish titles of *gobernador* and *alcalde* were ceremoniously bestowed on influential natives. Among the Pipatsje (Maricopas), the journals of Anza and Font provide a description of such an event (November 15 and note). A bit later, among the Quechán, Font seems to hint that the person known to the Spaniards as Capitán Pablo Feo[30] although a former enemy of theirs, might be a better candidate for their favor than Palma, who was Anza's favorite leader. That choice ultimately had severe consequences; Font may have been right.

The next step was so obvious that the viceroy (Bucareli), the army man (Anza), and the missionary (Garcés) never let it out of their minds: finding a way to connect the New Mexico settlements with the newly formed Pacific Coast settlements on the same latitude. When he reached the California coast in 1774, Anza hoped to return from Monterey by a more northerly inland route, but he had to give up the idea. The same wish, however, reappears as a leitmotif during his second expedition in 1775–1776. While he and Font were still on the Gila, Anza sent a scouting party due westward across the Colorado. Caught in the sand hills and Salton Basin on the other side, the scouting party was forced to turn south to the earlier explored route (November 16 and note.) Anza still hoped to bring his expedition northward by an interior way through mountain passes, desert, and the south San Joaquín to Mission San Antonio or at least to Mission San Luis Obispo. As Font later learned (April 3), this was actually a very bad route and this notion luckily was foiled by events. During the San Francisco exploration, Anza's wish to cross southeastward toward the Sierra Nevada obviously reflected his hopes of locating a gap through which to reach the Colorado. This last plan would almost surely have destroyed him and his party had they tried to return directly eastward across the Colorado Desert (May 8).

---
[30] Ugly Chief Pablo.

The California Expeditions

The accomplishments of Anza's first expedition in 1774 and his second in 1776 thus involved mainly what lay westward beyond the Colorado: the Sonora to California connection previously envisaged by Jesuit missionaries and now desired by the Mexico City government. At the time of the first expedition of 1769–1770, under the command of Gaspar de Portolá, various distorted rumors about the presence of Spaniards on the Pacific shore had already made their way through native groups to the northwestern-most Sonora missions. If news could travel, why not soldiers and missionaries? Several influences had converged upon the new Mexico City administration of Viceroy Bucareli in 1772–1773. One was the extraordinary arrival of the president of the Alta California missions, Junípero Serra, who abandoned his post in what seemed to be a desperate attempt to save the whole foundering California enterprise.[31] Serra brought news of a great river that seemed to reach the coast from inland at San Francisco harbor. Another influence was Captain Anza's already submitted official petition to carry out the old project of exploring past the half-mythical geography of the far northwest. And, of course, there were the desires of the frontier missionaries, desires that were impressively embodied in their representative, Garcés, and thoroughly shared by the Querétaro colegio administrators in their constant campaign for governmental support to expand the Spanish mission field.

As a result, a preliminary search for a way across to the coast seemed justified. Serra, from the Pacific missions, thoroughly approved the idea when the viceroy presented it to him. In mid and late 1773, plans were already being implemented for an effort to be led by Anza and Garcés. However, Apache attacks on the presidios delayed the expedition's planned departure and forced a change in the route. Since the Gila route was temporarily impossible, the only way to reach the Colorado was by traveling fast and light through the western desert of the Papaguería.

The second cause for delay was ultimately more favorable. This was the unexpected arrival in Sonora of a Christian native of Baja California, Sebastián Taraval. Father Garcés stated that Taraval, who was named after a former Jesuit missionary, appeared "as though dropped from heaven," although it was more like escaping from hell. Taraval was subsequently called *El Peregrino*[32] since, like a number of Spanish soldiers, he had run away from the starving time during

---

[31]The *Padre Presidente* was a missionary in a frontier field, chosen or elected to be in charge of certain administrative affairs because of the long distance from the ruling colegio. The position could rotate, but Serra held it lifelong when in California, and made such extensive use of his powers that the modern sense that we attach to "president" might almost apply to him. The title itself, however, had a more modest meaning in the eighteenth century.
[32]The Wanderer.

which governmental support for the Alta California settlements had lapsed. From Mission San Gabriel near the Pacific, Taraval and his family, including his wife and parents, found a way through the mountains and southeastward into the desert. Three of them died there.[33] After many more adventures, El Peregrino was passed on by the Colorado natives to the Spanish in northwestern Sonora. His story made the intervening desert more frightening. Yet, if a lone Indian without provisions could cross, so might a well-supplied group, especially with Taraval as a guide. He had experienced the country beyond where Father Garcés had visited.[34]

So in February and early March 1774, the small military expedition led by Anza and Garcés wandered through the desert beyond the Colorado. They nearly perished there, but before that could happen, in desperation they took a route along which Taraval recognized a mountain and was able to bring them to water. From there, following his tracks in reverse, they came through narrow ways up to the top of the main range of California. Anza bestowed the pretentious and politically favorable name of *Puerto de San Carlos* on a boulder-filled gap. This was his way of honoring his monarch, Carlos III of Spain. More fertile valleys and even lakes lay beyond. These were christened in succession after the Prince of Asturias who was heir to the throne; then San José, for the former expedition organizer and now politically rising future Minister of the Indies, José de Gálvez; and finally San Antonio, for the current viceroy, Antonio de Bucareli, who was both ultimately and intimately responsible for the current exploration.

Then the Pacific settlements were visited. By June, the expedition had broken into a number of parties and returned to Sonora via the Gila. The colonizing enterprise that already had been envisaged was now feasible. Despite the enormous delays caused by unavoidable communications difficulties, the Spanish government on both sides of the Atlantic moved with exemplary speed.

The River and the Harbor

Serra's report of a great river named San Francisco was the lever which moved that empire at its top. A river running out of the heart of the continent—a potential highway for British or French-Canadian or who knew what intruders—and emptying into an unrivaled harbor! As Font explains in his journal more than once, the Anza expedition was planned and carried out in response to the necessity of Spain's occupying and fortifying the harbor of San Francisco and

---

[33] Anza indicates that a brother also survived.
[34] This is a retelling of these well-known events, using the viewpoint of Barbastro's historical notes.

exploring the river of the same name that was supposed to empty into it.[35] The reconnaissance which Font and Anza carried out as their final contribution to this goal, and which Font regarded as his own chief accomplishment, is recorded in the most detailed portion of his journal (chapter 5 in this present edition). Serra had taken Crespí's report and map with him to Mexico City, and the journal was rapidly epitomized there for officialdom. The sketch map was elegantly redacted by Font's cousin at the Colegio de San Fernando, and the whole packet was rapidly shipped off to Madrid where the king and his ministers viewed it.[36] The Franciscans' eloquent pleas for further exploration and settlement seemed obviously compatible with already existing hopes for a connection with Sonora. Thus, the San Francisco Harbor and River project was born.[37]

The sort of claims that were being made by the party of expansion at the distant Madrid court under the rising Minister of the Indies, José de Gálvez, can be deduced from a counter-plea penned by a conservative Spanish government official.[38] He wrote, "It is unknown how many people must have perished in the sea and land expeditions to the harbors of Monterrey and San Francisco; depicting the excellence of those pleases persons who fail to reflect that they further the interests of Spain not at all; practical persons and good Spaniards can only regret the millions she [Spain] spends upon maintaining a quite large navy upon the coast of New Galicia on the South Sea for the sole purpose of struggling against the storms, elements, and wastes of the north of Monterrey.... Of what use to the Spaniards settled at the newly surveyed, famous harbor of San Francisco will their cochineal, cocoa, vanilla and even potable gold be, if its value does not cover the costs [of transportation] when it is brought to Vera Cruz?" (for shipment across the Atlantic).[39]

Cochineal dye had actually once been touted by José de Gálvez as a future product from his planned settlements in California. However, "potable gold" is merely a sarcastic reference to the fantasy goals of the old alchemists. This skeptical and narrowly mercantilist critique failed to quash the combined appeals of imperial

---

[35] In official correspondence, the terms "harbor" and "river" are used interchangeably in relation to the San Francisco project. See, e.g., Bolton 1930 5: 209, 210, 214–15, 220, 238, 252, 255, 256, 259, 261, 271, 278; Garate 1995: 72, 92, 118. During the reconnaissance itself, Commander Anza's journal refers to "the survey of the harbor and river" (March 12 and 22, 1776; cf. Bolton 1930 3: 120, 122).

[36] Credit for the drawing was naturally claimed by Pablo Font's superior, Rafael Verger, the Guardian of San Fernando.

[37] One of the eloquent representations by Rafael Verger to the Spanish government is translated in Stanger and Brown 1969: 129.

[38] Francisco Romá y Rossell, "Apuntes." These are points 47 and 49 of his notably Machiavellian position paper on internal Spanish Empire policy, composed as a qualification for appointment to office in Mexico. Later he was directly concerned in supplying the New California settlements—including San Francisco.

[39] Jalisco (and southern Sinaloa) on the Pacific, site of the new shipyard and port of San Blas.

defense and romanticism, and it was by royal invitation that the Franciscan Colegio de San Fernando addressed the king in a report dated February 26, 1776:

> Now annexed to your royal crown, Your Majesty possesses not only the harbors of San Diego and Monterrey desired and sought during the past centuries of the 1500s and 1600s, but also, indeed, the most important one of all, that of San Francisco: important for its capaciousness and beauty, as also because of its very full-flowing river, navigable for some forty leagues, [up to] where a plain of enormous size was seen, extending in a semicircle between northwest and southeast [and] capable of supporting many large cities, according to the journal written by Father Fray Juan Crespí . . . and the greatest likelihood is that the river can be navigated for over a hundred leagues, to judge by its flow of water, and that one can get very close to the Pimería Alta and perhaps New Mexico, with the advantage of having close at hand live and white oaks and pine groves to build boats as needed; whereby it is visible what serious harm the State would suffer should this river and harbor not happen to be, as they are, under Your Majesty's possession. If this harbor (God forbid) should come into the possession of another power, not only would the chain of conquests northward be severed, but also the hope would be lost of obtaining the great wealth promised by El Moqui and its other frontier provinces, and the peace and quiet of [the territory that] has been converted would be in extreme danger.[40]

Hinted at in this prospectus or offer of access to Sonora and New Mexico was a long-held geographic hypothesis which could indeed have been to the benefit of the Spanish empire. Vague or misunderstood native reports of the Colorado River's occasional overflow into the Salton Basin had given rise to the notion that at some point along its course the river split in two, with a western branch running toward the Pacific Ocean. This was an unlikely scenario, but not one that could be ruled out by eighteenth-century knowledge. In 1772, Francisco Garcés thought he might have come upon this "Yellow River" when he encountered the discolored water in the Laguna Seca drainage west of the lower Colorado.[41] Could the newly discovered Great River of Saint Francis on the Alta California coast, coming from the southeast, be the mouth of the rumored Western Colorado?[42]

On the ground, the progressive history of the exploration was naturally more complex than the theories. In 1769, the first overland exploration of the California coast had found its course blocked by an unexpected "arm of the sea" reaching inland. Those on the expedition, lost and practically starving, had disagreed as

---

[40]"Manifiesto que el discretorio del Apostólico Colegio de San Fernando hizo al Rey en 26 de febrero de 1776, sobre los nuevos descubrimientos de la Alta California." Printed in [Mexico,] Archivo y Biblioteca de la Secretaría de Hacienda 1914: 27–84; reprinted as [Apostólico Colegio de San Fernando] 1948. The quoted passage is on pages 31–32 of the 1914 printing. For manuscript locations, see Brown 1965: 375 note 1.
[41]As mentioned by Anza in his journal entry of March 5, 1774.
[42]See Brown 2001: 35.

to its significance: had they or had they not possibly found their goal, the desired harbor of Monterey? Captain Fernando de Rivera y Moncada, who was present on that expedition, sent his leather-jacketed scouts inland to find out. The first expedition's European contingent, guided by the engineer Miguel Costansó, decided that the new waters must be the "inlets" or *esteros* that were described in old accounts of the little-known coast as being at "San Francisco." By that term he was referring to the bay under Point Reyes, which he regarded as stretching out to include the entire present-day Gulf of the Farallones. In order to make this identification, Costansó had to stretch the usual meaning of the term. The inlets, he wrote, "shot an extraordinary distance inland," that is, they were bigger than the term normally would suggest.[43] The outer entrance from the sea into the inland waters was not visible, but the explorers suspected that it lay through a gap visible to the northward on the coast (present Bolinas Bay), and somewhere among the mountain ranges (San Bruno Mountain and Tamalpais) that could be seen from the south where they were.[44] On the sketch of the bay that he made at the time, and on the general maps that he drew of the coast, Costansó safely assumed the mouth's existence. The redrawn detail in figure 2, taken from the large-scale version of Costansó's general map, is undoubtedly very similar to the sketch that he provided to the viceroy in 1772 when called upon by him to plan the Anza expeditions.[45]

Captain Rivera never did agree with Costansó's interpretation. After the expedition was over, he opined that they might as well have settled down at the new bay and called it Monterey. Who would object? Again, when he returned to explore in 1774, Rivera's report to the viceroy expressed his conviction that "these waters were first discovered by our first expedition journey."[46] The more accepted interpretation, however, left "San Francisco" itself on the far side (north) of the "inlets." A quick reconnaissance in 1770 by Pedro Fages, the new Monterey commandant, led to four of his scouts having a view from the east side of the bay and out through the mouth of the waters.[47] But the strait's existence was no surprise.

---

[43] "Estuary" is a poor translation of *estero*, since the English word designates the discharge of a river into the sea, and there was no question of a river on the first discovery, nor does the Spanish word share that definition. By a strange semantic reversal, the later British naval explorers on the Pacific coast were influenced by how the Spanish word was used in this local application, so that as a result there are named "inlets" up to two hundred miles long on the British Columbia coast.

[44] This summary relies partly on the information in Stanger and Brown 1969 and Brown 2001, but presents new material. After the discussions in Treutlein 1968: 19–26, Stanger and Brown 1969: 11–13, and Brown 2001: 76–77, 92–94, there should be no doubt that the explorers of 1769 did *not* see the Golden Gate.

[45] Costanó 1940: 14.

[46] Brown 1962: 335; Stanger and Brown 1969: 143.

[47] The soldier Alejandro Soto has a two-thirds or better chance of having been one of the four discoverers of the Golden Gate. Fages had six soldiers with him, and we know that Corporal Soto was among them because, for the trip, he borrowed Carlos Rubio's brass- and silver-mounted musket worth 53 pesos and broke it. (Carrillo, "Noticias de algunas cosas"). The names of the five other soldiers on the trip are not known.

Figure 2. San Francisco Bay and River, 1770. By Miguel Costansó. Detail, redrawn, after Bibliothèque Nationale, Paris, Département des Manuscrits, fonds mexicain 156, from a photographic copy. © *BnF*.

It merely confirmed the existence of a barrier to any northward expansion. Boats would be needed to cross, but there were none available.

The president of the Alta California missions, Junípero Serra, had obtained tentative government funding for a "San Francisco" mission, and he was not a person who readily gave up such opportunities. In March 1772 he sent his assistant Juan Crespí back, along with Fages, to continue to look for a way by land around the difficulty. The results were unexpected. From an inland hilltop, the mounted Spanish party viewed an immense river, two-thirds of a mile wide at the mouth. It circled back through a vast plain bounded only by a high snowy range that was far in the distance to the southeast. Although it was too far to be sure, it seemed possible that the river came out through a gap from the other side. But at that point, letters caught up with Captain Fages telling of starvation in the settlements left behind. The commander made a quick return from his camp at present-day Pittsburg. He sent out scouting parties southeastward and southwestward to find a shortcut back between the mountains and then followed the southwestward route back through the Amador-Livermore Valley which was referred to by Crespí and afterward by Font as "Santa Coleta."[48]

When Captain Rivera arrived at Monterey in 1774 as commandant of the new settlements, he wrote that he would rejoice if this proved to be true, although he saw strong reasons against it. He was correct, of course. At least, he thought, the probability could be established by observing the river's direction, even if his planned exploration (which he had hoped to make ever since 1769) failed to reach the main Colorado itself.[49] However, he had a subsequent interview with two imprisoned deserters who had fled in that direction, and also with Sergeant Mariano Carrillo, who had scouted beyond the mountains in 1772 and had also pursued deserters there. Their only report was that a river a mere eighty paces wide joined the San Francisco fourteen or fifteen leagues—thirty-six to thirty-nine miles—above the latter's mouth. The deserters are said in other accounts to have gone up the river forty leagues—over one hundred miles—no doubt hoping to find the Colorado and escape along it to Sonora. The leagues are probably to be counted from the present-day Oakland/Berkeley region, where Commandant Fages had sent a party to hunt grizzly bears. Rivera was left confused as to the number and importance of the inland rivers, and uncertain about whether he should visit them.[50]

In the end, the captain decided to follow that part of his instructions which called for a further exploration northward to the inland waters that, by a slight shift of usage, were beginning to be regarded as part of the harbor of San Francisco. At the beginning of December 1774, he and Francisco Palóu from Mission San Carlos were part of a small group camped in heavy wind and rain among hills well south of "the mouth of the inlet." Arising before dawn, Rivera and four soldiers climbed the heights to the north—San Bruno Mountain and Mount Davidson—and viewed the complex topography ahead. Two days later, finding himself "less than satisfied" with the results of this viewing, he broke camp and headed northwest and north. Rivera journeyed through a large tract of sand dunes alongside the ocean shore to the "mouth of the harbor." He and Palóu both carefully described this from their viewpoint on top of the cliff at the extreme outer point of its southern side—not at the Golden Gate itself, whose inner shore they did not visit. Leaving any further exploration for "after the rains," they returned down the coast to Monterey.[51]

---

[48]Treutlein 1972: 351; Stanger and Brown 1969: 125–27.
[49]Treutlein 1968: 54.
[50]Rivera y Moncada to the viceroy, August 30 and 31, 1774, Rivera y Moncada Papers, The Bancroft Library, C-A 368.
[51]Brown 1962; Stanger and Brown 1969: 132–46.

The next year's exploring was preempted by expensive and ill-coordinated sea expeditions originally arranged from Mexico.[52] One result of the surveys was sailing-master Cañizares's equivocally expressed doubts about the great river, as reported to Font by Rivera.[53] From the ship anchored at Angel Island, Cañizares had been sent out twice with orders to make a boat survey of the uppermost waters of the "inlet." The chart resulting from his visits shows not just one river emptying into present Suisun and Honker Bays but four rivers. The accompanying report describes only two, with depths of less than two fathoms and with extremely shallow bars in their mouths.[54] This might conceivably have applied to what we know as the Sacramento River, but hardly to the San Joaquín estuary, Crespí's "Great River." There matters stood, or seemed to stand, when the expedition with Anza and Font set out for the coast at the end of 1775.

An Observer and His Instruments for Anza's Second Expedition

On January 2, 1775, Viceroy Bucareli at Mexico City had written to inform Lieutenant Colonel Anza (promoted to that rank on the strength of his successful exploration of 1774) that his proposed new expedition for taking families of colonists to California had received full government backing. Among the details was the fact that Father Pedro de Fonte [sic] of the Colegio de la Santa Cruz in Querétaro had been proposed to the Viceroy as someone who should accompany Anza all the way to Monterey and during the inspection and survey of the River of San Francisco "for observing latitudes, as one having understanding in the matter." Anza in one letter also uses the spelling Fonte, which presumably is how everyone in the New World pronounced his name. Accordingly, the viceroy "requested and charged" the Guardian at Querétaro to grant Font a leave of absence.[55] Thus Font received the unique chance to apply his mathematical, artistic, and literary talents to a single important goal.

The colegio authorities must have been the agency that put Font's name forward to the government. What personal lobbying the unimportant friar must

---

[52] There was also a brief land expedition, mentioned by Font several times, that included naval officers and the missionary Palóu.

[53] See above and under February 7.

[54] On some of the flaws in this survey, which were presumably due to Commander Juan Manuel de Ayala's injury caused in turn by his predecessor having become psychotic in the face of the dangers of the northward voyage, see Stanger and Brown 1969: 31–35. The chart has often been reproduced, e.g. in Galvin 1971, which correctly assigns its relationship to the improved version from the naval surveys of the following year (Galvin 1971: 101–106).

[55] Garate 1995: 198–99 (facsimile). In view of Anza's attitude toward Font, his own subsequent request for the friar's services was obviously a mere formality, placed upon him by his superiors.

have engaged in to receive this assignment can only be guessed at. According to his later correspondence, the colegio expected to receive from his participation in the expedition "an itinerary, if possible with a map."[56] Drawing maps and plans is an artistic talent as much as a mathematical one. Under extremely difficult conditions in the field, Font did produce drawings that impressed those around him. Anza and Junípero Serra both asked for copies and even Commandant Rivera expressed appreciation, as other viewers have done ever since. Also, the Franciscan superiors received considerably more than the "itinerary" they had requested. Font apologized for the large size of even the shortened text, which was far less than the literary monument that he had determined to produce for himself and for possible future readers.

The proper recording of locations in little-known territories was extremely important. Anza's first expedition had made its nearly fatal excursion too far south into the desert while looking for a way to California, largely because Jesuit publications had placed the confluence of the Colorado and Gila rivers a long way above the true latitude.[57] Once they had reached the Pacific Coast, Anza's companions, Fathers Díaz and Garcés, had ridden from San Gabriel to San Diego and back to acquire an astrolabe (a relatively primitive instrument) for use on the return journey. However, Garcés's take on such scientific subjects had almost nothing in common with his companion Pedro Font's passionate amateurism. For Garcés, "the world," by which he meant society and government, had a taste for "the curious and the rare" rather than for doing something really useful, which he defined as spreading the faith. But, wrote Garcés, the world's desires for idle knowledge had to be indulged in order to gain secular support for the friars' real purposes.[58]

According to the viceroy's letter, the instruments for Font's geographical observations were to be purchased for the expedition "in agreement with engineer don Miguel Costansó," who had accompanied the first expedition to California in 1769–1770 and was now rising to influence in the colonial military engineering corps.[59] In his journal, Font tells an admittedly unverifiable but lively tale about the important instrument to which Anza reverentially referred to as "the expedition's quadrant" (June 2). This device had a graduated quarter-circle, a level, and a telescopic sight, and was used for taking the height of the sun. According to the story, the viceroy had used his power in coolly extorting the item from a

---

[56] Brown 2006: 94.

[57] In his journal of that exploration, Juan Díaz penned a criticism of the Jesuit observations, although he later removed it from the copy that he sent to the government.

[58] Garcés, "Cartas," 201.18, January [no day date], 1775.

[59] "Costansó" was the phonetic spelling of his family name that the young Catalán engineer used at the time. He later altered it to a more formal orthography.

previous owner. The identity of the owner (the gossip varied) was either the head of the viceregal secretariat or a Mexico City nobleman who insisted that he would accept no other replacement than one that had been made in Paris or London.

Even this scientific device had limited practical value for geography. In England, the chronometer, a complex instrument which allowed the fixing of points east and west on the earth's surface, was being perfected. But quadrants, octants, sextants, astrolabes, and other current tools could only measure north and south positions. In 1767 the British government (which was not backward in taking credit for technical advances) had offered to send members of the Royal Society of London to Baja California to aid in the international observations of the transit of the planet Venus. The government offered to provide a quadrant, a pendulum clock (a primitive chronometer) and a reflecting telescope with a two-piece objective and an achromatic micrometer. Figure 3 shows largely identical equipment being actually used for that purpose by the French and Spanish scientists who were going to California to observe the transit. In return, the British had asked for extensive information about Spanish settlements on the Pacific. An anonymous Spanish "patriotic nobleman" already had written a treatise in which he warned his government against such requests by the French and British academies to observe the transit on Spanish soil. He believed that they would use this as a pretext to spy and would load their subsequent travel accounts with subversive remarks for a Spanish public that thought it was in vogue to read foreign books. Accordingly, the proposal from London got a ballistic response from the Madrid government, on the (certainly true) grounds that the British wished to spy on the Spanish coasts. In addition, it was an insult to the Spanish nation to suppose that it lacked competent mathematicians or even achromatic telescopes![60]

Clearly, both Font and Anza were suffering from what would be characterized today as "high-tech envy" caused by the expedition's instrument. Anza allowed special people such as the gentlemen and ladies at San Miguel de Horcasitas to examine and admire the fine engraving on the brass as well as the smoked-glass telescopic eyepiece through which the sun could be viewed directly. He also spoke of his "observations," although he had neither the requisite mathematical ability nor the requisite mathematical tables, as Font points out. Font, who possessed both, was regularly annoyed by the commander's refusal to trust him with the quadrant. Anza finally handed the costly instrument over to him at San Gabriel, with the irritating remark, "Since you seem to know something

---

[60]James, Earl of Morton to Prince Masserano (in French), May 15, 1767, and the July 9–13 proceeding of the Indies Council, Madrid, with the opinion of its *fiscal*, Archivo General de Indias, Audiencia de Guadalajara 369 (The Bancroft Library film, reel 544 frames 2–23; also Transcript Z–E 1). Bolton Papers 80, The Bancroft Library, transcript from Biblioteca Nacional, Madrid.

FIGURE 3. Solar observations being made at Mexico City, 1767. By Felipe de Zúñiga y Ontiveros. A quadrant is in use at the upper left of the etching. *Courtesy of the Sutro Library of the California State Library, San Francisco.*

about it. . . ."⁶¹ This did not settle the matter. Even after the expedition's end, the two of them were still quarreling over it. Font's scornful sentence in which he dismisses Anza as a "supposed man of honor behaving basely over a bagatelle" is undercut by his own admission in his correspondence that he hoped to keep the expensive "bagatelle" himself. "Instead of having the opportunity, through this journey [the expedition], to acquire an instrument that I might be able to use on a future occasion, I have lost something, because I gave Father Garcés a poor-quality quadrant that I had and he broke it."⁶² The disputed quadrant remained in limbo at San Miguel de Horcasitas until an order of March 12, 1777, was received, according to Father Barbastro's notes. The order was from the new Commandant General of the Interior Provinces, the Caballero de Croix. The order stated that the quadrant was to be delivered to "the frontier missionaries" for use in further expeditions. So, Font had won the issue, if not personally, at least for his colleagues. However, like so many of the Caballero's decisions, this one proved to be rather off the point. The age of advance was over and the long North American frontier stalemate was about to begin.

Font as Cosmographer

Pedro Font's reputation as a geographer (or cosmographer, in the term used at the time) is safe on the basis of his writings and his maps. His feeling for the land can be left to speak for itself, as it does in his epiphany at the limitless view of California's Central Valley: "The sky joins with the earth so that the eye loses its objective and there is no telling whether what follows beyond is water or land" (April 3). Near the beginning of his voyage (October 31), Font was the first modern person to conduct a detailed inspection of the palatial ruin found in an abandoned city of the ancient Hohokam. He is the only investigator who has collected, in their original detail, the related legends that were preserved by the local natives (October 31). In the below-sea-level basin of the Colorado Desert (December 9), he enjoyed the eerie sensation of treading over grounds that he could picture as being recently the floor of a sea, a notion reflected in the popular modern belief that the Gulf of California recently extended up through the Salton Basin.⁶³ Many contemporaries speculated on what the unknown interior of western North America was like. Some thought it contained great buffalo

---

⁶¹As described in Font's correspondence. The journal, on the other hand, suggests that Anza used the phrase earlier while visiting Font at San José de Pimas in 1775.
⁶²Brown 2006: 93–94; cf. Matson 1975: 266.
⁶³Current scientific opinion is to the contrary (Redlands Institute 2002: 17, 23, 25). The popular view gets some appearance of plausibility from considering the past effect of the enormous yearly buildup of the Colorado River delta in blocking off the Salton Basin which was far below sea level.

plains, while some French geographers maintained that there was a great "Sea of the West." Font's tentative answer at least was an imaginative one: perhaps it was all a vast tule swamp or a swampy lake. Four months after Font's return to Sonora, Francisco Garcés came back from his visit to the Grand Canyon, and poured cold water on that idea. The Franciscan Silvestre Vélez de Escalante's expedition from New Mexico in the same year also found the way to Monterey blocked by profound canyons and endless dry mountains.

To assist with Font's technical determination of positions, his colegio had sent him a small, rather outdated self-help geography manual and tables for latitude observations that apparently had been copied by a friar at Querétaro. Somehow Font got hold of the better tables by the well-known geographer Jorge Juan. These tables allowed him to produce roughly adequate records of latitude with the aid of a couple of additional calculations.[64] Font's accuracy definitely improved with practice along the way, between September 16, 1775, and June 2, 1776 (see the latter date's entry). Of course, most distances on the ground had to be estimated in Mexican leagues which were equivalent to about 2.6 miles each (see the note under October 1), but since Font was a relative newcomer to the far distances of the frontier, he is inclined to exaggeration. As he admits in a note (April 29), the distance figures for the return journey are more reliable than those that he gave during his first traverse of the route. Even so, he is far less accurate in his estimates than the vastly experienced Anza.[65]

Font subjected his estimates of courses and distances to a complicated further procedure. As he describes it (April 14 and 29), his observed latitude positions were entered upon drafts of the map that he was preparing. These positions formed the framework to which the daily estimates of course and distance were adjusted by a graphic procedure. As he put it, "the dividers will determine this." These data then had to be recalculated in order to be entered into the revised text of his journal. Only a dedicated scribbler like the author would have undertaken such an amount of refiguring, and in view of the enormous number of corrections even in the existing manuscripts of the journal, it is probably a good thing that his raw notes are not preserved. The problem with his method is its circularity, for, without any independent knowledge of the longitude positions

---

[64] Jorge Juan y Santacilia (1713–1773), a famous mathematician, traveler, and naval officer; co-author of a book (1748) that criticized Spanish colonial forms of government in Peru, and inspired attempts at reform.

[65] Font estimated the relatively fast pace of the return travel at the equivalent of about 3.9 miles per hour (April 14 and 29). Font, Anza, and other explorers did not use different "leagues" that were defined as being of varying sizes, as is claimed by Bolton (1930 vol. 4; 1931: xii), a conclusion which must have arisen from totaling the league counts for each explorer and then dividing the results into the corresponding distance as taken from twentieth-century maps. However, in all cases the league that was intended was the standard Mexican one. As part of this edition, Font's varying figures, along with Anza's, are summarized in the table of Days' Marches.

of his anchor points, his corrections of estimated directions as well as distances could be cumulatively and arbitrarily wrong. Yet he speaks regularly of deducing geographical relationships *por la cuenta*, "by the reckoning," referring to his cumulative running estimates of distance and direction. It is for this reason that his initial estimates of distance and direction, made from the saddle, are often better than the altered values that appear in various levels of revision in the successive texts of the journal.

All this had practical consequences. One of the arguments that Font used in order to persuade Anza to turn back from the exploration of the San Joaquín—just before the point where they might actually have gotten across the barrier of the tule marshes—was the offer of a straight course back to Monterey that he had deduced must be available from their current location (April 4.) Anza took his advice and the party spent over two days struggling in the roughs of the Mount Hamilton Range, which the soldiers named the *Sierra del Chasco*.[66] Anza's journal records this information but Font's journal does not. This fiasco led to a later confrontation at the edge of the desert (May 8) when Anza proposed to take a new and direct course across to the Colorado and Font failed to dissuade him by his positional deductions. In this case, although Font was correct about the situation, Anza did not believe him. If the experienced soldier who was appointed to guide them had not flatly refused Anza's orders, the party almost certainly would have died somewhere in the salt basin or beyond in the notorious Yuma sand dunes that had already claimed the family of El Peregrino. Font was somewhat less wise when he insisted that there was only a relatively short east and west distance between San Diego and the Colorado. This theory, based partly on soldiers' reports and largely on wishful thinking, produced an unattractive wasp waist at the top of the Baja California peninsula as shown on his maps, but it had no further immediate bad practical effects (February 2, May 15).

For the San Francisco reconnaissance with Anza (March 22–April 8), Font was able to use a level for measuring tidal changes, as well as a "graphometer" that Francisco Palóu had somehow brought to, or acquired at, Mission San Carlos. The graphometer was a fairly simple surveyor's instrument. It consisted of a graduated semicircle with a plain alidade. It could be used horizontally for plotting angles, as on a plane table, or vertically for trigonometrically deducing heights, as in the case of the Palo Alto redwood (March 30). It may have had some use in drawing the small hill profiles that Font scattered through the margins of his manuscript pages recording this part of the journey. But it is probably more likely that he returned the instrument to Palóu before he profiled the Santa Bárbara Channel islands on the return march (April 27).

---

[66]Disappointment Mountains.

Font on the Expedition

Even as the first elements of the expedition set out from San Miguel de Horcasitas, the capital of the province of Sonora, Font was told by a colleague that the commander had made "certain remarks" to his disfavor (October 9). What these were can be gleaned from a letter that Anza had written as early as the preceding January when he was first informed of the viceroy's detailed arrangements for the expedition.[67] Essentially, Anza felt that Font's frontier experience was too limited for the task. He worried further that the two friars, Font and Garcés, "belonging to a class very different from my own," might combine their opinions against him to the detriment of his command. He felt that Garcés had done this in 1774 and that the result had been a near disaster in the desert. No doubt this is why Font was especially enjoined by his superior, the Guardian, to keep good harmony with the commander during the expedition, as he later noted apologetically in one of his letters.[68]

Font the greenhorn does make it clear that beans and tortillas are not a good diet for him, even if he ultimately was unable to avoid them. It also seems clear, although he never states it in quite this way, that he was subjected to a prolonged hazing test from the military frontiersman commander, who was famous for being able to ride fifty or sixty miles in a day after drinking nothing but a cup of morning chocolate. Anza constantly provided Font with excuses for avoiding travel. And Font, just as constantly, expressed his determination to stay with the commander the entire way, as his original instructions required. In an entry as early as November 10, while still in the long, long reaches of the Gila River valley, Anza's journal acknowledges Font's ability to keep up while "battling a good many illnesses" including malaria attacks. However, the comment could have been added to the entry at some later point in time. Font later wrote that he was hardly free from health problems for a week during the entire journey and he wrote about them in self-fascinated detail in his journal. It is worth mentioning, however, that he actually removed a few of these passages on revision, as if he intended to have some sort of balance for his narrative. The diagnosis that he suffered from scurvy caused by a depleted frontier traveler's diet is strongly supported by one of the removed passages (December 30, cf. December 27), in which he speculates that his mouth affliction has been dramatically helped by eating wild-rose hips, a major source of anti-scorbutic Vitamin C.[69] The point at which the commander finally accepted the friar as a fit traveling companion seems to have been their departure from San Diego (February 9), when Font persuaded Anza to eat some bread and cheese for lunch while in the saddle. By

---
[67]Garate 1995: 33–35; 216–17.
[68]Brown 2006: 93.
[69]The diagnosis is made by Dr. Gastón Cano in Montané 2000: 480 on the basis of the final version alone.

the end of the journey, Font was matching Anza and his small group of picked soldiers during their amazing gallops across the desert at night in late May.

This companionship did not remove the other sources of interpersonal friction with Anza and with others, which Font chronicles in full, to put it mildly. After his return to Sonora, he admits that Anza had courted his friendship only for the purposes of the political campaign against Commandant Rivera. Then he had dropped him. As Font expresses it in subsequent correspondence, if he entered Anza's house upon the wrong foot, he left it in the same fashion.[70] Even when he was among his colleagues, it is hard to assess his claim (April 20) that both he and his California missionary contemporaries had a good sense of humor, since humor is often the most difficult element to pin down in writings from another century. Father Caballer's unexplained jest involving an ox (April 22), or his prank played on Font concerning the veiling of recently married couples, do not seem very promising. Although Font has abundant sarcasm, it is not clear how much humor he saw in the actually very funny account of his manipulation by the San Miguel de Horcasitas officers' wives (February 6). At the very least, the situation's potential for humor could not have escaped his consciousness. And, he obviously does not mind telling stories that cast him in a bad light, whatever the lessons are that he pretends to draw from them.

On the whole, it is impossible at times not to dislike Father Font. The same thing could be said about anyone who chooses to reveal so much about his or herself. The author's self-righteousness and critical attitude, his outspoken jealousy of anything that threatens his position or standing, and above all, his continual personal complaints make for some disagreeable reading, even though its details may seem lively after 230 years. He may have sincerely believed that he was recording his complaints only for their instructional value, but few contemporary readers will believe him. The nadir is certainly reached on December 17. That is when the young widow, María Feliciana Arballo, sang clever comic songs at the colonists' celebration of survival and reunion. This led to her being beaten by the man with whom she was traveling. Over Font's objections, Anza intervened to stop the beating. It would be safe to bet that Font himself was the subject of one of her spontaneously composed *glosas*, especially since it is on this same occasion that he refers to the colonists as "rabble."

Font and the Colonists

Font's commission as chaplain to the second Anza expedition meant that he was responsible for the religious needs of over two hundred parishioners on the

---
[70]Brown 2006: 93.

march. How thoroughly he was engaged with them as individuals is difficult to say, but his revisions to the table of personnel that he copied from Anza show that he had a certain acquaintanceship with the families He performed a suitable number of marriages and baptisms, since quite a number of women among the colonists were pregnant. He also heard confessions and administered the last rites, although his journal does not usually mention these.

He usually described his sermons as his "four words" and he often summarized them quite fully, sometimes not to his own advantage.[71] The low point in the sermons was his self-pitying introduction to the Christmas Day address to the crowd. The high point came after they had reached Monterey when Font recounted and summed up the great deed that they all accomplished together. He did this in straightforward terms that were well designed to appeal to the audience. His sermons often employed simple numerology. This was a preaching device that had been sanctioned since Saint Augustine. At times Font overused this technique. When at journey's end he was prohibited from giving a celebratory summing-up of the journey's accomplishment (June 2), it seems partly understandable that the stated reason was that "it would annoy the governor." Indeed the planned sermon was again going to involve much playing around with numbers. Also, Font's occasional deliberate use of unfamiliar terms like *"palpable"* seems as likely to have puzzled his audiences as to have impressed them.

The members of the expedition destined for California had been enlisted as volunteers from the old towns of Sinaloa and from thinly peopled Sonora. They were an interesting mixture of people from different classes and races. There was even one Apache in the group. The province of Sinaloa was originally founded two hundred thirty-five years earlier by an army forcibly levied at Mexico City by Nuño de Guzmán who was the last and worst of the conquistadors. He marched the force into the far northwest and left them there in a virtual state of abandonment, after almost all of the thousands of Aztec warriors who had been their original companions had perished by *chubasco*, flood, and disease. The survivors slowly mingled with natives of the area and with later arrivals, including settlers of African descent who came from the tropical shores farther south. These survivors built a viable Latin American society but this society was not immune to sickness and natural disasters. In 1770, five years before the second Anza expedition, the economy was severely damaged by another chubasco which destroyed fields and submerged towns. Twenty years later, the economy still had not recovered.[72] In 1775, the same year that the expedition was mounted,

---

[71] The Garcés journal's editor, Elliott Coues, went on record as saying that he *thought* he would be willing to listen to Father Font preach, for the sake of having the personnel list that Font preserved (Coues 1900: 1: 72).

[72] Gómez Canedo 1971: 99, a report by Grimarest, the intendant governor of Sonora, 1790.

an epidemic of disease thinned the ranks of the recruits and military personnel destined for the journey.

In one of his sermons, Font acknowledges that the people's motives for joining the expedition were good and bad. But he makes it clear that his marching parishioners had a common desire to better their lot through the opportunity that had been suddenly offered to them by this enterprise of the Spanish Empire. On the march, as they crossed from the desert over the wintery mountains of California, some of the women cried out ¡*Ay!* This was their way of expressing longing for the homeland they had left behind, a homeland without all that snow. Yet they and their families put up with the deprivations that Font had warned them would follow. While the officers feared that the colonists might revolt, the chief complaint that the colonists expressed (outside of a lack of soap) had to do with delays in getting to the site of the settlement they were to build. They also worried that their children were becoming spoiled for lack of meaningful work. They proved to be a durable folk, as Font constantly warned them that they would have to be. So perhaps his sermons did have some effect.

Of all the place names the travelers constantly bestowed along the way as a means of recording their odyssey, a few informal names have been preserved. Font mentions two such names near the beginning of the journey, *Puerto del Azotado* and *La Laguna del Hospital* (October 28 and November 7).[73] Unfortunately, he records none after that. Even his discussions of names given by earlier expeditions are very frequently inaccurate. Nevertheless, it is very likely that a number of names bestowed by the colonists during their march can still be found upon the landscape even where their origin is forgotten. In the summer of 1776, during the final march to their destination at San Francisco (this was after Font had left California for Mexico), the traveling settlers named a hill in present-day Gilroy *Lomita de la Linares*. According to her descendants, Gertrudis Linares climbed that hill holding her infant son so that she could watch the men hunt elk and antelope for dinner. The peak at present-day Morgan Hill may have been dubbed *La Oreja del Oso* because the sight of grizzly bears was a new experience for the travelers.[74] In their camp at what was to become San José, according to a later tradition "the children cried" because the provisions were running low again, hence the name *Lomas de las Lágrimas*.[75]

The personal history of María Feliciana Arballo, the "free *mulata*" already mentioned, and her posterity certainly is one encapsulation of the epic of the early peopling of California. After harder and lonelier times than any imperial

---

[73] Whipped Man's Pass and Hospital Lake.
[74] The Bear's Ear.
[75] Hills of Tears. Gudde 1969: s.v. Lomita; Brown 2006: 21–22.

official would have cared to predict for the new province, a nineteenth-century descendant of Arballo's became its last Mexican governor. In addition, his brother served in the constitutional convention for the new North American state after leading the most successful attack against the invading United States forces in the Mexican War. Even the Apache father of a family among the settlers became a well-remembered founding figure in the town of San José.

At the final parting from the colonists at Monterey on April 14, of which Anza gives a so thoroughly self-glorifying account, Font briefly mentions the tears which were shed. However, he gives more attention to his encounter with the corporal and the chicken droppings. Perhaps he knew or suspected that not a lot of the crying was for him.

Font and the Natives

Font's journal provides an epic running account of the nations and tribes encountered on his journey of two thousand miles, as seen through European eyes. First were the large agricultural tribes of the Gila and the Colorado, which had been in increasing contact with the Spanish. The River O'odham (Gila Pima) creation and flood stories were written down by Font after he had heard them told while he was riding. This, in and of itself, was a remarkable feat of memory and recording. Obviously, Font was not among those in the mounted party who laughed at the wrong time and provoked the teller of the tale into silence. Just as remarkably, this record forms a much more unified myth cycle than can be found in any later fragmentary versions of the same tales. In the same entry of the journal (October 31), the careful description of Arizona's *Casa Grande* and its attached traditions is also the classic discussion on the subject. However, the most developed of the many ethnographic essays which Font includes is the treatise (December 27) on the Quechán (Yuma) and Kohuana (Cajuenche, Cojat) nations. These were written from the point of view of a missionary who expects the work of their evangelization to begin almost immediately and who feels that he sees the problems and the solutions. It can at least be said that the writer's judgmental stance or Eurocentric perspective provides an easily understood platform for informational observations that a less rigid or more easily sympathetic recorder might have seen fit to leave out.

It is unquestionable that Font experienced a profound personal shock when he encountered non-agricultural groups living, as he saw it, at or over the edge of survival in the deserts and mountains. He memorably called them "children of night and of fear" (May 6). His reaction motivates the long theological consideration which he inserted into the final version. This entry, which fills the last portion of the December 7 entry, discusses the possible salvation of non-Christian native souls. To many readers this might seem either impossibly condescending to the natives or else simply bizarre. However, it is not difficult to translate Font's concern into more general terms. How many thousands of humans, during thousands of years, must have lived in isolation from the mainstream of humanity and of civilization, in small starving bands continually at war one with another? What significance could be attached, or could they themselves attach, to their lives? Poor Font. His own superiors would likely have disapproved of his attempt to solve the ancient and difficult theological question of non-Christian salvation. In the western Church, this matter supposedly had been settled long ago along strict Augustinian lines: no salvation outside of Christianity or outside of the Church.[76] In theological terms, Font's argument might be intriguing, even though the manuscript suggests that it was only at the last moment in developing his theme that he came upon the most relevant Bible text for his purpose. His hopeful conclusion concerning the fate of the natives of the desert and other natives is certainly more humanly appealing than the orthodox opposite. Seventy-five years after Font, North American exploring parties visiting the far southwest were appalled as Font was by the physical appearance and what they took to be the moral character of the non-agricultural mountain and desert groups, as compared to the well-fed vegetarian natives of the Colorado River.[77]

Font's reactions to the seashore, bay, and river groups of the California coast—hunters, fishers, and gatherers who only occasionally looked starved—are, appropriately, mixed. Among those natives who were beginning to relate to the agricultural life inculcated by the missions, the San Diego natives had just mounted their unexpected attack and revolt in which a fellow Franciscan was beaten to death. During the Spanish military's interrogations of captives after the event, it was said that a local chief who was on a hill watching the men and women laboring in the mission's corn field had said aloud, "They will do that with me," and then had gone on to plan the attack.[78] Of course Font had no sympathy with such motives for the assault, which he recorded at length from

---

[76]Cases of individuals, including some clergy, who expressed contrary views in the Spanish and Portuguese empires and were punished for them by the Inquisition are discussed by Schwartz (2008 passim), who also suggests that there was something of an informal loosening of such strictness after the middle of the eighteenth century (Schwartz 2008: 215, 237, 251). In fact, by the 1760s the Portuguese and Spanish governments had begun to rein in the excesses of their respective Inquisitions. Still, the risk Font incurred in writing down his thoughts on the subject was not nonexistent in theory, however slight it may have been in practice.

[77]Compare, for example, Font's December 23 and 24 remarks with those of Möllhausen ([1858] 1969 2: 244, 327), or R. H. Kern (Weber 1985: 171, 177).

[78]Burrus 1967 2: 473.

the viewpoint of Spanish eyewitnesses. He unemotionally mentions the brutal whippings that the soldiers later imposed on those "ringleaders" that they could catch (January 15 and 31).

Font completely approved (January 5) of the California missionaries' use of what was called the "Texas method," by which converts were required to live in a tightly regulated community and to labor in common. On the other hand, after his return to Sonora, Font argued vehemently that this treatment was valid only for groups not used to agriculture, and then only for a limited time. But if this method were applied to people such as the Quechán and Kohuana, who already practiced their own form of agriculture, it would be unpleasant, impractical, and finally, unjust.[79] The later history of the Colorado and even of the California missions would suggest that Font may have been correct.

The long, valuable description of the native towns of the Santa Bárbara Channel (February 24) stands out as being carefully factual. However, as might be expected from a missionary, Font's attitude regarding the bad behavior exhibited by the California leather-jacket soldiers toward the natives is appropriately severe. Later, as part of the shortened official version of Font's journal, his memorable depictions of the Santa Bárbara Channel natives' fear of the soldier Camacho (a habitual criminal often found in the stocks at the Presidio of San Diego) came into the hands of progressive thinkers of Commandant General Croix's entourage.[80] They immediately seized upon the account as a means of proving the evils of the Spanish Empire's treatment of native populations. Font, however, probably was more concerned with expressing his disapproval of the quality of the local troops under the command of Captain Rivera.

When he finds groups that he likes, Font is capable of enthusiasm, although he always tempered that with a willingness to criticize. His appreciation of female beauty is not off limits. As Vladimir Guerrero has recently pointed out, Font gradually seems to overcome some of his repugnance during the course of the northward journey and, by its end, to imply some respect for native societies even when he does not openly admit it.[81] In encounters with groups around San Francisco Bay, he disapproves of scalp collecting and of thievery and cannot be bought off with gifts of tasty food. "Not even that [food] made me approve of those

---

[79] Brown 2006: 88, 114–15.
[80] He was regarded as a carrier of venereal disease (Provincial State Papers, Archive of California, The Bancroft Library, C-A 1: 144). According to Garcés, the natives on the Channel referred to all Spanish soldiers as "Camachos" (Garcés, "Relación"). Garcés, however, had not visited the Channel himself.
[81] Guerrero 2006: 171. On the other hand, it is a mistake to suggest (Guerrero 2006: 125) that Font regarded *El Peregrino*, the Indian guide Sebastián Taraval, as being nothing more than a mule driver. Of course Font may have held such an attitude, but in this context he was merely nagging Anza over Anza's assigning to Taraval various inconsistent positions for accounting purposes (May 25). In this instance Font was not categorizing Taraval.

INTRODUCTION   45

Indians," he said on April 2. But the other wildly varying behaviors which Anza's party experienced at first contact—dissuasion through gestures, displays of prowess, courteousness, scientific curiosity, stubborn quiet refusal, sheer panic, ceremonious hospitality, rapaciousness, edginess with precautions (March 25, 26, 28, 30, and 31; April 2 and 3)—are described with an equanimity which suggests that Font knew that any or all of these reactions might be a rational response on the inhabitants' part to the overwhelming foreignness of the European strangers.

Font never did, however, approve of the Kumeyaay or any of their relatives, even on the way south toward the end of his journey. On his return, when he was again among the Quechán people, Font seems more relaxed, although on revising one entry (May 15) he seems to have slightly toned down the dubious story of the soaping of the chief's daughter.

Anza, Font, and the Harbor

Instructions for the San Francisco reconnaissance, with the full weight of Mexico City and Madrid behind them, required the explorers to find a site for the planned fortress as near as possible to the harbor mouth. At San Diego, Commandant Rivera claimed to be relieved to learn that some flexibility in the choice would be possible, since his own visit had convinced him that there were no resources at all for a settlement at the south side of the mouth. Although some of the correspondence did mention wind-bent scrub oaks along the hills toward the interior, the general picture conveyed by Rivera's report was, as Font says (February 7), only that of the sandy tracts through which he had traveled along the ocean shore.

When Anza, Font, and Lieutenant Moraga returned with far more favorable news, Serra immediately embraced the previously uncertain conclusion that the "inlet mouth" was "the true harbor of San Francisco."[82] Rivera, on the other hand, raised the lieutenant's wrath by suggesting that it might have been fairer to take some of the colonists along so that they could look at their future home themselves (April 19, note.) In fact, some of their descendants might have agreed with Rivera's opinion. Decades later, a long-suffering missionary summed up isolated San Francisco in four words: "sand in the brambles"—and not to mention the fogs and the winds.[83]

Anza, however, had found the unquestionably perfect spot for the harbor mouth's defenses, the hundred-foot-high projection of an elevated white cliff at the narrowest point in the strait, and all other considerations had to give way

---
[82]Treutlein 1968: 45, 85.
[83]The citation is from a letter of the second decade of the nineteenth century to another missionary, in the Taylor Collection, Chancery Archives, Archdiocese of San Francisco; I have lost the exact reference.

to this single strategic fact. The rest of the picture was filled out by Anza and Font in as favorable terms as possible. At times they went beyond strict fact, as is exemplified by the changes that Font made in rewriting his journal texts, such as in connection with the availability of timber.[84] Much emphasis was put on the agricultural and irrigation possibilities of a small pond close to the chosen garrison site. Anza's related correspondence does specifically admit that drinking water for the settlement might be a problem. But he tries to overcome this potential defect by mentioning a multiplicity of available if distant sources of water. He also raised the possibility of placing the garrison itself at the more favorable spot he and Moraga had found on the eastern, bay-facing side of the peninsula. They had named this spot *Los Dolores* (April 12, note). However, according to Font, the officers agreed with the missionary that this latter spot should be a mission site instead. Later, Rivera's last-ditch suggestion, that Los Dolores might be a preferable site where the colonists could settle, was severely rejected by Anza. Fortunately, a groundwater trickle reported by Corporal Robles near the future presidio ultimately turned out to be a reliable supply (March 28, note).

The peninsula on which San Francisco stands is only some six miles wide at the tip and for a long distance southward.[85] The favorable representation by Font and Anza undoubtedly was aided by the fact that the maps available to government authorities (the Costansó sketch of 1770–1772, the Pablo Font redrawing of the Crespí map of 1772, and the Cañizares chart of 1775) all showed the peninsular breadth as two or three times the actual distance. Indeed, on the map which Font produced in 1776, it is over three times as wide. As a result, the crowding of presidio and mission resources was a growing problem in later years. This tension was not solved even after the constantly mixing presidio and mission livestock began to spread southward of Lake Merced in the 1780s. The timber supply—a problem recognized, if much understated, by Anza and Font—had to be drayed from thirty miles away by using oxen. Lime for cement was brought by mule up a rugged trail from fifteen miles down the coast. During the period when the population of native converts at Mission San Francisco was still large, a station was built farther down the peninsula in order to house around half of the neophytes, with a church, and a cemetery. This potential additional mission was eventually disapproved by the civil-military authorities.[86]

---

[84]There are examples under March 27 and elsewhere.
[85]Even less wide when former coves and tidal inlets are allowed for. See figure 21 in chapter 5. In 1828 the missionary Tomás Esténaga estimated the distance between the head of "the San Bruno inlet" (the tidal and willow marsh running up the valley to present Colma) and Lake Merced as a quarter-league (under ⅔ of a mile). Taylor Collection no. 2048.
[86]Diez et al., 1979; Fages, "Informes particulares." Cf. Hoover et al., 1966: 393; 2002: 393–94. Cf. Brown 1962: 329 on the erosion caused by the crowding of herds on the northern part of the peninsula.

Font and the River

Already, early in 1776, while Anza and Font were still at San Diego waiting to go north, they found themselves involved in a three-way verbal dispute (February 7). The issue was whether or not a great river existed in the vicinity of the projected new settlement at San Francisco. On one side of the disagreement were some soldiers who claimed they had actually seen the reported feature. However, their superior officer, Commandant Fernando de Rivera y Moncada, admitted that there was some question as to the river's existence. He had heard the sailing master José de Cañizares, who had surveyed the bay, deny privately that there was any such thing. Anza himself ended that particular argument by making a public vow that, if the river actually existed, he personally would present the viceroy with a vial of its water upon his return to Mexico City.

Here, no doubt, Font was first alerted to the possibility of making a geographical coup. Plainly, he regards his predecessor in the field of recording Pacific Coast discoveries, Juan Crespí, as a rival whom he needs to outshine. During his daily entries for his and Anza's San Francisco reconnaissance, Font does not miss any opportunity to debunk Crespí's reports of finding fair-skinned, fair-haired Indians. He even attempts to diagnose the psychological traits that led Crespí to make such a mistake.[87] Destroying the legend of the great river of San Francisco now would have few or no practical consequences, since any decisions based upon its supposed existence had already been made and would not affect the outcome. However, to show the mistakenness of some of the reasons of state was, at least to Font himself, an impressive achievement. Besides, there was the fascinating chance of contributing to a solution of the nearly total mystery of western North American geography.

Where Font is most unfair to his predecessor is in his claim that Crespí identified the Carquínez Strait (the "canyon of waters") with the supposed river mouth. In 1772, on first approaching the strait, Crespí excitedly envisaged a connection with the enormous interior Sea of the West shown on many French maps: "I myself shall say it is no inlet but an arm of the sea, and will prove to be a strait lying up within the mainland." Once arrived within the strait itself, he wrote: "far away toward where it ran, there was a great opening in the land, and [tidal] flats, and off in the distance the horizon showed a sort of sea-blink; yet we could never be sure the sea had been seen. . . ." But disillusionment came right

---

[87] See Brown 1991: 62–63. Font had a copy of the famous 1772 Great River journal, presumably one of the shortened and redacted texts (there were at least three independent redactions) although he could have been shown the original draft by Serra or Crespí himself at Carmel. There, he might also have viewed the draft of Crespí's major record of the first expedition, 1769–1770, and also Francisco Palóu's possibly completed redaction of the same document, although he does not mention either. To see the final versions of either the 1769–1770 or the 1772 Crespí journals, he would have had to be in Mexico City before the Anza expedition, and there is no sign that he was.

afterward: "The scouts returned, after seeing from the height that it was only flats."[88] The final version of Crespí's journal, used for the summaries that were supplied to the government, did not apply the term river to the straits channel itself, but only to the branching and reuniting waters well above it, and to their dimly seen tree-marked course off to the southeast and south.[89]

This landscape was the Sacramento–San Joaquín "delta." It has sometimes been described as "perimarine" in modern times. In the eighteenth and nineteenth centuries, it was by far the largest tidal freshwater wetland in the world—a geographical anomaly. Font's repeated attempts at finding an adequate terminology for it began with "marsh," then "lake," and went on to "freshwater sea" and, in his final text, "*piélago*," a Greek-derived term so fancy as to be nearly meaningless (March 27; April 3 [twice]; April 4). It is not surprising that this question attracted the interest even of his own religious superiors, and that it led to discussions and arguments involving the behavior of currents, tides, salinity, and so forth, none of which produced better explanations than Font's own. "Who can say whether it may not rival the Great Lake[s] of Canada in size?" wrote one of his colleagues later, in a printed book.[90] Font himself cautiously suggested an indefinite extension inland, and, obviously just in order to cover all bases, in a last-minute addition to his final text he allowed that it might be "some matter of what they call the Sea of the West" (April 3).

Lieutenant Moraga, meanwhile, had second thoughts about the supposed barrier of the tule swamps that had turned Anza and Font back from further exploring. In September, as soon as he could leave the San Francisco colonists constructing the new settlement with their crowbars, axes, and shovels, Moraga led a party of eight soldiers eastward and retraced the steps of the earlier reconnaissance. At the same time, naval officers with a boat party discovered the mouth of the Sacramento ("San Roque"). As is indicated by a legend on the chart that they produced, a crewman whom they sent up a tall tree at present-day Collinsville, no doubt using a spyglass and sighting directly up the dead end that is still called False River, mistakenly reported that the San Joaquín ("San Francisco") was nonexistent. Moraga missed his appointed rendezvous with this boat expedition and as a result it failed to explore further in this direction. Reading between the lines of Palóu's account of his excursion, it seems likely that Moraga did this deliberately to reach the "San Francisco River" by taking

---

[88] Stanger and Brown 1969: 124–25 (substituting "inlet" for "estuary"). This is from the field draft of Crespí's journal, in which he was noting down the events almost as soon as they occurred.

[89] Galvin 1971: 114, 120–21 (in translation). The distances are exaggerated, probably because of a serious error in determining the latitude (Stanger and Brown 1969: 127; Brown 2001: 72).

[90] See Matson 1975: 280–81 and Brown 2006: 105–108 (Font answering Guardian Jiménez's objections); Stanger and Brown 1969: 165, translated from Arricivita 1792: 466–67.

a lower route across the eastern hills to the off-branch now called Old River, which he reported as being no great river at all.[91]

At the beginning of December, Captain Rivera finally came north to visit San Francisco and to found Mission Santa Clara. He then set out with Moraga to follow farther around the east side of the delta. Rivera's contribution to the geographical controversy is of some interest. "I believe that these tule swamps, of which so much is reported, originate from nothing more than the swelling of the rivers here in the rainy season, with their natural flooding being increased by that of the tides, which when added to it forces them to run backward." The reference is to the exceptionally high "spring" tides of December, which indeed must have inundated the entire delta. Rivera continues, "Although salt water does not reach this high or far up [and] the water is always found fresh enough to drink, still, what with the river beds being insufficient to contain the flow, it pours out and spreads over the land, which is low-lying and grows tule rushes just as it would have grown other plants."[92] Except for the arguments over Font's report back at the Querétaro colegio, the matter remained untouched for a long generation, until Moraga's son Gabriel effectively completed his father's work by exploring large parts of the Sacramento and San Joaquín valleys.

The Two Commanders

Font's recording of the disagreement that arose between Anza and Rivera at the end of the expedition is the major subject of chapter 6 in the present edition. It makes unpleasant reading since it involves the destruction of a career military officer. An examination of the topic is crucial to evaluating both Font's truthfulness and the nature of the surrounding historical events and personalities.

The two commanders, Rivera and Anza, first met under the threat of the San Diego uprising. Although both of them had been in California in 1774, they had missed meeting each other by a month, since Anza returned to Sonora just before Rivera took up his residence at Monterey as commandant of the "new establishments." Rivera was responsible for a narrow chain of settlements, somewhere between five hundred and eight hundred miles long. These settlements consisted of a very few, extremely wide-spaced encampments and incipient missions. To protect them, Rivera had the smallest imaginable handful of soldiers to set against countless numbers of natives whose character was mostly unknown and, he believed, not very peaceable at best. Ortega, who was his subordinate officer, expressed severe doubts about the feasibility of the San Francisco project

---

[91]Soto Pérez 1998 2: 1203–1205; Moraga, "Carta."
[92]Translated from Burrus 1967 1: 326; cf. Brown 1998: appendix 8.

when the first rumors concerning it reached California in 1775.[93] Anza, however, had thought otherwise even on his first visit in 1774. To him the danger from "Indians who are terrified at the braying of a mule" seemed small.

Early in 1776, when Rivera still thought he had gained a friend, he wrote to Anza that his life had been a torment ever since higher authorities had plucked him up and sent him north to the new lands.[94] At the same time, Rivera regarded himself almost the archetype of the man on the scene who appreciates the current situation better than distant superiors do. In his correspondence he emphasized his experience, which stretched back for decades in the Jesuit missions of Baja California. Even the Queretaran friar, who later referred to him in an obituary as "an intelligent rustic, short of understanding in delicate [political] affairs," admitted that he had known the character of the Indians well.[95] The native uprising at San Diego verified the captain's often-expressed worst fears. It struck, not coincidentally, just at the instant when the already thinly stretched garrison had been reduced by missionary and official demands: requisitions for soldiers to found Mission San Juan Capistrano and demands from the new governor in Baja California for an escort for official dispatches.

In a generous letter to Anza, Rivera wrote that no one could ever disparage nor could anything ever diminish Anza's accomplishment in bringing his people across the desert. As Rivera saw it, the arrival of two hundred soldier-colonists could represent the salvation of the entire Pacific Coast province. However, the one place where he did not need them to be was a hundred miles north of the farthest presidio and further isolated at the tip of a long peninsula which he himself had scouted and found barren. He made no secret of his desire to hold them in the south at San Gabriel as long as he could and permanently if possible. Even after Anza had moved them to Monterey, Rivera maintained that the colonists should know that their duty was to serve in the defense of the existing presidios rather than found a new one.[96]

The San Diego uprising had involved non-Christian groups from far inland and a possible realignment of interests among the desert tribes who were already disturbed by Anza's treaty-making. Rivera also believed that Garcés's wide missionary wanderings were destabilizing the frontier. Anza himself had once expressed similar views. In the wake of Anza's crossing from the Colorado River to the coast, individuals from the river groups had begun showing up at the southern California missions, claiming to have come to trade for shells or just

---

[93] Brown 1962: 328.
[94] Letter of March 28, 1776.
[95] For Rivera's background and career, see Crosby 1994: 333–45, etc.; Brown 1962: 327.
[96] Letter of April 2, 1776, postscript (Garate 2006: 40–41; facsimile, 228).

to visit. After his second arrival, fresh from making successful arrangements with Chief Palma at Yuma, Anza offered Rivera the services of several hundred Quechán warriors from the Colorado. Rivera replied that, if he himself had been upset at the arrival of a couple of Mojaves, Anza could imagine what enthusiasm he would have for five or six hundred Yumas![97]

Rivera made it clear that he would be forced to neglect a still serious situation at San Diego if Anza ordered one or both of them to proceed north to found San Francisco. Garcés, when he had traveled widely among the desert tribes, expressly denied that he had ever agreed with Anza that there was no danger from them. It was beyond doubt, he wrote, that the friendliness of the Colorado River tribes had kept the San Diego uprising from having consequences which would have imperiled even Anza's own expedition if they had spread. Indeed, if a Spanish garrison were not established on the Colorado, in a few years the Monterey settlements would become indefensible even with two hundred additional soldiers for the Alta California presidios.[98] Rivera was also quite concerned about Moraga's confrontation with rebel-allied hostiles in the desert mountains, although both Font and Anza seem to downplay it in their accounts.[99] Also, a year and a half later, in 1777, Rivera's replacement in Monterey, Felipe de Neve, the new governor of the Californias, reported a conspiratorial gathering of twenty-one villages at the instigation of the supposedly Christian chief of the village of *La Soledad* near Mission San Diego. This was evidently the same man whose loyalty Font and Rivera had earlier suspected.[100]

In the month that Rivera and Anza spent at San Diego, a friendship seemed to have developed, evidenced on Rivera's side by the tone of his letters after Anza had left.[101] When they parted, according to Font's description, there were "mutual regrets." (Font later deleted this from his revised account.) However, the supremely active Anza became impatient with the slow pace of Rivera's "campaign" and with his own unemployment. He recorded this impatience directly

---

[97]Letter of April 2, 1776; facsimile in Garate 2006: 226.
[98]Garcés, "Relación."
[99]It would be interesting to know more about this encounter with two hundred warriors while returning from his chase of the Spanish deserters (March 7). They had loot from the San Diego attack, a detail that might support Rivera's fears of renewed trouble; he pointed out to Anza, also, that one of Anza's own soldiers had recognized a San Diegan among the horde. The fact that Font breaks off his description abruptly, while other sources report that the soldiers charged and scattered the natives, suggests that there may have been fatalities among the latter.
[100]Provincial Records, Archive of California, C-A 22: 60. Cf. Bancroft (1886) 1963 1: 301.
[101]As Dr. F. Boneu reminds me, Rivera's signing himself as *su negro*, "your black man," in his letters to Anza does not mean that he himself was black. His descent from a Spanish Creole family seems well attested. The expression, however objectionable it may seem, was widely used in Latin America as a colloquial or more intimate equivalent of phrases similar to the polite formula "your humble obedient servant" found in eighteenth-century English. Cf. Real Academia Española 1994 s.v. negro, sense 13; Santamaría 1974 s.v. negro, sense 1; and other Latin American dictionaries.

in his journal. The same feeling is evident in other places in his daily entries, consisting of notes on the rain falling outside the door of his primitive quarters. The frustration he felt then certainly helped to animate his side of the subsequent correspondence with Rivera, who later claimed to have detected that the lieutenant colonel left San Diego with "a double motive." Rivera was presumably implying that Anza had hidden his intentions of taking the colonists north and carrying out the reconnaissance that would be the final preliminary step to founding San Francisco.[102]

Anza's intentions, whatever they were at the time, must have developed even more fully after he reached Monterey. As described in his journal (March 20), Font had a long interview with Junípero Serra, the already famous president of the California missions. Serra was reputed to have immense influence with the far-off viceroy, but he had been continually frustrated by the local commandants in his plans for new missions. In this interview, which radically altered Font's opinion of Rivera, Serra dwelled not just upon the obstacles he claimed the captain was presenting to his plans but upon what Serra thought was Rivera's thoroughly unreasonable behavior in general. Anza, who had his own closed-door sessions with Father President Serra, certainly received the same message: Serra would not be unhappy to see Rivera go. Almost immediately, Anza's letter of March 13 was dispatched to Rivera with a sergeant and seven soldiers as couriers (March 13 and footnote). The letter, which Anza completed even though he was suddenly stricken with extreme physical pain, contained a considerable number of friendly expressions. When Rivera received it on March 30, he was dismayed by the contrast between its tone and its contents, which he interpreted as a repudiation of the lieutenant colonel's earlier agreements with him. He composed his response during an entire day in solitude. The response was a long objection and an attempt to reach an understanding.

However, Rivera's attempt to maintain an adequate relationship with Anza was doomed. Captain Rivera's troubles had been multiplying in Anza's absence. There did not appear to be any increase in the threat of Indian attack which Rivera constantly invoked. Anza characterized this threat as a "straw man." According to the captain, his extraordinarily abrupt departure northward for Monterey toward the middle of April was due to a rumor that the viceroy at

---

[102] See the note to the May 3 entry. This interpretation is based on Rivera's reaction to Anza's letter of March 13 from Monterey (April 15, note) and Rivera's later claim (May 3, note) that he was surprised by Anza's move to take the colonists north, a statement that at first glance seems irreconcilable with Anza's journal entry about the consultation he requested with Rivera at San Diego (see the note to January 22). Anza's account appears to claim that he had notified the captain of his plans, but when read more closely it can be construed as saying only that he agreed to give Rivera soldiers and to wait for the outcome of the next sally against the rebels. The other details might refer to his own private resolve.

Mexico City had received sealed orders from Madrid. These orders were to be opened after it was known that San Francisco had been founded. In this light, the delay that Rivera had been proposing and which he regarded as justified and necessary now might render him culpable of disregarding orders from the highest imperial level. Both Lieutenant Moraga at Monterey and Anza in a letter to Rivera confirmed the existence of the rumor. Anza twisted the knife in the wound by writing that he had heard the story about the order the year before, while he was moving in court circles in Mexico City.

For Rivera's "disturbed head" (as he referred to it) there was a final cause. It certainly was the most serious one even though he could not publicly acknowledge it. Back in March at San Diego, the Christian "ringleader" Carlos had escaped from a guardhouse long enough to claim sanctuary inside a warehouse that was being used as a temporary church. The missionaries refused to turn Carlos over to Rivera, and what followed on March 16 was the scene described third hand by Font (April 15). The captain went into the building to remove Carlos by force. He did this over the objections of missionary Vicente Fuster and Rivera was declared excommunicated on the spot. The result was that when the garrison personnel next gathered for a religious service, most of the soldiers left the "church" rather than consent to their commandant's excommunication.[103] Whatever the personal repercussions, this situation was incompatible with order in the small local society.

All of these matters are relevant to the incident that took place on April 15 on the trail from Monterey. This is when the two commanders, accompanied by their respective soldier escorts and two missionaries, rode past each other without exchanging more than a few words. This was a scandal, of course. Two commanding officers sharing total responsibility between them for the vast, thinly held frontier and meeting in the midst of the wilds ought to have observed some protocol even if they had not had urgent and important matters to discuss and to decide. The accounts, including Rivera's, agree more closely than might be expected as to the details of the encounter (April 15, footnote). Perhaps the main difference is Rivera's point that after their initial disjointed and distracted exchange of words, Anza did nothing to help him out by continuing the conversation. Anza's management of the situation has to be admired on some level. He kept silent in the saddle while Rivera made a fool of himself and departed, saying, "Forward, everyone! And bear witness for me." Anza chose to treat the affair as a deadly insult. Following Rivera's swift completion of his visit to Monterey, soldiers and colonists were treated to the even worse scandal of the two commanders' groups leapfrogging past each other down hundreds of miles

---

[103] Geiger 1959 2: 92.

of Pacific coastline. The only communication that existed was written letters carried back and forth by overworked soldiers.

Rivera's state of mind quickly became the issue raised by Anza, Font, and Moraga. It is fairly easy to discount Rivera's own excuse, that is, the condition of his health. This could even seem to be an embarrassing attempt to imitate Anza's earlier heroism in disregarding the aftermath of kidney stone pain in order to complete his mission of the San Francisco reconnaissance. It is quite easy to understand the captain's other difficulties, such as being forced to abandon San Diego in the face of a threat he believed to be real, and attempting to repair what suddenly seemed to have been a serious dereliction of his own duty. But these do not explain why he arrived at Monterey carrying a sealed envelope addressed to the "Father President of the Missions" that he had perhaps opened (and read) on the way (April 19). Serra reported the affair of the letter to his colegio and stated that the captain had unequivocally sworn to him that he did not know the contents. Of course, opening a letter addressed to another person would be a breach of trust. In his journal, Font stresses this as much as he can. For Rivera to swear to Serra that he had not opened the envelope would be a far worse betrayal of his honor. However, according to Font's account—which also came from Serra and had been relayed through missionaries unsympathetic to the captain—Rivera tried to sidestep the issue of whether he had read the letter ("I would dare to swear that truthfully, I don't know, I don't know whether it was torn when I received it or if it got torn along the way") as he handed it over. The brief account in Serra's letter to the colegio, according to which Rivera denied under oath that he had intercepted the letter's contents, is not entirely compatible with this detailed story given by Font, whose origin he attributes to Serra. It is unfortunate, then, that a mistranslation of Font's account has potentially slandered the captain's character on this point (see the notes to April 19).

One of Rivera's traits that stands out is that he was sincerely religious, a statement that would not apply to all or perhaps even to very many of the military officers of his time. He had been enlisted as a soldier by the Jesuit missionaries of Baja California. They were an impressive group of employers. Rivera had been raised from the ranks by them to become the commandant of their little garrison. Even his written military reports have occasional evidences of his leanings toward piety.[104] At his death among the Quecháns at Yuma in 1781, Rivera's personal belongings consisted of little more than a chest holding religious

---

[104] In one document, after commenting on the war-like nature of the Santa Bárbara Channel Indians and the other natives in general, he adds, "But now their Saint Martin has come to them." Saint Martin was a Roman soldier who gave up his military career in order to undertake a mission of conversion to the inhabitants of Gaul (now France).

books.[104] Rivera wrote to the viceroy in 1776 and said that because of the circumstances, he personally did not consider himself excommunicated. However, the letter that he brought north to Serra came from the San Diego missionaries who were reporting their pronouncement against him. He must have known that the Father President's judgment of the case would determine whether the excommunication would be continued. The question affected not only his ability to command but also the fate of his soul. Perhaps from Serra's behavior during their interview, but certainly by an official notification through Father Peña after a day's tormenting delay, Rivera learned that the ban excluding him from the sacraments would be upheld. Maynard Geiger, Serra's official modern biographer, although highly sympathetic to the Father President, has been unable to conclude that the excommunication was valid.[105]

Following their meeting along the way, Lieutenant Colonel Anza's communications to the captain are more and more plainly designed to keep Rivera off balance. This can be the only explanation for the things that Anza said: that Rivera was a jumped-up common soldier whose claim to military experience was ridiculous; that Rivera ignored regulations and discipline; and that he could not even distinguish between a private letter and an official communication. On the other hand, Anza portrayed himself as someone born to the officer class and born to command. He also believed that he was someone who learned the manners and proper procedures used by aristocrats and powerful men at the court and capital. Finally, when Anza was already departing from the settlements and could probably not have been overtaken even by someone riding hard after him, he sent back a letter referring to his forbearance in not taking on Rivera physically, "at which you would undoubtedly have been the loser." If this implicit invitation to violence had expressed Anza's true feelings, it would be a serious stain on his character according to the values of that era. For it was the worst sort of cowardice to challenge a rival under circumstances which made it all but impossible to actually "come to blows" (as Font and others say they feared) or fight a duel (the forbidden word that they avoid mentioning). But Anza's purpose was more devious than this.

Thus, Rivera's final reaction to all of these assaults by message is a bewildered "For God's sake, what do you want from me?" But in his correspondence with the viceroy, in which he asks the same question about Anza's purpose, he also shows he knows that that officer's real concern is how matters will play out politically in Mexico City. And the tone of Rivera's letter indicates that he really

---

[105] Geiger 1959 2: 94–98, especially 97: "For that reason alone [the relationship of Spanish state and Church law, leaving aside other considerations], Rivera probably did not incur the excommunication."

does not care. In fact, the letter ends with what Anza had wanted from him—a request to be retired.[106]

It is undeniable that Font's record misrepresents the tone and some of the content of Rivera's correspondence with the lieutenant colonel. The venom (*veneno*) and the self-satisfaction that Font claims to detect, not just in the letters but everywhere in the captain's attitude and behavior, are simply absent from the original documents (see the notes to April 15, April 21 [twice], April 22, and May 3). It is unclear whether Font's account is based on his actually having read all the messages. We only know that Anza showed him one of his letters to Rivera (March 13). It is also possible that he was relying upon what Anza told him regarding the contents of the rest of the correspondence. In any event, misrepresentations are presented as facts. Font's personal responsibility for his immoderate partisanship overrides any question of what he actually knew or what Anza did or did not tell him.

No matter how much Anza exaggerated his low opinion of Rivera for the purposes of his calculated attack, he certainly regarded Rivera as unfit to command. Font's complaints that the captain was lax in command and "too fond of his soldiers" surely reflects the point of view of Anza, who believed that "an immense distance" must separate the officer from the common soldier.[107] Font's criticism does gain some support from the journal of a naval officer named Francisco Mourelle who visited San Diego in 1777 after Rivera's departure. Mourelle recorded that discipline was improving under Neve, the new governor, whereas before, it had been extremely lax.[108] But one has to take into account Rivera's problem of an impossible lack of personnel, so that he had to tolerate even the malefactor Camacho. Quite inconsistently, one item in Anza's long bill of complaints against Rivera accuses him of commanding "despotically." This was surely one of the grab bag of charges that Junípero Serra supplied to Anza for the purpose. Rivera's simple but adequate response was that he was sure that Anza commanded his own Sonora presidio in the same way.[109]

Anza's wider purpose was unspoken but can be deduced from the promises that Font describes him as making to natives at San Luis Obispo and at Yuma. In substance, Anza promised that he would soon return as the purveyor of Spanish favors and military support. With obvious hypocrisy, Font adds that he does not know what Anza meant. But it could only have been that Anza expected to become the commandant of the entire expanding northwestern frontier of New

---

[106]Rivera y Moncada to the viceroy, May 2, 1776, Huntington Library.
[107]Garate 2006: 106–107, 198, 245.
[108]Mexico, Archivo General y Público, Secretaría del Virreinato, Historia, Tomo 35, fols. 87–88.
[109]Garate 2006: 138, 274 (not 139).

Spain, once Rivera was removed and his own basis of power in Sonora and on the Colorado had been newly secured. Later, as the expedition ended, Font in his journal expressed disillusionment when the lieutenant colonel, having gotten all the use out of him that he could in the campaign against Rivera, abruptly dropped him. Font's journal records no other personal regrets, unless they are implicit in the tone of relief when he says the Anza party "tossed away the key" of the disagreements with Rivera on departing from California. Meanwhile, the colonists they had brought were still waiting for word to go on to their final destination.

Aftermaths

At the end of the expedition, Pedro Font retired from the Sonoran capital to the nearby mission of Ures. There, during three weeks, he drastically shortened his journal for official use. During another three weeks, he finished its illustrations and also wrote the first of his long and increasingly acerbic letters to the guardian of Querétaro colegio. In these letters he described the besieged condition of the province and branded the plan to advance the missions to the Colorado as impossible. A week later, he arrived at his original southern mission station of San José de Pimas. Six weeks after that, he turned it over to clergy from a different Franciscan administration. He joined eight other displaced missionaries from the Pimería Baja and traveled northward with them to the Apache-besieged Pimería Alta. He says his heart was already skipping beats from fear. On their arrival, the new missionaries were received by the friars at Mission San Ignacio and distributed among the surrounding stations as auxiliary clergy. Font spent two and a half weeks at Magdalena until the November 16 attack. By the end of November he was staying with five other displaced friars at the small settlement of Imuris, which was close enough to San Ignacio for him and his colleagues there to begin preparing the report and map of Francisco Garcés's wanderings. The early entries of the Garcés "journal" from Tubac as far as the Colorado are basically a summary of Font's shortened journal. Garcés was worried that Font's removal early in 1777 to the more isolated mission of Tubutama would leave the map undone, but in fact it was there that he completed it by adding the other padre's routes onto a map of the Anza expedition that he had already compiled at Ures. The result was a general map that was to have considerable influence on future geographers.

Garcés had succeeded in traveling most of the route that he and Anza hoped to discover. But what he described on his return to Sonora was a series of difficulties. The southern Sierra Nevada constituted a significant mountain barrier.

Then the native trade route leading from the Santa Bárbara Channel by way of the Mojave River and Desert over to the Colorado was especially difficult. There were enmities among numerous newly discovered native peoples. Finally, the way eastward from the Colorado across modern northern Arizona skirted "horrible canyons." At the bottom of one canyon, surprisingly peaceful Apaches (Havasupai) grew every sort of crop except wheat. Then, traveling across uplands where other "Apaches" (Navajo) herded sheep, Garcés came finally to the "Moqui" (Hopi) pueblo. Formally speaking, this was the westernmost pueblo of New Mexico, although it was closed to all Christians and particularly to Spanish Franciscan missionaries. After huddling for two nights in a corner between ranges of stone dwellings, the missionary heard a noise of music and dancing from an approaching crowd who proceeded, literally, to drum him out of town. Fortunately, he still had his mule for the long return through all the tribes to Sonora. There, as Font notes in his journal and letters, his colleagues had been in serious doubts of his survival.[110]

Garcés's reluctant conclusion from his travels was that the wished-for route from Monterey to the Colorado, and from there to New Mexico, was impractical unless a number of Spanish settlements were established along the way. Although a colleague of his did boast that Garcés had been the first Spaniard to have visited both provinces, Monterey (Alta California) and New Mexico, there was no immediate advantage to be gained from the routes he discovered.[111] As a result, a generation later the great geographer Alexander von Humboldt was still ignorant of the barriers of the Grand Canyon and the Sierra Nevada which Garcés had encountered. Humboldt marveled that "no traveler up until now has come from New Mexico to the Alta California coast" and that the Spanish nation, which had explored and conquered so much of the world in the sixteenth century, had been "unable, in two centuries, to find an overland road in New Spain between Taos and the harbor of Monterey."[112]

Garcés continued to be the chief spokesman for the advance of the colegio's missions to the Colorado, "running roughshod over everything," as he later expressed it, in order to get beyond Sonora.[113] Font, as spokesman for the contrary view, let minatory letters to the colegio flow from his pen while complaining rather contradictorily that the Querétaro authorities were never going to listen to him. This frustration seems to have led him to attempt a direct

---

[110]Garcés, "Relación." Cf. the corresponding part of the "journal" (Galvin 1967, 1971), a document which provides more details and also some slightly different points of view, since it was intended for the government.
[111]Gómez Canedo 1971: 79.
[112]Humboldt (1811) 1971 I: 316–17.
[113]"Si no hubiéramos atropellado con todo para salir de la provincia...." Civezza Collection, Legajo 201.2.

address to the Minister of the Indies in Madrid, and he no doubt warned of the threatened collapse of the frontier. Of course this was without effect.[114] At this period, the trauma of the November atrocity had not left Font. Confined by fear of attack to a single building and enclosure whose exact dimensions he gives with the same compulsiveness that makes his expedition journal so valuable, he writes that his life is a "drawn-out death" and that his heart still skips a beat at the slightest surprise. In another letter, he asks permission to retire before he is killed, since he has no valid missionary assignment to justify his death and consider it martyrdom.[115] It had been planned for Fathers Pedro Font and Juan Díaz (who had been with the first Anza expedition) to travel all the way to Querétaro to report personally on the explorations, but according to Font's last letter, the colegio authorities proved unwilling to support the trip. By that point, his relations with his superiors had deteriorated so far that he no longer hoped to retire there, since he felt he would be unwelcome at the colegio. Perhaps he had not been particularly comfortable there even before he came to Sonora.

While the missionaries prepared their reports, Anza delayed in Sonora to manage campaigns against the Apaches and Seris. Eventually, he proceeded triumphantly to Mexico City to introduce to the viceroy his Quechán ally Palma, and also, if all of the plans were successfully carried out, the Mission San Luis Obispo boy Pedrito (Pedro Regalado Cayuelas), who did at least return to live in California with the full status of a Spanish subject.[116]

Turning to Rivera, after his arrival at Monterey in April 1776 the captain ordered Lieutenant Moraga to go north with the settlers to begin the new settlement and fort. With this accomplished, the captain finally, if reluctantly, had become directly responsible for the founding of San Francisco. He received little credit for it then or since.[117] Later, in reporting on the matter to the viceroy, Rivera asserted in a stiff tone that had he received the direct order for the founding in time, he would have obeyed it immediately.[118] At the end of 1776, Rivera finally went all the way north and either chose or assented to the friars' choice of a site for Santa Clara, the second northern mission, before making his reconnaissance of the San Joaquín along with Moraga.

---

[114]This is probably the source of Barbastro's quickly withdrawn statement that Font had been in correspondence with Minister Gálvez. The representation is said to exist in the Ignacio Abbad Collection at the cathedral of Barbastro, Huesca province, Spain. I have been unable to verify the fact.

[115]Brown 2006: 87, 103; cf. Matson 1975: 277.

[116]For events in the later life of Pedro Regalado Cayuelas after his return to California, see the note to April 22.

[117]April 1776 (first of three of that date in Rivera's docket). Garate 2006: 78–81; facsimile 234; to viceroy, May 1, 1776, Garate 2006: 102–103, 158–60.

[118]Letter of March 2, 1777: "quedo instruido de lo que debiera haber practicado, que si lo hubiera advertido puntual, habría seguido la observación." Rivera y Moncada Papers.

High officialdom duly notified both Anza and Rivera of the viceroy's displeasure over their disagreements. Anza was reprimanded for leaving the province before completing his orders for founding San Francisco. Even though Rivera was sent back as commandant to his long-missed Loreto in Baja California, he apparently never saw his pay again. His family on the mainland had to be supported by a relative. At the end of the decade, possibly as a reparation or redemption, the government offered him the task of managing preparations for the new settlement of Los Angeles. Like Anza six years earlier, Rivera recruited settlers in Sinaloa and Sonora and brought them safely across the desert, past the new Spanish settlements at Yuma, to the coast. But in the immediate aftermath, both he and Garcés were killed in the Quechán rebellion.

Anza was removed from the immediate Sonora scene. However, he was not assigned, as he had hoped, to lead the advance of Spanish power into the northwest. Rather, he was appointed governor of New Mexico. Talk of finding a new route to California had dwindled into a mere pretext for his transfer to Santa Fe where his frontier military skills were exercised against the Comanches on the high plains. Meanwhile, he was forced to observe his old plans for Spanish expansion being mishandled by a new governmental entity independent of the viceroy. The treaties Anza had arranged between the native groups began to unravel and the new Colorado settlements were destroyed. Then, after some slight success in settling down the Apaches, there followed decades of political chaos in the former Spanish colony and the border tribes fell back into mutual hostilities and decimation from disease.

Font never did return to Querétaro in his lifetime. Perhaps his distinctive voice in history should be thought of as simply fading away into exile like that of the Biblical prophet Jeremiah in Egypt. The rest of his life in Sonora can be followed only in scattered entries in the registers of the churches that he served. Early in 1779 he was functioning as a parish minister at the *Cieneguilla* mining camp. A few years earlier, as a guest there, he had seen "how the Indians take out the gold." He was now burying and no doubt baptizing and marrying those same Yaqui and O'odham miners.[119] Then, through most of 1780 and 1781, Font served the mixed native and Spanish settlement of *El Pitiqui*, now *Pitiquito*, in the Altar Valley.[120]

A document dated some two decades later credits Font and a fellow missionary friar (who was soon to die in the Quechán rebellion) with building the stone church which still stands at Pitiquito.[121] As early as 1793, the building was

---

[119]Garate 2000—: Event IDs 9416–19, 9264, 8745–46.
[120]Garate 2000—: Event IDs 9264, 8745–46, 9259, 9266, 7801, 4537.
[121]Kessel 1976: 100, note 22.

Figure 4. The church at Pitiquito. By Hazel Fontana.
Courtesy of the Southwestern Mission Research Center, Tucson.

mentioned in first place among three stone and masonry frontier churches that the Queretarans had built, with "sword in one hand for fighting the enemy, and mason's trowel in the other."[122] Since Font was a capable mathematician who in California had even drawn up a design for the mission church and buildings at San Gabriel (May 4), the Pitiquito building can probably be regarded as his final statement.[123] The church completely eschews the lavish and rather cramped

---

[122] Officer et al. 1996: 66. Of course this does not mean that the missionaries physically wielded swords.

[123] That is, final unless the existing interior wall paintings should prove to have some connection with Font's design, as has been imaginatively speculated (Perry 2004). These remarkable dry frescoes (or tempera paintings—Giffords 2007: 425), discovered some forty years ago, commence near the church door with a much larger than life-sized Death standing below the words of the handwriting on the wall ("Thou art weighed in the balance and found wanting . . ."), and they lead, past an equally gigantic Mary as Queen of Heaven, toward the altar, near which, along with angels and other religious and ornamental motifs, there is a Lucifer wreathed with a serpent. (Cf., from another tradition, "Then I saw that there is a way to hell, even from the gates of Heaven": John Bunyan, *The Pilgrim's Progress*, First Part *ad finem*.) These wall pictures cannot be attributed to Font's time since they overlie other, unrecovered paintings that are presumed to have entirely different subjects (Schuetz-Miller 2000: 795). Until the time comes when these are revealed, it is still possible to be reminded of Font's skills as a draftsman and his minatory and sometimes morbid mindset. An unsuspecting twentieth-century congregation was horrified when the skeleton suddenly began to show through the covering whitewash (Officer et al. 1996: 72).

Baroque ornamentation that was greatly admired then and now. Such a style is found in the architectural works of Font's fellow Queretaran builders at nearby *Caborca*, at San Xavier, and elsewhere. But Pitiquito's plan is small though spacious. Its broad barrel vault and well-lit interior is matched by the modest adornment around the main door. This bit of decoration alludes architecturally to the more modern neo-classical style and is far better handled than the superficial attempts that were made at other churches on the frontier to imitate the style that was becoming standard in the far-off colonial capital of Mexico City.

The date of Font's death remains uncertain. It is usually given as September 6, 1781, although there is a record of his conducting a baptism two days later on September 8.[124] If somewhere there is a surviving parish register that contains his death entry, then that register has not turned up yet. But it appears certain that Font, at forty-three years of age, outlived only by a few weeks the slayings of his recent fellow-minister Moreno and of many others, including his old companions in a great enterprise, Francisco Garcés, Sebastián Taraval, and Juan Díaz. The Quechán rebellion was the same debacle that he had been warning against, over and over again.

Font's Legacy: The Maps

Font's reputation in his own century and that which would follow was mostly identified with his graphic works. Almost every item that he is known to have drawn has been preserved in one repository or another.[125] His overall map of the Anza expedition's routes, finished in two copies along with the shortened text in 1776 at Ures, has already been mentioned, as has the particular map of the Monterey–San Francisco reconnaissance.[126] However, his most influential work was the map in which he added Garcés's itineraries in the northern interior.[127] Garcés's *"Advertencias previas"* to his own journal explain that he directly oversaw Font's work so that the map did not reflect only the written record.[128] Three copies of the Font-Garcés map were sent with the Garcés journal to Querétaro at the beginning of 1777, along with Garcés's plea that two of the three map

---

[124]Garate 2000–: Event ID 4537. A printed text (Matson and Fontana 1977: 145) has Font baptizing on October 8, 1781. This may however be a duplication of the September date.

[125]Wagner's list of Font's maps (Wagner [1937] 1999: 171, 344) does not distinguish between the general expedition map and the Font–Garcés map. The engraved map was not directly known to Wagner.

[126]Mexico City, Archivo General y Público de la Nación, Secretaría del Virreinato, Historia Tomo 24; and accompanying the final text of the journal. Reproduced here, figure 5. The inferior version reproduced in Hayes 2007: 42 appears not to be Font's own work but a copy made for the naval explorer Felipe Bauzá and later taken by him to London during the Napoleonic wars. Its original is clearly the genuine map by Font now found in the Spanish archives. For a reproduction of the latter see Brown 2006: 167.

[127]Wagner (1937) 1999: no. 658.

[128]Translated, Galvin 1967: 2.

copies should be remitted to the Mexico City government.[129] According to Barbastro's notes the colegio later supplied both the map and the journal to Teodoro de Croix, the new commandant general of the north, when he visited Querétaro. These same notes contain a canceled statement—a "No" written opposite it in the margin—that Font himself had sent his journal (obviously the shortened text) along with his general map to Minister of the Indies, José de Gálvez, who replied to him with thanks. Barbastro must have been thinking of Font's known representation to Gálvez, which indeed might have been originally accompanied by the map. If the minister answered, the reply is not known, but at least two copies of the Font–Garcés map did reach the archives in Spain.[130]

In 1777 the local provincial government must have asked Font for a general map of the northwestern provinces, since he produced one. According to the title he gave, it used geographical information from Governor Francisco Antonio Crespo as well as the knowledge gained by himself and Garcés.[131] According to Father Barbastro, this Sonora map's accuracy was highly praised by the engineers Manuel Mascaró and Jerónimo de la Rocha.[132] In the mid-nineteenth century, the original form of the Font–Garcés map was known to and copied for the use of the North American surveyors and engineers who were engaged in mapping the international boundary and the Southwest.[133]

The most remarkable form of the general map, however, is an engraving dated at Mexico City in 1781, the apparent year of Font's death (fig. 6).[134] Humboldt referred to it two decades later, and at least three separate prints still exist, which indicates that it must have had some circulation. Henry Wagner speculated that this engraving, along with two engraved maps of the California coast dated in the same year, was intended for some never-achieved publication dealing with sea voyages as well as land explorations.[135] There are indeed hints that such a publication was planned by Brigadier General Miguel Costansó.[136] However, it is just as likely that the Font–Garcés map was commissioned by the Querétaro colegio for a planned publication of the travels of Garcés and Font. But such a publication was presumably derailed by the destruction of the Colorado missions that same year. Neither the Costansó nor Querétaro possibility is ruled out by

---

[129] Brown 2006: 94, 105, cf. Matson 1975: 267, 279; Garcés, "Cartas," 201.19. Cf. Wagner (1937) 1999: no. 655.
[130] Chapman 1916 opposite 364 and 366 reproduces the two manuscript copies.
[131] Wagner (1937) 1999, no. 657. Reproduced from a copy, Galvin 1967: facing 102. Crespo was the highly active, although interim, governor until later in 1777.
[132] Gómez Canedo 1971: 51.
[133] The copy by Edward O. Ord is reproduced in Coues 1900 1: frontispiece.
[134] Reproduced in color, Hayes 2007: 42, along with other Font maps (see above).
[135] Wagner (1937) 1999: 196. It is not necessarily significant, however, that the plates of all three maps were made by the important Mexico City engraver Manuel Villavicencio.
[136] Brown 2001: 117, 128.

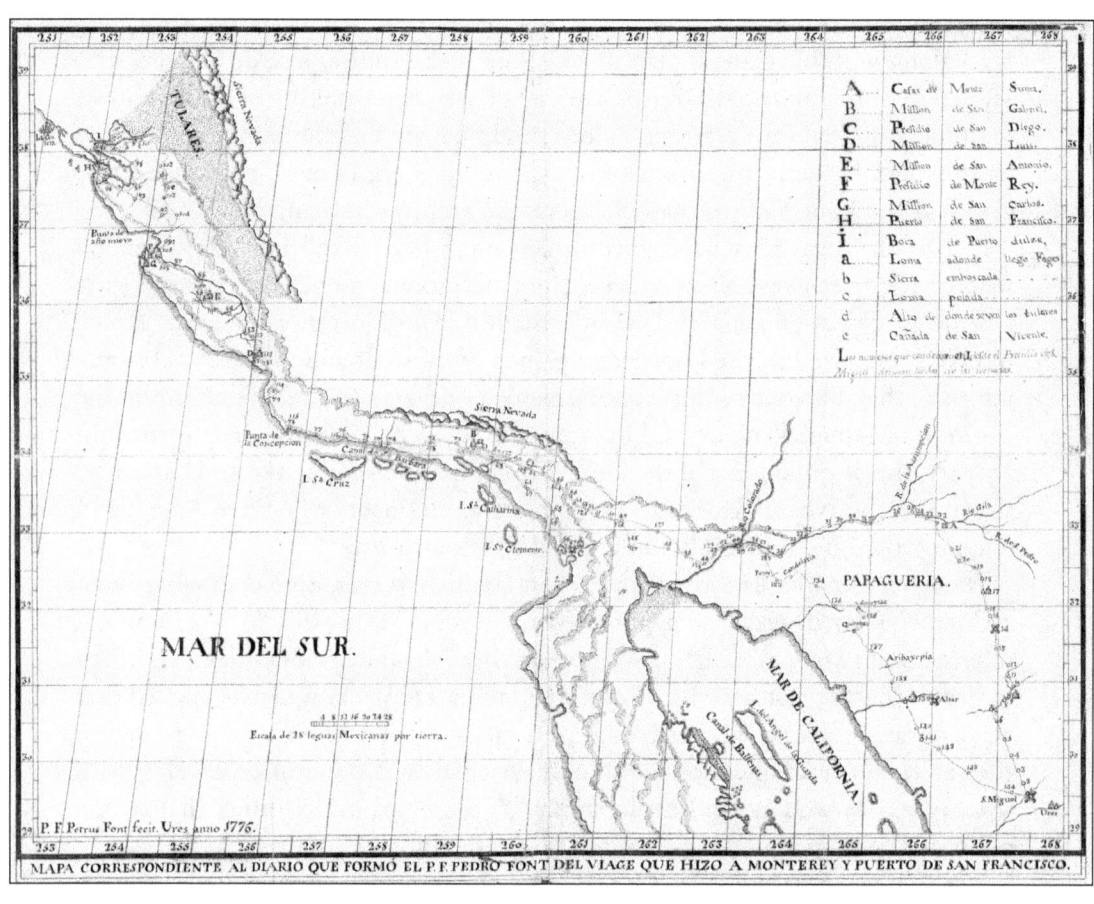

Figure 5. Map corresponding to the journal that Father Fray Pedro Font kept of his journey to Monterey and the port of San Francisco, 1776. Font's general map. *Reproduced courtesy of the John Carter Brown Library at Brown University.*

the fact that the engraved version reaches westward only to Mission San Antonio and omits Monterey and San Francisco Bay.

If the general map was the most influential example of Font's graphic work, the rather simple ground plan of the Casa Grande ("Moctezuma's Palace" as it was sometimes called then and since), along with its accompanying description in the journal, had the most varied later history. Exemplars of the Casa Grande drawing and of the plan of the mouth of San Francisco Bay accompanied Font's fair-copied manuscript of the shortened text.[137] Another original pair of the same drawings, very likely removed by Font himself from his draft of the shortened text, is inserted in the Querétaro calligraphic copy paid for by the municipality of his home colegio. In order to accompany his final text, Font later redrew both plans, with the map of San Francisco Bay showing some minor revisions.[138] In the early nineteenth century, the calligraphic manuscript's original Casa Grande plan had pencil notes of instructions for a woodcut added to it in an English hand. This was probably for the enormous Lord Kingsborough project concerning Mexican antiquities even though it does not seem to appear in the published volumes.[139] During the same period the Casa Grande description was translated in the French travel book compilations of Ternaux-Compans. As Coues pointed out, North American topographers used information from this source during and after the Mexican War.[140]

Font's Legacy: The Field Text

As already indicated in the preface, the main distinction of this present new translation is the use of material from the "field text" by Font that recently came to light in the Franciscan Historical Archive in Rome.[141] The manuscript is referred to in Font's two later texts as being the draft (*borrador*) that he wrote during the expedition. He describes it as consisting of twenty *pliegos*, that is, gatherings made up of two sheets of *papel común* folded into four folios (eight

---

[137] These are reproduced from the Rome manuscript in Soto Pérez 1998 2: 1293.

[138] The revised version moves Yerba Buena Island farther away from what evidently was intended to be Hunter's Point. It also does not clearly mark the sand district on the western side of the peninsula, as the earlier version does.

[139] Kingsborough 1830–1848.

[140] Coues 1900 1: 93; for information about other uses, see, for instance, Fort Sutter Papers, Huntington Library, volume 32, MS no. 137: "Notice of the Great House (Casa Grande) called that of Montezuma. . . . This notice is extracted from a journal . . . by the Father Pedro Font, of the college of Santa Cruz de Querétaro." The handwriting of one of the Kern brothers, Edward M. or Richard (d. 1853), seems to be scrawled upon the copy, which apparently is the one also used by the Mexican Boundary Commission (Bartlett 1854 2: 278–80).

[141] For the locations of the three texts on which this edition is based, see under Font, Pedro in the Manuscripts and Archival Sources section of the bibliography.

pages) apiece.[142] The field (Rome) text does in fact consist of eighty folios, and it is signed and dated on the June 2, 1776, the day of Font's arrival back in Sonora. The printed form in Father Soto Pérez's monumental edition of early California materials does not indicate the many authorial changes that were made in the text, between lines, and in the margins.[143] These corrections and additions show that the document was not written very continuously, although the truncation of some entries at the end, and the looser handwriting there, probably do reflect the exhaustion of the final gallop homeward across Sonora.

Despite Font's later description of it as "the journal or draft that I kept writing on the way," it is clear that he also added and removed pages in his work, though at present it would only be possible to ascertain the precise makeup of the document by unbinding it. Major portions of the manuscript seem to have been laid out for entries long before their text was actually written, so that the writing becomes crowded; the frequent thrust-in alterations of the spaced-out original marginal notations of league distances point in the same direction.[144] Occasional entries are dated earlier than events to which they refer. For example, at a position immediately following the introduction to a table under October 22, and occupying the verso (back) of folio 181 and the recto (front) of folio 182, appear the description and plan of the "Casa Grande de Moctezuma" which Font visited on October 31. This position must indicate that at least the following list of personnel and equipment and all the entries through October 31 were not copied into the manuscript before November. Again, under December 7, the remark about presents given to the Halchidhoma refers to events that Font could not have learned of until considerably later. This indicates that it is also one of the three cases (there is another involving the April 13 entry) in which portions of the field text could only have been written after the apparent date. Thus, Font may have written and inserted the whole of his long description of the Quechán nation quite some time after he had ended the visit there, perhaps even after his second visit. His usual procedure in writing the field text was to leave physical room for such additions, but in this particular case, manuscript clues as to his procedure are lacking.

Font's Legacy: The Shortened Text

A much shortened text of Font's account, although still in the form of a journal, exists not only in finished form but also in a preliminary draft copy, which was

---

[142] A note in the draft of the shortened text refers to "the general journal," apparently meaning the field text.
[143] Soto Pérez 1998 2: 1027–192.
[144] For example, the note to "I was left without learning it," April 13.

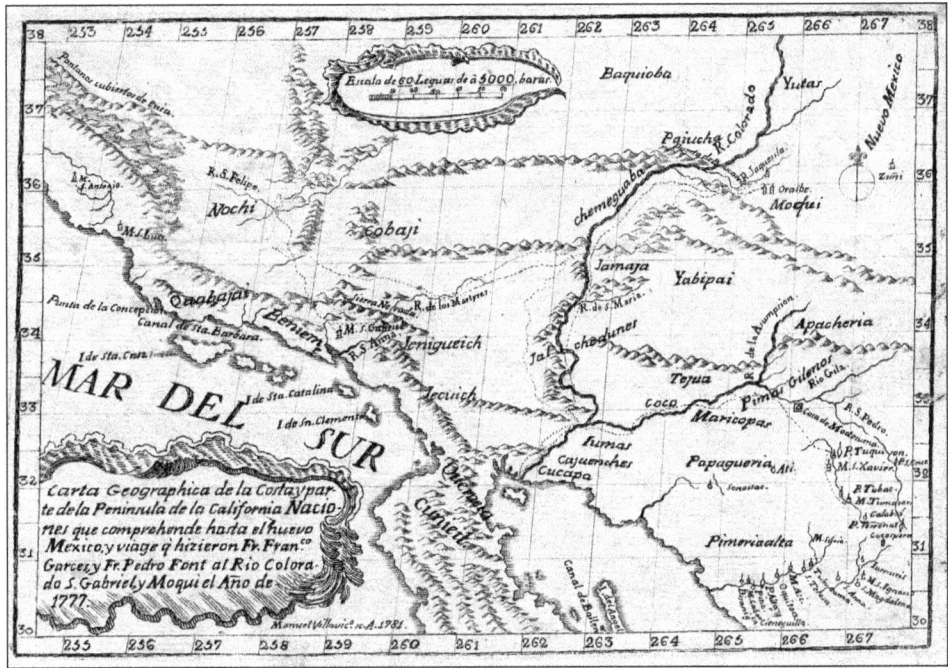

Figure 6. Geographical map of the coast and part of the peninsula of California, tribes in the area as far as New Mexico, and a journey made by Fray Francisco Garcés and Fray Pedro Font to the Colorado River, San Gabriel, and El Moqui in 1777. Engraving by Manuel Villavicencio, 1781. *Courtesy of University of Arizona Library Special Collections, Tucson.*

signed and dated at Ures on June 23, 1776. This manuscript, now owned by the University of California, Berkeley, is a very rough one and it is loosely written. However, it is not prior to the Rome field draft—as has mistakenly been thought—since it is not based on the original form of the field text but on that manuscript's state after extensive corrections had been made.[145] The shortened text is full of its own further corrections and additions, and, despite its relative brevity, many of these are changes from the words of the field text, in the direction of the wording found in the final text. A number of Font's inlaid, essay-like discussions, such as those on the Quechán and Kohuana natives, on San Francisco Bay, and on other topics, also first occur in this shortened draft manuscript.

A cleanly written holograph manuscript is now in the central archive of the Franciscan Order. It also bears the June 23 date. Plainly, it constitutes a fair-

---

[145] A glance at any part of the table of Days' Marches, following the translation, will prove this. There are countless further examples in the texts.

copied version of the messy draft just described.[146] This fresh text must be the one that Font sent to his colegio at Querétaro, along with a cover letter dated July 18, 1776, in which he explained that the delay from June to July was due to his work in making the clean copy of the shortened journal and its map.[147] Thereafter, despite Font's complaints about others' neglect of his ideas, he and his superiors proved themselves gifted as publicists, since other closely contemporary copies exist or have existed, in the forms of the calligraphic manuscript from Querétaro (now at Berkeley); one copy in the Mexican national archive; another at the Universidad Nacional Autónoma de Mexico; one reportedly in the cathedral library of Barbastro in northern Spain; and perhaps even one that reached early-day California.

Oddly, in more recent times it was the rough draft copy of the shortened text which had the more conspicuous history. According to Frederick Teggart, who was the manuscript's early twentieth-century editor, the draft and the calligraphic manuscript had "formed part of the materials gathered by General H. W. Halleck for his unfinished *History of California*."[148] It seems possible that an English translation was made for Halleck before he left California to become President Lincoln's chief of staff in the Civil War, since such a manuscript circulated in the 1850's and later and was partly published in San Francisco in 1877. This was when it was acquired by Hubert Howe Bancroft.[149] The original Spanish manuscripts owned by Halleck also came eventually to The Bancroft Library at the University of California, Berkeley by means of another private collection.

Despite its great accuracy, Teggart's edition (1913) of the Berkeley draft of the shortened text was like other printings of Font's texts, in that it marked rather few of the author's changes and additions as being such. Teggart, however, correctly deduced from such details that the draft manuscript could not

---

[146]Franciscan Historical Archive M/34, Mexico Missiones, Relationes et Epistolae, fol. 183r–201v. Title page plus 18 folios, i.e. nine *pliegos* of text. Font's map of the San Francisco harbor mouth is reproduced from this manuscript by Soto Pérez (1998 2: 1293)

[147]Brown 2006: 91, 94.

[148]Teggart 1913: 4–5. An anecdote in Angustias de la Guerra Ord's *Ocurrencias* (Beebe and Senkewicz 2006: 228–29) illustrates Halleck's forcible methods of collecting historical material during the Mexican War. Halleck used his position in the military government to borrow and not return to her family an old map that originally belonged to Mission San Carlos. The map is fantastically described as having been drawn by the Jesuit, Juan María de Salvatierra, and as already showing the gold deposits that were later discovered by North Americans (always a sore point with Californios). Possibly this was one of Font's maps, either the one left with Serra at Mission San Carlos in 1776 (April 11), or else (and possibly identical with that one) from a manuscript of the shortened journal text that seems to have left some trace in the early California archives.

[149]Cerruti 1954: 95 relates how he removed the English-language manuscript from the possession of an old Californio citizen of San José. Reference courtesy of G. Smestad; for Bancroft's association with it, see Bancroft (1886) 1963: 259 note. The Querétaro manuscripts from which the original was copied had evidently already been taken to the Franciscan colegio of Guadalajara.

be identified with the original field text draft which Font had mentioned in two of his texts. This false assumption had been made by the two chief scholars who dealt with the manuscript before Teggart, George Davidson (1907) and Zoeth Eldredge (1912). They based their conclusion merely upon the messiness of the draft manuscript, with an apparent neglect or misunderstanding of its clear statement that it had been taken or copied (*sacado*) from an already existing draft field text.[150] When Herbert Bolton published an independent translation of the shortened version and, separately, a full translation of the final version with each translation containing extremely limited cross-references to the other text, the erroneous conclusion as to Font's method of composition was adopted, repeated, and remained unchallenged until Father José Luis Soto Pérez (1998) published the true draft text along with an accurate description of the textual relationships.[151] This new understanding resolves many problems. Not least, it restores confidence in parts of Font's account, since one no longer has to believe that so many of the descriptions in his final text were composed months or a year later and from memory. At the same time, the relationship between the versions makes it possible to discover how many of his complaints and other personal discussions were, in fact, added later on. The present edition uses a difference in type size to make a distinction between descriptions that evidently are original, and digressive passages that are found solely in the author's later text.

Font's Legacy: The Final Text

This best-known version of Font's narrative has been called, variously, the "complete," "private (*íntimo*)," or "expanded" journal, designations influenced by the mistaken interpretation of textual relationships that has just been described. The manuscript is best referred to simply as "the final text." Containing 336 pages, it is dated considerably later than the other texts: Font signed it at Mission Tubutama on May 11, 1777. There are indications that most of it was completed as early as September 1776, which might suggest that after the November attack at Magdalena and the continuing personal trauma, which in his letters Font describes himself as suffering, had impeded his literary work. However, other explanations are also possible (May 11 and June 2, notes).

Despite Font's acknowledgment, in a letter, that his handwriting was rather ugly even though legible, this text is much less of a private journal or an official

---

[150]Thus, the final text's similar mention of a field draft was taken as referring to this draft of the shortened text. The coincidental fact that the number of folios in the shortened version (forty) could be interpreted as corresponding to the twenty gatherings (*pliegos*) that Font reported for his original field draft might have played a part.

[151]Bolton 1930 3: 201–307, and vol. 4.

report than it is a carefully and clearly written book. It has page numbers rather than foliation and additional endnote reference numbers in the text, although these are found only on the early pages, and the notes which Font must have intended at first to provide are entirely missing. The highly polished nature of this text raises the question of what his purpose was in writing it. A book publication would have been a dubious project in the secretive Spanish Empire of that time. However, changes were rapidly taking place in the political and cultural atmosphere. A decade and a half later, when the California missionary Luis Sales published his own account in Spain, he was able to do so with only minor official repercussions. Possibly, Font's enormous drive toward self-expression made him give his work the best treatment that he could conceive, just for whatever use his colleagues or later generations could find for it. In the end, a summary based upon the journals was published a few years after his death in a history of his colegio.[152] Only in the twentieth century was it recognized that the long final record of the Anza expedition was a significant work in the literature of travel and exploration.

In the document's colophon, Font explains that this final text replicates his long, original draft journal, but that it contains various "materials and clarifications" which he had been able to add. Font's additions to his original account include, somewhat notoriously, those in which he expressed his personal and often unfavorable views of other persons, including the expedition's commander. In fact, however, many details that had been recorded in the long draft were omitted from the rewritten final version in spite of Font's general disclaimer. Presumably, this was because they seemed less important than or inconsistent with the after-the-fact personal reflections which the author was introducing in his final text. At the same time, the final text does contain many descriptive details that complement those preserved in the field text. It is an open question to what extent these additions come from the author's original field notes (for whose existence there is abundant evidence), or from his memory; no doubt he drew on both.

What is known about the manuscript's later history is that toward the end of the nineteenth century it was in the possession of Dr. Nicolás León, a well-known physician, writer, bibliophile, and collector of materials relating to his part of Mexico; and that from him it came to the John Carter Brown Library of Providence, Rhode Island, where it remains.[153] A handwritten transcript of the

---

[152]Arricivita 1792: 461–69.

[153]A possible clue to its earlier survival is that at the Querétaro colegio, shortly before its suppression, Herbert Bolton was informed by the Guardian that "there was in the library not long ago a manuscript copy of the diary of Father Font's expedition to California" that could no longer be found (Bolton 1913: 393). León is said to have owned another manuscript of a Font journal, which he retained; possibly this is the second-hand copy of the shortened version, without drawings, that now belongs to the UNAM, Mexico City.

manuscript was made in the 1890's and used by scholars such as Elliott Coues of the Smithsonian Institution. Before his death in 1899, Coues had planned a published translation. The handwritten copy was turned into a typed text at the instigation of Charles Fletcher Lummis and others in the following decade. This typed transcript, which is at three removes from the original manuscript, is now in the Los Angeles Public Library. It is the basis for recent printed and on-line publications of Font's final text. The well-received English translation published by Herbert Bolton in two forms (Bolton 1930d, 1931), which is still in print, was evidently based on photographs of the original manuscript. The Bolton edition is mostly a careful work, if marred by some squeamishness on the translator's part so that Font's expressions such as "farts" became rendered as "filthy habits" and some of his frank descriptions of the Quechán people were not translated but left in Spanish. The translation was apparently done by Nellie Van de Grift Sánchez, who probably should not be blamed for the inaccurate rendering that (correctly or not) dishonors Captain Rivera.[154]

This Edition

The goal of the present edition is to provide a unified translation of Father Pedro Font's various versions of his account, incorporating all of the information that he found worth recording. This involves combining as well as choosing between the multitude of additions, corrections, and deletions that the author worked through on the way to composing his final manuscript. Wherever certain passages in the final version evidently were added in hindsight, they are presented in a smaller type size, using as a basis for the distinction either the final version's own wording or the combined evidence of the field draft and the shortened version. Where the field draft and the final version are nearly identical, the field draft's expressions like "now" and "here" are preferred to the rewritten final version's backward-looking "then" and "there." In the shortened text of his journal, Font introduced a strict format for his daily entries, starting with an abbreviated statement of the day's march and going on to other details. This format was partly kept in the final text, but so inconsistently that in order to incorporate the field text's extra details it has usually proved desirable to keep the original organization of an entry.

Font's reports of daily times, distances, bearings, and observed latitudes are a special problem, since they were changed so many times within and between the versions. In this translation, the field text's figures for hours of departure

---

[154]The translation is much better, both stylistically and in other respects, than that of the 1775–1776 Anza journal published in Bolton 1930 vol. 3, which fairly often misconstrues meanings.

and arrival are used in preference to those in the final text, where they have been rounded off. Similarly, the less accurate calculations of latitude reported in the field text as being made from the Gasco tables are entirely omitted here, as they were in Font's later versions. On the other hand, the text presented here generally does employ the field draft's originally estimated bearings and courses for the march. The basic reason for preferring these pristine data was discussed above: they are less influenced by Font's subsequent graphic recalculations which often are faulty. A table titled "The Day's Marches" is provided, following the translation, in order to give in a concentrated form all of the variant expressions of directions and distance that are found in the various manuscripts as well as in the parallel journal of the expedition's commander. Modern place name identifications for the expedition's camp sites can be found in the table.

Spanish text, including spellings of names, has been modernized unless there is some reason not to do so, as especially in the case of Font's renderings of words derived from Native American languages, which are given as he wrote them.

In the notes, biographical facts about persons mentioned in the text are limited to details that illuminate Font's account, and to events that occurred within a few years of it. Inconsistencies between Font's and Commander Anza's journals, particularly about details of the march, are usually not mentioned, for reasons of space.

The division of the text into chapters, with their titles, is my own contribution.

The small geographic profiles which Font inserted into his text, and the larger maps and figures drawn by him, are reproduced through the courtesy of the John Carter Brown Library of Providence, Rhode Island, and the kindness of the Franciscan Historical Archive, Rome.

Omitted from this book is the journal that the missionary Tomás Eixarch kept at Yuma from December 1776 to May 1777 and that Font preserved by copying it into his final text on pages 271 to 311 of his manuscript. The journal has been printed by Montané (2000) and is translated in Bolton (1930c).

CHAPTER I

From Sonora to the Gila

September 29, Friday. After the above-mentioned persons had been appointed, and a day after the soldiers had passed in review, everything was in order to begin the journey to Monterey from the pueblo and Royal Presidio of San Miguel de Horcasitas, where we were at the time. I sang a Mass attended by the people for the good success of the journey. Following the gospel, I delivered a sermon to them, concerning the journey we were about to undertake.

My sermon was based upon the very same gospel assigned to that feast day. I exhorted them all to endurance during the hardships of traveling, and above all to the fact that they must give a good example to the gentiles, so as not to shock them in any way, as a sample of Christian behavior. I also said to them that the chief patroness of the entire expedition during the journey would be La Santísima Virgen María de Guadalupe, chosen with special acclaim and good feeling on everyone's part by unanimous agreement of myself and our commander; a notion that the two of us had shared even before we spoke to each other about it, concurring in the fact that our patron must be the Sovereign Virgin Mary, Mother of God, under the title of Guadalupe, as being mother and protectress of the Indians and of this our America. And inasmuch as it was the day of San Miguel, and the holy prince is depicted as being at the feet of the image of Nuestra Señora de Guadalupe, we chose the prince San Miguel as co-patron of the expedition; and furthermore, on my own behalf and on that of our commander, who was a brother of the Holy Colegio,[1] we chose as a co-patron our Seraphic Father San Francisco under the title of his marvelous Wounds.[2]

After Mass, preparations were commenced for the march. Because so many people and so much equipment were involved, and because this was the first day, it was impossible to begin the march before the afternoon, and so it was decided that we should cross to the other side of the river and camp there before nightfall. Thus we set out from the Royal Presidio of San Miguel de Horcasitas at a half past four in the afternoon and halted on the other side of the San Miguel River, not very far from it, at a little after five o'clock, having traveled one short league, course northwest.

---

[1] Anza was an honorary lay brother of Font's mother house for Franciscan missionaries. This paragraph is an addition found in the final version.
[2] The stigmata miraculously imprinted upon Francis's hands and feet. The title or "style" is: San Francisco de las Llagas, or Las Llagas de San Francisco.

Figure 7. San Miguel Arcángel, 1774. By Florencio Ibáñez. From a manuscript partly written by Pablo Font (Pedro Font's cousin). *Courtesy of the Santa Bárbara Mission Archive-Library.*

I shall note here that, during the days I stayed at the Presidio of San Miguel de Horcasitas, I took four observations for the latitude of this presidio, employing the greatest care and the astronomical quadrant that had been sent by the viceroy and brought here by our captain-commander. But since the tables which were supposed to have been sent from Mexico City did not arrive, for the calculation I availed myself of tables made by don Jorge Juan[3] (which I acquired by chance, since I had not been given any instruments or instructions at all for the fulfilling of my function; and which, being made for the meridian of Cádiz and for the years 1756, 1757, 1758, and 1759, require two corrections) and also of other tables made by one of our own Religious,[4] between which two there are ten or twelve minutes' difference, in addition to which they require a further correction. Therefore, by averaging the two tables, I determined through observations made with the aforesaid quadrant that the Presidio of San Miguel de Horcasitas lies in 29° 40'.[5] And this is the method of calculation that I shall hold to, by using the aforesaid tables in all of the observations I shall make during this journey.

---

[3] Jorge Juan y Santacilia, the famous eighteenth-century mathematician and intellectual. Font regularly refers to him as "Jorge," apparently thinking that this is his patronymic and not his given name.

[4] In the field text, Font's latitude observations constantly include results "according to the tables of Father Gasco." Soto Pérez (1998 2: 1191 note) has tentatively identified this reference as being to Fray Matías Gasco, a resident of the Querétaro colegio. It is very likely that he merely copied the tables given in the mathematical work of Tosca referred to by Font three paragraphs further on. Since these were inferior to the Jorge Juan tables, Font omitted their results in his shortened and final texts, and they are normally omitted also in this translation.

[5] On his return to Horcasitas in the middle of 1776, Font repeated his observations and was surprised to get a different result (and a much more accurate one; see under June 2, below).

Thus, based on observations that I made, I shall record latitudes derived from don Jorge Juan's tables, first without any correction and then by applying to the said tables the two corrections that are required for the calculating. Then finally, the better to satisfy expert persons, I shall express the meridian altitude of the sun's lower limb as registered on the aforesaid quadrant by the horizontal thread in its eyepiece, in all of the observations that I made.

I note also that I may have experienced some amount of error in regard to the courses traveled, because I was unable to acquire a good compass and could only manage the loan at San Xavier del Bac of a very small, poor compass that could barely point. Therefore, for lack of an instrument, I am not completely satisfied with the courses that I record despite having used the greatest care in respect to them. In drawing up the map that accompanies this journal, I have attempted to correct them a bit further, by having reference to the observed latitudes.[6]

Finally, I shall note that in regard to the number of leagues that I record, I have calculated them based upon one measured league that I rode at the same pace as that at which the marches were made.[7] All of the leagues that I have estimated during the journey are Mexican ones, of five thousand *varas*,[8] or three thousand geometric paces, of which twenty-eight make up a league of latitude on the ground,[9] while twenty-three and one third do the same in a direct line,[10] corresponding to the seventeen and a half Spanish leagues by air and twenty-one on the ground given by Father Tosca, volume 8, treatise 24, book 1, chapter 4, proposition 23, which are composed of four thousand geometric paces or six thousand six hundred sixty six varas and two thirds of a vara, or two feet, according to Father Flores in his *Clave geográfico*, chapter 3, section 3, number 125.[11]

[September] 30, Saturday. At nine o'clock in the morning camp was raised and we commenced traveling upon a northwestward course. We set out from the

---

[6]The courses expressed in the present translation are mostly taken from Font's field text journal. See the discussion of his procedures in the introduction, and the appendix (table of Days' Marches), for the courses given in other texts.

[7]That is, distances are estimated by the time traveled. See Font's remark under April 29.

[8]A *vara* is 32.9 inches, or 33 inches for practical purposes in this document.

[9]In the manuscript, it looks as though Font started to write "twenty-eight and some. . . ."

The standard definition of Spanish leagues as 21 equaling "one degree on the earth's surface" is, of course, found in the eighteenth-century published mathematical tables that Font employed. Whereas the value for the Spanish league of 4,000 *pasos geométricos* is 5572.7 meters, the Mexican league, as defined by Font, is 3,000 *pasos geométricos*, which would be 4,179 meters, and his other definition of it as being one twenty-eighth of a degree of latitude gives a result very close to the same figure. However, a contemporary of Font's, Miguel Costansó of the Royal Corps of Engineers, who accompanied the first expedition to California in 1769–1770, produced a somewhat larger value for the Mexican league, equivalent to 4.19 km, through direct comparison of the Mexican *vara* with the international standard of the Paris foot (*toise*).

The length of a terrestrial degree of latitude near the northern limit of Font's explorations is actually about 110,985 meters (Bowditch 1975: 124), roughly one-twentieth shorter than the equivalent of the value used by Font for a degree "on the earth's surface," and thus a potential source of error in plotting his maps. On the value of Font's practical estimates of distances, see the introduction.

[10]That is, one that does not take account of the curvature of the earth's surface.

[11]The first volume of the well known work *España sagrada* (1747 and later editions) by Fray Enrique Flórez had such a title and contents. However, Font's letter of July 18, 1776, calls his manual a "little book," so that the reference is probably to an early edition of the extract of the first volume, *Clave geográphica para aprender geographía los que no tienen maestro*. The reference to "Father Tosca" is to Tomás Vicente Tosca, *Compendio matemático en que se contienen todas las materias más principales de las ciencias que tratan de la cantidad*. Font may have used the Valencia edition of 1757. "Feet" here means Mexican-Spanish feet of one third of a *vara*, almost exactly eleven inches.

spot near the San Miguel River and about midday, having traveled some four leagues, course north-northwest, came to the place called *Chupisonora*, formerly the ranch that belonged to Militia Captain Mesa. The spot has good grass and sufficient water. The way is a bit rough and rocky, and since the mules are frisky and the muleteers not very skilled, one pack train was left by the way with its loads cast off, mules straying, and with such hindrances that it was unable to get to our stopping place during the entire day.

October 1, Sunday. We paused here because the mule train that had dropped behind yesterday had not arrived. At a suitable hour in the morning, since it was Sunday and day of the Santísima Virgen del Rosario, I called the people together at my tent (which was serving as my church during our travel), using for a bell the cup or beaker[12] belonging to our commander. Inasmuch as, for lack of a vestment,[13] I was unable to say Mass, we prayed the Rosary, kneeling in front of the image of our patroness, La Santísima Virgen María de Guadalupe, that I had brought with me (and which was embellished and sent to me by Father Preacher Fray Francisco López).[14] I ended by singing the Litany and the *Alabado*.[15]

My baggage was limited to two mule loads. One of them consisted of a trunk to carry the tent with its poles and stakes, and a small chest in which I took some books and necessary papers. The other consisted of saddlebags called *cantinas*, with a pillion attached, used for carrying vestments for saying Mass and whatever else was needed for administering it, along with other necessary items for travel. Lying crosswise over the bags was a large portmanteau containing my clothes, and bedding or blankets to sleep in.

The mule train arrived at midmorning rather worn out from its hard day yesterday, and we delayed here in order to let it rest and to search for some missing animals. After midday, a boy came up saying that the Apaches had carried off some mares he was herding. Four soldiers and the ensign[16] went out and found the mares but not the Apaches, who were not there; all that was found was the tracks of the ones who passed by this spot a few days ago on their way to San Miguel.

I shall note that since this entire route lies through dangerous country, some residents came out from San Miguel to escort the expedition and went as far as the pueblo of *Santa Ana*, and others

---

[12]*Jarrilla o tembladera.* The words apparently refer to some sort of wide vessel made of thin metal, perhaps having two handles. An object similar to this description was found in the ruins of the Spanish mission at Yuma in the 1850s, when the United States Army reoccupied the site, but its use was unknown. Under December 5, Font refers to water freezing in "the *tembladera*," located apparently outside of his tent.

[13]Font received the necessary vestments for saying Mass four days later, on stopping at Mission San Ignacio.

[14]Soto Pérez (1998 2: 1190 note) supposes that this refers to Fray Francisco Antonio López, a long-term resident of the Querétaro colegio.

[15]A well-known hymn associated with the Franciscan missions of Mexico: "*Alabado y ensalzado / sea el divino sacramento...*," in praise of the sacrament of the Eucharist and the Holy Family. Consult Smestad 2005: 121–122 and the audio CD that accompanies it.

[16]José Joaquín Moraga.

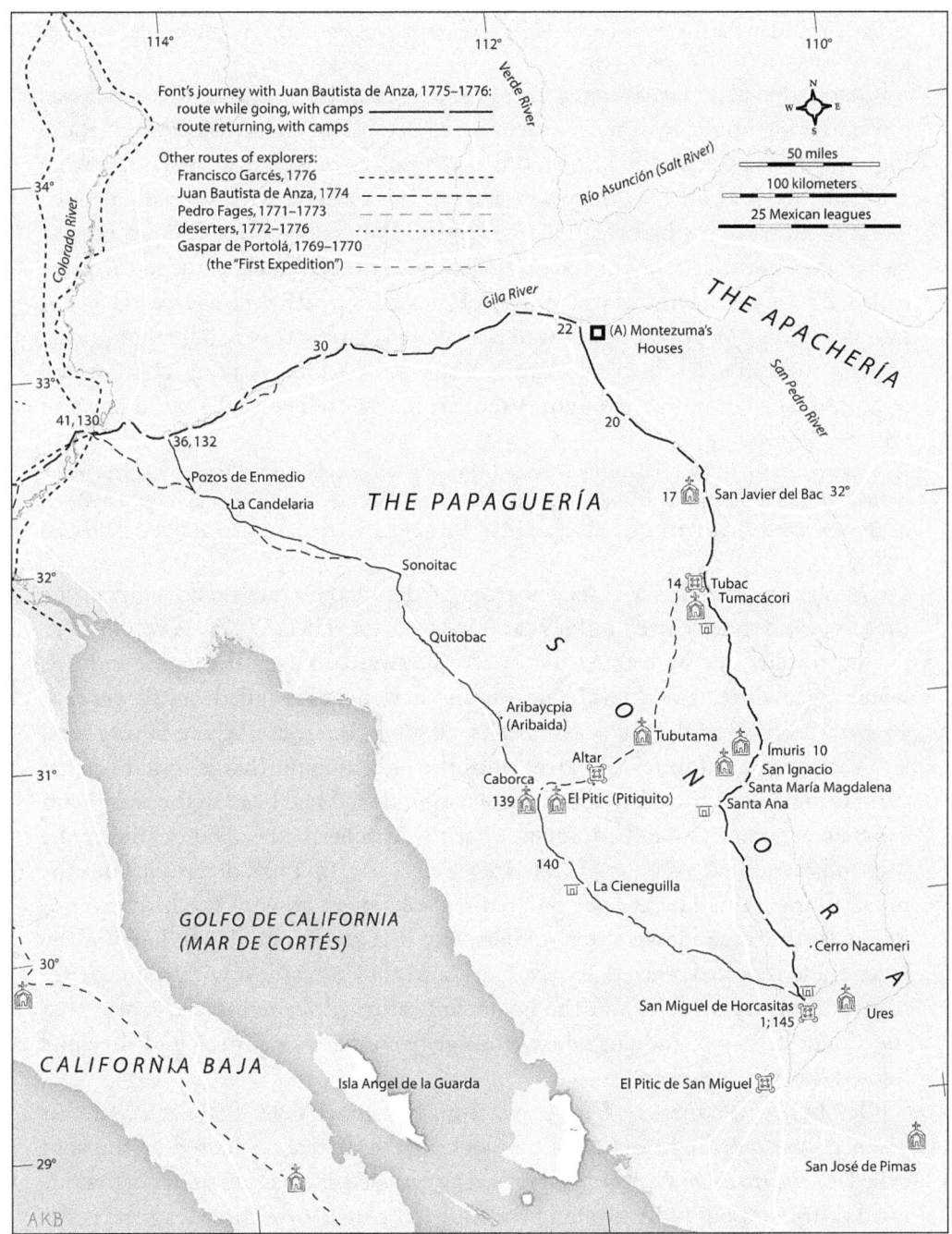

Figure 8. Redrawn and annotated version of Font's general map, southeast section: Sonora, the Papaguería, and the Gila.

came from that pueblo and escorted the expedition as far as the Presidio of Tubac. These men are not counted in the list at the beginning, as they were not part of the expedition and were not going to continue for the whole way.

[October] 2, Monday. Starting at eleven o'clock in the morning, the order was given to bring up the mounts in order to load up and to pursue the journey. Raising camp took no little time, the more so now at the outset; over two hours were spent at this, inasmuch as there was a great deal of delay with so many people; worst of all was how bad the muleteers were. We set out from Chupisonora at two o'clock in the afternoon, and at sunset, close to six o'clock, came to the place called *La Palma*, having traveled five leagues on a northwest course. The spot has plentiful good grass but not water, as there is only a very small amount that scarcely sufficed to let the people drink. Today's route follows along a hollow and is a bit brushy but not very rough. A mule train that fell behind arrived late and with packs lost.[17]

As I was rather ill, I had need of someone to help me fetch my effects and put up the tent when we halted, and although he offered to appoint a servant for me, our commander did not do so until we reached Tubac and after I had asked him for one several times; so that I had to do it all myself.

[October] 3, Tuesday. We set out from La Palma at a quarter to eight in the morning, and shortly after midday came to the place called *El Charco del Canelo*,[18] having traveled for six leagues on a northwestward course. This spot, and this whole area, which is very level here and further on and is called *Los Llanos de la Virgen*[19] has a good deal of grass (as also all along the route, which is very level and very open), but water is scarce, since the only amount that is found is what gathers in pools in the rainy season. The corporal who had been in the rear guard came up as soon as we halted, saying that six Apaches had sallied out along the way and carried off a she-ass, belonging to a soldier, that had departed from the route. Our commander at once ordered ten soldiers to go with the lieutenant to follow them. At sundown three soldiers who had gone yesterday to look for the laden mule that had strayed arrived back, and they brought it with them. After nightfall the ten soldiers and the lieutenant returned, bringing the report that they found tracks of Indians who seemingly were Seris or Pimas, and they had hunted down a deer there.

[October] 4, Wednesday. We set out from El Charco del Canelo at a half past seven in the morning, and at one o'clock in the afternoon halted at the spot called *El Puerto de los Conejos*[20] after having traveled six leagues on a northwestward course. About halfway along the route, at a little over three leagues, is the

---

[17]Or: with strayed mules. *Carga* meant colloquially "mule, pack animal" as well as "pack, load."
[18]Cinnamon Pool.
[19]Plains of the Virgin.
[20]Rabbit Pass.

spot called *Querobabi*, a year-round watering place with good water. The soldiers asked permission to go out and slaughter some of the livestock that runs wild in these parts and belongs to the residents of the pueblo of *Nacameri* and the pueblo of Santa Ana; they were granted it, and killed a few head, which supplied the people with meat.

[October] 5, Thursday. We set out from the El Puerto de los Conejos at a half past eight in the morning and at two o'clock in the afternoon halted at the spot called *El Charco de Gauna*[21] which is located between the two places called *La Piriguita* and *La Barajita*, having traveled for seven leagues on a northwestward course. It is a spot that has rain water in little pools and not much of that, but has a great deal of grass, as does the entire route, which is very level and open, with large flats. As they did yesterday, the soldiers again slew some wild cattle, of which there are a good many, all belonging to the ranches of Santa Ana.

[October] 6, Friday. We set out from El Charco de Gauna at a half past eight in the morning and at noon reached the bank of the river of the pueblo of Santa Ana, having traveled for five leagues on a north-northwestward course. This is a settlement made up of Spanish residents who own cattle ranches. Three soldiers remained behind searching for some strayed mules and did not come back during the entire day.

[October] 7, Saturday. We delayed here because of the three soldiers who had remained behind searching for some laden mules. They returned with one of them, but three of them, along with their loads, remained straying and could not be found. I observed for the latitude of this pueblo using the expedition's astronomical quadrant, and according to the tables of don Jorge Juan, using no correction, I found the pueblo to lie in 30° 46½', and with correction in 30° 38½'.[22] And for the sake of gaining greater clarity and accord, I shall, in all observations, record the sun's meridian altitude above the horizon as shown by the quadrant, to which must be added 16 minutes as being the semi-diameter of the solar disk. And thus I say: at the pueblo of Santa Ana, October 7, 1775: meridian altitude of the sun's lower limb: 53° 28'.

[October] 8, Sunday. I said Mass. We set out from the pueblo of Santa Ana at a half past nine in the morning and at two o'clock[23] in the afternoon we halted at the pueblo of *Santa María Magdalena*, a *visita* of Mission San Ignacio, having traveled some six leagues on a north-northeastward course. As soon as we reached here I sent word of our arrival to Father Preacher Fray Francisco Zúñiga, the minister of Mission San Ignacio.[24] He came over before nightfall.

---

[21]Gauna's Pool.
[22]Santa Ana is in 30° 32'.
[23]The field text has "one o'clock."
[24]Zúñiga had arrived from Spain in the 1769 missionary contingent, much later than Font.

[October] 9, Monday. I said Mass, and later, Mass was sung by Father Fray Francisco Zúñiga while I accompanied it upon my instrument

—the psaltery I had been carrying with me, which I had brought along at the behest of our commander; he persuaded me that it would be very suitable for pleasing gentile Indians along the journey, particularly the Yumas, who are very fond of entertainment.

We set out from Santa María Madalena[25] at nine o'clock in the morning and at a half past ten reached Mission San Ignacio, having traveled for two leagues on a north-northeastward course.

As Father Zúñiga had conveyed to me certain remarks that had been made to him by the commander concerning myself, I again requested him[26] for a servant to help me set up my tent when we halted—also the altar and whatever else I needed—; and although he promised to give me one, he still did not do so.[27]

[October] 10, Tuesday. I said Mass. We delayed at this mission in order to get together some loads of provisions that were taken on here. Using the quadrant, I observed the latitude of this mission and found it, by the tables of Jorge with no correction, to lie in 30° 55½', and with correction, in 30° 47½'.[28] And thus I say: at Mission San Ignacio, October 10, 1775: meridian altitude of the sun's lower limb: 52° 10'.

Father Zúñiga loaned me all the vestments needed to say Mass and administer [the sacraments] except for the cruets—which I got from Mission Tumacácori, where I also laid up a supply of hosts for the whole way—and except for the vessels of holy oils, which I got from Mission San Xavier del Bac. As a result, thenceforward I was able to say Mass along the way, and did celebrate it on most days.

[October] 11, Wednesday. I said Mass. Before we set out, Fathers Fray Felipe Guillén and Fray Manuel Carrasco[29] arrived at the mission here. Both of them had been ill and they were coming to convalesce here. This is a very fine, plenteous mission, and would be much more so, were it not for the damage done by Apaches who invade this country at every turn, and for that reason the road beyond here is quite a dangerous one. We set out from Mission San Ignacio at a half past ten in the morning and traveled, course north-northeastward, through a hollow for four leagues, and at a half past one in the afternoon we halted at the river bank, near the pueblo of *Imuris*, a visita of Mission San Ignacio, and about a league beyond the aforesaid pueblo. This whole route, since before San Ignacio, is not so open a road, and dangerous because of Apaches.

---

[25]"Madalena" is a phonetic spelling that Font uses twice in the field text.
[26]Commander Anza.
[27]On Anza's criticism of Font's lack of frontier experience, see the introduction. Font was soon going to have a servant assigned to him—José Miguel Silva—but with ultimately unsatisfactory results for both men, as will be seen later.
[28]The latitude figure is six minutes too high.
[29]Felipe Guillén would be killed by the northern Seris in April 1778; Manuel Carrasco, who had gone to the Sonora missions in August 1773, possibly at the same time that Font did, died at Magdalena in March 1776 while Font was in California. (Soto Pérez 1998 2: 1191 note.)

[October] 12, Thursday. I said Mass, the first one that I said in my tent, which was the expedition's portable church. We set out from the river near Imuris at a half past eight in the morning and at one o'clock in the afternoon halted at the spot called *El Guambút*, before entering into the canyon, having traveled four leagues on a northward course. A little before this place is the spot called *Los Alisos* because there are trees of that sort there.[30] El Guambút canyon beyond here is a very dangerous spot, where the Apaches and runaway Piatos have committed several slayings, and for this reason we delayed here in order to go through it tomorrow with everyone keeping together with the pack trains. Some people went fishing and brought back very good-sized catfish. Today's route is a rather narrow and brushy one.

[October] 13, Friday. I said Mass. We set out from El Guambút at eight o'clock in the morning and at one o'clock in the afternoon halted at the spot called *El Síbuta*, having traveled for four leagues on a northward course, going very slowly through El Guambút canyon so as to keep together and not break the column of people and mule trains.

[October] 14, Saturday. We set out from El Síbuta at eight o'clock in the morning and at three o'clock in the afternoon halted at the spot called *Las Lagunas*,[31] having traveled eight leagues, course northward with some veering northwestward. Earlier than halfway along the route is the spot called *El Agua Zarca*.[32] It is a very small-sized spring of water. The way goes along through among hollows between low hills, behind which lie quite high mountains, and the whole country is very full of good grass.

To the right, along the whole way, there run high mountains with a good deal of trees that continue in a chain from the pueblo of Dolores and even before there, extending up to and beyond the pueblo and Presidio of Tuquisón and ending before the Gila River. Low hills run on upon the left, and behind them a range of some elevation and steepness that starts from the pueblo of Santa María Madalena and runs up to *La Aribaca*, Arizona, and the place called *Las Bolas*, so named because of the balls of virgin silver that were yielded by the ground there; that entire range is said to be ore-bearing. All of these districts are very plentiful in grass, and out of them issues the San Ignacio River.

Ever since yesterday, there are no mesquite trees to be encountered; instead there are live oaks and walnuts, whose nuts, of which I ate a good few, are like those in Castile but much smaller and with a very tough shell and the meat— although very oily—very tightly enclosed.

[October] 15, Sunday. The place is exposed to danger from enemies[33] so our commander would not agree to my saying Mass in the field. Since it was Sunday,

---

[30] Sycamores.
[31] The Lakes.
[32] The Light Blue Water.
[33] "Apaches," in the field text.

in order to say it, I left the people without Mass and went on ahead, escorted by four soldiers, to the pueblo of *Calabazas*, distant two leagues from the stopping place and a little apart from the way. At that pueblo, which is a station of Mission Tumacácori (before, it was also a station of Mission Huevavi,[34] which was abandoned because of the Apaches), I encountered Father Preacher Fray Pedro Arrequíbar, and when I had said Mass I went off to the road to meet the expedition's people, who were now coming by. They had left the stopping place at Las Lagunas at eight o'clock in the morning, and had reached the Royal Presidio of Tubac at two o'clock in the afternoon, having traveled seven leagues on a northward course. I myself remained at Mission Tumacácori, which is on the route at one league before reaching the presidio. The two Fathers, Tomás Eixarch and Pedro Arrequíbar, were there along with the two Fathers of San Xavier, Félix Gamarra and Francisco Garcés, who were ill. I remained there with them.

People came out from Tubac to receive us, and so forth. The route is good, with a great deal of grass, though the water is not of the best.

[October] 16, Monday. In the morning I went to the Presidio of Tubac with Father Tomás Eixarch and returned to the mission in the afternoon, even though our commander had sent for me, I would not stay at the presidio during the days of delay that were needed in order to arrange whatever was necessary for pursuing the journey and to finish gathering all the people who were to go along on the expedition.

[October] 17, Tuesday, was taken up with that business. My illness of diarrhea worsened today and I had to spend the entire day in bed.

[October] 18, Wednesday, was employed for the same purpose. I continued ill, with no improvement, and in bed.

[October] 19, Thursday, was spent the same way. I stayed the same with very little improvement. Father Fray Tomás Eixarch went to the presidio and brought back the astronomical quadrant with which to observe the mission's latitude, but being ill I was unable to make the observation I had wished to.

[October] 20, Friday, passed in the same fashion. I spent the entire day in bed with no improvement.

[October] 21, Saturday. The commander called for us, and to me he sent a servant[35] to serve me along the way, after I had asked him for one for the third time. Thereupon I went in the morning to Presidio of Tubac in company with Father Preacher Fray Francisco Garcés and his companion, Father Preacher Fray Tomás Eixarch, who added themselves to our company in order to remain at the Colorado River to search out the intentions of the tribes that live there upon its verges and to await us there until our return from Monterey, as ordered by the most excellent señor viceroy. Father Preacher Fray Pedro Arrequíbar came along

---

[34]Usually spelled Guevavi.
[35]José Miguel (de) Silva, a native of the town of Sinaloa.

with us and returned in the afternoon. I observed the latitude of the presidio here, and found it, according to the tables of Jorge Juan, with no correction, in 31° 45½', and with correction in 31° 38½'.[36] And thus I say: at the Presidio of Tubac, October 21, 1775: meridian altitude of the sun's lower limb: 47° 16'. But since the day was a dull one I was not satisfied with this observation.

[October] 22, Sunday. I sang Mass, for a successful journey for the expedition, accompanied by Father Garcés, since there were no other singers at the presidio; all of the people attended. Following the gospel I said four words to the purpose,[37] and by taking the subject of the gospel for the day, which was: "Do not fear, little flock," *Nolite timere, pusillus grex*,[38] I exhorted everyone to perseverance, and to bear up under the hardships of so long a journey, and to hold themselves lucky and happy that God had chosen them for that undertaking. And by drawing a parallel between the crossing of the people of Israel through the Red Sea over to the promised land[39] and the present expedition's journey to Monterey and their crossing over the Colorado River, I proclaimed to them what punishments God might put upon them, if they misbehaved with the gentiles along the way or scandalized them with their actions, as He did with the Israelites who fell into that sort of misbehavior, or if—as those others did against their leader Moses—they complained about the head of the expedition and his orders, not holding him in due respect. And on the other hand, I assured them of God's protection and that of our patroness the La Santísima Virgen María de Guadalupe, the pillar that was to protect us all during the voyage, if we were to act as good Christians. And finally I promised them—after the great many benefits, even perhaps mingled with hardship as they were, that God was providing them in this life—the happiness of eternal rest in the land of promise and true homeland, the land of glory.

The day being clear, I returned to observing and found this presidio, according to the tables of Jorge Juan with no correction, to lie in latitude 31° 50', so that I found a difference of four minutes between yesterday's and today's observations, perhaps because the sky was very dull yesterday; and with correction, in 31° 43'. And thus I say: at the Presidio of Tubac, October 22, 1775: meridian altitude of the sun's lower limb: 46° 50'.

Here at this presidio were finally gathered all of the people and families belonging to the expedition, who were to go on to Monterey and the new settlement at the harbor of San Francisco, and all the provisions needed for the journey, with the mule trains, mounts, and livestock[40] were brought to completion; all of which, making up the expedition, are as follows, by entries.

---

[36]Just slightly high (Tubac is in 31° 36.8'), but not as high as the following day's observation.

[37]In the final text: "I gave a talk or brief sermon." From here onward, Font often refers to his (not so brief) sermons as "giving four words."

[38]Luke 12:32.

[39]This is the first mention of Font's image of the colonists' California as the Biblical "land of promise." His colleague Father Paterna's words of greeting when they arrived there (January 5) added strength to Font's promise.

[40]The short text here reads: ". . . in the entries for which, I do not record the number, as I did not succeed in learning it." In the field text, the figures for the number of horses are also left blank.

Persons

In first place, Lieutenant Colonel of Cavalry and expedition commander don Juan Bautista de Anza	1
Father Chaplain *de propaganda fide*[41] from the Colegio de la Santa Cruz de Querétaro, Fray Pedro Font	1
Fathers Fray Francisco Garcés and Fray Tomás Eixarch: these are coming assigned to remain at the Colorado River	2
Expedition purveyor don Mariano Vidal[42]	1
Ensign don José Joaquín Moraga, who, although married, came alone, not bringing his family as his wife, who was ill, remained at Terrenate.	1
Sergeant Juan Pablo Grijalva	1
Eight experienced soldiers taken from the presidios of La Sonora	8
Twenty recruit soldiers for Monterey, raised by the commander himself in the province of Sonora	20
Ten experienced soldiers from the Presidio of Tubac for protecting and escorting the expedition	10
Twenty-nine wives belonging to the sergeant and twenty-eight soldiers	29
One hundred thirty-six individuals of both sexes pertaining to the same soldiers and to four other volunteer families going in order to remain in Northern California, or Monterey.	136
Muleteers for the expedition's three pack trains and equipage of the commander, the cook, and so forth[43]	20
Three cowhands for the cattle	3
Three employees[44] for the three Fathers: a servant, a dependent, and a lad of Father Tomás's, to whom was added another who remained with the two Fathers at the Colorado River	4
Four of the same for the commander	4
Three Indian interpreters for three tribes: Yuma, Cajuenches, and Jalchedun on the Colorado River[45]	3

---

[41]"For the spreading of the Faith," i.e., a person dedicated as a missionary. The phrase came from the establishment of a Vatican congregation of that name in 1622, and it was regularly used in reference to the missionary colegios.

[42]The field text list Vidal's name in last place, at the end after the Indian interpreters.

[43]In the field text: "Fifteen muleteers." One of the muleteers was the Baja Californian traveler and guide Sebastián Taraval, who had proved (at great cost to himself) the possibility of crossing the desert between the Pacific Coast and the Colorado. Anza apparently had some extraordinary difficulty in fitting him onto the payroll, since Font reports later saying to the commander, "you have counted [him] as a muleteer, a cook, an interpreter, and at first as my employee." (May 25)

[44]*Sirvientes*, employees paid by the government to work, in this case, for the missionaries.

[45]From the final text. In the field text, "Five interpreters for the Pima, Yuma, Cajuenches and Níjora languages" reflecting Anza's claims about personnel, which Font later discredited; see under May 25.

Sum total   240

Included in this number is the woman who later died along the way.[46]

Equipment

Being driven are one hundred and forty mules laden with provisions, ammunition and baggage belonging to the commander and all the members of the expedition, other effects belonging to it, and presents in His Majesty's name for gentiles along the way	140
Idem, about twenty-five pack mules belonging to individuals among the soldiers	25
Idem, horses belonging to the expedition and to some individuals, including some saddle mules	500[47]
Idem, some thirty mares with a few colts, and burros	30
Total mounts[48]	695

Livestock

Idem, three hundred twenty-five head of cattle for the expedition's use on the way, with what remains at the end of the journey intended to provide breeding stock for the new settlement and missions at San Francisco harbor	325
Idem, about thirty head belonging to individuals	30
Sum total of livestock[49]	355

I shall note that the contents of these entries kept diminishing during our travel, inasmuch as some animals died, others strayed and were lost, and others were traded off as circumstances arose.

With the expedition's personnel all gathered, then, along with a few others who had joined, so that there must have been two hundred and fifty souls of us in all,[50] and with the necessities all provided, it was decided to pursue our journey on the following day.[51]

---

[46]A note added in the final text. She was Manuela Piñuelas; see the note under September 23.

[47]An official communication by Anza states that the recruit-settlers owned about sixty mounts, over half of them being mares fit for breeding. (Garate 1995: 155, 158; facsimile 304.)

[48]Horses and mules, including pack animals. Notice Font's disclaimer, above, about not knowing the number of animals.

[49]In the field text, just "Three hundred and two head of cattle" without mention of ownership.

[50]The number of "240" persons above in the list as found in the final text represents Font's later estimate made at Monterey in May of the following year, when he copied the commander's roster dated October 20, 1775.

[51]Two marginal notes by Font in the field text are for his guidance during revision: "Note: the escort that came as far as Tubac, etc. The *Alabado* and the order of marching &c." "Marches: the captain first then myself. The *Alabado* sung."

I shall note that the arrangement observed during marches was the following upon the whole way: At the suitable hour, the horses and mules were ordered to be brought up and each person proceeded to catch his own animals, the muleteers their mules and the soldiers and employees horses for themselves and their wives and the rest, and while loading and saddling went on I usually said Mass, as there was enough time for the purpose. When the pack trains were ready to set out, our commander would say ¡*Vayan subiendo!*, "Start mounting up!", and we all got on horseback and the march at once began, forming into a line in the following fashion. Four soldiers went in front scouting out the way; our commander rode on point in the vanguard; then came myself; and behind me followed the people—men, women and children—along with the soldiers escorting and watching over their families, and the line was closed by the lieutenant in the rear guard; afterward usually came the pack trains, then the loose mounts, and the livestock last of all: all of which together formed a very long line. As soon as we began to move, I would intone the *Alabado*[52] and all the people would respond, and this was done every day both in going and in returning. After all the people had dismounted on reaching the stopping place, the lieutenant would come up to report to the commander whether everything had arrived or whether anything had delayed behind, for whatever action needed to be taken. At night, family by family, the people prayed the Rosary in their family groups, and on ending it they sang the *Alabado* or the *Salve*[53] or some other thing, each group in its own fashion, so that, what with the variety of sound, it was a pleasant thing to hear. As there was a considerable number of people, the camp after we had halted resembled a settlement, what with the quarters which the soldiers built for themselves by using their capes, cloaks, and branches, and even more so with the field tents, of which there were thirteen, nine belonging to the soldiers, one for the lieutenant, one for Fathers Garcés and Eixarch, one for myself and a larger round one for our commander.

[October] 23, Monday. We set out from the Presidio of Tubac (after Mass had been said) at about eleven o'clock in the morning and after three o'clock in the afternoon halted at the spot called *La Canoa*,[54] having traveled some five leagues on a north-northeastward course. Along the way we had a great deal of wind and dust, ending with clouds and a little rain next day in the morning. All this country is cool, with mesquite groves and a great deal of grass. At night, the wife of a soldier[55] was overcome with labor pains and she gave birth to a fine boy, but the delivery was so crossways that it was born feet first and the woman died of complications before dawn the next day, and in the afternoon was taken for burial to Mission San Xavier del Bac and was interred on the morning of the 25th by Father Garcés, who had gone on ahead accompanying the body.

[October] 24, Tuesday. I said Mass. We set out from La Canoa at two o'clock in the afternoon and at five o'clock halted at what they call *La Punta de los Llanos*[56] having traveled three leagues upon a north-northeastward course. There

---

[52]A performance of the hymn can be listened to on the sound track of Smestad 2005.
[53]*Salve* is the well known *Salve Regina*, "Hail Holy Queen," addressed to the Virgin.
[54]The Canoe.
[55]This was Manuela Piñuelas, wife of Vicente Féliz. She left him six other children (see Font's personnel list, under April 13) besides the newborn, José Antonio Capistrano Féliz, who died not long afterward at San Gabriel.
[56]The Tip of the Plains.

is grass enough but no water at the stopping place and on the plains beyond it. To our left hand, we went along past some heights that already belong to the Papaguería, and to the right runs the range that comes a very long way, from before Mission San Ignacio and has several names before it ends a little beyond *El Tuquisón*, where they call it the Santa Catarina mountains, along whose slopes on the other side runs the San Pedro River until it joins the Gila River. Along the way I began praying the Rosary with the people, for the deceased woman, and ended it by singing the *Salve* of the Virgen de los Dolores.[57]

[October] 25, Wednesday. We set out from the La Punta de los Llanos at a bit after half past eight in the morning and at one o'clock in the afternoon reached Mission San Xavier del Bac, whose minister is Father Fray Francisco Garcés, having traveled six leagues on a north-by-east course. This is a pueblo of good[58] Pimas, or Sobaýpuris, and once was very populous but at present it has been brought very low by the hostile actions of the Apaches and even more so because of its water, which is very harmful because of its being thick and nitrous to the degree that a Jesuit Father proved that a vase of water when distilled left behind two ounces of niter and slag. In the afternoon Father Tomás baptized the boy that was born on the night of the 23rd.

[October] 26, Thursday. I said Mass, and before the Mass I celebrated three weddings of people belonging to the expedition, out of four that presented themselves to me at Tubac, and during the Mass I veiled the newlyweds.[59] Previously, I had named the servant whom our commander had given me, José Miguel Silva, as notary in order to publish the banns and so forth; and I had disallowed the other wedding because of having learned, on the 23rd, that there was an impediment on the part of the woman, she having promised another man first and the engagement not having been terminated by mutual consent.

We set out from Mission San Xavier del Bac after a half past eight in the morning and, as there were bad spots because of the ditches formed from the lakes there on the plains, we made our way around a height and halted, at one o'clock in the afternoon, one league beyond the pueblo of El Tuquisón, which

---

[57]This is presumably the "Devout song in reverence of the sorrows of Most Holy Mary, not imitating the *Salve* [i.e., the *Salve Regina*] of the Church," which if sung or said gained a hundred days' indulgence according to a decree of Cardinal Mendoza (1508–1566) (Anonymous 1806, fifteenth leaf verso). The refrain, sung at the beginning, and repeated at the end of each stanza, is "*Salve, Virgen pura, dolorosa Madre; salve, Virgen bella, Madre Virgen, salve.*" The verses are very penitential, e.g. stanza 2: "My faults add a new torment to your sorrow-filled, inconsolable soul." This tone would have agreed with Font's tastes, so that it was likely he who chose the song.

[58]Refers to the O'odham who had not rebelled against the missions. "Good" is found only in the field text, and "or Sobaýpuris" is added there above the line.

[59]The three couples were Ignacio de Higuera and María Micaela Bojorques (Bohórquez); Tiburcio Vásquez (Vázquez) and María Antonia Bojorques (Bohórquez); Gregorio Antonio Sandoval and María Dolores Ontiveros. (fig. 9) The identity of the pair who could not be married is not known.

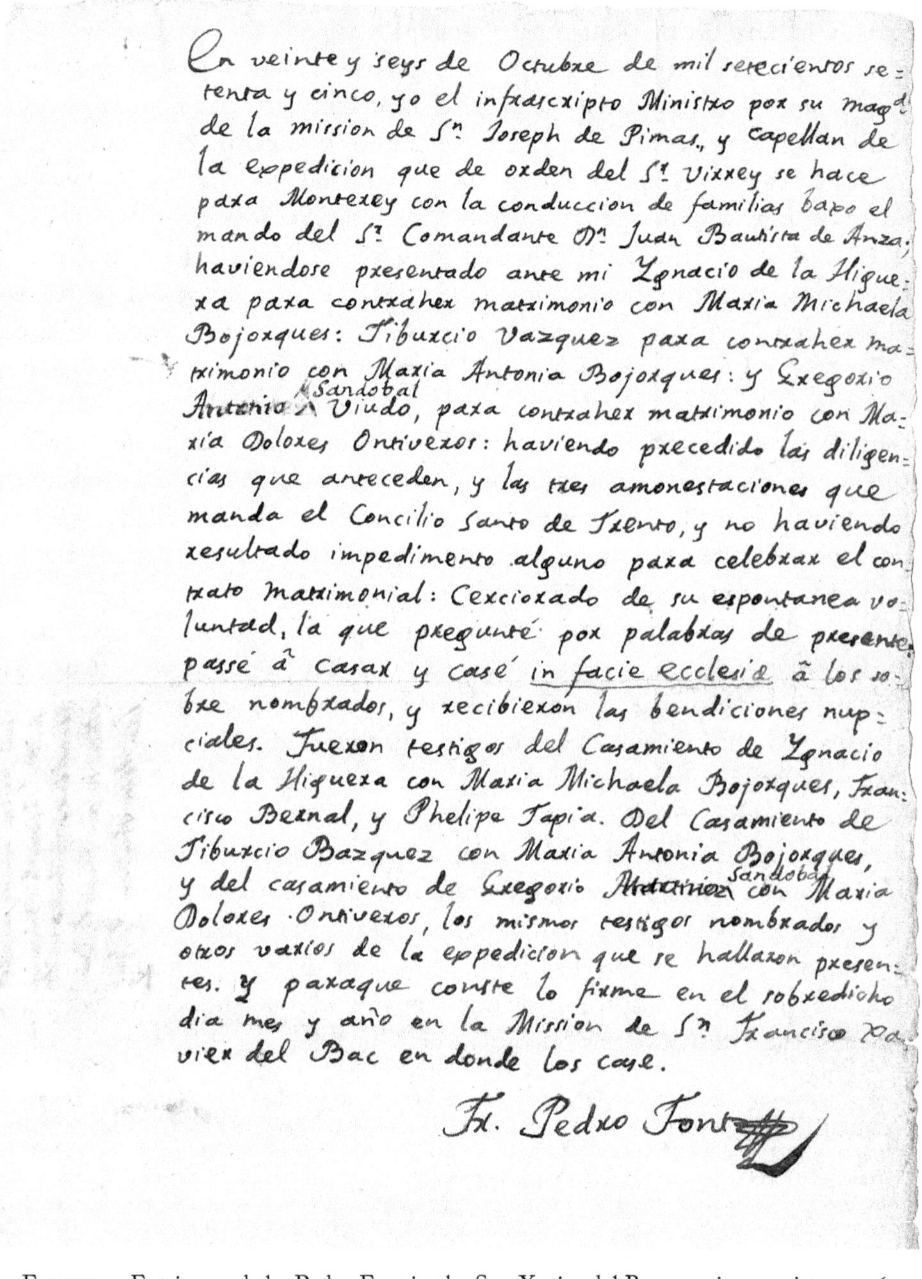

En veinte y seys de Octubre de mil setecientos setenta y cinco, yo el infrascripto Ministro por su mag.d de la mission de S.n Joseph de Pimas, y capellan de la expedicion que de orden del S.r Virrey se hace para Monterey con la conduccion de familias bajo el mando del S.r Comandante D.n Juan Bautista de Anza, haviendose presentado ante mi Ignacio de la Higuera para contraher matrimonio con Maria Michaela Bojorques: Tiburcio Vazquez para contraher matrimonio con Maria Antonia Bojorques: y Gregorio Antonio Sandobal Viudo, para contraher matrimonio con Maria Dolores Onriveros: haviendo precedido las diligencias que anteceden, y las tres amonestaciones que manda el Concilio Santo de Trento, y no haviendo resultado impedimento alguno para celebrar el contrato matrimonial: Cerciorado de su espontanea voluntad, la que pregunté por palabras de presente, passé à casar y casé in facie ecclesiæ à los sobre nombrados, y recibieron las bendiciones nupciales. Fueron testigos del Casamiento de Ignacio de la Higuera con Maria Michaela Bojorques, Francisco Bernal, y Phelipe Tapia. Del Casamiento de Tiburcio Bazquez con Maria Antonia Bojorques, y del casamiento de Gregorio Sandobal con Maria Dolores Onriveros, los mismos testigos nombrados y otros varios de la expedicion que se hallaron presentes. Y paraque conste lo firme en el sobredicho dia mes y año en la Mission de S.n Francisco Xavier del Bac en donde los case.

Fr. Pedro Font

FIGURE 9. Entries made by Pedro Font in the San Xavier del Bac marriage register, 1776. *Courtesy of University of Arizona Library Special Collections, Tucson.*

belongs to Sobaýpuri Indians, a visita of Mission San Xavier del Bac, and the last Christian pueblo in this direction. Not counting the turning, we traveled four leagues, on a northward course. This pueblo of El Tuquisón[60] is more populous than the one at San Xavier del Bac,
and during the following year, 1776, the Presidio of Tubac was transferred to it and is there today, now called the Presidio of *San Agustín del Tuquisón*.

It is a remarkable fact that although the whole route we traveled up to here is in great danger from Apaches, they have not attacked us nor did we see any of them along the entire way, and this is a favor that we must credit to the protection of the La Santísima Virgen de Guadalupe, since if the Apaches had attacked, doubtless we would have suffered losses, as our few soldiers were raw and inexperienced, and rode so constantly engaged with their little children that at times there would be one or another soldier carrying two or three young ones with him, and most of them rode with a child. But God is conveying us and our patroness the Virgin Mary; and with that said, everything is said.

[October] 27, Friday. I said Mass, and inasmuch as we were now leaving the last Christian pueblo and entering the lands of gentiles, I gave a talk to the people after the gospel, exhorting everyone to come to confession and to furnish a good example to the gentiles through whose country we were to go, as, being Christians and examples of Spanish Christianity, they were required to do. At noon, using the astronomical quadrant, since the pueblo of El Tuquisón is the final point of Christendom in this direction, I observed and found it, by the tables of Jorge Juan with no correction, in latitude 32° 30', and with correction in 32° 22'.[61] And thus I say: at the pueblo of El Tuquisón, outside the place one league to the north, October 27, 1775: meridian altitude of the sun's lower limb: 44° 26'.

We set out from El Tuquisón at one o'clock in the afternoon and halted at a little before six on a plain in sight of a low, steep mountain range the Indians call *La Frente Negra*,[62] and before entering a pass here that we will go through tomorrow, that they call *El Puerto del Azotado*,[63] having traveled for five leagues on a course of about two leagues north-northwestward, and the remainder northwestward. Before we set out two muleteers hid themselves in order to escape on foot;[64] the Indians of El Tuquisón were at once informed so that they would search for them, and at night eight Indians came over bringing one of them captive whom they had found immediately. He was given twelve lashes as a down

---

[60] In the field text, just "Tuquisón."
[61] The actual latitude of the camp was probably four minutes lower than Font's figure.
[62] The Black Forehead.
[63] Whipped Man's Pass.
[64] Stricken, in the field text: "one on foot and the other on a mule."

payment and was kept imprisoned in the guard post, and because of this event the Spaniards gave the spot the name El Puerto del Azotado.

[October] 28, Saturday. I said Mass. We set out from the plain at El Puerto del Azotado at a quarter past eight in the morning, traveling a west-northwestward course with some veerings to westward until half past one o'clock and at six leagues halted at a spot close to some lakes of rainwater that the Indians call *Oytaparts* and that formerly was a village of Pápago Pimas[65] that was destroyed by the Apaches. The way is all a very level, open one, but with little grass and less water.[66] The mountain range that we had been leaving upon our right and that I spoke of on the 14th ends before El Puerto del Azotado, and on our left today we are following at some little distance a rugged, low range that belongs to the Papaguería; lying to the right was very level open land that is Apache country.

Before we mounted up, Father Garcés took our commander to task over the animals he had asked him for and that had been promised to him by him, and when he had received an answer to the effect that he was not able to give him any since he had no animals to give, Father Garcés spoke to him rather plainly, which the commander showed that he resented very much and although I attempted to mollify him he refused to speak to us all day long.

[October] 29, Sunday. I said Mass, and during it I gave a hortatory sermon to the people.

Pima Indians[67] were sent out very early in the morning to inform the Pimas of the Gila River of our coming, and they reached there at night.

Following the Mass an edict was issued ordaining matters conducive to better behavior on the part of the people[68] and immediately twenty-five strokes were given to the other runaway muleteer, whom the Indians of El Tuquisón had brought captive.

We set out from the Oytaparts lakes at one o'clock in the afternoon and at a quarter past five halted a little beyond a height having a peak, which the Indians call *Tacca*, having traveled for some five leagues upon a course of about two leagues northwestward and the remainder north-northwestward. The spot has little grass and no water and the whole way is of the same sort, although very level, open country, the same as yesterday. Half a league from where we set out, there is a spot or abandoned village called *Cuitoa*, a Pápago settlement with a Pima name, which they usually live in at some seasons, and there must be about thirty-five to forty *jacales*[69] between good and poor ones; and a little over a league

---

[65]In the field text, "Otapars," and just "of Pimas."
[66]"Little grass," however, is emended in the manuscript to "some grass." The sentence is found only in the field text.
[67]"Pima" is only in the short text, and is crossed out there.
[68]The texts of Anza's journal say: "the Pimas call it Oit Par, which answers to 'Old Town' in our language, since it was one such belonging to those natives and was [all] [mostly] destroyed by the Apaches, our common enemies, because their dwelling places were so close by...."
[69]In the short and final texts, "some thirty." A *jacal* is a shed-roofed structure, thatched and often open-sided, although Font applies the word to other grass-built constructions in native villages.

beyond, there is a lake that is an overflow or sink of the river of El Tuquisón and San Xavier, which loses itself and ends here on these plains.

[October] 30, Monday. An attempt was made to rise early, and we set out from the *Picacho de Tacca*,[70] at eight o'clock in the morning and, traveling first for about six leagues northwestward, then three leagues north-northwestward and at the last some three leagues almost northward, at a half past five in the afternoon arrived near the Gila River having traveled some twelve leagues, and halted at the edge of a lake of sufficient size which is a bit over a league away from the river and seemingly is created by water on the plains running toward it whenever the rains come, or else by the Gila River itself when it rises and overflows its bed. The whole route between El Tuquisón and the Gila River is open country, most of it with large levels, but with scarce grass and very lacking in water for want of which we traveled going so far around, almost making a C; it is found only in the rainy season in pools in low spots where we saw a sort of ditches made by Pápago Indians to collect the water in. On today's march the footing is rather poor because of the great many gopher holes, and the soil, which does not contain stones, is whitish and very light, so that with the impact of so many mounts and people such a dust was raised that it was this more than anything else that caused us distress,

and the whole country beyond, downward all along the Gila River, is of the same sort, so that we had the same trouble in traveling.

In all this country there are no trees nor anything equivalent; there is only one or another very scrubby mesquite to be seen for long distances, and what is plentiful is the plant or weed they call here *la hediondilla*, or elsewhere *la gobernadora*,[71] and another useless little scrub bush that if eaten by horses scalds their mouth. In the end, I see nothing worth praising in this entire country of the Papaguería that we are crossing.

As a result of the message sent to the Gila folk yesterday, past noon we were met upon the way by the governor of the Pápago villages of *Cuytoa* and *Aquituni*, which we saw empty of people yesterday and today along the way, and who live at times on the banks of the river because their lands, which belong to the Papaguería (and they themselves being Pápagos) are, as I have recorded, so sterile from want of water. This governor came out, along with another man, on horseback and got down upon reaching us, and at once the governor of *Uturitúc*, a pueblo of the Gila River, came up along with his alcalde, accompanied by the governor of *Sutaquison*,[72] who had had the name of justices conferred upon them,

---

[70]Tacca Peak.
[71]Creosote bush, in both cases. *Gobernadora*, a reference to its medicinal qualities, was used in the Californias.
[72]In the field text, "the town of La Encarnación de Sutaquison."

bestowed by our commander in the King's name on the last occasion.[73] These justices were accompanied by eight or ten Indians, all of them on horseback and more or less clothed, the Cuytoa governor wearing old-fashioned breeches that were very wide and long, like a folded blanket, and colored as it were with a sort of red, black and yellow lines with a bit of white, made of the cotton that they gather and weave in their own fashion. They got down in order to greet us, and presented the soldiers with two scalps of Apaches they had killed a day earlier— they are continually at war with them—and at once got back up on horseback and went with us to the stopping place. These Gila Pimas are like all the other Pimas of Pimería Alta, fairly dark, and good-sized of body, courageous, and exceedingly bitter enemies of the Apaches. They inquired whether we were coming to live with them now and baptize the children, which it seems they greatly desire (and they have asked for Fathers several times, as when last year they requested them from provincial Governor Crespo[74] when he came inspecting the presidios), and they acted very happy with our arrival and the governor said that it would be good for the soldiers to come and live with them so they could fight together against the Apaches. The climate, I thought, was quite cold in winter and very hot in summer. It does not seem much plagued by biting insects, mosquitoes, and so forth; I saw only some very large yellow wasps.[75] By what I could tell, the district does not hold out the best advantages; a small amount of harvest can only be obtained, as the Indians do, along the river bank, by using a great deal of water, and the only wood for building with is in the grove along the banks of the river, and that not very large, and the countryside has only scarce grass for livestock and mounts. This spot is near the abandoned village of *San Andrés*, close to a height called *Comari*.

[October] 31, Tuesday. I said Mass, which a few of the Gila gentiles listened to with great restraint. Our commander decided to have the people lie by today, resting from yesterday's long march, and therewith we had a chance to go and inspect the Casa Grande that they call La Casa Grande de Moctezuma, located one league from the Gila River and distant some three leagues upriver, east-southeastward from the stopping place at the lake. We went there after Mass and returned after midday, accompanied by some Indians and the Uturitúc governor, who along the way narrated to us a story and tradition preserved by the Gila Pimas from their ancestors, concerning that Casa Grande, which all

---

[73] Refers to Anza's exploratory expedition of a year and a half earlier, on its return up the Gila valley from California and the Colorado, on May 22, 1774.

[74] Francisco Antonio Crespo, interim governor of Sinaloa and Sonora 1773–1777.

[75] Probably the oversize wasps now known in the country as tarantula killers, with bright orange wings on a blue-black body. In the eighteenth century, an orange color was usually described as a shade of yellow or red.

Figure 10. La Casa Grande de Moctezuma, 1934. By George A. Grant.
Courtesy of the National Park Service Historic Photograph Collection.

amounts to fables of the demon[76] mingled and tangled up with a few Catholic truths; I shall recount it later. We made a minute and quite leisurely survey of that ancient edifice, and then went back. The river, to judge by the groves that could be made out within the limits of the view and that throng its banks, runs from east to westward. At this spot in front of the door of the Casa Grande[77] I observed and found its latitude according to Jorge with no correction, in 33° 11', and with correction in 33° 3½'.[78] And thus I say: at the palace or Casa Grande and old edifice that they call Moctezuma's, on the Gila River, October 31, 1775: meridian altitude of the sun's lower limb: 42° 25'.

The only grass is on the shores of the lake where we stopped; everything else is infertile soil that grows nothing but useless, scrubby, weedy brush, and it is nitrous land for many leagues up and down-river except in the river's immediate vicinity, and it only rarely rains in summer. According to what they themselves say, its rains are from November onward in all of this Gila River country that belongs to the Pimas.

---

[76]In the final text, just "fables."

[77]The field text, here and later, refers to it as "the palace." The final text adds "marked with the letter A upon the map that I made afterward."

[78]The true latitude is 33°.

We inspected this edifice and its ruins with all care. I shall place here an ichnographic[79] plan of it, for the better understanding of which I shall give the following description and explanation.[80]

The Casa Grande, or Moctezuma's Palace, according to such histories and scanty information as exist or are given by the Indians concerning it, must date back for five hundred years or more, since it appears that it was established by the Mexicans during the time that they were led by the demon in their migration through several countries before reaching their promised land of Mexico.[81] During their stops, which were long-lasting ones, they produced settlements and buildings. The place where this Casa Grande is located is level in all directions and distant about a league from the Gila River, and the ruins of the buildings of which the settlement was formed extend for over a league[82] toward the east and to other directions, and scattered over the whole area here are pieces of pots, jars, plates and so forth, some of them plain and others painted in various hues, white, blue, red, yellow and so forth, an indication that it was a large settlement belonging to a different people than the Gila Pimas, since the latter do not know how to make such pottery. We made a close examination of the building and its site and did a provisional measurement with a lance, a measurement that afterward I converted into geometric feet and is very nearly the following one. The Casa Grande is rectangular[83] and lies perfectly square to the four quarters, east, west, north and south, and around it are ruins evidencing some sort of surrounding or wall that enclosed the Casa Grande and other buildings,[84] especially at the corners where there apparently was some sort of a construction like an interior castle or watch tower, for a piece of it is still standing at the southwestern corner with partitions in it and an upper floor.[85] The

---

[79]Ichnography is the drawing-up of ground plans; the layout of a building. In the first forms of the short and the final texts and of the plan itself, the false spelling *ignográphica* appears, later altered in both texts to *ichnográphica* (*icnográfica* in modern Spanish correct spelling).

[80]The Casa Grande is still so called, as are lesser ruins, found elsewhere, of the once extensive Pueblo-like culture that is now referred to as Hohokam, from the O'odham word for "old ones." Font's very rough estimate of the age is not inaccurate. Dating from his own time, there are some vague references to another *casa grande* located much farther west, in the Colorado delta, which was about to be visited by Font's expedition. But if such a site existed, it evidently was destroyed by the river before he had a chance to see it.

[81]This refers to the then already established legend of the travels of the Aztecs from their original home, guided by the god Huitzilopochtli, whom they carried with them in a box. Font evidently sees this as a blasphemous parody of the wanderings of Israel with the Ark of the Covenant.

[82]"For about two leagues," in the field text.

[83]In the field text, "almost square."

[84]On the first state of his drawing (Soto Pérez 1998 2: 1039), Font wrote: "A wall or enclosure with no recognizable door or entrance because so decayed."

[85]On his plan's first state (not reproduced here), Font had written: "A castle with traces of some partitions and stories but its entrance is not recognizable"; "this castle is smaller than the house and was not measured because of being very much decayed."

outer wall is 420 feet[86] from north to south and 260 feet east and west. The interior of the Casa Grande consists of five halls, three of them in the middle of the same size, and one longer one at each end.[87] The three halls are 26 feet north and south and 10 feet east to west. The two halls at the two ends are 12 feet north to south and 38 east to west.[88] The halls are some 11 feet high and, it seems,[89] are all the same height. The connecting doors are 5 feet high and 2 feet wide and are all almost the same size, with very little difference, save for the first four ones at the four entrances which were seemingly twice as wide. Thickness of the inner walls, 4 feet, and they are well plastered; thickness of the outer walls, 6 feet.[90] On the outside, the Casa Grande is 70 feet[91] north and south and 50 feet[92] east and west. The walls are bowed out[93] on the outside. Apart from the Casa Grande, in front of the eastern door, is another room, 26 feet north and south and 18 east to west not counting the thickness of the walls.[94] The timbering, by what appears, was of pine, and the nearest mountain range where there are pines is some twenty-five or thirty leagues away; it also contains *táscal*[95] or juniper as they call it in Spain, and a little mesquite. The whole edifice is built of clay and to all appearance is a pounded-earth construction using boxes of several sizes.[96] A very large ditch that supplied the settlement with water comes from the river, over quite a far distance, although it now is very much stopped up. Finally, the building plainly had three stories, and if what can be dragged out of the Indians is true, and judging by the visible signs, there were four of them, the floor of the Casa Grande being deepened as a sort of underground room. One sees nothing to light the rooms except for the doors and some round holes in the midst of the walls, looking eastward and westward,[97] and the Indians say that the ruler

---

[86]The field text originally read "420 and one-half feet"; the "60" of "260" seems altered from "50" (or possibly "80"). The following notes concerning Font's architectural measurements all refer to the field text.
[87]Main rooms.
[88]"12" appears to be altered, perhaps from "11"; "38," inserted as the final figure, has been altered several times, possibly from "28 or "30."
[89]"It seems" is only in the field text, and is stricken there.
[90]In both the short and the final texts, "6" is altered from "5." In the field text, "5."
[91]In the field text, "68 feet." In the short text, the alteration from "68" to "70" was done twice over.
[92]In the field text, "48 feet"; in the short text, "48" altered to "50."
[93]In the field text and originally in the short text, *escarzanas*, "bowed-out; having a batter, a tumble-home; bulging," but in the shortened text this word is then altered to *escarpadas*, "steep," which was repeated in the final version. *Escarzanas* was correct; cf. Bartlett 1854 2: 272: "The inside [of the walls] is perpendicular, while the exterior face tapers toward the top, in a curved line."
[94]"Not counting . . . walls" is added in the final text; the two earlier texts have "18" altered to "19" and "19" altered to "18," respectively, perhaps owing to some uncertainty over whether the walls' thickness had, in fact, been allowed for in the figuring.
[95]*Táscatl, táscate*, a Mexican word.
[96]Contrary to Font's conclusion, it is believed that moulding frames for the building material were not used.
[97]This is what the final text says. The field text states, "from east to westward"; in the short text, the same mangled phrase is altered from "to east to west," into "from east and west."

whom they call the Bitter Man used to look through those holes (which are of some size) to view the sun at its rising and setting in order to greet it.[98] No traces were found of stairways, so that we judged they were made of wood and were destroyed in the fire suffered by the building on account of the Apaches.[99]

The story that was narrated to us along the way by the governor of Uturitúc in his own Pima tongue and was relayed to us by our commander's servant, an especially good interpreter of that language, is as follows.[100]

He said that in very ancient times a man came to that country who was called the Bitter Man because of his ill nature and hard rule; that this man was old, and had a young daughter, and that another young man came along with him who was not related to him or anything; and that he married him to his daughter, who was very good-looking, and so was he, and that this old man brought the Wind and the Storm Cloud along as servants. That the old man began building that Casa Grande, and ordered his son-in-law to go look for beams to roof the house. That the youth went away very far off and, because he had no hatchet or anything else to cut the trees with, he delayed for a great many days and finally came back without bringing any beams. That the old man grew very angry and told him that he was good for nothing, that he would show him how he was going to bring back beams. That the old man went very far off to a mountain range where there are many pines and that, by calling upon God to help him, he cut down a great many pines and brought back many timbers for the roofs of the Casa Grande. That when this Bitter Man came, there were no trees nor plants in the country and that he brought seeds of all of them and gathered very large harvests with the two servants, the Wind[101] and the Storm Cloud, that he had. That he grew angry with the two servants because of his own ill nature and sent them away and that they went very far off and since he was no longer able to have a harvest because of the lack of his servants he ate up what he had gathered; and that he began to die of hunger. That he sent his son-in-law to call the two servants and get them back and that he was unable to find them however much he searched. That the old man went then to look for them, and having found them he brought them back again to serve him, and that, with them, he again had great harvests,

---

[98]This fragment of legend establishes that the Casa Grande served at least partly as a solar observatory. Many early monuments around the world have been discovered to have served this function.

[99]Font's comment written on the first state of his plan is more verbose: "No stairways or any trace of them were found in this house or palace, from which we inferred that the stairs to climb to the upper stories were made of wood, and must doubtless have suffered total destruction because of the Apaches having burned the building." This is perhaps a more definite statement that the wooden part of the building was actually destroyed by Apaches.

[100]Saxton and Saxton (1973: 349–57) give a much more recently recorded story, "A Mean Ruler is Assassinated," which begins, "It is said that long ago there were people [i.e., other people] living nearby," and identifies the good-turned-bad ruler as "Montezuma," a late Spanish form of the name, not a native one.

[101]In the field text, "the Air."

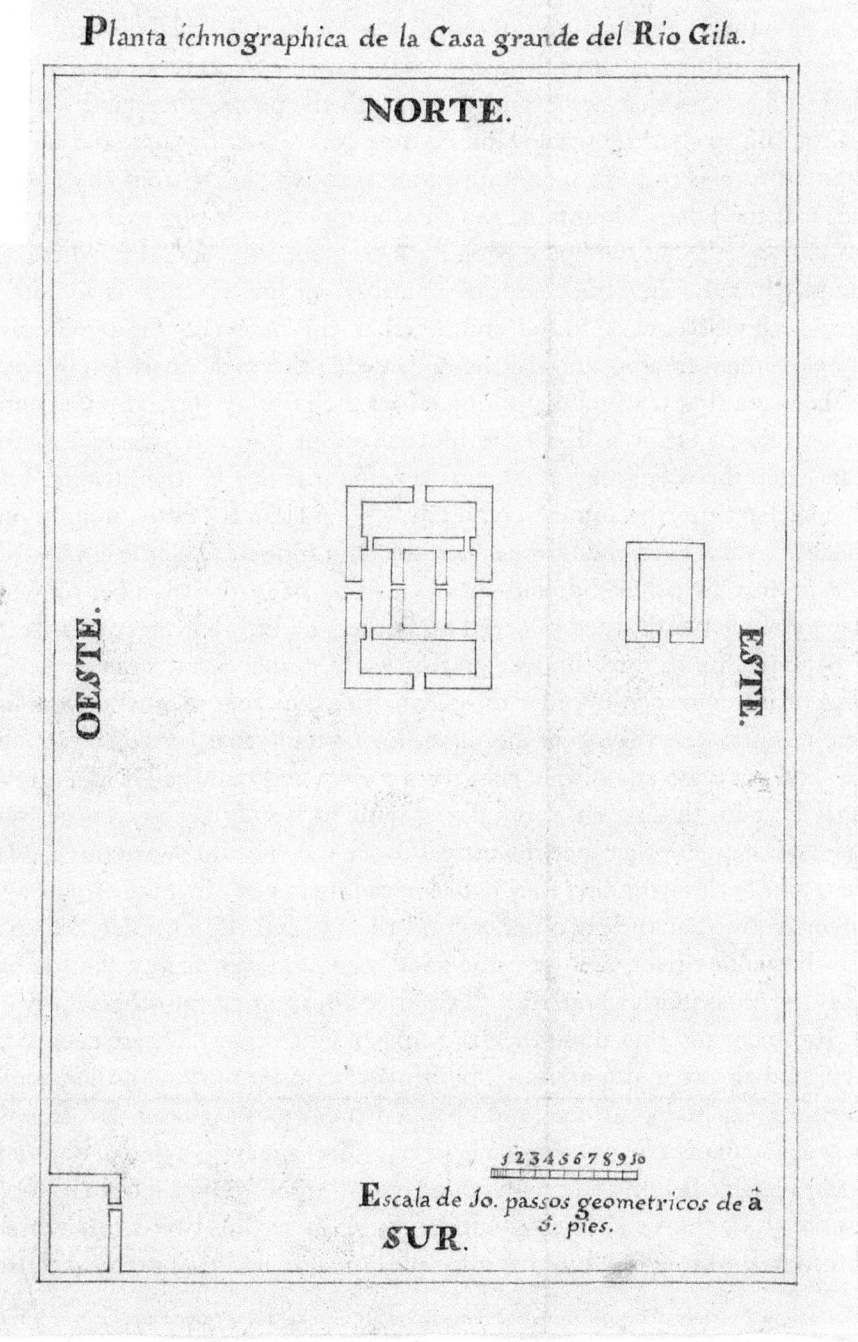

FIGURE 11. Ichnographic plan of the Casa Grande of the Gila River, 1775. By Pedro Font. *Reproduced courtesy of the John Carter Brown Library at Brown University.*

and that he kept on in that way in that country for many years, and that after a long time they went away and nothing more has been learned of them.

He said further that after the old man, there came to that country a man called the Drinker, and that he became angry with the people there and sent a great deal of rain so that the whole land became covered with water, and he himself went off to a very high mountain range that is in view from there and that they call the Foam Mountain, and that he took a little dog and a coyote with him. (They call that the Foam Mountain because at the end of it, where it stops abruptly in cliffs, like the corner of a rampart, at the top there is a white patch like a rock visible, close to the summit, that runs on evenly for a good distance along the mountaintop, and the Indians say that that is the mark left by the foam on the water that reached that far up.) That the Drinker stayed up there and left the dog down below to report to him whenever the water reached there, and that, when the water reached the foam patch, the dog let the Drinker know—since at that time, the animals could talk[102]—and that the latter brought him up. That after a few days, the Drinker sent the hummingbird and the coyote to bring mud to him; that they did, and out of the mud he made a number of men, and that some of them turned out well and others badly. That these men scattered throughout the country upriver and downriver; that after some time he sent some of his own men in order to see whether the other men who were upriver were talking; that they went and came back saying that they did talk but that they had not understood what they were saying, and that the Drinker grew very angry because those men were talking without having been given permission. That later he sent other men downriver to see the ones that were there, and that they came back saying that they had received them well, that they spoke another language but that they had understood them. Then the Drinker said to them that those downriver men were the good men, and that these were the ones as far as the Opas (with whom they[103] are friends), and that the others upriver were the bad men, and that these were the Apaches (of whom they are enemies).[104]

He said also that at one time the Drinker became angry with the people and killed a great many of them and changed them into saguaros and this is why there are so many saguaros in that country. (The saguaro is a green, watery trunk of considerable height and evenly round and straight from its foot to its top, with rows of thick thorns all the way up, and usually having two or three branches formed in the same fashion, that look like arms.) In addition to this, he said that

---

[102] All around the world, tellers of ancient tales traditionally introduce this comment.

[103] The Pimas. The words in parentheses were added in the final text.

[104] In place of the following two paragraphs, the field text adds, "He said other things, all of them a rumor and a fable, amounting in substance to this tale." A twentieth-century, much altered version of the Flood story, involving some of the same personnel and including Coyote's creation of unsatisfactory humans who talked differently, is found in Saxton and Saxton 1973: 55–59.

another time the Drinker grew very angry with men and made the sun come down in order to burn them, and it was beginning to destroy them entirely; that the men begged him very much not to burn them up and that then the Drinker said that he would not burn them any more, and commanded the sun to go up but not so far as it had been before, and he told them that he was leaving it lower in order to burn them with it if they caused him to be angry another time, and that that is the reason it is so hot in that country in summer.

He went on to say that he knew other stories he was unable to tell because time was coming to an end and he insisted that he would tell them to us some other day; but since we had laughed a bit during the tales that he was telling with considerable seriousness, we were unable later to get him to tell us anything else, as he said he did not know anything more. I have narrated all of this account or anecdote using the style of speech seen here, as being the one most appropriate to the manner in which the Indians express themselves.

November 1, Wednesday. I said Mass, attended with a good deal of attentiveness, calmness and quiet by a few Gila Indians who were there and, however poorly, did attempt to imitate the Christians in crossing themselves and the rest. We set out from the lake at a half past nine in the morning and, traveling four leagues to west-northwestward, at one o'clock in the afternoon reached the pueblo of *San Juan Capistrano de Uturitúc*[105] which is the first one belonging to Gila Pimas that is encountered while going from upriver, downward. It is a somewhat regular pueblo with little jacales of the sort that the Gila people make. By what I could see all along the way, the ground is barren just as I said earlier, and plentiful only in large gopher holes into which the horses stumbled quite a lot. Halfway along, there is a deserted settlement or village.

The Indians here had built a large *ramada*[106] outside of the pueblo to bestow on us, in front of which, gentiles though they are, they planted a large cross. All the people of the pueblo, whom I estimated as being a thousand souls, received us inside the ramada, lined up in two files, men on one side and women on the other, and as soon as we got down they all came in turn to greet us—our commander and the three Fathers—and shake our hands, first the men and then the women, big and little,

displaying a great deal of happiness at seeing us by setting their hands on their chests, naming God and giving other utterances of goodwill. This audience lasted a long while, since nearly all of them greeted us by saying *Dios ató m' busibóy*[107] just as do the Christian Pimas of Pimería Alta, meaning "God give us, ourselves, help," and a response had to be made to their greetings.

---

[105]In the short text, this seems to have an accent mark on the third syllable, "Uturítuc."

[106]A booth, an enclosure or shelter made of branches, etc.

[107]The phrase is analyzed as "God (perfective aspect) (future tense) you (plural) help/favor" meaning "God will help/favor you all." Versions of the phrase are recorded as early as the seventeenth century. This analysis is by courtesy of David L. Challe (Tohono O'odham Cultural Center, Sells, Ariz.).

They lodged us in the large ramada that they made for the purpose, in front of which they planted a large cross, even being, as they are, gentiles. And since it was some distance away from the river, the governor ordered his women to bring water and they did at once bring water to the camp for all of the people.

These Gila Pimas are well-behaved Indians and of good heart, and to mark our coming, they asked our commander's permission to dance and at once the women went dancing in a chain, in their own fashion, from one of the soldiers' messes on to another; and in sum, all these folk displayed great pleasure at seeing us in their country, and some of them immediately offered their little ones for us to baptize; which we would not do because we were here only in passing, but did attempt to please them by giving them good hopes.

In the afternoon I went with Father Garcés to inspect the pueblo and see the fields as far as the river, and we were accompanied by the Pápago governor of *Cojat* who had come along for the excursion. The fields, cultivated in sections, are surrounded with poles, with very good-sized, very clean irrigating ditches, and are close to the pueblo and the banks of the river, which is large only at flood time and now was carrying so little water that it came only halfway up the leg of an Indian whom I told to go into it and who got across its width of some twelve varas.[108] And this is the cause for their not having planted yet, as they told me when I asked them, since the water was unable to flow into the irrigation ditches because the river was running so low; and they said to me further that in order to improve this they intended to gather themselves together and had planned to drive a great many poles into the river bed and add a great many branches in order to raise the water so that it would go into the ditches: a proof of how dedicated to working they are and not given to vagabondage like other tribes, since they themselves have devised a way of damming the river in order to keep themselves in their own pueblos with their fields.

I saw also how they were weaving cloaks of cotton that they plant for themselves and spin, and most of them know how to weave. They have some large sheep with good wool, and Castilian chickens. They are quite well-built Indians but very ugly and dark, the women even more so, and, possibly because they eat a great deal of *péchita*, which is mesquite pods ground and made into mush, screwbeans and grass seeds and other coarse fare, when they are all gathered together one smells a really foul odor off them. This afternoon our commander gave all of them a present of tobacco and necklace and glass beads, with which they were very well pleased, and this distribution of gifts lasted until nightfall.

[November] 2, Thursday. We began saying Mass very early in the morning, and using the vestments that I had with me and the one that Father Garcés was

---

[108] 33 feet.

bringing with him for his stay at the Colorado River, we set up two altars and, as it was All Souls Day, we three Religious said nine Masses: an unusual and unheard of thing for so many Masses to be said during a single day, on the Gila River![109] They were attended, with calmness and quiet, by a good number of Indians. We set out from Uturitúc at eleven o'clock in the morning, and by travelling four leagues course west-northwestward with some veerings eastward, at about three o'clock in the afternoon we halted on the bank of the Gila River near the settlement of Sutaquison, entitled *La Encarnación*[110] which lies a half league away from the river and whose governor was accompanying us. The Indians belonging to the pueblo came out to receive and to greet us with displays of great joy; I judged it to be one of four hundred to five hundred souls, and when we had gotten down they greeted us with great affection, setting their hands upon their chests. These are Indians like the last ones, ugly in appearance, and dedicated to toil and to their plantings, and, as they eat a great deal of péchita and screwbean, quite ill-smelling.

At a little under a league along the way, we passed by the San Andrés village and, a league before here, the village of *Atizón*, both of them being smaller pueblos, and this small-sized district amounts to almost the whole of the country occupied by the Gila Pima tribe; all of it is a thin, white soil that raises a very clinging, befouling dust, with which, and their coarse fare, the Indians here are all the more disgusting. At this spot the Gila River was dry and water could be gotten from it only by making wells in the sand; it is of use only in flood season for the Indians' fields and plantings. It has a continuous tree grove along its banks but the cottonwoods are not very large ones.

In the afternoon, the Indians had tobacco handed out to them and the women were promised a distribution of beads for the following day. The question was put to the Indians why they lived so far from the river, since earlier they had had their pueblo on its banks and now had moved it to a spot away from it. They answered that they changed site because, what with the groves and wood there, things were going badly for them near the river, from the Apaches, and being distant from it they had a free field for pursuing and killing Apaches that came to their pueblo. After midday there arrived at the camp an Opa Indian all painted on his face with red ochre and with his bow and arrows, that are not as good as those employed by the Gila people, and he commenced making his very long speech and through the interpreters we gathered that he was saying, in substance, that the Opas now were friends with the Yumas and a peace council had been held between those tribes at the place called *Agua Caliente*. I shall note that

---

[109] On All Souls Day, priests were allowed to celebrate Mass three times.
[110] The Incarnation.

Opas and Cocomaricopas and Chuchumaopas[111] are the same tribe and are only distinguished in name, according to the places they inhabit. The Gila folk said that Palma[112] sent a peace message to the Opas and that it was received by the latter, who responded to the message by sending them crosses as a peace sign.

[November] 3, Friday. I said Mass, and after it Father Garcés and Father Eixarch went to the pueblo along with the purveyor[113] to distribute beads to the women and after that went on to join us at the place at the lake. We set out from Sutaquison at a quarter to ten in the morning, and at noon halted on a plain where there was a small lake shown to us by the Indians, and sufficient grass,[114] having traveled for two leagues west-northwestward. Lying about westward from this spot, and thereabouts, is a mountain range called the *Comars* mountains that comes out of the Papaguería and runs northward, ending around about three leagues off, at the end of which the Gila River joins lower down with the La Asunción River, which is a big one, larger than the Gila by some[115] three times. Grass is very scarce in all this land, which has very nitrous, thin soil so that when dry it sends up great clouds of dust and when wet it is slippery: quite an ugly country, all told, even though fertile within the Indians' fields because of their application to cultivating it and their use of irrigation channels that draw from the river.

It began to rain as we were about to mount up, this being the wet season here, without any thunder and lightning, and it rained for a little while and at once stopped, but we were caught by a downpour along the way that got us considerably wet and ended in quite a strong southwest wind, and since the soil is so thin the footing became quite slippery. The spot, like all the others, has little grass, and bad at that because the ground is so nitrous. The Gila River runs from east to west and all the abovementioned pueblos lie on the south side, upon its banks; on the opposite side to the north is another pueblo called *Nabcúb*, entitled *San Serafino*—so named by Father Garcés[116]—about a league upriver from El Sutaquison.

[November] 4, Saturday. As it was the feast day of San Carlos and the saint's day of our Monarch[117] we sang Mass with all possible ceremony; Father Garcés sang it and I accompanied upon my psaltery, and earlier Father Tomás and I

---

[111]The final text removes the words "and Chuchumaopas." Cf. "Tutumaopas," mentioned in the journals of Juan Díaz, 21 May 1774 (Díaz, "Diario," and Soto Pérez 1998 1: 728) and of Garcés, where the name Tutum- was applied to the settlements at Agua Caliente (the November 14, March 31 camp) (cf. Forbes 1965: 127). All of the groups mentioned were part of the Pipatsje (Maricopa) people.
[112]The Quechán (Yuma) chief who was favored by Anza.
[113]Mariano Vidal.
[114]The final text retrospectively adds: "a lake of bad water that we called La Laguna del Hospital because some people fell ill at it."
[115]Stricken in the short text: "by at least."
[116]During his earlier excursions, the last one having been with Anza in 1774.
[117]Carlos III of Spain.

said a Mass. The march was ordered after midday but not begun because of a woman's falling ill. To celebrate the feast day, following Mass our commander decided to give a ration of drink to the people of the expedition, the ration amounting to a *cuartillo*[118] of *aguardiente*[119] for everyone, with which there was more than a middling amount of drunkenness among the troops, to the extent that more than one of them stayed drunk until the next day.

[November] 5, Sunday. I said Mass and during it gave a hortatory address in performance of my ministry. We delayed because the sick woman was unable to go on, and at nightfall another woman fell ill with very strong pains in the lower side. I observed for the latitude of this spot, and found it, by the tables of Jorge with no correction, in 33° 21½', and with correction in 33° 14½'.[120] And thus I say: at some lakes two leagues distant from the Gila River and the pueblo of Sutaquison, November 5, 1775: meridian altitude of the sun's lower limb: 40° 40'. I occupied myself today with drawing an ichnographic plat of the Casa Grande of Moctezuma.

[November] 6, Monday. I said Mass. The first sick woman became somewhat better but the second one continued very ill, for which reason our commander determined to keep us here, and following midday another woman fell ill of the same lower side pains, and as for myself, in addition to the sickness I already had, I came over with shivering after dinner, and, over an hour afterward, was seized with a fever that stayed with me until midnight. I spent this morning in our commander's tent, busied with drawing a plan of the Casa Grande that he asked me for, and, what with the heat in the tent, I already felt ill when I finished it before dinner, and then I became seized with the fever chills.

[November] 7, Tuesday. At dawn the sick women were better and so was I, wherefore it was decided to pursue the march. The ground at this spot is so briny that it whitens as though someone had spilled flour on it, and this may be the reason the water was so bad—briny and thick—that even the horses fell ill.

The Gila Indians, whose tribe ends here, enjoy better health and are quite fat and strong, perhaps because they are native to these lands, although I did notice that among all those that flocked to us on our arrival I did not see very many old men or old women. They attempt to clothe themselves in their cotton cloaks that they process and weave themselves, and with some coarse cloth they acquire through the trade they have with the Pápagos and the Upper Pimas and the presidios of Tubac[121] and Altar, and they use the coarse cloth to make their clouts with. Those who have no breeches replace them with a folded, tied-up blanket, and the women

---

[118] About a pint.
[119] Fruit brandy.
[120] The camp may have been in 33° 10' or 33° 11'.
[121] Added in the final text, "or Tuquisón, now."

cover themselves with deerskins. The hair styling they employ is an unusual one, since they take a thin woolen cord, about a *dedo* thick[122] and as long as a lead-rope, and bunching it up they insert it through their hair and tie it all together with a long cord and wind it around their head from the left side to the right. Then they fasten it with the leftover end, giving one or two turns around their head, and a projection, like a sort of wreath, is left atop it where those who possess any feathers put in some, along with little sticks, and ornaments. The women wear their hair dangling over their shoulders and ears and cut it off in front as far as their eyes or their eyebrows. What I shall finally say of these Gila Pimas is that they are well prepared to have missions founded among them, not only because they are well-behaved but also because they live in regular pueblos, since within the scope of some six leagues[123] there are five pueblos, the four above-mentioned ones on this side of the river and the one on the other side that Father Garcés called San Serafino de Nabcúb; and for the reason that they attempt to support themselves by their toil in their plantings. But since they live so close to the Apaches, a good-sized garrison is needed for their protection, and here (in addition to the expense) lies the problem in supporting it, for all of this country has very little grass as I have said above, both for mounts and even for livestock.

Using the greatest deftness, an Indian today stole a small china pot belonging to our commander; however, he was made to give it back. This matter of thievery is a trait common to every Indian.

We set out from the salty spot, which because some people had fallen sick we called *La Laguna del Hospital*[124] at one o'clock in the afternoon and at a quarter past six halted at a dry stream, having traveled for some six leagues upon a course of southwestward a bit over one league; about two leagues west-southwestward; and the remainder to westward. It is a spot having a good deal of grass for the animals, but no water.[125] The turn at the outset of the march was taken in order to get around quite a steep, not very high mountain running southeast and northwestward, and at this end of it, around which the Gila River runs curving from its usual course, the La Asunción River comes in from the north, much larger than the Gila River since it is made up of two rivers, one called the *Salado* for its briny water, and another called the *Verde* because of its having a great deal of green grass on its margins and in its neighborhood, according to what the Indians say. Today's route is very level soil and not as dusty as the last march; especially with movement in the air, the dust is such that it hinders breathing

---

[122] 7/10 of an inch.
[123] In the field text, "of seven leagues."
[124] Hospital Lake.
[125] In the final text, "some grass, no water."

and, one way or another, such a thick cloud of it arose that we were unable to see the rest of ourselves a short way off.

[November] 8, Wednesday. We set out from the dry stream at a half past eight in the morning and traveled for some nine leagues. We went about two leagues west-southwestward over level ground, and at once came into a pass in low, steep mountains which are the Comars range that runs out of the Papaguería towards the river, and traveled about a league westward until leaving the pass and then came into ground that was level as far as the bank of the river, going west-southwestward, and at about four o'clock in the afternoon we halted at the river bank at the place called *Uparsoytac*. At the time when Father Garcés, who titled this settlement *San Simón y Judas*, saw these Opa Indians of Uparsoytac there were not so many folk there as there are now, but more of them have gathered because of the war waged on them by their enemies, who required them to live closer together than they had been accustomed to, and who belong to the tribe called Nanaxi in the Pima language and are the Tejua Yabipays that border with the Apaches upon the north, or else are Apaches. They[126] showed themselves very well-behaved and received us well, and three of them came on horseback to greet us.

Following midday, I was seized by chills and then the fever came on me more strongly than on the 6th so that it manifested itself as being a tertian, although my diarrhea had improved a bit. I had some trouble finishing the march.

The Opa Indians here support themselves by their plantings of wheat, maize and gourds and they seemingly do not eat so much péchita and screwbean as the Gila folk and they do not stink like them nor do they have rotten teeth. As they live next to their fields, the settlement or villages extend for about a league along the side of the river, from which they do not bring irrigating ditches since, due to the fact that the Gila and the La Asunción rivers come joined into one all the way from the end of the Comars range near La Laguna del Hospital, the river bed is very wide and carries a great deal of water, more so at flood season at which time it spreads out a great deal and waters a great deal of level soil, which is the irrigation that gives them their crops. It would not be hard, I think, to make ditches in order to improve the fields.

These Indians live mingled with some Pimas, and men and women use almost the same head styling as the Gila people and go dressed in their cotton cloaks and also the dark woolen ones with white streaks that they get from *El Moqui*.[127] They also are accustomed to paint their faces and bodies, even using soot if they cannot afford red ochre, and they work the painting so as to make rays, and this is their fancy dress. They are very fond of beads for collars and earrings, which

---

[126] The Opas.
[127] The Hopi pueblos.

they wear both in their ears and in their noses, the central cartilage of which they customarily have pierced. Their bodies are good-sized and they are as well shaped and brave as the Pimas, with small difference—not as ugly as those before—, though their bows and arrows are somewhat inferior. On one side and the other farther up the river, there are a number of small-sized villages of Indians belonging to the same tribe, and they extend to near the junction of the Gila and La Asunción rivers, which join about twelve leagues above this spot.

[November] 9, Thursday. I said Mass. As the mounts had reached here very exhausted from yesterday's march because they had been sick at our setting out from La Laguna del Hospital, so much so that three animals died and some were left behind unable to follow, it was decided to lie by today. I arose with no fever and improved, although dizzy-headed. In the afternoon our commander distributed to the Indians beads and tobacco, and I estimated that about a thousand souls or a bit less had come together, and the gathering of the crowd gave rise to no small stink from their windiness, which they let go without any reserve.

Here we commenced seeing women wearing little skirts made from cottonwood and willow bark, like those worn by the Yumas, this being their clothing along with a deerskin that they wear tied at their waist, downward. The men go about a bit more covered, with their cotton cloaks (those that have them), and whereas they go much laden with bead necklaces and pendants on neck and ears and, with some of them, on noses, we did not see a single woman wearing such adornments, something that one would have expected to be the opposite. As we were at the edge of the river, the people were able to get their clothes washed. I thought that, if a mission is to be established here, the best spot is on the other side of the river, by locating the pueblo at the foot of some small heights half a league distant from the river and running east and west, but this must be examined more closely.

[November] 10, Friday. I said Mass. We delayed here, because at dawn a woman who had miscarried a dead child on the 2nd was very ill from her childbirth, as was a soldier who suffered a kind of a stroke yesterday night and had been a bit ill for some days past. I myself after midday was seized with chills and fever more strongly than before and with vomiting, which I kept experiencing until nightfall.

From here onward, the river has small title to the name Gila, since the major portion of its water comes from the river of La Asunción. According to the Indians' report, the river, which is quite big going past here, increases in the following manner. The Gila River comes from the east and has so little water at this season that it stops short. Near El Sutaquison it is joined by a small stream that, because of its salty water, they call the Salt River, and it comes from about north-northeastward, and is joined by the Gila River about ten leagues farther up from this place, as I said above. Before coming to the Opas and the villages of San Simón y Judas it[128] is already a big stream because it is joined by the river called La Asunción, which the Indians call the Azul River, also Verde, and they say it comes from the Apaches or else they say that they do not know where it comes from since it comes from very far off. And they say that another small river joins this one and, so joined, they unite with the Gila River. Shortly beyond where they join, before the *Uparsoytac* villages here, an arm splits off and makes a loop until close to the small heights I spoke of yesterday.[129] That is why, whereas in the previous spots belonging to the Opas the river still runs low, reaching to the animals' flanks, yet after the branch has rejoined it further down, it becomes much bigger, as we experienced when fording it. I thought it possible for an irrigation ditch to be taken off it.[130]

[November] 11, Saturday. At ten o'clock in the morning we set out from the Uparsoytac settlement and, by traveling westward for a league and a half, arrived about noon at Opa villages located at the edge of the river. We halted here since there was some grass and stubble in the fields for the mounts. It began drizzling as soon as we had stopped and kept on in that way all the day until night, but after nightfall the rain stopped, and at daybreak the weather was better.

[November] 12, Sunday. I said Mass, saying four words of exhortation to the people. We set out from the Opa villages at a half past nine in the morning and halted at two o'clock in the afternoon at the river bank at some Indians' lodges. Since it was the feast of San Diego, we named the village *San Diego*, having traveled five leagues west-northwestward. There is some grass in its surroundings though a great deal of it had been burnt by the Indians. The route is not through such bad, salty land as on the previous march; some mesquite trees, but no grass,[131] encountered. As it was bad day for me,[132] I went on ahead and had the fever overtake me upon the way. Having reached the stopping place I lay down there and my fever lasted until nightfall. The river here was very deep down and with little of a flow.

[November] 13, Monday. I awoke relieved of my tertian fever. We set out from the San Diego village at a quarter past nine in the morning and halted a bit after one o'clock in the afternoon, shortly after fording the river, at a spot called *Aritoac*, having traveled some four leagues westward. The spot has very little grass and there is none elsewhere. The route is not a very bad one; on setting out from

---

[128]The Gila River.
[129]In the field text, "until close to some heights"; in the final text, "goes past the small heights I spoke of yesterday." The descriptions in the two texts are combined here into this paragraph.
[130]This last sentence is only in the final text, where it is added between lines.
[131]"Little grass," in the final text.
[132]Refers to the recurring malarial fever.

the camping place we went up over a small range formed of boulders and coarse black stones all heaped together, as it were, and there is level ground continuing on just beyond. A good ford was searched for along the river, which here runs very swollen, its flow coming not from the Gila but from the Azul River, so that it came up to a horse's flank. We crossed it without incident; however, it is quite formidable at the seasons of its rising as can be seen from the bed and overflowed places along it.

[November] 14, Tuesday. I said Mass. We set out from El Aritoac at nine o'clock in the morning and, following mid-day, came to the spot of *El Agua Caliente*[133] having traveled four leagues on a west-southwestward course. This place has a large hot-water spring and small springs of not very good cold water, and there also is grass—not, however, very much of it and fairly despicable at that—reaching as far as the river, which lies about two leagues away from El Agua Caliente and appears to be running southwestward. It is an open spot having a considerable view around, but very scant qualifications for a settlement.

On setting out from the camp we went over some little heights of dark rocks, heaped together, as it were, and over very bad land until going down to the river, and then we went along its shores or overflow spots, which are very broad and led us away from it. From the top of the little heights one can make out, very far in the distance, the mountain of *La Cabeza del Gigante*[134] that the Indians call *El Bauquíburi*.[135] I went on ahead and the tertian chills and fever came on me before noon and lasted until nightfall.

[November] 15, Wednesday. It was decided to delay here today to let the mounts rest as they were in a dreadful state from lack of grazing. A great many Indians who lodge on the river banks above and below here, Cocomaricopas, gathered to see us. In their manner, clothing, and even in language they are the same thing as Opas[136] and have a different name because of the district they live in. Our commander, in the name of our lord King, gave the title and staff of governor of the entire tribe to an Indian chosen by themselves whom we named Carlos, and to another, whom they chose and we named Francisco, the alcalde's staff.[137] When they had been instructed in their new duties and functions, the rest of the gathered Indians greeted the new justices in token of submission each in turn, by giving them their hand once they were confirmed in their positions. Afterward,

---

[133] Hot Water.

[134] The Giant's Head.

[135] See the December 4 entry below. The name is not to be confused with Baboquivari Peak in south-central Arizona.

[136] The field text adds, "and almost the same as Yumas."

[137] According to Garcés, one of the elders at first objected to the new offices on the grounds that since the Opas were not bad people—not thieves, not quarrelsome, not misbehaving with women—why did they need magistrates? (Galvin 1967: 10).

tobacco was handed out to all of them and beads to the women, and this spot and its governance were entitled *San Bernardino del Agua Caliente*.

I observed for the latitude of this spot (though the day was a fairly cloudy one and I could not make the observation precise, so that I am not very satisfied with it but will record it anyway) and found it according to the tables of Jorge with no correction in 33° 8½' and with correction in 33° 2½'.[138] And thus I say: at El Agua Caliente, November 15, 1775: meridian altitude of the sun's lower limb: 38° 4'.

The Indians whom I saw gathered here I estimated to be about two hundred souls at most, all of them unarmed and friendly, and in the evening they stayed until past midnight singing their own kind of music, quite a mournful one. El Agua Caliente is a very level open location with a very wide horizon, and the spring rises at the foot of some small rocky heights. It is not a very good spot, yet the least bad one that I saw for a mission belonging to the Opas here. At this season it is already very cold, and the water, although coming forth very hot, immediately chilled in the water bags, and even froze during the night.

[November] 16, Thursday. As it was a bad day for me, and so that the fever should not catch me upon the road, our commander determined that I should go on ahead with two soldiers, my lad and my two pack mules, and Father Fray Tomás came along with me for the same reason, as a few days ago he had a recurrence of the quartan fever that he had had before, and this was a bad day for him too. The march was supposed to be a four leagues' one, as far as the stopping place that they named San Bernardino in the last expedition, an islet formed by the river when it rises any amount where there is sufficient grass and some villages of Indians. However, the soldier who was acting as a guide lost track of where we were going and having passed it by, we traveled for about ten leagues at a good pace. Suffering as I was with the fever, and seeing that it was past two o'clock in the afternoon (we had set out from El Agua Caliente at a half-past eight) and that we were getting much farther away from the river, after I had several times reproached the soldier over our getting lost I at last took myself in hand and said that I was not going any further since it was not possible our commander had intended to make so long a march. And so I started off toward the river and as soon as I reached the cottonwoods, got down and said that I was not going away from there, back or forward. The lad with my pack mules got lost also and finally found us before sunset, and the three soldiers whom our commander had ordered out ahead to scout out the Colorado River and the bad route through the dunes lying beyond the river, arrived as well; and the soldier who had been guiding us went away with them and we were left alone.

Our commander, seeing that we had gone on ahead, supposed we had found a

---

[138] The latitude figure is about two minutes too high.

better spot than the one he had told us of to stop in, and so he continued onward with all of the troops. However, seeing that the day was coming to an end without his having encountered us, he halted at a half past four in the afternoon in the grove along the river not far from the water, where there was a little grass. He had set out at a half past nine in the morning and had traveled nine leagues. He sent the sergeant to look for us, and after he[139] had found us about one league below where the camp had been set up he returned and reported; and our commander sent two soldiers to be with us during the night, along with tablets of chocolate, some dried fruit and a bit of cake. Here we waited through the night—I and Father Tomás, through our fevers—and the pack trains and livestock reached camp very late at night with a great many delays and with worn-out animals. The whole route is quite level ground, but worthless, with a good deal of dust and no grass. The course of the march was west-southwestward with some veerings westward; and the river follows a southwestward course. The cottonwood grove along the river is taller now and very extensive, and to judge by the marks left by the river, in its flooding it must be a league in width, and in spots, more than that.

[November] 17, Friday. As our commander found himself in a spot that did not have very much grass, he decided to go ahead and make this little march, and he set out from near the river at about ten o'clock in the morning. We ourselves awoke somewhat improved though with teeth chattering, and downhearted from the already very raw chill that occurs in this country at this season, so much so that water froze within our water bags, and at mid-morning I decided to set off for the camp. I scarcely had left our spot when I met the livestock coming along the route, and they told us that the soldiers were on the way. We waited for them and in the meanwhile I dined upon a bit of cooked rice sent us by our commander, and shortly thereafter I and Father Tomás joined him and the people. We went on, following the route on a west-southwestward course, and on traveling about two leagues halted at the river's edge where there was some grass, chiefly a tough sort to which the soldiers gave the name *galleta* grass.[140] We reached here shortly after midday.

[November] 18, Saturday. I said Mass. We set out from the river's edge at ten o'clock in the morning and, by traveling for four leagues course southwestward with a little veering to one side or the other, we halted at about two o'clock in the afternoon near the river at the foot of the *San Pascual* height, a very steep rocky mountain of middling height that comes from nearly south, northward out of the Papaguería and ends at the river's edge; they gave it this name during the last

---

[139]The sergeant, Juan Pablo Grijalva.
[140]Literally, "hardtack" grass. In an annotation to Montané's edition of the final text (Montané 2000: 133), Professor Solana lists the several species of *galleta*.

expedition. Halfway along the route we forded the river for the second time. The way is very sandy, with dunes in spots, and after crossing the river the ground is very nitrous, so much so that near the stopping place the soldiers found a spot close to the water that was all granular salt and the people supplied themselves with a bit of it. Grass is scarce; there is nothing but some wretched cane-grass in a low spot caused by the river. Since it was a bad day for me, I went on ahead with Father Tomás and the chills came over me halfway along the route and afterward my fever lasted until nightfall. Father Tomás went off to fish and caught some of the sort they call *matalotes*[141] that are very full of spines, and presented me with some. It seems that the river has no other kind than these and few of them at that.

[November] 19, Sunday. I said Mass. After midnight last night a woman[142] successfully delivered a child, for which reason we delayed here today and after Mass I formally baptized the newborn and named him Diego Pascual, it being the octave of San Diego, and also for San Pascual which was the place where we were. As this was a good day for me, I took sufficient heart to say Mass. There is a very steep mountain range in view afar off from here (since this is mostly a very level country); as seen toward the north, it runs about east and west deviating to southwestward and the Indians say that the Jalchedun[143] tribe, which inhabits the banks of the Colorado River, is on the far side of the range.

The governor and alcalde who were installed as magistrates at El Agua Caliente came here accompanied by other Indians belonging to their tribe, in order to join and go on with us to visit the Yumas and, through our interposition, to confirm the peace agreement with them. The governor said that he was only happy to be going with us, as otherwise he would be very fearful as to his enemies' reliability, as they are bad people, etc. (for Indians always are accustomed to mistrust those who have been their enemies). This Opa, or Cocomaricopa, tribe, which reaches from the Gila people downriver to about as far as this spot, is so small-sized a one to judge from the number of people who have gathered together to visit us, attracted by the novelty and by the beads, that seemingly they do not amount to three thousand souls, a small number in comparison to the land that they occupy, for there is no other tribe in over fifty leagues' distance toward all four quarters. This is proof of how wretched a country it is, made almost uninhabitable by its barrenness and sterility, as is well shown by the hunger and poverty in which these Opa Indians live. From which I conclude

---

[141] According to Professor Solana (Montané 2000: 88), this would be the *matalote yubarta* (in English, razorback sucker). Under March 24 in northern California the same word is used for a fish whose mouth, as described, does suggest a sucker. The "spines," however, might also indicate a pikeminnow (formerly called "squawfish"). Under April 7, still up in northern California, Font possibly wanted to compare the fish to a shad.
[142] Ana María de Osuna, wife of Ignacio María Gutiérrez. They already had two daughters.
[143] The Halchidhoma.

that two missions would do for these heathen people, one at Uparsoytac—and this one might be some good—and another at El Agua Caliente or a better spot if one is found, which I judge it will not be very easy to do—and this one will be a mission with few people and with small prospects. So that by placing two more missions at El Sutaquison and at Uturitúc for the Gila folk,[144] all of the gentile people that occupy this great river will be under administration.

In view of our delay, since the grass or cane-grass here was insufficient, a place was sought for the animals to be pastured on stubble, and God saw fit that a large patch of grass or straw was found on the other side of the river about a league away from the camp, and the mounts and livestock were taken there. I observed at this spot and found it, according to the tables of Jorge with no correction, in 32° 54', and with correction in 32° 48'.[145] And thus I say: at the San Pascual height, November 19, 1775: meridian altitude of the sun's lower limb: 37° 20'.

[November] 20, Monday. I said Mass. We delayed because the woman who had recently delivered a child was unable to travel, and we felt the raw chill of the season even more. I had it[146] in feet and legs very intensely from dawn onward and it did not leave me until nearly noon, when the fever came on me and lasted until past mid-afternoon, which, what with the discharge of a great deal of watery diarrhea and a great lack of appetite, left me much weakened.

[November] 21, Tuesday. I awoke better off though much exhausted in strength; already on the day previous I had begun taking some medicine, such as can be had in this forsaken country. We did not travel today since the woman who gave birth was not ready yet to move. I again observed this spot, for the purpose of comparing this observation with the preceding one, and found it, according to Jorge, in 32° 54½', the same as on the 19th,[147] and thus I say: at the San Pascual height, November 21, 1775: meridian altitude of the sun's lower limb: 36° 52'. Today a soldier found a salt deposit on the other side of the river with salt in the form of salt froth as white as snow, so that, along with the other day's supply which was granular salt, the soldiers provided themselves with salt in plenty. This proves how salty the river and all of this country is, for it yields nothing else, not even firewood in any plenty for curing the intense chill of the weather here.

[November] 22, Wednesday. I said Mass. The woman who gave birth awoke improved and it was decided to pursue our journey. We set out from the San Pascual height at a half past eleven in the morning, and having traveled some six long

---

[144] The Akimel O'odham (Gila River Pimas).
[145] The figure is about a minute and a half higher than the actual latitude.
[146] The chill preceding malarial fever.
[147] That is, uncorrected. The recorded difference of half a minute is ignored because, in the field text, Font originally reported the two latitude readings according to the less accurate tables of Gasco as being exactly the same (32° 48').

leagues upon a west-southwestward course with a few veerings southwestward, at a quarter past four in the afternoon we halted on the river bank at the foot of a small low height, flat on its top, that the Indians call the *Cerro del Metate*[148] and we called the *Santa Cecilia* height. Today's route is almost level but quite fatiguing because it is thin sandy soil, with little hills and patches of dunes. The river goes along at a greater or less distance upon the right; it overflows onto those plains a great amount. A short distance away to the left is a dune that continues along between the San Pascual height and the stopping place, and the whole area is like all the rest of it, with no grass, or anything else to replace it. At the stopping place alone was there some small galleta- and dune-grass. For as far as the eye can see, the land seems to be of the same quality on the other side of the river, which comes very spreading and in bends, and runs a bit constricted past the stopping place.

The tertian fever attacked me so little today that I hardly felt it, perhaps because day before yesterday a soldier's wife named Francisca Ruelas[149]—his name is Pablo Pinto—gave me a very hot draft of water boiled with cilantro and oregano which is good for stopping chills and fevers, even when done with just cilantro.

[November] 23, Thursday. I said Mass. After the pack trains had already set out they were ordered to return since it was past eleven o'clock and it had not been possible yet to gather the mounts, who, because there was no grass, had gone straying a great deal; for which reason we paused here today, and also because at the same hour the livestock came up that had been left tired out along the way yesterday. Some animals[150] perished from tiredness and from all the raw chill felt here and because of lack of grass.

[November] 24, Friday. I said Mass. Last night a pregnant woman[151] fell sick, as though trying to give birth before her time was here, and since she arose still ill, our commander decided we should delay here, and when he had aided her by giving her a delicacy he had, which was a plate of food,[152] she improved. I observed the latitude of this spot and by the tables of Jorge Juan I found it, with no correction, in 32° 44½', and with correction in 32° 39'.[153] And thus I say: at the Santa Cecilia del Metate height, November 24, 1775: meridian altitude of the sun's lower limb: 36° 24'. The fever came over me, following midday, and lasted for about two hours although with some improvement and not so strong as it had been at the start.

---

[148]Mortar Hill.
[149]Later referred to as Tía Francisca when she gave Font a further herbal cure (December 21).
[150]Horses and/or mules.
[151]Gertrudis Rivas, wife of Ignacio Linares. See below, December 25, and in the introduction.
[152]Anza's journal says it was medicines to delay the premature birth. Either Font—and the woman too?—were not informed of the fact, or else Anza's entry prevaricated in order to enhance his image as being in control of the expedition
[153]Font's figure is, for a change, about three minutes too low.

[November] 25, Saturday. I said Mass. We set out from the Santa Cecilia del Metate height at a quarter to ten in the morning and by traveling four leagues southwest by west halted at a quarter to two in the afternoon at the edge of a briny lake about a league distant from the river, although it is an overflow from it. Along the way a Yuma Indian who was sent by Chief Palma and is one of his chief companions met us riding on a mare and told us how Palma with all of his Yuma folk and the Jalchedunes as well, who had come down to the river junction in order to see us, was awaiting us in peace on the strength of a message sent to them from the spot called El Agua Caliente. We traveled during the whole way over ground that is covered by the river when it rises, and a bit of grass was only to be found at the stopping place, where there were great amounts of drift or piles of timber and brushwood brought down by the river during its formidable floodings.

[November] 26, Sunday. I said Mass, during which I gave an address in which I particularly condemned an abuse that I had noted, involving some soldiers whose behavior with respect to their wives was so jealous that in addition to not letting them talk with anyone else, they had forbidden them to come to Mass.

We set out from the briny lake at a quarter past ten in the morning and halted at two o'clock in the afternoon at the edge of the river, having traveled some four leagues on a westward course, with a bit of—or mostly—veering west-north-westward. If yesterday's route was a poor one, today's was worse, keeping along the river within sight of it near or far, and traveling over sandy grounds and a sort of dunes that the river floods over when it rises. Father Tomás got a fish out of it today, a matalote of some size, and a lad caught an even larger one, and it looks as though the river does not produce any other kind of fish. At the stopping place there was a patch of straw for the mounts, and there were signs showing that Yumas had camped there a bit earlier, perhaps coming to eat péchita, of which there is a little bit here, and to walk about as they are accustomed to do. The country has no more trees in it than the cottonwoods growing on the banks of the river, and, in my view, nothing that is of any use for human existence.

A steep, rocky, and arid mountain range of some little height runs upon this side of the river, coming out of the Papaguería with apparently several short spurs that run in a number of directions to the dunes of the Papaguería; it ends upon the banks of the river, upon whose other side there runs, slightly roundabout from southeast to northwest, another range, not very high, with the same attributes and a bit red-colored, along whose skirts the river runs and in which an almost square peak with four points that we called *El Bonete*[154] can be seen opposite the stopping place.

---

[154] *The Biretta. A type of clerical hat used by (among others) the Jesuit Fathers who had previously had the Sonora missionary field.

CHAPTER 2

Yuma and the Desert

[November] 27, Monday. I said Mass. We set out from the river's edge at a half past nine in the morning and by traveling northwestward for two leagues we halted at a half past eleven on the edge of the river at a passage through which the Gila River runs constricted between the range on this side that I spoke of yesterday and another that lies upon the other side; plainly, whenever the river rises it runs very rapidly here. Along the way a relative of Chief Palma came to receive us, and as soon as we halted, Chief Salvador Palma himself and another chief whom we named Pablo, came to visit us accompanied by a number of Yuma Indians as we were dining. They greeted us with many a show of happiness, particularly Chief Palma, who embraced all of us and presented our commander with a small amount of *orimuni* beans,[1] and the latter[2] during the afternoon took him around the camp to inspect all the people, whom he proceeded to greet by giving an embrace to everyone, men, women and children, in token of goodwill.

This Chief Palma is the man presently in command over the entire Yuma tribe. He has come to rule because of his bravery and his speech-making, as among Indians is usually the case, and even more because of the importance that the Spaniards—Captain Anza now, and before him already Captain Urrea[3]—have most recently been attaching to him. This is the reason that he is acknowledged by Pablo, the other chief, to whom we gave this name because he is chief of the villages near the small height that Father Garcés had called San Pablo. Because of his ugly looks he was called *El Capitán Feo* during the last expedition.[4] The population of the villages belonging to this Pablo Feo is greater than that of

---
[1] Properly spelled *yorimuni*, a Yaqui and Río Mayo term, "white bean." A smallish, strongly flavored indigenous variety.
[2] Anza.
[3] Bernardo de Urrea, Anza's predecessor as frontier commander and negotiator with the native nations beyond the frontier; at this time he was semi-retired at Altar, Sonora.
[4] The Ugly Chief Pablo.

Chief Palma's villages, and I thought him possessed of a great deal of wit, as much or more than Palma has, even though he is subject to the latter. He is a great preacher, full-voiced (and they say he is also a sorcerer), and at nightfall he gave a big sermon, a long speech, to his people which amounted to telling them they should not steal from or do harm to the Spaniards as they were friends who did no ill. Our commander told me how last time, when he made his way here during the first expedition, this Chief Feo set to counting the number of soldiers, and seeing there were not many of them he commenced saying to his men that it would not be hard to slay them all in order to keep the horses and whatever else the Spaniards brought with them, and such were his intentions. When this was understood by our commander, he had him informed that if he wished for war he should gather all his own people and many more and he would see just how they[5] would defend themselves and how badly it would go with them.[6] And, with that he pulled back. And although at that time he attempted to oppose the expedition's passage by the Colorado River, this time he has been very serviceable and has shown himself very inclined to us.

[November] 28, Tuesday. I said Mass, which was heard by the two chiefs with a good deal of peacefulness, modesty, and attention. We set out from the passage and banks of the Gila at a quarter past nine in the morning and by traveling five leagues west-southwestward with some turnings, we arrived at a quarter to two in the afternoon at the shore of the Colorado River[7] after easily fording the Gila River for the third time, just before its joining with the Colorado. The Yumas accommodated us within a ramada that Chief Palma ordered to be made here as soon as he learned of our coming. A few people assembled; most of them, however, were on the other side of the river, and we were told they would come over on the following day.

A great many[8] Indians of both sexes came here to visit us, very pleasure-loving and happy and much painted in different manners and various colors. The Gila River joins the Colorado River about a league lower down from this spot, which is what was called *La Isla de la Trinidad*[9] during the last expedition because this piece of ground then was made an island by the Gila, the Colorado, and a branch of the latter that joined the Gila before the Gila joined the Colorado.[10] There was no such island now because of the shifting ground caused by the rivers when they flood.

On arriving here, the soldiers were ordered to fire off shots, something that the Yumas like very much, this salvo being a response to the pleasure manifested

---

[5] Anza and his men.
[6] With Pablo's side.
[7] In the short text, added and then partly stricken: "the Gila and Colorado river," as if they were a single feature here.
[8] Font's final text with its "great many" is obviously inconsistent with what the field text has just called "a few people."
[9] Trinity Island.
[10] Some of the wording is inserted here from the following entry in the field text.

by these people at our coming; and they responded to the musket shots with a great cheering and hubbub. Shortly after we had reached here, Governor Carlos of the Opas came in along with his alcalde Francisco and some others, in order to make peace. He commenced his speech from horseback, riding across in front of the Indians, of which Palma disapproved and gave him to understand that if he had come to confirm the peace and had a good heart he ought to dismount and speak to him on foot, just as he himself was, and not passing in front of everyone in this fashion; whereupon he got down at once. Carlos and Palma, who were holding their staffs while sitting down upon the ground with the rest of the people surrounding them, talked briefly with each other. Then the preacher-chief Pablo took the lead. He stood up in the midst of all of them, gave a big sermon all of which amounted to saying that they did not wish for any more wars since we had decreed so (and he pointed to those of us who were present, our commander and myself and the Fathers). And, pointing toward all four quarters and in all directions, he said repeatedly in a very loud voice and with gestures and movements and grimaces of great earnestness, that now they intended to be relatives and friends with every tribe and people or *queyé*[11] which means fellow countrymen. And to conclude, our commander ordered the two chiefs, Palma and Carlos, to embrace each other, which was done, and following the lead of the two chiefs, the rest of the people did so also.

The basis for this peace had been laid during the other expedition when the commander told them that the king did not wish them to be at war and that if any tribe attempted to harm another, the Spaniards would come to punish the offence.[12] Father Garcés before that had persuaded them of the same. And perhaps that is why they started trading with each other, for last year scarcely a single Indian was seen wearing a cloak. But now we are seeing some of them wearing cotton cloaks that are made by the Opas and one or two black wool cloaks of the sort that are made at Moqui and acquired by the Jalchedunes and other friends of the Moquis.

We went to dine, and in affirmation of the peace, after first asking for and getting permission from our commander, Chief Palma took Governor Carlos and all his people to dine at his house and on the following day gave him provisions of beans, péchita and other things of theirs for his journey whenever he should wish to go back. After nightfall, Yumas and Opas stayed around the fire until very late, lying stretched out upon the ground and half buried in the sand and

---

[11]In the field text, Font made several attempts at spelling this word, trying both *queyé* and *jeyé*, and ended with the latter.

[12]This time, Anza exempted from his order of protection the tribe belonging to the mountains in the west (i.e., those whom Garcés and Font call Quemeyá, the Kumeyaay [Dieguinos]), who had been stealing horses from "our new establishments of Alta California" and had killed a Spaniard (in 1769).

heaped together like swine, as is their habit, singing in their mournful fashion and using a basket to strike a drum. I spent some time with them myself.

At nightfall, along with an interpreter, I met with Chief Palma and had a long conversation with him inside the ramada concerning whether he wished me and other Fathers to come and live there with his people. His answer was that he would be very happy if we would, and everyone else would too. And I continued by saying to him that this would require their learning the *doctrina* in order to become Christians, and also that they would have to learn masonry, carpentry, tilling the fields and toiling, and so forth. And, they would have to live together in a pueblo that the people would build in order to live there together in their houses, not scattered about as they do now, and that a house must be built for the Father as well as a church. To all of this, Palma answered that they would be very pleased to do everything I said, although he himself had gotten too thickheaded to learn things, and that he only wished this could happen now and that we were not about to be leaving. And that insofar as building the pueblo, there was a hill or tableland on the other side of the river, not reached by it[13] which he had already scouted out as suitable for our dwelling there. I said to him that I would be coming back in order to report this speech of his to the king, and that since he and his people wished to become Christians and be on good terms with Spaniards, the king next year would doubtless tell us to return and live here with them. If I were to come back, I would teach them to work and also to sing. Palma listened to this with such pleasure that he set to singing the *Alabado* along with me, and took his leave with many embraces and displays of happiness. He concluded by saying that he was a Spaniard now and I was a Yuma, and queyé.[14] Chief Pablo Feo was present at this whole discourse, attending closely and agreeing to the same with great pleasure.

[November] 29, Wednesday. I said Mass inside the ramada, which was some four varas wide and about eight long[15] and in which we set up an altar with a portrait of the Virgin brought along by Father Garcés.

Because the Colorado River is so free-flowing and overflows so far over the plains here, just as we did not find the island of La Trinidad any more, so also the ford was gone that the expedition crossed by the first time. The Indians said that the Colorado ford was very deep,

because every year these two rivers, the Gila and the Colorado, flood so extremely and run so unrestrainedly over the level, loose ground here, it seems that they change their course a bit by forming gullies, and break out into branches according to the way in which the water shifts its force to one side or another. The evident fact is that the Gila alone, during its highest flood, occupies over a league; one can imagine how much the Colorado must do, since it is so much bigger.

---

[13]Not flooded by it during the high water season.
[14]In the field text, Font's attempts to re-spell this word left it illegible, with *queyé* added in the margin.
[15]So, about 11 by 22 feet.

It was proposed, therefore, to cross the river with rafts, but when our commander considered that ferrying all that assemblage over on rafts would be a very long and costly task, he went instead with some soldiers to survey the river and returned saying that with some trouble he had found a ford across the Colorado River, a little above the old one and the place where we were, that was not very bad. During the afternoon, once that had been found, a way was cleared through the woods and trees in the bottom land for crossing the river on the following day.

A great many people of both sexes came here today, all of them very pleased as to our coming, and passing from one of the Spaniards' messes to another, visiting them with an excessive amount of friendliness and a curiosity to see and inspect everything, to the point of becoming importunate and tedious. A Jalchedun came to see us also, and went back with a message for him to give to his people concerning our arrival and the affirming of the peace. Word went out that in the evening our commander would make a present of beads to those persons gathered, but this was not carried out until after we had crossed the river.[16]

[November] 30, Thursday. I said Mass, which was heard by Governor Carlos and other Indians, and afterward he made an address in which he said his heart was very happy because the peace had been made and because he saw that we were staying among the Yuma people here with such pleasure and satisfaction. And he and the alcalde had been entrusted with sending on to Tubac some letters that Father Garcés passed to him. The aforesaid Cocomaricopa, Governor Carlos, left for his own country after Mass, having come with us in order to affirm the peace with the Yumas, and he went back quite happy. And we ourselves went off to the river, following a route that the muleteers, to the amazement of Palma and the other Yumas, had opened the afternoon before through the woods and brush, which are very dense for a great piece before reaching the river.

We set out from the shore of the Colorado River[17] at nine o'clock in the morning and at one o'clock in the afternoon the entire expedition, people and mule trains, finished fording the river with no particular accident. We crossed it where it split into three branches and a small side channel, and having traveled around a short league northward we stayed upon the Colorado River bank. I estimated the river's width here where we forded it to be three hundred varas and perhaps a bit more,[18] and this is at the present season when it is at its lowest; when it rises its width extends for leagues on this land which is so flat. We were fortunate

---

[16]In the field text, "In the evening, our commander made a present," etc., canceled by adding "but he did not do so."

[17]Stricken in the short text: "of the Gila and Colorado River," as earlier.

[18]In the final text, "between three hundred and four hundred varas." 300 varas is 825 feet; 400 varas is 1100 feet.

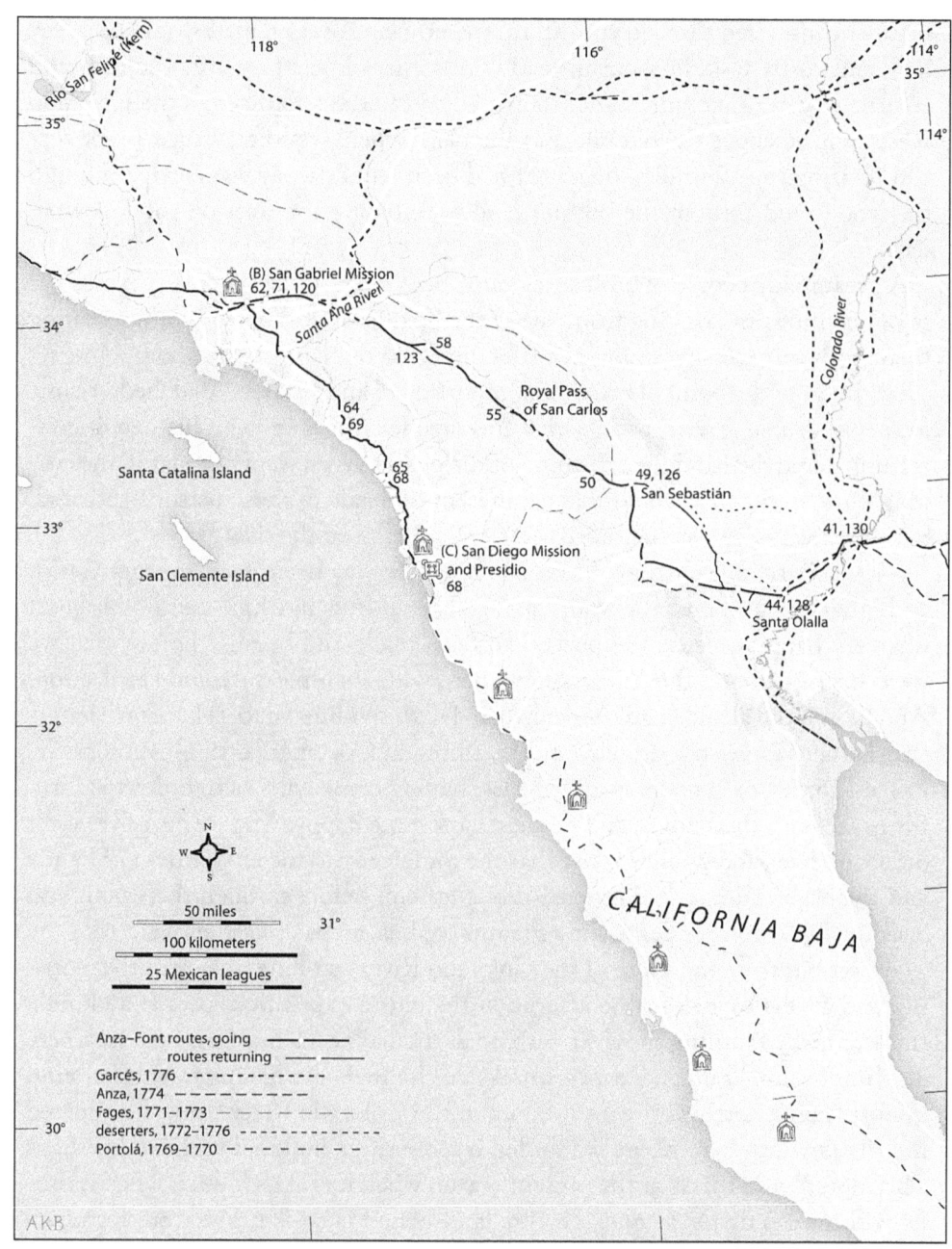

FIGURE 12. Redrawn and annotated version of Font's general map, south-central section: the desert, southern California.

to find the river here split into branches, for this eased the crossing of it which otherwise would have been difficult. The first branch was narrow and deep, the second not so deep and more constricted, and the third branch also deep and much broader than the first. The people all crossed without accident, although there might well have been one, because the animals were swimming while getting across the ford and one man, acting as though he were unafraid of the river, turned aside and at once went under, so that the water took from him a blanket and some baskets and a small child he was carrying in front of him began to slip from his grasp. But the Virgin willed for us to get to the other side with no other damage other than getting a bit wet, since the water reached up to the backs of even the tall horses, such as mine, and thus I was wet up to my knee.

The pack trains were sent across then, by dividing loads or sending one *tercio*[19] across with each mule, and thereupon all the livestock, mounts and pack beasts got successfully across.

The only load that got wet was one of mine in which I was carrying holy oils and vestments. Since so little attention was being paid to me and to whatever I said, despite my charging the muleteers to be careful not to let it get wet and my begging the same thing of our commander, it may have been for that very reason that this was the load with which they used the least care. Three Yumas carried Father Garcés across on their shoulders, two of them at his head and one at his feet, stretched out face upward like a dead man. I myself crossed on horseback and, as I was feeling ill and light-headed, I was accompanied by three servants, unclothed, one in front leading the horse and one on each side holding me up to keep me from falling off.

As the assemblage was a big one, we spent about three hours fording the river and we stayed right on its bank in order to dry out our wet things. One can imagine, from what I have said about fording the Colorado River, how monstrously large it is when it rises. For a ford where the animals did not have to swim was only found with difficulty, even though this is the season now when it runs lowest, and we crossed it before it joins the Gila River, and it split into three branches where we forded it, not counting another branch that remained for us to cross, How formidable it must be down lower where it joined with the Gila and when it is flooding!

Our commander went in the afternoon along with Father Garcés and Father Tomás to Palma's house, and to see the place next to it where a ramada or jacal was to be built for a dwelling for those two Fathers, who had come in order to remain here at the Colorado River to catechize the Yumas and explore the willingness of other tribes, and so forth.

December 1, Friday. We delayed for the purpose of building a jacal at Chief Palma's village for a dwelling for Fathers Garcés and Eixarch who were to remain here at the river. Our commander went there with the Fathers and returned at

---

[19]A portion of a mule load; the word literally means "a third," but it came to denote a part of a quantity of material, often one half.

sunset, and the muleteers worked on the building the entire day. The location of Palma's house was a bit over a league away from the camp. We had a very tedious day because a north-northwest wind arose at dawn, so strong that we scarcely were able to keep the tents standing, and it ceaselessly raised the soil under our feet, a very fine sand, made foul and sticky by fine dust from the dried slime left by the river, allowing us neither to breathe nor to see and fouling our clothes and everything else; this hardship lasted until the sun went down. Some Jalchedunes came in peace to see us in the afternoon.[20] Our commander said that he would make the Indians a present of beads and tobacco if they gathered at Palma's house, but inasmuch as they live so dispersed, he thought that too few of them had gathered, so that he put off giving presents.

Palma put on the clothing that had been presented to him on behalf of the most excellent viceroy, which was a shirt, breeches, and a yellow suede jacket with a bit of decoration, a cloak or sleeved cape made of blue cloth with braid on it, and a black velvet cap decorated with fake stones and a palm-leaf-shaped plume. This chief is called Palma because of the friendship he formerly maintained with a steward of Mission Caborca who was named Palma and whose name he took; and he is called Salvador because he was given this name by the Indian Sebastián Taraval at the time the latter left California for here in Sonora and stayed at the chief's house for some days. On behalf of the viceroy, our commander brought the clothing and gave it to him at nightfall and had him put it on there in his tent, the two of them together, without our being present or informed of it. This is because he is so fond of appropriating all of his accomplishments to himself and of winning respect that he refuses to let anyone else have a part in them, nor does he let anyone into his fellowship who might in any way attract people's appreciation, which he desires all for himself. For this reason, although it would have been normal for the presents of beads and tobacco that he brought in His Majesty's name to have been distributed to the Indians by the three of us Fathers who were on the expedition to gain their goodwill, since it is the Religious, after all, who are to be their ministers, and the Indians show favor and respect to those who give to them, the commander nonetheless made those distributions himself and would never allow us to do so. Nor did he ever, during the whole way, give me so much as a string of beads in case I should take a notion to give any Indian a present, save when we were at Mission San Luis upon our return, where he gave me a small number of bead strings because I asked him for them.

I proposed to our commander that this would be a very proper place for taking an observation. However, since he was unwilling for the observations to be made in my name or to have it said I was making them, he was present at all of the ones I had made so far as though it were he who was making them, although not even for that purpose would he turn over to me the astronomical quadrant sent me by the viceroy, or anything else needed for fulfilling my duty. And since he could not be present at the observation today because he was busy with the building of the shed, he replied that an observation should be made on another day at the *Puerto de la Concepción*[21] so

---

[20] Garcés reports that this group told a wild story: their people, the Jalchedunes (Halchidhoma), were being terrorized by a great wizard—a man who had run away from the new California missions and had been killed and burned to ashes by the tribes he met but who had had the skill to revive himself in the form of a whirlwind. Anza could not help showing annoyance at this tale. (Galvin 1967: 13–14.) Possibly Taraval himself, on whose epic flight it was based, was also listening.

[21] Conception Pass.

that I was unable to observe as I had wished. From the time when he first came by my mission, San José de Pimas, he strove to have me bring my musical instrument, convincing me that the psaltery was very suitable to attract Indians, especially the Yumas, who are very fond of celebrating. Although I considerably resisted taking it along, because of the danger of losing it during so long a journey, I finally had to agree to his demands. And now that, to my own considerable disadvantage, I have been bringing it along, he has said nothing more to me about it nor suggested my playing it nor desired to hear it nor wished any people to gather in my tent; while I have been dragging this useless burden along without its doing any good for the Yumas, or anyone.

Our commander wished to have the shed finished in one day, but this was not possible, and at nightfall, following dinner, I asked him whether we would be leaving the following day, since in the morning he had said that we would; and he replied we would not. I then said to him that since we were going to delay, I begged him to shift camp over to where the shed was being built so as to free us from the discomfort we suffered today with all the dirt and wind, which had been so bad that even cooking was impossible. However, he refused to agree with my request; although in the end, on the next day, he carried out, without being asked, that which I had been asking him to do tomorrow, thereby causing us one more day of torture.

I asked him, was this how he was leaving Fathers Garcés and Eixarch there at the river—leaving them with no guard, among the gentiles? And I asked him other questions concerning the way in which these two Fathers were being left there, for I wished to learn about it. He resented this a great deal and replied in this way: To what purpose were those queries of mine? He did not need to account to me for his decisions. He was doing more than he had to, in building the shed for them, which he was not required to do and had no such order to do. No one had charged him with the duty of overseeing the way in which the two Fathers were going to stay there, since they had freely chosen to come without being sent by the viceroy, and since they had opted in this way to come they would learn to manage their stay. What he said was based upon the fact that, when the viceroy decided that Father Garcés should go to the Colorado River, as witnessed by his decree given at Mexico City on November 28, 1774, the latter[22] portrayed certain difficulties involved in it, for which reason the viceroy replied that should Father Garcés not wish to go and should he perceive great difficulty in remaining at the Colorado River, he would not require him to do so. But His Excellency made very clear his desire for the Father to go, as he signified to him in the letter he wrote to him dated March 20, 1776, by which he remitted to him a copy of the letter written from New Mexico by Father Preacher Fray Silvestre Vélez de Escalante in case the information given by the Father should be some use to Father Garcés for his journeys and explorations.[23]

In the end, our commander said that the three interpreters, two muleteers, and their two servants should remain with the two Fathers. The three interpreters were three Indians who were so worthless as to be good for nothing, not even as interpreters, since their Spanish was very bad. Of the two muleteers, one was the Indian Sebastián Taraval, who is the one who served Father Garcés and accompanied him in his voyages as he says in his journal.[24] The other was a lad who

---

[22] Garcés.
[23] Compare Font's argument with Captain Rivera, May 1 and footnote. Font discusses Vélez de Escalante's letter, below, in the April 3 entry.
[24] Font's frequent references to Garcés's journal were all written after his return from the expedition, and so they involve backward-looking mentions of events that took place long after Font had left the Colorado. Late in 1776, in Sonora, he himself assisted with the final composition of the Garcés journal (see the introduction).

came as the dependent of a soldier and remained because he did not have a mount or any way of continuing.[25] Although he served Father Tomás very well and was the only one who was of any use to him, he was not repaid for his service and toil nor given anything, as the commander said he was not liable for him and had no such obligation. The two servants were a useless lad who volunteered to go with Father Garcés, and who was not given anything and went back to Sonora from the Colorado River.[26] The other was a small boy brought voluntarily along by Father Tomás with his horses, to serve him as a page.

I note all this down so that what usually occurs with commanders during such expeditions should not pass unknown and should provide guidance in order to show that the way things are to be managed must be established at the start, without trusting to offers and fair words; as happened to Father Garcés, who trusted the general offers that our commander gave him, but afterward had the experience of their not being fulfilled in particular. For, since these gentlemen who lead such journeys, and even the ones in command in these remote countries, have no one over them to curb their behavior, they are so absolute in their proceedings that one has to have a great deal of patience dealing with them. However good they may be, they still give one a good deal to bear, and after all, that supplication that our venerable Father Fray Antonio Margil de Jesús, so experienced in these matters, was accustomed to utter still holds true in one way or another: "From soldiers, deliver us, O Lord," *A militibus libera nos, Domine*.[27] However, there is no rule without an exception.[28]

[December] 2, Saturday. Since the work on the jacal continued, we delayed here, and the lieutenant went over to it along with the muleteers. Following midday the tertian fever came on me (perhaps I had relapsed because I had gotten wet crossing the river on the 30th), and it was the final one. About three hundred Indians of both sexes gathered in the afternoon, and tobacco and beads were given out to them by the order of our commander. The weather today was quite tedious what with the wind and dirt that arose, but not as bad as yesterday.

Father Garcés went to the building site of the jacal, and when he returned he and Father Tomás spoke to me of the small amount of provision that had been ordered to be left for them, and I advised them to speak plainly and fearlessly concerning what was proper.

[December] 3, Sunday. Our commander decided to do what I had asked on the 1st, not however through respect for my request or moved by my petition.[29] Father Tomás said Mass and the rest of us heard it, and following Mass we set out from the edge of the Colorado River at a half past ten in the morning and arrived at noon at Chief Palma's village. We halted near Palma's house at the house built for the Fathers, having traveled downriver for a short league.[30] The

---

[25] See May 25, below.
[26] Garcés describes the seven as including—besides the small boy, two Spaniards (the muleteers) and three interpreters "on the expedition's rolls"—"another Indian lent us by Captain Bernardo Urrea [of Altar presidio]" (Galvin 1967: 14), so that this last person must be the same as Font's "useless lad."
[27] An imitation of a petition in a litany. Margil (1657–1726) was a famous Franciscan missionary, once affiliated with Font's colegio of Querétaro.
[28] This cautious afterthought was added to the final manuscript, partly in the margin.
[29] To move camp to the missionaries' new jacal.
[30] See the note on the distance under November 30.

remainder of the day was occupied with finishing the jacal, which though not quite completed was left in a good state.

And the Fathers also were left sufficiently content with what was left for the two of them and the seven others with them, namely: a tercio[31] of tobacco; two boxes of beads; one *arroba*[32] of chocolate; one arroba of sugar; one arroba of lard; five head of cattle; three tercios of dried meat; one *carga*[33] of beans; one carga of milled flour; a little fine flour; one *almud*[34] of chickpeas; a box of cake; three hams; six cheeses; a frying pan; a griddle; an axe; twelve cakes of soap; twelve wax candles; and one jug of wine that could not be used for saying Mass since it was so bad that it did not even resemble wine in color or flavor and they had to send to Caborca for some.[35] This was something, but, not much in relation to the nine mouths that had to be fed or to the fact the provisions had to last until our return.[36]

At nightfall I called Chief Palma and Chief Pablo, whom I understood to be somewhat related to him, into my tent, and addressed them through an interpreter, urging upon them what attention and respect they must use toward the Fathers remaining there and that when I returned, if they had behaved well toward them I would go to the king and report it all to him so that he would esteem them, and then we Spaniards would actually return to live with them. To all of which they answered that I might leave with no worry; that once Palma had obtained the staff and now the clothing that had been given him, it would be perceived that he stood in the stead of Captain don Juan and that he would care for the Fathers just as I would do myself and that he would punish misbehavior should anyone try to do harm, etc.

And Chief Pablo added that if anyone attempted to harm them or steal anything he would kill them himself. I answered that as for killing, I did not wish it nor did God, for it was not a good thing and that if anyone did anything bad he should tie him up and whip him, and this pleased him so well that he cast himself lengthwise on the ground, stretching out his arms and legs and saying with great depth of expression "*Ajót, ajót*," which means "good, good."[37]

While I was in the midst of this conversation, our commander sent calling for Chief Palma with no other purpose than to get him out of my tent, since he was not pleased to have anyone else involved in conversing with the Indians, especially not with the chiefs, and in giving them directions. Afterward, he had the Indians dance for a while in the firelight in front of his tent, in order to keep them there, so that I had no chance to talk further with them.

---

[31]A tercio of tobacco was approximately 5 arrobas, about 125 pounds.

[32]Approximately 25 pounds.

[33]A double-hundred weight.

[34]Probably somewhere between 5 and 10 quarts. Measurement equivalents for the eighteenth-century Sonora frontier are very difficult to determine.

[35]Eixarch, in his journal, says that it made him nauseated.

[36]The field text says only, "The Fathers were left provided by our commander with what was necessary, as far as was possible."

[37]In the field text, the equivalent passage is found later on, and part of it is attributed to Palma: (The Yumas) "are considerable thieves, which is the propensity of every Indian, and when I told Palma to take care that the Indians should steal no animals or anything else, he answered that if anyone stole anything he would kill them, to which I answered he should do no such thing but punish them with whipping after tying them up; which greatly pleased him, and Chief Pablo answered very happily, 'That good, good, good,' and so forth."

[December] 4, Monday. I said Mass in the ramada and dwelling place of the Fathers, the first one that was said in it, and with everything in order we took our leave of Fathers Fray Francisco Garcés and Fray Tomás Eixarch who were remaining along with those mentioned above. We set out from here at Chief Palma's village at a half past nine in the morning and by traveling west-southwestward almost along the bank of the river, with a number of twists and turns, we halted at a half past two in the afternoon at Captain Pablo's villages near a lake where there was some grass, one league this side of the pass on the San Pablo height, having traveled some five leagues. Chief Pablo stayed with Chief Palma in order to live with the Fathers.

As soon as we set out, we forded a remaining branch, not a very deep one, of the Colorado River, which comes, divided from it, from some four or five leagues above and by following along the foot of some heights joined the river here again. At about a league past the stopping place we came to the pass that on the previous occasion was named La Concepción, which is a narrows between two small heights through which the Colorado River, joined now with the Gila River, goes greatly constricted. We paused here for a little in order to survey the very extensive landscape that opens up from the small height on the northern side, and by which flows the river, whose course here seemed to me to be from east-northeast to west-southwestward; Northeastward at a distance of about ten leagues the rock that they called El Gigante the last time, which the Indians call El Bauquiburi, is clearly seen, a great round rock on the top of a steep mountain located between the Gila and Colorado rivers; and northward at about three or four leagues is the other rock, closer by and on this side of the Colorado, that they call *La Campana*,[38] atop another mountain, also a steep one.[39] I did not think that the little height on the northern side was at all good for a settlement, not just because it is small and uneven but because so far as I could see it becomes isolated when the river rises. I liked the hill on the south side better because it is more spacious and because the way to get off it is always available if needed, even if the river rises.

At four leagues, we went by the pass of the San Pablo height, along the foot of which the river goes; it also has a very pleasant view but its extent is so short that everything is gullies, and I did not see a single level piece of ground on which even one church could be built. The route, although almost entirely level, was a very toilsome one because of being so dense with brush that, during many

---

[38]The Bell.

[39]"Last time" refers again to the expedition of 1774. In the final text, "The Giant's Head." The remarkable heights since have been called Castle Dome (The Dome) and Picacho Peak (Chimney Rock, Sentinel Mountain), respectively.

Figure 13. A View of the Colorado River from the height at Yuma, 1858. By Heinrich Balduin Möllhausen. Castle Dome Mountains ("El Bauquiburi") in the background. A *jacal* in the foreground. *Courtesy of the Amon Carter Museum of Western Art, Fort Worth.*

portions of it, nothing showed but a little path that had been opened, with the rest all a thicket of totally useless brush and other thorny bushes that yield the screwbean, with a few mesquites that yield péchita, so that the pack trains, mounts and livestock reached here with considerable delays and with strayed animals. The brush so plentiful on today's route and in this country is called *cachanilla*.[40]

Father Garcés had some polite discussions with our commander over why he was not leaving him the animals that had been promised him for his journeys. He decided to come with us but delayed in order to arrange his affairs and provision himself for traveling down to the mouth of the river.

What Father Garcés explored during this and other journeys that he made as far as San Gabriel and El Moqui will be found in his journal.[41]

---

[40]The plant is also called arrow weed. In the field text, "We reached here . . . with some toil; the pack trains, horse herd, etc., with more, and with loss of animals."

[41]Again, a reference in the final text to future events of 1776. For Garcés's journal, see Galvin 1965, 1967, and Coues 1900.

[December] 5, Tuesday. At dawn a mule and a horse had died of the cold, which was so severe that water froze in the water bags and in the beaker.[42] I noted that even my urine had frozen in the pot inside the tent. We set out from Chief Pablo's villages at ten o'clock in the morning and traveled for some four leagues southwestward with a number of turns in several directions, to west-southwestward, south, south-southeastward, etc., following the low spots that are drowned by the river's rising, even though we went at what seemed a great distance away from the river, leaving it upon the left. After one o'clock in the afternoon we halted near a lake belonging to the villages of El Cojat, who also are Yumas. Beyond the San Pablo height the river takes a swerve almost to the southward and plainly gives many a bend on its way, although in substance I thought its course was west-southwestward; no more of it can be seen from there because it flows very far away from the route, which goes through its bottomlands and leaves quite far upon the right a hill of sand dune that seems to be reached by the river when it floods. The route has a good deal of cachanilla, screwbean, and mesquite brush but was not half so tedious as the one yesterday, and we went by some villages of Yumas who came out to receive us and were very happy to see us and all wanted to lead us to their houses. There are large pieces of ground to be seen that would be very good for cultivation and so forth; I shall speak of this at *Santa Olalla*.[43]

Today among other Indians who accompanied us for some stretches, there was an Indian half Pima, half Yuma who insisted on going ahead and guiding us on foot; he was the son of a Yuma chief of great authority who lived here on the river and had a great command and authority at it[44] and by whose death Chief Palma made off with the command, and who was married to a Pima Indian woman who was still acknowledged by the Yumas. And therefore during the first expedition, our commander (as he told me himself) named the Pima Indian woman The Queen, and the boy he called The Prince. The latter served them at that time as an interpreter since he understood and spoke the Pima language; at present the same Indian is known as The Prince and was so called this time by our commander and the others.

Yesterday night this Indian came to the tent of the commander, who did not recognize him at first sight because he was so covered with paint, until, when he began to speak, a servant of his named Manuel Barragán,[45] who was versed in the Pima tongue, said, "Sir, this is The Prince," and I, hearing him named thus, asked why they called him The Prince. The commander then said to me, "Father, inasmuch as the Jesuits were so fond of enlarging on their accomplishments, in the reports they made after they came to explore the Colorado River here, they dwelt a great deal upon the size of this Yuma tribe, and to make the news the more talked about they said it had

---

[42] *Tembladera*. See the note to October 1.
[43] See the note on the name below, under December 6.
[44] In the final text, "who commanded within the whole tribe."
[45] Later, a prominent citizen of Tucson. His name is added in between the lines of the manuscript.

a kind of civilized government, acknowledging one person as a king over all of them, and this king was none other than the chief who was this boy's father and is now dead. And it occurred to me last time to call this Indian here The Prince and his mother The Queen, by way of playfully alluding to this report."[46]

We halted upon a plain with a good deal of grass near one of the many lakes in the bottomlands, left filled by the river when it drops, and a great many Indians resorted to the camp and brought gourds, beans and other crops that they grow, bartering with soldiers for beads our commander had given the people for that purpose.

A steer was killed close to the commander's tent (today's slaughtering, that was to be rationed out to the people, as was done every six days) and I was sitting there along with our commander near the steer drinking chocolate, when the Indians gathered so thickly, and they are so foul, that what with the pestiferous windiness they let out they did not allow us to catch a breath, and in no way would they withdraw. I stood up, and asking an Indian for his staff that was some ten *cuartas*[47] in length, one of those that they use for their hoop-rolling game, I grasped it crossways and started moving them backward, gently and graciously as though I were smiling. However, one Indian immediately looked very angry and by pulling the staff upward pushed himself back inside, and the rest followed his example and the owner of the staff snatched it out of my hands, and the irate one continued to look angry, not letting me out of his sight until I went into the tent. I deduced from this that all of their friendliness, which is more due to the gifts of beads than to their docility, might turn to arrogance when it becomes a matter of subduing them into catechism and subordination,[48] all the more so if we consider their habits and their way of living, of which I shall speak later.

[December] 6, Wednesday. The Indians were a bit boisterous last night and proved themselves to be greater thieves than others by stealing a sword, a griddle that was returned afterwards, and some clothing from people who were careless. We set out from the El Cojat villages at ten o'clock in the morning and halted at two o'clock in the afternoon at Santa Olalla Lake, the name given it during the first expedition[49] having traveled some five leagues mostly southwestward and

---

[46] The Jesuit reports were widely circulated and appreciated in Europe in the eighteenth century, chiefly in the form of an elegantly edited and published series under the title of *Lettres édifiantes et curieuses* (Paris: N. Le Clerc, 1702–1776).

[47] 6 feet 10½ inches.

[48] In the field text, "that these Indians, as docile as they are, will be stiff-necked at entering into God's Law and into subordination."

[49] Santa Eulalia (St. Eulalia). "Santa Olalla" or "Olaya" is a phonetic spelling of a mispronunciation of the Spanish name. Anza, who was from a European family, decided to imitate this mispronunciation in writing when he named the lake in 1774, remarking "y así la llamáis" "and that's how *you* say it," meaning that he said this to his soldiers. Font and Díaz also found it appropriate or mildly amusing to write the place name in this way. In 1776 Garcés insisted on spelling it correctly (Galvin 1967: 15 etc.).

south-southwestward, the course varying almost anywhere between south and west because of the great many turns in the route. Father Fray Francisco Garcés arrived after we had stopped, coming along in order to pursue his journey downriver as far as the mouth and visit the tribes dwelling along its bottoms. I had a little recurrence of the tertian fever today and was brought very low from diarrhea.

The route is not a heavily wooded one although there is a great deal of brush, and pieces of it are sterile ground. The edge of the dunes is visible in the distance, and very far off, always on the right hand, a steep mountain range, of which the San Pablo height is a spur, is visible. It seems that this mountain or range starts out from the range in which lies the rock called La Campana—or even from the Bauquiburi mountain—and runs to join the range that they called *San Sebastián* during the last expedition; this is a range seen opposite us far in the distance and that comes from Baja California, being the main range that runs about northwestward and west-northwestward[50] throughout all of California.

The Santa Olalla Lake is narrow, like a slough, and over a league long, lying along almost the same course as does the river but about two leagues or a bit more away from it; it can be deduced from this how many leagues the river extends over when it rises, since it fills it and the water even rises more than two varas,[51] as shown by the trash that we saw upon the trunks of the willows that line its shores, left by the river when it overruns that ground during its floods and even reaches a great deal further. The soil accordingly is moist and has a good deal of grass, and there is also a good number of quail within the woods and along the water's edge and some fish in the lake; within a short time the Indians got a good amount of small matalotes out of the lake, and they also caught a mullet and two tiny *corvinas*.[52] We were accompanied by the Pima Indian we called The Prince and by another Indian who lives here and is the one who first came out to receive us, as I say under November 25.

From the barrenness of this country, all level as it is and yielding nothing beyond the salt bush they call *chamizo*[53] and from the look of the dunes, I have come to suppose that this entire ground was occupied by the sea in ancient times and that these salty fields and dunes were left exposed during one of the sea's great withdrawals that histories tell us of.

[December] 7, Thursday. I was feeling very oppressed today due to the diarrhea. In order for the mounts and mules, which were very poorly off, to regain strength from the good grass at the lake, it was decided we should remain here.

---

[50] In the field text, "about westward or west-northwestward."
[51] 6 inches.
[52] Matalotes, see footnote above under November 18. Corvina is the saltwater corvina, sometimes called "sea trout." Mullet is also a common intruder, upstream, from the Gulf of California.
[53] Brush.

A great many Indians belonging to the Cajuenche tribe that lives from here on down the river came to us, very pleased and raising a great deal of hubbub as though happy to see us; they brought to the camp a vast number of watermelons, gourds, and food that they bartered for beads, so that the soldiers provisioned themselves well and also managed to get some black cloaks from El Moqui and so forth. These Cajuenches are no different from the Yumas in their habits, and are almost the same in their language or at least they resemble them in the sing-song pronunciation that one hears from them.

In our pleasure at having reached this spot, the expedition's people were issued a refreshment yesterday evening, which amounted to giving them aguardiente, so that there was a sizeable degree of drunkenness and shouting among that crowd last night. In the morning, although I was sick, I forced myself to say Mass and then went to see the commander in his tent and said to him, "Sir, apparently there were men drunk last night." He answered me that there had been some. And as I thought this disturbance such a disgraceful one, to the point that even his cook had left us without supper because he was not up to cooking, I said to him, "Well, why give them aguardiente if they are going to get drunk?" He answered me that that was not why he gave it. "Fine, so be it," said I, "since if it had been done for such a purpose it would have been with a double bad intention. Since drunkenness is always an evil, the drinker and the one who aids the drunkenness of others both sin; and the only excuse for sinning is lack of awareness and you are not unaware of these people's intemperance when they have aguardiente." He answered me with a bit of restraint although a bit resentful and with no sign of regret. Afterward he said to me, "Would Your Reverence like for us to observe today?" I answered that he might do as he wished as the decision was not mine as to when to observe, but only when he wished; that I had wished to observe at the meeting of the rivers, a better spot for it, as I had proposed to him on the 1st, but since it had not been done there it should be done whenever he wished. He said that measures would be taken to observe there on our return; and thereupon I went to my tent. And he came to it at eleven o'clock and said to me, "Where will Your Reverence arrange for the instrument to be set up?" I answered, "Sir, wherever you please." He said to me then, "Your Reverence must arrange it, since you understand it better than I do, and Your Reverence is the one to do the observing." This is the first time I ever heard him use any such expression and with that I arranged the instrument. The commander was present and obliging although a bit grave, no doubt because I was being grave as well. He could see that I was wasting few words and not going off into politeness and niceties over matters that lay within my responsibility. I do not record this out of any ill will or to preserve affronts in memory but for the one and only purpose of letting it be realized what caution and patience is required toward these gentlemen with absolute power.

I observed, then, the latitude of this place and found it, by the tables of Jorge with no correction, in 32° 37′, and with correction in 32° 33′.[54] And thus I say: at Santa Olalla Lake, December 7, 1775: meridian altitude of the sun's lower limb: 34° 28′.[55]

---

[54] The latitude may be nearly correct, even though it is considerably north of the position implied by Font's courses and bearings.

[55] In the field text, the calculation according to the inferior Gasco tables is given as "32° 34′," with the correct remark: "This observation is the same as was made by Father Díaz [on May 9, 1774], 32° 34′."

And inasmuch as this is where the Yuma tribe ends and the people of El Cojat, who are also called Cajuenches (some of whom came to see us) begins,[56] I shall tell what I have learned concerning this tribe during my passage through here, and concerning their country which they inhabit; noting that whatever I shall say concerning the Yumas may be understood in almost the same way of the Cajuenches and other tribes downriver, and also of the Jalchedunes or Soyopas[57] from up the river, since all of these Indians are nearly the same in customs and in all else.

The Yumas' dwelling place is on the bottomlands of the Colorado River above and below the meeting of the rivers, and on the banks on both sides of it. The waters of this river, although always more or less cloudy, are fresh and good and not briny like those of the Gila River, which has thick water because of the La Asunción River. Therefore the Colorado River, after being joined by the Gila River, becomes somewhat infected by it. The bottomlands extend for about two leagues on either side of the river, and in places more, and have on them a great deal of cottonwood groves and mesquites and other scrub trees as well; the cottonwoods, from being very dense together, are commonly thin ones although very tall, and a great many ones among them and among the willows are dead from the Indians' removing their bark, which they use in making the women's little skirts, as I shall tell.

The river holds a good many fish, more of them in the hot season and larger and larger ones the closer to the sea, while it holds few in winter since the water is very cold.[58] It spreads out over the bottomlands a great deal each year during its floods, which arise from snow melting in the summer in northern mountains very far upcountry, and for this reason it rises not suddenly but stealthily and takes almost the entire year to rise and fall, so that it begins rising in March and April and increases every day from then on until July, when it commences to drop and decreases each day until the end of the year. The land watered by it commonly is good soil, particularly that right next to it, and since the water overflows it so gently it does not destroy it but rather leaves it quite well fertilized by the watering and moist enough for the plantings that the Indians make

---

[56] In the field text, Font originally wrote: "and the El Cojat people begin, very far down, and afterward the Cajuenches." Later, he crossed this out and replaced it with the description given above, which identifies the El Cojat people with the Cajuenches. In a letter of January 1775 Garcés explained that "between Santa Olalla lake near the San Francisco villages and those [villages] that I called Santa Rosa [this is not identical with the Santa Rosa de las Lajas of Font's journal] it is about seven leagues by a straight route; the Santa Rosa Indians are Quíquimas, who [showed me? guided me to?] the river [in 1771], while those belonging to San Mateo lake and Las Llagas, Merced and San Jácomo are Quegüenes or Cajuenches."

[57] According to Garcés, these were the Mojaves.

[58] After returning in "the hot season" (May 1776), in the final text Font revised his opinion: "The river seemingly holds few fish, and spiny ones at that."

upon it when the water draws back and for the plentiful harvests they gather. In a word, the Colorado River here strikes me as being very similar to the Yaqui River both in its flooding and other qualities and in the temper of the Indians who dwell on it; however, it far exceeds it in everything, and is its superior in having tree groves, which the Yaqui River does not. In winter the climate is a considerably cold one, and quite heavy freezes and frosts are experienced in the mornings, and this goes on for three or four months, from November until the end of February. It is a very hot climate for the rest of the year, with excessive heat spells in the depth of summer, which is usually the rainy time; in winter it rains little or not at all.[59]

The Indians' crops are wheat, the sort of maize called Apache corn that ripens within a short time, *yorimuni* beans, *tepary* beans,[60] muskmelons, watermelons, and very large gourds from which they make a dried food called *bichicoré* in Sinaloa, and other sorts of grass seeds, so that they have enough to eat; they also gather a great deal of screwbean and péchita, though this is done more to vary their diet than from any necessity.

The district occupied by the Yumas must be about twenty leagues in length, the center of which falls at the La Concepción passage, which is the best spot that I saw and near which Chief Palma has his dwelling and village.

This chief, as I said, is the one having at present the most authority among the Yumas, and is acknowledged as such by Chief Pablo despite the latter's being a chief over more people and a larger village. No doubt this is because he has seen Chief Palma being so favored by Spaniards: by Captain Urrea, Captain Anza, and even by the viceroy. This Chief Palma came to power through the death of another chief whom they acknowledged previously, and whose son was the Indian we called The Prince as I said above. And so far as I could determine his rule has not been acquired through inheritance, since he is not the preceding chief's son and I believe not even a relative of his; but only through his thrusting himself forward and being valiant and a good speaker, as among the Indians is usually the case, where the one who speaks best and vaunts his bravery makes himself the chief or commander and is acknowledged by the rest of them as being such. A proof of this is the fact that lands previously owned by Chief Palma, inherited from his parents, lie upon this side[61] of the river and close to the Gila River before it joins the Colorado River; Palma himself showed them to us when he accompanied us as we went by them on November 28 and they are not very good land, and that which he possesses at present at his village on the other side of the river, and which is better, was granted him by the Indians only a few years ago. This being in command and superior must not be taken in the full sense of the term, since the Indians, being so free and living in a brutish and uncivilized fashion as they do, often pay no attention their chief even when he gives orders, as I saw to be the case on occasion. I believe that the main reason they do acknowledge him is in order to avenge some offense or to go to war against other surrounding tribes, the Jalchedunes, Cajuenches and others—who are

---

[59]From the field text. Again, the final text holds a revised opinion: "summer, in which there is usually some rain, as there also is in winter."
[60]Pinto beans.
[61]The southeast side toward Sonora, where the author was writing the final text.

not in any way subject to Chief Palma nor do they acknowledge him, for they hold themselves to be as valiant as the Yumas.

These Yumas (and also the Cajuenches and others) are well built, tall, strong and not very ugly, and good-sized in body and normally most of them approach eight cuartas in height, many of them nine and some are over nine according to our measuring of them.[62] The women are not so tall but are also quite full in body and of very good stature.

Their customs, so far as I could ascertain, are the following.

As to religion, no particular cult of idolatry can be recognized among them, although apparently they do have some sorcerers or charlatans and medicine men who exercise this office by shouts, gasps and shakings. They say that there is a God and that they know this because the Pimas have told them so, and that these and the Pápagos, with whom they are at peace and have some trade, have explained to them that there are good people up there in the sky and that under the earth there are dogs and other very fierce creatures, but that they do not know anything else because they are ignorant and that therefore in order to get to know something they will be glad to learn whatever we will teach them.

And since religion, even though it be a false one, is the foundation of any ordered monarchy, government, or republic, and there is no religion to be found among these Indians, they live in very disordered fashion, brutishly, completely without civilization and with as little subordination as I said earlier, each one ruling himself according to his own whim, like vagabond people.

Their wars and campaigns regularly last for only a few days and amount to this: a great many of them gather with their chief or someone commanding them, they go to an enemy village, they give the shout or whoop to make their adversaries flee or to terrorize them if they have caught them by surprise, they usually slay some woman or other or some careless person, and they attempt to catch some children in order to take them out to Spanish countries to sell them: in Sonora, we call these *níjoras*,[63] wherever they come from, and this very unjust trade in níjoras is the reason their wars have become so filled with slaughter. Their weapons are a bow that is taller than themselves, poorly strung, and a few arrows, most of them carrying no more than two or three so far as I saw (and a very few of them carry quivers, if in fact they do, so since I saw none), and these are somewhat long, poorly made and thin.

Their houses are so many huts built of sticks, raised a bit and covered in earth upon the roof and the sides, and a bit sunken in the ground, like a rabbit hole, and twenty or thirty or more of them live like swine in each house; and these

---

[62] 5½ feet. 9 cuartas = 6 feet 2¼ inches. A slightly more specific passage in the field text, under May 11 below, is apparently the source for this information.

[63] In the field text, here and elsewhere, níforas. The *f* and the *j* are often pronounced similarly in some varieties of Spanish.

are not built together in the shape of a settlement but scattered over the bottomlands, making villages of three or four buildings, sometimes a bit more or less.

Their clothing is, in the case of the men, none; although with the attempt to establish peace that was being made from the time of the first expedition onward, they have plainly had some trade with other tribes, so that we began to see Indians wearing cotton cloaks and another black woolen sort that come from El Moqui, which they were able to acquire through the Cocomaricopas and Jalchedunes.[64] They wear these from halfway up their bodies upward, leaving the rest exposed, including their most shameful parts, because they say the women are not pleased to have them cover them up. But the normal thing is to go entirely naked, and they are so shameless that they constantly have their hands on their indecent parts, playing with themselves and distorting the organ, and so uncouth are they that if one scolds them for it they do it even more and start laughing, as I myself experienced. And if they feel like urinating, whether they are standing or walking, they do what is necessary, just like animals do, but at least the animals stop to piss.

Likewise when they are gaseous they let it out with great impertinence, in front of everyone, and since they eat so many beans and other seeds they stink from their windiness, and if they are sitting upon the ground all that they do is to lift their haunch a little on one side, and since the farts they emit are such long, strong, full-formed ones, they raise dust off the ground with the gust. Our commander on one occasion asked an Indian to bring him a light for a cigar. The Indian did so, and while the commander was lighting his cigar, the Indian, standing very seriously in front of him with the match stick in his hand, let out a formidable fart, and although the commander told him that was not something that was done, he kept smiling quite undisturbed. Chief Palma, who previously behaved like the rest, had already begun to improve in this respect. At first, when he was told this was not a good thing to do in front of people, he answered he could not do otherwise, since if he did not, he would burst. I do not know whether this free behavior can be attributed to their ignorance, innocence, and frankness, or whether it is the result of their great savagery. In respect of incontinence, they are so indecent and excessive that I do not believe there is any tribe in the world more so than they. It can almost be said that the women are held in common, and the courtesy that they bestow upon guests is giving them a woman to sleep with. And, although there is seemingly some type of natural matrimony among the older ones when they acknowledge one or another of the women that they have, or had in youth, as a lawful wife, still I believe that there is no marriage among the young ones, as they live with whatever women they wish and leave them when they see fit; or at least polygamy is very general and freely used among them.

The women, even the very young ones and including babies in arms, wear little skirts they make for themselves out of willow and cottonwood bark, which they beat to a certain degree. They tear it into strips and then string or interweave it on one end and make a kind of apron out of it that they tie about their waist with

---

[64]In the field text, "which they have acquired through the upriver Indians, Jalchedunes and so forth."

a cord, one of them in front and the other behind. The one in the rear is longer than the front one which reaches to their knee. As these consist of so many strips or ribbons of the narrowness of a *dedo*,[65] they make a rustle with their swaying as they walk. I saw men among the women who were dressed like them and regularly go about with them, never joining the men, and our commander called them *amaricados*, perhaps because the Yumas call effeminate men *maricas*.[66] I asked who these were, and was told that those were not men such as the others, which was why they went about covered in that way, from which I deduced they must be hermaphrodites; but from what I learned afterward I understood them to be sodomites, dedicated to the unspeakable deed. Wherefore I conclude that they[67] will prove troublesome in this matter of licentiousness whenever the Holy Faith and Christian religion is established among them.

Some women, although few, also are accustomed to covering their back with a kind of cloak or small cape that they make out of rabbit and otter skins with the fur on it, cut into strips and interwoven using tree-bark thread; but normally they go about with their whole body exposed save for what is covered by their little skirts.

On cold nights, especially in winter, they make a fire and around it they entwine themselves with each other, lying down jammed together, and even half buried in the sand, like swine; in the daytime they usually go about with a firebrand in their hand and bring it toward their body wherever they feel the coldest, in back, in front, on the chest, on the back, on the belly; this is all the blankets they have, and when the fire burns out they throw that brand away and look for another one that is burning. The men are much accustomed to painting themselves red (using ochre) and black (using a shiny black earth of a leaden hue) so that they appear like something hellish, especially at night; also with white and with other colors. They paint not only their face but their whole body as well. They glue the paint to themselves with an ointment made of marrow or other substances in such a way that even when they go into the river and swim a great deal, as they are accustomed to doing, the paint does not come off them easily. Those who cannot get anything better blacken themselves with charcoal from top to bottom with several rays and patterns so that they look like devils; and this is their party dress.

---

[65] A measurement equal to the length of a finger; about 7/10 of an inch.

[66] This is not a native word but a well-known Spanish term, as the website of a signore Giovanni dall'Orto (http://www.giovannidallorto.com/testi/indie/font/font.html#2a) is the first to point out in this context, with the further inference that Font did not recognize the word as being such when he heard it from Anza. This last clause in the sentence, like most of the content of the surrounding sentences, is only in the final text, where the clause is added between lines.

[67] The Yumas (Quechán). What Font wrote proved to be true. Just before he died in the Yuma revolt of 1781, Garcés wrote that the custom of "taking concubines" meant that few converts of between the ages of twenty and sixty could be made. (Garcés, "Cartas," 201.23.)

The women paint themselves only with red, which is a very general thing among them. I saw only a single grown-up girl who between the top and the bottom of her face had round white dots in two lines. The men have their ears pierced with three or four large holes (the women, not so much), and in them they wear little dangling strings of wool or *chomite*,[68] or other pendants. They also wear, around their necks, good-sized necklaces made of dried heads of small insects, found here, that look like those of scarabs. And they are very much drawn to glass beads, for which they barter away their few blankets (which some of the expedition's people obtained themselves) and also their seeds and other objects that they brought, so that around five hundred watermelons must have been sold in camp yesterday along with a great amount of gourds, maize, and so forth, and today over twice as much was sold.

Besides this, almost all of the men have the cartilage in the middle of their nose pierced, something that I did not notice with the women, from which they—the richest of them such as Chief Palma—wear suspended a small stone between blue and green in hue; others wear a small half-round piece of something like marble or bone, as did Chief Pablo; others, some sort of a bead or other trifle, and although I saw several of them without anything, others that I saw contented themselves with wearing a stick thrust crosswise through it.[69]

The men's hair styles are unusual: most of them wear their hair cut short in front as low as their eyes and the rest down as far as the neck, and others wear it somewhat long. They usually brush or dress their hair by painting their head with white clay and other dyes to stiffen it—which they are accustomed to doing at the edge of the water, and at great length—and they lift the hair in front straight up like a crown or like horns, and leave the rest much smoothed with paints and clay, and they also usually use other colors to make some patterns in it. The women employ very little of all this and only an occasional one presses and arranges her hair with clay.[70] The normal thing is for the hair to be cut short in front down to the eyebrows, and the rest somewhat long, hanging over the shoulders and the back.

They are very fond of smoking[71] and very slack at working. Were this not so, they would have many more plantings. But they are satisfied with having enough to eat in plenty, which, since the land is so fertile from being watered by the river, they achieve with little labor. That amounts solely to this: before the river rises they clear the piece of land that they wish to plant and leave the trash

---

[68]Tangled wool fibers, as used for making native dresses (a Mexican word). Santamaría 1974: 416.

[69]Through the septum.

[70]This last statement is from the field text. It reflects the writer's experience during the first visit, and is inconsistent with the final text, which says: "and their common hairdo is to press and arrange their hair using clay, just as is done in Europe with flour powder."

[71]Eixarch, staying among the Quechán, later wrote: "besides constantly asking for tobacco, they put it into a [piece of] cane as thick as a finger and taking a good-sized fistful in order to fill it, and that is how they smoke, and are not satisfied with a cigar."

there on it; the river floods and carries away the refuse from the clearing, and as soon as the river drops and withdraws they make holes in the ground using a stake, plant their seeds and give it no further cultivation. And they are also considerable thieves, a characteristic of every Indian.

As to language, Yuma and Cajuenche, Jalchedún, and the rest are one and the same, differing only in pronunciation and in some terms. Their speech is not as unpleasant as is that of the Pima tongue and I even thought it to be less difficult to pronounce; it has a slight lilt on every clause, or something that sounds like a person asking a question. At present, because of our persuasions, the Yuma tribe is at peace with all the ones surrounding it except with the Indians at the river mouth, because of a war that Palma made on them a little while ago in which he killed about twenty of their people.[72]

On the strength of our message some Jalchedunes came down to the river junction bringing cloaks from El Moqui and so forth in order to barter with the expedition's people, but they found us already gone, and Father Tomás, who was staying there, received them well and gave them presents.[73]

In sum, they[74] are normally a well-behaved, pleasure-loving, happy people, and, because they are ignorant, they marvel at everything they have not seen, so that they were surprised by whatever they saw and made themselves bothersome, annoying, and even tedious, fatiguing us by their approaching our tents and inspecting everything. They liked hearing the mules and hinnies braying, and as they had not seen such animals the other time, they especially liked a male and a female burro that had come along with the expedition. These animals sing or bray longer and louder, so that when they heard them they would imitate them in their own fashion, with a considerable uproar and hubbub.

To conclude all that has been said, since I have lingered a bit in speaking of the Yumas and their customs, I wish to record here a problem or reflection that often came to my mind during this journey, when viewing the ignorance, misfortune and wretchedness in which the Indians whom I saw all along the way as far as San Francisco harbor live. Without question, the Yumas can be regarded as the most fortunate, wealthy and comfortably situated of all of them, since after all they have enough to eat and live on their land with fewer discomforts. But the rest that I saw

---

[72] The final text adds, referring to a later event, "but this breach of unity was repaired by Father Garcés when he went there, as he tells in his journal." Garcés's visit to the mouth of the Colorado took place in this same month of December; his journal record (composed mostly after his return in 1776) describes only his attempts at preaching peace, especially following an individual violent incident that involved two downriver groups, not the Yumas. (Galvin 1967: 18–21.) However, in a letter of January 1776 to the viceroy from "San Pedro de los Yumas," he writes: "Although the Cucapás were at war and presently very sad because of the great mortality inflicted on them by the Yumas, Cajuenches and Jallicuamais otherwise called Quíquimas, nonetheless (thanks to God) the blessing of peace has been achieved, and on this very day Palma tells me that some of the Indians who have been enemies will come in." Garcés, "Cartas," 201.25.

[73] This passage, which occurs in the field text as well as the final text, refers to events that Font could not have learned of until considerably later than the date of the entry. See the introduction.

[74] The Yumas.

upcountry, besides the fact that they live in a continual warfare between villages and thus live in constant fright and go about like Cain, fugitive and wandering, seized by fear and trembling at every step, seem to have the curse that God set upon Nebuchadnezzar placed upon themselves, eating, as they do, grass of the field like beasts and living on plant and grass seeds along with a bit of game consisting of deer, hares, gophers, squirrels, mice and other vermin.[75]

Given this supposition, just as the apostles asked Christ the question concerning the man who was blind from birth, "Rabbi, who was it who sinned, this man or his parents, that he was born blind?" *Rabbi, quis peccavit, hic aut parentes ejus, ut cæcus nasceretur?* (John chapter 9),[76] we might ask, what sin must have been committed by these Indians and their ancestors so that they were born in those remote northern countries to such misfortune and unhappiness, such nakedness and discomfort, and above all in such blind ignorance concerning everything that they are not even acquainted with the passing comforts of the world so as to seek them, and much less (or so I thought from what I could ascertain concerning them) do they have any inkling of the existence of God, living as they do like beasts without employment of reason or logic and being distinguished from them only by corporeal or human shape but not by its proper operations? And this same question, and all the rest that I shall say, applies to many other tribes that dwell in unknown countries belonging to the two poles, Arctic and the Antarctic and in other parts of the world.

I know well that the answer is: "Neither has this man sinned, nor his parents; but that the works of God should be made manifest in him," *Neque hic peccavit neque parentes ejus, sed ut manifestentur opera Dei in illo*;[77] and therefore, since God created them, His Divine Majesty knows the high purposes for which He willed them to be born in such wretched estate and to live so blindly, and it is not ours to attempt to ascertain such high mysteries, for: "The judgments of God are a great deep," *judicia Dei abyssus multa*.[78] But, considering that God's mercy is infinite and that He, for His own part, wills that all men should be saved and come to knowledge of eternal truths—as the apostle St. Paul says: "Who desires all men to be saved and to come to the recognition of truth," *Qui omnes homines vult salvos fieri et ad agnitionem veritatis venire* (First Epistle to Timothy, chapter 2)[79]—I can do no less than piously imagine, in favor of those poor Indians, that God must be entertaining some special providence, hidden to our inquisitiveness, by which they can be saved and not damned one and all.

For, as the theologians say, if a man were to exist in the woods, without a knowledge of God and entirely removed from acquiring the necessary instruction, God would avail Himself of His own angels to give that man the knowledge required for his eternal well being; and that man "in the woods," *in silvis*, whom the theologians posit as an hypothesis, is without any doubt the Indians that I saw and other ones who must exist further upcountry whom I have not seen. For, if God has allowed those people to live for so many centuries and indeed millennia in such ignorance and blindness that they scarcely are aware of themselves and, I believe, do not know themselves to be rational humans, what can we possibly think? Is not this all the more so, in view of a God so merciful that "His mercy triumphs over judgment," *misericordia ejus superexaltat judicium*?[80] Are we to believe that God created those men to be destined solely for Hell after they

---

[75] Daniel 4:33.
[76] John 9:2.
[77] John 9:3.
[78] Psalm 35:7 (36:6). At the end of his discussion, Font returns to the same passage of this psalm in order to prove his point.
[79] 1 Timothy 2:4.
[80] James 2:13.

have spent so wretched a life as they do in this world? By no means! Shall we say that the Devil can do more than God, by lording over so many souls living in the shades of a negative faithlessness, without God's conveying to them any light to let them be freed from the Devil's tyrannous and eternal rule? Even less!

We must then think that God has some hidden means of saving those souls which He redeemed at such a price with His own most precious blood; and this can be supported by that text of the prophet Joel, chapter 2 verse 32, "And it shall come to pass that whosoever shall call upon the name of the Lord shall be saved, for there shall be salvation in Mount Zion and in Jerusalem as the Lord has said," *et erit omnis qui invocaverit nomen Domini salvus erit quia in monte Sion et in Hierusalem erit salvatio sicut dixit Dominus*:[81] The children of Holy Church in grace shall be saved "in Mount Zion and in Jerusalem." Now follows what is to the purpose: "And in the remainder (remnant) whom the Lord shall call," *Et in residuis quos Dominus vocaverit*,[82] which literally means that the remainder belonging to the bosom of Holy Church shall be saved, whom God will call by some other hidden means.[83] And more so, if what the enlightened and venerable Fray José de San Benito says is true, which is that the number of those who are saved is more than those who are damned and that on Judgment Day we will see many, whom we thought to have damned themselves, entering Heaven by a back door, since this is more in keeping with the purpose of man's creation.[84] It is certain that "It is impossible to please God without faith," *sine fide impossibile est placere Deo*, Epistle to the Hebrews 11.[85] And, that "Unless someone is reborn from water and the Holy Spirit he cannot enter into the kingdom of God," *nisi quis renatus fuerit ex aqua et Spiritu Sancto non potest introire in regnum Dei*, John chapter 3,[86] but likewise it is certain that invincible ignorance makes the Law unbinding.

The apostle St. Paul says that he who shall call upon the name God will be saved: "For, whosoever shall call upon the name of the Lord shall be saved," *Omnis enim quicumque invocaverit nomen Domini salvus erit*, Epistle to the Romans chapter 10.[87] Then, presupposing a knowledge of God, the converse of the proposition is true: since I shall now say, along with the same apostle, "How, then, shall they call upon him in whom they have not believed? And how shall they believe in him of whom they have not heard? And how shall they hear without a preacher? And how shall they preach, unless they are sent?" *Quomodo ergo invocabunt in quem non crediderunt? aut quomodo credent ei quem non audierunt? Quomodo autem audient sine prædicante? Quomodo vero prædicabunt nisi mittantur?*[88] Then, lacking the knowledge of God, it seems they have some excuse while remaining in their negative faithlessness which no one has offered them any reason to doubt, since in order for Holy Baptism and belief in the chief mysteries of our Holy Faith to be binding, it is required that some notice or recognition of such obligation must first come about through preaching of the Gospel. "So then faith comes by hearing, and hearing by the word of Christ," *Ergo fides ex auditu, auditus autem per verbum Christi*.[89]

---

[81] Joel 2:32.
[82] Certainly, Font's claim that this "literally means" what he says it does would be regarded by many interpreters as a great overstatement.
[83] The whole argument drawn from the Joel text, beginning with "and this . . . ," is added partly between lines and partly in the margin
[84] José de San Benito (1654–1723). His theological works went through four editions up to 1738.
[85] Hebrews 11:6.
[86] John 3:5. Font has added the word *Sancto*, "Holy," to the Bible quotation.
[87] Romans 10:13.
[88] Romans 10:14–15 (continuing from the last quotation).
[89] Romans 10:17.

And shall we perhaps be able to say that they have been lacking this notice and recognition? "But I say: *Have* they not heard?" *Sed dico: Numquid non audierunt?*[90] It is certain that the Gospel was promulgated to the whole world by means of the apostles, so that the case on God's side was justified:[91] "Yes, verily, their sound went into all the earth, and their words unto the end of the world," *Et quidem in omnem terram exivit sonus eorum et in fines orbis terræ verba eorum,*[92] but it is certain likewise that when the apostles divided up the world among themselves in order to preach the Gospel in the whole earth, it does not appear that they included America, as it was a portion then totally unknown to everyone and perhaps even to the apostles themselves, enlightened though they were by the Holy Spirit. And even though it is supposed through conjecture and claimed as certain that the apostle Saint Thomas preached in the two Americas, it is not known that there were any other preachers between then and now, except since the time of the conquests[93] in the conquered territories, and in so many hundreds of years it is natural that the preaching and teaching of the holy apostle was not known and completely forgotten.

So, then, I argue thus: Ignorance entirely invincible exempts from fault; those Indians live in utter ignorance, even concerning God; therefore it is not their fault that they live plunged in the darkness of their negative infidelity. That they live in utter ignorance is not hard to believe, in consideration of all the ignorance one experiences among the converts and old Christians here in America even with the instruction that they have; such ignorance not only in the positive sphere but even in the natural one[94] that the theologians of Europe cannot easily realize it as being so great and so widespread as it is. And as these Indians are of such limited understanding, and without any education, it follows naturally that their own ignorance is incomparably greater.

But what shall we say, in view of this? Shall we say that God damns them without any fault of theirs? This cannot be, it would be an affront to His justice, and it is certain that "Your damnation comes from yourself (is your own fault)," *perditio tua ex te*.[95] Shall we say that God saves them without any merit of theirs? This seems contrary, for "It is a man's business to prepare [his own] soul," *hominis est præparare animam*.[96] What, then, shall we say? With the apostle Saint Paul, we shall be able to exclaim "Oh the depth of the riches both of the wisdom and knowledge of God! How unsearchable are his judgments, and his ways past finding out!" *O altitudo divitiarum sapientiæ et scientiæ Dei! Quam incomprehensibilia sunt judicia ejus, et investigabiles viæ ejus!* (Epistle to the Romans chapter 11).[97] And since this mystery of predestination is such a hidden one, on man's part it would be very presumptuous to seek to ascertain this sovereign secret by use of his own limited understanding. "For who has known the mind of the Lord? Or who has been his counselor?" *Quis enim cognovit sensum Domini? Aut quis consiliarius ejus fuit?*[98] I shall say, only, with David, "Men and beasts of burden thou shalt save, O Lord, even as thou hast multiplied thy mercy, O God," *Homines et jumenta salvabis, Domine, quemadmodum multiplicasti misericordiam*

---

[90] Romans 10:18 (continuing).

[91] Meaning that God was justified in condemning faithlessness in those areas in which the apostles preached the Gospel.

[92] Romans 10:18.

[93] The European arrival in the New World from the end of the fifteenth century onward.

[94] That is, not only in terms of being "educated" but in terms of what conventional European theology would have regarded as some of the elements of natural human reason, such as the existence of one God.

[95] Cf. Hosea 13:9, "*perditio tua, Israhel*" "Your perdition is your own, O Israel."

[96] Cf. Proverbs 16:1.

[97] Romans 11:33.

[98] Romans 11:34.

tuam, Deus (Psalm 35),[99] and shall piously believe that those "beasts of burden" whom God shall save are those ignorant Indians and abandoned gentiles that without doubt are the beasts of burden of the human race; how many of whom shall be saved, and how, and when, God alone knows, "to Whom alone is known the number of the elect who are to be lodged in eternal bliss," *cui soli cognitus est numerus electorum in superna felicitate locandus.*[100]

[December] 8, Friday. I said Mass. In view of the scarcity of grass and water during these many leagues' distance, in order to keep from hindering ourselves by such an accumulation of pack trains and people were we to proceed together, our commander decided to issue orders to divide the expedition's people and pack trains into three sections for the long and hard marches that lay ahead. The first section, in which I myself went and which consisted of our commander's equipment, one pack train, twelve soldiers with their families, and some mounts, was led by the commander himself; the second, which consisted of another dozen soldiers, another pack train and a group of the mounts, was led by the sergeant; and the third, consisting of another twelve soldiers with another pack train and the remainder of the mounts, by the lieutenant in the rear guard. All three were to set out each one day after the other, while the livestock with the remaining soldiers and cowhands should set out on the 10th and travel straight to the watering place of San Sebastián saving some leagues by crossing through the midst of the dunes. Among other matters, it was decided that everyone should carry along a hundredweight of grass.[101]

A great many Indians came to our camp from downriver: Cajuenches, mountain Indians, etc., all of whom are like the last ones in clothing, disposition, good behavior, noisiness, friendliness and all the rest. They brought a great many watermelons, gourds, maize, and so forth.[102] And although I was unable to see the whole amount of people gathered together, nor the Yumas either, as they live so scattered apart, I estimated by what I could see that the Yuma tribe is not under three thousand souls, and it may be that this Cajuenche tribe is larger.[103]

In the afternoon Father Garcés gathered the people, distributed a few beads and a little tobacco among them, and then showed them a large painting of the Most

---

[99]Psalm 35:7–8 (36:6–7). Here Font triumphantly sets down his positive conclusion, by citing the same verses which he had used near the start of his discussion apparently to negate the possibility of his wish for the salvation of the gentiles.

[100]The phrase is familiar from the Mass for the dead, where it is followed by "Grant, we pray, that the book of blessed predestination may hold written the names of all those whom we raise in prayer, or of all of the faithful." (Information from Robert M. Senkewicz.)

[101]Tercio, half a muleload.

[102]Other members of his expeditions found the local watermelons to be small and poor. They may well have been an old, unimproved variety, since watermelons had been introduced to this area as early as 1540 by Alarcón's expedition.

[103]In the final text, after the second visit: "the Yumas must amount to about three thousand souls, and the Cajuenches a bit more."

Holy Virgin with the child Jesus in her arms; on seeing the image, they displayed great happiness and jubilation and, according to the interpreters, said it was good and that they wished to become Christians in order to be white and beautiful like the Virgin and that they would be very willing to be baptized. To this, they were told that at present it could not be, it would happen at another time. The painting was turned around, and painted on its back was a damned person; and they raised a great cry, saying they did not like that, and so forth. The same had been done with the Gila people, Opas, and Yumas, and they all responded the same, showing no aversion to Christianity. Rather, many of them wish and have asked to be baptized, but no one has been baptized because they are not instructed. And the people are clearly quite well disposed to entering the Holy Church, as soon as resources are provided to that end, and they are not averse to subordination to God's law and to our sovereign, since they say they would like to have Spaniards and Fathers come to live with them. I believe that one might achieve a great Christian population among these tribes. However, given the inconstancy of Indians, I judge that a rather large garrison is still needed so that fear of weapons[104] may suppress whatever offense they might wish to commit while subordination is being established among them. Since last year, they have become accustomed to saying the names of Jesus and Mary, and the greeting of many of them is, *Queyé, Jessús Marría*.[105] They repeat it a good deal, noisily, and with very little respect.

On the 6th as we were eating dinner, Father Garcés arrived here along with two interpreters, a lad, and his little pack mule load. He intended to go on down river, view the tribes dwelling there, and settle a peace between them and the Yumas, especially the ones at the mouth, who had been hostile. However, he had already been frustrated in this purpose. The interpreters refused to go with him on the grounds that some Indians had told them not to go down there because they would be killed. Even though the Father would not be harmed, they themselves would be. Therefore they fearfully refused to go onward. Father Garcés told me of the matter and I advised him not to go alone if his interpreters did not go, since he would be gaining nothing in terms of viewing tribes that he had already seen, whereas his journey was directed toward going with interpreters to determine their willingness with respect to religious instruction and to being Christian, and he could not achieve that without an interpreter. Therefore, the best thing would be to go back with Father Fray Tomás and go to the Jalchedunes after Christmas and determine their willingness and gather information concerning the bordering tribes and other lands, and so forth. The downriver tribes could still be reached and viewed when missions and a garrison

---
[104] Firearms.
[105] The doubled consonants are meant to indicate how the natives pronounced these Spanish words.

were established at the meeting of the rivers. Father Garcés was on the point of following this advice when last night an Indian came over saying that Palma and Pablo intended to go downriver on the other side to observe without being seen how the Indians there received the Father, and that he[106] was on his way, with some of his people going on horseback and some on foot. I said that this was not good, because if Palma went in this manner, the people downriver would think he was going fighting and this could be bad for the Father. So the Indian should be told to go to Palma and tell him not to go there, or if he did wish to go, to go with the Father, openly, since he who has a good heart ought not to hide. The interpreters were engaged in this talk after I decided along with Father Garcés to send Palma a message by means of one of his relatives to tell him not to leave his village. The Indian, who is another of Palma's relatives and came to greet us on November 25, said that what he[107] was going to do was to send two women ahead of Father Garcés. The women would be either from among the slaves here in the Cajuenche tribe or from the ones belonging to that tribe that are here and married. These two women would carry the message of how the Father who visited them the other time was coming to see them again, that he was bringing presents for them, and was coming in order to settle a peace with the Yumas. This idea pleased the interpreters so much that they at once decided to go, thus Father Garcés had his purpose granted.

Father Garcés is so well suited to getting along with the Indians and going among them that he seems to be very much like an Indian himself. He acts stolid in everything, like an Indian. He sits with them in a ring or at night around the fire with his legs crossed and will stay spellbound that way for two or three hours or more, thinking of nothing, chatting very calmly and slowly with them. And even though the Indians' foods are so disgusting and dirty, as unclean as they themselves are, the Father eats them gladly and says they are good for the stomach and quite delicious. In sum, as I see it, God has created him wholly suited to seek out these unfortunate, ignorant, and rustic people.

Last night the Indians were having a party with their dancing and uproar that sounded like singing, and something hellish, and the outcome was that they stole clothing and whatever else they could get from any soldiers who were careless.

[December] 9, Saturday. We set out from Santa Olalla Lake at a half past nine in the morning and at a half past three in the afternoon we reached the briny well of *El Carrizal*,[108] having traveled some seven leagues upon a west-

---

[106]Palma.
[107]Palma.
[108]"The Cane-Grass Patch" in the final text. In the field text, it is "the spot belonging to the El Carrizal stream." Elsewhere in the field text and in the original form of the shortened text it is always referred to in the plural: "the briny wells" (or "stream") of El Carrizo.

DECEMBER 9, 1775

northwestward course. It is a dreadful place, with no more grass than a bit of cane-grass growing at the water's edge downstream and extremely bad water that appears to be here year round, but very salty. Nearby is the largest well. This well had been opened up last time and was immediately repaired again. And after it, so were others.[109] Therefore, somewhat acceptable water, springing afresh, was obtained from them and used to water the animals. This was done by hand, using baskets. Father Fray Francisco Garcés left by another route for downriver, intending to get as far as its mouth, having taken his leave of me, for the reason I spoke of yesterday.

To the south from here and some fifteen leagues[110] distant there is in view a rather long, steep mountain range that Father Garcés called *San Gerónimo*, opposite which lies the dark *San Jácome* height. Behind it and much farther off a very even and long range that comes from Baja California and seems to be the main mountain range, is visible, very high, running about southeast to northwestward. Northeastward and very far away the San Sebastián range can be seen, and to the north, on the other side of the dunes and quite far off, the steep range that comes off from the La Campana mountains and runs circling around these plains and dunes from east to westward to join the main range of California.

At a bit over a league along the route there is located a salt lake with no grass, and at about four leagues, a little well of briny water that Father Garcés called *El Rosario*. The route is a level one but a poor terrain, saline and barren, growing nothing except brush, creosote-bush and another bush they call *parrilla*,[111] and other salt scrub. Because of the infertility of this country, which is so level, and from the look of the dunes and most of all from the bounty of mussel and sea snail shells that I saw today—lying in heaps in places, and so aged and ancient that they are easily broken by squeezing them between the fingers—I felt confirmed in the notion that this entire ground was occupied by the sea in ancient times and that these salty fields and dunes were left exposed during one of the sea's withdrawals that histories tell us of. Favoring this is the fact that marks of a similar withdrawal can be noticed on the Yaqui River more than ten leagues before it reaches the sea; and its coast, which along with that of the Pimería Alta and that of the Pápagos is barren for many leagues, is the same as this country as far as the mouth of the Colorado. For along the way there, as one goes from the *San Marcial* camp to Yaqui, a great many heaps of oyster shells, mingled with earth and half buried, are found along with other shells and signs of the sea, and it is impossible that such piles of shells were made by men who would bring

---

[109] The final text here, as it does elsewhere, speaks of only a single well.
[110] 39 miles.
[111] The term is not familiar ("little grapevine" or else "grate, grill"). Professor Solana (Montané 2000: 129) plausibly suggests it is a Franseria bush ("Ambrosia": a ragweed relative).

them from the sea, so far away, merely to bury them in heaps. All of this is no more than a conjecture, albeit one that is quite likely.

[December] 10, Sunday. I said Mass, they began loading up, and we set out from the briny well of El Carrizal at a half past eleven in the morning and halted at a half past five in the afternoon at a dry ravine or gully with no grass or water, having traveled for some seven leagues on a west-northwestward course. The only thing in the ravine was some dead mesquites, which we used to make fires. At Santa Olalla Lake, our commander, who foresaw this from what he had experienced during his first journey, ordered everyone to furnish their water bags with water and to have maize brought along with us, and also that everyone should carry an amount of grass with them, which we, from himself on down and including myself, did, and the animals dined a bit upon this grass and maize. A number of ravines are encountered and crossed along the route, which is fairly level and has no dunes because we were avoiding them to one side or the other as we went along; the ravines appear to be formed by the force of water when it rains, although it seems, on the other hand, that it rains very little, as along the way we met with the droppings left by the cattle and mounts during the last expedition. From this I deduce that either because the ground is so dry and thin, it swallows up the rainwater, or else that there is little rain, or else that the ravines are caused by rain falling in the steep rocky mountain range in the distance that circles all this large plain and dunes and the water seeks its path through here downward to the sea, toward which the ravines lead; or else that the only rain is an occasional cloudburst, very heavy, as happens in California.[112] The route is visibly strewn with little marine snails and mussel shells, which confirms my conjecture noted down yesterday. Halfway along the way we found in a ravine the little well of *Las Angustias*,[113] over a vara in depth and with very little water, bad but not as bad as at El Carrizal. All of this country makes difficult traveling because of the utter lack of grass and water and its being almost entirely dune sand.

[December] 11, Monday. The loading up started very early in the morning, before daylight, and we set out from the dry ravine a little after seven o'clock in the morning and at six o'clock in the evening reached the little well that last time they called *Santa Rosa de las Lajas*[114] having traveled for fifteen leagues, a varying course, west-northwestward before deviating west-southwestward a little before stopping. They are wells which contain good water but very little of it, so that two wells were opened at once, and afterward four others, and they were

---

[112]Baja California. The remark about ravines running toward the sea seems uncharacteristic of the topography of this march, unless soil fill from the New River overflow has made great changes in the landscape.

[113]Distress, so called during the first Anza expedition in 1774. For the explanation of the name, see the note under May 8, below.

[114]The Sandstones.

worked upon from the time we arrived until noon on the following day in order to get water; six wells were opened and the animals were watered using baskets, which is the way it is done in such places. At first we found ourselves in difficulty because no water came out, but with hard work the wells were deepened a bit and our patroness La Santísima Virgen María de Guadalupe willed that water should flow. Had this not happened, the expedition was at risk of perishing for lack of water, on her own feast day, which was tomorrow.

This spot called Santa Rosa is a stream that seemingly flows beneath the sands and is the runoff from some little low hills, spurs departing from the steep high range that comes up from Baja California and lies near here; and in the neighborhood there is some of the grass they call galleta. One sees from here a big-headed height very far away about to the east-northeastward that our commander thought was El Bauquiburi, although I myself did not think so and doubted that it could have been seen as it already lies a great distance off. Near here on the left hand along the way lies the *Cerro del Imposible*,[115] which is quite a high steep height, separated from the San Gerónimo range behind which are the stranded fish seen during the first expedition.[116] The route is a not very bad one, had it been only not so long, for which reason we reached here quite tired. Along it one encounters a good many heaps of mussels and countless numbers of very tiny, spiral-shaped sea snails that in spots show as white as flour, a fact that confirms this to be maritime country and, even, that the sea once reached to there; however, no gullies were found like yesterday's.

It was only in the afternoon, as we drew opposite the Cerro del Imposible (so called, since last time, because the soldiers found it impossible to reach it), which we were leaving upon our left, that we came into some very unpleasant land because all the ground was full of little mounds of hard soil that we called *almondigones*,[117] meatballs, very well suited for tiring out the animals, and later

---

[115] The Hill of the Impossible.

[116] Signal Mountain. The shoals of dead fish were encountered on March 5, 1774, as recorded in Anza's journal: "On rounding the dune a sea inlet [the modern Laguna Seca] starts out [with] countless stranded fishes of sorts and sizes that belong to the sea and not to lakes and rivers, however large those sorts are. This inlet is the one that Father Garcés two years ago thought was made by the Río Amarillo, a misunderstanding he did not perceive because he did not taste the [salt] water." The "Yellow River" was a mythical stream reputed to run west off of the Colorado toward the Pacific (cf. Brown 2001: 35). The journal of Francisco Díaz, at the same place and time as Anza's entry, says: "About ten or twelve leagues lower down in this same valley is where Reverend Father Francisco Garcés saw the yellow water he speaks of in his journal [of his earlier excursion in 1772]. I have deduced from this information, and from a very large beaching of sea fish that we have found all along the lake's edge at this spot together with a great many other signs plainly demonstrating that seawater is what it holds at times, that the Father's 'yellow water' is some large inlet or other that at times of a great amount of rain or of the sea's having made an unusual incursion, has, aided by the drainage from the mountain range here, extended all the way across this valley and has then withdrawn back to its normal state." (Díaz, "Diario"; Soto Pérez 1998 1: 718.)

[117] *Albondigones*.

Figure 14. A train of explorers, mules, and horses approaching Signal Mountain in the desert, 1853. Pacific Railroad Surveys. *Reproduced from Williamson 1856.*

we passed through a dune for about a league. This route from El Carrizal to Santa Rosa was discovered by soldiers sent ahead by our commander from the Gila River on November 16, and along it one avoids the dunes by leaving them to one side and the other, passing through only an occasional small piece that has them. At this season it turns really quite cold here in these plains and we had a cloudy sky: on the 9th there were clouds like spider webs, a bit thicker ones on the 10th; the 11th was cloudy all day with thicker clouds, and the 12th dawned with low thick clouds touching down upon the mountains, which led me to suppose that perhaps we were approaching a country where the rains fall in the winter.

[December] 12, Tuesday. I said Mass, preparation began for the march, and we set out from the Santa Rosa wells at a quarter to two in the afternoon and at a quarter to five halted at a sort of a dry creek, having traveled three leagues upon a northward course (with a quarter point's worth of deviation to one side and the other). We left the six wells at Santa Rosa open for those who would be coming behind. This dry creek here comes from a range not very far away that seems to be a spur of the long mountain range of California and runs toward the plains we are leaving to our right and the dunes, keeping the range upon our left. It has no water but does have a good deal of galleta grass, some of which is also found along the way; there is likewise some firewood to warm ourselves with, which is lacking at Santa Rosa. The route is a fairly good one and it is only at departing from Santa Rosa that it has hilly ravines from hills of sandy, hard ground with a great many black rocks, which are not very large, and sandstones.

Following midday, a very strong cold west wind arose coming from the main range of California, where rain seemed to be falling as it was all covered with thick clouds; it kept on through the afternoon, getting stronger, so that we were compelled to halt, and it kept on blowing almost the same all during the night until dawn. This strong wind, which must be a feature of these plains here, is what forms the dunes into their various shapes. They are heaps of fine sand that the wind shifts from one side to another, as I noticed today, since, under the wind, dust clouds were seen in the distance very thick and low, and even right next to the ground.

[December] 13, Wednesday. At daybreak the weather was as cold as though it were snowing, which continued, and even worse, until after midday, with a small thin air that pierced one's face. We set out from the dry stream a little after nine o'clock in the morning and at a half past three in the afternoon, having traveled some seven long leagues on a north-northwestward course and mostly almost northward, we reached the spot that was called San Sebastián last time.[118] This is a small village of mountain Cajuenches, or more properly speaking, of Indians of the Jecuiche tribe.[119] It is a level route, without dunes, but the ground is treacherous in places so that when one's animal treads on it, after a few paces its hooves suddenly sink in. The badlands with dunes and so forth seem to be coming to an end here. Since we are drawing closer to the mountains, it seems that there will be better grass up ahead.

This place of San Sebastián is a spring of water that on issuing forth is a bit hot or lukewarm year round, and deep, a sort of a swamp as it has very little flow. Last time, the animals cleaned themselves out here from eating the nitrous grass. It did not happen as much this time and there is cane grass and some grass. But it is not very good because the soil is very nitrous throughout this low spot here. In spots the salts appear as white as flour. The water, however, does

---

[118] On March 10, 1774, Anza had named it in honor of Sebastián Taraval, "the Wanderer" (El Peregrino), who, during his earlier flight from the coast, had discovered the way which the expedition was now following.

[119] This is one of the ethnic terms employed by Garcés in 1774 and afterward, somewhat confusingly, like the other names, Cajuenches, Jahueches, Apagüeches, Jenigüechis, etc., used by the Quechán for their various neighbors to the west and south. "Jecuiche" was most properly applied to the far-spread Takic (Shoshonean)-speaking group later known as Cahuilla, as well as to the smaller one known as Cupeño. (Cf. Forbes 1965: 37, 345.)

not seem to be very bad, all the more so as it is very lukewarm while the weather in this country is so cold; although near the spring there is a slough that is very miry and has a little water in it that is very bad and harmful. There is also some firewood from scrub mesquites. A few mountain Indians, or Jecuiches, live here, who judging by what I saw must amount to about twenty or thirty souls, very wretched and hungry, thin, stunted, and poor-bodied, who came out to see us on our arrival even though they had fled when they saw the soldier who was going out in front as guide. They ceased their flight on seeing that the soldier was calling to them.

What with the cold weather here, it is a wondrous thing to see these Indians in the buff,[120] and themselves so unbothered that the first thing they do in the morning is to go bathe in the spring, as we have seen being done. They employ bows and arrows, although not many, and poorly made ones, and they have another weapon or kind of war-club, a hard, thin stick about three fingers wide in the shape of a half-moon or sickle, and about two tercios in length. They use this stick to hunt hares and rabbits by throwing it in a particular manner so as to break their legs, and they also are accustomed to hunt them using the nets they have, made from a very well spun thread, so soft that it seems made of hemp and I was unable to recognize or to learn what they make it from, because there was no interpreter. Their speech is different from that of the Yumas although somewhat similar to that of the Cajuenches, or so I thought.[121] Their food is a hare or two when they can catch them (there are not many of them), mescal at times, which they go far into the mountains to search for, and more normally mesquite pods and screwbean[122] and the tule rush that grows at the lake belonging to the spring, and therefore their teeth are very dirty and rotten. And so starving are they, that in all haste they scooped up, dirt and all, some grains of corn left on the soil from what was fed to mules. I thought these Indians, who—judging by what Father Garcés said and by the ones I saw later at the *Puerto de San Carlos*[123]—I imagine must belong to the Quemeya tribe, were the most unfortunate, unhappy people of any I have seen. At nightfall there were clouds and a good deal of chill, and rain was threatening.

[December] 14, Thursday. The weather at daybreak was very cold, cloud-covered sky, and with a very strong wind, which at ten in the morning turned to snow. While it was snowing the livestock arrived. It had set out on the 10th from Santa Olalla Lake heading straight across for here from El Carrizal. Since

---

[120]*En pelota*. The Spanish phrase is equivalent to "in the buff," in English.
[121]Thus in the final text, revising the field text: "is like that of the Yumas with small difference."
[122]"And screwbean" is not in the final text.
[123]San Carlos Pass.

they had not been watered in five days, they threw themselves into the water like lightning. Only eleven head were lost along the way.[124] Along with the stock came the cowhands and soldiers who had been driving them. They were perishing from cold and hunger, as their food supply had run out. It snowed for about an hour, the wind died down, and it kept on raining all day until long after nightfall.

The second group of people, with the sergeant, was to have arrived here today; seeing that they had not come, we supposed that the rain had caught them at Santa Rosa yesterday morning, judging from the clouds that we saw in that direction while on the way, and therefore they had not set out from that spot. God grant it is so.

When the livestock arrived, I happened to be in the commander's tent, where I spent most of my day because the tent was better sheltered and had a fire in it. Seeing how raw the weather was I said to him that in view of the fact that grass did not seem to be very poor at this spot and that water was plentiful, I thought it would be better to wait here for the two sections of people that had stayed behind, and then join together rather than go and wait for them at the *Santa Catarina* stream three days' marches onward as previously had been decided, since it would be easier to send them aid from here rather than from farther ahead in case some need arose. And our commander replied that he had decided to do that. Therefore it was decided to remain here until all the expedition people, who were split into two sections behind us, should come together.

[December] 15, Friday. At daybreak the weather was clear although with a few clouds, and the main mountain range of California made its appearance whitened with snow, with the San Gregorio[125] range, which we have opposite us and which links up with the California mountains, being entirely snowy from its summit to its skirts. And crowned with snow also was the steep range which we had been leaving very far away to our right surrounding all the other side of the dunes and plains since before San Pablo; it appears to join with the main California range farther up from here, above San Gregorio; so that we find ourselves surrounded, here in this plain, with snow and with such a chill as can be imagined. Eight head of cattle[126] and a mule belonging to the cowhands were found dead of cold at dawn, killed by all the heavy chill last night because on coming here they had been so thirsty and had gorged themselves with water. The sergeant, along with the second section of the expedition's people and the second pack train, arrived at noon. They came perishing from the cold from the cruel day which caught them traveling yesterday. Some of their animals had become tired out and crippled. Following midday, the fog rising from the snowy

---

[124]Guerrero (2006: 136) in essence attributes a disagreement between the details of Font's record and Anza's journal entries for December 14 and 15 (Anza says the cattle were too worn out to water) to Font's failing to check his facts with the commander. This is a possible suspicion, but hardly provable.

[125]In the final text, "San Sebastián."

[126]Font's field text originally said "nine"; Anza says "six."

California range spread across the whole horizon and the day became overcast, foreboding a bad night and renewed snow or rain.

[December] 16, Saturday. At daybreak the chill had moderated but the whole horizon was cloud covered and stayed so for the entire day, without raining. We were expecting the third section bringing up the rear with Lieutenant Moraga[127] to come up today, but it did not arrive, perhaps because they encountered some delay.[128] At noon the sergeant came up, saying that at least two horses were missing from among the mounts. It was plain from the tracks that they had been stolen by mountain Indians who came to visit us yesterday and were driving them toward the steep mountains we had been leaving to the right upon our way. He said that the man who had been on horse guard had followed the tracks for a good stretch until the mule he was riding gave out and he had to return. Our commander at once ordered the sergeant to go out with four soldiers and chase them, with orders that if they did not overtake them today they should pursue the endeavor until tomorrow and that he should make the Indians understand they had behaved badly. He should show them some boldness in order to inculcate fear and awe, but not use firearms unless in self-defense, should the Indians try to resist.[129] These Indians are of a worse nature than those of the Colorado River in every respect and were accomplices in the San Diego uprising that I shall speak of at the right time. Because of what they did during the last expedition,[130] our commander called them the Apaches of this country.

The soldiers did not return during the entire day until nightfall, and then came back with three horses that they had taken from the Indians, whose villages are in the steep mountain range mentioned, which the soldiers reached and which must be some four leagues distant from the place of San Sebastián here. This gave the soldiers the opportunity of seeing that this range lies a bit of a distance away from the other snowy one that was opposite us. There is a pass between the two that perhaps would allow a way to be opened that, at least, would come out at the San José valley. By leaving the Puerto de San Carlos off to the left, this way would cut off the bad spots lying ahead while crossing the

---

[127] Font sometimes called Moraga *teniente* (translated here as lieutenant) and sometimes, as on December 17, *alférez* (translated there as ensign). *Teniente* was roughly equivalent to first lieutenant and *alférez* was roughly equivalent to a second lieutenant. These distinctions in rank tended to be more flexible on the frontier.

[128] In the final text (with hindsight), "because it was delayed by the snow."

[129] The orders as described in Anza's journal were that the soldiers "should demand three times of them" (this being the historical Spanish *requerimiento* directed to the enemy before engaging in battle) "that they return the theft, letting them understand that if they did it again they would undergo the force of our weapons"; however, the soldiers should not actually fire unless the natives used their own weapons in refusing to return the horses.

[130] Attacking the Spaniards' horses and mules with arrows in 1774.

main range—this might be verified by sending out a few men traveling light—and the route then would be made shorter or at least better.[131] They also saw that there is a marsh, a bit of a cane-grass patch, and a stream, although with bad, briny water, farther down at the foot of the range at the villages belonging to the Indian thieves. They said that as soon as the Indians saw the soldiers they ran away and hid themselves and they were only able to catch one of them and three women, whom they threatened should they steal again, and asked them for the horses. And although they at first denied the allegation, the soldiers followed the tracks and came upon them, finding two of them hobbled and one tied up to a mesquite, in different places. Thereupon the Indians, seeing themselves caught in the act, excused themselves by saying that those horses had come by themselves and by very helpfully and obligingly offering to drive back to our camp any horse that might run away. A poor showing these unfortunates have made of themselves!

[December] 17, Sunday. I said Mass and after it our commander sent some twenty animals[132] to meet Ensign Moraga and his people, supposing he must have met with some delay as he did not come in yesterday. I observed the latitude of this spot and found it, by the tables of Jorge with no correction, in 33° 10½' and with correction in 33° 8'.[133] And thus I say: at the San Sebastián village, December 17, 1775: meridian altitude of the sun's lower limb: 33° 10'. At a quarter past three in the afternoon Lieutenant Moraga arrived with the third section of the expedition's people, after they had experienced a great many problems on the way. These were that the cold required them to take three days' march to get from El Carrizal to Santa Rosa, where they arrived on the 14th perished with hunger and with cold because of the snow that caught them upon the road, which, together with the chill, struck so hard that, between mules and horses, there are fifteen animals left lost and dead along the way. And God be thanked that the people escaped with their lives, it being no small wonder that no one died or fell ill. They stayed at Santa Rosa on the 15th, and set out from there yesterday, and their arrival today has been a great pleasure for everyone, so that we have managed to rejoin each other now in order to continue the journey, if God favors it.

Had we delayed for some two weeks at Santa Olalla Lake to pasture our animals on stubble as the lieutenant and the soldiers said we should, perhaps the hindrances would not have proved so

---

[131] The actual existence of the San Gorgonio pass, farther north, justified Font's and the soldiers' suspicion that there was a better back door into Southern California. His description of the farthest mountain projection of the Santa Rosas has led, in modern times, to the bestowal of the name "Font's Point" on its summit. In 1774, Garcés, on the same route, had less correctly persuaded himself that the intermountain valleys to the northward would provide the desired shortcut across to Monterey.

[132] Herded by two soldiers.

[133] The latitude figure is barely a minute too high.

great, as there was a great deal of good grass there and good water. I suggested as much to our commander on December 1. However, he replied that at Mexico City they had assigned a limit of only seventy days for the travel, a fact which I found difficult to believe.[134] Thus, in order to get to Monterey quickly he was unwilling to delay. In the end, he missed doing that, for haste is never good in such cases. It is no wonder there were such problems with the animals, since because the commander did not go to Tubac in August, as he was supposed to and had earlier decided to, there had been some disorder there during his absence and that was the time the Apaches fell upon the presidio and carried off the mounts, some five hundred animals. What with this and the animals he lost in a stampede at San Miguel, he was left with few animals for so long a travel and one so devoid of grazing, and he refused to buy more, saying the ones he had were sufficient and if not everyone could go on horseback, they would go on foot; which is why most of them have been riding on a single horse with no change of mounts between San Miguel and here, and doing so with a thousand toils.

At nightfall, what with the joy of all the people's having arrived, some rather unruly partying broke out over there. A woman, a widow who was traveling with the expedition, quite brazenly sang some glosas that were not so nice. Her singing was acknowledged by the applause and shouting from the rabble.[135] Her companion, that is, the man with whom she was traveling, became angered at this and punished her. Our commander overheard this and it caused him to come out of his tent and scold the man for punishing her. I said to him, "Let it be, sir, he is doing the right thing," and he answered, "No, Father, I must not allow these excesses in my presence." He was strict about this excess and not strict about the excess of the party!—which went on until quite late.

[December] 18, Monday.

I said Mass, during which I spoke four words concerning the party last night, condemning the act, since in place of giving thanks to God for their having reached here alive and not having died, as the animals did, during all those hardships, it seemed they were thanking the Devil with that kind of festivity, and so forth. I imagine that this did not sit very well with our commander, who all during the morning did not speak to me. I shall stipulate that this happened to me many times, since, being of a sensitive and proud nature as he was, anything served to annoy him and he would appear very sober and offended and sometimes would even go two or three days without speaking to me or else wasting very few words on me—and those occasionally not particularly pleasant ones—, not accepting any conversation with me even though I attempted

---

[134] The claim was true. The provisions that had been issued were intended to last for seventy days after leaving Tubac. Anza obviously had been counting on being able to draw upon the new mission settlements, once the expedition had reached California.

[135] The performance evidently required talent, since *glosas* are song lyrics adapted to the occasion, and humorously "feeding into" a set refrain. ("A composition at the end of which, or of each of its strophes, are inserted one or more previously set forth verses, rhyming and making sense"—*Diccionario de la Real Academia Española*.) There are familiar examples of similar comic songs in English. The woman was (María) Feliciana Arbayo (Arballo), a recent widow whom Font later describes in his roster of personnel as traveling alone with two little daughters. According to Anza's personnel roster, the younger child was only a month old in October, and the three were traveling with the soldier-settler family of Agustín Valenzuela (the husband, wife, and young daughter). Other records show that she was from Culiacán, a "free *mulata* (mulatto)," her age given as twenty-five in October 1775 and twenty-four [*sic*] in April 1776 when she was married by Fray Francisco Garcés to Juan Francisco López. Her descendants in the third and fourth generations included leading families of late Mexican California.

it. Combined with the illness of diarrhea I was having, this provided me with a sizeable cross to bear, God be thanked.[136]

Following Mass, a start was made on preparing for the march, and as a great many of the mounts were fatigued, the extra packs were emptied of grass and the pack train mules that had been coming along without loads, some twenty of them, were provided for the people:

not all of the people, however, and starting today a number of them began traveling on foot, since up until now, two or three children or even two children and a soldier had been riding on one horse, so that the animals were worn out and a great many horses and mules had been left tired out and dead along the way.

We set out from San Sebastián a little before one o'clock in the afternoon and at a half past four halted at a low spot near some small heights where there was a good deal of galleta grass but no water, having traveled for some four leagues on a course west by north. The route is level, and the soil is sandy and firm, with some mussel shells and little sea-snails. It is only on setting out from the low spot at San Sebastián that there are some ravines and sticking places, and that whole low spot is so nitrous a soil that there are large pieces of it as white as though it had snowed on them or as though flour had been sprinkled there. Excepting the small cane-grass patches which the animals lived on during these days, there are no trees or grass other than salt weed and the creosote bush or gobernadora, which grows over all of this plain as far as the spot where we halted today. We were keeping the same heights and the long range of California upon our left, and the mountains that encircle all of the plains behind us upon our right as well, and closer by, a tall height that became snow-covered during the last few days. And tomorrow we shall advance toward the San Gregorio pass. On going about two leagues we came upon a very small-sized deserted village, and along the whole way there is nothing more than an occasional scrub mesquite, and creosote bush; our route lies close to some hills, as we search for a hollow to cross the main range.

[December] 19, Tuesday. I said Mass. We set out from the low spot at nine o'clock in the morning, and by traveling west-northwestward for five short leagues, at a quarter past one in the afternoon we came to the spot called, last time, the well of San Gregorio. It is a place that has little grass and less water, lying at the entrance of the little valley formed upon the west and north by the high mountains of California, and on the south and east by little heights of small elevation. The route is a fairly level one, with sandy soil that is like a dune or a little thicker, but more solid, whether because that is its nature or because

---

[136]As a matter of religious conviction, Font is trying to be thankful for the difficulties with which he is faced, since they allowed him to imitate Jesus who carried his cross.

it is moist from the recent snow. The tall heights, or San Sebastián range, that we are leaving to our right are the ones we saw all snow-covered on the day it snowed, and they, together with other heights reaching out from the main range of California, form the pass that we shall go through tomorrow.[137] To our left are small heights of very slight elevation close to the road, a good piece of which is a stream, dry on top, that is the runoff from the hills or small heights when it rains. Both these and the tall heights are so arid that neither appears to contain bush or weed, and the plains have just what the ones earlier had. This sad plight concerning grass extends as far as San Gregorio, for there is nothing but a bit of creosote bush in the low spots. The stopping place has little grass—good, however—and a well of good but scarce water which issues from the foot of small heights upon the left forming a little valley. The water in the little well ran out quickly which is why our commander ordered other wells to be opened to water the mounts and livestock. Although they toiled at this operation the whole day until nightfall, no water could be gotten from the wells, so that the majority of the animals went without water. Necessity made some of them drink a sort of salty, bitter water found lower down. This did them a good deal of harm.

[December] 20, Wednesday. I wished to say Mass but was unable to, due to the great chill in the weather and even more to the bad night I had because of my diarrhea. We set out from the San Gregorio well at a quarter past nine in the morning, and by traveling northwestward (very slowly, because the mounts and mules were very beaten down) for four leagues, at a half past one in the afternoon halted at the bank of the stream issuing from the hollow and spot that was called Santa Catarina the other time, where the stream spreads, loses itself, and comes to an end out over the plains here. The route is level although a bit full of dune sand and there is nothing save brush and creosote bush all along it, and here at this spot there is a bit of galleta and *cholla*, which the livestock occupied themselves with. Beyond San Gregorio the hollow formed by the arid mountains I spoke of yesterday commences to narrow and runs onward to reach the top of the main mountain range.

Last night, for lack of water and perhaps oppressed by the cold, the livestock mounted a stampede and part of them went back toward San Sebastián. The sergeant along with the cowhands and some of the people went in the morning to get them back and did not return during the entire day. The remainder of the stock, which had stayed, reached this place at nightfall quite tired out, with eight head and some other animals left worn out and lying down along the way.

Here at this spot were three mountain Indian women belonging to the Jecuiche

---

[137] Font's final text reads, "To our left are hills and middling-high mountains, both the one and the other already belonging to the main California range."

tribe that lives hereabouts, who were gathering a small lentil-like seed yielded by a slightly sweet-smelling scrub plant. The moment they saw us they fled in all haste, leaving their *guaris*[138] and baskets behind them there. Although a soldier went after them on horseback to bring them back, he was unable to catch them, for they hide in the gullies and scamper away like deer because they have never seen any people. None of the women appeared all day long. Our commander ordered that no one should touch their effects where they lay, and later he gathered them together near his tent so as to give them back to the Indians undamaged in case they came here. They are a people poor in body, very miserable, and stunted.

[December] 21, Thursday. I said Mass. We delayed because the men who stayed back to collect the scattered livestock had not come in, and during the morning our commander sent two soldiers with a change of mounts to meet them, but they did not return during the entire day, which caused us some worry.

Since the pack trains set out from San Miguel[139] so overburdened and large, with forty beasts in each one, and with the muleteers who handled them so little skilled that there was only one who understood his trade well, while the rest began learning it along the way, the mules received rough treatment. Thus, mules and horses were constantly straying and dying, just in order to save paying the salaries for good muleteers. And because we did not pause where we could have, we must now linger in these bad spots so that the mounts can regain strength and rest. These delays and losses perhaps caused the commander some mortification, and so he stayed inside his tent today, and I in mine. We did not speak to each other or see each other except at the dinner hour.

I was a bit improved with regard to my illness, perhaps the effect of a drink I took yesterday that Tía Francisca[140] had given me for an upset stomach. Also, yesterday and today were rather mild, although at the end of afternoon the whole horizon clouded over as though the weather were readying for another snowfall.

[December] 22, Friday. The day continued very cloudy, although with little chill, as though it were about to snow or rain, and I awoke and remained all day long brought a bit low with my diarrhea, which became much more severe. After midday three of the mountain Indians from hereabouts came by, perhaps drawn by hunger and need, very stunted, thin, and sooty. They were given something to eat and one of them collected her guari which was full of small seeds that they had left behind when we came and they had fled. She gathered the rest of the effects that belonged to them and went away. After a little while, other Indians made their appearance among the camp's messes.[141] Perhaps they

---

[138] Guari is a local Mexican term (also *huari*, *guare*) for a basket.
[139] San Miguel de Horcasitas.
[140] See the note near the end of the November 22 entry.
[141] The expedition personnel's group gatherings for meals around their fires and tents.

were beginning to lose their fear seeing that we were not harming them. In my opinion, they are among the most unhappy people that exist in the world: their dwelling, among arid cold rocks in these mountains; their clothing, none (and the women, some very wretched covering made of mescal fibers);[142] their food, tasteless roots and grass seeds and worthless mescal, and little enough of everything, so that their food is fasting; their weapons, some few and poor bows and arrows;[143] and in sum, so savage, wild, dirty, unkempt, ugly, small and stunted that it is only because they have a human form that one must believe that they are men.

Shortly before nightfall, the sergeant came up with the men who had stayed behind to collect the livestock, some of which was lost and others perished. One group had gone toward San Sebastián, and between herding it and bringing it back they had had a good deal of hardship; a great many head died, some at San Sebastián and others along the way and some seventy reached here, many of them thoroughly fatigued.

[December] 23, Saturday. A very fine rain started during the night and kept falling at intervals. The weather at daybreak was very cloudy, with the clouds pressing upon the heights though raining less, which is why our commander decided to continue the journey. Loading up took place following midday, and about one o'clock in the afternoon[144] we set out from the Santa Catarina stream. By traveling up the hollow course northwestward with an occasional turning, for a bit over a league, we halted a little before three o'clock in the place called Santa Catarina the other time, at the foot of the big willow tree upon whose trunk Father Garcés had written the attempt made by the mountain Indians to shoot his animals with arrows during the last expedition, and near the spring from which the stream that we followed up the hollow arises.[145]

This spot lies within a hollow that runs on upward and through which the route across the main California range passes. The hollow is formed between a

---

[142] The phrase about women's clothing appears only in the final text.

[143] Again, the final text expresses a reevaluation, since the field text had read, "their weapons, none." But the abandoned goods had included a bow, and the next entry mentions bows also. The original notion that the inhabitants had no weapons may have arisen with Anza's first visit in March 1774 when the only one seen was "a man with an arrow, no bow." The Spaniards learned differently shortly thereafter—see the note below on Garcés's and Díaz's experiences.

[144] In the field text, corrected from "about two o'clock."

[145] On April 18, 1774, Garcés and some soldiers were on their way through to the Colorado and were distributing gifts to the natives when one of them secretly wounded "the fattest horse." Just after dark, some of them returned and slaughtered it without being caught—"it looks like a craving for horseflesh," wrote Garcés. Father Juan Díaz's party had had the experience of two or three arrows being shot at the mounts near the same spot two or three weeks before, and on May 6, Anza's party returning from California had found Garcés's carved note and right afterward, two or three of their own mounts were shot from ambush. Anza had one native whipped. The name "*El Pie del Sauce*" "Foot of the Willow Tree" which Font records for the spot seems to be a sort of a pun—it was also the foot of the way through the mountains.

number of pretty high, very rocky heights, or, say rather, great piles of rocks and boulders of greater and lesser size, seemingly shoved and piled up there as if that were the dustbin of the world, and accordingly they are barren, arid and without trees or any green thing. There is no grass here,[146] and only along the way are there a few small willows on the stream banks; in spots it is a bit broken and bushy with weeds or rockrose and some of the creosote bush, which, being an ill-omened plant, is never missing in these nitrous lands—and worthless as well.

We saw a number of Indians high up on the hills and in among rocks, so wild they seem fauns,[147] and very stunted and sooty and diminutive in body and wholly naked. However, since they saw that we did them no harm yesterday and today, as soon as we had halted our commander went to a village to visit them, two of them came over with a bit of firewood and presented it to our commander (who they and the Jenigüechis further on ahead call Tomiár),[148] a piece of mescal head, which I tasted and thought very fine. Since this is the season for gathering mescal, perhaps it is for that reason that there were more Indians seen here this time than the other one. However, they were so distrustful that they would not come out from up there in the rocks, behind which they had scrambled up, and not one woman showed herself.

A fine rain began as soon as we came into the hollow's narrows and it lasted until we had come near the stopping place; the remainder of the day continued very overcast and rain began again after nightfall and continued more heavily during most of the night. The Indians who did show themselves did so unarmed, even though they make use of their wretched bows and arrows and their sickle-like stick, as I said at San Sebastián. And they are ill-willed, mean-hearted and evil-intentioned people, and they are also very cowardly.

[December] 24, Sunday. I said Mass. We set out from *El Pie del Sauce*[149] at a half past nine in the morning, and by traveling up-hollow for about some four leagues, course west-northwestward, we halted at about two o'clock in the afternoon in the same hollow at a dry stream that receives the waters from the heights whenever it rains, and not very far from a small spring of water. The spot is scarce in water[150] with very little galleta grass and less firewood. About halfway along the route is a middling-sized spring which, running down-hollow loses itself among the sands before joining the water from Santa Catarina. The hollow runs still sloping upward, though gently so, and is of fair width along all of today's route. There is some mescal plant in it, not as sparse as at the start,

---

[146]In the draft text, "there is little grass here [altered to 'little or no'], and galleta at that." The final text denies it categorically.
[147]The "wild men of the woods" in classical literature.
[148]Chief or lord in the local Takic languages. This parenthetical remark is only in the final text.
[149]The Foot of the Willow Tree.
[150]In the field text, "a spot with no water."

and some creosote bush and galleta grass in spots, and we also saw horns of wild sheep, perhaps hunted by the Indians, but the soil is all sandy and rocky. The heights forming the hollow are positive heaps of rocks or boulders much like the stones found in rivers—all sizes of them—along with some sand or arid ground, so that no trees to be seen upon them nor anything of note for human comfort.

Close to the spring we encountered along the way, we saw a village of Indians who had scrambled up among the rocks, from which they were watching us pass by. When our commander called to them and showed them beads, only one single woman was bold enough to approach. Our commander gave her a string of beads. Near the small spring, shortly before halting, we saw another village whose houses were half-underground grottos made between rocks and covered a bit with branches and earth, like rabbit holes. And the Indians came out of their grottos, angered, as it were, signaling to us with their hands that we should not go forward and talking very fast with a great deal of gabbling, bumping with their haunches and with such movements and leaps, like those of kid goats, that they have been called *Los Danzarines* ever since the other time.[151] One of them in particular, who must have been some sort of a petty chief, began to talk very fast as soon as he saw us, shouting a great deal and in a great rush as though offended and unwilling for us to go through his land, and making frantic haunch swingings, little jumps, leaps, and sways. The women did not show themselves, but the men were unarmed, ugly, stunted, disheveled and sooty, as are all those who live here in these mountains. Their tongue is totally different from that of the Cajuenches: they talk very fast, and it seems an uglier speech, just as ugly, headlong and laughable as they themselves are. Their dress is to go naked. The women wear their little skirts made either of mescal, some deerskin, or something else.

Ever since the snowfall, the livestock were so weakened that three head gave out yesterday during such a short a march, and another one today. The dead animals were hauled to the camp and distributed among the soldiers; two animals also appear to have been lost, if the Indians did not hide them and steal them. The chill was not a very heavy one although it was damp.

I learned that the troops were being given drink, since this was Christmas Eve night. To see

---

[151] The Dancers. However, the name may also have been bestowed for better reasons. On April 16, 1774, north of this location, Francisco Garcés saw a performance: "A very crowd-pleasing [*chusco*] Indian came on with a very fine-sounding song and a well-measured step, and then, while keeping up the beat, he adopted the posture of someone sitting upon a small chest, finished the song, and followed it by a shriek and heavy breathing in which he continued the beat, entertaining us very much." Further south, on April 17 at San Patricio hollow, "there was a dance in this form: the Indian man shouted out as though exhausting himself, shaking his arms and legs excessively, while a woman with her body bowed over circled around him as he acted like a raging madman. The woman made a calling motion with her hand, like our Spanish women."

whether I might stop this drunkenness, after dinner I said to our commander, "Sir, even though my bringing up the matter is useless and I have no role to play here, I have learned that there is to be drinking today. He replied, "There is." "But sir, "I continued, "I say that I do not think it good for us to celebrate the birth of the child Jesus with drunkenness." "Father," he said to me, "I am not giving it out for them to get drunk on." "Surely that must be so," I said, "since if you did, the evil would be all the greater; but if you know they will get drunk, don't give it to them." He said to me in reply, "It is provided to me by the king, and they give it to me so that I can give it to the troops." I responded, "Fine, but that must have meant in case of need." "But Father," he said, "better they should get drunk than commit something else." I answered, "But sir, getting drunk is a sin, and he who cooperates with sin also sins, and thus if you are aware that someone gets drunk upon thus-and-so much, give him less or don't give him any." He did not utter another word. I went off to my tent without having been able to hinder this disorder, since he had already decided to issue it. So, drink was at once given out to the people, a cuartillo[152] to each one. Our commander said loudly, "Make sure that you don't get drunk, for if I catch you drunk outside your own lodgings I'll punish you myself." He quieted his conscience with this and the people went on loudly singing and dancing during the night as a result of the drink ration—untroubled by our being in the midst of such hard mountains, in rains, and so set back by worn-out and dead animals and cattle. Such is the rule, there, of these absolute gentry. I have narrated this event to prove it!

In the evening they called me to hear the confession of a soldier's wife who had been having birth pangs since yesterday. She was the one I spoke of on November 24, who had the treat, and she was very fearful of dying. Having comforted and encouraged her as well as I could, I retired to my tent and at a half past eleven at night.[153] In a very short time she successfully gave birth to a boy child.

[December] 25, Monday. Because during this holy night of Christmas Eve a soldier's wife (the one I spoke of yesterday) had successfully given birth a little before midnight and since the day was a very raw, foggy one, it was decided to delay here. So, since I found myself a bit better, I had the opportunity of saying the three Masses, and following them I solemnly baptized the newborn child and named him Salvador Ignacio.[154] During the first Mass I said four words to the audience concerning this day's mystery. The weather continued foggy until afternoon, when the sun showed itself a little, and nightfall was somewhat clear and without much of a chill. Since the spot had very little grass and water, the livestock went on ahead, following the route onward little by little. I was somewhat less ill today.

The Indians of these mountains are so savage and wild that they left their huts last night and climbed up into the rocks. Perhaps they were afraid because they saw that we had delayed and did not go onward as they had indicated we ought

---

[152] About half a liter (or half a quart).
[153] At the beginning of the next entry, the field text says it was "at a quarter to eleven," as does Anza's entry. Did Font exaggerate the nearness to midnight and Christmas for the sake of effect?
[154] Salvador Ignacio Linares was born to Gertrudis Rivas, wife of Ignacio Linares (see note under November 25). Salvador means "Savior."

to do. And even though they have seen that none of them has had the slightest harm done to him, only a very few of them have come down to the floor of the hollow, while some have shown themselves up there atop the heights among the rocks. From this, I deduce that should it be desired to establish one or two missions at the valley of *El Príncipe* or in this area for this Jecuiche tribe—supposing it were possible to do so—, to subdue these Indians into a settlement would be as hard as subduing wild sheep into a tame flock. And, unless God performs it all, it is no easy matter to get them out from among the rocks, as they climb up with the same ease and agility as deer do.

This being so important a day, during the first Mass I gave a talk concerning the mystery,[155] and, in view of the drunkenness that had taken place, I could do no less than say something in disapproval of such uproars and disorders, the more so under our present circumstances. It seems that this did not sit well with our commander, judging from the reserve and small favor he revealed by staying vexed with me during the entire day. So that what I said should stand on record in case it should be required, afterward I made some notes of what I had preached, which in substance is the following.

I am well aware of what small profit I shall gain from speaking, given how I have no role to perform here and how little attention it will receive, etc.,[156] and with St. John I can say, "The voice of one crying," *Vox clamantis*, etc.[157] And, though the Holy Spirit tells me that "Where there is no hearing do not pour out your speech," *Ubi non est auditus non effundas sermonem*,[158] still, St. Paul tells me also "Fulfill your ministry," *Ministerium tuum imple*, etc.,[159] and days exist which, as St. Gregory says, although they may be much taken up with ceremonies, etc., cannot be allowed to pass without something being said, etc. What day is this? You will say, *Nochebuena*.[160] And why is it called that? Was not Nochebuena the night of the Supper? The Resurrection?[161] Why is it called *Nochebuena*? Because this is the night of much eating and drinking, dancing and drunkenness, uproar and shamelessness? O world, world, how dost thou alter everything! The most sacred days are turned to days of greatest profaneness, etc. No, faithful ones! The reason it is called *Nochebuena* is that it is the night during which Christ, so long desired by the ancients, etc., was born to free us from slavery, etc., and to open Heaven for us, etc. We were slaves because of original sin, etc. And to prove that He came to all of us to free us in order to save us, look at the conditions of the time in which He is born. He is born at the time of Caesar's edict, etc. (St. Gregory's exposition upon the gospel of the first Mass). But, just as the emperor intended to take a census of the entire world yet many remained unaccounted for, etc., so God "wills all men

---

[155] The Incarnation, the Christian belief that, in Jesus, God became human .

[156] More or less what he had said the night before to Anza, who of course was listening to the sermon.

[157] This quotation from Isaiah 40:3 ("*Vox clamantis in deserto*"—a voice crying in the desert) is applied in John 1:23 to John the Baptist, who announced the coming of Christ. At this Christmas Mass, Font sees himself as doing the same thing.

[158] Sirach 32:4 (Ecclesiasticus 32:6).

[159] 2 Timothy 4:5.

[160] *Nochebuena* means "Good Night." The phrase literally refers to the night before the dawn of Christmas Day, since according to Luke 2:8, Jesus was born at night.

[161] Not exactly the diplomat, Font was telling his congregation that they did not even know the difference between two central Christian feasts, Christmas and Easter. In many Hispanic countries, the time before Easter, Holy Week (*Semana Santa*), is a time of celebration and pageantry.

to be saved," *omnes homines vult salvos fieri*,[162] and yet there still remain so many heathens, as we are seeing, outside the Church and many Christians who, etc. He is born in Bethlehem, "home of bread," *domus panis*, etc.,[163] and though being born as bread, yet there are few who savor Him, satisfied as they are with taking Communion once a year, or, if they can, even less, etc. (I said this in reference to getting the people to go to confession, which I was unable to achieve during the whole journey although I urged them to do so even before we set out. Some of them had not complied with the Church[164] because I and whatever I said were held in small regard.) He is born, not in His home nor in His own homeland, etc., so that we may understand that the whole world is our homeland; or, better, an exile, etc.: "We have no enduring city here," *Non habemus hic manentem civitatem*.[165] How many of those who are coming along are sighing for their homeland, Sinaloa, Culiacán, etc., and not sighing for their true homeland, Heaven! etc., etc. St. Leo: "Let us therefore give thanks to God the Father, through Jesus Christ, in the Holy Spirit," *Agamus ergo gratias Deo patri per Jesum Christum in Spiritu Sancto*, etc; and it concludes, with the same St. Leo: "Acknowledge, O Christian, thine own worth, and having been made a spouse of the divine nature, do not return unto thy former baseness through degraded companionship," *Agnosce, o Christiane, dignitatem tuam et divinæ factus consors naturæ, noli in veterem vilitatem degeneri conversatione redire*,[166] etc. (Explain and apply.)[167] I anticipate, thereby, a happy Easter for us all; which may God grant us with grace in this world, in order to praise Him eternally in the fatherland of glory. *Ad quam*, etc.[168]

Because I was so sick, I was unable to adapt myself to the pattern of meals that was kept by our commander, which was chocolate in the morning. He would not eat anything else during the entire day until concluding the march, and sometimes not until night. For this reason I would often ask for something to carry along to eat during the day, even while on the move. Usually, with a bit of trouble, I would get it and therefore often would go without supper. Since supper consisted only of chile and beans, I was better off without it, and would go to bed early rather than wait for this sort of late supper. While I was getting ready to go to bed, I was visited in my tent by the purveyor with a message on behalf of our commander, in this manner: "He says, sir, to ask whether Your Reverence has anything in mind for San Gabriel." I said to him, "What? For San Gabriel?" He answered, "Yes, as soon as we reach the stopping place tomorrow he is sending mail to that mission by means of some soldiers." "Indeed I would like to write," I said to him, "but how am I to write now when it is so late? It must be that he decided this days ago" (he had decided, back at the Colorado River, to send this mail when we reached the Puerto de San Carlos, but had not told me so), "and now, at last, he finally lets me know. So tell him, I will write tomorrow when we reach the stopping place, if there is time, and if not, I will be patient." I record these matters so that they may serve as guidance and that through them it may

---

[162] 1 Timothy 2:4.

[163] The traditional interpretation of the Hebrew name. Font adopted this concept, like the earlier idea that Jesus was appropriately born during a Roman census, from the Christmas sermon of Gregory the Great. See http://catholicism.org/stgregory-christmas.html.

[164] Church law mandated annual confession and communion.

[165] Hebrews 13:14.

[166] Pope Leo the Great, Sermon 21:3, the first Christmas sermon in the collection (Freeland and Conway 1996: 79).

[167] This, like the "etc.'s" used in Font's reports of his discourses, is a note to himself of the sort found in collections of model sermons, indicating a topic to be developed.

[168] "*Ad quam gloriam nos perducat*" (to which glory may He [God] lead us) was one traditional ending for medieval sermons.

be recognized that during journeys like this, and with such gentlemen as this, it is imperative to arm oneself with patience.

[December] 26, Tuesday. I said Mass. We set out from the dry stream at a quarter past nine in the morning. The course on setting out was northwestward, and after a little more than a league we changed to west-northwestward, westward, and during the narrowest part of the hollow we twisted about until at the foot of the grade we took up a northward course and, from the top of the grade, turned back north-northwestward, and finally ended with a northwestward one on coming down. At a little before two o'clock in the afternoon we halted in a low spot that lies beyond the top of the range, next to the rocks forming, in the main California range, the pass which last time was called the Puerto Real de San Carlos, having traveled for about three leagues or a bit more, but very slowly and with many delays. The route goes along the main stream, which is dry, in the hollow, which goes on narrowing greatly until reaching the foot of the grade and where there already are some bad spots. The grade is divided into two portions; the first is a bit of a hard and long one, the second not so much, and in between the two is a semi-level piece. Beyond the top, one follows along a rather narrow dry stream, and, on coming to large round rocks, goes down a short, gentle slope until reaching the low spot where we halted.

A very thin sleet began to fall shortly before we came into the narrows of the hollow, and lasted until after we had halted. The day and night continued rather moist and chilly, but the woman who had just given birth was better enough to be able to continue the journey. Creosote bush, an ill-omened plant that alone is capable of living in lands so bad—and so well suited for it—as these are, went on as far as the summit of the pass. Then at once I was aware of a change in the country, since already we saw scrub oaks with acorns and other shrubs, and they say there are pine trees with pine nuts in the mountains hereabouts, although I did not see any. The spot here has a spring of water and a small stream nearby farther on, and a sufficient amount of good grass. The range hereabouts seems already quite fertile and well-watered, by contrast with what lies behind, which rather seemed rock piles than mountains.

We came upon an abandoned Indian village here in this low spot, where the signs made it plain that they had left their huts or gopher holes as soon as they detected our coming, and, to judge by their fresh tracks, they had gone climbing up away. So savage and surly are they that the moment they saw the livestock coming on ahead of us God knows what they must have thought of it. And thus we were unable to see a single Indian. It must have been five o'clock in the afternoon when I was sitting on the ground and we felt a shaking, an earthquake to all appearance, that commenced with an instantaneous strong rumble like thunder, that everyone heard, and although lasting a very short time, was a bit strong, and came again, very feebly, a few minutes later. At night a very fine rain fell, but even though from the rain and the cold it appeared that it would be snowing at dawn, instead the weather at daybreak was quite clear.

Late in the evening when I was beginning to go to bed, the purveyor came to my tent and said to me, "Father, the letter?" "What letter?" I answered. "For San Gabriel," he replied. I said to him, "Come inside and listen to this. What then? Was I supposed to know there would be time for writing? Last night you said to me that when we reached the stopping place today our commander would be sending out mail, to which I replied that I would write if there were time at our arrival, and if not I would drop the matter and have patience. You have not told me whether or not there would be time, nor has our commander informed me of such a thing nor has he even spoken a word to me regarding the matter during the whole way. The mail already could have traveled four or five leagues since two o'clock in the afternoon when we reached here. And the reason for my not writing is that it would give me much satisfaction to imagine that the mail would have to be delayed, waiting for my letter, when I see that I have not earned less important favors than this one from our commander! Therefore, as he had said nothing to me concerning this delay—for I am never informed of anything, and the servants and even the lads in the expedition know about decisions before I do—I assumed that the mail had already gone." "But, no, sir," he answered, "the mail will leave tomorrow at dawn." "Then I shall write a few words to the Fathers," I said, "even though it is very late, and I do so with difficulty." I wrote my letter and went over to hand it to our commander, who acted even more annoyed than he had been, having heard what I said to the purveyor. After giving it to him I went to rest and did not waste any words on him.

CHAPTER 3

Alta California and the San Diego Diversion

[December] 27, Wednesday. I said Mass. The mail was dispatched for Mission San Gabriel early in the morning, to give notice of our arrival and request animals from there in order to relieve our own ones.[1]

We set out from the low spot of the Puerto de San Carlos at a quarter to ten in the morning, and, by taking up a northwestward course which at three leagues we changed for a west-northwestward one, at a quarter past two in the afternoon

---

[1] The communications included two by Anza, dated December 28, for the California commander Fernando de Rivera y Moncada at Monterey, announcing the expedition's arrival from Sonora. (Garate 2006: 162–70; 2–9.) Anza explained that the losses of livestock and horses along the way, due partly to the delays caused by the people's frequent sicknesses as well as other problems, meant that only a little over a hundred head of cattle could be delivered to the new settlements, out of the two hundred originally intended for that purpose. The same delays and danger of further losses had caused him to arrive by the route he had chosen, a choice which the viceroy's orders permitted him to make, rather than attempting to find a way straight to Monterey. (Anza had originally requested this freedom for the sake of finding a direct route there; see Garate 1995: 28–31.) Since higher officials had not allowed for so long a period of travel, the expedition had no more than a week and a half's worth of supplies left. (Cf. the note to Font's statement under December 17.) Anza's journal entry also explains his decision to defer the attempt to find a shorter inland route, and instead to go by way of the coastal missions, where the horses and mules could be attended to and not all of the cattle would be lost.

The main letter reports that help with provisions and animals for transport are being asked from the Mission San Gabriel military garrison and those of the other missions. The commandant, however, is put on notice ("which will serve you as a notification for your guidance") that Anza will be taking aid from the missions themselves along the way in his own right, rather than through Rivera, at least until the latter issues his own orders. If delay in bringing the whole expedition to Monterey means that the supply ship will be unable to take part in the survey of the San Francisco River, Anza proposes to go ahead on north himself for that purpose. The colonists then will be left at San Gabriel for Lieutenant Moraga to bring on later, since there would be fewer problems along that route than the one they had just completed. A postscript mentions that the expedition's people are in most need of soap and shoes. (Soap was still unavailable after they had gotten to Monterey; see under March 17.) The second letter has an urgent request for new underclothing for the travel-worn members of the expedition, who otherwise need just a few new blankets in order to be able to last it out. Anza also advises Rivera that the expedition is bringing the wife and children of the soldier Duarte who belongs to the Monterey command, since back at the Real de Álamos in Sonora "she had asked me to do her the favor of transporting her to her husband's side." The soldier Duarte was possibly José María Duarte of the Mission San Gabriel guard.

we halted at the beginning of the canyon or stream called *San Patricio* the other time, close to where its stream rises, having traveled some six leagues.

The land here is better than that before, and after passing the Puerto de San Carlos this country entirely changes its appearance by comparison with what lies behind on the other side. From a height next to the spot we set out from formed by great rocks, boulders, and crags between which one travels and which form the Puerto de San Carlos, one sees, like a change of scene on a stage, the main California range in two entirely separate ways: green and lush with good grass and trees upon the side looking toward the South Sea, and, on the side looking toward the Sea of California,[2] as dry, barren, and arid as I have described it.

On setting out from the spot, we traveled over a very short, rocky gap, which is the true Puerto de San Carlos through the range here and at once entered onto level good soil. From the gap, to north-northwestward and northwestward one sees a range, very lofty and at present white with snow, that appears to be a spur of this main California range we are crossing, which also has snow on the summits and in its crannies.[3]

After a league, we came into a valley that last time they named the valley of El Príncipe,[4] formed between the snowy range I spoke of, along with others, upon the right, and upon the left by another spur of mountains, very high, and full of pines, that seems to lead toward San Diego. The entire valley has a good deal of good grass and all this soil is very moist, of good color, and appears fertile.[5] Beyond the valley we came into scrub woodland—about a league's worth of scrub plants the leaves of which were grayish and fragrant like lavender or rosemary, or more so, when crushed between the fingers, and other shrubs whose buds smell a bit like anise—, and then onto a dry stream that forms from the drainage of the nearby hills, which shape a quite narrow canyon that we followed downstream until reaching a spot having a spring of water, beyond which, even with no rain, the stream begins running. On coming into the hollow, we saw the snowy range to the west-northwestward, which is the direction we took.[6]

---

[2] Respectively, the Pacific Ocean and the Gulf of California.

[3] In the final text, "one observes the same main range, very lofty and white with snow, and this snowy range continues on to a point beyond San Gabriel mission."

[4] The name San Carlos was bestowed by Anza on the pass that the Baja Californian Sebastián Taraval led him to in 1774. The name honored King Carlos III according to the prevailing Spanish fashion, that is, by invoking the king's saint's name. The following, lesser natural feature was named El Príncipe in honor of the heir to the throne, the Prince of Asturias.

[5] The field text describes two valleys rather than one, possibly an accidental duplication that was deliberately removed from the final text: "Then we came into a small-sized valley that has good grass, and beyond it, there followed about a league of scrub plants [etc.]. . . . After this there followed a larger valley with a great deal of good grass, and all this soil is very moist, of good color, and appears fertile. This valley is formed by two ranges of sizeable elevation and with a great many pines visible upon them, and in the distance to the left is seen another very high range, very full of pines and trees, that it appears runs on to near San Diego. We set out from the above-mentioned valley, which was called the valley of El Príncipe the other time. . . ."

[6] In the final text, "we took to the hollow, which is very narrow and formed by the same hills and branches of the main range."

Close to the stopping place we found three little jacales or huts of Indians with a great many shells of acorns, which are what they eat and which are plentiful in the mountains hereabouts. Since they are so dirty the surroundings of their huts were full of their excrement, filthy with it in the way of all of these mountain people. We saw in the hollow a great many plants that were good to look at and fragrant, and at the stopping place were a great many rose patches, like those of Castile, which are the first ones that I saw in that country. The roses are small and have only five petals, but are very fragrant, withered at this season, and they bear their variety of small fruit,[7] a little red bud with their seeds, having a slight, pleasant flavor. I ate some few of them, which tasted good to me and perhaps would have been better when not so dried up as, to judge by their wrinkled appearance, at present they were. There are live oaks and other trees, as well. The weather today was fairly good.

[December] 28, Thursday. I said Mass. The woman who recently gave birth was a bit ill at daybreak, perhaps from the heavy chill last night here in the hollow and from being jolted along the way and from the moisture of the day before yesterday. Thus, we delayed today. A soldier brought in rocks that seemed to be ore, and some moderately skilled persons with the troops were inclined to say that there would be deposits here in these mountains and lower down, since the samples pointed to that. I observed the latitude of this spot at the spring or source of the stream in the San Patricio hollow, and found it, according to Jorge Juan with no correction, in 33° 37½', and with correction in 33° 37',[8] and thus I say: at the San Patricio hollow and the source of its stream, December 28, 1775: meridian altitude of the sun's lower limb: 32° 48'.

[December] 29, Friday. We set out from the San Patricio hollow at a half past nine in the morning, and by following down the hollow on a west-northwestward course and some veering northwestward, winding about, at a half past four in the afternoon we halted at the bank of the San José stream where the hollow we had been following ends, at the beginning of the valley that was called San José the last time, having traveled a good seven leagues. The hollow, or rather ravine, is a very narrow and quite rocky one, having trees in spots more or less, and through it there runs water issuing from several small springs located in crannies or hollows next to it. At about four leagues, the hollow begins widening out and the water in the stream, which splits into two branches at the last in order to go out into the San José valley, loses itself in the sands. The hollow is shaped by a number of small heights running down from the high mountains to one side and the other that I spoke of yesterday. The mountains upon the right-hand side are

---

[7] A rose hip.
[8] A minute or two too high.

the snowy range, white and snow-laden upon its summits, and the high range upon the left side had scarcely any snow on it, both of them being very lush with pines and live oaks bearing fine, large acorns. There are also a good many of both of these kinds in the hollow, along with sycamores, cottonwoods and other sorts of small trees. The snowy range seemingly is an offshoot of the main California range that we crossed, and runs northwesterly; from its skirts arises the river, or very crystalline year-round stream, upon whose bank we stopped, and which has a good deal of cottonwood groves on it.

The stream splits into two branches, one going westward and another one which we followed, and all of its waters cease within the valley, which is formed by these small ranges here upon the east; by another range, a bit more elevated, upon the south; by a range apparently running across from south to north, not very high and having gaps in it, upon the west; and by a bit of the snowy range, which closes it off upon the north. All of the land and hollow here are very moist, fertile, and lush, and here I saw a number of plants that I recognized, similar to those in Spain, as I also did while in the hollow, in which, in addition to a great many rose patches, there are several fragrant herbs that look to be useful, among which I saw and plucked some lavender. In the hollow we saw some abandoned little jacales, and a little before we halted, a few Indians showed themselves at a distance where they were encamped at the river's edge, carrying their bows and arrows, but they refused to approach even though we called to them.

These Indians are members of the Jenigüechi tribe, and very similar in every respect to the Jecuiches of the mountains.

I shall speak concerning the wide-reaching valley of San José and its pleasantness, once we are passing through it.

[December] 30, Saturday.

The weather at daybreak was fair and without the chill we had expected to have from being next to the snowy range. I was feeling considerably better from my sicknesses. The moment we crossed the Puerto de San Carlos an improvement set in and the crystalline, excellent water of the San José stream here agreed very well with me.

The stream issues from the snowy range and comes through so lush a hollow that we called it, because of its handsomeness and beauty, *La Cañada del Paraíso*.[9] On coming out from it, the stream goes for some few leagues through the San José valley, a bit close over against a bare mountain or low hill range lying in front of the snowy range and whose appearance and composition, according to those skilled in the matter, is an indication of ore everywhere. The stream, having flowed for about four leagues, disappears into, or helps to form, the large lake lying in the bottom of the valley here, close over against another hill that

---

[9] Paradise Hollow.

Figure 15. A native *kish*, San Jacinto, 1888. By Charles Edwin Kelsey.
Courtesy of the Alan K. Brown family archive.

follows beyond the ore-laden one. On its banks the river has a good deal of not very tall cottonwood groves, up to where it disappears into the lake. I thought the place a very good one for a settlement.

We set out, then, from the San José stream at a quarter past nine in the morning, and by traveling a west-northwestward course for a long five leagues through the valley, at a quarter past two in the afternoon we halted in the San José valley at the foot of a somewhat stony hill and not very far from the lake. Between this lake and another one lying a little farther on there runs a small stream of very good water.

The San José valley is a very large and handsome one, with very good moist soil, to the degree that even in this winter season we saw the entire land putting forth little grass shoots across most of it wherever it might, or in stretches, and the soil is very soft, so that it becomes a bit miry during rains. Placed at intervals in the valley are small heights having a few rocks, with some scrub plants upon them but no trees, and their soil is soft like that in the valley. There are no trees in all the valley save for the cottonwoods on the river, but pines and live oaks are visible upon the high and snow-covered mountains, and it may be they hold other trees in their skirts and hollows, since they are very moist. There is a large lake in the valley, formed from the San José River and other streams which issue out of a number of sources and springs within the ranges lying around. Since it does not have another outlet in any other direction, as is plainly shown by marks, the lake grows much larger during rainy seasons. There are a vast number of geese on it in very large flocks that show white in the distance.[10]

The valley is formed, upon the east, by the ranges of the San Patricio hollow, on the west by a chain of not very hilly low knolls, on the south by a range of middling elevation called the *Sierra del Trabuco* which extends toward the road to San Diego, and on the north by a range of low hills that runs along in front of the snowy range.[11]

Finally, the sky is very clear and the view is most delightful, and it appeared to me that there may be some site or other, excellent for a big settlement, on the other side of the lake and river, with fine prospects for large plantings and horse breeding and stock raising of both cattle and sheep. This would be a very advisable thing at this spot, since it lies in the midst of so much unsettled country.

As we set out from the stopping place, a few Indians appeared in the distance and fled like deer as soon as a soldier went out, calling, toward them. We saw some ten of them along the way and they started to flee even though they were armed. Our commander called to them, and I did, and we went toward them; they approached us, and were given a cigar or two and were told by our commander, using signs, to come along with us to where we were going to halt, in order for them to be given beads. However, they drew back again at once and did not show themselves any further. Their bows are quite long and their arrows of middling size, rather poor, and without a flint. There is no firewood at this spot, or anywhere in its vicinity. To our good fortune the chill was not very bad even though we were in view of the snowy mountain range.

The commander was a bit agreeable with me today, and we talked some along the way (whole days used to pass without our saying anything to each other except what was strictly necessary). However, he became a bit unhappy during the conversation that arose, because he insisted that the snowy range we had been seeing to the westward very far off was the same snowy height we came in view of at the Puerto de San Carlos. I made it clear to him that that could not be so, since, although the snowy range that extends along from here is the same one as far as San Gabriel and farther, still, what we were leaving to our right today was the first snowy height upon it, which we saw from the pass. This was like another talk we had had earlier, in which he told me that during the first expedition, he had come in view of this snowy range from the briny well of El Carrizal. When I said to him that I found this very hard to believe and that for it to have been seen from there was impossible, not only because of the great distance but chiefly because lying across between there is the broad high main range which we went through up to the Puerto de San Carlos, he answered me, somewhat aggrieved, "It must be as Your Reverence intends, but I am not lying and am very well aware of what I am saying." I record this in order to show the

---

[10]Anza had previously named the lake San Antonio de Bucareli, in honor of the viceroy.

[11]Blunderbuss Mountains. This description in the final text replaces the account of the valley given earlier in the field text.

presumption which such individuals and gentlemen are accustomed to use in speaking, wishing to have everything they say believed and no one disagreeing with them.

Today I was better off from my attack of diarrhea than on any day since I left San Miguel. The improvement began day before yesterday, perhaps due to the small red fruit I ate from the rose patches in the San Patricio hollow on the 27th. I began to feel better the following day. And yesterday, as soon as I drank water from the stream I recognized how good it was and I drank it to quench my bodily thirst.

[December] 31, Sunday. I said Mass. We set out from the foot of the hill at a quarter past nine in the morning, and at a quarter to five in the afternoon came to the bank of the Santa Ana River, having traveled some eight leagues on a westward course with some brief veering at times west-northwestward. As soon as we set out from the stopping place, we left the first expedition's route so as to avoid an amount of winding about and bad spots in the pass that leads out to the Santa Ana valley. We crossed over the hill range that hereabouts encloses the San José valley by going through a small pass in the little range next to the stopping place. When we got down to the other side of the pass we traveled for about a league over level land and continued on for about three leagues more through a valley that connects with the San José valley and is quite far-reaching and has good soil. We then came to hills and went up to an easy pass and down to a rather narrow hollow which broadens out until it comes out to the Santa Ana valley and must be about a league in extent. Afterward we traveled for about three leagues across that valley until we came to the bank of the river. In the first and second range of hills and their hollows, which have moist soil, I saw very plentiful amounts of rosemary and other fragrant plants and, in the long second hollow, a great many sunflowers in bloom and grapevines and vine shoots of such good size that it seemed like a vineyard. Perhaps given a little cultivation, they would yield good grapes. In sum, all of this land seems very good, and if only the little heights here in these valleys had trees instead of some rocks on them, there would be nothing more to wish for.

Yesterday and today we found no water along the route, although there is some to the sides at some distance off. I saw quite a deep, round pit full of water yesterday next to the route. Since it was in the midst of the plain, I suspected that it might perhaps be the result of an earthquake that had caused that piece of ground to sink, and the water in it seems to have kept at the level of the water in the lake. Along the route today I found and gathered some shells belonging to snails like those that live in the woods in Spain, a thing which does not exist elsewhere in other parts of this America nor do they know of them there.

All along the way, we kept the snowy main range upon our right, and upon the left a long range, not so high, along whose skirts on the other side goes the road from San Gabriel to San Diego. On Commander Portolá's expedition which came overland from California to these new discoveries during these past years[12] the first explorers named it La Sierra del Trabuco.

The Santa Ana River is one with a good deal of water, and sunken very deep in, so that it must have a width, in all these surroundings, of some four or five varas, or at most six,[13] but so deep that it has very few fords, and these, difficult ones because of the rapid flow of the water. For this reason, the livestock (which reached the stopping place at midnight) had some trouble crossing to the other side in the morning the next day, and a bull was drowned in the ford. A horse also drowned. The horse had stepped into a bad spot in order to drink. The horse was caught by the current and was unable to escape. The river's waters are very crystalline and fine, and it seems to rise in the snowy range and runs from northeast to southwest with some variation and deviation, or west-southwest, among little hills and small heights until it empties into the sea above San Diego.[14] Upon its banks it nourishes a few cottonwoods, the only trees that are to be found on all of these plains. Only upon the snowy range are there some pines in view; in its hollows there may be other trees that cannot be seen because they are too far away. We did not see a single Indian today.

January 1, 1776, Monday.

I said Mass and, during it, four words to the people concerning the solemnity of the day, exhorting them to renew good habits because we were commencing a new year, etc.

What with the frost that fell in the early dawn, the soil at daybreak was as white as though it had snowed, although the cold was not too great. Since yesterday's march had been a long one and the livestock had reached here so late[15] it was decided not to do anything more today than ford the river, which though narrow has a good deal of water and is very swift and with its bed sunken very deep down as I said yesterday; for which purpose the ford was gotten ready, with work being done upon it during a good period after Mass. At about ten o'clock in the morning the post that had been sent on December 27 arrived with a reply from Mission San Gabriel, a soldier from there[16] and seventeen animals sent by the Fathers to aid ours which had become quite worn out. They brought the awful news that around two months ago the Indians of the harbor and mission

---

[12] In 1769–1770.

[13] The measurements correspond respectively to 11, 13¼, and 16½ feet.

[14] In the final text, "runs . . . westward to the sea and most of it goes sunken deep among hills."

[15] Anza's December 31 entry explains that the unusual length of that march was because firewood, which was absolutely necessary, was not to be found onward from the San José River (the camp of the 29th), except for what they carried to the next stop. The cattle had not arrived until midnight, with the most worn-out ones being driven separately.

[16] Corporal Guillermo Carrillo.

of San Diego had risen, killing a Religious and wounding soldiers. When we reach the mission I will learn better concerning these reports.[17]

The order was given to ford the river and we commenced to do so at two o'clock in the afternoon, some on horses, and it was successfully forded by a little after three o'clock. Most of the people crossed upon a bridge formed by a thick cottonwood that had fallen crosswise over the river; near it was the other cottonwood that had been used to make a bridge during the last expedition. This spot is the same as all the rest, moist and fertile land with rose patches, vine shoots, blackberry brambles, and other plants whose greenness is a pleasure to view. In one word, all of this country from the Puerto de San Carlos onward is a land that does not produce thorns and prickles, not on trees nor on plants nor on bushes. Nor, in all the land I traveled through all the way to San Francisco harbor, did I see any thorny trees or bushes such as exist outside the country, save for prickly pears and some thistles that I saw near San Diego harbor; nor is there a thorn to be found upon the plants, outside of the brambles and rose patches. In sum, it is a totally different land than the rest of what I have seen of America, and very similar to Spain in its plants and the floweriness of the fields, as also in the fact that the rains come in winter.

[January] 2, Tuesday. I said Mass. We set out from the Santa Ana River at a quarter past eight in the morning, and at a quarter past two in the afternoon halted at the bank of the *Arroyo de los Alisos*[18] having traveled for six long leagues upon a westward course. The route is very level the whole way except that upon setting out from the Santa Ana River we passed some long smooth hills which, like all the rest of the route, were full of good grass both dry and green: a very suitable country for small stock[19] because so clear and not having anything that might damage the wool. The mountains alongside it are the ones already mentioned, and at the halting place we were now closer to the snowy range. The entire horizon was very cloudy at daybreak, and halfway along the route we began to have very fine, gentle rain that was not much of a bother; however, it rained more heavily as soon as we halted and continued in that way until far into the night. The *Río de los Alisos*[20] is so called because it produces a good many of them along its borders, and this is the only sort of timber or firewood that exists on these plains. Its waters are crystalline, extremely fine-appearing, and very good

---

[17]Anza's journal summarizes the report as being that a missionary and two employees were killed and all the soldiers of the mission guard wounded. For this reason, and because he had information that the Indians around his own mission were gathering to attack it, Carrillo had not sent on Anza's letter to California Commander Rivera, whose arrival and orders he was expecting. Rivera later wrote a letter in which he reminded Anza that on hearing the report, Anza had immediately thought of marching directly from the Santa Ana camp to San Diego in aid of the settlement there, but that when he heard the second piece of news that Rivera had been notified and was expected to arrive at San Gabriel, he continued on to there instead. (Rivera to Anza, April 2, 1776, Rivera y Moncada Papers C–A 368: 19; Garate 2006: 222.)

[18]Sycamore Stream.
[19]Sheep and goats.
[20]Sycamore River.

to taste. It arises from the snowy range and normally carries only a little water, but does so year-round. Upon its banks I came across an extremely tender, very fine-flavored plant somewhat like lettuce sprouts though having a more slender and longer leaf. I gathered a good-sized serving of it and brought it to our commander's tent. We ate it as a salad and were all very pleased with it. I named it *lechuguino*.[21] I found another plant having a leaf a little like parsley and a taste and a shape very like a plant called *murritórt*[22] in my own Catalán language. We did not eat any of this plant because there was very little of it and it was too small, perhaps because it was out of season. There are also other handsome plants; and rosemary, etc. Ever since the San José valley, along the way I have been hearing birds singing that are a bit larger than sparrows. They say they are larks though I did not think they were; their song is not a long one, but sweet.[23]

I left word of our coming here, carved with the point of a knife upon the trunk of a large sycamore near which we halted, with this inscription below an HIS[24] that our commander had carved on it during the last expedition: YEAR 1776. The San Francisco expedition came here.

[January] 3, Wednesday. We set out from the Arroyo de los Alisos at a quarter past nine in the morning, and at three o'clock in the afternoon halted at the edge, on the other side, of the stream that joins along with others to form the San Gabriel River, having traveled some six leagues on a westward course. The whole way is very level, and at about a league after the stopping place we went through a pass or a gap formed by the skirt of the snowy range upon the right and by some low hills on the left that extend westward; at its foot there is a lake when it rains. Last time, they called it *El Puerto de los Osos*, from having seen some few of them there.[25] One then comes into a country very level on all sides; we found it very green in spots, and the blossoms already bursting forth. The ground is very moist, not only because the wet and rainy season is now, in winter, just as it is in Spain, but also because of the heavy dews that, as I have noted, fall during clear nights. The rains are soft, fine, and continuous, and with no thunder. Live oaks are to be seen in some places, and there seem to be more of them in the mountains along with pines. Before coming to the stopping place we came into an open wooded area with several sorts of bushes, among them a great many

---

[21]Lettuce Sprout.

[22]*Morritort*, common cress.

[23]The final text adds, "and I afterward saw many of these, everywhere we went." Just as Font says, meadowlarks are not really larks.

[24]The first three letters of the Greek spelling of "Jesus," and a common abbreviation for the name. Font includes a small cross extending above the middle letter, not reproduced here. The symbol, although familiar elsewhere, may have had some special meaning as representing his colegio of the Holy Cross of Querétaro.

[25]Bear Pass. The field text, through a grammatical gender reference, applies the name to the lake itself.

junipers[26] which we call *ginebre* in my own Catalán language. The river issues out of the snowy range and runs about westward; its water is very crystalline and excellent and fairly full-flowing even when not flooding[27] while the size of the ground that is occupied by its bed plainly shows that it carries a great deal of water when it rises. Having learned that Mission San Gabriel had been moved to the spot where they had their fields, somewhat nearer to the snowy range than previously, we left the old route, the one followed last time, at a point halfway along and, opening a new route, directed our march straight toward the new site; however, since our animals had become fatigued, we remained at the bank of the river and did not reach the mission today.

There was a great deal of fog at daybreak today that at once rose up into clouds hiding the snowy range, into which they withdrew, leaving us with quite a clear day. We did not feel a great deal of cold last night despite being so close up to the snowy range, and perhaps the climate is a more kindly one because the sea is not far off, since even though there is a sizeable chill, it is not so raw nor as greatly felt and painful as what one experiences upon the Gila and Colorado rivers.

[January] 4, Thursday. I said Mass. At daybreak there was heavy frost and clear weather. We set out from the San Gabriel stream at nine o'clock in the morning, and arrived at a quarter to eleven at Mission San Gabriel[28] having traveled some two leagues upon a westward course.

Mission San Gabriel is situated at about eight leagues' distance from the sea, in a spot with splendid features, with a good deal of water and very good soil. The site is a level and clear one, and about two leagues away from the snowy range, which lies to the north of it and which we have been leaving upon our right ever since the Puerto de San Carlos. Here, apparently, is where the snow covering stops although the range itself does not. It is the same main California range that continues on ahead very far upcountry; and by all indications is the same range that Father Garcés crossed during this journey and which he called the *Sierra de San Marcos*.[29]

On setting out from the stopping place, we passed through the bed of a big river that had no water in it and a good deal of small cottonwood trees. This is apparently the river that goes to San Gabriel, to the mission's former location, at which it always holds enough water, flowing past there with a good deal of water bestowed on it by the river at which we stopped and by other springs farther down.

We found here at this mission the captain commandant of Monterey, don Fernando de Rivera y Moncada, who had come here because of the uprising of Indians belonging to Mission San Diego. Those Indians, together with the mountain gentiles, (there were about a thousand of them gathered together,)

---

[26]*Enebros o juníperos*, using the two standard Spanish words for the juniper.

[27]So in the field text. A different (later) judgment in the final text: "but with no heavy flow, although...."

[28]The final text adds, "marked upon the map by the letter **B**."

[29]This event, Garcés crossing the San Marcos (Tehachapi) range into the southern San Joaquín, took place in April 1776.

attacked the mission. They murdered Father Preacher Fray Luis Jaime, a Mallorcan, and wounded the soldiers, a report that we found very grievous.[30] Rivera had come from Monterey to go on to the presidio there. He reached this mission at night on the 2nd.[31] Shortly before we arrived, Commander Rivera and the mission's Father Minister Fray Antonio Paterna came out to receive us. Our arrival was one of great rejoicing for everyone. The mission's guard received us with a salute of firearms and the two other Fathers who were there, Father Fray Antonio Cruzado and Father Fray Miguel Sánchez, did the same with many pealings of the bells and with notable displays of pleasure. This mission is in a better spot than before, with water right at the walls of the building which they built of adobe brick and a tule-rush roof, etc.

[January] 5, Friday. We remained here to rest, and the commanders conferred as to the business concerning the rebellion of the San Diego Indians.[32] I went

---

[30] The final text shortens this to "they destroyed the mission and slew its Father Minister Father Fray Luis Jaume." Jaume is the Mallorcan and Catalán spelling of the name. Subsequently, Font will give a reduced estimate of the number of the rebels.

[31] Rivera, who had paused on his way to San Diego at San Gabriel to meet Anza, was just getting ready to ride forth with Father Paterna to encounter the travelers on their way, when they actually arrived. The two quickly mounted anyway and went out to greet them. Rivera was pleased that he had managed to meet Anza in health and without misfortune. (Burrus 1967 1: 225.) Anza in his journal notes that Rivera feared that further events just as serious, or worse, might still happen at San Diego.

[32] Anza's journal records that Commander Rivera gave him a full report of the San Diego revolt (no doubt as reported by Lieutenant José Francisco Ortega), which was generally said to have involved six hundred Christian Indian converts and gentiles. Rivera asked Anza to aid him with the soldiers under his command, since under the circumstances these would not be able to go immediately to Monterey, and even less to the planned survey (in the company of Rivera) of the San Francisco River. Also, the rainy season would not allow them to reach there, because of the terrain and the intervening rivers. Anza in return offered not only his soldiers but his own services, on the assumption that the viceroy would approve of his doing so, and the commandant accepted, asking Anza to join him in resolving on whatever led to the service of both Majesties (i.e., God and the king). Anza agreed that they should proceed jointly, reporting on the matter to the viceroy.

Captain Rivera in his letter of April 2, 1776 gave Anza his own more detailed recollection of the command discussion: "We spoke together, and when I said to you that, since I was unable to return [to Monterey], you should proceed on north if you saw fit to do so, you answered that that would be only on condition that we both went [to San Diego first], since four eyes see better than two do; that this place [San Diego] was also a harbor [just as San Francisco was] and since it ought not to be left at risk of ruin [either], we should go together if I thought well of it. I agreed without hesitation and with thanks, judging the occasion to be such a great one and knowing well that I had considered requesting the governor of the Californias [at very distant Loreto] for men and horses."

In reply to Rivera, Anza reminded him on May 20 that it had been his own wish to proceed to Monterey immediately but this was frustrated by the poor condition of the expedition's animals, by Rivera's failure to provide the previously requested provisions and mounts, and by his advice that the flooding rivers would impede the journey. Because of the events at San Diego, according to Anza, Rivera had felt it impossible for himself to "join in the examination of San Francisco harbor so that we should agree upon taking possession of it as stated in our orders." Anza had then announced to Rivera that, since in any case the expedition was forced to delay at San Gabriel while its mounts recovered, they (the two commanders) should go to San Diego to chastise the rebels, and if this could be done soon they would both return to fulfill their assignment, "it being clear that I went for not over a month." If it took longer than that, Anza would return alone in order to do the task. Rivera y Moncada Papers C–A 368: 19. Cf. Garate 2006: 222–23; facsimiles 257, 32; transcription 58–60.

with Father Sánchez after dinner to view the spring from which they brought the irrigation ditch for Mission San Gabriel here. This has provided it with the best advantages. In addition to the fact that the ditch is a sizeable one and runs in front of the Fathers' house and the little jacales of the Christian Indians who make up this new mission—amounting to what must be some five hundred souls of new converts both old and young—, the site overlooks all the plains in the immediate locale that are suitable for planting. Thus the fields lie next to the settlement and it is a mission that possesses such fine advantages for agriculture and such fine grazing for livestock and horses that nothing better might be wished for. The cows which the mission owns are very fat and yield a great deal of delicious milk with which they make a great number of cheeses and very good butter. There is breeding of swine, and a small-sized flock of small stock from which they slaughtered three or four of the sheep that they had, at our arrival. The meat was particularly good, and I do not recall having ever eaten richer and finer mutton than this. They also have some chickens. There is a good deal of live oak and other timber for building, and accordingly a great deal of firewood. The only thing lacking is limestone, which so far has not been found, but perhaps a good search will find some so that the buildings can be improved.

a small number of which are, at present, made of adobe, and most of them are of palisade construction and tule-rush,[33] which is why they are very dangerous and liable to burning. The buildings at present amount in their entirety to one very long, large jacal of one single room with three compartments, and this serves as the Fathers' dwelling, as a granary, and as everything else. A bit aside from this is another jacal, square, that serves as a church; and near this, still another one which is what they call the guardhouse or soldiers' quarters for those eight of them who are guards at the mission; and then some small jacales made of tule-rushes which are the Indians' huts, between which and the Fathers' house the irrigation ditch goes.

Celery grows naturally at the spring where I found other plants that seem to be passably good little lettuces. There were also roots that in shape and flavor seemed to me like the parsnips in Spain; and I found thereabouts a great many turnips that, from a few seeds the Fathers cast down there the previous year, have taken over the ground. Near the mission's former location, distant about a league southward from this new one, there grows a very plentiful amount of watercress, of which I ate a great deal. In sum, it is a country which, as Father Paterna says, seems like a promised land[34]

although the Fathers have undergone a great deal of want and hardship in it, inasmuch as beginnings are always hard, all the more so in those lands in which there was nothing to be had and they suffered being abandoned without supplies for two years.

The converted Indians of this mission, who belong to the Beñemé tribe and also the Jenigüechi one,[35] appear mild-mannered and more or less well inclined; they are of middling stature, the

---

[33]Bulrush thatch for the roofs.
[34]Shortly after his first landing at Monterey in 1771, Paterna had already become enthusiastic about the new country, which he thought might someday become famous (Brown 2001: 89).
[35]These are two of the ethnic terms first recorded or applied by Garcés in his journal.

women a bit smaller; round-faced, snub-nosed and a bit ugly. In their gentile state, the men's clothing consists of going entirely naked; the women wear one or more pieces of deerskin with which they cover themselves and also some sort of blanket made of otter or hare skins, even though the Fathers attempt as best they can to clothe the converted people in some fashion. The method observed by the Fathers in making conversions is not to require anyone to become a Christian. They accept only those who present themselves voluntarily and they do this in the following way. Since these Indians are used to living like beasts in fields and mountains, they warn them that if they wish to be Christians they can no longer go to the woods but must live at the mission. If they leave the *ranchería* (this is what they call the Indians' little jacales and housing) they will go after them and punish them. Thereupon, they begin to instruct those gentiles who voluntarily come in, by teaching them to cross themselves and all the rest that is needed. If they persevere in the instruction with the same intent for two or three months, then once they are instructed they go on to baptize them. The everyday management is this: Mass is normally said in the morning when the sun rises, and during it (or without it, if it is not being said) all the Indians gather and the Father recites the Christian doctrina[36] with all of them, which ends with singing the Alabado, which in all of the missions is sung in one single manner and tune, and the Fathers sing it even if they lack a good voice, since conformity is the best thing. They then go to break their fast upon the *atole* that is prepared for everyone, and before taking any they cross themselves and sing the *Bendito*.[37] Afterward, they go to work, so far as possible, with the Fathers using their own example to sway them to the toil and direct them. At noon they eat their *pozole*, which is prepared in common for everyone, and afterward they work again for another while. And at sunset they once again recite the doctrina and finish by singing the Alabado. The Christians are distinguished from the gentiles by the attempt made to have them go more or less clothed or covered, to the extent that the shortages in the country have permitted, and the catechumens are not included for the pozole ration but are given a bit of whatever is left over. If any Indian wishes to go to the hills to see his relatives or look for acorns, they give him permission for a set number of days; normally they do not fail to return, and sometimes they come back with a gentile relative who remains for instruction, either because of the others' example or else attracted by the pozole, which they like better than their plants and wild foods, and therefore those Indians are usually "caught by the mouth."[38] The doctrina recited in all of the missions is the short one by Father Castañi[39] done in total conformity without any Father changing a word of it or adding anything else to it. This is recited in Spanish even though the Fathers may know the Indian language. This is the case at Mission San Antonio, whose Father Minister Fray Buenaventura Sitjar understands the language of the Indians of that mission and speaks it well, yet, for all that, the doctrina still is recited in Spanish. Inasmuch as the Father had turned the

---

[36] Catechism.

[37] A prayer praising God as the source of the food which is being consumed and asking blessing on the food and on those eating it.

[38] A common expression among missionaries; also "caught by the stomach."

[39] Bolton 1931: 181 footnote has information from a secondary source: "The reference is evidently to Father Bartolomé Castaño. In 1840 Juan Romualdo Amaro printed in Mexico the *Doctrina extractada de los catecismos mexicanos de los Padres Paredes, Carochi y Castaño, autores muy selectos: traducida al castellano para mejor instrucción de los indios, en las oraciones y misterios principales de doctrina cristiana*. I have not learned the exact title of the work by Castaño on which this catechism [i.e., reference] is based." Doctrinas (catechisms) were very similar one to another. Presumably someone, Fuster, Caballer, Serra, or Dumetz mentioned Castaño's name to Font in a Catalanized form, *Castany*, which Font then re-Castilianized as "Castañi."

doctrina into the Indian language, the most that happens is a recital once a day in the Indian language and once in Spanish, thereby conforming with what has been so many times prescribed ever since the First Mexican Council[40] and is well handled by Señor Solórzano.[41] The Indians should be taught the doctrina in Spanish and the attempt made to have them speak Spanish, since all of the Indian languages are barbarous and very wanting in terms.[42]

An attempt is made in the missions to have the unmarried grown girls sleep separately in some place apart, and at Mission San Luis I saw a married soldier serving as a sort of superintendent of the mission, giving the Father some relief, and the soldier's wife was in charge of the unmarried girls who were under her care. They called her *la maestra*.[43] They were at her side during the day. She taught them how to sew and other matters. At night she locked them in a room where they would be protected from any assault. That is why they were called "nuns," which I thought was a very good thing. In sum, I thought the method observed by the Fathers in those new missions to be a very good one, and I shall note that the same thing that is done at one mission is done at all of the others, which is what pleased me most of all—except for Mission San Diego. Because it is the poorest mission and because of the disadvantages of the land, there are no fields held in common or even individually. Pozole is not given out communally and the Indians have been allowed to live in their villages. However, they are obligated to come to Mass on Sundays in shifts, as is done in Lower California. This is the reason why this mission is so backward, besides which its Indians are the worst ones at the new missions.

[January] 6, Saturday. I said Mass, and afterwards a Thanksgiving Mass was sung in thanks for our arrival. I accompanied it upon my instrument, and Father Paterna sang it at the altar and, after the gospel, preached a sermon about the mystery of the day. It was very well delivered and very much to the purpose. Our Commander Anza offered to accompany Commander Rivera in going on to San Diego with twenty soldiers from the expedition to collaborate in punishing the Indian rebels should it be necessary, and to take the field against the gentile Indians who made the attack on Mission San Diego.[44] The decision was

---

[40] The acts of the First and Second Mexican Provincial Church Councils (1555, 1565) had been recently (1769) published at Mexico City by Archbishop Francisco Antonio Lorenzana.

[41] The reference is added between the lines. The *Política indiana* of Juan de Solórzano Pereira (1575–1655) went through a number of editions; Font might have used the Madrid one of 1736–1739. The question pursued at length by Solórzano (book 2, chapter 26) was whether the natives of North and South America should be made to adopt Spanish to the point that their original languages would be forgotten. Solórzano pointed out that it was "the oldest thing in the world" for the conquered subjects of empires to abandon their own language; this had happened both to the original Spaniards, so that now no one knew what tongue they once had spoken, and many times before and since, such as during the Aztec and Inca empires in America. It was a change necessary for the amalgamation of different societies; as Augustine said (*The City of God*, book 19, chapter 7) people in general relate better to their own dogs than they relate to other humans who speak a different language. As for the crucial question of teaching religion, Solórzano quoted with approval a royal writ directed to Peru in 1596: "it has become understood that [even] in the best and most perfect of the languages of the Indians, the mysteries of the Faith cannot be well and properly explained save with great absurdities and imperfections." (Madrid edition of 1647–48: 216–20.)

[42] "Barbarous languages" literally means languages that are unlike the European ones whose terms and concepts are derived from the Classical tongues.

[43] Teacher. This is repeated below, during the first visit to San Luis Obispo (March 2).

[44] The mention of campaigning against the non-Christian attackers is not in the final text.

made to set out to San Diego the following day. I myself was to go there and the expedition's people and all the remainder were to stay at San Gabriel until we returned. And, when our commander told me of his decision, he said that in view of my poor health I could stay here if I wanted to. I answered that if it was his pleasure, I would be glad to go with him, since the people remaining at San Gabriel had a minister there for whatever should arise and would not miss me, and thus it would please me not to leave his side; whereupon we agreed to set out for Mission San Diego the following day.

This journey had been determined upon ever since yesterday. However, they did not say anything to me nor was I told, in the event that I might wish to go or to stay here, and I only learned something this morning from a servant. At nightfall, then, a little after vespers, Commander Anza came to tell me how he was leaving for San Diego the next day and for this reason he was about to bestow the key of the astronomical quadrant on me. If I required anything I should ask the purveyor don Mariano, who was staying behind. I replied that it seemed hard that I was always the last to learn of his decisions to stay or to march, that he never took me into account, etc.; that despite the fact that I had said to him at San Miguel even before we set out that I would not depart from his side during the entire journey and would go with him wherever he went, since this was what I chose to do. Nonetheless, since his choice was to leave me here, I would comply with what had been decided and would have patience, just as I had had with other matters. Thereupon we commenced a long private discussion that proceeded in friendly, quiet terms. However, I spoke to him very clearly concerning the manner of his behavior with respect to me and the little regard shown me before now, as though I were in the expedition as a favor and at his will, and not by higher command as in fact I was, etc. And as for the key to the instrument, I had refused its acceptance because he had not entrusted me with the instrument from the start as had been ordered, and even ignoring the fact that my duty while I was along was to make observations—still I had only been able to do so whenever he wished, as though his desires were the command over everything and my only function was to hinder him and cause him difficulty. And so he was doing the right thing by leaving me here, thus freeing himself of this useless baggage. The commander attempted, as much as he was able, to satisfy me and in the end, besides almost forcing the key upon me, which I had to accept in order not to appear obstinate and rude, he finished by over and over again asking my pardon for whatever might have offended me, excusing himself on the grounds of its being his own failures of attention, and telling me that he would be very pleased if I should wish to go to San Diego. So I should decide the matter myself and should consider it tonight so as to inform him tomorrow. I said I had no decision to make nor anything to consider regarding the topic, as it was my choice to go with him everywhere and during everything, as I had told him from the start—only, not on a campaign were he to sally out against the San Diego rebels[45]—and so I would comply with whatever he might wish. The expedition people staying at San Gabriel would not miss me since they had three ministers there at the mission for whatever might arise. Thereupon we agreed that I would go and take the quadrant along in order to observe the latitude of that harbor; and our commander was so changed thenceforth that the Fathers at San Gabriel recognized the change from that very hour on, as thenceforward he behaved a bit more amicably and very differently toward me though without giving up his gravity and air of command. I record this to show that when the occasion arises, one should speak plainly

---

[45] Since as a friar and missionary he would not want to join a military action.

with such gentlemen, for if it is done politely and using fair words, one normally does not lose anything by having done so but rather very often can gain a great deal; for respectfulness and forbearance are not always suitable and usually make them all the more arrogant.

[January] 7, Sunday. I said Mass, and during it I made an exhortation to the people remaining at the mission, taking my leave of everyone by four words from the altar and charging them to show good behavior in their actions so as not to give a bad example to the new Christians there, and encouraging them to bear up under their hardships, etc. Afterwards, order was given for the journey and for the requirements for those of us going to San Diego. These were Señor Comandante Rivera with ten soldiers, Señor Comandante Anza with twenty of the expedition's soldiers, and me, and a pack train (with no load) to bring back provisions.[46] We set out from Mission San Gabriel a little after midday, traveling light, and after seven o'clock at night halted at the bank of the Santa Ana River after fording it, having traveled twelve leagues southeastward with some variance. The route is a level one almost the whole way, save for some hills at about the middle of the route, all of it very green and covered with grass, and a number of plants among which is found a kind of very small onion-set that in shape and flavor and effects is the same as the garden onion; I had some of it to eat at Mission San Gabriel. At a league and a half[47] we passed by the mission's former site, where the jacales are still standing. At three leagues, one crosses the San Gabriel River, which carries a good deal of water here and runs about westward toward the sea. At seven or eight leagues the hills begin and there is a well in a hollow among them. Then follows level land as far as the Santa Ana River, which flows wide here and with a good deal of water, running seaward about west-southwesterly, although seemingly, by what they said and what I saw the following day, it forms large lakes close to the shore, without reaching to the sea.

The Santa Ana River is so called because Commander Portolá's expedition arrived there on the feast day of Santa Ana gave it that name. It also bestowed the rest of the names along the whole way between San Diego and Monterey, and they called Mission San Gabriel "*San Gabriel de los Temblores*" because the ground shook on the day they arrived at that place.[48]

---

[46]Seventeen of the expedition soldiers, and twelve of Rivera's, according to Anza's entry. There is a discrepancy of at least one between Anza's and Font's totals, whether or not the commanders are counted as being among the soldiers.

[47]In the final text, "at a league."

[48]The first expedition (of 1769). From about here onward, unlike earlier references in Font's journal and reflecting the terminology that was in use by the California soldiers and their later descendants (cf. Brown 2001: 51), the mentions of "the expedition" and "the first expedition" frequently refer to Portolá's expedition rather than to Anza's later one of 1774. It seems that it was the scouts of the first expedition, under Sergeant Ortega, who bestowed the name Santa Ana on July 27, 1769 (Brown 2001: 121), and not the expedition's missionaries and officers, who called it *El Dulcísimo Nombre de Jesús* and *Los Temblores*. Despite what Font says, the latter name was only identified with Mission San Gabriel while the mission itself was being planned. The intended site was then moved far north of the river, leaving the name Temblores behind to compete with Santa Ana; the latter designation was obviously the soldiers' preference, since it survived. San Gabriel de los Temblores means San Gabriel of the Earthquakes.

Today was clear, but a bit bothersome with the northwester that prevails greatly here and in these South Seas.[49] The wind dropped as night came on, with a great deal of a chill, and very little firewood, as the whole country, and the river, is very lacking in trees—which is the drawback that it has.

[January] 8, Monday. We set out from the Santa Ana River at a quarter past seven in the morning, and having traveled an east-southeastward course with some variation, at a quarter past four in the afternoon halted at the Santa María Magdalena stream,[50] having forded it (though at this time it had no more water in it than a big spring does). It was named by Portolá's expedition and was otherwise called *La Quema*[51] because of a fire in the grass patches that put them in some danger and that was caused partly by accident, partly by the gentiles.[52] And we had traveled about fifteen leagues.

At the start, the route is a level one; at about seven leagues, having already come into the hills, we reached the spot called *Los Ojitos*[53] where we had a bite of lunch and drank water. Winding about during the entire stretch because of the hills lying out from the mountains here, at four leagues further southeastward we came to the El Trabuco stream, issuing from the mountains of this name, which I mention under December 30 and 31. They were given this name on the first expedition because they lost a blunderbuss at this place.[54] There is a small stream there. The remainder was to the southeast by south over rather level land, a sort of a hollow of some width, halfway along which we found gentile Indians hunting mice and gathering prickly pear fruit from a small cactus patch there. I ate some of the fruit, which is very mediocre and bony, when they invited me to; there are no nopales hereabouts.[55] And then came the river where we stopped, at which I found a plant that the Monterey soldiers call parsley since its flavor

---

[49]The Pacific Ocean.
[50]In the field text, "the Santa María Magdalena River."
[51]The Fire.
[52]This incident is not mentioned in the records of the first expedition, although the journal of Costansó in January 1770 seems to indicate some such event since it refers to the place as *El Incendio* (Boneu 1983: 294).

In my edition of the Juan Crespí journals of the first expedition, the expedition camp sites of July 24 and 25, 1769 are misidentified as having been at "San Juan Capistrano" and "El Toro," respectively (Brown 2001: 294–306, headlines of alternate left-hand pages). These are also the locations given by Bancroft (1963: 142), Engelhardt (1922: 11–12), Bolton (1927: 136), Hoover et al. (1966: 259), and Browning (1992: 13, 206). The locations as identified by Stephenson (1930) and Meadows (1965) were more nearly correct. The correct locations, as Font's account and other records show, are as follows: the July 24, 1769, camp was at the northeast corner of the intersection of the *Cañada Gobernadora* and the San Juan River (which was also the "La Quema" Anza-Font camp site of January 9, 1776); the July 25 camp was on the *Plano Trabuco* a short distance southwest of the present-day Santa Margarita Parkway bridge over the *Arroyo Trabuco*.

[53]The Little Eyes.
[54]There is no mention of this incident in earlier records, but of course the name survives.
[55]The better (Mexican) kind of prickly-pear.

lies between parsley and celery, and that the people from the expedition who went on to San Diego last time[56] call water lettuce, and it has neither the form of lettuce nor of parsley but it is a little bit like celery. The land is all green with good plants and grass, and nearly all the way consists of hills, up and down. At intervals from the top of the hills one discovers a great portion of sea, with the San Pedro bight which lies almost directly opposite San Gabriel and, closer by, a middling-sized island concerning which they were unable to tell me with certainty whether it is called *Isla de Santa Catarina* or *Santo Tomás*, a name given during the first expedition by sea (I learned afterwards that it is called Santa Catarina).[57] The course was east-southeastward until halfway along; changed to eastward as far as the El Trabuco stream; and from there we descended from the hills to a long hollow and changed course to southeastward.

Close to this spot of La Quema, between it and the sea about a league downriver from the stopping place,[58] is the site of the new Mission San Juan Capistrano that the San Fernando Fathers[59] started to establish two months ago; but they withdrew and abandoned the work after hearing about the uprising at San Diego.

[January] 9, Tuesday. We set out from the La Quema stream at a half past seven in the morning and by taking up an east-southeasterly course varying at times between east and south because of the turns in the route, at five o'clock in the afternoon we halted at the San Juan Capistrano River (the name given it by the first expedition)[60] having traveled for fifteen leagues. The route is entirely hills and hollows and therefore a considerably broken one, though without rocks and with the soil very moist and green. A number of streams are encountered, having no water in them, however, as they only carry it when it rains. At eight leagues we came to a small lake at a stream, and the soldiers call it *Las Flores* and it seems to have water year-round.[61] At two further leagues, we came to the Santa Margarita River at two o'clock in the afternoon, where we saw a great

---

[56]Refers to those of Anza's Sonora soldiers who had been to San Diego in April 1774 with the missionaries, and who were also with this party in 1776.

[57]"(I learned afterward . . .)" is a later addition in the field text. The final text has: "and also the island called Santa Catalina, which lies out at sea some six leagues." As Font perhaps should have known, the name Santa Catalina had actually been given 174 years earlier, by the Vizcaíno sea expedition. "Santo Tomás" may be a late reflection of the sea voyages of 1769, whose sailors, suffering from scurvy, were misled by the inaccuracy of the Vizcaíno latitudes when they fatally confused the Channel Islands with landmarks that were actually located much farther south; "Santo Tomé" was a reported island off Baja California.

[58]Anza's entry says the distance was three quarters of a league (1.95 mile) below his camp site.

[59]The California missionaries sent out by the Colegio de San Fernando de México and led by Serra.

[60]The 1769 expedition. See Brown 2001: 276–79.

[61]"The Flowers" seems to have been the soldiers' version of the name *Los Rosales* [rose-patches] *de Santa Práxedis*, bestowed by Juan Crespí during the first expedition, July 21, 1769 (Brown 2001: 288 column b).

many white geese, perhaps coming there from the San José lake that I speak of under December 30. Close to this spot, before reaching the halting place, we passed close by another lake of some little size that is seemingly formed by overflows from the San Juan Capistrano River here, which had no water in it at present. There was hardly any water at the stopping place, though the river usually carries a great deal during rains, and we had a very strong chill here at night from lack of firewood, which is what the land and hills here are scarcest in. We were so near to the sea that we heard the noise of it all night long; it often comes in sight from the hilltops along the way, and today, from a height, we also saw clearly the rocks that form the Puerto de San Carlos that we went through on December 27 and the snowy range as well.[62]

[January] 10, Wednesday. We set out from the San Juan Capistrano River at a half past seven in the morning, and at a half past three in the afternoon we stopped at the spot called *La Soledad*, having traveled some fourteen leagues on a southeastward course with a number of veers to east-southeastward and a great many more of them as far around as to the southward.

As soon as we set out from the stopping place, I saw a village of Indians downriver from the spot. At about six leagues there is the spot called *Los Batequitos*, a small watering place a bit off the road on the side opposite from the sea.[63] Two leagues further is the Indian village and spot called *San Alejos*, and before and beyond it two inlets from the sea are encountered. Then one comes into hills having a growth of—besides rosemary and other plants I was unable to recognize—a variety that they call *bruc*[64] in Catalonia and which they use to make brooms, and another that they call *arbós*[65] there; and still others like very scrubby

---

[62] The party was following the inland route opened by the first expedition of 1769, east of San Onofre Mountain and roughly along the present-day Basilone Road. Their view must have been from Horno Summit and the slopes immediately below it, from which a line of sight extends past the north side of Wild Horse Peak, twenty-six miles away, onward to Table Mountain, which lies between Horse Canyon and Nance Canyon at a distance of just over fifty miles. The clarity of the atmosphere which was normal in those days must have given the travelers the ability to pick out such distant details; and probably they were passing a spyglass (a low powered, hand-held telescope) around among themselves. The head of Nance Canyon is usually identified as Anza's San Carlos Pass. However, Müller's formula for intervisibility (Kowalczyk 1968: 376–77), when applied to government map information about the terrain, indicates that the Anza party could not have seen anything farther to the south than a point in Terwilliger Valley about a mile north of the canyon head.

At the end of the sentence, the field text adds: "the snowy range as well, ending in a point that it makes in its midst, concerning which I spoke on December 15." Since in this version of Font's text the references to earlier entries are dated one day too early, this refers to the December 16 entry, when the soldiers' report of "Font's Point" led him to suspect the existence of what is now called the San Gorgonio Pass.

[63] The name Batequitos (Batiquitos) apparently dates from the first expedition. Those "small waterholes" at which the 1769 expedition camped were at the northeast head of Batiquitos Lagoon, just toward the ocean from the natural route ("El Camino Real") that was followed then and since. Font's description of them as lying on the other side of the road may be mistaken.

[64] Broom heather.

[65] The arbutus bush. Usually spelled *arboç*.

live oaks with a small leaf, that yield acorns. From the hills one descends to the stream and spot of *San Dieguillo*.[66] The route is, like yesterday's, a broken one, all up and down hills and hollows and treeless and very scarce in firewood, but the countryside as green as all the rest with a great deal of grass. Plainly, whenever it rains a great deal this route is a very tedious one and almost impossible to travel because of the mire and the water carried by the many flooding streams in the hollows. Now we find them dry, since very little rain has fallen and the rainy season is just beginning. The village of La Soledad is now attached to Mission San Diego and in it there are some Christians. And their governor, who came over to visit us along with other Indians bringing firewood, was shot with arrows by the runaways in the late uprising and showed me his three wounds
—but I learned afterward that they were bullet wounds that he received in the skirmish, since he was with the insurgents, an accessory in the affair along with the others. He spent a while with us, and some Indians brought firewood, but Señor Rivera exhibited a great deal of distrust toward them and seemed to be feeling some fear.[67]

After dinner, the Indians came over from fishing, crying *Cassau, cassau*, which is what they call every sort of fish, and they brought to our tent extremely fine sardines[68] they had just gotten from the water, such large ones that they seemed to be the salted sardines called herrings in Spain. I immediately took a few of them and at that very hour set myself to cleaning them, and we tasted them. I ate one that had been broiled on the coals and three that were fried. They were very tasty, but as it was already late, Señor Anza ate less than an entire one.

[January] 11, Thursday. We set out from La Soledad village at a half past seven in the morning and traveling a southeastward course for four leagues, through hills as always and along the shore of the *Puerto Anegado*[69] during most of the last two leagues, at about ten o'clock we reached the Presidio of San Diego.[70] By my own count, this makes sixty Mexican leagues between San Gabriel and San Diego. However, Constanzó, who came with Commander Portolá and Captain

---

[66]The normal form of the name, already in use at that time, was and is San Dieguito. Both forms mean "Little San Diego," although the reason for the name seems not to be known.

[67]Rivera records that before dismounting he rode by or through the village to check on its appearance. Anza mentions that a number of Christian converts belonging to the mission turned out to have musket-ball wounds, showing that instead of fighting the attackers they had been among the most vigorous enemies in the fray. After the attack, Sergeant Ortega released the chief because his wounds, one in a wrist and two in a leg, were said to have been accidentally received as he sat on a hill near the mission. The story seems to have changed, since Rivera later was told that the chief was wounded while sitting beside his hut in the village, i.e. had not been at the assault—which Rivera found difficult to believe, but perplexing to disprove. (Burrus 1967 1: 234; 2: 468, etc.) Font's January 27 entry reports that the chief was severely warned again; however, a year afterward, in 1777, the same man was accused of trying to foment a new anti-Spanish conspiracy.

[68]Rivera says that the fish were brought over while the party was dining (Burrus 1967 1: 226).

[69]Flooded Harbor.

[70]The final text adds "marked on the map by the letter **C**." Font refers to Mission Bay as "Flooded Harbor," Puerto Anegado, because of the half-submerged marshy islands in it.

Fages, said there were only forty.[71] Extraordinary was the joy in the presidio at Commander Rivera and Commander Anza's arrival with the soldiers, what with the reinforcement these troops were bringing to those there.

The Presidio of San Diego is located in a very bad place, a small and uneven hill overlooked by other hills. The river goes by the foot of the hill and is dry for a great deal of the year; drinking water can scarcely be gotten by digging wells right into its sand. It comes from the main California range lying not far off about to northeastward; and turning southward around the hill it empties into the harbor, which is some two leagues away from the presidio, southward.

We found here Father Minister Fray Vicente Fuster of the destroyed Mission San Diego (which was situated about a league up the river)[72] and Father Ministers Fray Fermín Lasuén and Fray Gregorio Amurrió of Mission San Juan Capistrano who were beginning to establish it near the place of La Quema but left it upon the uprising by the Indians. The Fathers along with the entire garrison took particular comfort from our arrival.

On the shore of Puerto Anegado and about a league from the presidio is the village of *La Rinconada*.

This presidio has no agricultural possibilities at all and consequently neither does the mission and therefore very few Indians live at the latter and most of them are allowed to dwell in their own villages even though they are Christians, as it is done in Baja California. And that is why they have so much contact with the gentiles, and are themselves more gentile than Christian; and with the destruction and attack here, everything was left very impoverished and backward. They were just beginning to get some planting done at the mission that was being established up the river, which was why the Fathers had moved their mission away from the presidio, as well as to keep from having to live so uncomfortably at the presidio which, besides the scarcity of water, allows them no way of enlarging at all.

However, with what has happened, they again took refuge at the presidio, where they are subsisting at present with a great many toils and needs for lack of buildings and a dwelling place, and even more for lack of provisions, since all that the warehouse contained was a little rice and wormy corn.[73]

The harbor is a very fine and secure one, formed upon the land side by a strip of flats that comes from the main range and runs east and west, and on the side of the sea by a low range running southeast to northwestward as far as Puerto Anegado, which at times is connected with the harbor, leaving the range nearly an island; its point or extremity is called *Punta de Guijarros*,[74] near which is the

---

[71]Miguel Costansó, the military engineer (who later spelled his name as Font gives it here). His journal account gives about 41½ leagues between San Diego and the original point where Mission San Gabriel later was founded, a figure that is much more accurate than Font's.

[72]In the field text, "about a league and a half distant from the presidio, and the gentiles destroyed it."

[73]The warehouse that now was serving as the mission house and church.

[74]Ballast Point.

entrance or mouth, extending due northward, of the harbor, which is quite large, of considerable depth, and nearly round. At the end of the range, about northward from said harbor, is a different, false harbor that I think was called *San Dionisio* by Vizcaíno. It is not a good harbor because it has a great many reefs in its entrance and Vizcaíno, it seems, called it the Puerto Anegado on the shore of which lies the village they call La Rinconada or El Rincón.[75]

Opposite the harbor mouth and at a distance of some six leagues lie islets named *Los Mártires* or *Los Cuatro Coronados*; while to the west-northwestward and very far off, about fifteen leagues from land, a large island, called San Clemente, can be seen. Upon the land there is grass enough, although not so good or as plentiful as elsewhere, and it is scarce in firewood and, much more, in timber. In sum, Mission San Diego is the worst of all those that the San Fernando Fathers possess among the new establishments there, and its Indians are also the worst; they belong to the Quemeya tribe, very similar to the Jecuiches both in their evil purposes and wicked hearts, and in their being poor-bodied, ugly, dirty, disheveled, sooty, stinking, and flat-faced. They made plain their nature during the first arrival into that country with Commander Portolá's expedition, for only shortly after the Fathers founded the mission there, they rebelled and wounded Father Fray Juan Vizcaíno in his hand with an arrow, and they have ever shown themselves as undesirable.

[January] 12, Friday. I awoke with my diarrhea rather dreadful, but the weather was somewhat calm, unlike yesterday when as soon as we arrived here there arose so strong a northerly that it was rather remarkable, and it lasted until nightfall. Using the astronomical quadrant, I observed the latitude of the presidio here, and found it, according to the tables of Jorge Juan with no correction, in latitude $32° 38'$[76] and, with correction, in $32° 44½'$.[77] And thus I say: at the presidio and Mission San Diego harbor, January 12, 1776: meridian altitude of the sun's lower limb: $35° 24'$.[78] Both harbors here are very plentiful in fish of various kinds, all of which the Indians call cassau, such as bream, sole, shad, *viejas*,[79] large sardines, and many other sorts, all of them very good, and caught by the Indians using hooks and gaffs from their little canoes made of tule-rush. Because they eat a great deal of fish without cleaning any of it, this makes them stink more than others do. However, they show so little gratitude toward the Fathers and they are so ill-mannered that for the Fathers to get any fish, they are required to pay them for whatever they ask for in beads or corn, and so forth, and then the Indians give whatever they normally have left over.

[January] 13, Saturday. I climbed a small height next to the presidio and had a better view from there of the harbor, the sea, and the islands, six or seven of

---

[75] Mission Bay (False Bay). This discussion—which understandably occurs only in the field text—seems confused; Font altered it later and here as elsewhere, the references to Vizcaíno are mistaken.

[76] In the field text, "$32° 42'$, the same in which Constanzó placed it": another reference to Miguel Costansó's *Diario histórico* (Costansó 1771). Cf. Brown 2001: 253 (with 786 n141).

[77] Font's latitude figure here and on February 2 is extremely close to being accurate.

[78] Again a disagreement with the field text, which has "$35° 20'$."

[79] The name is applied to a wide variety of quite different Pacific, Atlantic, and Mediterranean fishes.

which are in view to the south-southwest of the harbor mouth at about six or eight leagues. The smallest of them are called Los Cuatro Coronados. Others are to the west-northwestward, among which I saw a large one about twenty leagues out to sea, called *San Clemente*, and they say it is inhabited. Today the two captains began the inquiry concerning the recent uprising, destruction of the mission, and death of Father Minister Father Fray Luis Jaume,[80] by examining Indian ringleaders who were imprisoned in the presidio—those who could be captured at that time—and taking reports concerning their crimes.

I shall give an account of the uprising and dreadful event just as it was related to me by Father Vicente Fuster,[81] noting at the start that since the San Diego presidio and mission has no possibilities at all for planting—it hardly has enough water for basic necessities—the Fathers proceeded to baptize a number of Indian converts, which I believe amounted to over five hundred of them, and allowed them to live in their own villages with one person who had learned how to pray so that they would do the same; and with the requirement that the villages come to Mass in rotation on feast days, as had been established in Baja California. Thereby, the Christians were such only in name, and more or less the same as gentiles, being as new to Christianity as they were, and living in so free a manner with so little teaching, since the Fathers were unable to do otherwise. They,[82] therefore, ill pleased with their subordination (as normally does happen with Indians)—and possibly wishing to make off with whatever had arrived at the mission shortly before in a good-sized shipment of supplies, which had caught their eye—conspired, like household spies, with the mountain gentiles to do away with the mission and the presidio. They expected to achieve this by seizing the opportunity when they would see the Spaniards' few forces being divided up, especially the small number of soldiers who left to form the guard for the new Mission San Juan Capistrano which Father Fray Fermín de Lasuén and Father Fray Gregorio Amurrió were going to found near La Quema, as I mentioned on the 8th. The gentiles thus determined to split up, some of them going for the presidio and others for the mission. The group that went to the mission was not supposed to commence the attack until they saw the presidio burning. The fire or light would be visible since it was a short distance away. The soldiers at the presidio were so off their guard that the Indians would have won their gamble just as they expected, as the presidio is overlooked by a very nearby hill from which they were going to give the war whoop and, after seizing the cannons or

---

[80] The original Mallorcan-Catalán version of the missionary Jaime's name.
[81] Fuster had written an account of the rebellion both in the mission's new register of deaths (the old one was destroyed in the fire) and in a letter to Junípero Serra of November 28, 1775, quoted extensively in Geiger 1959: 430–33 notes; translated in Tibesar 1956 2: 449–58.
[82] The baptized Indians.

JANUARY 13, 1776

culverins, to set fire to the buildings, which was easy to do as they were made of tule thatch. But God so willed that the Indians at the mission did not wait for the signal but commenced attacking and setting fire to it before the presidio began to burn, so that those who were going to the presidio feared they had been detected and at once pulled back to join the others at the mission; even though the soldiers were so sleepy-eyed that they did not hear the shots or the shouting nor see the light of the fire which was in sight of them.

And in his statement the sentinel on duty at that time excused himself by saying that while it is true that he saw the light, he thought it was the light of the moon. And it is to be noted that the moon that night was one day before the full and consequently was in the west at the hour when this happened, while the light from the fire must have been visible to the east of the presidio, since this is where the mission was. But it is no new thing for soldiers to fulfill their duties in this way; it happens like this most of the time here on the Sonora frontiers, where many harms inflicted by the Apaches catch the presidio soldiers by surprise, off guard, and unprepared, either sleeping or playing cards.

On November 5, 1775, then, at about one o'clock at night, the whole group of Indians who were to mount the attack fell upon Mission San Diego, joined by those who were to attack the presidio and did not do so because of the failure to await the signal I spoke of above. Although it is known that some forty villages joined and convened for this, the number of enemies could not be ascertained exactly, large though it was, as there would have been four hundred of them even if there had only been ten Indians per village, whereas many villages were capable of contributing twenty or thirty combatants. They were all from the Quemeya and Jecuiche tribes, and possibly some others joined them. As it was nighttime and the soldiers of the mission guard were asleep in the guardhouse (that is how those scandalous good-for-nothings fulfill their duty), the Indians first robbed from the church whatever they pleased, and so forth, smashing with a stone the chest holding vestments and carrying them away along with two images, one of the Immaculate Conception[83] and the other of San José, and sent their women off to the heights with the plunder. And then, seizing some firebrands right from the guardhouse, they began to set fire to the guardhouse, the church, and the Fathers' houses, since they were built of tule-rush (in Catalonia they call it *balcade* and make everyday chairs from it) and of palisade, they easily caught fire. At the noise, Father Fray Luis Jaume

came out of his house and then realized the uprising that was under way—which several times he had been advised of previously but never chose to believe it as he thought it to be impossible that his Indians should do such a thing to him, since he loved them very much and was as good to them as he could be, and had even gotten angry with the Indian who had told him of it last, threatening him with having him whipped if he ever came to him with that again.[84] It is not

---

[83] The Virgin Mary.
[84] This was said by some of the natives interrogated in the military inquisition that was made just after the attack.

good to have too much confidence in Indians, since in the end they are an unfaithful, ungrateful, and inconsiderate people.

He then went over to the stream where the Indians were. They caught him there and stripped him of his habit and underclothes, leaving him with only a reliquary which he wore around his neck. They shot him with arrows until they were fully satisfied, driving over twenty arrows into his body. Then they smashed his head and face with the sickle or saber-like sticks that they use or with rocks.[85] He was only recognized as being the Father by the whiteness of his body and a bit of his fringe or tonsure.

Of the four soldiers of the guard who were awakened by the fire in the guardhouse, one went out without his leather jacket on to see what was happening. He and another soldier were immediately wounded and unable to use weapons, but they did not die. The other two fortified themselves among some adobe bricks close to the house and some bushel baskets that Father Fray Vicente Fuster had pulled out of the flames. He himself took protection behind them, and using his cloak and his habit protected the gunpowder sack from the horde of burning firebrands raining down—a great wonder that the powder did not burn.[86] Although they shot an arrow through his cloak his wound was no more than that of a blow from a stone on his shoulder. In the struggle, the carpenter and the blacksmith both died. They were artisans who were paid and maintained at the mission by the king.[87] The two soldiers fought back and managed to fire off some very good shots. After the fight had lasted a long time, God willed that they, such a throng of Indians, withdraw at daybreak, after they had been unable to do away with two soldiers,

which is proof of what wretches they are and that they would never have done such damage if the soldiers had been awake. In the end, they withdrew, fearing that when daybreak came, help would come from the presidio. The presidio was far from doing that. They did not even know what was happening there until the dead bodies were brought to the presidio.

The four soldiers of the guard were not charged in any way for having been asleep, either because they emerged wounded from the fray or because Commander Rivera is very fond of them. I have already related the excuse given by the sentinel. He thought the light he saw was

---

[85]"And with rocks," in the final text. During the inquiries after the disaster, the natives tended to assert that Jaime had been killed by their war clubs and arrows; the Spaniards, that it was done with rocks. The claim propagated by Francisco Palóu that Jaime's last words were "Love-God" or "Love-God, children" (the Franciscans' slogan) was originally made by the Fathers' house servant, himself suspected of complicity in the attack. When some gentiles who had been involved were interrogated, they asserted that the missionary "was saying something in his Spanish, which they could not understand," or else that before dying, he only had time to say "¡Ay, Dios! ¡Ay Jesús!" (Burrus 1967 2: 469, etc.)

[86]According to Fuster's letter to Serra, the missionary himself entered a burning building to bring out the full sack of gunpowder, gave it to the soldiers, and kept snatching the burning brands away from the open mouth of the sack. Font may be deemphasizing Fuster's activities because they seemed to him a little too warlike for a missionary.

[87]The blacksmith was José Romero and the carpenter was José Urselino.

that of the moon. When pressed as to how he could not have realized the difference, seeing that that light was arising from the ground, he answered that he had not seen it because when going on guard duty he had only been charged with watching the prisoners, and since he was facing them while looking at them, and the mission thus lay at his back, he did not turn to see where the light was coming from even though he saw it to one side. Now this would be an excellent proof of how thoroughly the soldiers fulfill the orders given them, were we not, on the other hand, aware of how little care they give to carrying out not only specific orders, such as that one, but orders from higher up that are very pertinent and, at times, of great importance. But men can reconcile anything when they wish to, and so Señor Rivera thought this excuse a sufficient one and let the sentinel go free. He did not even confine him. Instead, he blamed the uprising on the lieutenant of the presidio don Antonio Francisco Ortega[88] and his poor conduct. He in fact was entirely without blame in the matter, and at the time had been occupied in founding Mission San Juan Capistrano. Because he got along well with the Fathers, he was much disliked by Señor Rivera, who cares more for the soldiers than for the Fathers, and hence predilection had the opportunity to do its work here. The fact that Señor Rivera likes the soldiers better than he does the Fathers is evident by the words uttered from his own mouth, because when the news of the uprising here reached him at Monterey he went immediately to Mission San Carlos Borromeo to convey it to the Father President, and went in saying this: "Father President, I have just received dreadful news from San Diego that requires me to start for there immediately, and it is that the Indians have risen, burned the mission, and killed Father Fray Luis. The only thing that pleases me is that they haven't killed any of the soldiers, thank God." I heard him say this very same thing while on the road and he later certainly reaffirmed it by the measures he took for the soldiers' healing, chiefly for the one who was wounded worst. He kept saying how much he would regret it if he should die. When speaking of the Indians and the event that happened he would often say, "Thank God, thank God I have the comfort that so far they haven't killed any of my soldiers." Let this serve as guidance to show what the ministers have to suffer from gentlemen commanding in remote countries who have no one over them, as has happened to the poor Religious there, who amid all the hardships they have been having, have their greatest one in the poor regard Commander Rivera has shown them.

In the morning, Father Fray Vicente Fuster withdrew to the presidio with the dead and wounded. The fire had turned everything into ashes, so that the censer, chalice, and wedding coins, which I saw,[89] had melted and pooled, leaving this mission without possessions and the three Fathers thoroughly needy in every way. What they were left with was the ashes of their mission and of its furnishings and of their books, papers and so forth—all of which was burned up—and with their proximity to the Presidio of San Diego, the presidio of hunger and wretchedness.

It is to be noted that although many of the Indians in the uprising were gentiles, many of them also were from among the converted Christians; and it is clear that the mountain Indians here, who are very like the ones we saw between San Sebastián and San Gregorio and our crossing of the mountains, are more ungrateful and fierce than those belonging to San Gabriel and further on

---

[88] *Sic*; José Francisco Ortega.
[89] Thirteen coins symbolically given by the bridegroom to the bride at the marriage ceremony.

—the lowest sort of people that there are thereabouts, and I would almost even dare to say that just as the California range seems the dustbin of the world through its infertility and stoniness, so the Indians who inhabit it are the dregs of the human race.

[January] 14, Sunday. I said Mass. I officiated at the Mass, which was sung to the Most Sweet Name of Jesus for the successful pacification of the rebellious Indians, and I accompanied myself upon a poor spinet that Father Fray Ángel Somera left here at the mission when he visited this presidio.[90] Though it is the rainy season here, it has been noted that the weather is so clear that not even clouds have arisen, and the fear therefore is for a dreadful year from drought; if so, there will not even be any grass, which is the only thing that exists hereabouts for mounts and livestock.

[January] 15, Monday. The inquiry concerning the uprising was pursued by Commander Rivera, to allow him to decide whether to go to punish the rebels who are at large. He was also concerned about the disorder that had occurred among the soldiers. I shall note that in addition to the five Indian ringleaders held prisoner at the presidio, two who belonged to the mission were captured as they were going to join the gentiles who were preparing a third attack upon the presidio. The lieutenant ordered them whipped. The whippings given were such that one of the Indians died from them and the other one was very ill. With great clarity and forbearance, Father Fray Fermín[91] undertook to treat the second one, but today the Indian, showing little gratitude and less courtesy, vanished upon finding himself better. He did not say anything to the Father nor did he ask for permission. They say he went to his village.

[January] 16, Tuesday. I said Mass. After nightfall last night Commander Rivera dispatched the sergeant of the presidio with fifteen soldiers[92] and an Indian interpreter to go to the San Luis village and fall upon it today at daybreak to catch rebel ringleaders—important Indians and apostate Christians—whom he had learned were there, through an account given by an old Indian woman. And this afternoon, from the top of the presidio hill here it was observed that there were a great many smokes visible in the mountains. This is how the Indians inform one another when they have some happening to report.

[January] 17, Wednesday. The weather was fine in the morning, but at daybreak

---

[90]José Ángel Fernández Somera was from a Mexico City family that had supplied two very different brothers—a Jesuit missionary and a military officer—to the Baja California mission field before the expulsion of the Jesuits. In 1771 he landed in Alta California at Monterey and went south to found Mission San Gabriel. In 1772 he retired to Mexico, necessarily by way of San Diego and the peninsula. On June 2, 1772, he was at San Fernando de Velicatá in Baja California, no doubt on his way south. (Information from Harry Crosby.) A spinet is a smallish keyboard instrument.

[91]Fermín Francisco de Lasuén.

[92]Rivera's daybook agrees that there were fifteen soldiers. Anza says seventeen soldiers were to be sent with the sergeant. The interpreter was not entrusted with the purpose of the sally.

on the side toward the sea, there was a fog on the horizon. With the northwest wind blowing, the fog spread above us in the afternoon so that before sunset everything was covered by fog.[93] Therefore, we put off our intention of going to view and examine the site of the destroyed and burned-down mission. As for myself, although I felt a bit relieved from my diarrhea, today I became very bothered by very painful small sores that broke out in my mouth, especially on the tip of my tongue. I could hardly speak or eat, except with great trouble; it is a sickness that they call *fuego marcial*,[94] in California.

[January] 18, Thursday. The weather continued very wet and depressing with the very thick low fog. I was drooling a great deal. The sores in my mouth and on my tongue were no better and I was having great trouble talking. A word came during the afternoon that a whale had beached itself at Puerto Anegado; later, that there were two but they were not whales, but rather two large fish, about three varas long.[95]

It is to be noted that it is quite normal for an occasional whale to become stranded on those shores every year, and whenever this happens the Indians at once inform one another and gather like flies to devour it. They remain there on the shore until they finish it off. And, since the whale usually is so fatty, and they themselves are so filthy, in eating it they oil and smear themselves disgustingly with the fat. They stink so badly that the foul odor they give off is revolting.

[January] 19, Friday. The weather continued very foggy and wet, and I was still ill; I took a bowl of hot lard with sugar in it in the morning, in case my sickness was due to indigestion. The sergeant and soldiers came in at nightfall with four gentile culprits they had captured, and with the news that the rebellious Indians with their leaders had gone back up into the mountains, where, they said through the interpreter, they had the images and the rest of what they plundered still intact. However, an apostate Indian and leader of the rebels, named Pablo, had shown himself brazenly among them as if mocking the sergeant, trusting in the roughness of the mountains into which they had climbed—by which, one could imagine the amount of trouble it would take to subdue these Indians.

[January] 20, Saturday. I was better at daybreak but the weather was still gloomy and cloudy as on the days before. Our commanders began questioning the new prisoners to obtain the information they needed to pacify and secure the country. They were given fifty lashes apiece as a welcome.[96] In the afternoon I witnessed a vivid reproduction of the burning of Mission San Diego, when a

---

[93] In the final text, "but in the afternoon the horizon became covered by a large amount of fog that rose from the sea and had been forming upon it ever since the morning."

[94] Burning in the mouth which caused mouth ulcers, probably due to scurvy, no doubt. Cf. the note to the February 6 entry, below. "California" refers here to Baja California.

[95] 8¼ feet.

[96] Rivera released two of the gentile prisoners because of their whippings and since they had denied being guilty. (Burrus 1967 1: 227.)

middling-sized jacal built of tule-rush that was serving as a smithy accidentally caught fire. The fire could not be put out by any means even when all the people assembled tried to do so. I saw then what I had realized already, how dangerous buildings are that are made of tule or grass, and of palisades.

Therefore, the first thing that ought to be attempted when a mission is founded is not to be satisfied with merely any kind of building or jacal, as were the Fathers at the missions there, where they were unable in fact to do anything else for want of resources that should have been provided right from the beginning for buildings and for other matters. Instead, from the very beginning one must insure a well-made construction, free from fire, for at least the church and the ministers' main dwelling. For one must not be too trusting when living among gentiles and new converts who have to be considered enemies. In addition, an occasional malicious person sometimes will seize the opportunity and, by picking up a firebrand, put an end to the mission and everything else, in a single night; and this is without taking any consideration of the accidents that can occur in such buildings.

Commander Rivera continued pursuing the acts and interrogations concerning the rebelliousness of the soldiers belonging to the presidio here, who disobeyed their lieutenant, don Antonio Francisco Ortega.[97]

The reason for this disobedience was that he indicated to them that they were to go to found Mission San Juan Capistrano, and appointed those who were to go. Although they did not utterly refuse, they showed considerable reluctance to go, either because they are a lazy, no-good lot or else because they judged they would have to undergo greater hunger and deprivation at the mission than at the presidio, as the supplies that had been arranged for and provided for the mission's support and founding were so small that the whole of it, once the provisions for the days they spent there were consumed, amounted to four cargas[98] in all including the vestments and other things for the church and household—I saw where they had them deposited at the presidio, in the corner of a small room.

Here, in passing, I wish to point out how improper it is to proceed to found a mission without the necessary resources.[99] Doing so causes it to be ill-established, founded badly, and with twice the hardship; and since in such circumstances the ministers require the greater amount of protection and support from the troops, and possess nothing to reward them with, it follows that they are poorly esteemed and that, for many years, the mission progresses very little or not at all and even is liable to fail from poor support, as in the case of San Juan Capistrano here. Thus sparing a few necessary expenses at the start will cost double later, and with less result. All of this can be learned from experience at those missions[100] where the Religious would have liked to possess what was needed and to have had good resources provided for the founding of the missions. Still, since they desired to have missions there, they were satisfied with whatever provision was made for them at the time and directed it all toward saving expenses. This is the reason that they have advanced very little during what is going on seven years now, and have endured a vast amount of hardship and neediness. It is most certain that the provision was scant both for buildings and for

---

[97] Again, José Francisco Ortega. Both the field text and the final text have the mistaken form of his name here.
[98] Mule loads or an equivalent measure by weight or volume.
[99] This was a favorite theme of Font's, especially regarding his own colegio's plans for founding new missions out beyond the Sonora frontier. See Brown 2006: 85–118.
[100] The Alta California missions (San Diego included).

the development of the missions. Without specifying every item, let the fact that each mission was provided only nine cows and a bull as a basis for stock-raising suffice for proof.

The lieutenant then determined that to establish the mission it was necessary to at least build a jacal to serve as a church and dwelling for the Fathers. Seeing that there was no one able to do it except for the soldiers, he indicated to them that they should work on the building. This they utterly refused to do. The lieutenant said to them that going there and not working on the building was the same as doing nothing, since if they stayed there in the open there would be no progress on the mission, and so since the Fathers themselves had offered to work, he himself would work as well; and if he did, everyone else would have to follow his example and work. The soldiers resisted this and the lieutenant went on to order them specifically and then they refused to obey him, telling him that the king was not paying them to do that and thus they would not acknowledge him as being their lieutenant. He finally threatened them a bit and patched the matter as well as he could and eventually went there with the more tractable soldiers. Señor Rivera commenced investigating this rebelliousness or disobedience as soon as we came into the presidio, and being, as he was, fond of the soldiers and an enemy of the lieutenant's, in the end he found none of the soldiers guilty nor punished anyone, putting the fault for those doings upon the lieutenant, who tended to favor the Fathers, and characterizing his conduct as poor. Indeed that ancient proverb of Spain proves true everywhere, "Laws extend where kings intend."[101]

[January] 21, Sunday. I heard Mass, which I was unable to say because of my poor health and also because the Fathers possessed so little wine that they only said one Mass each in turn on feast days; so that what they had would last a little longer, I gave them a vial of wine that I had with me. It had begun raining during the night and kept on in that way all of this day, (but softly and with no thunderclaps, which are rarely heard there), and the rainy season is the same as in Spain, in the winter, and usually lasts from November until March, and during that time the roads become very bad, with the mud and mire that develops.

[January] 22, Monday. The weather was very wet and overcast though with no rain, and I was somewhat better with some medicine that Lieutenant Ortega requested for me from the presidio.[102]

---

[101]*Allá van leyes a dó quieren reyes.*

[102]According to Anza's journal, a meeting between himself and Commander Rivera took place on this date at Anza's request or insistence. Anza had decided that the campaign against the rebels was going slowly and could not be effectively completed until the end of the rainy season, or until the soldiers' horses had recuperated. But this would require over a month's delay, which in turn would require him, if he stayed at San Diego, to disobey his orders as to taking his expedition to Monterey and reconnoitering the river of San Francisco. Therefore, Anza offered to leave ten of his sixteen soldiers with Rivera while he himself would go to Monterey with the colonists and then on to survey the river. Rivera, in return, stressed the supreme importance of securing San Diego, since the rebellion might spread to the other settlements. He asked Anza to leave the soldier-colonists at San Gabriel where, in the middle of the frontier, they would be at hand for the commander's use in case of (military) necessity, adding that they would not be "burdensome" there. (As Anza soon learned, this would prove to be untrue.) Rivera assumed that the project of settling San Francisco was suspended by events and could not be carried out until the settlements were entirely secure, or at least until the viceroy, after being informed of the troubles, might re-order its being done. Anza decided to give in to Rivera's request to the extent of letting him have the soldiers, and of awaiting the results of the next planned sally against the rebels. Then, if possible, Anza would leave immediately to manage the journeys to Monterey and San Francisco harbor. Rivera would not take part in these, although he agreed to have the expedition handed over to his control before new orders were received. Anza's entry adds that he thought Rivera intended to spend many months in settling the San Diego situation.

[January] 23, Tuesday. I said Mass. The weather continued chill, and raining for most of the day.

During these days work was done on making the presidio secure, which had been so mishandled that there were neither separate quarters nor a guardhouse for the soldiers, nor even a stockade to mark it out for its security and protection.

[January] 24, Wednesday. During these days, questioning continued as to the uprising, and so forth. The weather stayed cold and drizzling and I continued improved from my diarrhea although tormented somewhat by the small sores in mouth and tongue, which were helped a bit by a gargle they prepared for me from *yerba de la golondrina*[103] with a little alum and sugar in it.

[January] 25, Thursday. This morning an Indian said that there was a whale stranded on the shore, and since the weather was clear at daybreak and we had a desire to see this sea monster, after dinner our commander don Juan de Anza and we four Fathers went with a small guard of soldiers and don Rafael[104] the presidio storekeeper to see it. However, we made the two long leagues' journey in vain, because what had stranded was not a whale but another sort of fish, some three varas long, which the Indians immediately fell upon and butchered so that when we reached the sea, nothing was left but a piece of the rib bones. Therefore, we returned home without achieving the purpose of our excursion. I did have this opportunity of seeing the spouts or whistlings of water that whales shoot through their nostrils into the air; there is a great amount of this in these seas and they call them *ballenatos*.[105] I also noted the unusual character of the shore there, which for a long distance consists not of sand but of middling-sized and small loose stones like those found in rivers, so that it is impossible to ride across it, and the sea with its waves constantly breaking over that endless amount of stones made such a noise that, next to it, we could not understand or hear each other even by talking very loud.

At nightfall, with great quiet and concealment, Commander Rivera dispatched the sergeant of the presidio with fifteen soldiers and a gentile Indian, one of those whom they had brought in on the 19th, to go to the San Luis village to seize Indian culprits staying there, by falling upon them in the morning.[106]

[January] 26, Friday. Perhaps because of the excursion yesterday, which was a bit hurried, my illness in the mouth was worse and I was quite sick today with that fuego marcial. At nightfall, the sergeant and soldiers came in with

---

[103] Swallow-wort: a folk-pharmaceutical item denoting astringent Euphorbia (spurge) sap.

[104] Rafael Pedro y Gil. He had written an emotional letter on the occasion of Father Jaime's death.

[105] Elsewhere in the Spanish-speaking world, the word is applied to the young of whales, not to their spouts. Font seems to be aware that this sense is an unusual one.

[106] Rivera's daybook says that there were fifteen soldiers and an interpreter; the gentile captive was sent along as a guide, tied up.

nine Indian captives, two of whom had been lesser ringleaders[107] and with some women. Among the women was one from the presidio who had fled a few days earlier. They were captured without hostile action even though the Indians of the village grabbed up their weapons when they saw the soldiers. However, on perceiving how large a number of them there were, they chose rather to flee and went up into the mountains along with the chief leaders named Carlos and Francisco. They took with them half of a stole, a humeral and a piece of a pallium with the lining torn away.[108] Señor Rivera began at once to question the captives and ordered the most culpable of them to be secured heavily and for all of them to be handed a serving of fifty lashes on first arrival. And although he was unable to ascertain where they might have put the images that they carried off of the Immaculate Conception and San José, the commander learned from the captives that another of the main leaders had gone to the village of La Soledad village; and at that same hour, he secretly dispatched the sergeant and soldiers to go there to seize him in the morning.[109]

[January] 27, Saturday. The weather continued clear, but I was worse off with the mouth sickness and a swollen inflamed tongue so I scarcely could speak with difficulty. The sergeant and soldiers returned at noon without any captive, because the Indian they went to look for at La Soledad village had fled the night before.[110]

[January] 28, Sunday. Nothing special occurred. At daybreak my tongue and mouth were no better, so I was unable to eat or swallow anything except for liquids and even that with difficulty; but in the afternoon, after drinking some chocolate, the diarrhea came back. After I was able to relieve myself, the swelling in my tongue went down and I began to feel much better but I still had some pain from the sores. This reaffirmed the suspicion I had been having that the illness in my mouth was due to my not being able to relieve myself.

Seeing that the two commanders were not taking the field and that the sergeant alone, during so many days, had been the one performing the sallies described above, last night, not having

---

[107]"Lesser" is found only in the short text, stricken. According to Captain Rivera's daybook and Anza's journal entry, the captives included three chiefs (*capitanejos*): one of San Luis, another Christian, and a heathen. The two chief suspects were put in irons and under guard. After the whipping of the men, they were turned over to the chief of the local *ranchería*, with warnings not to hide the major ringleaders, but one of the Christians and most of the women escaped that night. More whippings followed.

[108]Church vestments taken from the burned mission by the rebels, and regarded as symbolically important by both the Europeans and the natives.

[109]Instead of a single main leader, Font's field text speaks of "some culprits (apostate Christians mingled with gentiles)"; the short text reads, stricken, "other ringleaders and culprits." In the next entry, however, the field text speaks of only a single Indian as the soldiers' quarry. Anza's entry identifies him as Carlos, the main rebel leader, still spying on the Spaniards' movements.

[110]The village chief (the same one who told Anza, Font, and Rivera that his bullet wounds were from arrows) denied Carlos had been there, but others admitted it, and Sergeant Carrillo had the chief whipped and warned that the next time, he would be treated as a total enemy.

heard them discuss whether they were going to sally out or not, I asked Señor Anza what his decision might be, explaining to him that by our staying at the presidio without sallying into the field and ending this business of the uprising—besides the fact, which seemed to me a pity, that we were consuming what little the Fathers possessed[111]—the days were running out for making the long distance that we still had to go in order to reach Monterey. To which Señor Anza responded that up to the present, Señor Rivera had not spoken to him concerning sallying out; so that, unless something else arose, he had decided to leave upon the following Sunday, one week from today. He said that we would leave the expedition people at San Gabriel and travel light in order to reach Monterey and investigate the San Francisco River, which was said to be a very large one. I had asked our commander this because, although we had been getting along better ever since the 6th and at San Diego the two of us had slept in a small room (though this was more by necessity than because of friendship, since there were no other rooms), I had never been worthy enough for him to convey his decisions and thoughts to me, even by way of conversation, although he talked them over with others, and at times I would have wished to know about them—if not for curiosity's sake, at least for my own guidance and so as not to be caught by surprise.

[January] 29, Monday. Nothing in particular happened, and I continued with the improvement I had first gained the evening before, gargling with barley water mixed with rose of Castile and a bit of vinegar in it.

[January] 30, Tuesday. Still nothing to comment on today. I wrote a letter to the Reverend Father Guardian of my colegio[112] and another one to the Father President of Sonora, Fray Juan Díaz.

[January] 31, Wednesday. The day passed with nothing in particular to note. I saw how poor a state an Indian, who was among the captives and had been whipped, had been left in by the lashes. Based on this occurrence and through what I have experienced of this San Diego vicinity, I recognized that it is an extremely poor climate for the healing of sores and wounds. The Indians are so infested with sores, scabs, and pimples, even from their infancy, it is as if though they were rotten, which perhaps results from infected blood and the dampness; I also noted this among the gentile Indians I saw in the mountains. This poor constitution, taken together with the choler[113] that the prisoners must have developed and their not being well adapted for whipping, perhaps led to the bad outcome of their buttocks becoming ulcerated. The sores on the Indian I saw were black and horrifying. He had come to see whether the Fathers could give him a cure.

---

[111]Serra, in a letter of April 18, reported that Font had told him that on this occasion he had said to Anza, "Sir, what are we doing here, using up whatever this poor Father doesn't have?—since he has neither any chocolate left, nor candles to light us with, and you are not doing any campaigning or anything else" (Tibesar 1956 2: 434).

[112]In a later letter, after returning to Sonora, Font complained that he had received no acknowledgment or answer from Fray Diego Jiménez, the Guardian, who was engaged in negotiating and planning for new missions on the Gila and Colorado rivers, subjects on which Font had what he thought were useful suggestions (Brown 2006: 91–92).

[113]Yellow bile, one of the "humors" (secretions) which it was thought needed to be in a good balance for health.

February 1, Thursday. The correspondence being directed by way of California to Mexico City was dispatched by don Fernando Rivera at noon with six soldiers, giving His Excellency the viceroy notice of the occurrences here and the state of this presidio, by sending him the proceedings and statements.

[February] 2, Friday. The day broke clear and I was much improved; I said Mass and the blessing of candles took place, using the small amount of wax that existed there. And I shall note that the church was a very poor, old jacal of tule. It had previously served as a warehouse. I again observed the latitude of this presidio to see whether it would agree with the previous one that I made on January 12; and by the tables of Jorge, with no correction, I found it in latitude 32° 37½', four and a half minutes less than on January 12 and with correction in the same latitude 32° 44½'. And thus I say: at the presidio and harbor of San Diego, February 2 of the bissextile year 1776: meridian altitude of the sun's lower limb: 40° 14'.

By the sergeant's report, it seems that this presidio is nearly parallel with the mouth of the Colorado River, for he said that on the occasions when he has made excursions eastward toward the California range in search of gentiles or for other reasons, he has recognized that the river lay directly in front of his road, although he did not see it. However, he thought the Colorado River might be some fifty leagues distant from the presidio here[114] and not along a very bad route. In the account of the voyage that he made through the California Sea, from the cape and harbor of San Carlos located in 28° as far as the mouth of the Colorado River, as found in *Afanes apostólicos*[115] book 3, chapter 8, page 388, Father Fernando Consag says that the said mouth lies in latitude 33°. Don José Cañizares, a sailing master of these seas and a very skilled one, on a map he made of his voyage from the harbor of San Carlos to San Luis Gonzaga Bay, places the Colorado River mouth in a little under 33° latitude; from which I deduce that my own observation is in some agreement with Father Consag's and Señor Cañizares's map, which I have in my possession.[116]

[February] 3, Saturday. Three soldiers bringing mail arrived in the morning from San Gabriel with letters from Lieutenant Moraga for Commander Anza, advising him that the Fathers of that mission had discontinued food distribution

---

[114] It was at least seventy leagues, and extremely difficult ones as Font should have known from his own crossing of the Colorado Desert.

[115] *Apostólicos afanes de la compañía de Jesús, escritos por un Padre de la misma sagrada religión de su provincia de México* (Barcelona, 1754), a published official account of Jesuit missionary activities and explorations in northwest Mexico.

[116] This entire sentence is found only in the field text, along with a later marginal note explaining its non-appearance in the other texts: "I say that Cañizares made a map, etc., because that is what I was told; but later I learned that he made no such voyage nor such a map, and only copied the map found in the third volume of the *Historia de la California*." The map is found between pages 236 and 237 of Miguel Venegas (ed. Marcos Andrés Burriel), *Noticia de la California, y de su conquista temporal, y espiritual hasta el tiempo presente*, Madrid, 1757. In reality, the mouth of the Colorado is in approximately 32°, not 33°.

to the people of the expedition and were only giving out half-rations, which upset the troops. And, Mission San Gabriel did not have enough provisions for our people. Therefore, he should come to some decision concerning the matter. They also reported that an Indian belonging to the mission and three gentiles were held captive there because they had stolen and slaughtered two cows and two hogs belonging to the mission. So provisions were taken from the warehouse and preparations were made to transport them there by the pack train that had come with us that was not carrying supplies. And, our departure for Monterey was prepared.[117]

However, ever since the 1st, after the mail was dispatched, it had been decided that Commander Rivera would stay at San Diego and not leave there until he had the country secure and at peace, and consequently, when Commander Anza returned, he would turn over the expedition to Rivera at San Gabriel, where they agreed to meet at that time if it were not possible earlier.[118]

[February] 4, Sunday. I said Mass, and following it the expedition's long pack train set out for San Gabriel, laden with provisions—consisting of wormy maize—for the people staying at that mission. The decision was made for us to set out tomorrow for Monterey, although nothing was said to me nor was I given notice of this departure, which should have been today according to the inquiry I made on January 28 and the answer to it; for I was never able to learn this in advance. It was cloudy at daybreak and commenced raining at midday, although it did not continue long.

---

[117] Anza's entry for this date admits that even the full ration that had been issued at San Gabriel fell short of what the government had prescribed for the settlers.

[118] Retrospectively, the decisions taken by the two commanders up to February 1 were summarized in Anza's May 20, 1776, letter to Rivera (see note to January 22) as follows: ". . . We [Anza and Rivera] agreed that all of my expedition [was this meant to include Font?] would remain at San Diego and San Gabriel in order to continue in assisting you; that Lieutenant Moraga would go along with me on the San Francisco inspection; that in the interim, should you successfully have concluded matters concerning San Diego, you would go up along with my whole expedition until we met at San Luis [Obispo], for me to [be able to] open a route from there straight toward La Sonora. And if not, I would advise you of my return to San Gabriel, for [the two of] us to confer concerning what I had inspected, for the purpose of [my] carrying an account of everything to His Excellency, whom we would thus have kept informed up to this point." Anza says that he then went on to warn Rivera that the viceroy would find regrettable any report of a delay in occupying the wished-for harbor [of San Francisco].

Then, with this news (on February 3) of the expedition's problems in surviving at San Gabriel, it was agreed that Anza would take most of the personnel up to Monterey, and just as Anza was departing from San Diego, Rivera bestowed all of his own powers of command upon him for whatever purpose he might wish, powers which Anza states that he had used with the greatest gratitude. (See also the note to the January 22 entry.) Anza's journal entry indicates that his plan at this point (not recorded elsewhere) was to lead the colonists north past the numerous and potentially hostile population on the Santa Bárbara Channel and to leave them at the following missions where they could wait out the rains in safety and be well supplied, while he went on to see whether he might get past the rivers that he supposedly might not be able to ford in order to survey the harbor of San Francisco. The wording of the entry reflects a careful concern for balancing Anza's own concerns with Rivera's, noting, for the record, that both officers were equally unhappy that the situation had required upsetting their arrangements for pacifying San Diego, where none of the rebels had yet surrendered, and for fulfilling Anza's orders.

[February] 5, Monday. It rained a good deal during the night and was raining at daybreak although it did not continue. However, as the footing was poor and the weather threatening rain, we put off the march that had been ordered and remained here.

[February] 6, Tuesday. The animals were brought up for our journey—that is, for Captain Anza and myself, since Commander Rivera was staying at the presidio until he could leave it in order—but we put off the march and remained here because it was very cloudy at daybreak and then a very strong south wind came up, the one which causes rain and bad weather here. It lasted until noon when it began to rain. In the middle of the afternoon the rain stopped and the wind continued strong. At daybreak, I was ill in my mouth, which had been getting better the last few days. The lieutenant's wife[119] told me that my sickness was called fuego marcial[120] and that it was a debility that afflicts people at Loreto in California and from which she had suffered when she was there. She made a remedy for me which consisted of spreading verdigris ground to a powder over the flayed part, using a feather, both morning and afternoon. This caused me to drool a great deal and feel a bit better.

At night after dinner I saw a light in the little room where Señor Anza and I slept. I went to see who had lit it, since candles were in as short supply at the presidio as everything else was and we were careful not to light them unnecessarily. I found that the cook had lit it because he was waiting for Señor Anza to ask him whether he should pack up the cooking pot to march out the following day as he had ordered him to do; and since it was raining, he did not have it packed. I returned to the room where we all were, in which the three Fathers and Señor Rivera slept, and where we ate and passed most of the day since there were no other quarters in the presidio. I mentioned who had lit the candle and why, and with this opportunity I delivered my complaint to Señor Anza there in front of everyone. I told him that I found it difficult that he never told me about his decisions whereas he told them to the servants with whom he discussed these and other matters and sometimes very familiarly. However with me, he always employed great gravity and reserve. He answered, "What, then? Would Your Reverence like me to report my decisions to you? I have no such obligation." "I am aware that you have no such obligation," I said to him, "and I do not suggest as much, but I should think it to be normal for you to tell me, as a fellow traveler, what you decide, so that it should not take me by surprise, since I also must travel and therefore would be happy to know of it, not so as to intrude into your giving orders. For you well know that I have not intruded, until now, in delaying or in marching, since those are your decisions as I said to you the day we reached Santa Ana on October 6, which is when you asked for my opinion concerning whether we should stay at the pueblo or on the river, after you had ordered a halt at the river. I know you, and I am aware that you do not like to take advice from anyone. I also know that you are not about to do whatever I may ask of you, as I learned on December 1 when I requested that you move the camp to Palma's village and you would not do so. And so,

---

[119]María Antonia Victoria Carrillo, spouse of Lieutenant José Francisco Ortega and sister of the Carrillo brothers, Sergeant Mariano Carrillo and Corporal Guillermo Carrillo.

[120]This repeats what is said under January 17; see the note there.

since you do not share your thoughts with me so that I can give my views, and since neither am I inclined to do so, nor, as I recognize, would you receive them, it would at least be a good thing for you to tell me, in conversation, as a friend, what you decide, for my own guidance." To this, he told me that I was complaining without cause, since he did notify me of what he had decided. To which I replied, "It is true that you do inform me, but this is after the fact, when everyone already knows it or when I see it happening, as was the case with the mail you dispatched from the Puerto de San Carlos on December 25, and with the decision to come to San Diego, which you told me about on January 6 at nightfall when everyone already knew about it. "But Father," he said, "let me tell Your Reverence that my delaying here is because I saw that Your Reverence was ill, but in so far as it concerns me, I would already have gone." I answered that I thanked him for this favor although he had not indicated any such thing to me before this moment, but he should understand that I had no desire for him to delay because of me, because ever since before we departed from San Miguel, I had told him that I did not wish our marches to be delayed even for a day on my account. And so I concluded with: "If that's the only reason for delay, let us go right now or tomorrow even if it is raining."

I said that, because several times at San Miguel he had decided to start the march and it was thwarted through a number of excuses that were produced in order to cause the journey to be put off, according to his wife's wish and his own wishes to please her in this way. Eventually, during those days, I fell ill and Señor Anza decided to start the journey on September 28. He asked me whether I was fit to travel, because if not, he would put off the departure until I was well. I answered that he must not delay because of me; that I trusted in God that I would begin to improve while on the way. The lady wanted a little more delay and thought she would get it if I were sick, which is why she asked doña Catalina Ortiz, don Manuel Monteagudo's wife, in whose house I was a guest, to persuade me to express my displeasure in leaving until I was better.[121] To this suggestion, I answered that I in no way would go against what had been decided, and therefore, since Señor Anza had decided on the departure, it would not be thwarted on my account. Doña Catalina said to me: "But doña Ana Regina Serrano would be very much pleased if they delayed just one day longer. That would easily happen if only Your Paternity would say so, since you are ill." To which I answered: "I, too, would be pleased, not so much because of being ill but for other reasons. But since the decision has been made, I do not wish to say anything." Doña Catalina urged me on, saying, "But Father, clearly state Your Paternity's opinion." Supposing that we were having a personal conversation, I said to her, "Señora, my opinion is that since we are at the Presidio of San Miguel and have delayed here so many days for other reasons, we might delay for a day longer and thereafter set out from the presidio and begin our march on the Holy Prince's[122] day after the people had heard Mass. Perhaps we might have a sung Mass and perhaps I would be ready to say four words to the people, and"—as I had already suggested to Señor Anza—"I think that would be better. But if he has already decided otherwise and not heeded my suggestion, I have nothing more to say other than that I do not want it said that we are delaying because of me." This discussion came to an end and doña Catalina immediately went to the Anza house to narrate what I had said. Shortly afterward, Señor Anza came to see me and said, "So, Your Paternity has decided for us to go on the feast day of San Miguel?" I answered, "Sir, how could I have decided that? Doña Catalina asked me for my opinion, conversationally, and I told her what I thought, but without objecting to your decision." "So then, Father," he said,

---

[121]See the June entry 1, and note.

[122]That is, the feast day of the Archangel St. Michael (one of the three "patrons" Font named for the expedition).

"it will be done just as Your Paternity says." "You will do as you please," I answered, "but let us understand that this is no requirement of mine and I do not wish you to delay the march a single day on my account." "No, Father," he said, "but I, too, think that what Your Paternity says seems better." Señor Anza then went away and after a while doña Catalina came back and said to me, "Doña Ana and I thank you because they are delaying for a day longer." "But what part do I have in that?" I said. She answered, "A great deal, because don Juan did not wish to delay and now he will because Your Paternity wishes so." "Señora," I said, "I do not wish one thing or the other, but only what don Juan wishes." "But Father," she said, "the moment don Juan reached his house he said, 'Well there, I am staying a day longer because the Father has to be indulged, and he has decided it this way. What it is, is that he wants to promote his affairs before leaving'"—referring to the sung Mass and exhortatory talk that I had suggested and he had rejected.[123] I have retold all this at length in order to have it understood by what means these gentlemen are accustomed to cover their dealings with the Religious, by becoming their friends when it suits them and having no regard for them on other occasions when they do not have need of them.

As a result of my reply, everyone began trying to persuade me not to go to Monterey but to stay, as the weather was bad and, with my sickness, I would risk death. They had, however, different purposes in mind. The Fathers were moved with pity and felt sorry for me at seeing me sick. Señor Anza was not very pleased having me in his company. Señor Rivera, as I learned afterwards, did not want Señor Anza or me either, to go on to Monterey and San Francisco harbor for reasons which I shall state tomorrow. I resisted their suggestion, saying that I desired to fulfill the instructions I had been given, etc. Finally, after a number of disputes, I ended by saying, "Don't tire yourselves, I have no intention of staying. If Señor Anza leaves me here with no supplies, then I will have to stay because I possess no animals nor any way of getting them, but if Señor Anza will give me some supplies, I will go with the gentleman wherever he goes and accompany him in all of his hardships and travel, since I still can ride a horse. If I become disabled along the way and am unable to go any further, I am content with him leaving me at any point." The conference ended and we went to retire, with the harmony that we had been enjoying a bit disturbed because of the plain speaking, as usually occurs.

[February] 7, Wednesday. Setting out was not possible because it had been raining all night long with a very strong south wind, and the day went on in the same fashion until afternoon, when the rain stopped with the wind continuing.

We spoke about Monterey a great deal during all of these days, and concerning San Francisco harbor, even more, with Señor Rivera constantly saying that we might spare ourselves this journey as we would not attain the goal for which we came. It is requisite for this purpose to specify that it was on the strength of the survey of San Francisco harbor made by Captain don Pedro Fages in company with Father Fray Juan Crespí during March in the year 1772, and of the report made concerning it accompanied by a map upon which they drew a large river they claimed to have found and which they called San Francisco River, that an order came from Madrid for that harbor to be at once taken possession of and settled. And for this purpose, the viceroy ordered Commander Rivera to proceed to survey that harbor and seek out a good spot where a presidio and settlement might be founded to serve as a basis or a beginning for future plans. And this

---

[123]The suggestion was that Font wanted to use the more solemn Mass and sermon to promote his own stature among those going on the expedition. Anza, in a communication to the Mexico City government from Tubac, October 20, did blame Font's "serious illness," although not his expressed wishes, for a four day delay in setting out from Horcasitas. (Garate 1995: 174, 176; facsimile 318.)

was the purpose to which the present expedition, that of Commander Anza, for transporting families, was aimed, as appears by His Excellency's decree issued at Mexico City on November 28, 1774. By virtue of that order, Commander Rivera, accompanied by Father Fray Francisco Palóu, went to survey said harbor at the end of that same year 1774, but since it rained on them at the time, they spent some days delayed near *La Punta de las Almejas*[124] until one morning when Señor Rivera went all alone to survey the harbor, which was close by there. He got as far as the outer part of the mouth, where he set up a cross, as I shall recount at the proper place. And, because the entire stretch he traveled across is sand dunes and he did not see anything else, he then returned to Monterey and wrote to Mexico City informing His Excellency that there was no spot at the harbor or in that entire vicinity that was at all suitable for establishing a presidio or the two missions which even then had been funded and decided upon for that harbor.[125] It must be added that Señor Rivera immediately declared himself to be opposed to this new founding, and therefore his report stated that the matter was not feasible; besides which he was very reluctant to carry out the new orders he had. These orders were for the two of them as soon as Señor Anza had arrived. They were to proceed to explore the harbor and by mutual agreement choose the best site for the settlement and presidio, and the people belonging to this expedition were to proceed there immediately. For, in this matter of not regarding others' opinions, Señor Rivera surpasses Señor Anza. Rivera is so pleased with his own self and with the experience he possesses (as he himself puts it) that it does not suit him to ask anyone else's opinion on any matter. The San Diego uprising, then, arrived very conveniently for his intention, because he was able to cite it to show why it was not possible for him to proceed to the harbor of San Francisco (even granting that the harbor there would be good for what was planned) until he had left the harbor of San Diego secured and at peace.

Ever since the 1st, for this reason, it had been decided that even if we ourselves went to Monterey, he would not leave San Diego, and in that event he would receive the expedition—which Señor Anza was to deliver to him—on our return, at San Gabriel where they agreed they would meet at that time. Yet, still continuing to persuade us not to go there, and fearing perhaps that we would survey the harbor better than he had done and would therefore report the contrary of what he himself had done, he was accustomed to say to us, "What is the purpose of your wanting to go there and tire yourselves out, since I have already told you that I have thoroughly explored everything there and have reported to the viceroy that there is nothing there that is of any use for what is being planned?" At the time, I imagined that this argument was given straightforwardly and based upon fact and I did not understand his hidden intentions until I had learned a great many things at Mission San Carlos Borromeo[126] and had witnessed the encounters that I shall be telling about.

But even before coming to San Diego, I always had believed we would go there—to the extent that the day after arriving at San Gabriel, the purveyor came to me and said, "We're all right

---

[124]Mussel Point, so named in 1769, i.e. Point San Pedro. However, they were actually inland, at San Andreas Lake.

[125]In Captain Rivera's judgment, there was "no firewood or one stick to build with." Font points out here, and also later on, that the captain had seen at close hand only the sand dune country on the west side of the tip of the peninsula. His journal of the excursion, however, shows that he also viewed the larger area, from the tops of Mount Davidson and San Bruno Mountain. (For a translation, see Rivera 1962. The missionary Palóu's journal of the same trip received two totally independent translations in Bolton 1927 3: 249–307 and Bolton 1930 2: 393–456. Cf. also Stanger and Brown 1969: 132–146; Brown 2005: 50–55.)

[126]This must refer to his receiving Junípero Serra's views on Rivera and on other matters. Below, Font will briefly describe the interview.

now, Father, now that we've found Commander Rivera here, since that lets us off from having to travel further." "But why?" I said, and he answered, "Because once the expedition's people are handed over here to Señor Rivera, there is nothing more to be done." "Well, but why are we to be let off from going to Monterey," said I, "if doing so is Señor Anza's duty?" "And what need is there for that," he replied, "with Señor Rivera being here? Isn't it best for us to deliver the people to him and return and thereby be back in Sonora a month from now?" I answered, "No, sir, it is best to fulfill the charge and duty that we have, which is to go to Monterey and proceed from there to survey the harbor of San Francisco." Although Señor Anza was at first a bit inclined not to proceed onward, he nonetheless always demonstrated a desire to continue the journey, to which my own opinion perhaps contributed. Although he did not ask for my thoughts, I believe he was aware of them, as the purveyor certainly must have told him of the reply I had given him when he came to seek out my intentions.

During these days, therefore, all talk revolved around this topic, with Señor Rivera being questioned as to what he had learned and was saying he had seen. There was much harping about the continuation of the journey, the result being that Señor Rivera came to accept that Señor Anza should go on with the people to Monterey[127] leaving ten soldiers and their families for him at San Gabriel. I learned of this yesterday. And, I also learned that we would not be traveling light, as Señor Anza told me we would do on January 28.

A still greater disagreement arose concerning the great river of San Francisco because Señor Rivera told us that there was no such river. This was contrary to the report that seemed already so deeply rooted and was certified to by the soldiers there. Yet it was the truth, as we saw afterward and I shall recount. This, he said, had been told to him by don José de Cañizares, sailing master of the frigate *San Carlos*, the ship that sailed into the harbor late last year.[128] And he recounted this report for us several times, in the following fashion. The ship *San Carlos* came to the mouth of San Francisco harbor and upon anchoring it sent its sailing master Cañizares with the launch to go inside and survey all of it. He came back after a week, and when asked by his captain[129] about the great river, he answered that he had not found any such river. He[130] then asked him whether he had reached the farthest end of the harbor, and on hearing the response that he had not, told him, "Then take provisions for two weeks and survey the whole thing again leaving nothing out." That Cañizares went away again, and during that time the ship raised anchor one night in order to moor itself more securely because it was drifting landward. The currents began carrying it into the harbor without their realizing it and by the time they noticed it, they were inside and they anchored near *La Isla del Angel*. This is where Cañizares found the ship when he returned; and that he said he had followed the entire shore of the harbor and had found no great river anywhere along it and had seen only a number of streams and small rivers.[131] It is to be

---

[127] In a letter to the viceroy, Rivera later denied that he had been properly informed by Anza about the decision to move the colonists to Monterey. See the note under May 3.

[128] See the introduction.

[129] Frigate-Lieutenant Juan Manuel de Ayala.

[130] Ayala.

[131] This account is not in complete accord with the record of the harbor survey according to the log of the *San Carlos*. Cañizares's first small boat exploration, lasting a week just as Font says it did, was sent out only after the ship had anchored behind Angel Island (La Isla del Angel), and the incident of the anchor dragging had occurred a week before that, near Sausalito. The second exploration to the head of the bay, lasting ten days (with two weeks' supplies), produced an apparently ambiguous result: a chart showing four waterways running into the head of Suisun and Honker Bays, and a written report that seems to attempt to single out the two separate mouths of the Sacramento ("formed from quite small branches") and the San Joaquín—both of them stated to be closed off by shallow bars. (Stanger and Brown 1969: 150–52, 158; Galvin 1969: 82–85, 97.)

noted that perhaps in order to avoid getting on the bad side of the Fathers, who were committed to their view and through Father Fray Juan Crespí's report and journal had provided the news concerning the river and produced the map, Cañizares told them while at Monterey and Carmel that there was such a river, that he had seen it and had been into it and had taken on water inside it. Such are we men, that often the truth gets hidden just in order to accommodate others!

Hereupon there arose a long disputation as to whether or not there was such a river, to which I contributed my opinion as well, although they did not give me much opportunity to do so. At one point I said, "Sir, it may be that river is very large in flood season because it comes from snowy mountains and that Señor Fages saw it during that period, and that it is an everyday sort of river at its own natural flow, and that is how Señor Cañizares saw it." Señor Anza answered me very sharply. He was still annoyed by what happened between us the night before, "Father, I don't know about that." "I can see that you don't know," said I, "but I am saying it as a reflection upon these two contradictory accounts." Señor Anza said to Señor Rivera, "Please draw the harbor for me on paper." During previous days, I had copied a drawing of the Bodega harbor that the sailing master of the schooner[132] had given to Señor Rivera after they discovered that harbor, and also a drawing of the San Francisco harbor made by the same sailing master without his having seen it. It was very poorly drawn, to which I had added whatever I thought good for my own guidance, according to what Señor Rivera had described for us. Señor Anza knew this, as he saw me doing it. Then Señor Rivera began drawing lines, but since his hand and arm tremble a great deal he failed in his purpose. Although not asked, at that point I took out my own drawing and completed informing myself as well as I could concerning the subject.[133] It had now been decided that we were to go visit the harbor, and Señor Anza said, in order to finish off the problem of the river, "Is there not some soldier here who went with Captain Fages?" Señor Rivera answered, "There is. The sergeant is here.[134] If you wish to satisfy yourself we shall call him." "Call him then," said Señor Anza. Thereupon Señor Rivera called for the sergeant and as soon as he had come, he[135] said, already vexed, "Here you have the sergeant; talk to him until he tires." The sergeant was asked whether he had seen the great river, and he answered that he had seen it, had stood on its bank, and drunk of its water. He finished by saying he would swear to it.[136] (This was a mistake on the part of the soldiers, who came upon fresh water in the tule swamps, as I shall tell in the proper place; they characterized it as a river without considering whether it was flowing, or other matters.) Señor Anza finally concluded this topic by saying, "Friend, I am going there, and if we come upon the river I shall take a vial full of water out of it and seal it very thoroughly. And I ask Father Fray Pedro, right now, to be prepared to give me a certification to the effect that the water in that vial comes from the great river of San Francisco so that I may present it to the viceroy. And if there is no such river, then we will have confirmed the report by Cañizares."

Señor Anza still insisted upon the people being taken to the harbor of San Francisco, and said that the viceroy had laid this charge heavily upon him. The viceroy had told him that if there were no suitable spot next to the harbor mouth, the settlement should be placed wherever seemed best to him even if it were some leagues away from the harbor, as long as it could be used to assure that

---

[132] The *Sonora*, in which Juan Francisco de la Bodega y Cuadra had just performed his extraordinary reconnaissance of the Northwest Coast all the way to Alaska, anchoring at Bodega Bay on the return. See the depiction of the vessel on Font's maps, at that place.
[133] Presumably by asking Rivera for details.
[134] Mariano Carrillo.
[135] Rivera.
[136] "And finished . . . swear to it" is added between lines.

the harbor there was in Spain's possession. Señor Rivera answered that that was a very different matter, since he had been instructed that the settlement should be next to the harbor. Therefore, he had reported that this was not possible since there was no good place there. However, he did not deny that spots could be found at a distance from it, and, the case being such, his heart felt much more at ease. At last, seeing that Señor Anza was determined to and that he could no longer hinder our going to survey the harbor there, he ended by saying, "So, friend, go, do go and survey it to your heart's content, and decide what seems best to you. When you come back you will inform me of what you have seen, and I will agree right now with whatever you decide." Señor Anza was in Señor Rivera's disfavor from this night onward since he[137] was so opposed to the new foundation there. This decision on the part of Señor Anza, along with whom I earned my own share of Señor Rivera's hatred, was the source of the incidents and quarrels that occurred afterwards and that I shall tell of further on.

[February] 8, Thursday. The night continued with the wind very strong, and veering around until it turned into a northwesterly. So the daybreak was a bit clear, with no rain. However, as the weather was not settled, it was decided we should remain here today,

and this delay was blamed on me, in the following way. The animals were brought up. As we were beginning to saddle up, the weather was still very unsettled, with a very troublesome cold wind, so the two commanders asked me for my opinion regarding whether to march or to delay. They told me that I must decide. I spent a little while making excuses but finally said that my opinion was that we should go. But if the weather along the way would prevent our traveling, as they were saying it would, we would gain nothing by setting out. Thereupon Señor Rivera, who leaned toward having us stay (and Señor Anza did not contradict him), said, "The Father has spoken; well there, his view is for remaining here today"; whereupon they ordered the animals to be led back and we delayed until the next day.

[February] 9, Friday. The river here at the presidio ran quite high with the recent rains; it comes from about northeastward, from the main range, and on passing by the small hill with the presidio it goes southward and empties into the harbor.[138] We took our farewell of the three Fathers and of Commander Rivera, who remained (to our mutual regret) at the presidio.[139] Commander Anza and I turned back toward San Gabriel in order to transport the families to Monterey.

I attempted, as well as I could, to comfort Lieutenant Ortega, who was suffering considerably from the slights put upon him, with little or no cause, by Señor Rivera, who was remaining, as I said above, determined not to move from here until he had finished capturing the culprits and had left the presidio secure. However, at the time, still unaware of his intention, I urged him a good deal to come with us.

Then Commander Anza and the rest of us set out from the Presidio San Diego at a quarter to nine in the morning, traveling a northwestward course

---

[137]Rivera.

[138]In the field text, the river "comes from the mountains in an east-northeastward direction."

[139]So in the field text. In the final text, reflecting Font's change of opinion about Rivera, just: "I took my farewell of the three Fathers and the gentlemen" (i.e., the officers).

varying north-northeastward as far as San Dieguillo, where the river was running high. At a quarter past five in the afternoon we came to the spot called *El Agua Hedionda*[140] (which is a stream with little water at this season), along the way leaving the same spots that are recorded above. And we had traveled about fourteen leagues.

Along the way, I said to Señor Anza, "Sir, how far are we going tonight?" He answered, "To Los Batequitos, or however far we get." "Fine," I said, "but why don't we eat a little something? Once you are on horseback you don't think of eating anything, or of our doing so either." He said to me, "Inasmuch as we snacked this morning, I had enough so that I'm not hungry." (Our snack had been a couple of eggs.) I answered, "But what are a couple of eggs? I'm forced to admit I'm a man and I need to eat when I'm hungry. Isn't there anything at hand?" (At the presidio they had packed up some provisions for us for the road.) A servant replied, "There is bread and cheese here." "Bring it on, then," I said, "that's just fine." I took and ate it, and so did Señor Anza, who had just told me that he had had enough but right afterward was hungry enough to eat some cheese! He was somewhat displeased with what I had said, but did mend his ways. From that point on he always ordered a servant to carry boiled meat, bread, and cheese to have at hand, and after midday he would ask me if I wanted anything to eat, and we would eat a mouthful even while riding, which had not been the case earlier.

[February] 10, Saturday. We set out from El Agua Hedionda at seven o'clock in the morning, and by following a northwestward course, with a number of veerings to westward and otherwise, because of hill turnings, at a quarter to six in the afternoon we halted at a pool of water we found in a small stream, one league before reaching La Quema (from where the pack train that left San Diego last Sunday set out today; they left firewood and fire here for us)—having traveled eighteen leagues. All the streams were now carrying water, and the river at the place called San Juan Capistrano was running very high; we supposed that its waters come from the slopes of the El Príncipe Valley and the Puerto de San Carlos over the mountains, which lies directly eastward opposite that spot, and, from the hilltops, is seen not very far off. There are so many hills to be gotten past during this route that yesterday I started taking the trouble of counting them. We went over twenty-one hills yesterday not counting the smallest ones; today we went over fifty-four of them.

[February] 11, Sunday. We set out at seven o'clock in the morning from the small stream, and by traveling northwestward with a number of turns, we went by the same places as on coming and reached the Santa Ana River, which we easily forded as it was not running high, at a quarter past four in the afternoon. We camped at its edge after fording it, having traveled sixteen leagues. Here we found the pack train that set out from the presidio on the 4th. It had been held back by the rains and reached this river just a little before we did. I counted

---

[140] Smelly Water.

twenty-seven hills that we went over today. Among the endless variety of flowers, such as tulips and others of all sorts of colors and very lovely, with which the fields, heights, and valleys of this country are just now beginning to clothe themselves, I saw a number that were like those in Spain. Among the flowers were some very pretty, tiny ones with five petals that have the shape of a face, similar to flowers called *pensamientos*[141] that I saw in some gardens in Catalonia. The only difference is that the ones in Catalonia are yellow with a bit of purple on the tips of the petals, whereas these are yellow all over, and they have no smell.

[February] 12, Monday. We set out from the Santa Ana River at seven o'clock in the morning, and by traveling a northwestward course with the usual veerings west-northwestward, and so forth, at a half past one in the afternoon we came to Mission San Gabriel, having traveled twelve leagues. The mule train came in before sundown. We went over twenty-three hills today, making one hundred twenty-five together with the rest.

We had the surprise at this mission of finding that a soldier, from among the ones belonging here[142] and who had been one of the mission guard, had deserted last night, along with four others—two lads and two muleteers from the expedition, with thirty animals belonging both to the mission and to some individuals[143] and with other items stolen by them from the camp.[144] Lieutenant Moraga (of the expedition) set out after them with nine soldiers right away in the middle of the morning—news which Señor Anza and I regretted very much, as we had come here to pursue our journey to Monterey immediately. This occurrence delayed us until the lieutenant's return,

---

[141] Pansies. Font cites the Castilian form instead of the Catalan, *pensaments*.

[142] Belonging to the Alta California garrisons, not to the Anza expedition. In the final text, "of Monterey," meaning the same thing (all of the new settlements).

[143] According to Anza, the expedition personnel involved were three muleteers and an employee of Sergeant Grijalva's, and about twenty-five of the best mounts were taken, mostly the mission's, but including two expedition mules.

[144] Anza's account in his journal is as follows: A muleteer returning from the soldiers' mess to take his midnight lie-down noticed that some packs had been untied, and reported a probable robbery to Moraga and Vidal, who immediately asked the *cargador* (baggage-train handler) for the name of the person to whom they had been assigned. That man proved to be missing, along with an amount of beads, tobacco, and chocolate suggestive of a desertion. An inspection of the troops revealed who else was gone. They had taken with them two muskets, a saddle, and possibly other small items. In the morning, the loss of mounts that had been turned loose in nearby fields was noted. Other ones were brought in from the expedition's herds further off, and Moraga and *ten* soldiers set out for a chase of two days, which was all that could be expected of the horses that they had chosen, even though they were the best. As was learned afterward, the hunt turned into a much longer one than that.

Anza attempted to find out how far the deserters' conspiracy extended, but decided that none of the settlers were involved. The general belief was that the soldier had persuaded the others; it was said that he had tried to desert from Baja California earlier, by embarking in a tule float, in which he was blown about by the wind during one entire day and on the next was blown back by it to the shore from which he had tried to leave.

all the more so in view of the fact that the mission did not possess enough provisions to support the people there any longer, and Father Paterna was refusing to provide rations or anything else. Added to this was the fact that we found the expedition's soldiers very discontented. They said that Señor Anza had brought them under false pretences, and they were refusing to go onward. They said that they had been promised three hundred sixty-five pesos worth of pay and rations. But now they were here without rations, perishing from hunger, with no cows or any of the other things they had been offered when they enlisted. In addition, their pay was given in poor-quality goods and there was a surcharge of one hundred fifty percent. Señor Anza now found himself in hard straits because of the lack of provisions, since he had scarcely brought the amount that he required for transporting all those people. And here was the proof of what I had said to him on the night of December 1, in that talk we had when he showed such resentment and told me that it was only out of respect for the Fathers that he was remaining for one day to build their jacal for them, since he already had very limited provisions for remaining any longer. To which I answered that this was the purpose for which they had entrusted him with this commission, so that he with his experience would provide what was required and foresee what might happen; that he must realize that, in this expedition, he was like a ship's captain, whose duty is, if he has to make a voyage of four months, to lay up provisions for six, and that that was what he should have done, and could have done since he would be granted whatever amount was required from the king's treasury.

[February] 13, Tuesday. It was overcast with fog at daybreak and continued so all day, which was rather a gloomy one, what with this and with the affair of the robbers yesterday. In view of the unexpected event, it was decided to wait here for some days until the lieutenant returned. In the afternoon, I went with Father Paterna and don Juan to see the mission's very good-sized, new wheat field. I was pleased with the sight of how the recently converted Indians belonging to this mission were applying themselves to plowing and work. The Fathers' labors seem to be succeeding with them. Through their own example, the Fathers persist in teaching them to toil—and lo, Father Paterna with his hand upon the plow!

Shortly before noon it cleared up a little and I decided to observe, but was unable to make the observation precisely. I shall record it notwithstanding, as I do not know whether I shall be able to make another. Using the table of Jorge Juan, then, I found this mission of San Gabriel in 33° 38' latitude, and thus I say: here at Mission San Gabriel on February 13, meridian altitude of the sun's lower limb: 42° 40'. Father Díaz observed at this mission and found it in 33° 46½' latitude, making a few minutes' worth of difference from the observation made by Constanzó near this spot when he was with the first expedition.[145] And so, although I was unable to make a precise observation because the point of noon had gone past because of cloudiness, I judge nevertheless that the discrepancy may be of only a very few minutes.

---

[145] The observations on August 1, 1769, yielded latitude 34° 10', according to Juan Crespí (Brown 2001: 72 and 334–35). Font's later observations (February 17 and 19) of 34° 5½' were entirely accurate.

[February] 14, Wednesday. The weather continued misty, cloudy, and with a very wet fog until afternoon, when it cleared a little and the sun came out. Father Paterna gathered all his neophytes belonging to the mission and asked me to play my musical instrument a little for them, by which they were very much pleased. At nightfall two of the soldiers who had gone with the lieutenant came back. He sent them back because their horses gave out. They said that the lieutenant was on his way, determined to catch the deserters whose fresh track they had been pursuing during the whole way.

[February] 15, Thursday. It was raining at daybreak, continued so until noon, and then cleared a bit in the afternoon. Nothing special occurred.

[February] 16, Friday. Continued rain and fog, creating quite a depressing day. We continued without any special occurrence, other than the fact that don Juan has been indisposed in the stomach and has been throwing up his food every afternoon ever since we reached the mission. God grant that it becomes nothing greater.

[February] 17, Saturday. The day broke clear and fine and I again observed the latitude of this mission and achieved better success than on the 13th; I found it, using the tables of Jorge Juan with no correction, in 33° 58½', and with correction in 34° 5½'. And thus I say: at Mission San Gabriel, February 17, 1776: meridian altitude of the sun's lower limb: 43° 42'.

[February] 18, Sunday.
I said Mass, and during it following the gospel I preached four words to the expedition's people exhorting them to endurance and resignation in hardship, using the example of Jesus Christ, who gladly accepted the Passion that he knew he was to undergo in Jerusalem, etc., since after suffering and death there follows revival and rest, etc.

The weather continued fine and there was no occurrence of note other than that don Juan was worse today with his indisposition. His sickness was caused by the food provided at the mission. The cooks were boys who were so dirty that they did everything in an unclean and very uncouth manner. They themselves were rude and not at all particular about anything. Added to this was the fact that we ate without tablecloths, on top of an old door that served as a table. The door was so greasy and dirty that the filth on it could be scraped off with a knife. However, I think that the vomiting came mainly from depression caused by the shocking occurrence with the deserters and from seeing the expedition's people upset about the hundred fifty percent charge upon the goods they were paid (something Señor Anza had not known about when he left Mexico City, or so he said, since he was of the understanding they would be paid in cash). He was also depressed because the people were asking him for food because they were suffering from hunger and were selling everything they had to the mission in order to help themselves. He had nowhere to go to obtain provisions to give them, since everything that could be gotten from the San Diego warehouse had already been brought by the pack train. For all of these reasons, don Juan was very gloomy and melancholy during these days, and even I attempted to improve his mood by seeking conversation with him and also by entertaining him for a while with the instrument.

[February] 19, Monday. I said Mass. The weather continued very fine and don Juan was better. For my own satisfaction I again observed, and the observation yielded the exact same latitude as on the 17th, 34° 5½' with correction, and with no correction, with half a minute's difference, 33° 59'. And thus I say: at Mission San Gabriel, February 19, 1776: meridian altitude of the sun's lower limb: 44° 24'. It was decided not to wait for Lieutenant Moraga beyond tomorrow morning. If he did not come by that time we would continue on our way on Ash Wednesday, in view of the fact that days were passing by and the conclusion of the expedition's journey to Monterey was being delayed.

I had a large part in this decision, since I went to visit Señor Anza this morning following Mass. Finding him a bit better, which I was very happy to see, I approached him and said that if delaying here was going to cost him some of his health, it would be better for us to go onward. His health must come first and if he fell ill, what were we to do, because then everything would be hindered and lost. The best thing was to set forth, since once out on the road the people would be content and quiet, whereas if we stayed here longer, the people would become more dissatisfied each day and the few provisions that existed would eventually be used up. Then we would be unable to go on to Monterey. Hereupon we agreed that whether or not the lieutenant came back, we would go on Ash Wednesday after Mass. And from this day onward, Señor Anza behaved in a more friendly way with me than he had up until this time.

[February] 20, Tuesday. I said Mass. The weather was very clear. The lieutenant did not come, so things began to be put in order for continuing the journey toward Monterey. Ten soldiers and two settlers were left here at Mission San Gabriel along with the families belonging to them, as Señor Rivera had ordered at San Diego. They were assigned today, and we were to continue the journey tomorrow with the rest of them.

CHAPTER 4

Northward to Monterey

[February] 21, Wednesday. I did the blessing of ashes; I said Mass, and during it, four words to the people who were remaining and to the rest of them who were going (who wept a bit since they regretted this separation), by using the gospel of the day to reaffirm what I had been saying to them in the talks I gave them. That is, that they had come in order to suffer and give an example of Christianity to the gentiles, etc., the whole of it amounting to exhorting both groups to repent for their faults and patience in hardship, etc., etc. We set out from Mission San Gabriel at a half past eleven in the morning and halted at a half past four in the afternoon at the spot called *El Portezuelo*[1] having traveled for five leagues following a west-northwestward course with some veering to one side and the other. At two leagues we crossed the Porciúncula River[2] which carries a good amount of water and runs toward the San Pedro bight, and spreads out and loses itself upon the plains shortly before reaching the sea. The land was very green and flowery and the route had a few hills and a great deal of miry grounds created by the rains. This is why the pack train fell far in the rear. At the stopping place there is year-round water, although little of it, and sufficient firewood. As one goes along, far off on the left hand, upon the sea, lies the hill range forming the San Pedro bight, and on the right rises the snowy range, with another steep, steep range lying in front of it.

[February] 22, Thursday. We set out from El Portezuelo at eight o'clock in the morning and halted at a quarter past three in the afternoon at the spot called *El Agua Escondida*[3] which lies before the spot called *El Triunfo*[4] where we hoped to arrive today. We traveled nine leagues on a westward course with some veering.

---

[1] The Pass.
[2] Named by the first expedition (Portolá Expedition) on August 2, 1769, because of the religious feast day honoring St. Francis's gaining a "small parcel" of ground (*porziuncula* in Italian) on which to build his first church.
[3] Hidden Water.
[4] The Triumph.

Shortly after setting out from the stopping place, we came into a very spacious valley called *Santa Isabel*, at the middle of which and at a little over three leagues is the place called *Los Nogales*[5] which is a small spring of water like a little lake, issuing in the midst of the plain, near which there are small walnut trees. And at about seven leagues we came to the foot of the mountains, which together with the range which we crossed through the gap yesterday, and today have been leaving upon our left, and with the other range running in front of the snowy range of mountains, which we had been having on our right, make this valley and it ends here. We went into a hollow which has a very small amount of water and then spent about two leagues going over grades as far as the stopping place, which is also a hollow with little water and a good many live oaks. It is formed by a number of hills belonging to a mountain spur that departs from the main range and extends toward the sea. Because of the windings about, our course turned as far as southwestward. Along the way we saw gentiles, although just a few of them and they were naked and entirely weaponless. Even so, they refused to approach us.

[February] 23, Friday. I said Mass. We set out from El Agua Escondida at eight o'clock in the morning, and by traveling a westward course with a good amount of veering to southward and as far around as north-northwestward we reached the Santa Clara River after nightfall, later than a quarter past six, having traveled fourteen leagues. At the start the way consisted of a good many hills and grades; there then followed a level route for some leagues, ending with a very steep grade, the big grade from which the sea and the first islands of the Santa Bárbara Channel can be seen. On going down it one finishes crossing the mountains I spoke of yesterday that depart from the main range and end on the sea, and enters upon a plain extending for five leagues as far as the river and beyond.

The mountains hold a great many white oaks, live oaks and other trees, and also some watering places, such as the ones at El Triunfo and at Los Conejos, and we saw four small-sized villages in the range. At a little over a league on the way is the place of El Triunfo and an Indian village, and afterward we came upon three other villages at intervals. Each of them has the qualities for a stopping place, with water, grass, and a great deal of firewood from live oak and white oak trees with large acorns. At a little over eight leagues, we came to the steep grade. At its foot there is another village that has a spring; and with a bit over five leagues more, we came to the river. The stopping place is a bit scant

---

[5]The Walnuts. It seems quite possible that this is an error for the name El Encino (live oak), attached to the famous spring ever since 1769. "Santa Isabel" is also probably an error, since the San Fernando Valley had been named Santa Catalina by the first expedition in 1769.

in firewood and the river very miry and hard to ford when it rises a little, but it was now low. Close to it was a village of some size.[6] The Indians there had fish because the sea is close by here. At the river there were a great many geese, ducks, cranes, and other sea fowl. Upon the plain before reaching the river, we saw an exceedingly big herd of antelope close by, who fled like the wind as soon as they sighted us and seemed like a cloud moving over the ground as they vanished from our sight. We saw a number of Indians in the course of the day, all unarmed and naked, but the Indian women observed great caution and hardly a one came forth from their jacales, because the soldiers stationed hereabouts[7] are unmarried and have made them wary due to a number of stupid acts that their unbridled passions caused them to commit with them.

And I noted the same caution at all of the villages along the channel. Close to a small village at the foot of the big grade there is a spring of water like a well, and twelve paces away from it is a sizeable spring of tar that issues there upon the spot. I learned afterward that there is another, larger one near Mission San Gabriel.

At sundown a very thick fog arose off the sea and hid the entire horizon from us, so that the day ended very overcast and the night was a very dark one; up until here, we had had clear weather.

This matter of the fog is a very common and constant one on the seas and coast there, but not harmful.

[February] 24, Saturday. At daybreak it was very cloudy, dim, and damp with fog, and stayed that way all day long although the fog lifted. We set out from the Santa Clara River at a half past nine in the morning[8] and by traveling a westward course, at a half past three in the afternoon we halted on a small height at the edge of the sea, close to the village of the spot called La Rinconada, having traveled seven leagues. At three leagues, all of which is a level way, we came to the edge of the sea and the river and place called *La Asumpta* or *Asunción*,[9] where there is the first village of Indians belonging to the channel, which begins here (unless one counts the one at the Santa Clara River as being first). It is called *La Carpintería* village, because they saw launches being built at it, on the first occasion.[10] Two leagues farther on there is another village which is a place where hospitality is extended to mountain Indians coming down to the sea when both of them are at peace,[11] the *Los Pitos* village,

---

[6] In the field text, "on its bank we found a large Indian village."
[7] In the final text, "of Monterey." Again, meaning the original California troops.
[8] In the field text, "at nine o'clock"; in the short text, "at a quarter past eight" [*sic*].
[9] The two terms (Latin and Spanish) are roughly equivalent, referring to the Assumption of the Virgin.
[10] During the first expedition, 1769. But the name was actually given then to the place that is still called Carpintería, further west along the Channel.
[11] That is, when mountain natives and shore dwellers are at peace with each other. This description was later overwritten in the field text by the following account (unfavorable to Rivera) of the first expedition's experience. Only that passage is in the final text.

FIGURE 16. The Canaleño town at Santa Bárbara, 1792, detail. By John Sykes. Font's La Laguna village, vastly reduced in size and population since 1776. *Courtesy of the Hydrographic Office and National Archive, United Kingdom, London. Reproduced with the permission of the Hydrographer of the Royal Navy.*

so called after the pipe the men of Commander Portolá's first expedition heard being played in it all night long; which is why Señor Rivera, who led the vanguard at that time, kept the people under arms all night long, fearful of some ruse on the part of the Indians, only to see at daybreak that it was a very small-sized village of four little jacales, very wretched, and without any people.[12]

This whole way as far as the stopping place lies along the seashore and almost treads on the waves, which makes it a very pleasant route. It would have been more so had the day been a clear and fine one and not as murky with fog as it was. The expedition's people, who had never seen the sea, were in awe of it.

The Santa Bárbara Channel, which is a very long one, is so named because out at sea at a distance of some six or eight leagues there are a number of islands that, with the mainland, make a channel. And I would say that another reason for calling it a channel is that all along it the way goes channeled between sea and land, along by the shore, since the land ends here in mountains that are very

---

[12]Engineer Costansó in 1769 spoke of "highly discordant shawms or pipes" (Boneu 1983: 186). But as usual, Font seems somewhat unfair to Rivera, since the size of the village ("eight or ten houses") had been obvious from the start (Brown 2001: 400) and on other occasions the captain felt he had some special reason to be suspicious of native intentions when pipes were being played.

steep and as it were chopped off in the midst, so that almost it is not feasible to go over them, since they are so lofty and steep,

although not rocky but having soil well covered in grass and green. In places the only way through is along the shore, and in other spots, although there is a route that they call "along the heights," it is one going along the abrupt edge of the hills, with great plunges down to the sea visible below.

The Indians of the channel belong to the Cuabajay tribe, and they and the Beñemés trade with the Jamajabs and others on the Colorado River, using their beads or bead strings of little flat, round, small shells. They have great cords of these bead strings hanging around their necks and on their heads. Their clothing is, in the men, complete nudity and it is only for adornment's sake that they usually wear a little rope or other trifle around their waist which does not cover anything. Around their heads, using their hair, they tie a little lead-rope into which they drive some sort of small stick or feather. This is like what I related concerning the Gila people on November 7. However, the main item around their head is a knife, which is a thin stick some two fingers broad and about a tercia long.[13] Using tar, they fasten a flint that is somewhat long and sharpened so it can cut on both sides. It is pointed down to the end of it. Or else they use the blade of a knife or some other similar piece of iron if they can acquire any. They all place this knife upon their head and tie it crosswise using their hair. They are also accustomed to carrying a sweat-scraper, which is a filed-down piece of bone or similar substance, of some size, with which they scrape their body when in a sweat and get rid of it, and they say it is a very good thing because in this way they get rid of tiredness. Some of them have the cartilage of their nose pierced. All of them have pierced ears with two large holes in them, thrust into which they wear little tubes that look like two horns, thick as the little finger on one's hand and over half a cuarta long.[14] They are accustomed to carrying powder of their wild tobacco or some other little thing inside these tubes. Their speech is totally different from that of the mountain Indians and others behind us. They call the chief whom they acknowledge in the villages, *temí*[15] just as the Jenigüechis and Benyemé call him *tomiár*. The women cover themselves with deerskins around the waist and an occasional otter pelt blanket on their backs. I saw few of them, however, because as soon as they saw us they quickly shut themselves up inside their jacales, particularly the young ones, while the men stayed outside, keeping their doors shut and taking care that no one went inside.[16]

Once I approached a jacal that I saw standing open to examine its construction, which is the best kind among the jacales that I saw anywhere on the journey. Its shape is round, quite roomy, large, and tall, like a half orange, with doors and partitions inside, and it has an opening in the middle of the top to let in light, serving as a chimney to let out the smoke from the fire they make in the middle of the jacal. In some, there are two or three holes like peepholes, at the sides. In all of them, the framework is of bent poles, quite solid, and the walls are made of very closely interwoven grass. There is a mat at the doors which is drawn across within what is like an inner portal, and another one on the outside that they usually bar with a whale bone or some sort of pole. I went to the door, then, and although I made no request to go inside, since I was aware

---

[13] 11 inches.

[14] 4⅛ inches.

[15] Members of the first expedition (1769) recorded the terms *temi* (for the chief of El Cojo) and *pirotomi*, translated as "village chief," which apparently is the literal meaning of its elements. However, in later years it was admitted that the Spanish never had come to understand the exact organization of Canaleño (Chumash) society, with multiple "chiefs" in every village and district.

[16] The degree of trust had indeed changed drastically since 1769; cf. Brown 2001: 788.

of their reluctance, before two minutes had passed they shut the door on the inside against me and I withdrew disappointed. What caused these reactions are the seizures and acts of violence committed by the soldiers during their journeys when they have traveled along the channel, particularly at the beginning. One, who was immoderate even among them, was a certain Camacho, whose reputation became so widespread among the Indians that they call every soldier Camacho. We had nothing but questions from them asking about Camacho: Where was Camacho? Was Camacho coming?[17]

I saw a few of the men wearing a little cape like a doublet. It was made of bearskin, reaching to the waist. I understood by that emblem that these were owners or masters of the launches.

These Indians are great fishermen and very clever.[18] They make baskets of various shapes, and other things that are very well carved, such as wooden bowls and boxes and other pieces that are made of stone. And above all, they build launches, very elaborate ones, in which they go to sea. They are made of a number of boards which they carve without using any more tools than their shells and flints. They close the joins by sewing them together with some very strong threads that they possess, and tamp the joints with tar so that they become very strong and secure. Some of them are decorated with little shells. And all of them are painted red with ochre. The shape is like that of a small open boat, narrow at the ends and wide in the middle, without a frame and ending with the two points a bit raised and bowed upwards, the two sides not being closed together but left open at the end in the shape of a **V**. Raised somewhat in the middle is a board which is laid across from side to side. It serves as a little bench and preserves the convexity of the hull. Each of the launches consists of some twenty boards, long and narrow. I measured one and found it was thirty-six cuartas long and a bit over three cuartas high.[19] Normally, so far as I could see, no more than two Indians ride in each launch when they go to sea or go fishing, with one of them at each end. They carry poles about two varas long[20] that end in paddles. These are the oars with which they paddle, alternately thrusting the ends of the pole into the water first on one side of the launch then on the other. In this way they steer the launch wherever they wish and head out upon those high seas with speed and great audacity. I counted nine launches here at this spot of La Rinconada and one was being repaired, and determined in my mind that, given some instruction, these Indians would become great seamen.

All of the settlements or villages on the channel have a place for playing sports in common, a quite smooth, leveled piece of ground with low walls surrounding it, like a bowling ground, and they play upon it by chasing a half-round small

---

[17] See the introduction.
[18] The sailing master Miguel del Pino, after visiting the Channel from 1769 to 1771, called these people "the hardest-working Indians I ever saw, and the most civilized, on any coasts" (Brown 1969: 4). "Indians" in this context would include natives of the Philippines, with whom Pino was conversant.
[19] 24¾ feet long and a bit over 24¾ inches high.
[20] 5½ feet.

stick. Close to the villages they also have a place we called the graveyard, where they bury the dead. They make it with a number of poles and planks that they paint with different colors, white, black, and red, and drive them upright into the ground. On very tall, straight, thin poles that we called the towers because they were visible some distance off, they set baskets that belonged to the dead persons along with other things that perhaps they valued, such as small skirts, shells, and in some places arrows as well. Over the dead, they set ribs and other large bones of the whales that regularly become stranded on the coasts there. They have, also, a common sweathouse, which is a closed, hot room to sweat in, which they make somewhat underground and very solidly built with poles and earth, and above in the middle is an opening like a trapdoor that serves as a vent and as a door through which they go down in, using the ladder, which consists of poles, straight and joined together, thrust into the ground, with one of them being shorter than the other. I went up close to a sweathouse and felt a great deal of heat coming up from it. They make a fire in the middle of the sweathouse and the Indians come in to sweat while sitting around it. As soon as they are thoroughly sweaty with their sweat dripping onto the ground, they come running out and hurl themselves into the sea to bathe in it, since it is right at hand there.

These Indians are well-formed and good-sized of body, although, in my judgment, not very sturdy[21] because of sweating themselves so much. The women are of a somewhat agreeable appearance; they use some earrings in their ears and have their hair in front cut short and standing up like a forelock, and the rest falling over their shoulders. The weapons used by these Indians, like all the rest, are the bow and arrow, but the arrows are of wood, very well made and elaborate, not made of cane like the ones commonly used by Apaches, Pimas and the rest, and the bows are small, about a vara long, but very strong and all of them wrapped with sinew and of a graceful shape. Their customs are like those of all the others: they live without law or king and without any particular knowledge of God so far as I could perceive. They are devoted to fishing, by which, with grass seeds, they get along without much hunger or starvation. They are also clever, I thought, and not very backward, since even though we had no interpreter through whom we could talk with them, we made ourselves understood in the way dumb people do, by using signs, by which they explain themselves clearly.

—But, quite thievish, which is characteristic of every Indian. As we passed through the village of La Asumpta[22] we stopped for a bit, since it was the first one, to look at their launches, graveyard, and so forth. Señor Anza, I, and others dismounted. In front of all those people, an Indian had the guile to take off

---

[21]The field text has, "they are healthy and sturdy and good-sized of body—peaceable Indians, however."
[22]"Of La Carpintería," in the final text.

a colored kerchief cloth from Señor Anza's saddle. He had left it there while getting down. We got back on, and after we traveled a short way Señor Anza noticed that the cloth was missing. One of his servants went to the village to look for it. He asked for the cloth and they denied knowing about it but immediately told him to go to thus and such a jacal, for it might be there. From there they sent him to another jacal, and from this to another. Seeing that they were refusing to give it to him and were continuing to conceal it, he drew his musket and went to the third house they had pointed him to. He told them he would slay them if they did not give him the cloth. It was only a threat, but immediately one fearful Indian told him he would look for it for him, and then sought out the cloth and handed it to him without delay.

They showed themselves to be well-mannered and peaceable to us everywhere and I did not think them very warlike, but it will not be easy to subdue them, because they dislike Spaniards because of what the latter have committed among them. Sometimes the Spaniards take away their fish and foods for their own provisions when they travel along the channel, sometimes they take their women and abuse them. They are very attached to living upon the coast. Although there are more than thirty streams along the coast there is no spot for locating a good mission because of the small amount of water carried by the streams, many of which dry up during the course of the year, and mainly because of the lack of any extent of level land fit for planting. As for grazing, there is good grass everywhere, and there is plenty of timber and trees in some places. In sum, the tribe that holds the channel is quite a big one, and the land is the most populated of all that I saw, as may be gathered to be the case from the villages I shall name. But I am not in agreement with the population count that was first made, which was of over twenty thousand souls. For, although it is true that there are villages that may amount to over a thousand souls, I considered that most of them did not reach a thousand and I think some of the ones which are small do not reach five hundred souls.

There is a stream here at this spot of La Rinconada, in the same corner where the village is. After we crossed it we stopped upon a small height right next to the sea which possessed a very wide view, although the fog prevented us from seeing the islands lying in front of us. Among the Indians who came over to the camp, I saw one wearing a cotton cloak like those made by the Gila Pimas, and I deduced he must have acquired it from so far away through the trade they have with other Indians. And they showed and pointed out to me an Indian there who they told me was from the large channel island called *Isla de Santa Cruz* and had come for the trip (it is a wonder how they go sailing over the seas there). Even though the color of this Indian's hair was between red and black, while those on the mainland have black hair, I thought he was very similar to the Indians of the channel. The Isla de Santa Cruz is nearly triangular and must be some twenty leagues long; they say it is very populated and lush,
but I was scarcely able to make it out, because of the fog. The Fathers told me that the viceroy had charged and commanded the officers that an attempt should be made to keep the islands from

being abandoned, especially that one, and that the Indians should not be asked to leave it just because of their being subdued and converted to Christianity.[23]

[February] 25th, Sunday. I said Mass. We set out from La Rinconada village at nine o'clock in the morning, and by traveling a westward course with very slight veering northward, at three o'clock in the afternoon we halted at a spot[24] having sufficient water and firewood, called the vicinity of the *Mescaltitán* villages,[25] having traveled for seven leagues. The route was, as I said yesterday, following the shore. At a little over a league we came to the place of *San Buenaventura*, which is a plain a bit over a league long.[26] At each end there is a village at the edge of the sea. Here it was planned to establish the mission of San Buenaventura, which is funded but was not founded because resources were not provided.[27] There is some grass and a good many live oaks, but little water. At two more leagues we came to another village, and upon a further league came to the village of *La Laguna* where a few baskets were bought for beads and we supplied ourselves with fish because a launch happened to be coming in to shore right then from fishing and brought a number of very good and different sorts of fish of various colors and shapes that I could not recognize. And we had this chance to see how they take the launches out of the water. Ten or twelve men approach as it comes to shore and take the launch, along with its catch, upon their shoulders and carry it to the house of the launch's owner or chief, who, by all indications, is distinguished by the little bearskin cloak that he wears tied over his shoulders. The tools they use for fishing are quite large fish traps, and hooks that they make from shell, and also one or two small nets made of a very strong thread like hemp.

At the stopping place, Señor Anza offered me a choice of his baskets, saying I should pick whatever ones I liked, but inasmuch as I had nothing to carry them in, I answered that I would take them when we ended the journey if he would give them to me then. He answered that he would do so, with however many I wished. However, he gave me none of them later, since I finished the journey out of favor with him.

[February] 26, Monday. I said Mass. We set out from the stopping place[28] at

---

[23]At the end of the century, however, all the island inhabitants were removed to the mainland missions.

[24]In the short text, stricken, "at a watering place one league before coming to . . ." (an unfinished phrase).

[25]So named by the explorers of 1769, after the town of Mescaltitlán in Jalisco, New Spain, because both were isolated settlements that filled the round islands on which they were located. Font's spelling is a phonetic one for the common pronunciation of the name. After the North American conquest in the nineteenth century, it came to be called Mescalitán Island.

[26]In the final text, "of about a league long."

[27]The actual reason was Commander Fages's unwillingness to carry out the founding: his last-minute decision upon hearing of troubles at Mission San Gabriel in 1771 (see Brown 2001: 90) and his renewed refusal in 1772 caused Serra to make his epochal voyage to Mexico. Font's "San Buenaventura" is the present Carpintería Valley, since there was a continual vacillation over the choice of sites for the proposed mission.

[28]In the final text, "from the vicinity of Mescaltitán." Font often designates stopping places by descriptive phrases that he then uses as names.

a quarter past eight in the morning, and by traveling about a league southward came to Mescaltitán, a fine spot and one I thought good for a mission. It consists of three big villages, two of them a bit apart and located next to the sea—one on each side of an inlet opposite which is a small island next to the land, a good spot for a settlement—with the largest one being a little inland, upon the route which we were traveling.[29] Afterward, heading to the west, we came at three further leagues to the villages of *San Pedro* and *San Pablo*, two of them, one at the foot of a hill and the other atop another hill, between which goes a stream, and both at the edge of the sea, along whose shore the route begins to go here. At a little over two leagues we reached *Ranchería Nueva*[30] so called because when the expedition[31] came here it was a large one and located in a different spot, and it was burnt by the gentiles during a war that they had, and afterward they moved to where those who survived it are now. Shortly afterward, at a half past three in the afternoon, we stopped at the edge of a stream, one of a number along the way that come down from the quite high mountain range we were bearing upon our right, and on which are visible some pines yielding good large pine-nuts with a husk so soft that it breaks between the fingers. We halted upon a small height at the edge of the sea close to Ranchería Nueva. And we traveled a bit over seven leagues today.

From the stopping place, I saw a number of spouts out at sea, cast up by whales passing by there. Found along the sea shore at the water's edge from the San Pedro and San Pablo villages onward is a great deal of tar coughed up by the sea, stuck to the rocks and dried, and fresh pellets of it as well. Perhaps there are wells of tar that run into the sea, as it could already be smelled along the way yesterday. From Mescaltitán onward today the odor was as strong as what one can smell aboard a ship or in a warehouse full of naval rigging and tarred cordage.

The Indians we saw in today's villages, of which there are six, are like what I spoke of yesterday, and the women, who are not ill-featured, immediately shut themselves up with their little ones and only an occasional one showed herself. The Indian men all go entirely naked save for one or two wearing small otter skin blankets, while the captains of launches wear one of bear skin. I imagine that although the reserve shown by these women may result from outrages committed among them by the first troops that arrived here, the fact that they so universally shut themselves up with their little ones and that the men, even though unarmed, sally out, may be an effect of fear or else something customary

---

[29]This description was rather thoroughly rewritten between the field and final texts, which are combined here in the translation.
[30]New Village.
[31]The 1769 Portolá expedition.

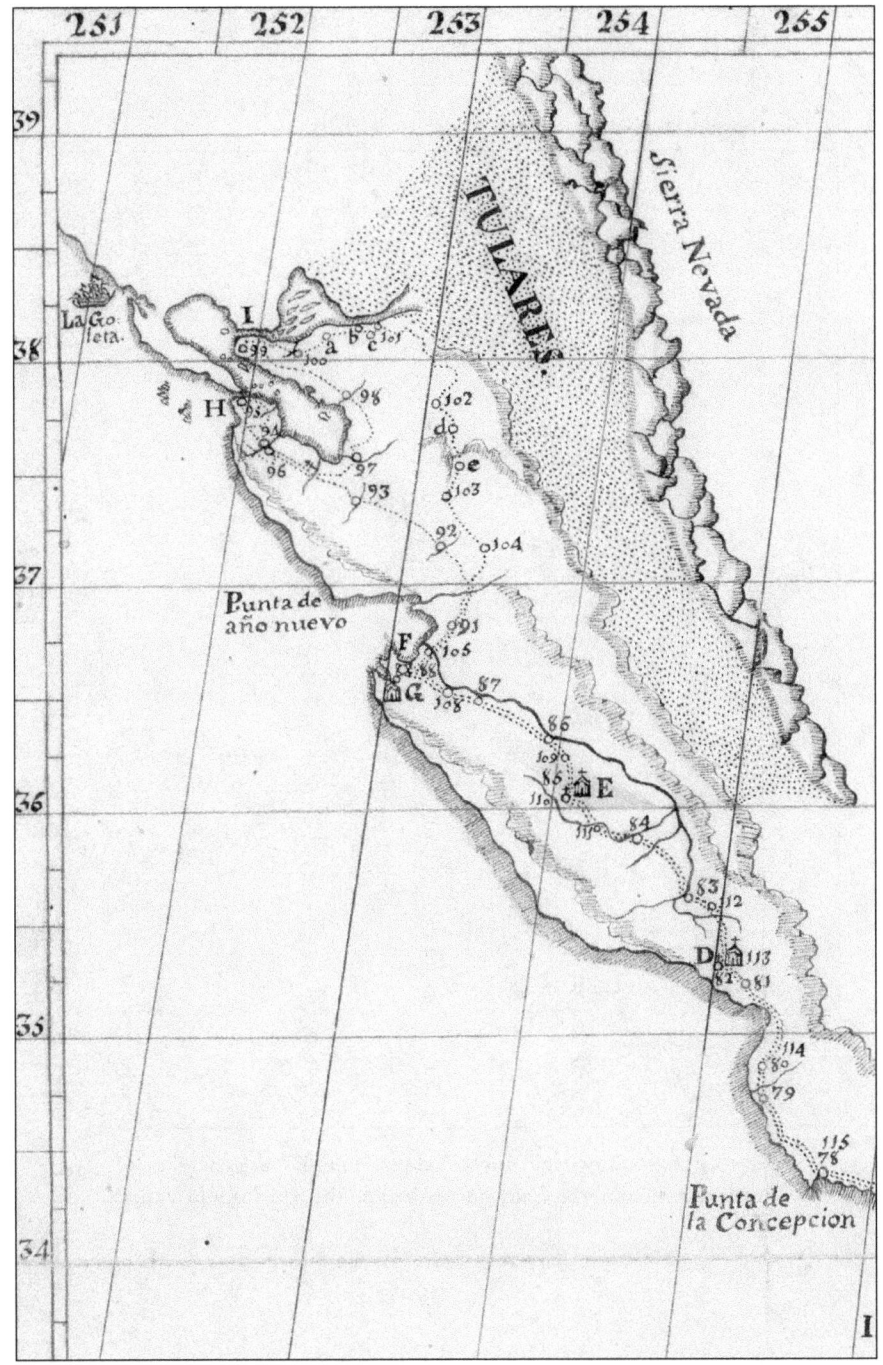

Figure 17. Font's general map, northwest section: the California coast and the San Joaquín Valley. *Reproduced courtesy of the John Carter Brown Library at Brown University.*

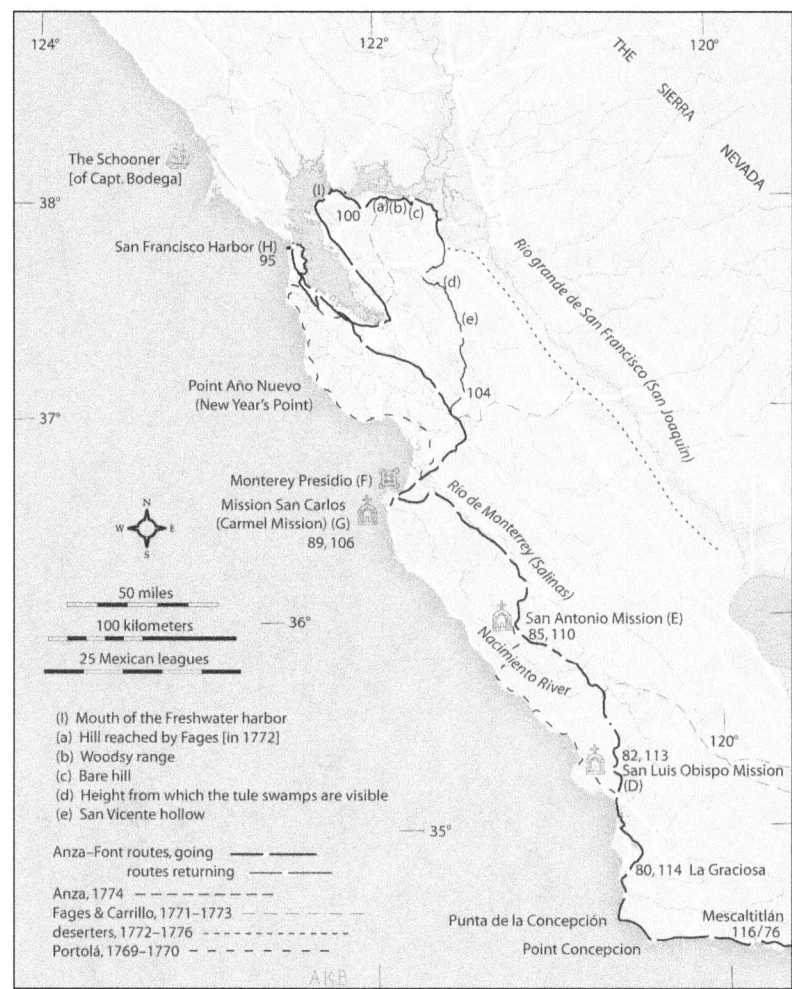

FIGURE 18. Redrawn and annotated version of Font's general map, northwest section: the California coast and the San Joaquín Valley.

with them. A number of baskets, cups very well carved out of stone, and wooden bowls of various forms and other elaborate pieces of work were collected today in return for beads at the villages we passed through. I suppose that these Indians, being as clever as they are and devoted to toil, would do splendid things if they had suitable teachers and tools or instruments, since they possess nothing other than flints and making what they can make with these is a very slow process.

Today the entire route was a very pleasant one and would have been more so had it not been for the fog, which is very constant there. At daybreak today the fog dampened us as much as though it had rained. It cleared after we had gone a little way but a patch of low fog stayed upon the sea, preventing us from seeing the large island all day long. Fog arose again at midday from under our feet along the shore, as though it were smoke, so thick it kept us from seeing even the people coming along behind us, and disappearing and regaining body from one moment to the next. But despite all this, the weather was quite good.

[February] 27, Tuesday. I said Mass. We set out from near Ranchería Nueva at eight o'clock in the morning, and by traveling a westward course with some veering west-southwestward, at a half past three in the afternoon we halted at the edge of the sea close to the village of *El Cojo*,[32] having traveled eight leagues. There was fog at daybreak that dampened us like a drizzle and kept up until midday on land; it lasted, however, out at sea, and did not let us see the islands. The route was a tedious one during the morning, as we headed over the top of the hills, all of them ending very abruptly at the sea, so that it was all up and down until halfway along the route, when we headed back along the shore. Shortly after our setting out, we came to the abandoned village[33] whose Indians went to Ranchería Nueva because of a war waged upon them by their enemies. Afterward we passed by a small-sized village; then there followed another abandoned one where there was only the graveyard. Later, on descending a grade, we came to the village of *La Gaviota*[34] and headed along the shore. There followed, then, another small village; afterward we came to the village of *El Bulillo*[35] where the launches currently were coming in from fishing, heavily supplied with large sardines about a cuarta long, and all the expedition's people provided themselves with fish in such plenty that a portion of what Señor Anza had bought for everyone was left there since there was no one willing to carry it.

And finally, we went by the village of El Cojo and stopped shortly afterward at a small stream with very little water and very scant in firewood, having gone

---

[32] The Lame One.
[33] Tajiguas Creek.
[34] Sea Gull.
[35] Usually called by the equivalent form, El Bulito.

by five villages and two abandoned ones. The spot here is already close to *Punta de la Concepción*,[36] where the Santa Bárbara Channel comes to an end. The Indians we saw, their fashions and devotion to fishing and making baskets, and so forth, are as I have described above. This whole coast is very scarce in shells; we saw a few today, some of them unusual ones.

Some people belonging to the village came to the camp and offered to clean the fish that we had, using their own knives. Our commander loaned one of them his pocket knife, which had a handle and sheath made of silver. The Indian undoubtedly was better pleased by that knife than by his own flint knife, so he waited until no one was paying attention and then made off with the knife without anyone ever noticing it. Señor Anza later missed his knife, and calling to another Indian who was there told him to go to the village and say they should return the knife. Otherwise, he would be going back to punish them. The Indian went and returned a short time later with the knife, apologizing for the other Indian who had carried it off by saying that he was afraid to come and had taken the knife unintentionally. He thought it had been given to him. This occurrence is a proof of every Indian's propensity to theft, and also a proof that the Indians there are not very warlike.

[February] 28, Wednesday. I said Mass. The weather was clear at daybreak with no fog on land but some at sea, so we left the channel without seeing the islands. We set out from near the El Cojo village at eight o'clock in the morning and followed a northwestward course which we kept altering west-northwestwardly and finally westward over a stretch of six leagues until cutting across the Punta or Cabo de la Concepción. We then followed a northward course and at four o'clock in the afternoon halted, four leagues farther, on the shore close to the Santa Rosa River, having traveled twelve leagues. And since we waited for the pack trains in order to ford the river together with them, the tide rose and we were unable to cross, and at a quarter to six we remained on this side of the beach or shore, returning back a bit.

On going a bit over three leagues we came to the village of *La Espada*[37] and two leagues farther to the village of *Los Pedernales*.[38] The two villages are somewhat wretched, with fewer people, and the last of those on the channel, which ends at Punta[39] de la Concepción, where the sea and its coast run westward and where, beyond there, they turn northward and northwestward. The northwest wind was strong and a bit chilly from morning onward, and with some fog, but following midday it turned into a northerly with the day very overcast by high fog that caused us a very cold, unpleasant afternoon. The whole route keeps along the top of the hills—the shore being impossible because of reefs[40]—and in

---

[36] Point Conception.
[37] The Sword.
[38] The Flints.
[39] In the field text, "cape." Punta de la Concepción, which the earliest navigators called Cabo de la Galera, marks a major turning of the coast and should probably always have been designated as a cape, but for some reason "Point" has stuck.
[40] Font uses this term for shoreline rocks.

sight of the sea a very short distance off, until, getting very close to the river, one goes down to the shore or dune that lies between the sea and the river. Before reaching the shore, one travels for a good while over dunes and sandy hills.

The mountains that we were leaving upon our right end at Punta de la Concepción, and beyond it the land changes its appearance greatly, with all of the country very much abloom and green with many sorts of grass, with good grazing and fragrant and useful plants. Ever since we first set out today and until we halted, I saw a great amount of sea fennel, entirely the same in leaf and flavor as the kind that grows among rocks and on walls on the seacoast of Catalonia, the only difference being that its stem rises about a half vara above the ground, it has a narrower leaf, and it was blossoming with yellow flowers like little sunflowers, which in their plenty provided a handsome sight all along the way.[41] The Santa Rosa River is not a big one but is so bushy along its banks and in the middle, and has such a bad bed, that the only way to cross it is by its mouth, and that only when the sea is at low tide, For when the tide rises it comes up the river, which swells, and a large flat or tule rush marsh lying along the river banks between the hills on either side becomes even fuller of water, and when the tide ebbs, it goes out at considerable speed. For this reason we were unable to ford the river today and had to delay here at this spot, which is quite scarce in firewood and good water, since the river water is brackish and turbid.

The soldiers told me that the tule marshes, which I shall speak of in the appropriate place, extend as far as this river, or else that this river, being as miry as it is, is a part of the tule marshes.

[February] 29, Thursday. At daybreak there was fog, which had lasted all night long, and vanished at midmorning. However, even though we were stopped at the edge of the sea, the fog rose so thickly before noon that the sea was invisible. Because the tide had risen we delayed until it lowered, and we set out from near the Santa Rosa River at a half past twelve, successfully fording it at one o'clock in the afternoon. By keeping upon a northward course with some veering northeastward, at a half past three we halted at *La Graciosa*[42] lake, so called from its being small and having very fine water even though it is ponded up, lying nearly between dunes and close to the sea.[43] We had traveled only a little over three leagues. Before the river, the route lies along the shore; after it, it departs a little from the coast, which is full of rocks and reefs, and one crosses dunes or hills of sand and also goes through a low place between two hills, one that is a bit wide and turned halfway into a lake by water that is ponded up all over it.

---

[41] A half vara is 16½ inches. Evidently a goldenbush, Haplopappus species [*Ericameria ericoides*] (fig. 19.)
[42] Graceful, pleasing.
[43] Francisco Palóu, in his redaction of the Crespí journal of the 1769 expedition, suggests that the name was given because a soldier (a Catalán?) misused the word *graciosa* in describing it. There might, however, have been still another reason for the bestowal, that the explorers witnessed native women dancing there. (Brown 2001: 122).

Even though it has no outlet to the sea it is not very miry. Here in this low spot we saw a band of six bears, since there are a great many of them in this country, very large ones.

March 1, Friday. I said Mass. We set out from La Graciosa Lake at eight o'clock in the morning, and at a quarter past five in the afternoon we halted at the spot called *El Buchón*[44] village, having traveled ten leagues. The course was such a changeable one that it ran between northeastward and westward in the following manner. Upon setting out, we headed northeastward and traveled for some three leagues about two or three leagues away from the sea, up and down over sandy hills and dunes. We then headed northward and traveled for a bit over a league until coming down a long grade to the village of *Laguna Grande*[45] which I thought to be a bit like an inlet, but it is good water and can be camped at. After that we headed northwest and, traveling some three leagues, crossed quite a long, wide valley that ends with a stream having no water in it but miry mud instead. We then headed westward as far as the seashore, traveling about a league through hills and dunes where there are some lakes of not very bad water, ponded up without outlet to the sea save for a small amount when they become very full at the time of rain. While one is in these last dunes one must pick one's way along because there is no mark or trace of a road in that stretch since the wind constantly shifts the sand about. Finally, we traveled for some two leagues along the shore, partway along which we forded a little river that empties out there, and then left the shore, and going a little away from the sea we came to El Buchón.[46] The weather was foggy at daybreak and continued with overcast all day long and with a very strong cold west wind that gave us quite a difficult day after it arose. The village of El Buchón is so called because when the first expedition, of Señor Portolá, arrived here a very important Indian chief called Buchón, famed upon the whole channel for his courage and the harm he had done there by his wars, lived at this village.

I learned that one of his principal wives was still alive (while another concubine of his had become a Christian and was at Mission San Luis, married to a soldier) and she was acknowledged by the gentiles, who paid her a tribute of some amount of their seeds. The chief, however, had already died.

This is a spot having very fine water and a great deal of firewood that served us very well. The shoreline that we followed during this whole way is very scarce in shells and I saw very few along it although there were, nonetheless, a few rather unusual, exquisite ones. I imagine that this must perhaps be because the

---

[44] Named after an Indian chief named Buchón.
[45] Large Lake.
[46] The final text heavily rewrites details of the march, adding the information about the dune lakes that is incorporated here with the field text's account.

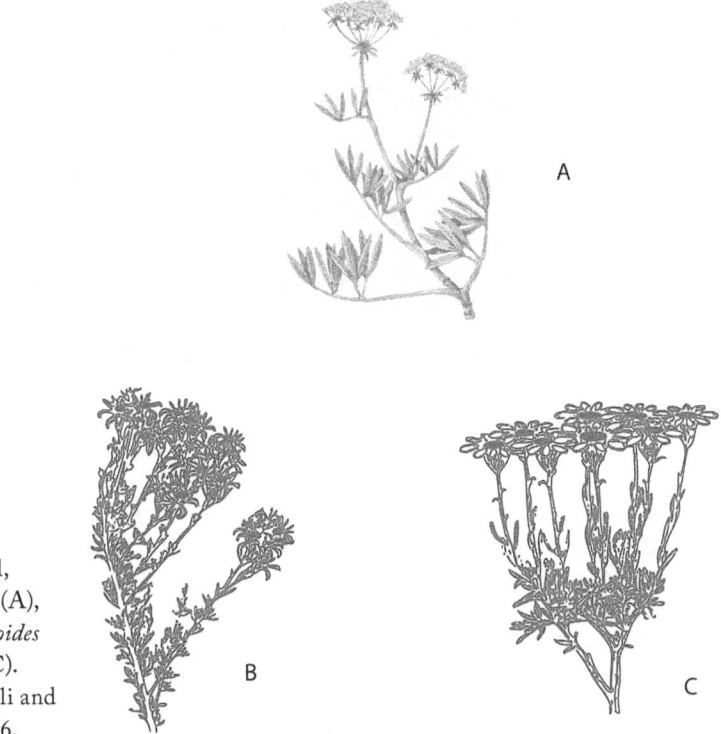

FIGURE 19. Sea fennel, *Crithmum maritimum* (A), with *Haplopappus ericoides* (B) and *linearifolius* (C). Redrawn after Fenaroli and Tosco 1964; Smith 1976.

seas here are very heavy upon the coast, by what I have seen so far, and the tides quite high. A point of land goes out to seaward from here, having a good many mountains which are spurs of the Santa Lucía range.[47]

[March] 2, Saturday. I said Mass. We set out from El Buchón village at eight o'clock in the morning, and by traveling three leagues, one northward and two northwestward, at a quarter to twelve we came to Mission San Luis Obispo.[48]

The weather was clear but cold, for this country is a colder one than that behind us. The difference was clear as soon as we doubled Cabo de la Concepción, for the country from Punta de la Concepción onward, although it is healthy, alters greatly in appearance and climate. A message was dispatched to the mission at daybreak, announcing our arrival. Upon coming out from a hollow at about a league from the stopping place, we passed by the foot of a hill among whose

---

[47]In the final text, five sentences earlier: "Then . . . some three leagues, until arriving near a point of mountains that goes out to seaward and is the Santa Lucía range, very high, steep and long, which begins here and ends at Mission Carmel near Monterey; and the sea is already in view from here."

[48]The final text adds "marked by the letter **D** on the map."

rocks we saw, right upon the way, some springs of tar arising there. After this we came onto what they call the San Luis plains, upon which there are some boggy spots with ponded water; at one, the worst of them, the mules became mired and some people fell off, so that we had a certain amount of delay. The Father Minister of Mission San Luis, Fray José Cavaller, along with Father Fray Pablo Mugártegui, came out to receive us upon the way. As we reached the mission, Father Fray Juan Figuer was awaiting us at the church door, vested with cope and holding a censer. We entered the church singing the Te Deum, being all the while received with pealing of bells and musket fire from the guard, and our arrival was one of mutual and very great joy.

Mission San Luis is situated in a handsome spot: a little height next to a stream of most excellent water, close to the Santa Lucía range and three leagues from the sea, with extremely fertile soil and fine fields and a great deal of timber.[49] The mission building consists of a big, rectangular jacal with a square hall[50] in the middle and four rooms or compartments, one at each corner of the hall. The latter has two doors that let light into it, one through which the hall is entered and the other going out to a small courtyard containing the kitchen and pens. Separate from this one is another jacal that serves as a church. There are some little jacales or compartments to one side that serve as dwellings for others, and in which the unmarried girl converts, whom they call "the nuns," sleep shut in and are under the instruction and care of a soldier's wife of some age, whom they call la maestra. She teaches them to sew and to be clean, which they already do very nicely just as though they were little Spanish girls. And opposite the mission is the guardhouse and the small jacales, or village as they call it, belonging to the Christian Indians, all of this forming half of a central square. Yet all of these buildings, carefully constructed as they are, are made of tule rushes, palisades, and a bit of adobe brick, since no resources were provided for doing anything more, and consequently they are at risk of fires.[51]

The Indians belonging to this mission are clean, tidy, and with better features and better looking than those of any other tribe among those I have seen.[52] The women wear a forelock that they make by cutting off their front hair and leaving it short so that it projects out a little above their forehead and around the face, and the remaining hair they tie back in a tail or, as I said concerning the Indian women of the channel, they leave it loose over their backs, which makes them quite attractive. The women there, however, are not so well featured and clean as the ones at San Luis. With the women at San Luis, what most stand out are their eyes, which are generally quite almond-shaped, lively, shining, black, and rather large. Their color is an agreeable one between dark and pale, and there are some of them who are almost as finely featured as Spanish women. Both men and women are neat and clean, so far as is manageable for this type of people,

---

[49]"And . . . timber" is added from an equivalent sentence in the next day's entry in the field text.
[50]A main room.
[51]Font was prescient here. Late in the following November, the mission buildings were damaged when hostile natives shot fire arrows onto the tule thatched roofs.
[52]In the short text, stricken, "better-looking than those of the Channel."

and they do not stink like other Indians. In addition, the women are friendly and fond of Spaniards, who are pleasing to them, which is why the soldiers so misbehaved with them when they stayed in this vicinity for some time slaying bears, in order to satisfy the hunger they suffered there during Captain Fages's time because their supplies failed them.[53] The men have their ears pierced but do not, however, wear very many pendants in them. The women wear earrings.[54]

These Indians belong to the Nochi tribe, and I thought them more cheerful and sociable than others.[55] In the gentile state, the men are naked like the rest of them, and the women wear blankets made of deer and otter skins. They understand how to make baskets with a great variety of patterns and in any shape they are asked to produce, even hats, just as they made one for Señor Anza, which he asked them to do.[56] I was unable to fix with certainty where all of that abundance and variety of basketry found on the channel is produced, and am inclined to think most of it is made in this Nochi tribe, the one that inhabits the tule marshes that are close to this mission. Certainly I did not see any basket being made anywhere on the channel, which perhaps I would have done were they produced there, unless it is that they make them inside their jacales into which I was not able to enter. As I said, they did not allow it. Some of the Fathers are of the opinion that they produce them on Santa Cruz Island and that the Indians there bring them to the channel and mainland in order to market them. Some soldiers who went to the other side of the tule marshes in search of deserters—whom they were unable to catch, and only succeeded in taking away their weapons—said when they returned that they had seen more baskets over there, and finer ones, than on the channel. Thus it follows that they are made by these Nochi Indians, who are the ones who inhabit the tule marshes, concerning which I shall speak at the proper place.

[March] 3, Sunday. I said the final Mass and during it preached four words to the people
upon the gospel, which was that of the Transfiguration, applying the glory of [Mount] Tabor to the pleasure we all felt upon reaching so fine a mission as the one here and resting there for a day, and encouraging everyone to persevere in enduring whatever might occur afterward, since that was no more than a transient rest for recovering our breath in order to persevere until reaching the end, just as Christ gave His disciples that day of glory in order to encourage them to undertake the career of apostleship He had set them aside for and to suffer the hardships that awaited them, etc., etc.

---

[53] This was in the spring and summer of 1772, shortly before the mission was founded.

[54] The last sentence is found only in the final text. In the field text, a similar description of the San Luis Obispo natives appears in the following entry, March 3, and again under April 22, when Font visited the mission on his return and rewrote the description, pretty much as it is here in the final text.

[55] "More cheerful and sociable" are terms applied to the natives in the field text's briefer remarks. "Nochi," which applied primarily to the San Joaquín Valley ("Yokuts") peoples, is one of the ethnic terms recorded by Father Garcés in his 1776 journal (to which Font had access only after the return from his own voyage). However, the two groups were quite distinct in language; the San Luis Obispo tongue was related to that of the Channel.

[56] Speaking of the Channel natives' *coras* and *bateas*—globular and flat baskets for storing and cleaning seeds respectively—the Dominican missionary Luis Sales wrote, "they make all this from rushes of different colors and are so deft at design that they copy whatever is set before them." (Sales 1960: 69.) A broad-brimmed, crowned basketry hat made at Mission San Buenaventura was given to the navigator George Vancouver in 1793 and is now in the British Museum.

Following Mass, I solemnly baptized an Indian boy about seven years old, whose godfather was our Commander Anza.[57] The christening was done ceremoniously with peals of bells and with musket fire; and we delayed here this day. I observed the latitude of this mission and found it, by the tables of Jorge with no correction, in 35° 8½' and with correction in 35° 17½'.[58] And thus I say: at Mission San Luis Obispo, March 3, 1776: Meridian altitude of the sun's lower limb: 48° 4'. Here, even with the cold, we began to feel fleas, which are extremely plentiful in all this country. Up until now, ever since crossing the mountains, we only had felt one or two of them.

[March] 4, Monday. I said Mass and took my farewell of my countryman Father Cavaller and his two companions, who were very demonstrative in every way. We set out in good weather from Mission San Luis at nine o'clock in the morning and traveled on such a changeable course that, starting with northeastward, it ended west-northwestward, and at a quarter to five in the afternoon we halted at a spot called La Asunción, on the bank of the Monterey River, which has already been joined here by the Santa Margarita River[59] having traveled some ten leagues. On setting out, we traveled northeastward for about a league, then, turning almost northward, went into a long and very lush hollow. A fine stream runs through it and all along it there are different sorts of trees, among which very handsome laurels were noted.

Going up through it, we crossed a mountain spur that departs from the Santa Lucía range and interconnects with other mountain country that we commenced leaving on our right, behind which lie the tule marshes, and which runs on to the mouth of the freshwater harbor at the end of the San Francisco harbor, where it comes to an end.

After climbing, we went down northward through rather spacious little hills and very green meadows, with their streams. At about five leagues we came to the spot called *Santa Margarita*, a plain that is very miry when it rains, though not so now, and reaches onward between the Santa Lucía range and a smaller one, with two rivers that run for a good distance, one upon either side, and then join with other, small streams to form the Santa Margarita River. Here there is a small village. Afterward we went over fairly level land, bit by bit changing course from northward to west-northwestward until we ended the march at the stopping place, a sort of a valley having the Santa Lucía range on the left and the other range on the right. The whole route, and the plains here, are full of very thick, tall white oaks with fine large acorns, and there are also a great many sycamores and pine trees with good-sized pine nuts. There are birds thereabouts

---

[57]The boy was christened Carlos Antonio de Anza, for his godfather. Anza also stood as godfather to five adults whom Font baptized on the same day. (Mission San Luis Obispo Libro de Bautismos nos. 172, 176–180.)

[58]This is only very slightly too high.

[59]In the field text, "on the bank of the Santa Margarita River or, say rather, the Monterey."

that they call *carpinteros*[60] which make round holes in the trunks of the oaks and thrust an acorn into each hole so thoroughly that it can hardly be gotten out. They lay up their provision and harvest in this way and there are trees that are entirely studded with acorns on their trunks. Atop the mountains, a good many pine trees are visible, so lush that their branches on the trunk start from near the ground, and, diminishing as they go, end in an almost pyramidal point.[61] The pine nuts are hard-husked and not as large as the ones we saw on the channel. In sum, a fine country and lovely waters.

[March] 5, Tuesday. I said Mass. The weather was fine at daybreak, with a chill that warmed up as the day came under way. A little before our setting out, a courier arrived from San Luis with letters written by the Fathers for us to carry to Mission San Carlos. For, in order to chat with us, they had not written the letters during the day we were there. Living so alone and far from each other as they do, the day when they see any company is an unusual one. The courier riders went back immediately.

We started out from the spot of La Asunción a little before nine o'clock in the morning. On setting out, we successfully crossed what they call the Monterey River, which is the same Santa Margarita River combined with the aforesaid Monterey one, and they issue from the Santa Lucía range. It goes northward, then northwestward, and empties into the sea near Monterey. It had little water in it since there had been very little rain this year; it has few fords, and is usually miry. We traveled a northward course, close to the river, for some three leagues then changed course to northwestward. The route continued through low hills, and hollows of some little length, with level portions, and with some turns west-northwestward. About five leagues further, we came to Nacimiento River, which joins lower down with the San Antonio River, and the latter with the Monterey.[62]

And finally, after two further leagues on a west-northwestward course, we came to the stopping place, which is at the edge of the San Antonio River and the beginning of a long hollow through which the river comes, issuing from the Santa Lucía range, as do the others that I have named.

We saw only four Indians along the route, which is all full of white oaks, not, however, such large ones as those we saw yesterday, and very little grass, because it has not rained and the soil, which is a bit rough and thick although not bad, is dry. They call this spot *el primer paso*[63] of the San Antonio River.[64] We were

---

[60]Woodpeckers.

[61]In the final text, "spruces," the term that Font later decided should be used for redwoods, which, however, these were not. The description of the shape might fit the distinctive Santa Lucía fir.

[62]This statement, added in the final text, is erroneous, since the two streams empty separately into the Salinas (the "Monterey") River.

[63]The First Crossing.

[64]In the final text, earlier in the entry: "halted . . . at the spot called *el primer vado*, the first ford." *Paso*, more often than *vado*, was the term used by the Hispanic settlers.

bothered a bit by fleas at this spot. We had felt them already while at the missions, but not as much as here, where they were numerous, very hungry, lean, and their bites stung.

and this is seemingly a plague in that country, especially when the weather warms a little, so that they are to be found not only in houses and jacales but also in fields and along the roads—wherever one halts, they are found.[65]

[March] 6, Wednesday. The day broke fair and I said Mass. We set out from the first ford at a quarter to eight in the morning, and by traveling west-north-westward, with variations, at four o'clock in the afternoon we came to Mission San Antonio de los Robles having traveled a long ten leagues.[66]

Upon setting out from the stopping place, we traveled a very short way southward, then continued on westward through the canyon of the river, which we forded three times and which runs from west to east (a proof of how high the mountains are from which it rises).[67] At about four leagues, where the canyon already is widened out, we followed a west-northwestward course, up to the mission. The whole way goes in sight of the river, which has a good amount of cottonwoods upon it, and almost all the route, the farther one goes along, is a level one and open country with hills to one side and the other and with a great many white oaks. One league before coming to the mission is the former mission site, from which they moved because the river usually dries up down below; afterward, it runs northward and joins with the Monterey River. This is a cool spot, and—although I did not expect it since there had been no rain—a very pleasing one.

Yesterday along the way we saw a good many white oaks but today there were a great many more of them, very large ones, which is the reason why that hollow is called *La Cañada de los Robles*.[68] The river runs through it and we forded it three times. The hollow is a bit narrow at the start but afterward widens out considerably, and the former mission site lies about a league before arriving.[69] They moved it to where it is now because it is a better spot and possesses a more assured year-round supply of water from the river.

Mission San Antonio is situated at the foot of the Santa Lucía range (which begins, as I said, a little below Mission San Luis and follows along the coast to its end close to Mission San Carlos Borromeo del Río Carmelo), and within a not very broad hollow some ten leagues long and very full of large white oaks, for which reason the mission is called San Antonio de la Cañada de los Robles.[70] And the spot is a very good one, with fine lands and

---

[65] Professor Solana (Montané 2000: 229) thinks that Font exaggerated and in fact had brought the fleas with him, since they could hardly have infested the countryside without having their warm-blooded prey at hand. On the contrary, those who remember California before the use of DDT can testify to Font's truthfulness.

[66] "Marked by the letter **E** upon the map" is added in the final text.

[67] Since the location is, in fact, not very far east of the coastline.

[68] The White Oak Hollow.

[69] Arriving at the mission.

[70] San Antonio of the White Oak Hollow.

sufficient water from the river flowing through the hollow. However, it is some distance away from the sea, since although it must be some eight leagues by air, to reach the coast requires a long day's journey[71] because of the great roughness of the route in crossing the Santa Lucía range, which lies in between and is very high and broken, running very nearly northwest and southeast and forming high precipices and large reefs upon the coast. And thus the mission lies almost at the hollow's beginning before it goes into the mountains, which contain an abundance of white oaks, live oaks, and pines and consequently a great deal of pine nuts and acorns. For this reason the mission has a large herd of swine.

The Fathers of the mission, who were Father Francisco Dumets,[72] minister of Mission San Carlos—who had come here to this one because Father Fray Miguel Pieras,[73] who was ill, had gone to that one to be cured—and Father Minister Fray Buenaventura Sitjar, both Mallorcans, received us with particular rejoicing, and offered whatever they possessed with great openhandedness. They immediately gave the escort soldiers from Tubac a pig, along with another one to our commander's muleteers, and also brought forth a great deal of lard that was shared out among the people, who had not tasted any in a long time.

The construction at this mission is better than at the others. It is adobe with a good earthen roof and good-sized beams since they have plenty of wood. It has a main hall with two small chambers at one end and another room at the other end, through which one comes into the church, which lies right beyond. From the main hall, one goes out into a court where there is an adequate courtyard with a kitchen, oven and other workshops and pens. The kitchen-garden and fields are next at hand, around which, with the assistance of the Indians, the Fathers have made a very large fence enclosing all of it, very well built, of good-sized posts, and most of it is made of what they call *palo del Brasil*.[74] In sum, I thought it a very good mission with excellent qualities and advantages.

The Christian Indians composing this mission (of whom there must be some five hundred souls by now) are totally different from the rest that I have seen before here.[75] They belong to the tribe inhabiting the Santa Lucía range, and I did not learn what the tribe is called or whether it has a name. Both men and women are small in body, stunted and ugly, and in their gentile state they live scattered through these mountains and ravines without any particular knowledge of God. The men go naked, and the women wear one or another blanket, although the Fathers attempt more or less to clothe the Christians, as I said. The women do not wear a forelock like the ones of the channel and San Luis and neither sex takes care of their hair. I saw a number of women with their faces striped and marked up a bit in the way the Pimas are accustomed to doing. Their

---

[71]In the field text, "almost a day's march."

[72]Dumetz, a Mallorcan with a French family name (pronounced Dumé). The field text refers to him wrongly as "the reverend Father Minister of the mission" (San Antonio)

[73]Font consistently misspells Pieras's name, rendering it as "Prieras."

[74]This term, "Brazil wood," was used for a variety of tropical or exotic hardwoods. It is hard to tell what it refers to here. Possibly manzanita or madrone?

[75]Added and then stricken in the short text: "but tractable"; "a bit ugly."

language is a very rough one, hard to pronounce because of all the clicking in it. Through constant application and noteworthy toil, Father Fray Buenaventura has learned it.

He also has written the doctrina in the language, but as there are no letters to express all of that clicking, whistling and guttural, barbarous, laughable pronunciation. Use has been made of the letter **K**[76] and a number of accents and marks so that the resulting doctrina is as hard to read as it is to pronounce. The Indians, however, are already praying in Spanish, and use this language for prayer at least once a day.

I believe that the greatest hardship lies in the fact that there is such variety of uncivilized, barbarous languages to be found in gentile parts, and here I am reminded that it may be possible to attribute to this fact the reluctance which the apostle St. Thomas felt toward coming to preach the faith of Jesus Christ in the Indies, as is recounted by the Venerable Most Honorable Señor Don Fray Julián Garcés, in the letter which he wrote in favor of the Indians to Pope Paul III. In the letter he says that the saint was accustomed to saying to Jesus Christ, "Send me anywhere but to the Indians," *Quocumque mitte me præterquam ad Indos*; this letter is printed in the first volume of the Mexican Councils.[77] And in this sense, I imagine that that passage of Psalm 104 can, without violence, be understood that speaks of the pain afflicting the chaste heart of Joseph when he found himself a captive in Egypt and unable to speak, or else deprived of speech for a time: "A sword pierced his soul until his word should come," *Ferrum pertransiit animam ejus, donec veniret verbum ejus*,[78] since he found himself in a land and among people whose speech he did not know and could not understand: "He heard a language which he did not know," *Linguam quam non noverat audivit*; Psalm 80, verse 6. For there is no knife of pain that more greatly torments the heart of a minister wishing to serve God in the ministry and conversion of souls, nor any greater hardship, than to find himself among peoples having such diverse and barbarous tongues and to have no way of being understood by them, as Father Vieira so well emphasizes in the Sermon concerning the Holy Spirit, volume 1.[79]

[March] 7, Thursday. I said Mass, and afterward accompanied, upon my instrument, another Mass which we sang with all possible ceremoniousness to St. Anthony for the success of our journey and the discovery or survey we were going to make of the river of San Francisco. We and the Fathers there all the more so, were all wishing for this survey to learn the truth, given what Señor Rivera had told us concerning the report by sailing master Cañizares that there was no such river. Here they assured us that there was one, since they had heard the Indians of this mission say a number of times that there was a great deal

---

[76] The alphabetical letter K is rarely used in Spanish. Sitjar's translations into this local (Salinan) language survived in manuscript and were published in 1861 in New York City in Shea's Library of American Linguistics. Examples of his complex Salinan orthography are also found in the mission's register books.

[77] Lorenzana 1769 1: 28. The basic quotation is from the apocryphal Acts of Thomas, Act I (James 1924: 365). According to church tradition, St. Thomas had preached the gospel in India. Starting in the sixteenth century, some mission chroniclers and others occasionally argued that he had also preached in "the Indies," i.e. the Americas.

[78] Psalm 105:19.

[79] Bolton 1931: 281 footnote: "The reference is evidently to Father Antonio Vieyra, author of several volumes and pamphlets of *Sermones* and *Sermones varios* published between 1660 and 1691 (see Palau y Dulcet, *Manual del librero hispanoamericano*, tomo séptimo, p. 180 [Barcelona, 1927])."

of water on the other side of the range that I said during the journey we kept leaving upon our right hand. There was so much water that it was impossible to go further up on the other side. In this they were correct because that is where the tule marshes lie. However, since Indians do not usually distinguish between what is a river and what is not and are accustomed to express themselves, after their own fashion, by saying there is a great deal of water, this was what led to the Fathers' error. The error was based upon the report which they thoroughly believed, that is, that such a river existed.

We remained here today to rest. I observed the latitude of this mission, and using the tables of Jorge I found it, with no correction, in 35° 53½', and with correction in 36° 2½'.[80] And thus I say: at Mission San Antonio de los Robles, March 7, 1776: meridian altitude of the sun's lower limb: 48° 52'. Saint Anthony brought us Lieutenant Moraga![81] A little after midday, Moraga, the lieutenant of the expedition who had gone in pursuit of the deserters, arrived at the mission here. He had overtaken them and captured them a little beyond the briny well of El Carrizal heading toward Santa Olalla Lake[82] and had left them thoroughly imprisoned at Mission San Gabriel. Everyone was very much pleased with his arrival.[83] He said that he had recovered all of what had been stolen except for some animals that went astray and a few others of his that had been slain in the main range and at San Sebastián by mountain Indians. They are culprits of the crime at San Diego, who are at large in the mountains and as far away as the stopping place at San Sebastián. He found over two hundred of them gathered together. They faced him with weapons as though intending to hinder his passing.[84] He brought back from that spot a number of the stock that had been left worn out there during our coming when they mounted a stampede away from the stopping place of San Gregorio. He left them at San Gabriel along with the animals.[85]

---

[80] Only 1½ minutes too high.

[81] The sentence is only in the field text. Anthony of Padua, the Franciscan saint who sponsors the recovery of lost things (here, the Lieutenant), was also the patron of the mission at which Font and the others were staying, and had already been invoked for the discovery of the San Francisco River.

[82] On February 16, four leagues short of reaching the Colorado River and Santa Olaya (Olalla) Lake. (Anza.)

[83] Anza's entry adds that the muleteer who was chiefly implicated had taken the road toward San Diego, so that Moraga ordered the sergeant at San Gabriel to arrest and imprison him when he returned.

[84] He and his men charged after them (so say Anza's entry, recording Moraga's oral report, and Francisco Palóu's *Noticias*) and that was sufficient to chase them off. They wounded three of Moraga's mounts from hiding, repeating what they had done three times before (see December 23 and note), a crime which the Spanish had, until now, deliberately ignored in order to seem more favorable to the natives (*"por justificar nuestra causa"*). But items in the possession of the defeated group indicated that they had taken part in the sacking of Mission San Diego. See also the introduction.

[85] Mules and horses. But seven mounts had been lost during the pursuit.

He related for us the manner in which he had caught the prisoners and what happened on that day, and their reason for committing theft and flight, just as the prisoners themselves had immediately declared to him. What happened was that while we stayed at San Gabriel mission, the corporal of the San Gabriel guard fell in love with a girl among the expedition, and since he did not possess anything to give her in order to gain favor with her, he persuaded the muleteers to give her some of the things they had in their charge and they, agreeing, gave her chocolate and other items. From this, it follows that the first mover of this abuse, and the most culpable, was the corporal. After some days had passed, the muleteers and lads realized that they had stolen a good amount and were bound to be discovered so they began to think about fleeing.[86] For that purpose they made common cause with a soldier belonging to the guard there who was ill-contented and who also had already begun thinking how he might run away. He, then, told them to provide themselves with a good supply of tobacco, beads, and other items from among the effects, on the night that he was to go on horse-guard duty; and then they would leave with the animals from the horse herd in the quiet of the night with the assurance that, since they were under his care, no one would stop them. And that is how they carried it out. And, they said, the beads they took with them were meant to be bestowed on the Yumas so that they would take them across the river, and their intention was, upon reaching Sonora or at La Cieneguilla, to divide the animals among themselves and cover their flight with the excuse of the San Diego uprising, by spreading word and claiming that the Indians had slain all of us and they alone had been able to escape.[87]

They also said that the night before the lieutenant captured them, one of them said, "Fellows, my heart tells me they'll catch us tomorrow," and that they were unable to sleep all night long for fear, and began traveling before daylight, but that they lost their heading and only went in circles without advancing anywhere so that three times they came back to the campfire that they had made where they had stopped.[88] And they remained there for a long time once more until, long after sunrise, they decided to set forth again and had scarcely begun to travel when the lieutenant fell upon them. At first sight they had it in mind to show him some resistance, using the muskets

---

[86] Anza's entry says that the total theft committed by a single muleteer amounted to about two arrobas (presumably as much as fifty pounds) of chocolate out of a locked chest, and some aguardiente from a closed barrel.

[87] The background to the affair was reported by Anza in a letter to Rivera from Monterey six days later. "Lieutenant Moraga has not undertaken any judicial measures, but he assures me that all the verbal testimonies concur in asserting that the aforesaid desertion arose from—what I regret having to inform you of should the matter prove true—the fact that the muleteer José Ignacio Amarillas, after repeatedly selling an amount of chocolate and aguardiente which was in his charge to Corporal [Guillermo] Carrillo at [the latter's] instigation to the theft, and after realizing that what he had stolen would be missed and that I would punish his dishonesty, chose the course of inviting the soldiers and the others to desert. And once they had agreed upon it, Amarillas changed his mind when they were on the point of acting; [but] since they had made up their minds to do so, the five men who were caught by [Moraga] proceeded to carry it out." Font does not mention Amarillas's backing out of the plot. However, the summary of Moraga's report in Anza's journal confirms that on the night of the planned desertion, with the horses for their flight already secreted where they could get them, the original muleteer told the others he was afraid of the journey and of being caught by the Sonora authorities even if he made it successfully; he would, however, keep the others' plans secret after they went. This caused them to fear discovery even more, so they fled as planned.

[88] The report that reached Rivera was that the capture was made four leagues (about 10½ miles) short of the Colorado (not of Santa Olalla). The name of the soldier who was involved was José Mariano Yépiz (Llépiz).

they carried; however, they were stunned at the sound of his voice crying, "Stop, in the King's name!" and surrendered immediately.[89] Quite a remarkable, miraculous affair!

These prisoners were held for the time at San Gabriel, and although, for his part, Señor Anza assigned them as laborers for the construction at San Francisco harbor, Señor Rivera decided to leave two of them at San Gabriel and ordered two others sent to San Diego, from where one of them ran away and afterward overtook us at the Colorado River, as I shall tell. And since he[90] is so fond of the soldiers, he gave no further punishment to the deserter, who was guilty of a capital crime of having fled while on sentry duty, other than to remove his position as soldier, so that he escaped being court-martialed. And the corporal, who was most chiefly at fault, he did not charge with anything in the slightest, as he was distantly related to him.[91]

[March] 8, Friday. I said Mass. The weather at daybreak was very fine and clear. We set out from Mission San Antonio de los Robles at a quarter to nine in the morning, and at a quarter after three in the afternoon halted upon the bank of the Monterey River at the spot called *Los Ositos*,[92] having traveled some nine leagues.

At the start the route goes over a spur of mountains, until it comes down to a broad hollow called the *San Bernabé* hollow. Afterward it continues on, level, through a very long valley formed by the Santa Lucía range upon the left and the mountains reaching toward San Francisco harbor, upon the right.

The course was a varied one: upon setting out we headed northeastward and traveled for about two leagues up through a hollow; we then began turning northward, and went down a long descent[93] and went on through a level hollow of some little width for about three leagues, until getting past a spur of the Santa Lucía range, which, together with it[94] is what forms the Los Robles hollow; we traveled northwestward over level land for the remainder, as far as the stopping place. This plain, which is of some extent, is formed between the Santa Lucía range and another one, very high and long, which we started seeing on the day we set out from San Luis; it runs, with small difference, southeast to northwest,[95] and seemingly ends upon the sea in the vicinity of the San Francisco River.

---

[89]Two of them made a slight attempt to flee, says Anza.

[90]Rivera.

[91]Rivera's daybook explains that with the shortage of soldiers, it seemed impossible to punish Yépiz properly. According to Anza's letter to Rivera, it was Moraga who first condemned the captives to labor at San Francisco. The Carrillo brothers were related by marriage to Lieutenant Ortega, but evidence of a family relationship to Rivera has not been found; Font may have been wrong about this.

[92]The Little Bears.

[93]The field text has "by which one gets across the Santa Lucía range which we had been leaving to the right," i.e. the Jolon Grade. Font had first identified the hills east of the San Antonio River as being part of the Santa Lucía mountains, the main range to the west.

[94]With the main Santa Lucía range.

[95]As Font mentions in his March 24 entry, "southeast to northwest" is a correction that he had written in after crossing out his original (incorrect) phrase, "east to west," *de oriente a poniente*, one of the few times in which he uses Mediterranean direction names instead of compass points. (Cf. Brown 1978: 221–23 and *passim*.)

Through the midst of this plain flows the Monterey River, already joined by the San Antonio River and carrying a good deal of water and having a deep bed, with its banks very wooded for some distance upon one side and the other with cottonwoods and other, scrubby sorts of trees and a great amount of blackberry brambles. It runs about northwestward, to the sea. Along the way we saw a good deal of Brazil wood, and at San Antonio it exists in such plenty that they have made the fence around their cultivation out of it. The whole country is quite grass-covered and good. We saw a few Indians along the way.

[March] 9, Saturday. I said Mass. It rained a little about midnight, and at daybreak there were some clouds and the air cold, but no further rain. We set out from the place of Los Ositos at eight o'clock in the morning, and by traveling a west-northwestward course for ten leagues we halted at a quarter past three in the afternoon on the edge of the Monterey River at the spot called *Los Correos*,[96] having traveled ten leagues. The whole way lies over quite wide-reaching levels—the valley I spoke of yesterday—in sight of the Monterey River and not very far from the Santa Lucía range, with this to the left and the river to the right, mostly deep down in its bed and having a good deal of cottonwoods and other woods, which it waters when it rises out of its bed during floods. At about six leagues lies the spot called La Soledad. They told me it was called thus because in the first expedition, Portolá's, they asked an Indian for his name and he answered, "Soledad," or so it must have sounded to them.[97] There are usually Indians at it. Here and along the way a number of Indians came out to see us, different already from those of San Antonio and the Santa Lucía mountains, and some of them were able to say a few words to us in Spanish. One of them asked after Captain don Fernando by name and asked where he was.[98] Our commander decided to send a message to Monterey from here tomorrow after Mass, to advise them of our arrival, and both of us wrote to Father President Fray Junípero Serra, asking him to send a Father to the presidio so that we might sing a Mass of thanksgiving.

[March] 10, Sunday. I said Mass. It began raining before dawn and rain continued at intervals, light or heavy, all day long, so that we reached Monterey very wet. The rainfall ceased for a bit only at our arrival, with the horizon staying very cloud-covered.

After Mass the post I spoke of yesterday was dispatched. We set out from the stopping place of Los Correos at a quarter past nine in the morning, and at about

---

[96] The Couriers.

[97] The first expedition, however, traveled on the other side of the river and did not talk to any natives. The story is more plausibly attributed, by Palóu, to a slightly later visit by Serra, who reported that the Indian was a woman. Tibesar 1956 2: 140–41.

[98] Rivera.

a half past four in the afternoon we came to the Royal Presidio of Monterey harbor,[99] having traveled some ten leagues. On setting out we kept following the Monterey River for some four leagues west-northwestward until coming to the spot called *Buenavista*, where one leaves the river upon the right, and then kept on through hills and low spots westward, for the remainder. Halfway along this stretch is another spot called *El Toro Rabón*.[100] It is a good watering-place. From here onward, one commences to descry the *Sierra de Pinos*[101] that forms Monterey harbor. Like everywhere else, the route was lovely country, green, lush, flowery, fertile, handsome, and splendid. Despite being so wet that we had not one dry item, we reached the presidio to everyone's great joy and they received us with ordnance fire from some small cannons they possess there, and with the soldiers firing off their muskets.

The Royal Presidio of Monterey is situated upon a plain formed by the Sierra de Pinos, which ends here next to the sea and is about a quarter of a league from Monterey harbor. The presidio is composed of a stockade and some few buildings of wood and mud and a bit of adobe bricks. The construction consists of a square upon one wall of which is the commandant's house and the warehouse in which the quartermaster lives; a small chapel is on another wall with the barracks or guardhouse of the soldiers, and along the two other walls there are some jacales and small dwellings of the families and people living there, all made of palisade and mud and a bit of adobe. The presidio square or plaza, which is not a large one, is enclosed by a wall of poles or stakes. The whole thing amounts to very little, and the people live in a good deal of discomfort from lack of lodging, and it is not for lack of materials, since there is lime and wood is abundant, but for lack of support provided for this purpose. Our commander had to lodge in the warehouse, I myself in a very dirty little room full of lime, and the rest of the people accommodated themselves in the plaza, with their tents or however they could.[102]

Monterey harbor amounts to a little nook with small shelter under the Punta de Pinos, which stretches about three leagues out to sea and, with *Punta de Año Nuevo* which reaches about twelve leagues to sea, forms a large but very open bight, and therefore what is called a harbor possesses very little shelter, almost none against the northwester, which prevails greatly there; besides which, it is so small that it is filled by two ships and also has small depth. The Punta de Pinos lies nearly northward with respect to the Presidio of Monterey, from which it is about three leagues distant, and Punta de Año Nuevo lies about northwestward with respect to the harbor, from which it is distant some ten or twelve leagues.

---

[99] The final text adds, "marked on the map by the letter **F**."
[100] The Short-Tailed Bull, later known just as El Toro.
[101] The Range of Pines.
[102] In the field text, "Our people accommodated themselves in the plaza in their tents, and we stayed in the warehouse, another room, and the tents, and so forth." Font's "we" refers to the officials and to Font.

The presidio is named after San Carlos and is called San Carlos de Monterey. And this title is shared by the mission next to it, called, on this account, San Carlos. It is also called San José for the Visitor General Gálvez, because the Most Honorable Señor don José de Gálvez decided that San José should be the patron and protector of the new Monterey missions, to which end he contributed an exceedingly handsome image of San José, which is here now[103] and it is called "of the Carmel," because this is its original name dating from the time of the first discovery, made by sea by General don Sebastián Vizcaíno.[104]

[March] 11, Monday. About seven o'clock in the morning the Very Reverend Father President of the missions, Fray Junípero Serra, came over from Mission San Carlos del Río Carmelo to welcome us, with four other Religious, who were the ones designated for the two missions to be founded at San Francisco harbor and river: namely, Father Fray Francisco Palóu, Father Fray José Murguía, Father Fray Pedro Cambón and Father Fray Tomás Peña, along with the king's surgeon.[105] Remaining at Mission San Carlos were one of the mission's two ministers, Father Fray Juan Crespí (Father Fray Francisco Dumets,[106] the other one, was as I said at San Antonio) and the Father Minister of Mission San Antonio, Fray Miguel Pieras, who was ill. The joy which we all received at his[107] arrival was a great and very special one. After greeting each other with many displays of affection, we proceeded to the singing of the Mass. We sang Mass, then, in thanksgiving for our successful arrival, I sang it at the altar and the five Fathers who were co-officiating sang very finely and with the greatest possible ceremoniousness. The presidio and the expedition troops joined in with repeated salvos and musketry fire and together it all brought forth tears of joy.

Following the gospel, which because the feast of Saint Frances of Rome happened to be today was the one "concerning widows," *de viduis*,[108] I gave the audience a brief sermon, applying the gospel to the expedition as appropriately as I could, for which purpose I took as my theme, "The kingdom of heaven is like a net put into the sea and gathering every sort of fishes," *Simile est regnum cælorum sagenæ missæ in mare, et ex omni genere piscium congreganti.*[109]

And I began at once by exhorting all to give thanks to God for our arrival and for the success we had during the journey: Thanks be to God Who has behaved so kindly toward us, filling us with benefits and favoring us, during so long a journey, just as He did his most favorite people of Israel, etc. However, in order to make this all the more plain, let us proceed to recount the benefits we have more particularly experienced, so that we may better learn thus to return due thanks to God. I do not take into account those benefits that our own slight capacity does not extend to

---

[103] Portions of this passage are supplied here from the field text three entries later on.
[104] "Of the Carmel" refers to the Carmel River.
[105] The military physician (army doctor) José Dávila.
[106] Dumetz.
[107] Serra's.
[108] St. Frances of Rome led a community of devout women after the death of her husband.
[109] Matthew 13:47.

the realization of, which no doubt are countless in number, but I do consider the most palpable and perceptible ones of all, those which we all recognize and which cannot be denied, etc. We set out from San Miguel and traveled to Tubac through dangerous country where, if the Apaches had attacked us, we would certainly have had losses. From Tubac we continued on to the Gila River, and even though that is so dangerous a passage that soldiers and brave men feel their flesh tremble traversing it, we ourselves passed through without fear, without alarm, and without seeing any enemies' faces, even far off. We came into gentile country on the two rivers, the Gila and the Colorado, with the satisfaction and sense of security as if we were entering Christian lands, and without the least harm forded the formidable Colorado River. We crossed through the dunes, which the Indians themselves hardly dare to pass through because it is such bad country that not even birds dwell there, and reached the pools of Santa Rosa, where the expedition would have undoubtedly perished for lack of water, having found the pools dry; yet our patroness the Virgen de Guadalupe did not wish that such a harm befall us and so, through the slight toil of opening some wells, she provided sufficient water for everyone upon the day and eve of her feast day. We all met together at San Sebastián; was it not miraculous that no one perished in the snow and terrible blizzard that we had? Might we not ourselves have died, just as so many of our animals died of the cold? But why do I say died? No one even fell ill! In the California mountains, might not those Indians who had just destroyed Mission San Diego have attempted as enemies of Spaniards to hinder our passing and given us trouble and grief? But since Most Holy Mary, pillar of light and our defense, was guiding us, we reached San Gabriel successfully. No less success was ours in getting from that mission to this presidio here, for we passed through all that gentile country, particularly along the channel with all its inhabitants, and have found them, everywhere, at peace and allowing us free passage. Above all, we made this portion of our journey at the worst time of the year, since as those with experience know, this is the rainy season in these lands and this route becomes impassable with rainfall. But God did not will it to rain on us, so that we might reach this presidio successfully and in a short time, completing this portion of the way within as few days as though, almost, we had been traveling light; etc. "But Father," you will say to me, "didn't it rain a great deal on us yesterday? Didn't we get quite wet yesterday on the way?" It is true we did; but herein we find the finest touch of the benefit God gave us, by His arranging that we should get to know Him better through this means. For, tell me: if we found ourselves in straits at yesterday's rainfall, what would it have been, had it rained on us during the preceding days? But God willed it should rain on us only yesterday when we were already reaching the end of our travel, so that through experiencing this one hardship we might recognize how many of them God had spared us, etc., since a benefit is the better recognized through experiencing a single hardship and seeing the danger, etc. Through his sickness the sick person recognizes the benefit of health, etc. etc.

God gave us these benefits; through whose means? Through the means of our patrons, La Santísima Virgen María de Guadalupe, the prince San Miguel and our Father San Francisco, and so certain is this fact that no one can doubt it, and so clear that anyone can perceive it. Even the very number of the days that we have spent during this long journey encodes our three patrons, under whose protection we have ended our travels. Consider it thoroughly: between September 29 when we set out from San Miguel, and the present day, March 11, when we ended our travel—rendering God thanks by this due worship—we have spent exactly one hundred and sixty-five days on our journey. Who does not recognize that our patrons are enciphered in this count of days? The number 165 consists of three figures, the 1, the 6, and the 5. By itself the figure 1 is worth only one, but combined with other figures, even zeros, it is worth a hundred, a thousand, many thousands, etc. Whom can this number more appropriately signify than our chief Patroness La Santísima Virgen María de Guadalupe? She is the One, sole and elect, chosen among thousands to be the Mother of God and shelter of men, and, under the title of Guadalupe, the chief patron of this America, worth one hundred; and her patronage is enciphered even in the rays of light that we see here upon her image which has been the banner of the expedition and our comfort upon the way. Upon this sovereign image that we have present here, there are to be counted one hundred one rays of light between head and feet (this was the image of Nuestra Señora de Guadalupe that I had brought along, with which I set up the altar whenever I said Mass during the journey); in which number is encoded the patronage of this sovereign Lady so that we may realize that she, our chief and first Patroness, the one who is worth one hundred, is signified in the number one hundred, etc. The second figure is 6, which in combination with any other is worth sixty, and our second patron, the prince San Miguel, is signified in this figure 6, he whom we see portrayed at the feet of the sovereign image of Guadalupe and whose name Miguel, if you consider it thoroughly, consists of six letters. This prince, then, it was who—submissive at the feet of that wondrous sign which appeared in the sky and on the soil of Mexico City[110]—in obedience to God's precept rendered to Him the due worship that was denied Him by the evil angels whom he opposed, making fierce war upon them until he left them vanquished. With what weapon did he vanquish them? With that so famous and widely repeated *Quis ut Deus*[111] which consists of ten letters. Here then you see our patron San Miguel portrayed in the number sixty, because that is the number made by the 10, which is *Quis ut Deus*, repeated 6 times, which is Miguel. Even more plainly, in the number 6: In that wondrous and spiritual battle, it is recorded in the Apocalypse[112] that the third part of the whole number of angels who made up the seven choirs was lost along with their leader Lucifer, leaving Miguel commanding the rest of the good angels. Now, one who removes from nine the third part, which is three, leaves six behind; then this number 6 stands for our patron San Miguel, prince and head of the whole angelical militia, etc.

The third number is 5, a simple and lone number.[113] And what number more appropriate than this to signify that humble, sublime and holy single one, our Father San Francisco, our third patron under the title of his five wondrous wounds? etc.

So with the protection of our saints, we have reached Monterey with the success we have experienced. And for what purpose have we come? To reach Heaven by suffering hardships in this world, and by setting a good example as Christians in this country, cooperating in the conversion of gentiles, whose souls are the precious pearls sought by that heavenly merchant Jesus Christ.[114] Happy are you if you are fitted for so high an assignment as this one to which you are called and for which you have been chosen, etc.

Now you shall understand what Christ tells us in today's gospel. He says that the kingdom of heaven is like a net thrown into the sea, by which all varieties of fish are caught: *Simile est regnum*, etc.[115] Consider what happens concerning the net, which applies very well to this expedition. The fisherman casts the net into the sea and immediately a great many fishes begin to come into it,

---

[110]Refers to the sixteenth-century appearance of the Virgin of Guadalupe to Juan Diego the Indian.

[111]This is the traditional Latin interpretation of the elements of the Hebrew name Michael: "Who as God."

[112]Apocalypse (Book of Revelation) 12:4, as traditionally interpreted.

[113]A prime number. One wonders whether anyone in the audience appreciated this fact.

[114]Another reference to the gospel read during that service, Matthew 13:45–46.

[115]Matthew 13:47–48, as above.

but with different purposes: some are drawn by the bait, others carried away by curiosity, others following the others' example and to keep company with them; still others, perhaps, stirred by their inborn evil to disturb and tear the net; in sum, some of them because they are naturally good; others, and the majority, because they are unwary. Then the fisherman takes the net ashore, chooses the good fishes and throws the bad ones away, etc. In this expedition it also happens that way. Our commander cast the net of the recruiting that he was carrying out in Sinaloa in the name of the king our lord, etc. I do not doubt that you entered the net and enrolled with a good purpose of serving God in this way; who knows, however, whether many may not have been moved by the bait of wealth and comforts being sought? Who knows whether some joined the expedition being attracted, perhaps, by evil example and bad company and with the purpose of tearing down rather than building up, seeking a freedom of conscience, etc.? I do not suppose this of anyone, but I do say that if anyone came to Monterey with a wrong intention, let them try to rectify their purpose, and since they are among those who are called, let them be among those who are chosen; let it not be that at the day of judgment they should find themselves as fishes rejected by God after having had the trouble of coming to a land where the only comfort is suffering, etc. etc. Let us then give thanks to God, etc., and, in the name of God and our lord the King, I give thanks to our commander don Juan Bautista de Anza for the patience, wisdom, and courtesy which he as leader has had in guiding this expedition, and I promise him that God shall reward his work, etc. And I charge all of you, do not forget your obligations as good Christians, and keep in mind what I said to you in a number of addresses along the way, so that you may have patience in the hardships that shall come to you in the future, and by becoming deserving through them, you shall live in God's grace so that when we die we shall come to meet again in Heaven, etc.

God willed that all of this would turn out so well and to His purpose that I was unable to conclude without tears.[116]

Following Mass, the Fathers decided to return to Mission San Carlos, but we ourselves were unable to go there before the afternoon because of necessary business. So, while agreeing to have the four Fathers return, we successfully entreated the Reverend Father President to remain to dine with us. Even though it was somewhat overcast at daybreak and the day was a cloudy one, I made it my purpose to observe at this presidio here and succeeded in doing so, although with some trouble and not with the precision I had planned, even though I took the greatest care doing it. I found it, according to the tables of Jorge with no correction, in 36° 27½', and with correction in 36° 36½'. And thus I say: at the Royal Presidio of Monterey harbor, March 11, 1776: meridian altitude of the sun's lower limb: 49° 52'.

It was decided we should go on to Mission San Carlos, to accede to the Reverend Father President's requests and, chiefly, because there was no place for us

---

[116]Anza notes that "with considerable energy, our Father Chaplain Fray Pedro Font . . . exhorted our people to the end that they should demonstrate Catholicism by the good example of their lives, as a mirror sent by His Majesty's piety to these realms in order to convert their heathen people—the chief purpose for which they have been brought." This seems much less like the sermon that Font says he preached than like a reminiscence of the sermon on October 27 at Tucson, and a message that would be much more likely to please Anza's political superiors at Mexico City.

to stay at the presidio. And in the afternoon, leaving the affairs of the expedition in order and Lieutenant Moraga at the presidio with the people who had been transported, the commander and I, and a few other soldiers, set out from the Presidio of Monterey along with the Reverend Father President, the purveyor, and the presidio's surgeon at four o'clock in the afternoon. At five we reached Mission San Carlos del Río Carmelo,[117] keeping on a southwestward course and traveling one league. Here we were received by the Fathers, seven of them in number, with special joy and festive peals of the good bells there (particularly one large one that they had had brought by sea), which were answered by the soldiers with their gunfire and salvos, repeated over and over during the Mass by all of the troops there, and reaching as far as the presidio. We were accompanied by them[118] to the church. Father Fray José Murguía awaited us at the door vested in a pluvial cope[119] and there I gave holy water to our commander, etc., we venerated the holy cross, and, entering the church in procession, we intoned the Te Deum with great joy and tears of happiness over our arrival. And after giving thanks to God, we went on to the rooms and hospitality that had been prepared.

Mission San Carlos del Río Carmelo is situated upon a little height next to the sea and up closer to the Río Carmelo which empties into a small bight formed at this spot by the Santa Lucía range, which comes to its end here and at *Punta de Cipreses*.[120] Vizcaíno called it the harbor of El Carmelo.[121] East of and close to the mission lies the steep Santa Lucía range, ending here. It is an excellent spot, with very fertile soil; the climate a cold one, in a good way, and very healthy although rather foggy as is the case all along that coast. The mission has a church that is somewhat roomy and well built, although most of it is made of palisades and tule rushes and decorated somewhat with paintings. Separated from it are three adequate rooms that are the Fathers' dwelling. The rooms are well made of adobe. To the side are a kitchen, smithy, and two or three other rooms. Even though it has the mountains right beside it since it lies between the end of the Santa Lucía range and the range of Pines, it is, all things considered, an exceedingly fine spot, with a pleasing view due to its being so next to the sea and in a country that is so handsome and full of bloom that it is a wonder. It has a good-sized plain in sight which stretches upriver, between the river and hills upon which there are a great many pines, from which is named the Punta de Pinos

---

[117]Added in the final text, "marked by the letter **G** upon the map."
[118]Apparently meaning the Fathers.
[119]Evidently this formal greeting for any visiting clergy had been adopted from a custom followed in the most remote Jesuit missions of Baja California (Brown 2001: 172–73).
[120]Cypress Point.
[121]Apparently not true as regards the bay. The sailing master Miguel del Pino reported that he himself bestowed the name *ensenada del Carmelo* in 1771.

that forms Monterey harbor; also a great many cypresses, which give the name Cipreses to the other point which is on the side toward El Carmelo. All of the plain can be irrigated by the river, but the soil is so fertile that they obtain excellent harvests without irrigating. In the kitchen garden they get plenty of lettuce, cabbage, and whatever they put in, merely by watering the plantings once or twice with a little water. And this is very close up to the mission buildings.

The Indians belonging to this mission, now some four hundred Christians in number, I thought to be fairly sociable, not very ugly nor foul-smelling like those at San Diego. They are dedicated to fishing, and they do get a great many good fish at that spot. Besides sardines, which are plentiful and are caught at times without any toil because great numbers become stranded, there is a great deal of good salmon taken as they enter the river to spawn. The fresh water for this activity goes up so far that they assured me that some of the fish that ascend the Monterey River have been caught as far up as Mission San Antonio. We ate some of this kind of fish almost every day we were here. In addition as much fish was gathered as possible so that it could be dried for our commander to take along and hand out as presents. In sum, as good as the other missions are, I thought this the best one of them all.

[March] 12, Tuesday. We stayed to rest here at this mission. The weather was very cloudy at daybreak, and drizzling at intervals during most of the day. The expedition's Lieutenant Moraga came over to the mission in the morning. I went for a stroll to the garden, which is a stone's throw from the mission, and it was a delight to see how fine it was and full of vegetables.

Father Palóu was caring for it with such dedication that he spent the entire day working in it, and had it very well plotted out. It is square and has a border of pinks around it that are already in bloom, and its compartments are full of cabbages, lettuce, and other produce and plants. The finest thing about the land there is that such fine vegetables are gotten from it without irrigation that there are no better ones in Mexico City, such that a single cardoon[122] lasted regularly two or three days. It is not irrigated, because, so far, for lack of hands to make an irrigation ditch, they have had no way to bring one from the river—which can easily be done—with the result that they only water the plantings by hand. Afterwards, at transplanting time, they throw a gourd full of water on each plant, and this suffices.

I went in the afternoon with our commander and two Fathers to inspect the fields of wheat, barley, beans, chickpeas, peas, and lentils, and the sight of such handsome fields was a godsend, all of it. Along the edge of the fields goes the Río Carmelo, so called—as is this place—ever since the expedition of Sebastián Vizcaíno, when the name was given by the two Carmelite Religious who came with him and went here on foot from Monterey.[123] Also today, I saw the pole that had been brought by the sea and beached on the shore here not many years since. It is fairly thick, some four varas long,[124] round, and of a very hard wood I did not recognize, and all studded over with iron nails like hooks, of which it

---

[122] A variety of artichoke.
[123] An interesting detail but apparently not recorded anywhere.
[124] Eleven feet.

still held some[125] after about a half an arroba of iron[126] had been taken from it by having pulled out the ones that could be pulled. This pole came from very far off, since there is no iron anywhere in this country, nor is it known what purpose might be served by a pole of this shape.[127]

The small bight, which Captain Vizcaíno called the harbor of El Carmelo,[128] does not deserve the name of a harbor, since besides its having bad anchorage, everywhere rocky, it is totally open to the northwestward, which is the wind that most prevails here, and it is only sheltered a bit upon the east and south, by a point.[129]

The Fathers were very eager for the people to go on to San Francisco harbor, since this was why they had come, and four of the Fathers who were here had been here since two years ago, in storage, as it were, having been assigned for the two missions that were to be founded there. They were tired of waiting any further, for which reason I spoke to our commander concerning pleasing the Fathers, suggesting that he should select the most timely method for the people transported here to go on to San Francisco harbor, as the Fathers were displeased with so long a stay and even more with the delay they now feared because of Commander Rivera's absence and his reluctance with respect to this foundation. I said they would be satisfied with the people's going there even though the missions were not founded immediately, and if this were not done they were resolved to return to the colegio.[130] And he was so kindly with me that he shared with me his intention of seeking Señor Rivera's consent for the purpose by sending a message to him, and told me he would read me the letter once he had written it.

[March] 13, Wednesday. I said Mass. I wished to observe the latitude of this mission but was unable. Even though the weather was clear at daybreak, the sky clouded over with fog at midmorning. It cleared following midday; afterward the fog came back; and that is the way of the weather hereabouts, more in summer than in winter, so that one gets few days that are entirely clear.

This morning, our commander was in the course of attending to some letters to make up a post to Captain don Fernando Rivera and inform him of our coming here, etc., and he was suddenly attacked by so strong a pain in the groin of his left thigh that it scarcely allowed him to walk.[131] After dinner it grew

---

[125] In the field text, "many."

[126] Around 12 pounds.

[127] As described by Serra, the mysterious object, found in 1773, was originally 5½ varas (about 15 feet) long, tapering from 1⅔ vara (55 inches) circumference down to 1 vara (33 inches), all randomly studded with broad- and narrow-headed nails. The mission carpenters declared the wood to be *sabino* (apparently meaning redwood). Naval officers who examined it denied it could be part of a ship. (Tibesar 1956 2: 84–85.) In April 1774, when Anza saw it, those who had some experience of ships were maintaining that it was from a recent wreck, since the nails were not rusted; the points at the ends were not rounded off or decayed, and it was judged to be the broken-off third of a larger piece.

[128] See the note under March 11.

[129] In the final text, "by the Santa Lucía range."

[130] The Colegio de San Fernando in Mexico City. Font's information to Anza about the missionaries' threat provided Anza with material for a threatening postscript in his letter to Rivera of March 13 (Rivera y Moncada Papers C–A 368: 17 and 19; Garate 2006: 179, 220–21, cf. 20–21). See below.

[131] Anza had been planning to leave for San Francisco harbor and river on the following day. According to him, the pain, extending from the top of his hip to the knee on both sides of the leg, was so severe that it stopped his breath and he thought he was suffocating. Fever was also involved, then and in the following days. According to Captain Rivera, Anza said that he would rather be left crippled for life than have to suffer such pain again.

so much stronger that it forced him to be put to bed. He left the table with a great deal of trouble and almost had to be carried in the arms of others. The pain stretched down to his knee and put him in hard straits and this occurrence caused all of us no little regret.

The pain struck him as he was writing the letter to Señor Rivera, which he showed me afterward. He told him in it that he was going on to inspect San Francisco harbor, and that if he found a good place he would be proposing, on his return, to go back there transporting the people, if he [Rivera] would agree to that, even though he [Anza] were to delay another month for this purpose. He exhorted him to agree with this decision inasmuch as the viceroy would be greatly gratified with having that harbor taken possession of immediately and with this being done by placing the people there, who themselves desired to go there as that was their assigned destination and were showing themselves displeased at Monterey because of the discomfort they were in there. And, finally, that if this did not take place promptly, the Fathers were determined to go back in the first ship that arrived because they were unwilling to wait any longer. This was the letter that caused so much enmity on Señor Rivera's part against Señor Anza, since the latter declared himself on the Fathers' side and in favor of that founding which he himself so much resisted.[132]

[March] 14, Thursday. The weather was very overcast at daybreak and drizzling most of the day. Don Juan was a bit better on waking, though not greatly so, and thus was in pain all day, in bed and unable to get up. I myself had a return of that sickness and inflammation in my mouth that I first had at San Diego, and it gave me some trouble but was almost entirely cured by the lettuces that I ate here every day, very large good ones.

[March] 15, Friday. This country has a great deal of moisture, though one gets very fine days as well, at times. It is a good climate, however. Don Juan was in the same way as before and had not a very good night. I was a bit hard off with my mouth but said Mass to San Juan de Dios for Him to give us health if that were proper. The weather was as turbulent as yesterday's though without any rain.

---

[132] The letter is referred to again in the entry for March 17, below. As Font indicates, this was the communication which first disillusioned Rivera as to the understanding between himself and Anza. Anza's letter demanded ("you will be pleased to give me") a reply within twenty days, authorizing Anza's return to San Francisco with the settlers, "if you see fit," "as I do not doubt [you will]." Supposing Rivera's reply to be "that which I request," "we [will] rid our people of the discontents that they have been having, fearing their children's becoming spoiled from [their] having nothing to give them to do while transients; and [also] of the common claim that unless through extreme urgency, San Francisco harbor will not be taken possession of—which has been so much desired by the incomparable piety of our Sovereign and the Most Excellent Lord Viceroy," etc. Anza himself would be returning swiftly to Mexico City, rejoicing at "being able to say during my audience with His Excellency that [San Francisco harbor] has now been occupied, if not entirely." (Evidently, "not entirely" is a reference to the two planned missions, now regarded as Rivera's responsibility). The colonists would be left with Lieutenant Moraga and with the tools brought by the expedition, "a crowbar, three axes and as many shovels, or a few more additional [tools]," to commence building the new settlement. The postscript, as mentioned in the preceding note, describes the missionaries' threat to leave—"and I do not doubt that Religious who have been eagerly waiting so long for this assignment will do as they say." Anza's journal summarizes the main points as being requests, not demands: even without the eight soldiers he is sending to Rivera at the latter's request, there are sufficient forces for the occupation of the harbor, "even offering to him [Rivera] to lead the said force there myself if he cannot come to do it; or else to entrust it to the officer [Moraga] who is coming with this assignment."

[March] 16, Saturday. The weather at daybreak was good—clear, with fine sunshine—but with don Juan almost in the same way, and myself ill in the mouth without much improvement. I observed the latitude of this Mission San Carlos de Monterey (or del Carmelo) and using the tables of Jorge Juan found it, with no correction, in 36° 25½', and with correction in 36° 34½'.[133] And thus I say: at Mission San Carlos del Río Carmelo, March 16, 1776: meridian altitude of the sun's lower limb: 51° 52'.

[March] 17, Sunday. The weather was good. Don Juan got up for Mass, but it was with great difficulty, and other people had to carry him back to bed. I went to say Mass at the Presidio of Monterey, one league away, and returned to the mission after saying it. When I reached [the presidio], some of the expedition's people came to see and greet me, and to complain of the destitution they were in there, with bad drinking water, no water, and no soap for bathing, and so forth,

since Señor Rivera had ordered that no one should leave the presidio and that the mounts should be kept at the Punta de Pinos, were there grass there or not.

To this I responded with consoling words, as though reaffirming and crediting what they were telling me (and what, patently, was the case). The sergeant,[134] who had barely greeted me upon my arrival, overheard what I had said. He came out of his little room and told me, "Father, don't discourage the people." I answered him that I was not discouraging them by talking with them about the conditions and discomforts at the presidio which is what I had been preaching to them all along the way, etc. To which the sergeant responded to the people in an insolent fashion, "You're already here so tough it out or suffer!"[135] And he went back into his room again.

I saw the mounts penned up in the corral, and asked him why they were not being kept out in the fields all day as Señor Anza had ordered. He answered me that it was because Señor Rivera had ordered it so.

After the gospel during Mass, I gave a talk based upon the day's gospel and said some consoling words to the people concerning the multiplication of the five loaves of barley bread and two fishes which Christ bestowed upon those who were following Him with good intent, etc.,

by which He gave us to understand that the bestowals which God makes upon His own are not of temporal prosperity and plenty but of what is needful, and at times, unwelcome—figured in the loaves, which were of barley, not wheat, and in the fishes, which were not delicious meat, etc.

As soon as I returned to the mission, I communicated this to don Juan and

---

[133]Two minutes and a fraction too high—closer than his later observations (March 19 and 22).
[134]José María Góngora.
[135]Perish. Obviously, Góngora's opinion about the new country did not coincide with Father Paterna's vision of the "Promised Land."

what the sergeant had said to me concerning the mounts, whereupon he ordered that the animals should not be harmed by being penned up daily.[136]

Returning to the mission after Mass, I went to see the harbor that is close by the presidio there, and I saw that it scarcely deserves to be called a harbor given how small it is and how little shelter it has, even though the bight formed between Punta de Pinos and Punta de Año Nuevo is very large. I saw the marks that are given for it by Captain General Vizcaíno: the live oak to which he moored his ship, which at present has been cut down and only the trunk remains, and the stream next to it, on which a small dam has presently been made. A warehouse is being built not far from all of this, to enclose the provisions that are brought to the presidio by the yearly supply vessel.

Some soldiers that had been requested by Commander Rivera were dispatched to him today, along with Señor Anza's communication advising him of the expedition people's wish to go on to their destination at San Francisco harbor, so that he might ponder this matter. He personally offered to cooperate in order to take possession of that harbor in short order, by the settlement that was to be established there and that the Viceroy was so desirous of having take place quickly, and he indicated to him a time limit for the answer he was requesting, which he expected to have upon his return from the survey of the harbor there that we were about to go upon, so that he might proceed according to however he might answer.[137]

[March] 18, Monday. I said Mass. It was clear weather at daybreak, but afterward our wish for observing—Father Crespí by using his astrolabe and Father Palóu using his graphometer—was defeated by some fog. Don Juan had a bad night, though he improved some during the morning. I awoke with my mouth improved.

[March] 19, Tuesday. Fine, clear weather at daybreak, and our commander continued to improve a bit. I said Mass, and the last Mass was sung to San José, accompanied with deacons and all possible ceremoniousness, at which we Fathers sang and officiated, with myself at the organ. Following the Mass, the Father President preached a good sermon. Since he was feeling better, Señor Anza was present at all of this. I again observed this mission's latitude, and found it, according to the tables of Jorge, in latitude 36° 26½', and thus I say: at Mission San Carlos de Monterey, March 19: meridian altitude of the sun's lower limb: 53° 2'.

[March] 20, Wednesday. I said Mass, and the day was fine. Don Juan awoke

---

[136]"Whereupon . . . daily" is only in the final text.

[137]See the footnote to the March 13 entry, above. There were actually two letters of the same date, one of them dealing with the soldiers being sent (Casimiro Varela in place of Gerardo Peña, whom Rivera had requested) and with Moraga's verbal report on the desertion (already quoted in the note to March 7, above).

so much improved that he decided to pursue the journey for inspecting San Francisco harbor day after tomorrow, two days from now,

for which he wished—and I wished as well—that one of the four Fathers who were assigned to go there would come along with us, and they also were eager to come and would have gone with us willingly. But the Father President was not in agreement. Among other reasons that he cited, the main one was fear lest this might lead to delay in founding the two missions there, knowing as he did how slightly favorable, or entirely unfavorable, Señor Rivera was concerning the matter, and apprehending that he would be even less so if a Father went along since he might possibly think that the examination of the locales that Señor Anza was about to undertake was influenced by the Fathers. Thus, through his conduct, Señor Rivera has given great cause for regret to the Fathers and to the people bound for there as well.

I occupied myself today in copying the map of the harbor and river of San Francisco that was drawn up in Mexico City by my cousin Fray Pablo Font based on the information in the journal kept by Father Fray Juan Crespí during that journey which he made with Captain Fages.[138] I talked at length during almost the entire morning about the affair of Captain Rivera with the Reverend Father President, who did me the honor of sharing with me several problems which the commander has caused him and the Fathers, what with an unwillingness for founding missions or for supporting those that are founded, going contrary to the viceroy's decisions, and what with his being seized by excessive temerity accompanied by a complete self-satisfaction, paying no attention to the Fathers nor valuing their toils; and so forth. This is a trouble which occurs again and again with officers in far-off places, who find themselves in control and with any recourse a long way off. They do whatever their own opinion tells them or whatever suits their purposes.

This talk arose from my having said to the Father President that at San Diego, while speaking of how little basis there had been for the decision to found Mission San Juan Capistrano, Señor Rivera said: "I myself, Father, have not seen anyone more given to the founding of missions than this Father President; he thinks only of founding missions by any means whatever"—as though he were crediting the Father President with that founding which was done with such haste and so little precaution and foresight! This news which I gave him[139] caused him a certain amount of annoyance and displeasure, and in order to relieve himself, he told me the whole affair, which was a very long one, but in substance amounted to the fact that when Señor Rivera received an order from the viceroy for a mission to be founded between those of San Diego and San Gabriel without doing harm to the other missions and while still carrying out the founding of the two at the harbor of San Francisco, he immediately went to see the Father President in order to see that that founding should be carried out as soon as possible. And on the Father President's representing to him that the two missions of San Francisco harbor came first, he replied: "No, Father, those will be carried out when Señor Anza arrives; their affair belongs to him, and who knows

---

[138] The map was based upon a sketch by Crespí (reproduced in Galvin 1971: 118) but it was strikingly redrawn and introduced a serious distortion caused by the reviser's use of an erroneous latitude figure given in Crespí's journal (Brown 2001: 93). The name of the draftsman is recorded only here, by Font. See the introduction.
[139] Serra.

when he will arrive? And since I am entrusted by the viceroy with this one, I want it carried out as soon as possible since I desire to serve him,"—and so forth. This shows how these gentlemen perform their duties with respect to the friars whenever it suits them to do so. Certainly the Father President has always urged the founding of missions that were already endowed, but he did this with proper support, and in order to obtain this he went to Mexico City in the year 1773 to request it; and it was to these efforts that Señor Rivera was now attributing the founding of that mission, which failed. And, if the Father President had withstood it, he would have said it was not being founded because the Fathers refused.

I also learned, on this occasion, the reason for Señor Rivera's grudge against Lieutenant Ortega of San Diego, with whom he had previously gotten along very well and had been his compadre[140] when the two of them were in Baja California. As it happened, when the Father President left for Mexico City to petition for arrangements conducive to a better institution and regime for those missions, he also requested that Captain Fages be removed, not only because of his covering up the soldiers' licentious behavior with Indian women, especially when they had been slaying bears near Mission San Luis—not controlling their excesses lest they desert him because of the hunger and starvation they were suffering—but mainly because he took the entire command upon himself, wanting to deprive the Religious of any secular jurisdiction with respect to the Indians. The viceroy, then, told him to suggest someone else to be captain, which the Father President resisted doing, until finally the viceroy, after having urged him several times regarding this matter, asked him whether he knew of any individual over there who was of good conduct; to which the Father President answered that he was acquainted with Señor Ortega, who at the time was a sergeant and who had behaved very well on the first expedition. At that very time, Señor Rivera happened to be in Mexico City, about his own petitions, and the viceroy said to the Father President that Sergeant Ortega could not become a captain because he was not yet commissioned; however, Señor Rivera was there and if it seemed fine with him, he would name him captain. To which the Father President responded that he would concur in whatever His Excellency should command, since once this duty was entrusted to him, naturally he would be fit for it. Out of this, then, came Señor Rivera's anger with the Father President and with the Fathers, and his being their enemy though without any fault on his[141] side, since it was only a straightforward suggestion on the Father President's part, without his pressing it at all.[142] From this one must deduce that it is never a good thing for the Religious to get involved with the naming of officers even if it is required of them, since they generally repay them with ingratitude. Besides which, if the officer who is chosen or is replaced on account of their requests turns out poorly, the Religious have no recourse for claiming redress, for they will be described as malcontents. This is what was now happening to those Fathers, who at the sight of Captain Rivera began longing for Captain Fages, wanting to have him back. But they did not dare call for someone else who would show better behavior and would not disrespect them or oppress them like this man. Fearful of being refused, they did not dare to do so.

[March] 21, Thursday. I said Mass. The weather was clear. Don Juan continued to feel better, as did I.[143] I continued copying my map, onto which I added Monterey harbor and Bodega

---

[140] Literally, his fellow godparent, which no doubt was the case during their long service together in the small garrison at Loreto, Baja California, but here presumably implying close fellowship.

[141] Serra's.

[142] This seems inaccurate since, in proposing Ortega for commander in his formal recommendations to the viceroy, Serra provided a glowing, thousand-word tribute to the sergeant (Tibesar 1956 2: 300–304).

[143] Anza's journal reports that he was still unable to walk, although with others' help he got out of bed.

harbor, and finished it before noon. I observed once again, and along with me, Father Fray Francisco Palóu using his graphometer and Father Fray Juan Crespí using his astrolabe made their own observation, myself using the astronomical quadrant, and we found it: Father Crespí, in 36° 44', Father Palóu, in 36° 35', and myself, using the tables of Jorge, in 36° 26', so that we all came out nearly the same, and thus I say: at Mission San Carlos, March 21, meridian altitude of the sun's lower limb: 53° 50'.[144] In the afternoon I went with Fathers Cambón, Peña and Pieras (whose sickness was now better) to walk along the beach and the mouth of the Carmelo River, and there I saw the sea-wolves that are so plentiful along this sea and coast here, and heard them barking.[145]

---

[144] The final text says merely: "And I shall not note this observation because it is the same as that of the 16th with one-half minute more; although the three of us made some difference in the minutes."

[145] Sea lions rather than seals, although the Spanish term was applied to both.

CHAPTER 5

The San Francisco Reconnaissance

[March] 22, Friday. I said Mass. The weather was fine at daybreak, and so was don Juan.[1] And it was decided to begin our march this afternoon and that Lieutenant Moraga was to come along with us to the examination, with the expedition's purveyor don Mariano (who accompanied us as far as the presidio) remaining at the mission to manage the people's rations. The three of us Fathers observed again, as we did yesterday, and Father Crespí using his astrolabe found it in latitude 36° 40'; Father Palóu, in 36° 37'; and myself, using the tables of Jorge, in 36° 23½',[2] and thus I say: at Mission San Carlos, March 22, meridian altitude of the sun's lower limb: 54° 16'.

In the afternoon we took leave of the Father President and the rest of the Fathers from the mission, and at three o'clock in the afternoon the commander and I set out from Mission San Carlos del Río Carmelo to go (along with the expedition's lieutenant) onward to San Francisco harbor. At four o'clock we reached the Presidio of Monterey, having traveled one league to the northeast by north. Before entering the presidio, we went to look at Monterey harbor, and went on about half a league farther until we made out the end of Punta de Año Nuevo, which is hidden from view from the harbor[3] by the Punta de Pinos because it reaches far out to sea. We traveled for about two leagues in all, and don Juan felt no new trouble on the way, although due to the pain in his groin he was unable to move entirely freely and had to be helped when mounting and dismounting, which he was unable to do by himself.

[March] 23, Saturday. The weather was cloudy at daybreak and with quite a wet fog, no doubt resulting from the south wind which yesterday had blown with a clear sky, and it stayed cloudy all day. Don Juan got up with no setback in his improvement, and decided to pursue the journey, though unable to get onto or off the horse by himself because of the pain he still felt in his groin. I

---

[1]"Able to take a few steps," according to his journal. Although the surgeon Dávila had advised against riding, Anza felt no worse after mounting, and so rode to the presidio.
[2]Actually, about 36° 32.2'.
[3]In the final text: "from the presidio."

FIGURE 20. A map of the journey we made from
Monterey to the port of San Francisco, 1776–1777. By Pedro Font.
Reproduced courtesy of the John Carter Brown Library at Brown University.

said Mass, and in the meantime they were preparing the mounts and the provisions required for those of us who were going to survey San Francisco harbor, the great river, and the locations suitable for the two missions and the fort or settlement near the harbor mouth. This was the goal of the present expedition commanded by don Juan de Anza.

We set out from the Presidio of Monterey at a half past nine in the morning: commander Anza and myself, with Lieutenant Moraga; eleven soldiers, eight of them being escort soldiers from the Presidio of Tubac; and two being from the Presidio of Monterey,[4] who had been on the journey with Captain Fages,[5] along with the corporal from there named Robles,[6] who had been on the journey with Captain Rivera, so that being familiar with the way they might guide us to the harbor and the river; and the requisite number of muleteers and employees, which were six. These totaled twenty souls in all.[7]

On setting out from the presidio we went toward the harbor and at once took up an eastward course through the dunes along the sea, leaving upon our right two middling-sized lakes of brackish water. On going a short way, keeping on a course northeastward and a bit north-northeastward at the start, we went up and down through some hills

in which a very unusual odor, like that of amber, could at times be smelled but then would disappear. I could not tell where it came from. I smelled this same odor several times along the way, particularly between San Luis and Monterey, and occasionally I dismounted to smell some of the many different flowers that are found in those fields. However, I never found any that smelled similarly or so sweetly. From this I guessed that either there is amber along those shores that is cast forth by whales—since they are very plentiful in that sea—or that it is some kind of soft vapor sent forth by the ground there, since at times it is a strong smell and at others a weak, small one, abruptly noticed and then vanishing abruptly without a breeze to carry it off, as I noted every time that I smelled it. The Fathers there told me they had experienced it often and they too had been unable to learn what cause produces such a wonderful, fragrant effect.[8]

---

[4] The field text, before being corrected, gave the number of Tubac soldiers as seven and the Monterey contingent as three.

[5] One of the two was José María Soberanes. He was a native of Sinaloa, son of Ignacio Soberanes and María Petra de Pinto. Five weeks after his return from the San Francisco reconnaissance, he applied to marry Ana Josefa, daughter of Joaquín de Castro, from a family that had arrived with the expedition. See Font's mentions of him below and a footnote to April 23.

[6] Juan José Robles, who accompanied Rivera to San Francisco in November 1774, and also died with him on the Colorado in 1781. For his career, see Crosby 2003: 164–65. He may have had a brother or a cousin also named José.

[7] Anza's journal mentions provisions for twenty days.

[8] Dr. Greg P. Smestad, from his own experience, suggests that the odor described by Font was from a flowering plant, one of the Everlastings of genus *Gnaphalium*, probably lobogordo (cudweed, *Gnaphalium californicum*). The odor is very amber-like. *Gnaphalium beneolens*, named from its attractive smell, also seems possible. The flowering season may have been advanced into March because of the very dry winter or else the powerful fragrance might come even from the previous season's dried blooms, which remain on the plants in the way that the common name Everlasting suggests. Font's reference to whales is based on an old mistaken belief concerning ambergris; amber, of course, is hardened pine sap, with a resinous odor when heated (cf. Cornelius Tacitus, *Germania* 45: 6–8).

The hills end in a hollow that is not very long and there are no trees anywhere. At about four leagues we came to the Monterey River, which empties into the sea about two leagues away from here and which we forded easily since the rains this year were slight. Our course had altered at one point to the northward. We then took up a northeastward course, with a short veering to northward in order to get around a lake, and crossed over a plain of grass with not a tree on it, long and not very wide. It is called the *Santa Delfina* valley. In it, upon one side and the other, are several lakes or tule rush swamps, and it stretches for many leagues to the south and northward, ending at the sea bight formed by Punta de Año Nuevo, which is a mountain range that comes to an end there. It was at the foot of this range that we halted. This plain is the same one that I speak about on the 8th of this month, with the Monterey River running through it; it has the Santa Lucía Mountains upon one side and a very long high mountain range upon the other, and I thought today that this latter one runs from south to northward. At a quarter to four in the afternoon, having traveled eight long leagues, we entered into a hollow formed by some hills or not very tall heights running from south to northward. We halted along the way at the foot of a round hill where there are some sycamores and live oaks, and a small stream with some little lakes. Today's stopping place is called *La Natividad*.[9] We saw not a single Indian during the whole way; all that was seen was some smoke over toward the shore. The sea is not very far off from here, since the sound of its waves could be heard.

The whole route is a fairly level one, most of it grassy soil, with no trees except the cottonwood grove on the bank of the river.

[March] 24, Sunday. I said Mass,
and suggested to our commander that during this journey I should say Mass every day so that this land might begin to be sanctified and so that God would give us success and fortune in our discovery, and he thought my proposal a very good one.

The weather was clear at daybreak, which I credited to the northwesterly, a wind which in these lands is the prevailing one and which we had during the entire day, blowing a bit strong and cool. We set out from the spot of La Natividad at a quarter before eight in the morning and traveled upon a very changeable course. First we went in to the northeastward through the hollow; at one league we went uphill, eastward, along the hollow, and then at once went down quite a steep descent, course northward, for about a league, and crossed the *Arroyo de San Benito*, near which among some large rocks there is a cave[10] of some size having a separation in it, or divided into two chambers, that is very well suited for a life as a hermit.[11]

---

[9] The Nativity.
[10] The cave is said to be nowadays considerably fallen in. (G. Smestad.)
[11] San Benito Stream.

We continued on through another small hollow that ended immediately, and then came, on a northeastward and north-northeastward course, into the *San Pascual* valley, which must be about two leagues wide north and south, and more than the same again in length, and has no trees in it except for what can be seen—not many, and they are small in size—in the distance on the slopes of the hills. Crossing the San Pascual valley, we then forded the Pájaro River[12] very miry although it had very little water in it. Yesterday, in the quiet of the night, the noise of the sea could be heard, but not today. Because the Pájaro River has a great deal of water lower down and is so miry that it cannot be forded all the way to the sea, we came to make the detour shown by the courses given, by which we drew away from the sea.

We then came into some hills, and on going a short way we encountered the *San Bernardino* valley, which is very flat and must be about three or four leagues[13] wide and is very long. This valley is shaped on the north by the chain of treeless mountains which I spoke of on the 8th and yesterday, and today I assured myself of the fact of its running from southeast to northwestward, though since it does not run straight but forming as it were a circle, when seen from different spots it seems sometimes to run northward, other times westward, as I thought it did on the 8th but later crossed out.[14] This range runs onward to join with others that at the sea form Punta de Año Nuevo. On the south, the valley is shaped by the hills of the La Natividad gap—which in places have a considerable amount of trees on them—pines and what they call *palo colorado*[15]—similar to those hills that we crossed in order to get into the valley and that separate it from the San Pascual valley. Coming together, the hills run to the sea where they form the spot called *Punta del Pájaro* on the Monterey bight, named from the Pájaro River which empties out there.[16] We traveled north-northwestward about three leagues through this San Bernardino valley, over muddy ground. Clearly, it is mostly lakes during the wet season or whenever rain falls. Trees are visible in the distance along lakes or streams, wherever water forms pools with tule rush

---

[12]In the short text, "the Pájaro stream." This is the San Benito River wash, not the present Pájaro River, whose upper course hardly existed at that time.

[13]Altered from "four or five leagues."

[14]See the note to March 8.

[15]Redwood. The final text here, and afterward, consistently refers to redwoods as spruces: "The long mountain range that I spoke of on the 8th goes along upon the other side of the San Bernardino valley, and this valley is muddy ground, and most of it is lake when rains are heavy. There are few trees upon the whole way, but a great many spruce trees, and other sorts, are to be seen upon the mountains, and there are also some trees in the distance in the San Bernardino valley which must belong to the shores of the streams and lakes in it. In it we saw a great many antelopes and white and grey geese."

[16]There is no conspicuous point that answers to this description on Monterey Bay. The river was named Río del Pájaro by the first expedition soldiers in October 1769, because of a stuffed condor that was found in the remains of a native village.

marshes, to judge by what we saw and what was reported by the soldiers who went off to chase after antelopes—of which we saw several herds, along with a great many white and grey geese. We forded a stream in the valley that had little water but very miry, and at once came to a village in which I counted about twenty jacales of tule rush. However, with regard to people, we saw no more than two Indians who came to meet us on the way and presented us with three fish over a tercia long,[17] which we did not recognize though they have a mouth like the matalotes of the Gila River.[18] It seems they must be a type of freshwater fish that perhaps are caught in the lakes or ponds here in this valley.

We passed by a grove[19] of sycamore and alder[20] trees and followed the valley on a northwestward course over better soil than at the start and with better grass. At about two leagues at the foot of the hill range on the left hand we saw a great many Indians apparently running away. One of them approached to visit us on our way, and following his example, as many as eighteen of them immediately came up, while the rest of them stayed very far off so that we could not distinguish whether there were any women among them. They clearly were out hunting and they offered us some of their quarry. Our commander accepted a hare along with an arrow which they offered him as a sign of peace. They then immediately offered us their arrows and their quivers made of wildcat skins and other kinds of hides, as though trading them in exchange for beads. They had a great deal to say but we could not understand any of it. We judged them to be Indians who were very poor, as the ones whom we saw were quite thin. In addition to being rather dark, they had their faces soot-stained. I saw one of them who had his body painted in white rays; they wear their hair cut short.

We kept on through the valley for about two more leagues, as far as some low knolls where it seems to come to an end. Upon the plain itself, near the knolls, there are some small white oaks. We went west-northwestward over the knolls, and on coming down from them crossed the *Arroyo de las Llagas*.[21] And here we stopped a little after four o'clock in the afternoon, having traveled some twelve leagues in all. Here at the stopping place at the Arroyo de las Llagas we found standing the poles of the little ramada that was built during the journey made during September of last year by ship Captain don Bruno de Ayala[22] along with Father Palóu, when they went to survey San Francisco harbor for the second

---

[17] 11 inches.
[18] In the final text: "they were of the same variety as those that in the Colorado River we call *matalotes*—very spiny, and which live in the lakes there." A pike minnow or sucker. See the note to November 18.
[19] In the field text, "groves."
[20] *Alamillos*, possibly meaning, instead, "little cottonwoods."
[21] The Wounds.
[22] *Sic*; an error for Bruno de Eceta (Heceta).

time, and in which Father Palóu said Mass. We found that the Indians had made a fence of little sticks around the poles, and in the midst of it had placed a thick straight pole, set upright and about three quarters of a vara long[23] It was decorated with a great many feathers tied up in a sort of net, as if it were dressed. An arrow was thrust through it. Tied upon a pole were a great many arrows and hanging from another pole three or four balls of grass, like tamales filled with gruel. These were made from their seeds and acorns or foods that we did not recognize, and with a tuft made of a number of goose feathers hanging upon a long staff in the middle. We were unable to understand what mystery was cloaked in this decoration.

On passing by the village that I spoke of along the way, we saw a sort of graveyard at its edge, formed by a number of small poles—not, however, like the ones that we saw on the channel—and hanging upon them we saw such things as small snail shells, tule rush skirts that the women wear, arrows driven into the ground, and some feathers, all of which must have been treasures belonging to the dead persons buried there. I thought this place at the Arroyo de las Llagas—supposing that the stream runs year round—a very good one for a settlement since it has a good amount of level, good soil and sufficient timber of sycamores, white oaks and other trees. And I say, by what I saw afterward, that it is a very good spot if one goes on up the course of the river, which runs about northwestward, since seemingly it issues from among hills lying very close to a range of red pines and another large sort,[24] which is very well wooded. That plain, which holds a good many white oaks, terminates upon the south at the range's skirts; it is the same range that begins here and, running onward, forms the San Andrés hollow[25] and afterward ends at point *Las Almejas*.[26] As we continued on we kept this range to our left hand, while leaving upon our right, and at some distance off, the mountains that I spoke of on the 8th. The plain is closed on the north by these mountains running northwestward, which are all quite bare.

[March] 25, Monday. I said Mass. The weather was fair at daybreak although with the northwest wind blowing a bit chill and some scattered overcast, which turned into rather thick clouds after midday, from the wind's having ceased. Don Juan continued to be better. We set out from the Arroyo de las Llagas at a

---

[23]Nearly 25 inches.

[24]"Red pines" is another attempt at naming redwoods. The final text: "the range of spruces."

[25]"San Andreas," now well known as the name for the major earthquake fault line that runs through the valley from Daly City to Portola Valley, is a misspelling fostered by government agencies. The whole valley is referred to simply as El Cajón by Francisco Palóu and others in early San Francisco mission records, so that the name San Andrés (this was the spelling that was used locally until the twentieth century) probably already referred just to the area of present San Andreas Reservoir, and Anza and Font applied it somewhat wrongly. (See Brown 1975: s.v.)

[26]The Clams.

little before eight o'clock in the morning and traveled a northwestward course for about two leagues through the valley in which we had spent the night. It holds a great many white oaks of all sizes and some live oaks and other trees. We then went over some small-sized hills and down to another plain, most of which is a lake when rain is plentiful and now was dry except for one portion of it. The white oaks and trees continue along the foot of the bare northern range, which runs onward, and we traveled about one league upon the same course with some westward deviation. We went over some other small-sized hills and down to a good-sized plain that at first was very much grown over with white oaks and then had the trees running onward close up against the northern mountains. Everything else as far up as the foot of the southern hills that form the valley here is very level soil with lakes which, because of the mire, we circled around a bit in order to get past them even though they were dry.

Here is the *Llano de los Robles*,[27] which begins a little beyond where we set out from camp, and we kept on through it during the entire way. There are many white oaks here in this valley or plain, more in some places and less in others, some of them very large and others not so. Along the way we also found pools of water that turn into ponds during the rains. The water comes from the streams issuing out of the mountains on both sides and flows toward the harbor inlet[28] and disappears upon the flats and low spots there. The entire way is pretty level and good going, excepting when one comes upon some mire and has to circle about a bit to get past it.

Here about ten Indians came to meet us as we went. When they saw us, they shouted from among the white oaks there and out they came like fauns in the buff, running and shouting and making many gestures as though trying to make us stop there and indicating we should go no farther. But even though they came out carrying bows and arrows, they did no hostile act. They seem to be very impoverished Indians, but not as thin as the ones from yesterday. Some that I saw were bearded and one or two had long moustaches. Several of them were somewhat bearded and had a moustache. Many of them wore their hair tied up with a branch that went around their heads that held their hair in place, while others wore their hair short. They had their ears pierced like those behind us and on the channel, with little reeds in them. Although unwilling to approach us, they finally did so, and our Captain gave them some beads. Immediately some twenty or more of them came out from the hills on the south, armed with bows and arrows and some of them with long poles. We saw more people in the distance whom we thought must have been women, as seemingly there must be a village here, according to the paths and the number of people, although we did not see it. To judge by their shouting, motions, and gestures we were being told to turn back and go no farther onward.

---

[27] White Oak Plain.
[28] See the discussion of this term in the introduction and the note under March 27.

I think that today I must have seen over one hundred Indians. Of those who came to meet us, some thirty, seeing that we paid them no attention but were continuing on our way—or perhaps just because of the novelty—decided to follow us for a good stretch. The way they did this was to run one behind another in a line until they got ahead of us. They they would stop and commence shouting until they were hoarse, all the while making a great many motions and gestures as though they were angry and were not allowing us to continue on. Seeing that we were continuing on our way without paying any attention to them, they went back to running and getting ahead of us and then, though we were utterly unable to understand them, they performed the same actions of shouting and speaking very loudly and fast. They kept this up for about a league, until they finally departed. A few of them lingered and little by little they left us. We did not see them any more.[29]

We must have traveled somewhat over two leagues on a west-northwestward course, when we went over a hill or pass and then came into a large plain or valley some four or five leagues in width, and, in length, seeming to finish with the sea or inlet since we could not see its end nor any heights in front of us. From one side and the other a number of Indians came to meet us in this valley, clothed in the buff like all of them, and with motions and gestures like those of the ones behind us.

This valley, that I call the *Valle de los Robles* because it has so very many white oaks and quite large ones too, is formed on the south by very grassy hills and by mountains full of woods and red pine which run about westward and west-northwestward, and on the north side by the same chain of mountains that make the San Bernardino valley and others and that follow the same northwestward direction on the other side of the harbor inlet, and by what I could see of them today, go very far up. We traveled about six leagues through this valley, which in places has only a few white oaks and in some spots none; however, trees are always in view in the distance, in no small amount. We crossed two rivers of some little width, two narrower ones, and two streams[30] with deep beds, but all of them dry, and seemingly they issue from the mountains upon the south and run towards the inlet. All the plains here are very green, the more so wherever there are no white oaks, as it is better soil there; but the ground is rough wherever there are oaks.

We traveled through this valley, course west-northwestward, for a bit over four leagues and then traveled about two leagues westward until coming to the foot of the mountains on the south, near which we came upon the route that had been taken during the previous journeys. And a little before four o'clock in

---

[29]The final text, in which this paragraph occurs, omits much of the content of the surrounding paragraphs, perhaps out of a concern that the initial version inadvertently duplicated details of the landscape. This may well be the case, to judge from the parallel entry in Anza's journal (see the table of the Days' Marches), and from the actual topography.
[30]Altered from "three streams."

the afternoon we stopped at the edge of a stream of good water called *San José Cupertino*, at which there are a great many sycamores and which comes out of the mountains on the south through very small-sized hills and runs toward the inlet, and in the dry season has running water only as far as this spot. The place is at the start of a very dense wood of prickles that they call the *Bosque Espinoso*[31] although it has no thorns. From here, or a bit before here, we could see the San Francisco harbor inlet in the distance and a large number of trees in those surroundings. Today we went some twelve leagues.

This spot is a very handsome, lush one with plentiful firewood and timber, but it is not well suited for a settlement because of a lack of water, unless more of it could be found than what is in the stream. Perhaps some may be found among the hills on the south, which we did not go into, and planting ground as well, of which there is none at this place because it is all little hills.[32]

[March] 26, Tuesday. I said Mass. The weather was fair and a bit cool at daybreak although there were some clouds. We set out from the *Arroyo de San José Cupertino* at a little after a half past seven in the morning. From a hilltop on leaving the spot, we saw a great part of the southeastern inlet of the harbor, on whose shores there are visible a number of little inlets and a large piece of bad, muddy, nitrous ground before the water is reached. During some seasons, it seems that the inlet stretches out all across this margin and flat when it rises. We traveled a bit over one league, course northwestward with some veering to north-northwestward and crossed a stream with water in it called *Los Laureles* because it has a good many of them.[33] We then kept on northwestward through little hills and plains and came to the edge of a very dense wood of what they call *bruc* in Catalonia and I believe is called *abrojo*,[34] in Castile, and which, over a good distance, stretches to the inlet. And a little later, on going a little into the thornwood, we came upon a stream or slough with a great deal[35] of water that was in pools and barely running. We were delayed there for over a quarter of an hour looking for a ford across it and clearing the way out. And I shall note that this and all of the streams one comes across between the hollow or valley of San Bernardino and the harbor issue out of the mountain range to the south—which is full of redwood[36] and which I spoke of on the day before yesterday—and

---

[31] Thornwood.

[32] In the final text: "This spot of San José Cupertino has good water and a great amount of firewood but is not suited for a settlement in any way, lying as it does among hills very close to the spruce mountains I spoke of yesterday and having no level ground."

[33] The field text: "some."

[34] Thistly or thorn bushes.

[35] In the field text, "a good deal."

[36] In the final text, "full of spruces." From this point forward, the final text continues to employ "spruce" for the field text's "redwood" or "red pine."

flow toward the flat and the inlet. Close to here, before crossing this stream, we saw in the distance some sort of structure and went to see what it might be. We found a very round enclosure shaped out of laurel branches; it was woven together well and was about six quarter-varas tall[37] with a somewhat higher door upon one side in which to enter. On the opposite side there was another smaller door close to the ground, like a little window, a third of a vara in size.[38] Atop the fence were four tufts of dry grass beaten like hemp, and within, to one side, was a bundle of poles with no points, about two varas long,[39] driven into the ground and having feathers at the end like arrows, along with other shorter poles, all of them tied together. There was, however, not a single Indian about. We supposed that this enclosure was a place for dancing since there was evidence that there had been a fire in the middle.

We then traveled for about three leagues to the west-northwestward and came to the *Arroyo de San Francisco*, where we saw a village upon its bank whose Indians came to meet us on the way, and our commander went with me to the village and gave the women some beads and I counted about twenty jacales.[40]

We crossed the stream and came upon the cross that Father Palóu planted last year at its edge,[41] where there are a number of laurel, ash, and other trees. There are also eight redwoods, certainly a most useful sort of tree since they are very straight, long, and thick. I estimate that one of the trees must have had a trunk four to five varas wide. Below the crossing there is another larger one.[42]

We went on over a very beautiful plain full of white oaks, the ones which we saw along the entire way yesterday and today and which are also visible in the distance. It seems that they exist on the whole plain surrounding the inlet, which is a level area continuous with yesterday's plain. For this reason, this spot is an excellent one for a mission if only the stream did not dry up.[43] Perhaps by going a little closer to the range from which it rises on the south, which is the one so plentiful with redwoods, it is possible that water could be obtained there year

---

[37]Just short of 50 inches.

[38]11 inches.

[39]5 and ½ feet.

[40]By an error, the old translation (Bolton 1930, 1931: 326) reads "twenty-five." Anza agrees on "about twenty." The stream was called San Francisco because when camped there in 1769 the first expedition officers had come to an almost unanimous agreement that they had reached the "San Francisco" of the old navigators. Now San Francisquito Creek; the diminutive ending was added to the name by 1786 (Brown 1975: 82).

[41]The cross had been planted in November 1774. According to the Anza journal, it had been found subsequently (in September 1775) that the stream did not have enough water in the dry season, so that the spot, despite all of its advantages, was unsuitable for a mission settlement.

[42]In the final text, "some few spruces of the sort they call redwood, certainly a handsome sort of tree and, I believe, very useful for its wood, since it is very straight and tall, as I shall tell later on." "Later on" refers specifically to the triangulation measurement that Font carried out on the return, on March 30.

[43]In the final text, "I thought the San Francisco stream to be a lovely spot for a mission, if the stream is a year-round one."

round. We traveled northwestward about three leagues, level ground having a good many white oaks. Twenty-three Indians came to meet us at a league's travel across the plain, and then many more came out. Most of them were bearded and shouting. Closer to the village some women came out and our commander gave them beads. These Indians, whose long-bearded chief recognized Corporal Robles, were called *Los Gritones* the other time.[44] At about another league we came to another village where there was a large garbage dump of mussels. They get the mussels from the inlet and the villages commonly fight each other for them. We stopped there and our commander made the women a present of beads. We traveled a little bit farther, and the white oaks that are found along all the way up to here since the other side of the Arroyo de las Llagas came to an end. We traveled a bit farther still and arrived close to a village where several Indian men and women came out. Our commander presented them with beads and we stopped for awhile with them. One man had been wounded in the leg by an arrow. Another man stood with his bow and arrows making a great many motions and gestures as though he were fighting. He was pointing to the wounded man so we deduced that he was telling us they were at war with other villages up ahead and was encouraging us not to go there because they were very fierce.

We kept going, course west-northwestward, for some five leagues, and about a short league before halting we came to a village which was not small. It was located upon the bank of the *Arroyo de San Mateo*[45] which has a great many laurels and ash trees on its banks. Over this whole stretch, which also is level land, there are a good many laurels and some live oaks and an occasional white oak. This is not a bad spot for a settlement if the water is year-round, for besides enjoying a very lovely view it is level ground and has sufficient trees and timber, and more of it in the redwood mountains which are nearby here. Finally we halted at a quarter to four in the afternoon on the bank of a gully or little stream with very little water, not running, which is somewhat close to the hills on the south, having traveled about twelve leagues. We have been keeping the pine mountains upon our left, and there are some hills lying along in front of it which together with the mountains (which, across from where we stopped, have no pines visible on them and run on as only high green hills) form the valley or hollow of San Andrés; and seemingly not far from where we stopped is the spot between the hills where Father Palóu along with Captain Rivera was held up by rain.[46]

---

[44] The Shouters, probably in 1775. Rivera's exploration of 1774, which Font says Corporal Robles was part of, met only natives from the other side of the hills in this vicinity—evidently, the Lhamshín tribelet which also occupied the San Carlos area. The Shouters, south of Redwood City, would have been a different group, the Put·shón (Brown 1973; Milliken 1995: 34, 38, 79), who evidently were first encountered by Eceta's party in 1775. Robles therefore probably accompanied the latter expedition also.

[45] San Mateo Stream.

[46] November 30–December 3, 1774, before going on to the end of the peninsula.

At sunset some Indians appeared upon a hill, and then some others came out, drove the first ones away, and then came to the camp. To judge by the signs that they were making with their bows and arrows, it seems they wished to tell us that those former ones were enemies and that we were not to be afraid because they had scared them off.[47] These Indians stayed with us; they were very pleasant. I think they were asking me whether we would be staying. I could not, however, understand them. By using signs, I tried to tell them that we were going on. At nightfall we sent them all away. All of the Indians we saw today are quite ugly. Their ears and nostrils are pierced and a little stick is stuck through them. All of them were naked. The Indian women were wearing little grass skirts—not very thin folk, however. Most of them are bearded and their hair is cut short, although some of them wear it long and tied on top of their head like the Yaquis. They appear to be very docile Indians. A good, developed mission could be formed with them.

From this spot the inlet can be clearly seen as well as the mountains that form the harbor's mouth. Though very large, the inlet has very bad shores, since it is all surrounded for a good distance with marshy ground and little inlets leaving it and penetrating more or less into these margins and flats. However, outside of those flats, the land is level and fairly green.

[March] 27, Wednesday. I said Mass. The weather was very fair and clear at daybreak, with a sizeable mass of clouds remaining far in the distance behind us—a favor given us by God during all these days and the more so today, so that we might see the harbor we were going to survey. This would not have been possible if the fog had not lifted. We set out from the small stream a little after a quarter to seven in the morning and halted a little after eleven o'clock at the edge of a lake or spring-fed pond of excellent water next to the mouth of San Francisco harbor.

At the start we traveled on a northwest course for some three leagues over level green land with some rolling hills, but without a single tree. Only on the south side did we see a nook of live oak woods, not very far from the stopping place. The soldiers said there was a lake there, which according to the reckoning seems to be the one they call *La Merced*, where Captain Rivera was delayed.[48] Those hills on the south, continuing onward from the redwood mountain range, are

---

[47] The skirmish possibly was a charade designed to impress the Spaniards, since this location was at the center of the powerful Shalshón tribelet.

[48] No other record states that a lake at Rivera's and Palóu's campsite was named *Laguna de la Merced*. That camp was beside a sag pond which is now under the San Andreas Lake reservoir. Palóu's own account of the Eceta party's visit (Soto Pérez 1998 2: 961–62) appears to state clearly that the name was bestowed—no doubt by Palóu himself—on September 22, 1775, one or two days before the calendar feast dedicated to Our Lady of Mercy, *Nuestra Señora de la Merced*; and that it was given to the present Lake Merced, so that Font's location for the name is also mistaken.

very green but treeless, and that chain of mountains ends at Punta de Almejas. Hereabouts we saw a good many bears but they were unable to kill any even though they gave them chase. We then took up a northward course and traveled three leagues through somewhat broken, sandy country with a good deal of grass and brushwood and areas of small scrub live oak but no large trees. By detouring around the dunes on the shore—next to which we saw a sizeable lake of fresh water—and leaving them to our left, we came to the lake at which we halted: at eleven o'clock, very close to the mouth of San Francisco harbor, at the edge of a sizeable lake with very fresh, good water that appears to be spring fed, since a stream runs out of it with about a buey of water, issuing out onto the shore of the harbor.[49] I wanted to observe for the latitude, but as the pack beasts were a little late in arriving, by the time I set up the instrument the hour had already passed, and I was unable to perform it and left it for the following day. Today we traveled some six leagues. Since it had been impossible to observe, our commander decided to go and survey the harbor, and I was to do the observation tomorrow. So our commander, the lieutenant, four soldiers, and I went on to the survey. I saw a harbor of harbors, a prodigy of nature, one that is not easy to explain.[50]

First we went to the point of land at the mouth, where Captain Rivera had been (as I said on February 7) and where he had set up a cross, which we found lying on the ground. It was no longer in the shape of a cross perhaps because Indians had taken off the cord by which it was tied together and shaped. Here, using a graphometer that was loaned to me by Father Palóu, I engaged myself for a bit in taking bearings on the harbor mouth, *Punta de los Reyes*, Punta de Almejas, and the *Farallones*[51] that lie out to sea, and the whole length of the mouth up to where it enters the inlet.

On our way, we went down to a stretch of beach located among cliffs, onto which issues the harbor stream which no one had seen up until now.[52] The sea there is quite peaceful enough for a boat to land to safely take on water, since the waves do not break there in the same way as upon an open seashore.

We went down from here[53] to the seashore, very sandy, running toward Punta de Almejas, in order to see the *cayuco*,[54] that had been brought by the ship *San*

---

[49] According to Charles Lummis, a *buey de agua* was a unit of the old Mexican system. It is the amount of water that will pass through an orifice one vara square. Eldredge 1912 1:43.
[50] The final text adds, "the description of which I shall give later on." The final text also reserves the expression "a harbor of harbors" for this later formal description.
[51] Steep Rocks. They are now called the Farallon Islands.
[52] Anza's journal likewise says that the lake "had been till now held to be such," that is, without an outlet. The reference must be to the ill-recorded Eceta–Palóu reconnaissance of 1775.
[53] From the headland.
[54] Dugout canoe.

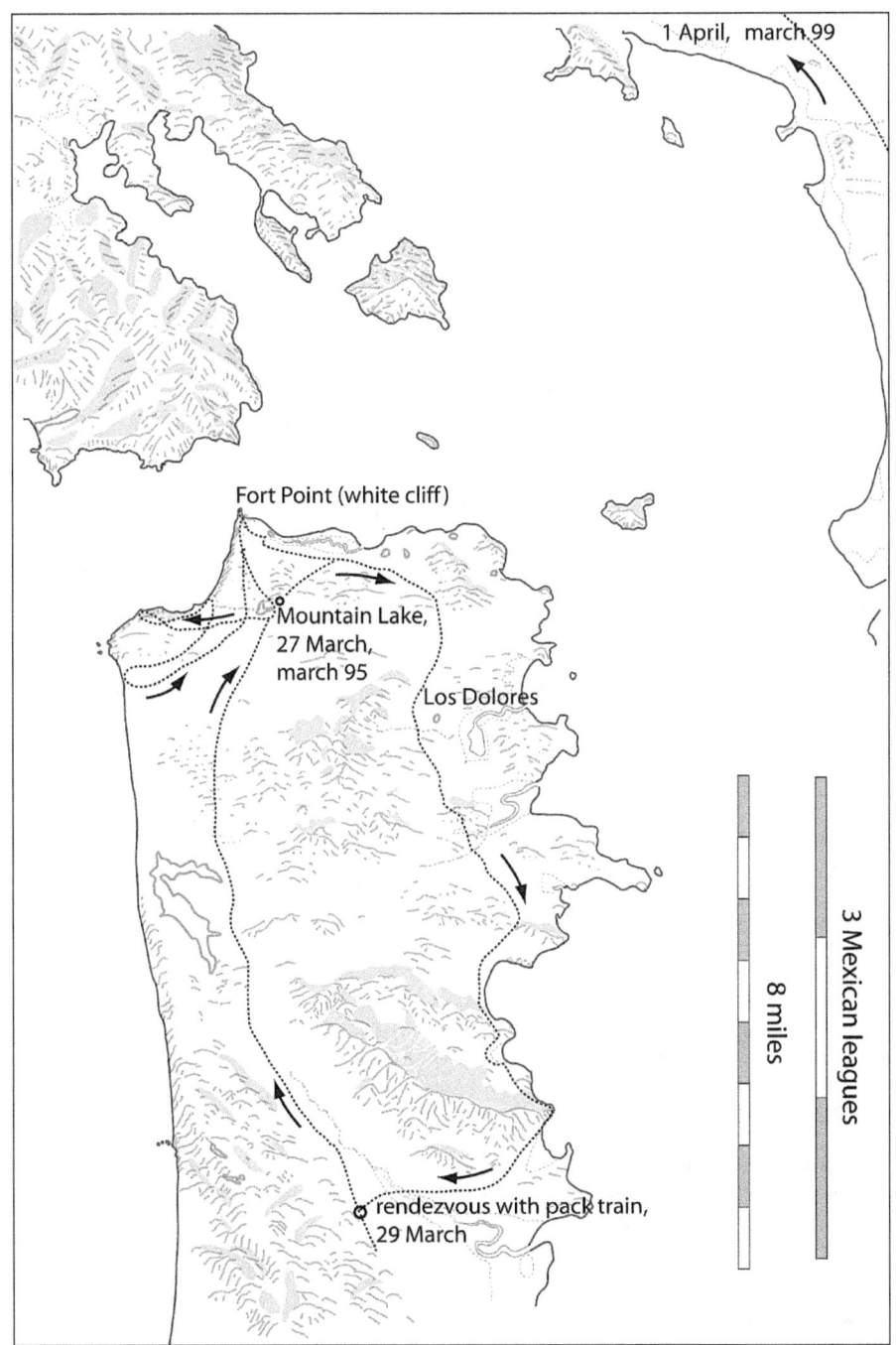

FIGURE 21. A reconstructed map of the San Francisco vicinity as it actually was in Font's time. *Drawn by Alan K. Brown.*

Carlos when it returned from surveying the coast above and entered this harbor, as I said on the February 7. We found it broken into bits and our commander brought two fragments from it away with him.

The cayuco is a vessel that resembles a canoe or small boat, like those on the channel, and is used by the Indians of the coast farther up. It is built of several boards, without nails, and the ends finish in a point made of a board that is hollowed out as though by using a chisel, to judge from the cuts and marks that were visible inside the point.[55]

We again climbed the sandy hills, went down to the stream and crossed over high hills until we came to the very edge of the white cliff that forms the end of the harbor mouth, and beyond which begins the large inlet with islands. The cliff is very high and straight-to, so that one can spit into the sea from it, and from here we could detect the outward force and resistance that the water of the inlet makes against the sea water on its way out, forming in the middle a kind of patch like a low wave,[56] and seeming to have a recognizable current. We saw whale spouts, a school of dolphins or porpoises, and otters and sea wolves.[57] Our commander decided to set a cross on this height. He ordered that it be made at once so that it could be set up the following day. So we returned to the camp, which was not far off, and reached there at five o'clock. We had gone some three long leagues during all of this. There is a great deal of grass at this spot and in its surroundings, sufficient wood, and good water, fine qualifications for founding

---

[55] It is untrue that the ship *San Carlos* had ever been engaged on the coast north of San Francisco, but Anza and Font evidently regarded the wrecked dugout as an artifact of the Northwest Coast cultures recently encountered for the first time by the Spanish. On August 13, 1775, during the second Northwest Coast exploring expedition, Captain Bruno de Eceta, in command of the frigate *Santiago*, had purchased a native *canoita* (a little canoe) "with two sharp prows, and extremely thin and narrow" (journal of Miguel de la Campa, in Soto Pérez 1998 2: 919, 948), near 49° of north latitude on modern Vancouver Island. Eceta brought the small craft back to Monterey on his ship and, once there, had it loaded upon a mule in order to carry it with him to San Francisco to aid in the survey of the bay being carried out by the *San Carlos* and its *pilotos* Cañizares and Aguirre. The overland party, which included the missionary Francisco Palóu (Palóu, "Noticias" IV cap. 4, etc., in Soto Pérez 1998 2: 922, 961), reached the bay mouth on September 22, where Eceta failed to connect with the *San Carlos* and turned back on September 24, having "engaged myself no further . . . than to inform myself of [the bay's] shape" (Stanger and Brown 1969: 36). Nothing is said in Palóu's record as to whether the Vancouver Island canoe was carried back to Monterey during the return trip. If it was abandoned and left behind, as Font seems to assume, then his and Anza's interest in the wreck they found may have been justified.

On the other hand, according to Palóu, a *cayuco* (a dugout) had been built by Spanish naval carpenters on the Carmel River flat in August 1775, to be used for the *San Carlos's* exploration of San Francisco Bay ("Noticias" IV cap. 2; Soto Pérez 1998 2: 904). During the actual survey, the makeshift boat was used only for minor ferrying tasks (journal of Vicente de Santa María, Galvin 1971: 32–33, 64–65). According to Palóu, a decision was made not to leave it behind for the overdue land expedition, but then it broke loose on September 17 during the *San Carlos's* difficult departure out of the Golden Gate, and five days later Eceta's and Palóu's arriving overland party found the cayuco on the beach somewhere south of the harbor mouth, "full of water and sand and with the oars cast away not very far from it." It seems likely, then, that what Anza and Font saw was this Spanish-built dugout and that the marks in it were actually made by steel chisels.

[56] The field text: "some small waves."

[57] Sea otters and sea lions (or seals).

Figure 22. Plan of the mouth of the port of San Francisco, 1776–1777. By Pedro Font. The early and late stages of the map. The commander's tent and another tent (Font's or the lieutenant's) are depicted at the camp site.
Reproduced courtesy of the John Carter Brown Library at Brown University.

the planned presidio or fortress here. However, timber for buildings is lacking, as there is not a tree in all those surrounding areas, and the woods of white oaks and other trees that we saw in such plenty along the way are quite distant.[58] The soldiers gave chase to some deer but caught none of them; we have seen a great many today, and also found antlers of some large deer.[59] Along the way we saw an antler that was over a vara in length, and the soldiers said that was a small one, as the large ones are over two varas.[60] Here at the mouth, at the harbor, the sea is so peaceful that the waves scarcely break, and their noise was hardly perceived from the campsite which was so close to the shore, even during the silence of the night. Here, in the vicinity and along the way, there are a great many lilies,[61] so I had them all the way inside my tent; with a great deal of wild mint close to the lake.

We only saw one Indian today, far off on the shore of the inlet. Two Indians came to the camp as soon as we had arrived. They were well-bodied and bearded. They made themselves useful and serviceable. They brought firewood and stayed a while. Our commander gave them beads and then they went away. According to what the soldiers said, while we were standing on the cliff with the cross at the mouth, Indians shouted to us a few times from the other side of the harbor, but I myself neither saw nor heard them.

The harbor of San Francisco, marked by the letter H on the map, is a wonder of nature and may be called Harbor of Harbors because of its great size and the number of coves it encloses on its margins or shore and at its islands. The harbor mouth, the entrance to which seems to be a very easy and safe one, must be about a league long and a bit less than a league wide[62] on the outer side facing the sea, and about a quarter league[63] on the inner side, facing the harbor. The inner end of the mouth is shaped by two very high, straight cliffs, on this side a white cliff and on the other side a red cliff, and they lie almost south-to-north of each other.[64] The outer end of the mouth, on the other side, is formed by some large rocks, and on this side by a high, sandy hill that ends in an almost round point and on its skirt has some white rocks within the water, like small island rocks. Commander Rivera reached the point when he came to survey the harbor here, and he set a cross upon it. On the other side, the shore of the mouth, which runs from east to west deviating southward[65]—a fact I observed on April 1 from the other side of the inlet or harbor when I traveled along there—appears to consist entirely of red rock. On this side, the shore of the mouth

---

[58] The final text significantly alters this to: "The only thing wanting is timber, there being not a tree on those hills there; however, the white oaks and other trees along the way are not very far off." Anza's first San Francisco journal entry likewise says "timber is lacking since in what was inspected there is none even for [building] barracks; I shall continue tomorrow in seeking it in the directions that are left."

[59] The final text adds, "which are so plentiful on the other side of the inlet."

[60] Over 33 inches, and over 5½ feet, respectively. Although 12-foot spans are recorded, Font repeats the 2 vara measurement on April 3 as referring apparently to the total span of the horns.

[61] Poppies, unquestionably.

[62] One league equal 2.6 miles. In the short text, stricken, "a bit over three fourths of a league" (just about 2 miles)

[63] Just under ⅔ of a mile (a considerable underestimate).

[64] The short text: "they lie straight south-to-north of each other."

[65] The short text: "east-northeast to west-southwest."

runs from northeast to southwestward, not in a straight line but making a cove. From its shore there empties out a stream issuing from the lake where we camped, and we called it *El Arroyo del Puerto*.[66] A boat may land there to take in water, since the seacoast turns tranquil along the whole distance of the mouth and the waves do not break upon the shore as they do on the coast outside. Punta de Almejas lies southward with respect to the outer point of the harbor mouth on this side, and must be some three leagues distant in an air line from it, with the shore, which is very sandy, forming almost a half circle. On the other side, Punta de los Reyes lies northwest by west with respect to the outer point of the mouth, and the coast going up to that point must be some twelve leagues[67] in length and does not run straight but forming at about three or four leagues,[68] by what I was able to see, a cove or a not very large bight. Visible at sea, at about some six or eight leagues,[69] are some rather large farallon of a sort of white stone, in this shape:

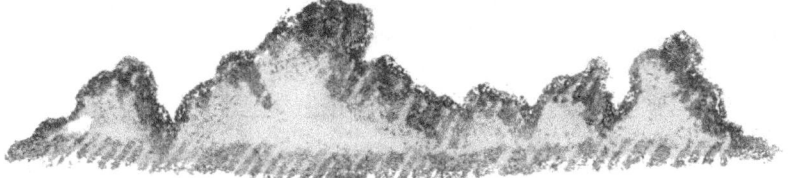

FIGURE 23. South Farallon. *Pedro Font sketch.*

—lying west by south with respect to the outer point of the mouth; and westward from the point farther out to sea four other island rocks are in sight, seen as having this shape:

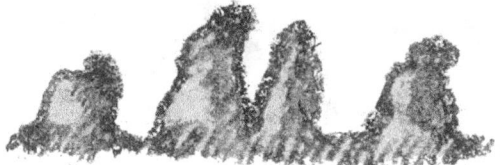

FIGURE 24. North Farallon. *Pedro Font sketch.*

According to information I received, Bodega's harbor[70] was discovered on October 3, 1775, by the captain of the schooner *Sonora*, don Juan de la Cuadra y Bodega.[71] It is situated in latitude 38° 18'[72] and lies some four leagues[73] north of Punta de Reyes, its mouth is formed by *Punta del Cordón*[74] on this side and by *Punta de Arena*,[75] on the other side. One league northwestward of the mouth is *Punta Murguía*, past which the coast runs on.

---

[66]The Harbor Stream.
[67]About 31 miles.
[68]About 8 and 10½ miles, respectively.
[69]About 15½ or 21 miles.
[70]In the short text, stricken: "Captain Bodega's harbor."
[71]*Sic*; Juan Francisco de la Bodega y Cuadra. Font reverses his family names.
[72]The sea captain's latitude is accurate.
[73]About 10½ miles.
[74]Point of the Cord.
[75]Point of Sands.

Beyond the inner point of the mouth, there follows the famous[76] harbor of San Francisco, and this consists of a large embayment or inlet as they call it.[77] It must be some twenty-five leagues[78] in length, and that viewed from the mouth runs about southeast-and-northwestward, halfway along which is found the entrance or mouth. Most of the harbor's shore, by what I saw when we passed around it, is not clear but muddy, miry, full of sloughs, and, accordingly, bad. The harbor's width is not equal throughout, since at the southeastern end it must be a league and in the middle four leagues. At the northwestern extreme it ends in a large bay somewhat more than eight leagues in size, as far as it appeared to me. I saw that its shore was clear, not miry like the one before, and it has an almost round shape although several coves can be observed on it. This is why I was unable to make out its shape very well at such a far distance. About halfway along the bay on the shore on this[79] side lies the outlet or river mouth of what up until now was thought to be a very large river and was called the river of San Francisco. From here on out I shall be calling it the mouth of the Freshwater Harbor because of the tests that were made when we went to survey it and which I shall tell about hereafter.

I counted eight islands inside the harbor and am unable to vouch for whether there are more of them. On coming into the harbor, the first island encountered, the center of which as viewed from the outer point of the mouth on this side bears northeast by north with respect to it, lying about a league[80] from the mouth, is called *Isla del Angel*, or *de los Angeles*[81] behind which the ship *San Carlos* anchored, as I said on February 7. It must be a short league in length, and viewed from the mouth it has this shape:

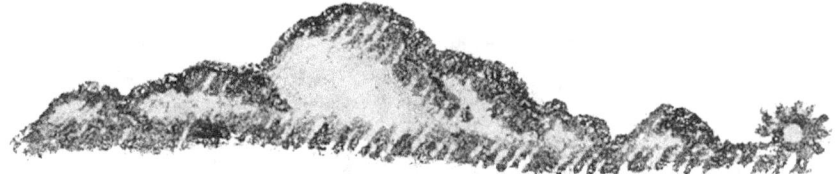

FIGURE 25. Angel Island. *Pedro Font sketch.*

Opposite the mouth there is a very small one like an island rock and another one, not so small, and still another, larger one about to the southeastward. Another quite large island can be seen at the southeastern extremity, very close to the land; I demarcated it later while passing close to it.[82] Another, around three leagues long, also close up to the land, is seen to the northwestward,[83] and near it are two other small ones, which I saw when we passed around the harbor, and on the way I demarcated the large one.[84] These seem, upon this side, to form the beginning of the

---

[76]"Famous" is added between lines, in the short text.
[77]So called since the first expedition of 1769, which confused the bay with the inlets (*esteros*) described as lying under Punta de Reyes. See the introduction and March 25, with note.
[78]In the short text, stricken: "some twenty-six leagues." About 65 or 67½ miles respectively.
[79]The east side (toward inland, on the way back to Sonora, which is where Font, after the expedition, thinks of himself as writing).
[80]In the short text, added and then stricken, "about a league and a half within the mouth."
[81]Angel Island or Island of the Angels.
[82]"Demarcating" indicates taking bearings, either by compass or by the graphometer. Here the final version inserts the profile of the Coyote Hills, placed below in the March 30 entry in the field version.
[83]*Sic*; "northeastward" must have been the originally intended word.
[84]Here the final text places the profile of the Richmond Peninsula, which will be seen below in the April 1 entry.

large bay which is the terminus for this immense gulf[85] of waters which, enclosed as they are and surrounded by mountains, are as peaceful as though within a cup. Finally, and in addition to the aforesaid islands, there is a middling-sized one in the bay and opposite the mouth of the Freshwater Harbor.[86]

As soon as we had arrived back from the survey, I said to Señor Anza, "Sir, since you intend to set up the cross at the harbor tomorrow, have it made right now, so that I can bless it after Mass tomorrow, if you think this is a good idea, before going to set it up." He answered me, "It will be done *there*, Father." And turning his back on me he went into his tent, snorting, and muttering between his teeth: "He's always coming around with 'if you think, if you think'." The thing was, he was unable to bear my giving him my opinion on any matter, and he was still rather put out by yesterday's annoyance, the cause of which I am about to tell. What happened was that I was bringing him the journals of Father Crespí and Father Palóu which they kept during their journeys and the map that I had copied of the harbor. Señor Anza had not wanted me to bring any of these items along, saying that what they had told him in conversation was enough for him. After we had stopped at the small stream, I brought out the journals and went over to where he was, leaning half-backward because of the pain he was still feeling in his groin. I began to read and the lieutenant sat down beside me to listen. Shortly after, Señor Anza stood up and leaving me with the portfolio in my hands he went off and sat down a bit away from me. (The same thing already had happened to me at the Arroyo de las Llagas when, on my having brought out the map, he stood up without trying to look at it and went off to take a walk a little way off.) Thereupon I went over to where he was and said to him, "Sir, it appears that you don't like me to read the journal to you since you have come to sit over here, leaving the place where you were seated empty. And this is not the first time that you have walked away from me while I was reading." He answered me that he had changed places because he was just as fine sitting there as here. I said to him, "No, sir; you don't have to admit it to me, but it is quite clear that you moved so you would not have to listen to me. If I take out the journal, it is because we have come to survey the harbor and the places that are suitable for the two missions. And the journal, which I am bringing along because you did not want to bring it, can enlighten us." He answered me that he had no need of the journal and that he was not stopping me from reading it. If he had any questions, he would ask me. He said that searching for places for missions was not part of his assignment since that matter pertained to Señor Rivera. His only responsibility was to survey the harbor for the purpose of locating the garrison there. He himself would see to it that he fulfilled the orders he had and would do whatever he thought best according to what he thought of the terrain. And so forth. In the end, we chatted for a while, man to man in a friendly fashion, but he still appeared to be rather put off by my having brought up a topic of this sort, as though it were exclusive to him. He could not tolerate my giving my opinion about anything. I record this in order to show what tact one has to use when dealing with individuals who are of a sensitive temperament and who have a high opinion of themselves, for we had been getting on well together, and this alone was enough to upset him. However, we got along well again afterward because of how deeply engaged he was in wanting to make the survey of the harbor and river and in carrying it out. And, because of the set-tos that we had with Señor Rivera during our return, we continued to get along until the end of the journey, when I lost his favor again, either because he no longer needed me or because he had hidden his dislike until then.

---

[85]*Piélago*. A gulf, sea (perhaps with islands). See the introduction.

[86]The final text continues: "it takes this shape," and inserts the profile of Mare Island which I have moved to the April 2 entry, corresponding to the description in the field version.

FIGURE 26. Topographic plan of Fort Point and vicinity, San Francisco, 1847. By W. H. Warner. North is toward the bottom.
Courtesy of the U.S. National Archives and Records Administration, Washington, D.C.

[March] 28, Thursday. I said Mass. The weather was fair at daybreak though with a few clouds that almost kept me from observing, although in the end, by using care and patience, I did manage to make the observation. Our commander decided to erect the holy cross, which I blessed following the Mass, upon the tip of the white cliff at the inner point of the harbor or inlet mouth where we had last been yesterday afternoon. About eight o'clock in the morning he and I went there with the lieutenant and four soldiers and erected the cross, which was left set up at the end of the white cliff at a sizeable enough elevation to be seen from the whole harbor entrance and from quite a good distance away. And our commander left written on a paper placed beneath some stones at its foot the notice of his arrival and the survey of this harbor. While on our way, we went up a small-sized knoll and at once came onto a very handsome, green, flowery tableland with a great many field violets, of which there are a great many hereabouts and which I had not seen anywhere until today in any of the country I have been traveling through.

The tableland is a very open one, of considerable extent, and level with a bit of a slope toward the harbor. It must be about half a league wide and a bit more in length and becomes progressively narrower until it ends right at the white cliff. This tableland affords a most delightful view, since a good part of the harbor and its islands lie open to view from it, all the way to the other side, and the harbor mouth and as much of the sea as sight can take in, out to beyond the island rocks. Despite the very good spots and fine country I have seen in the places I have been through, I have seen none that has pleased me so much as this one. I consider that nothing in the world could be finer, were it possible for it to be as well peopled as in Europe, since it has the best advantages for having a most beautiful city established at it, with every desirable access both by land and by sea, and with that harbor, so remarkable and spacious, where there can be constructed shipyards, dry docks, and whatever more shall be wanted. Our commander designated this tableland to be the site of the new settlement and fort that was to be established here at this harbor, since it lies at such a commanding height as to make it possible to defend the entrance of the harbor mouth by musketry. The water to supply the people can come from the spring-fed pond or lake where we camped, and that is only the distance of a musket shot.

Using the graphometer I again surveyed the harbor mouth and its configuration; we turned our attention to the water currents;

and I attempted to demarcate it.[87] And from here, our commander decided to go inspect those hills which run to the inner part of the harbor, to see whether he might find any good advantages in the vicinity for accommodating the new settlement.[88]

We then descended a slope and came to the shore of the inlet, which is clean here because of its nearness to the mouth. We found a small jacal on the shore with four little children in it; this must have been where the Indians who came to the camp yesterday were from. Four of them, very docile and courteous, also

---
[87]The final text continues, "The plan is the one that I shall set at the end of this entry." See figure 22.
[88]Here the final text inserts the profile of the San Bruno Mountain, found below in the field text.

came by today. We kept on beyond here along a level lying within a nook made by some hills, all of it very good soil full of grass and other plants, and in the midst of the level is a little lake, a sort of spring-fed pond or freshwater spring, with tule rushes which had been used to make three tule balsas that we saw there. And if a ditch is dug to the shore of the inlet this water here can flow to it, and then the whole level, which is no small one, is rendered very good for planting.[89] There appears to be water year round, since it is very green and lush and there are a good many bushes in the little hollows where the hills end. We again went up a hill and came into a very dense wood of scrub oak and other bushes and shrubs. It goes on for a good distance over the hills here at the edge of the inlet.

It had been intended for us to go on and inspect all of those hills and nooks, in the flat parts of which, seen from afar, there had been some patches of water and level ground, but our commander told me it would be better if I returned to the camp so as not to miss making the observation, since it was after ten o'clock and he had resolved not to return until he and the lieutenant had finished noting everything good about this place and its surroundings even if he spent the entire day at it. And that is how it was done. Just with what I saw yesterday and today, I was satisfied that this spot has very good potential for the planned settlement. It has a great deal of wood, water and grass for horses and stock, all close by, which is the main thing needed. And it only lacks timber for building; this is not very far away, for, once measures are taken to get it, either by using oxen on land or canoes over the inlet, even masonry structures can be built. There is a good

---

[89]Anza's judgment in his journal was more qualified: "at about a little over half a league eastward from the camp here there is quite a large lake that can be no less than a permanent one at all seasons . . . and, be it as it may, with a week's labor and a stockade and earth-stopped weir it can be made to provide to the utmost. It has no soil that can be irrigated [for cereal crops], as the rise of the tides fills the low-lying land, but good gardens can be gotten from the shores of the aforesaid lake," watered as they will be by the continual dews and fogs. Yet in his letters of May 1 and 2 to Rivera, Anza speaks of having soldiers' gardens at "a lake in between the fort and mission, where by stopping its flow at a proper time, enough water will be collected for [even] greater purposes." Further, Rivera's first and most important step respecting the new settlement ought to be to send Moraga there (in advance) to impound the water. Anza enumerates for Rivera the available sources for the presidio. (1) An unfailing supply even in deepest dry spells from shallow wells to be dug at the foot of the White Cliff (Fort Point). (2) The lake where he camped, with a *buey* of water issuing from it (Mountain Lake). (3) A small amount of water southeast of the chosen presidio site, reported by Corporal Robles, perhaps running, perhaps not, but "found even far into the recent dry spell"—the unusually dry winter and spring, of which Font repeatedly speaks. ("Y está corriente o no, me dijo el cabo Robles vio [agua], aunque largo en la seca pasada, al sueste" [es decir, sureste].) In the event, this became the presidio's main water supply, known as El Polín, after it was dug out by Lieutenant Moraga and the recruited settlers later in 1776 to improve the flow (Rivera to the viceroy, February 26–March 3, 1777, Rivera y Moncada Papers C-A 368). (4) Another lake about a league [*sic*] away, also with a flow which, as Anza had already told Rivera, can be held up with a very little labor, having only enough land for livestock and for making a few gardens (toward the Marina). (5) In addition, two other lakes between the same one and the fort, as well as other little spring-fed sources, although Anza estimates that they are not year-round ones. (Cf. Garate 2006: 104, 110, 198, 201–202.)

deal of quarry-stone and rock close by.⁹⁰ I returned to the camp, having traveled some two long leagues.

I observed the latitude of this harbor, and using the tables of Jorge Juan I found it, with no correction, in latitude 37° 40' and with correction in 37° 49',⁹¹ and thus I say: at the mouth of San Francisco harbor, March 28, 1776: noon altitude of the sun's lower limb: 55° 21'. Afterward I occupied myself by making a plan of the harbor according to the bearings I had managed to take yesterday afternoon and when we went to view it today, using the compass that our commander loaned me at the time and the graphometer I had with me. At a half past four in the afternoon our commander and the lieutenant returned from the inspection, very well pleased from having found more than they expected within the fold of these hills, whose extent does not reach three leagues.⁹² In them and in their hollows, they found a great deal of woods and firewood, a great deal of water in several spring-fed ponds or lakes, a good deal of land for growing crops, and, in sum, a vast amount of grass in the whole countryside. There are also a good number of docile Indians who are encamped at the foot of these hills at the shore of the inlet, so that the new settlement can have a great deal of wood, water and grass for their mounts, all of it close by. Only, they did not come upon any timber to build with; but the rest is extraordinary for a town and mission.⁹³

And as much timber as shall be wanted may be gotten through taking some small measures, since there is a plain of about fifteen leagues, extending all the way from some six leagues on the other side of the Arroyo de San José Cupertino to some three leagues this side of the Arroyo de San Francisco, and called the Llano de los Robles because it is very thick with oaks of all sizes. Very good timber can be obtained from these trees. In addition to this, a very high mountain range extends from the vicinity of the Arroyo de las Llagas all the way to Punta de Almejas, most of it dense with spruces and other trees which come as far as the San Andrés hollow which I shall speak of tomorrow. As much timber of all sizes as shall be wished for can be obtained from these places and with not a great deal of trouble. Getting it out is not very difficult. This is in addition to the timber that can be seen on the other side of the harbor in the mountains leading toward Punta de Reyes, and also what is in the woods and mountains on the other side of the inlet or harbor.

The Indians we saw on the way from Monterey to the harbor seem docile, healthy, and very poor. By the unarmed way in which they presented themselves, they showed no signs of being

---

⁹⁰This somewhat confused sentence is not in the final text.
⁹¹Font's result was less than half a minute too high with this observation.
⁹²The last phrase is not in the field text but is in the short text. In the final text it is altered, optimistically, to "must be some three leagues."
⁹³A judgment again modified in the final text, in the optimistic direction: "It lacks only timber for large buildings, although there is a good amount of tree timber in the woods for jacales, barracks and for the presidio's stockade." Anza's entry speaks of "endless amounts of wood for barracks, mostly green and dry live oak of a good thickness but bent over toward the ground because of the northwest wind so incessant on the coast; and [on] the inlet to the southeast a good spot for planting with irrigation, taken from a good-sized spring or source even if the present flow lessens by a half."

war-like or of having any bad intentions. And those who live in the vicinity of the harbor are quite bearded, but they are no different in color than the rest of them. I am stating this reminder here and later on, in opposition to the information given by Father Crespí in his journal where he says that he saw white, redheaded, and bearded Indians during his journey. We were traveling with hopes of seeing Indians of this type. However, even though the Indians we saw were the same ones that Father Crespí saw and, as the experienced soldier[94] assured us, we had been passing through the same villages, we saw no such white Indians, but instead only dark Indians like all the rest of them. Upon returning I took Father Crespí to task over this report he had given which we had found not to be so. He, being as candid as he is, responded to us with great simplicity and no self-importance: "They probably are not white since you clearly saw them; if that is what I said, then that was how it appeared to me." This was probably because the Father is so good and fond of Indians, and since he saw that those poor Indians were docile and friendly—just as they appeared to us—they seemed like angels to him.[95]

[March] 29, Friday. I said Mass. The weather at daybreak was fair though with a bit of a strong, cool south wind that after midday turned into a little drizzle which was no matter. We set out from the lake or spring-fed pond from which the stream that was first encountered arises, the one that we called the Arroyo del Puerto, at a quarter past seven in the morning. In view of yesterday's inspection, our commander decided to set out from the harbor by going around the heights that surround it in the vicinity of the mouth, and which viewed from the plain of the Arroyo de San Mateo here make the shape and to follow its inner shore until we came out to level land. This is why he sent off the pack train to return by the direct route with orders to halt at the Arroyo de San Mateo. We took a different direction and traveled eastward for a bit over a league. After crossing through a great deal of woods we came to a lake from which a stream issues that runs toward the inlet. We then kept on to the southeastward for a bit over a league[96] and came to a handsome year-round stream of extremely fine water, so adequate that the one at Mission San Gabriel cannot improve on it. Because it was the Friday of Sorrows[97] we called it the *Arroyo de los Dolores*. On its banks we found a great deal of very fragrant chamomile which had a yellow leaf and bud, and a great many field violets and other plants and flowers.[98] There is a good amount of soil for planting. Close to the stream the lieutenant sowed some grains of corn and chick peas to test the soil here, which we thought to be very good. And so I thought that this place would be very suitable for a mission,

---

[94]Corporal Robles.
[95]See Brown 2001: 62–63 for a commentary on this passage.
[96]In place of this passage, the final text sums up this first part of the march as being "over wooded hills and low spots with good soil in which we came across two lakes and some spring-fed pools with good water and with a great deal of grass, fennel and other good herbs."
[97]The Friday of Sorrows is the Friday before Palm Sunday and Holy Week.
[98]At the end of the entry, the field text adds "Among other good plants, lilies, violets and other flowers that I saw at the Arroyo de los Dolores, I saw great deal of chamomile. "

once the step is taken of bringing the timber for it from that hollow we inspected today.[99] It has a great deal of firewood, sizeable amounts of very fine water, sufficient and very good soil, and a good many docile Indians dwelling here.[100]

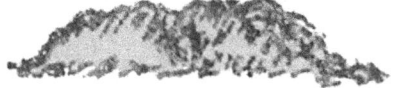

FIGURE 27. San Bruno Mountain. *Pedro Font sketch.*

We rode a little way, and I viewed the inlet from a small height (which must be three leagues from the point of the cliff at the harbor mouth). From that spot I could see almost to the end of the inlet and, by looking along the center of the water, I observed with the compass that the median of its end extends southeast by east or even nearly east-southeastward, and that the pine or redwood mountain range seen upon the other side of the inlet lay northeastward with respect to this place.[101] I noted also that the third island that I saw yesterday from the harbor mouth is a bit over a league long. And I saw that a very tall redwood tree, viewed from very far off, standing out like a large tower in the midst of all those oaks on the Llano de los Robles, and situated on the bank of the Arroyo de San Francisco, bears southeastward.

Close to this small height, at the end of the hill on the side toward the harbor is a good-sized piece of level ground overlooked by the Arroyo de los Dolores, which as it issues from the hills comes into it over a waterfall, and which can be used to irrigate all of it. Right at the fall a mill could be built, since it is very well suited for the purpose.

Some Indians belonging to the villages here, bearded and very docile, came to meet us. They followed us for a little way and then left us.[102] We traveled over slopes, hollows, and hills, changing course almost in a circle nearly as far around as west-northwestward before we turned around the mountain and came out onto the plain. Everywhere we went we saw very good soil, a great deal of woods, a bit of tree timber for making temporary huts or barracks, and a number of springs and little gushes of water. And in this stretch we came upon a small

---

[99]Cañada de San Andrés.

[100]This last sentence is found at the end of the entry in the field text. The final text here reads: "I considered this to be a very lovely spot, the best one for establishing one of two missions at, thinking that the other might be founded at the Arroyo de San Mateo, which would achieve having the two missions lie near to the harbor, as was planned, and the Fathers were inclined to this opinion." This last phrase was obviously composed after Font's return to Monterey, when he reported to "the Fathers," that is, Palóu, the other three missionaries who had been assigned for the two San Francisco missions, and of course Serra as well. Anza's views were slightly different.

[101]In his April 1 entry, below, Font refers to this mention of the East Bay redwoods.

[102]In the final text, the mention of natives appears later, at the end of the description of "this stretch" (the ride from the Dolores site along the bayside hills to the San Bruno area).

spring similar to a well, on a little height up very close to the water of the inlet at some ten or twelve varas away from it. Afterward, about midday and already beyond the hills, we stopped to have a bite to eat at a little stream with hardly any water that Father Palóu named the *Arroyo de San Bruno*.[103] Near it was the trace of a sizeable abandoned village. After we ate here, we continued on and took the route we had taken to get here, and we traveled a little way on it on a southeastward course.

Here our commander decided to go over and inspect a hollow that was close by named San Andrés, which lies in the mountains ending at Punta de Almejas.[104] As I have said, the purpose was to see if it had any good timber for the settlement at the harbor. To do this we left the southeastward course that we had started to take and took up a southwest course and came into a small hollow with a little stream where there were some little jacales belonging to an abandoned village. Then after crossing some hills we came to the Lago de la Merced[105] where Señor Rivera was delayed along with Father Palóu for some days when he came to survey the harbor and was rained upon as I said above; and then we came into the hollow, having traveled for about a league and having already changed our course. From here onward we took up a southeastward course, traveling through a long narrow hollow formed on its north side by hills, green but without any wood on them, those on the south side having a great deal of woods. As we followed it along we saw a great amount of woods in the hollow, the thicker it got the farther we rode along, with a great deal of different sorts of good timber trees such as live oaks, madrons, redwoods, cottonwoods, and other kinds as well. There was also a great amount of brush shoots on the bank of the stream or long narrow lake that lies along the hollow here and out of which the Arroyo de San Mateo arises and issues out to the plain through narrows made by some hills; it is made up out of two streams that join before it issues forth.

We must have traveled a bit over three leagues[106] when we were met on the way by a very large bear, which they managed to slay.
In that country there are a great many of them, and when the Indians go hunting, the bears usually attack and hurt by them. We saw many who were horribly scarred from the attacks.
The bear walked toward us quite undisturbed, but the instant I saw it so near and

---

[103]Apparently this was during Palóu's visit in September 1775. The saint's day does not occur until October 6, so that, according to F. M. Stanger's speculation, the name was likely given in honor of Bruno de Eceta, the ranking officer in the excursion (Brown 1975: 79).

[104]The field text says only: "to inspect the hollows in the southerly direction." The short and final texts read "that lies in the Spruce mountains," to which the short text added and then deleted: "which they also call redwood."

[105]On Font's error with this name, see the note under March 27.

[106]In the final text: "And about a league before there," that is, before crossing the Arroyo de San Mateo. The figure of a league is probably derived from figuring from the other distances mentioned in the field text.

standing there undecided, looking at us, I feared some tragedy, since it came out at us from so nearby and on a hill slope where getting away would be difficult. Corporal Robles fired a well-aimed shot at the bear which struck it in the throat. The bear immediately hurled itself down the slope, crossed the stream, and ran into the woods. However, it was bleeding so heavily that after going only a short way it fell over and it was dead. The soldiers then skinned it and butchered as much as they wanted. We delayed for over an hour here while doing this. Our commander took the skin to give it to the viceroy. I measured the bear. It was already old. Its fangs were very worn down and it had a tooth missing. It was quite fat even though its flesh smells a great deal[107] like musk or like that of a fox. It was nine cuartas long and four tall.[108] It is a fearsome beast, ferocious, very large, and corpulent. It was very tough; in between the skin and the flesh several gashes were found from shots that were fired at it while it was fleeing. The shot that went into it through the throat was found in between the skin and the flesh of the chest, with streaks on it and a small piece of bone stuck in it. There are a great many bears throughout these woods and we saw a number of them.

We traveled about one league farther and came to cross the stream, which goes in between hills here and out toward the inlet. We then crossed another stream coming from another lake and joining with the one we had crossed before; the two of them, joined, go in through hills and, so joined, formed the Arroyo de San Mateo where we camped. We kept onward upon an east-southeasterly course, going along the edge of a very long lake that forms the second stream we had crossed, in order to view the end of the hollow. But, after we traveled for over two leagues we perceived that there was nothing more worth seeing in it. According to the reckoning this is the San Andrés hollow in which there is a great deal of woods and redwood, and beyond it, upon this same southern side, there begins and runs along the long redwood mountain range out of which the Arroyo de San Francisco rises. So our commander decided to go toward the camp that he had ordered to be made at the bank of the Arroyo de San Mateo when he had sent off the mules along the direct route. By crossing over high hills, we traveled some two leagues upon a nearly northward course, went down to the plain, and came to the camp and the bank of the Arroyo de San Mateo at a half past six in the afternoon. The Indians belonging to the village here were quite attentive and courteous and even bothersome, as they had so thoroughly attached themselves to the camp that very late in the evening it became necessary to eject them in order to get them to allow us any sleep. And I believe that with a mission here, they would be easy to convert.

---

[107]In the field text: "a bit."
[108]About 6 feet 2¼ inches long, and 2 feet 9 inches tall.

[March] 30, Saturday. I said Mass. We had a bit of rain last night and at daybreak the weather was very overcast and drizzling at times. At midday it grew a little heavier, and a thin rain kept up until a little before we came to the stopping place.

The Indians of the village on this stream came very early in the morning to our camp and were very courteous and kind. We set out from the Arroyo de San Mateo at a quarter past seven in the morning, and halted at four in the afternoon upon the other side of a river that we called the Guadalupe River (which empties into the end of the harbor, and is very deep at about a league before it empties out, because of having its water backed up with no current in it), having traveled some twelve leagues on a varying course.

Upon setting out we followed the same route as on coming, on the corresponding course, and traveled about three leagues east-southeastward passing by the three villages within this stretch, all of them kind, docile Indians. Those belonging to the third village came out shouting to greet us and were left saddened, as it were, because we did not come to their jacales, which they were inviting us to go to. We traveled about two leagues farther, slanting a bit southeastward, until reaching the Arroyo de San Francisco where the cross is, and turned northward downstream for about a quarter league in order to measure the height and width of a redwood tree that I spoke of yesterday, standing at the bank of the stream (which is dry here) and visible from very far off to all quarters. We arrived at its trunk and saw that it was not a single tree but two trees very close together. From a distance they appear as one, and the thicker one has two small ones close up against it. I took this thicker one's measure, and using the graphometer they loaned me at Mission San Carlos del Río Carmelo, I found it to be fifty-five and one-half varas high, that is, fifty-six, if I succeeded in the procedure.[109] It was done in this fashion: I planted the graphometer thirty-six varas away from the foot and a vara and a half from the ground,[110] and then on sighting its top through the vanes of the alidade the latter read fifty-two and one-half degrees, which then, by forming the triangle of those degrees using the graduated semicircle and adding the height of the graphometer's stand, one and a half vara, yielded the total of fifty-six varas by using the dividers. The trunk was five and

---

[109] 56 varas equal 154 feet. In the short text and final text: "... found to be, according to my calculation, some fifty varas [137½ feet] more or less ..." (indicating caution on Font's part about his calculations). Anza states the height of the "red pine" as being successfully calculated as 156½ varas "despite [the tree's] being off center since it stands on the bank of the arroyo San Francisco." One of the two trunks (see fig. 28) fell into the deep stream bed in the later nineteenth century. The name for the tree and its vicinity is first recorded in 1853, in both Spanish and English: "el rancho San Francisquito 'Palo Alto,'" and "Ward's ranch, near the Tall Tree" (Brown 1975: 31). Several other tall redwoods, now gone, also grew along the creek banks.

[110] 99 feet and 4 feet 1½ inches, respectively.

FIGURE 28. The *palo alto* a century after Font, 1876. Photograph by Carleton Watkins. *Courtesy of the Palo Alto Historical Association and City Historian, Guy Miller Archives.*

one-half varas[111] in circumference at its foot, and the soldiers said that there were even larger ones in the mountains. The Indians of the village, who came to see us and who dwell here, were present at all of this, very quiet and attentive, and, as it were, struck with wonder at seeing what I was doing.

Here, deciding to go onward to inspect the great river they had been calling the San Francisco and that was said to empty into the harbor upon its north side, we left the route we had taken on coming, in order to head around the inlet and reach the other side;

and, altering our course, we traveled toward the water, keeping, however, about a league away from it, and more in places because of the mire. We continued for some three leagues on an eastward course; then, commencing to go around this end of the harbor, we went about three leagues northeastward, finally winding about from the west to the eastward in order to ford the river and as far as the stopping place.

We took up an eastward course and traveled thus for a bit over two leagues and came to a village whose Indians had a great deal of fear of us and the Indian women hid inside their huts although our captain gave the men beads.[112] This village is on a large plain at the end of the inlet. From here I viewed the island

---

[111] 15 feet 1½ inches.
[112] Anza's journal places the "dwelling" of about a hundred Indians at a large spring some 1½ leagues beyond the Arroyo de San Francisco (San Francisquito Creek).

that lies about halfway along the arm of the inlet that runs in this direction, and it makes the shape which I am representing here.[113]

FIGURE 29. Coyote Hills. *Pedro Font sketch.*

We continued on a northeastward and then north-northeastward course over that plain, which being such low ground is somewhat miry in spots, and plainly becomes impassable whenever it rains very much, for which reason the experienced soldiers told us it would be necessary to go around as far nearly as the Arroyo de las Llagas in order to get to the other side; but God granted that we should succeed in cutting across here, by which we saved some leagues and came upon the Guadalupe river, of which the soldiers had had no knowledge.[114]

Almost in the median of the plain there is a small grove with water, from which I saw that the inlet's direction corresponds to southeast by east, as I saw yesterday.[115] And upon traveling a bit over two leagues we came upon a big river, big not so much because of how much water it carries as because it has it backed up, with a very deep bed, for the reason that it runs to empty into the inlet, which holds back its flow.[116] Because of finding it so deep, we were delayed for over an hour in seeking a ford over it. We wished to cross it where we had come onto it since there was a bridge there made of a tree lying across, and on the other side there was a village whose Indians displayed a good deal of fear as soon as they saw us, and four of them who were on this side were soothed by our commander's giving them beads, and did not flee. But this[117] proved impossible because of the banks being so high. A ford was sought farther down, and for this purpose we continued down-river for about half a league on an almost westward

---

[113]Actually, "in the margin." In the final text, the remark (not accompanied by the drawing) is transferred to the location of the village at the end of the march, "two leagues and a bit more" further on. See the note below.

[114]As Rivera pointed out in subsequent correspondence, it had actually been crossed, although not named, by the scouting party that he had sent out under Ortega in 1769.

[115]Apparently altered from "east-southeast." The final text gives what seems to be this same remark in connection with the location, over two leagues onward, of the camp at the end of the day's march; there the bearing appears as "east-southeast." The alteration could have been made in order to allow for the change in locations, since it is relatively more accurate for the direction from the earlier position, which was west-northwest of the later one.

[116]The field text adds, "And here we got around the head of the aforesaid inlet and passed about one league, or a bit more, away from the end point of its waters."

[117]Making a crossing there.

course, but we saw that the farther it went toward the inlet and its mouth, the worse it became, through having much more water in it, even more backed up. We returned eastward to the village where there was a bridge made of a tree lying across and thereupon it was decided to have the people, the packs, and all, cross over by the bridge and have the animals cross by swimming. As the gully was so deep and wooded, it was necessary to fix the edge of the bed to give them a path in and out. Work was begun on this by cutting branches to open a way and digging out the edge of the bed to make an access. Meanwhile, a soldier set out to look for a ford higher up, and in a short while he came back saying he had found one. Thereupon, leaving the work just begun, we went that way, traveling northeastward with small difference, for about a quarter-league, and it turned out that without unloading the river could easily be forded there by only cutting a tree and a few branches. And having forded the river we halted on its bank at four o'clock in the afternoon, after traveling some ten leagues, which, what with the turnarounds we had made in order to ford the river, amounted to a bit more than eleven.

The river here did create something of a setback for the march, but nevertheless we gained a great deal through the measure that we took of coming this way, both because by crossing over the plain there we have avoided making a large circuit which the soldiers said was necessary in order for us to get to the other side of the inlet (which perhaps we could not have done in a single day's march), as also because we discovered that river emptying into the end of the inlet, and although some doubt was raised as to the possibility of its being the Coyote stream which we had had on our left[118] hand during the way up, it seemed on the whole to be a different one; for which reason we gave it the name *Río de la Virgen de Guadalupe*.[119] This river winds through the midst of a great and wide-stretching plain. This spot has very good soil, very level and well covered with grass but somewhat lacking in wood, there being no more than the trees along the river, which is very dense with cottonwoods, willows, sycamores, some ashes, laurels, and other trees; and nowhere in this entire country is there a single stone. Our camp was at once visited by some very docile, polite Indians,[120] and they brought across some sticks and brush and fire, etc., and were not so much afraid as at the start.

During this travel we went leaving upon our right hand the white-oak grove through which we passed while coming, which begins at the second village that we passed this morning and extends as far as the Arroyo de las Llagas. A little

---

[118]This must be a mistake. It should have been to their right—on the east as they went northward.
[119]River of the Virgin of Guadalupe.
[120]In the final text, "Later, the Indians were a bit courteous, brought over . . ." etc.

beyond the tree that we measured we found three very fine springs of running water on the plain (the whole of what we traveled today is level land).

On starting to go around the head of the inlet, we found another village whose Indian men and women showed great fear as soon as they saw us, which was reduced a little by giving beads to them. And one old woman, from the time that she saw us until we went away, stood in the door of her hut stirring about making crosses and lines upon the ground while all the time talking to herself as though praying.[121] She remained constant in her prayer, paying no attention to the beads that our commander was offering her.

From here I viewed the direction of the inlet, and saw that it was east-southeastward just as I had seen it yesterday, and also I demarcated the island that is visible, close to the land, at this end, as I said on the 27th.[122] At this spot we still felt a good deal of chill, and we have had the same thing during these past days even though we already are in the springtime. We were also somewhat bothered by small mosquitoes that sting a bit and breed at the edge of the river, which seemingly has fish in it which perhaps must come into it from the inlet, since the Indians make stake weirs for fishing and use a sort of fish-traps, and a small *mojarra*[123] about four fingers long was found on the bank. But we have noted that the Indians who live on the shores of the inlet are no fishermen; one only sees, at their villages, piles of mussel shells, which must be what they fish for and eat the most of nor do they possess boats or canoes, or floats other than one or two at the harbor.[124]

I shall note that these last courses in getting around the inlet's head and fording the river are not very exact since most of it has been done while winding about.

[March] 31, Sunday. I said Mass. The weather was clear at daybreak, with a frost making the grass, tents, and everything else very white. There was a good deal of chill all night and during the day also, what with the northwesterly[125] wind prevailing; it cleared the sky, but afterward it turned to a westerly and with this the horizon became somewhat obscured, although it was no great matter. We set out from the Guadalupe River a little after eight o'clock in the morning. At the start we took up a northward course and then, on going a short way,

---

[121]It is possible that the woman's stance and actions suggested to Font a Spanish expression denoting rejection *"con cruz y raya."*

[122]In the field text, as already seen, the bearing along with a view of the "island" appears earlier, attached to the description of the village a little over two leagues *before* the end of the march. The bearings on the direction of the bay as given there and here are perhaps derived from the same demarcation, altered to allow for the different positions.

[123]A fish, of course, here perhaps meaning a chub, or possibly a roach.

[124]In other words, at the mouth of the bay. However, in 1775 south of the Dumbarton strait the boat pilot Juan de Aguirre had found decorated poles driven in, "which, being in the midst of the water, I conceive are fishing markers" (Stanger and Brown 1969: 159; Galvin 1971: 97).

[125]The field text originally read "northeasterly."

north-northwestward, and traveled thus for about one league. But as we were close to the end of the inlet, we were faced with a miry slough in front of us, one of a great number that exist here in the lowland where the inlet extends, and that reach inland. It caused us to go back around in order to get past it, and at once we came upon a stream with a small amount of pooled water, not running, and by the reckoning it seems to be the stream that Father Crespí, in his journal, names as *La Encarnación*, which he crossed farther up and we crossed it where its tree grove ends.[126] We then came at once upon other sloughs that caused us to wind about and go in all directions for around about a league. In one of them we saw that the water of the inlet was running upwards in the slough as though the inlet was at the flood, while at the spot where we crossed it a small stream of water was running downward toward the inlet. In the end we drew close to the foot of the bare hills that run along this side and do not have a tree on them, and they are the same chain of hills and mountains that run to the San Bernardino valley and beyond. By all that we traveled during these windings, one may estimate three leagues: eastward, northeastward, and a bit northward. Being now on higher ground, we took up a north-northwestward course and traveled thus about two leagues. Afterward, we turned northwestward and continued in this course until we halted.

After getting out of the sloughs and reaching higher ground and before coming to the first stream[127] we went along the shore of a fairly big, rather briny lake, which we left upon our right. It has deposits of salt on the shores and a good deal of tule rushes, and it lies in between the high ground—over which we were traveling very far from the water—and the hills, out of which, to judge from trees that are visible in a small hollow, a stream apparently flows that becomes pooled up in the lake here. Most of the route is entirely very flat, green, flowery ground reaching as far as the inlet, but not having any more timber or firewood than what is offered by the trees along the streams that we came across, five in number.[128]

The Indians that we saw hereabouts are entirely different from the earlier ones in their speech, rather bearded, mild-mannered and very poor, but the same as all the others in their color.

We have seen a number of Indians all across the plain, some of whom fled from us and others who would pause and whom our commander attempted to

---

[126] The small stream named La Encarnación in 1772 was Calera Creek or Scott Creek, at the foot of the mountains. Here, instead, Font is at the lowest end of Coyote Creek, probably west of its present course (Brown 2005: 18 and fig. 7 there). Anza's journal entry makes the identification clear.

[127] Of the five streams that were crossed during the last part of the march.

[128] The description in Anza's journal of the first stream hollow coming out of the hills (the later *Zanjón de los Alisos* or "Sycamore Slough") leaves no doubt that at that time it formed the lower course of Alameda Creek. "It has a good many [trees] all the way to its joining with the Inlet, and water in plenty."

please by giving beads to them. The ones we saw before we reached the first stream appear to be very poor, wretched Indians since they do not even have firewood with which to warm themselves and they go naked like all the Indians found in this country. They eat grass, plants, and a kind of root which is very plentiful in these plains. They are like medium-sized onions and are called *amole*.[129] An Indian carrying his provisions on the end of a pole invited us to share some of them.

About halfway along the way, having gone about six leagues, we came to a stream having little water, with most of it, however, quite pooled, and with a great many sycamores, cottonwoods, and some live oaks and other trees on its banks. It seems to flow on westward to empty into the inlet (as all the streams do), in which direction there runs a growth of trees—either the stream's course or a bit of woods, I could not tell which. About thirty Indians came out of these trees to meet us, carrying bows and arrows (rather poor ones), but peaceably, since it seems that all the Indians there are docile. Their speech seems to be a different language from those we have heard up until here, and it is quite an ugly one. With the babble of them all speaking at once, it was very disagreeable to our ears.

Their method of greeting us was this: they came running up and before reaching us they would lift an arm and, with their hand stretched out gesturing us to stop, they uttered in a shout and very quickly "au, au, au, au; au, au, au, au; au, au, au, au, áu," and then stopped immediately, giving themselves a hard slap on the buttocks. There seemed something hellish in the way they came on, shouting, one behind another, and how they kept right on talking, still shouting, at great speed.

We stopped with them for a little while and our commander gave them beads. It may be that these Indians belong to that tribe mentioned by Father Garcés in his journal, saying that they talk in this manner while they are greeting.[130]

At a bit over two leagues we crossed two small streams having trees on them and separated only by a hill that was not very large, and in between them we saw a village with no people in it. We traveled about a league farther and crossed another stream, at which we saw an abandoned village and, in a jacal, a great many grass-stuffed birds that the Indians have in order to do their hunting. Here the soldiers gathered wild tobacco, of which there was a good deal.[131] Traveling about another league farther, we came to the fifth stream, which Father Crespí called *San Salvador* and where Captain Fages stopped; and we, also, halted at its

---

[129] The Mexican word for soaproot or soapweed (*Chlorogalum*).

[130] On May 3, 1776, three days later than the date of Font's entry here and over 150 miles away in the southern San Joaquín, Garcés met a village who "as soon as they saw me . . . began to shout 'Ba! ba! ba!,' slapping their thighs hard." (Galvin 1967: 49.) Font read Garcés's entry after June 1776. The linguistic groups involved in the two separate encounters were Miwok and Yokuts. Speakers of the two language groups were in contact with each other in the northern San Joaquín Valley.

[131] Very likely originally planted by the native inhabitants.

bank, at four o'clock in the afternoon, having traveled about twelve leagues in all, seven of them to the northwestward. In order to cross the stream we circled around a bit, since, although it has only a little water, what it has is pooled up in large pools and in a pretty deep bed very grown over with sycamores, cottonwoods, live oaks, and other trees. As soon as we had crossed this stream we happened upon a poor Indian who was coming along quite unconcerned and as soon as he saw us displayed the greatest fear describable. He was carrying a bundle of a plant that they eat, like what they call *morrén* at Mission San Carlos,[132] and he had no other recourse than to cast himself down flat on the ground, hiding among the grass to keep us from seeing him and only raising his head a bit to view us out of one eye. Our commander approached him to give him some beads, but he was so flustered that he could not even reach out to take them. The lieutenant had to dismount and put them in his hand, all the while that he, entirely dumfounded and almost without words, held out his morrén to him as though hoping by this offering to redeem the life he feared he had lost. He must never have seen Spaniards and that is why we startled him and caused him so much fear.[133]

This spot is nearly parallel to the Arroyo de San Mateo from which we set out yesterday, and the whole route lies some way off from the inlet, about a league away at the start, but we then began getting farther and farther away, so that the place where we halted here is about three leagues[134] from the water of the inlet. It is all level land up to the foot of the bare hills here which we have been passing along, and which continue ahead. The soldier Soberanes, who came this way with Captain Fages, said he did not know the name of the stream here where we stopped. When I replied that it was named the Arroyo de San Salvador, he said it was called the *Arroyo de la Harina*.[135] The soldiers had given it this name because a pack of flour had fallen into the stream, but that he did not know the saints' names that the Father[136] kept giving.

---

[132]The word does not seem to appear in available lists of native terms once used in the Monterey–San Francisco area.

[133]Anza's account is also graphic. "The last man we met was about forty paces off when he discovered us, and although he had a place about five paces away where he could hide, his terror was such that he let himself drop upon the spot, or rather, I think that he dropped involuntarily from the shock. Since he and we were following the same path, I went up to where he was, looking more dead than alive without noticeably stirring in speech or limb. I attempted to encourage him and make him stand, but was unable to do so [even] after a good amount of time, at the end of which he had the courage only for a poor grasp of some beads most of which he dropped. On seeing this, I thought best to leave him, for otherwise I think this poor soul would have died. We attributed his shock to the fact that clearly he did not have any information, even remotely, about us or about any other people than his own kind alone."

[134]In the final text, "a bit over two leagues."

[135]Flour Creek.

[136]Juan Crespí, in March 1772.

During the entire day today, our commander and I wondered whether the island at the end of the inlet, which I demarcated yesterday, is or is not an island, since it is quite a long hill and in addition to its having altered its aspect today, we were unable to see water this side of it—even when we climbed up the hills—except for a bit around the point that looks toward the inlet, while the whole rest of it is very close up to the plain, so that we guessed it may be the same mainland as the plain. If it is an island, surrounded by one of the many sloughs that the inlet creates upon the flats, then either the mire of the slough or whatever small amount of water it holds, which we were unable to see, will hinder crossing to it.

We had the same thing happen with the other large island I demarcated in the morning; I judge that either there is only a little water surrounding it that cannot be seen from a distance, or else that the way across is so miry that, being inaccessible from the mainland, it can count as an island. I was unable to ascertain whether there are any Indians living on the islands.

April 1, Monday. I said Mass. The weather at daybreak was very foggy and wet, but we felt no chill, as it seems this country is a more temperate one and, judging from the heat we felt during the march today, there is still more heat as one goes onward. This place could be considered *tierra caliente*[137] because of the combination of the heat and the plague of mosquitoes that began stinging us from the camp here at this stream onward and that pursued us the whole way to our halting place, particularly in the low spots and at the streams where there were trees. The fog lasted halfway through the morning and then proceeded to clear, leaving the sky open and the sun rather hot. The route was varied, now plain, now hills—the whole country, however, was very green and flowery and with lilies in plenty. The course likewise was varied, all the way to the stopping place.

The route lay along the hills of the range I spoke of on March 8, which has very few trees along its outside save for a patch of spruces[138] lying opposite to the harbor mouth, though its interior holds a great deal of woods and is quite broken, as we saw when we crossed it on our return. At the mouth of the Freshwater Harbor, where it comes to an end, it finishes in a sort of rather high, very round hills.

We set out from the Arroyo de la Harina at seven o'clock in the morning and traveled about two leagues course northwestward over level land at the foot of the bare hill that continues on in this way[139] to the mouth of the great river of San Francisco, except for a small piece of mountain range or hill that is thickly grown with redwood, which I spoke of on the 29th. I judged that the bareness of this entire range might perhaps be from its being so open to and beaten upon by the northwest wind. At two leagues we came to a stream with little water and a

---

[137]Hot land. The term refers to the tropical coastal areas of Mesoamerica.
[138]Redwoods.
[139]Bare.

Figure 30. The Alameda Peninsula, 1776. Pedro Font.
Reproduced courtesy of the John Carter Brown Library at Brown University.

very deep bed wooded with cottonwoods, live oaks, laurels, and other trees. We crossed it at the foot of the hill by circling around a bit, and before crossing it saw four bears upon a slope. We surmised that there are a good many of these here also, since we have seen a number of[140] Indians upon both sides of the inlet who are heavily marked by bear bites and scratches.

At about two farther leagues going west-northwestward we crossed a little stream with no water and almost not a tree on it, and shortly went up a hill lying directly across from level mainland that runs toward what seems to be a pretty thick, rather large white-oak and live-oak wood lying upon the shores of the inlet and nearly made an island by two of its branches. From that spot I demarcated the wood and two arms of the inlet there.[141] On coming down from the hill we at once crossed another stream with almost no trees and with a little pool of water, not running, in it. This seems to be the stream that Father Crespí called the *Arroyo del Bosque*[142] emptying into the end of one arm of the estuary. The Father took the latitude at it and found the spot to be in 37° 54ʹ.[143]

---

[140]In the field text, "many."
[141]The final text adds: "[the result of] which demarcation I am placing on the reverse of this page" (fig. 30).
[142]Creek of the Woods. "Woods" in reference to the view of the live oak wood of the Alameda Peninsula.
[143]Crespí's latitude was too high by nine minutes.

We kept on our way over hills and hollows and crossed two more streams with little water and deep beds and a good many trees. The second one has more of them and it goes out to a cove upon the inlet arm on this side of the wood. We must have gone about two leagues upon a course now northwestward, now west-northwestward. Afterward we came onto a plain and traveled northwestward; on it we crossed two small streams with no water in them. From the plain here, we saw the harbor mouth clearly: and when the point of the red cliff on the inner side came in line with the mouth's outer point, I watched for the direction in which they ran and saw they did so west-southwestward.[144] I thought the inlet must be four to five leagues[145] wide in front of the mouth, and the route passes along about two leagues away from the inlet. We then crossed a stream with a small growth of trees and very little water which seems to be the stream Father Crespí called the *Arroyo de la Bocana*.[146] Downstream there is a wood or thicket, not a large one, and the soldiers, who had seen tracks of the great deer—whose hoof print on the ground is almost as large as cattle—went off to the wood to search for them, and though they found some they were unable to get any of them.

We then continued upon the same northwestward course, over level land though with one or another little hill and along here we saw an Indian upon the plain. He was so afraid when he caught sight of us that he ran up a hill and hid behind some rocks. At around a league we went up some hills and on through them for about two leagues and came to a rather deep stream with trees and not much water, where we saw an abandoned village on its banks. From here we traveled a little farther, over plains and then through hills. Seven Indians came to meet us. Our commander gave beads to them and they followed us as far as the next stream, not very far away. We had some trouble crossing it as it had a very deep bed with a good deal of trees—live oaks, sycamores, and other kinds—and here we came to a village where we saw around twenty-three Indian men and some seven women, the others having gone to the woods to look for tule rushes, plants, and roots that they eat. Our commander gave them[147] beads, and they were very pleased and kind and gave us *cacomites*[148] that were half-roasted or barbecued.[149]

---

[144] In the final text, "westward with some deviation to southward."
[145] The final text: "some four leagues."
[146] Harbor Mouth Creek.
[147] The field text seems to refer only to the Indian women at this particular point.
[148] A Mexican word, originally referring to the edible bulb of the large, showy Mexican Tigridia flower-plant. In California, it always meant *Brodiaea* bulbs, as it does in this case. See Font's description, just below.
[149] "Toasted," in the field text.

Along the way, I demarcated the large island lying on this side, which presented this shape. It is quite a long one, very close to the land, and beyond its end the large bay begins. And from here we traveled over hills, up and down, following a northwest course for a little way, and then north-northwestward, going for about three leagues. And having crossed two or three little streams with no water in them we came to one with very little water on whose bank we found a middling-sized village whose Indian men and women were very pleased to see us, and kind, presenting us with a great many cacomites, a root that they eat which is a small, flattish, nearly round plant head, of the size and shape of a half-flattened musket ball; and also a good-sized string of barbecued amole which is another kind of a root resembling a larger version of a small onion, all of it well roasted or barbecued. I ate some and thought it tasted good, and our commander made them a present of beads.

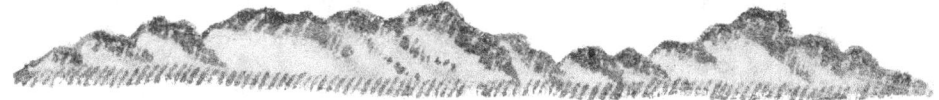

Figure 31. Richmond Peninsula. *Pedro Font sketch.*

Amole is their most normal food. It tastes a little like mescal, and is most plentiful, since the fields hereabouts are full of it.

We kept onward on our way, through hills and hollows on a northward course though at times changing to northeastward and slightly eastward for a short stretch. After we had traveled about three leagues in that direction we stopped at the edge of the next stream, which had very little water in it and the water was not as good as in the previous ones, even though we had shortly beforehand crossed an even smaller stream. We stopped at a little after a half past four in the afternoon, having traveled in all about fifteen leagues. This spot seems to be about one short league from the mouth of the San Francisco River, which we hope to see tomorrow, if God favors us.[150]

As soon as we had stopped, thirty-eight Indians came to visit us, unarmed, peaceable and very pleased at seeing us.

They proceeded first to stop and sit on a knoll near the camp, then one of them came over and after him another one, and thus they came, filing one after another like a band of goats, leaping and talking, until all of them had arrived.

They were very courteous, bringing firewood, and are great talkers. Their speech

---

[150]In the final text: "one league before reaching the mouth of the Freshwater Harbor or the mouth of what they were calling the 'Great River of St. Francis,' which I was very much wishing to see, and in the end did not, because there was no such river, as I shall say tomorrow."

had a great deal of babble and we could not understand anything they said. They go naked as do all of them—not, however, being at all white-skinned but just like all the others we have seen along the whole way. Very few of them are bearded, and those not so heavily as the ones we saw on the other side and near the harbor mouth.[151] After they had been with us a while we sent them away, signaling to them to go and bring fish. They seemed to understand this quite well and used two fishhooks that I gave them.[152]

The noise of the sea could be heard a little from the stopping place here, since waves in the bay do break upon the shore a bit, although it is no great matter. All of these hills that we have been passing through since this side of the *Río de la Bocana*[153] are the same ones which on this side, and together with the hills that extend from the mouth of the harbor along the other side, form the large bay in which the inlet terminates. The bay must be about a long eight leagues in breadth, and appears nearly round, although by what I can see on this side it has a good many coves on it, and what the other side is like is unknown, since it cannot be distinguished clearly at such a distance.[154] The inlet, on the other side, has visible several coves and sounds between the hills, but whether there are any more islands is impossible to make out.

Before reaching the stopping place, we stood viewing the bay from a high hill from which most of it lay open to view. I saw that it is surrounded on all sides by hills and mountains, except for a large gap bearing about west by north where a strip of flats extends along for a good distance, behind which, or farther on, a whitening as of water could be made out, stretching as far as another mountain range lying blue and very far off at the end of the view. I guessed the bay might perhaps connect in that direction with Bodega's harbor, as, when he was there, Captain don Juan de la Cuadra[155] was unable to tell from the currents that he

---

[151] Another reference to Juan Crespí's earlier description of the local inhabitants. Anza's journal specifies, "in color and skin they are not distinct from the ones we have seen until now, and on the Santa Bárbara Channel and much more so on the Colorado River they have a lighter color than these do here." Anza also mentions the beards that are scantier than across the bay, and long hair tied on top of the head, "as was noted upon those yesterday."

[152] Again the final text anticipates the result (see the next entry): "However, they did not bring back anything nor did they show much appreciation for the hooks, since using nets is their way of fishing."

[153] Harbor Mouth River. This should be "stream," as above in this entry. Font seems frequently to confuse *río* and *arroyo*.

[154] Font's term "the bay" as used here and elsewhere refers only to San Pablo Bay. "The inlet" is San Francisco Bay south of San Pablo Bay. The field text goes on to provide the listing of islands in San Francisco Bay as a whole: "I have clearly made out six islands in the midst of the inlet, two on the south side near the mouth and four northward from the mouth; besides those, there is the other long one at the southern end of the inlet and another, about three leagues long, on this northern side, beyond the end of which the bay begins, and these latter two are up very close to the land on this side."

[155] Juan Francisco de la Bodega y Cuadra. The guess that the Petaluma River might be connected with the ocean was disproved by a nautical survey the following summer.

experienced in it whether it was sea or a river; and that harbor lies in that direction not very far from the bay or so I understand. However, this is no more than guesswork.

[April] 2, Tuesday. I said Mass. The night passed with very little chill, and it was clear. There was very bright beautiful weather at daybreak, which lasted all day long, with a little heat that was moderated by the coolness of the softly blowing northwest wind. The two Indians to whom I gave fishhooks made their appearance but without any fish, and according to what I saw afterwards, they place no value on hooks since they fish by using nets.

We set out from the little stream at about seven o'clock in the morning and traveled for a little while northward and then northeastward and went by a village, a little way off of the route, to which we had been invited by some ten Indians who came to the camp very early in the morning, singing. We were received there by the Indians of the village with special displays of joy, singing and dancing.

The way in which they invited us was this: at sunrise the ten Indians came up one behind the other, singing and dancing with a great deal of jubilation, one of them carrying the tune and making music with a small stick of some length and split down the center, which he shook against his hand so that it rattled somewhat like castanets. They reached the camp, kept up their singing and dancing for a little bit, and then ended the dance, all giving a foot stamp and a shake of their body to the beat, and uttering in unison, and drily: Ha, Ha, Ha. They then sat down on the ground and indicated to us that we should sit too, and our commander, the lieutenant[156] and I sat down across from them. And at once one of them stood up and presented our commander with a string of cacomites and sat down again; shortly after he stood up and gave me another cacomite string, and again sat down; and in this manner they went on giving us their little presents. Another Indian gave me a very large *chuchupate*[157] root that he started to eat, telling me by signs that it was something good. Following this round of courtesies, they invited us to go to their village, indicating that it was close by which is why our commander agreed to give them that pleasure. As we started to journey, they kept us company with their singing and dancing. I interrupted them by singing the Alabado, as we had been doing every day on starting the march, and as soon as I had finished, they continued their singing and shouting more strongly and on a louder note, as though intending to respond to our own song.

On going a short way, we came to the village, which lies within a hollow on the bank of a small stream, and the Indians received us with indescribable jubilation. Three of them met us on the way into the village carrying long poles with feathers on the end and long narrow strips of hide with the hair on it that I thought were rabbit skin, like a banner,
—which is their sign of peace, and they directed us to the midst of the village where they had a flat spot like a little town square.

---

[156] The text reads "the purveyor" (*el proveedor*), an obvious mistake, since Purveyor Vidal had remained at Monterey. Lieutenant Moraga must be the one who is meant.

[157] The Mexican name has a number of applications, but here no doubt it is used either for a *Lomatium* ("wild parsnip," Parsley family) or else for balsam root (Sunflower family).

And they at once set to dancing along with other Indians belonging to the place, with a great deal of noise and jubilee. Soon thereafter an Indian woman of some age came forward and in front of us—on horseback as we were, without any of us having dismounted—she began to dance by herself, making motions very expressive of happiness. She would stop at intervals to talk to us, giving hand gestures as though making us welcome. After a little while, our commander said that that was enough. He began to present all the women with beads, they presented us with their cacomites, we took our leave of them all in order to be on our way, and they were left seemingly saddened at our departing. I myself was moved by seeing how happy these poor Indians were to receive us. Their color and their other traits, such as nakedness, not much beard, and so forth, are like all the ones seen so far, and those that we saw farther on ahead are just the same. Some of them have long hair, others short, and a few have beards of some length and size. Judging by the number of people I saw, I estimated the village must have held three to four hundred souls.[158]

We traveled over hills for about one long league northeastward and at nine o'clock we came to the water's edge, at the mouth of the great river of San Francisco, which, split into two branches, forms an island right at its mouth.[159] Here our commander decided to pause until after the noon hour in order to observe the latitude of this spot.

FIGURE 32. Mare Island. *Pedro Font sketch.*

From the moment we saw the river here, we began to doubt whether it is a river, or instead an inlet arm, since we perceived scarcely any current in it, and if there were any flow to be seen, it is apparently upward. Nor had the water any more motion than that which we observed at the mouth of San Francisco

---

[158] The final text, earlier in the entry: ". . . the village, which I estimated at some four hundred souls." Anza: "a village of about five hundred souls." The estimates of 400 or 500 agree well with the accounts of visitors in 1772 (Fages–Crespí) and in 1775 (Cañizares), when the survey boat's crew apparently were exceptionally well entertained here (hence it was labeled "Ranchería del Socorro").

[159] In the final text (denying the river's existence): ". . . and very near to the mouth leading into the Freshwater Harbor, marked on the map by the letter **I**, which up to the present has been believed to be a great river, which it is not, as shown by the tests that we made and the arguments that I shall be giving." The profile of Mare Island is found only in the final version, in the April 27 entry where the "islands" in the bay are enumerated.

harbor, where we noted a very gentle, disguised movement undoubtedly caused by the tide. In addition to this, we saw no sign of flooding upon its edge, and less still of trash or driftwood which would naturally be brought down by its floods—were it a river, and furthermore so full-flowing a river. And only on traveling farther up in the afternoon did we see an occasional stick that had been carried down and cast up on its banks.

And even were it to be said that its not carrying trash is due to its rising not very far away and running through a clear country from which it is unable to gather any driftwood or other things because there are no such things there, it would at least have to be granted that it must flood; and if it did so, it would have left marks of flooding along its margins. But the margins here have no visible marks, and its beaches, in places where it has some, are like the ones we saw on the harbor. Therefore, this Freshwater Harbor is a gulf of fresh water enclosed within a canyon with middling high hills upon both sides, running nearly eastward over a distance of some six leagues and then opening out vastly, across enormous plains which I shall tell of tomorrow and thereafter.

Its margins are very steep with cliffs in some places, and in others it forms a small piece of shore upon which, near the mouth, there were large heaps of little freshwater mussel shells. The hills forming this canyon have no trees on them, but the ones on this side do have a good deal of grass, while those upon the other side appeared rather bare, with very little grass, and soil of a rather reddish color. I tasted the water and found it salty although not even half so much as out at sea, so that it did not leave any sharpness or bad taste in my mouth and I thought it might even be drunk in case of need.[160]

In the river we saw four small boats very well-fashioned of tule rushes with their bows or points raised a bit higher, moored near the shore using stones for anchors, and in the midst of the water there were some Indians fishing in one; for the Indians catch large amounts of excellent fish, including extremely rich and plentiful salmon, in the whole gulf of the Freshwater Harbor here. I saw they were fishing with nets and were anchoring the boat with very long thin poles, to which they had their nets lashed. However, the way in which they had it moored confirmed for me in my already arrived-at suspicion or judgment that the water had no flow toward the bay, for I noticed that they moored their boat facing in the upward direction, toward the side away from the mouth, while the opposite seemingly would have had to be the case, were the water flowing downward. Given the fact that they were using those poles to anchor the boat, naturally these must have reached to the bottom. I therefore measured one of the poles using a lance. By converting the lance lengths to varas, I found it was eleven and a half varas long[161] so that by this conjecture and leaving out a good portion that sticks out of the water above the boat and to which the Indian

---

[160]Unlike Font, Anza found that "the water is undrinkable because of the saltiness."
[161]31 feet 7½ inches. But Anza says 13 varas (35 feet 9 inches).

FIGURE 33. A tule-reed boat on San Francisco Bay, 1816. By Louis Choris. (Background removed.) The central figure is wearing a mission-style blanket. *Courtesy of The Bancroft Library, University of California, Berkeley.*

fishermen have themselves lashed, I estimated that the water must have a depth of some nine or ten varas.[162] And its waters are very calm and peaceful.

I shall give another proof that the water there has no flow toward the bay. Among other fish that the Indian fishermen caught, they pulled out two very large ones about two varas long.[163] Their method of doing so was that as soon as they perceived by its thrashing that the fish was within the net which was attached to the two poles, they began raising one of the poles bit by bit. As soon as net and fish came near them they gave it a great many blows on the head with a club (I counted fifteen straight blows one of the times and twenty-odd ones the other) without taking the fish out of the water. When it was dead and had stopped thrashing they took it out of the net and into the boat. We called to these Indians, wanting to buy the fish from them, and though they paid no attention to us at first. But as soon as our commander showed them a colored handkerchief, they came rapidly to shore. They produced the two very large fish of a very unusual shape. We were unable to recognize what type it was. I was unable to tell whether they were the sort called *tollos*[164] although from their

---

[162]Approximately 25 to 27½ feet.

[163]5½ feet. Anza reports the one that was bought as being 2⅛ varas long (just over 70 inches).

[164]The term *tollos* is unfamiliar, but as Professor Solana indicates (Montané 2000: 263), the description applies fairly well to a sturgeon. Anza's journal adds that the eyes were golden "but extremely small," and the spots or marks were perfect stars. It is somewhat surprising that Font did not call the fish a sturgeon, *esturión*, if it was one, but on the other hand, the Spanish term was so unfamiliar to the descendants of the San Francisco colonists that they used the local native word, *urac*, for sturgeon. (This native term was misunderstood by Cook 1960: 259–60).

shape I thought they were, as they had quite a large head, small eyes, a small mouth resembling a tube that pushed in and out, no scales on its body, and thick skin with spots like little stars and other shapes on it caused by small bones between the skin and the flesh. Their flesh was very white and flavorful, without spines and with spongy bones resembling sinews.

Our commander offered beads in exchange for the fish, but they would not sell them at all for beads or for fish-hooks. They only wanted clothing. I never saw any Indians anywhere as desirous of and greedy for clothing as these were. It astonished me that they preferred any scrap of it to all the beads we had, which others value so much. In the end, our commander refused to give them clothing. Then a soldier bought a fish from them in exchange for an old article of common cloth. However, before handing it over they opened the fish and took the roe out of the belly and ate it raw on the spot and put the remainder into the gut. They then went on to devour the other fish, which they finished off quickly by instantly making a small fire, setting the fish over it, and then, while it was barely hot, devoured it raw, like animals. The soldier gave me a piece of his fish and so we ate some of it and found it very delicious, with fine flesh, yellow fat, and without spines or bones; all it has are a backbone and ribs like sinews and like the rumen of cattle, while in areas along the back and sides between the flesh and the skin, which is very rich and tender, there are some small soft bones, sometimes round, sometimes almost oval.

Now comes the proof. As soon as the Indians had devoured the fish they got into their boat and others of them got into the other boats which were close to shore, and raising their anchors, which were stones tied to a cable, they went off to the other side of the water with great ease, calm, and skill so that we could only see them paddling a bit in the middle. And they proceeded to land upon the opposite side a good way farther up, with respect to the side here from which they had set out, whereas the opposite would seemingly have had to be the case had there been a current in the water, for if the water had been flowing toward the bay, however much they paddled they would naturally have had to reach the other side below where they left from this one.

I observed the width of the mouth from a point of a hill next to the water about a quarter-league[165] from the mouth going upriver, where there was a clear overview of the entire width of the mouth, with the island in the midst of it, and from the observation that I made, converted to a triangle, I calculated that it must be a little under a quarter league wide.[166] In the bay and opposite the mouth is an island that must be over a league in length[167] from east to west and about a quarter league wide lying close to the mouth, not center to center with

---

[165] In the field text, this is corrected from "about half a league."

[166] In the field text, "one quarter of a league minus an eighth part, very nearly." About 3,000 feet.

[167] In the field text, "must be about two leagues long extending inland toward the bay." The short text: ("about" stricken) "a bit over a league."

it but over toward the northern shore so as to shape the body of water into two branches, one larger than the other.[168]

All of which I observed using the graphometer, in this way. I set the graphometer up upon the small elevation about a quarter league away from the mouth, from which point all of it was in view, and on sighting through the vanes upon both points of the mouth, the alidade registered forty degrees of clearance, divided in this way: six between the point on the other side and the island; nineteen between the island and the point on this side; and these twenty-five degrees were of water which was split as it were into two arms; and the remaining fifteen degrees were taken up by the island, which was to be seen in between, a bit out beyond the mouth, toward the bay.

The main branch of the river as it comes into the bay runs to the west by north, and the other, northern branch runs northwestward, and the island I have mentioned lies in between them.

The canyon with the water runs eastward, not straight but making bends and coves, and its width for three leagues inward essentially is the same as that of the mouth, after which it commences to open out more.

At noon I observed the latitude at this same spot and found it, according to Jorge with no correction, in 37° 56½', and with correction in 38° 5½',[169] and thus I say: at the mouth of the river of San Francisco,[170] April 2, 1776: meridian altitude of the sun's lower limb, 57°. Following midday, we continued the day's march and traveled eastward up close to the river for a bit over a league, up and down over the height of the hills close by the river; then about one league east-southeastward up through a hollow having a good many[171] white oaks, live oaks, and other trees, coming out again through it to the top of the hills next to the water.

From that height we saw that the water makes a bend here on this side and widens to about once again as much as the width at the mouth, and that at its margin on the other side directly across from this spot there is a point of land projecting a little out, with a rock or islet close to it in the water at its outer end. Looking northeastward, we saw a boundless plain without any trees on it, from which the river, which turns here and mounts northeastward, seems to draw its flow, and we saw that it splits into branches, going upward, in which direction the water widens out in the distance and forms a number of small island flats within it. And at the far end of all this wide-stretching plain, distant about some fifty leagues upcountry[172] we made out a large mountain range, very

---

[168] The field text, contrariwise: "The island lies with its beginning nearly level with the two ends of the mouth." Evidently Font had revisited his triangulation calculations.
[169] In the field text the figure has been written over and altered several times. The latitude is about 38° 3.5'.
[170] The final text: "the mouth of the Freshwater Harbor."
[171] In the final text, "some."
[172] 130 miles. In the final text, "some forty leagues," 104 miles. "Upcountry" (*tierra adentro*) usually means "north," but in this passage it indicates northeast, since the party, on an easterly course, was rounding the southward bend of the Carquínez Strait. This was their first view of the Sierra Nevada.

snowy and white. I thought that it seemed to run from south-southeast to north-northwestward.

We came down from the hilltops and traveled about half a league to the northeast, and then upon an eastward course because of hills and some lakes or inlets there (and having crossed the stream where Captain Fages halted then during his journey, which lies upon coming down from those high hills from which we sighted the snowy range) we came into a plain where after a short while we traveled east-southeastward and finally a bit southward, making what must have been three leagues in all, most of it east-southeastward. We came to the stream that they called *Santa Angela de Fulgino* in Captain Fages's expedition, which lies at the start of a large plain about three leagues in length having a good many white oaks and other trees and surrounded by not very high ranges upon one side and the hills that border the great river upon the other. We stopped at the edge of the stream here, which we found had only some little pools of not very good water, at a little before five o'clock in the evening, having ridden in all about seven long leagues today.

From the hilltops in the beginning of the afternoon, we saw Indians shouting to us on the other side of the river, and a little before halting, after we had come down to the plain, several Indians came to meet us. To us they appeared as being pleasure-loving, happy, and kind, and they were great talkers while following us to the stopping place; however, I changed my mind about them afterwards. A great many Indians came to the camp who we surmised belonged to a village not far from there down the stream. Though seemingly docile they became a bit impertinent and proved to be a bit[173] thievish, particularly with respect to clothing, which they were greatly drawn to and attracted by, and showed themselves desirous of acquiring and possessing it. They revealed themselves to be great thieves, and insolent, to the degree that when one stolen item would be taken from their hands they would steal something else. There were not enough eyes to watch and guard our things, so that the measure was taken of putting them out of the camp and taking leave of them nicely. But this had no effect, for one of them even somewhat misbehaved with our commander, who had had considerable patience with them up until then. Therefore, half in anger, he seized a stick that the other was carrying in his hands, gave him a little blow with it and threw his stick away into the distance. Thereupon they all went away, talking a great deal and putting forth a great amount of gabble, which I imagined involved some threat for us.[174]

---

[173] Successively crossed out, in the short text: "very"; "no small amount."

[174] They were "robbing hand over fist," according to Anza, "wherefore, and since night was falling, I had them dismissed, which they resisted." The man "had the temerity to threaten me with a stick he was carrying in his hand. Taking it away from him, I struck him with it twice over, and this was enough to cause them to decamp, and for the bold fellow to allow me to understand that he would be going off to sleep."

Some of them had come to visit us carrying their bows and arrows, which were all very elaborate and well wrought, the bows being made of good wood, small, and laid with sinews like the ones we saw on the channel, and the arrows being very smooth little staffs, well made and with very sharp, transparent flints. One man came with a scalp dangling on the end of a pole, which I did not think well of and which smelled like warfare to me. What these Indians were most drawn to was clothing. Eventually after they left, some was found to be gone—for, in order to qualify themselves as being great thieves, they had laid hands on everything—and we were missing the little mill for beating chocolate and a fillet that our commander used for tying up his horse's tail; which was why I formed a poor opinion of these Indians.[175]

The soldiers purchased four fish a bit over a vara in length and over a tercia wide[176] which at first sight we thought were sea bass but on opening them, seeing how red the flesh was, and even more when we ate them, we recognized it to be salmon much more tender, richer, and more delicious than what we had dined on while at Mission San Carlos del Río Carmelo. Perhaps it grows larger bodied and richer and more flavorful because of all the fresh water it has here. However, its shape is very different from the salmon that we saw and ate while at Mission San Carlos.[177] Where it is distinct is in having such a large body, since in its head it is very similar to the kind at El Carmelo.

The mosquitoes, still sucking our blood, bothered us a bit along the whole way today.

The Arroyo de Santa Angela de Fulgino lies on a plain of considerable extent, well grown over with white oaks and other trees, and would be not a bad place for a settlement, as Father Crespí says in his journal, if only the stream were a year-round one. But evidently it is not, as we found it having no flow and with only small pools of a little, not very good water. This spot is a bit over a league distant from the shore of the Freshwater Harbor, or from the fresh water, and the plain in that direction is surrounded with a middling range of hills, while on the opposite side it has quite a high mountain range with a good many trees on it, which we surmise is the same range that ends at the mouth of the Freshwater Harbor and which we crossed afterwards, and which I told of under March 8. As long as the range is, it is also very wide and encloses some not very large valleys, one of which is the valley of *Santa Coleta* so named during Señor Fages's journey when they crossed through by way of it on their return. It lies on the other side of the mountains that are seen from this spot.

[April] 3, Wednesday. I said Mass. The weather was very clear and without chill at daybreak; we would even have had a hot day save for the northwest wind's blowing soft and cool. We were not bothered by mosquitoes during

---

[175] The field text reports the thefts only in the next entry, as having been discovered the next morning, and ends the passage with: "and if they did not steal more it was because they were put out of the camp."
[176] Over 11 inches broad (a tercia is a third of a vara).
[177] El Carmelo.

today's travel, and we noted that all of the country we rode through today was very dry either because there has been no rain this year or because it only rains in summer in these parts, and for that reason the grass was almost dry.[178] We set out from the Arroyo de Santa Angela de Fulgino at a quarter past seven in the morning and upon an east-northeasterly course crossed the plain upon which we had stopped, which is much grown over with white oaks and through the midst of which goes a stream, much overgrown with cottonwoods and other trees, but which we found wholly dry. There is good soil there. We traveled through it for some three leagues, which is the size that it has both in length and in width between the edge of the stream and the foot of mountains that have two high peaks, and with a good deal of trees visible on them. As we started out, a number of Indians from the thieves' village met us as we went and presented us with cacomites and a small dried fruit strung on cords, a bit larger than a hazelnut, grey-colored and having a hard little pit inside. The soldiers said it was what they call *tascal*[179] but larger than the kind that grows in Sonora, and it is fairly sweet. Yet not even that made me approve of those Indians, as thievish and ill-willed as they had shown themselves yesterday.

We then came into hills and a hollow leading out upon a large plain at the edge of the river, and having traveled through the hollow for about a league northeastward we came to the top of the hill marked on the map by the letter **A**, which was the final end of the expedition and discovery made by Captain don Pedro Fages when he went to survey the harbor of San Francisco, accompanied by Reverend Father Apostolic Preacher Fray Juan Crespí, from which point that captain viewed this gulf of waters, which I call a Freshwater Harbor because of its calmness and depth and because the water already is found fresh and good farther back. I shall note that the said Captain Fages was at this hill in the year 1772 on almost the same days as ourselves, since they were at the Arroyo de Santa Angela de Fulgino, which we set out from today, on March 30, and Father Crespí gave it that name because that is that saint's feast day in our calendar,[180] and so I judge that this water that they described as a river must have been now in the same condition as they saw it in, since we saw and surveyed it in the same season as they did. It was from this hill, which must be round about a league[181] distant from the water, that Captain Fages and Father Crespí viewed its extent and saw that it became split into branches forming islets of flats. Since the soldiers previously had tasted the water along the way behind them and found it to be fresh, they[182] no doubt judged it to be a very large river that split here into three branches coming, separately, from farther up,[183] making two islands, and then joining each other again a little below here

---

[178]In the final text, "considerably dry."
[179]Tescal, i. e., tescalama, ahuilote, fruit of the Mexican uvalama tree.
[180]The day given to the Franciscan St. Angela of Foligno in the Franciscan Order's calendar of Church feasts.
[181]Stricken in the short text: "a bit over a league."
[182]Fages and Crespí.
[183]Stricken in the short text: "from very far up."

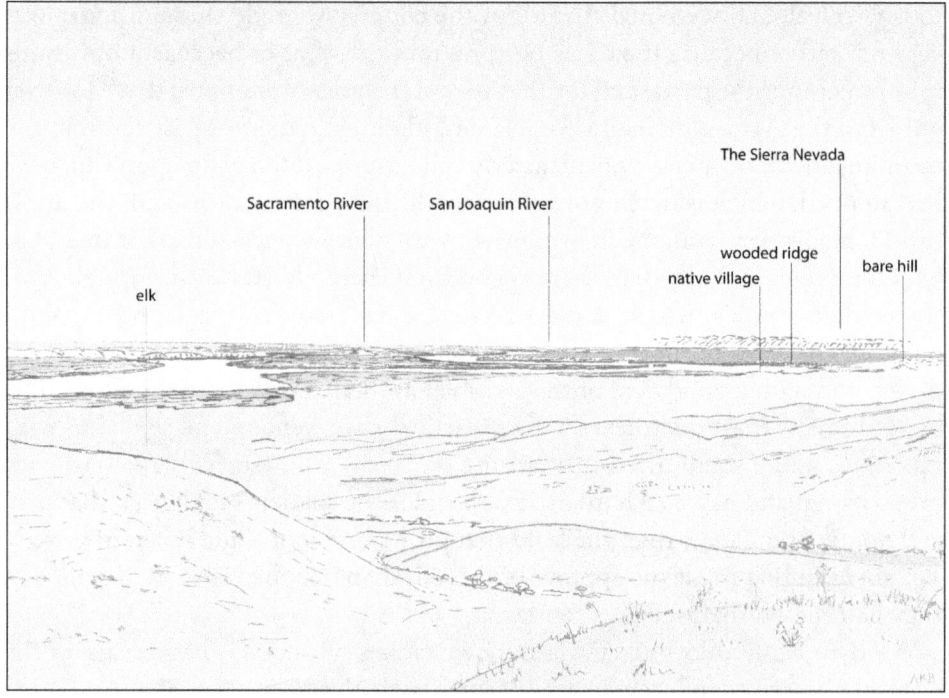

FIGURE 34. A reconstructed sketch of the view from the hills near Willow Pass. The mouth of the San Joaquín ("San Francisco") River is to the left, the low bare hill at Antioch to the extreme right, and the Sierra Nevada in the background. *Drawn by Alan K. Brown.*

where they enter the canyon—this, however, without noticing whether or not it had a flow in it, something that was not easily done from the hill, which is far from the water.

I myself saw the river split, not into three branches but into many, making several islets of which I counted as many as seven, some of them of some size and others small, all of them consisting of flats and appearing long and narrow.

That I saw so many islands when Captain Fages and Father Crespí saw no more than two of them must undoubtedly be due to the fact that they would have seen this body of water at high tide, while I saw it at low tide. The tide here in the Freshwater Harbor has a good deal of flood and ebb as I shall tell tomorrow. They saw the level country through which this flow of water stretches, the plains I spoke of yesterday, and they must also have seen the great snowy range on the far side of the plain. And finally, they saw that farther up the water circles northeastward and even eastward, up to a low range, with trees upon it, which hides the water farther up from being viewed. We ourselves saw the same range, to which our commander determined to go so as to have a closer view of the water and its circuit and to prove to ourselves whether it was a river or not. Although we were almost convinced it was not one, there was still some doubt, as we were far off and unable to make out its motion if by any chance it had any. Also, the soldier Soberanes, who had made this journey with Señor Fages and had come along as an experienced guide, was still holding on to his earlier impression and persisted in saying that the water there was a river and that this was the great river that they had seen.

A portion of water visible in the farthest distance seemingly was coming as a branch from the north, turning or ascending eastward, while closer by, the other portion of water, or larger branch, extended east-northeastward until it became hidden behind hills grown over with trees, and we saw that the tree growth continued onward across the plains. Upon the other side, nothing was to be seen but low bare hills, such as those we saw yesterday, following the margin of the river.

Up until here we had traveled for about four leagues, at a distance from the river of around a league or a bit more. We came down, then, from the hill and directed our way on a course east by north, going toward the range that was hiding the river's course from us, and upon which and beyond it about southeastward we saw a good deal of trees extending onward.

As soon as we had come down to the plain, of which there must be about two leagues between the foot of the hills and the water, we saw on the plain not very far from the water and at a distance of about one short league[184] a big herd of the great deer that I think are called *buras*[185] in New Mexico, which are some seven cuartas in height[186] and have antlers about two varas wide[187] with a number of branches. Although an attempt was made to get one, it failed because of their great speed in running, particularly at the present time when they happened to be without their big horns, which they undoubtedly shed seasonally judging by the great amount of antlers that we saw cast off thereabouts. Along the way we had already seen many of their tracks and likewise had found a number of their very large horns. I was moved to measure one and found it six cuartas long, with five branches each about a tercia in size.[188] We stopped here for about two hours. The soldiers, as soon as we had seen them, wanted to go and chase them to see if they could get one. Our captain gave them leave and they changed their horses and followed after the great deer until they were tired; but the deer were faster and they were unable to catch any. These animals are nearly gray colored, and as large as a two-year-old calf. They[189] got as far as the stream from which we had set out and when they came back, reported they had found over twenty Indians returning from fishing, each man laden with four or five salmon; and near the

---

[184] In the short text, stricken: "a distance of a bit over a league."
[185] This means mule deer, not American elk. In the final text, *buros* [*sic*].
[186] Roughly, 4 feet 10 inches. For the animals, Font uses the more appropriate word *ciervos* (the European deer that are closely related to American wapiti, though smaller)
[187] 5½ feet.
[188] Nearly 50 inches and 11 inches, respectively.
[189] The soldiers.

spot we had set out from they had met Indians coming from the mountains to hunt in the plain who were carrying a stag head. One Indian had been painted the color of the great deer. These Indians went along with them for a little while but as soon as they began getting near the thieves' village in the *Llano de Santa Angela*[190] they refused to go farther with them, indicating by signs that those people were their enemies. These great deer are very plentiful in this entire area; it has entirely the appearance of there being some extremely large *estancia* of livestock thereabouts, because of the tracks that we encountered this day and the next and which are like those of cattle.[191]

After the chase, we continued on all across the plain,[192] leaving to our right hand at the foot of the hills the brackish stream that was the final end of the expedition made by Señor Fages when he came surveying this river. And upon traveling some four leagues on an east by north course we came to a rather large village (whose Indians, who are like the others in their hue and in every way, received us peaceably and even fearfully) that was located in the plain at the foot of the small ranges[193] that we were coming in search of, and so close up to the water that there could not have been twelve paces' distance between water and the huts.

We stopped for a bit here at this village, in which the huts were not grass-built and wretched like the ones we had seen during this journey, but rather large, round and well built like the ones on the channel, made out of good, large tule rush mats with a framework of poles inside to maintain their roundness, and a door; and with the usual sweathouse for everyone. Our commander sought to treat them to a present of beads to remove the fear they had shown the moment they saw us, to the degree that the Indian women went and closed themselves inside their huts and the men stayed outside talking loudly (none of which we could understand)—not, however, with any weapons. One of them went in great haste to set a long pole on top of the sweathouse, with a plume of feathers at its end and a long piece of rabbit skin in two strips, with the hair on it, hanging from the pole like a pennant, which we supposed to be the sign of peace under which we were being received. At the same time, however, the little children and some women put out into the water, boarding their tule balsas. They have a great many of them, and very well made of tule rush with raised sides and a bow and stern terminating in a high point, and furnished all along the side with poles bent as though to provide a railing or backrest. The Indians paddled away with

---

[190] Santa Angela Plain.
[191] Captain Rivera, visiting nearby country later in the same year, made the same comparison between elk herds and the cattle on great Mexican haciendas.
[192] The final text adds, "straight toward the woodsy range marked on the map by the letter **B**."
[193] So in the field text. In the final text, "a little before coming to the range."

great ease and speed using small paddles. The Indian men responded to our gift by giving us feathers, small sticks, and other trinkets in token of their esteem, to the point of insisting that we take them. These Indians are just as ugly and dark as all of the ones we have seen up to here—not bearded, however.

Here we no longer suspected but became convinced that what was being called a river is no river but a very large lake[194] of fresh water, with no flow, that reaches throughout these boundless plains in a number of branches and bends. Our animals went down on foot to drink from it and we ourselves tasted it and found it very fresh and good.

I say that here we became convinced that what was being called a river is no river, because if it had been one, it would naturally have had some flooding; and if it did have some, it would not be possible for this village here to subsist so close up to the water in such a flat country, because, however little the river rose, it would necessarily spread and inundate the whole plain over which we came, and consequently would annihilate the village and its huts. And it cannot be claimed that this village had been newly established there and that its Indians withdraw elsewhere when the river rises, because, in addition to the fact that it was plainly shown by the signs not to be a new village but one of some age, one must grant that it has been in existence for at least some time over two years. This is because when Captain Fages came here and surveyed this water[195] from the hill where he stopped and from which he turned back because of letters he had received, he sent the sergeant and some soldiers to continue their search farther and they came as far as the village. According to the account of the soldier who came along as a guide[196] they found it in the same spot as we did. And from it they turned back without going any farther on or making any further inspection, either because they felt content with that, being convinced that it was a river there, according to the notion that they had formed at first; or else because they had no resources for continuing onward and staying longer, perhaps for lack of food and drink. For that was the time of great need in these parts because there was a lack of supplies.[197] Therefore, this village has been established here for at least two years, and two years there would have been more than enough time for the river to have carried it off in its floods—had it been a river.[198]

We were intending to keep on along the river or shore of the water in the same direction from here in order to go up to the top of the small wooded range—which is not very high—to get a view of the land and the course of the water. However, we had scarcely left the village when a swamp or small water arm with a tule rush marsh lay directly in our way, forcing us to change course. Therefore, heading east-southeastward and leaving to our left the little ranges we had been

---

[194]The final text: "a great piélago." See the introduction. From here on, the final text regularly uses this term.

[195]By an obvious oversight, quickly corrected by a strikeout since it contradicted the opinion that Font had already developed, the short text here referred to "this river."

[196]Soberanes.

[197]Fages's reason for turning back was that couriers reached him with news that the new southern settlements (San Diego and San Gabriel) were in danger of being abandoned because of the failure of supplies that Font mentions.

[198]"Two years," as repeatedly mentioned in this argument, must be an error, since the 1772 Fages–Crespí exploration was four years earlier.

in search of, we traveled over the ridge of a little low hill and came at once onto a rather large plain—although the soil was dry, it had a good many white oaks which were the trees we had seen about southeastward from the hill.[199] And having traveled thus for a bit over one league we came to a very bare hill that was not very high.[200]

In order to get a good view of the land we went up to the top of this hill, which overlooks the entire plain, and from there, we saw a tangle of water, tule marshes, a bit of woods near the mountains on the south, and an enormous stretch of flat land, never in my life I have seen so great an expanse of horizon, nor do I expect to see this again.[201]

Looking eastward, we saw a large and very long, snowy mountain range upon the other side of the plain and some thirty leagues away,[202] white from its summit to its skirts, running crosswise from south-southeast to north-northwest.[203] I judged by what I could demarcate of its bearing that upon the south this range might possibly have some connection with the snowy range that comes off from the main California range above the Puerto de San Carlos, or to put it better, that it is the same main range extending about northwestward as far as Mission San Gabriel and beyond,
and I even am convinced that this snowy range is linked to the large mountain range seen by Father Garcés which he calls the San Marcos mountains in his journal.[204]
But we were unable to make out either the one end of it or the other.

Turning westward, we could see along the course of the river the hills that we had been leaving behind us as we traveled, and in among which the gathered waters shot in or entered; and that on the other side of the water, the ranges open out a great deal, as though running northward, as far as the final end of them that can be made out, which is very far in the distance.[205]

Looking southward, we could see very far off a long high mountain range running about from southeast to northwestward, and this is the range that I talk

---

[199] From the hill earlier in the march (Willow Pass).

[200] The final text adds, "marked on the map by the letter **C**."

[201] In the field text, "we saw what we had not expected, and became still further perplexed, upon seeing the river now turning into a lake and a maze of water, tule marshes, woods and flat land." Font's following description as given here follows the order of the final text. The field text starts with the southern view, then goes to west—east—north.

[202] About 80 miles.

[203] The field text has these directions, less accurately, as "southeast or ["east-," stricken] south-southeast to ["west-," stricken] north-northwest or northwest."

[204] This is correct. On this same date, April 3, Garcés while still at Mission San Gabriel was about to leave on his San Joaquín exploration, during which he used the name San Marcos for both the Tehachapis and the main Sierra Nevada.

[205] The final text has: "on the other side of the water there was a low hill range the end of which, seen at a distance of some fifteen leagues, bore about northwestward, while onward from there nothing could be descried except plain."

about under March 8 and that we left upon our right hand during the whole way we came, all the way from the vicinity of Mission San Luis until the mouth of the river[206] where it ends, the whole of it being formed by a chain of mountains and hills that are bare upon the outside but have a great deal of trees in their center and on whose skirts lie the valleys of Santa Delfina (through which the Monterey River runs), of San Bernardino, and still others, including the Llano de los Robles going toward the mouth of San Francisco harbor. A Monterey soldier declared and affirmed that he recognized a peak that was visible to the southeastward at the limit of what could be seen of this range, and said that it was not very far from a spot they call *Buenavista* which was scouted by the soldiers when they went to the tule rush swamps which lie toward Mission San Luis in search of some deserters, and that if we were to head that way we would come out in the vicinity of Mission San Luis or Mission San Antonio.

Looking back northward, we saw that between the snowy range and the low hills northwest on the other side of the river, there is a great emptiness of horizon with no end to be seen to it, the sky joining with the earth so that the eye loses its objective and there is no telling whether what follows beyond is water or land.[207] We saw a boundless plain, that seemed to run in the same direction as the snowy range on its far side did, but opening out on the other side about to westward, so widely that it took in almost half the circle of the horizon. This is the great plain whose edge we stand upon, in which can be seen nothing except water in branches, tule rush marshes, and flat land without mountains or hills standing out anywhere in all this wide portion of the world's extent.[208]

And this is the plain through which that freshwater gulf extends, not continuously but by stretches, leaving large portions un-submerged or with not much water upon them, on which there are formed those great green tule rush marshes that begin close to Mission San Luis and, to judge by their course and by this reckoning, must be over a hundred leagues long up to here, not counting how far they extend farther up, the end of which we could not see, and they must be some twenty-five or thirty leagues[209] in width. I supposed that these tule marshes run on as far as the vicinity of Bodega harbor[210] and that the "green field" that Captain don Juan de la Cuadra[211] saw extending eastward from his harbor must be tule marshes like the ones we saw here, or else must be the same ones, continuing all the way over there.

Here a dispute arose with the soldiers who were along as guides, with their attempt to maintain that what we were viewing was a river, a thing that I could not agree with. To that end they

---

[206]In the final text: "the mouth of the Freshwater Harbor."

[207]In the final text, Font shifted this passage to the following day's entry, describing the view across the San Joaquín Valley.

[208]Although this passage refers to the view from the top of a knoll next to the municipal water tank at Antioch, the description must owe part of its effect to the prospect from higher up, in the hills near Willow Pass, which Font had viewed a few hours earlier (fig. 34).

[209]Stricken, in the short text: "twenty leagues." (65, 78, and 52 miles, respectively.)

[210]Stricken in the short text: "Captain Bodega's harbor."

[211]Captain Bodega himself.

alleged that there was a very large river on the other side, emerging onto this plain through gaps in the snowy range: a river, split into two branches, that had been found by the soldiers when they went searching for the deserters, and they were able to ford the first branch with difficulty, but in no way the second, and the Indians they saw there refused to let them pass and so they returned to San Luis.

According to all the signs this is the river encountered by Father Garcés which he called in his journal the river of *San Felipe*.[212] I had already had news of that river through a letter written to me from a Religious of San Fernando[213] who had served as a minister at Mission San Luis, a copy of which I shall set here because of the information that it holds about those lands—even though somewhat confused since the Father learned it only by hearsay, especially concerning the three rivers he mentions, where he supposes the water in the long canyon that runs up from the mouth of the Freshwater Harbor to be a river, and takes this San Felipe River, split into two branches, to be two further rivers. The letter is from Fray Domingo Juncosa, dated January 30, 1775, and runs in this fashion:

"Through the occasion offered by don Juan Bautista de Anza's telling me that he is going there to Sonora with orders to proceed along with Your Reverence to our Monterey missions and San Francisco harbor, I decided, seeing that this was such a good opportunity to write this letter to Your Reverence, informing you, etc. I have understood that Captain don Juan Bautista de Anza intends and has the goal to set out from Sonora for that country during the month of September, and to proceed across to San Francisco without stopping either at the missions or at Monterey until he returns from founding the settlement he is to make at San Francisco and from surveying that country. If the goal is indeed to do so in the way indicated, then, by the experience and information that I have about that country, I regard it as more than slightly risky, and they may be thoroughly misled. For, since the rains in that country are from November or December until sometime in April, it will necessarily happen that if they arrive at San Francisco before or at the beginning of the rains they will have to spend until April enduring the rains out in the open. As much as they may wish to go to Monterey, they will be unable to do so unless there are only a few of them traveling light, and that, with great effort because of the country's many mires that hinder any traveling, most of all with pack trains, as I myself have experienced. And even two or three persons traveling light have found themselves in no small manner too exhausted for the road, especially if the rains are at all plentiful. And supposing they choose to stay and dwell there at San Francisco without going down to Monterey, they will still, because of the rains, be unable to do anything toward founding a settlement except perhaps a very small amount of work—not employing beasts of burden to transport any timbers needed for buildings but, in that case, with the people themselves serving as the transporters on their own backs, facing heavy mud except during a few days that usually provide an interval between rains when, to be sure, people can achieve something in the way indicated; but it is very hard to manage to use beasts of burden because of the mires.

"In addition, they face another considerable danger if they proceed by cutting straight across from the Colorado River to come out at San Francisco, and that is that they no doubt will arrive at the end and innermost portion of the San Francisco inlet where three rivers or branches empty into it, which when they join into one close to that inlet" (this is the confusion about the river, which they imagined as split into three branches,) "empty into it. One of these has its course

---

[212]The Kern River. The soldiers' river was probably actually the Kings.
[213]Refers to one of Serra's colleagues, pertaining to the colegio of San Fernando of Mexico City.

from the east and the others, with slight difference, from the north, and therefore it is very possible, even unavoidable, for them to arrive somewhere in between the eastern and northern rivers, which cannot be forded, particularly the northern one, according to the account given by deserters from Monterey who reached it a long way up and at a distance of over forty leagues from the inlet where they empty out, at a point where they were unable to ford it and the gentiles refused to carry them over on their floats. On the other river coming from the east, the only ford that has been found is also at some forty or fifty leagues from its mouth. Therefore, supposing that you arrive as I have said, in that tract in between rivers, you will have to go back for at least those forty or fifty leagues in order to ford them and escape from that maze. It seems to me that because of these dangers the safest thing would be to go from the Colorado so as to arrive at one of the missions, and should you decide to go to the one at San Luis, which lies at 35° 28', you will have a good route if you choose a sort of hollow or valley that runs, with slight difference, from east to west over the whole distance of our missions between San Gabriel, or near it, and San Francisco" (this was the route traveled by Captain Fages one time when he went from San Diego to San Luis, refusing to stop at San Gabriel because at the time he was annoyed with Father Paterna, and we learned that it is a very rough, poor route), "which is located inland from the missions at a march of three or four days. The soldiers who accompanied Señor Anza from Monterey to the Colorado at the time of his return to Sonora perhaps could give him some information about it. Supposing that you follow the hollow and wish to arrive at Mission San Luis before you reach the parallel of 35° 28' the Indians will inform you as to where the mission is located and perhaps you will find the track of the animals left from the several times that that hollow has been traversed by soldiers going to San Luis at the period when they pursued deserters who were staying in immense tule rush marshes at more or less the same parallel as San Luis. Now when you arrive out at the missions you will be assured of at least having shelter and a better chance for supply at one of them or at Monterey, in case of your being unable to travel because of being trapped by the rains. And if you wish to take or to seek a direct way across between the Colorado River and San Francisco, or the reverse, you may take your return directly to the Colorado River from the aforesaid San Francisco after inspecting it and accomplishing the founding and all the rest of your affairs, without touching at the missions." He then goes on to ask me whether I can arrange to have some small stock and mounts brought along for Mission San Luis, which has none, doing this favor for his countryman and mine, Father Fray José Cavaller, the Catalán minister there. And he concludes by complaining of how little effort his colegio of San Fernando has put into petitioning the viceroy for such provisions, because the well-off Fathers in Mexico City do not feel or recognize the neediness of the poor Religious out there.[214] Etc.

I did not doubt from the information in this letter that there might be some river or rivers on the other side of the snowy range. I did not, however, agree with what the soldiers held to be true, since I did not see the river they said was there nor was there visible anywhere in the mountain range a gap through which it might reach the plain that lay before us. Thus the way they maintained their statement was only a piece of guesswork through which they wished to argue and convince us that the water in front of us was the great river of San Francisco. Because of my denying the existence of such a river, or at least the fact that we were seeing it, our commander said, "Father, isn't it enough for the gentlemen to say that they have seen the river that they say issues onto the plains here?" I answered him, "Sir, it's not enough, because the river that

---

[214] A rare expression of resentment by a missionary in the field. However, Font himself later expressed some not dissimilar views regarding his own superiors at the Querétaro colegio.

the gentlemen spoke of is one that they saw very far away from here, and no such river, nor the gap through which they say it issues, can be seen from this hill. Here and now we must not judge by guesswork and by what may be, but by what is and what we see; and what we see and have in front of us is not a river but a great deal of pooled water." And with that, the dispute and my own speech concluded.

In view of this our commander decided to go down and camp at the water's edge, having in mind to keep on ahead for a few days' march and cross the plain and approach the snowy range in order to prolong the exploring (which during the previous expedition was carried out only so far as the vicinity of this spot) as far in that direction as might be before exhausting the provisions we had with us—or, rather, for whatever distance they would reach while still enabling us to return. Therefore, coming down from the hill, we traveled about a league over the plain on a northeastward course through a level, fairly dense wood of small live oaks and some white oaks, but before reaching the water, already close to it, we came upon a small tule marsh and bog that barred our way; so we changed course and, by traveling about a quarter-league westward, reached the water's edge at a spot having an abandoned village, where there was a good deal of grass and enough firewood, and here we camped at a little after a half past four o'clock in the afternoon, having traveled about ten leagues in all.

Here finally we came to the realization that the river is no river—unless it becomes one farther up—but instead a great lake of fresh, very good water that, because it has very little drainage into the sea, keeps fresh the water that reaches inland. As soon as we had halted we went to view the water and to taste it, and we found it very crystalline, fresh, sweet, and good; and our animals went down to water at it without any trouble. We noted that it has a shore like the beach of a small sea, with little waves, and plants and some trees growing all the way down into the water. And we saw that, caused by the wind, it had a soft motion striking upon the edge or shore with gentle waves; we could perceive no current in it, however. In order to test whether it did have any, our commander seized a middling-sized stick that ended in a knob and threw it as strongly as he could out onto the water. Yet we soon saw that instead of drifting downstream, it was brought back to the shore by the little waves in the water, so that we recognized that it has no flow, or if it does have any it must be a very little one and out in the middle of the water, the width of which is almost the same as at the mouth. However, we at once noticed a more unusual fact, which was that it has a flow and ebb like the sea, and that the tide was going out. There were no deposits of flooding on the shore or trash, except for a bit of dried tule rushes, from which we deduced it is not a river. If it had been, it would have deposits of timber and signs of its having flooded—as naturally it would do, being as it is within view of the snowy range.

APRIL 3, 1776

Our captain set a marker on the shore at the point that was being reached by the little waves on the water. An hour and a quarter[215] went by and we returned to view the water and noted that it had uncovered a distance of over four varas away from the marker that had been set up[216] and that the water had dropped about two tercias[217] judging by the uncovered trunks of some trees there on the shore, ones which we had seen submerged earlier. We concluded from this that the water has its own ebb and flow like the sea and that the tide was going out at that time. From all of this it results that the river is no longer a river, so that henceforth we shall call it a lake until God pleases for us to discover otherwise. For this reason, our lieutenant, along with a servant, was charged with taking care to observe when the tide should be at its lowest during the course of the night and with measuring whatever amount of the beach or shore it uncovered, and with later observing how far up it came at high tide. As I shall tell, this was performed during this night and the morning of the following day.

To conclude this day's entry, I want to reflect, here, upon the information sent to Mexico City by Reverend Father Fray Silvestre Vélez de Escalante, minister of the Zuñi mission, that he had acquired in his journey between New Mexico and the Province of El Moqui,[218] made during last year, 1775. As I mentioned on December 1, the information was sent on by the viceroy to Father Garcés. While traveling on May 20 we received the cover letter but not the copied information, which had been misfiled within His Excellency's[219] secretariat when the letter was sent. So the information, addressed by the secretary don Melchor Peremás[220] to the governor of these provinces[221] don Francisco Antonio Crespo and advising him to remit them at once into the hands of Father Garcés, came one mail delivery late, and His Excellency had been unable to understand this oversight that had occurred in the secretariat. By chance, I happened to learn of this information and to read the copy at San Miguel[222] in the governor's house on the same day that I arrived there returning from this journey.[223]

This Father says that he reached Oraybe, the last town belonging to El Moqui and some fifty leagues distant to the west from the town of Zuñi that belongs to New Mexico. There he was informed by a Cosnina Indian that the land inhabited by the Cosninas lay six days by a bad route westward of Oraybe and that at nine days' travel beyond Oraybe was a very high mountain range running northeast to southwestward trending westward and over one hundred leagues in length, at whose northern skirts the great *Río de los Misterios* runs westward, not crossable by the Cosninas and their neighbors.[224] Consequently, the Cosninas do not know what people there

---

[215]In the final text, "about an hour."
[216]The final text: "a good-sized piece of shore."
[217]Over 11 feet from the marker, and dropping about 22 inches; the field text has, for this, "about a vara" (33 inches).
[218]The Hopi pueblos.
[219]The viceroy's.
[220]*Sic*; Melchor de Peramás.
[221]Of Sonora, Ostimuri, Sinaloa.
[222]Horcasitas presidio.
[223]June 1776. This paragraph of course was written after that.
[224]River of the Mysteries

are on the other side of the river or whether there are any, since they never cross over nor have they seen any signs of them.[225] He says further that on this side, at the edge of the mountain range nine days' travel westward from the Cosninas, there is located a tribe that speaks the same language and is called the Tomascabas and fourteen days' travel from these there are others called Chirumas[226] who are warriors, robbers, and inhuman, because they eat the human flesh of people they have killed in their campaigns; and that the Cosninas have learned from these Chirumas that there are Spaniards in that direction although a long way off, etc. And he ends by saying that this report that the Cosnina gave him was the same as what he already had been told by the Moquinos.[227]

First, we must assume that Father Fray Silvestre received his report from the Cosnina through signs, which is how the Indians usually express themselves, or else through an interpreter, possibly a poor one as normally is the case, unless the Father happened to know the languages belonging to that area. If he employed an interpreter or had recourse to signs in order to understand the Cosnina, he might easily be mistaken as to the information, since many times it happens that when one thinks he has expressed himself clearly with the Indians by these means, one finds out afterward that they did not understand him, or else understood the contrary of what he said. That being granted, and leaving aside the distances and directions which the Father records in connection with the tribes he names—in reconciling which, I find problems in accounting for the high mountain range that he says lies across from southwest to northeastward—where I find the most difficulty is in the river he calls the Río de los Misterios, not so much because of the name, which is a considerable surprise to me, but in how he describes it as being so full-flowing that it is not crossable by the Cosninas. The Father says that this Río de los Misterios flows to the westward. But then, since it is so full-flowing, it would be normal for it to go and empty into the sea. If this were the case, we would naturally have encountered it, because we reached a latitude of 38°, which is far enough for it to have come out upon the seacoasts that we traversed since I think that this latitude or even a lower one is what answers to the course of the river the Father speaks of, considering in what location he received the report. However, during the whole way, we have hit upon no river besides the Colorado River, which, as we experienced, can be crossed even when flooding and even can be forded when it flows within its natural bed. Neither can it be said that the Río de los Misterios is the Colorado River itself, and that it changes its name farther up, for if the Colorado is not so full-flowing as to be not crossable even where the rivers meet and below the Puerto de la Concepción—since the Yumas, both men and women, swim across it there—naturally it must be less full-flowing higher up above. Even were it so full-flowing, one is not easily convinced that the Cosninas and their neighbors are so much inferior to the Yumas that they would not dare fording the river however large it was—all the more so because they are born upon its banks, for we see that Indians raised on the banks of a big river, such as the Yaquis

---

[225] Escalante's "River of the Mysteries" referred to the Colorado in the vicinity of the Grand Canyon and above. Garcés, whose travels allowed him to interpret the letter far better than Font could, explained this report convincingly on the ground that "The river [Colorado] forms a great rampart for the Yavapais and the [Rocky] Mountain Indians because no one dares to cross unless he is taken over by the people of the region." (Galvin 1967: 86.)

[226] In the short text, the first attempt at copying the first reported tribal name was "To(b)asca(u)as" and in both examples of the second name, "Chirumas," the "r" has been altered from some other letter. Garcés, after his travels during this summer, was able to identify the reported "Tomascabas" with the Mojaves, and the "Chirumas" (both names are variously spelled in copies of Escalante's letter) with the Halchidhomas.

[227] The Hopi.

and the Yumas and even those on the seacoast, are all of them great swimmers. Whence I infer that they perhaps must have said to Father Fray Silvestre that there was a great deal of water on the other side of the mountain range, and since they told him it was fresh water without distinguishing whether it was flowing or not, the Padre decided it was a river, since its waters were not salt and they had not told him of there being a sea there.

Based on all this, I say that perhaps the great Río de los Misterios spoken of by the Father and reported to him must be a kind of very large pool of fresh water, running in the same direction as the tule rush marshes that we ourselves saw, or it must be those very same tule marshes and water that extend over the boundless plains I have spoken of, the water reaching inland as far as the other side of the snowy range through a gap or gaps and covering a great area east and west just as it does north and south; unless it is some matter of what they call the Sea of the West.[228] And this being the case, it may easily be believed that it is not crossable by the Cosninas, for crossing it from one side to the other is very difficult, I may almost even say impossible, and in consequence the Cosninas cannot know what people exist on the other side nor even whether there are any there, just as those on the other side cannot know, either, whether Cosninas exist.

From all of which, I conclude by saying that it appears to me to be a very difficult matter to open a direct route from New Mexico to Monterey as has been planned. Besides the information given by Father Fray Silvestre concerning the river or body of water lying in between, the tule swamps are also in the way and the route must pass through them before it reaches the seacoast. However straight one tries to make it, at best it can only arrive in the vicinity of Mission San Luis or farther down from there, in my opinion. *Salvo meliori judicio*.[229]

[April] 4, Holy Thursday. The weather was quite clear at daybreak although with a very strong northwest wind that had begun about midnight and continued all day until sunset, troubling us a great deal. After dinner, before midnight, our lieutenant went to see whether the water of the lake had gotten lower, and he found it had drawn back so far that we determined from the measurement he made that it had uncovered sixteen and one-half varas' width[230] of shore. My servant Silva, who was charged with going after midnight to see how much it had risen, went before dawn and saw that the water had risen so far that it lifted the dry tule rushes that it had washed onto the bank. At sunrise our commander and I went and saw that the tide was already beginning to ebb and that, what with the northwest wind blowing so hard today, the water was a bit more disturbed, with the little waves out on it turning white the way they do at sea, under the gales (as they are called), and with rather big waves along the shore. Using a level (I had a level along with me for whatever occasion might arise), I took the difference in the water's height, and determined thereby that the water had gone

---

[228] "Unless . . . the Sea of the West" was added in the final text at some point after the following passage had already been written, and it is not in the earlier version of this essay in the short text. See the introduction.

[229] A Scholastic phrase, roughly meaning "allowing for the possibility that this conclusion will be altered by a more competent authority." Garcés, returning from his own travels in the interior, expressed justified skepticism about Font's theory of vast swamps.

[230] 45 feet 4½ inches (the same as reported by Anza at 10:15 P.M.). In the final text, "some sixteen varas."

down a bit over three varas[231] from its height at high tide, measured down to where it left the shore bare at low tide. I shall note that the water was pooled up here[232] and must have had very nearly the same width as at the mouth, and the shore was not steep in the way it is elsewhere but very low-sloping, and along it we saw some little shells, almost flat, and as shiny as though made of mother-of-pearl, but thin and in fragments. I took the difference in the water's height in the following way: I measured two varas' worth of the shore down from the highest point on it reached by the water at high tide, and by leveling this portion I read off, by the level, one and one fourth cuarta[233] at the farther end of the distance, so that by estimating this amount against the sixteen varas of sloping shoreline uncovered at low tide, I determined by the triangle that the water had dropped some three varas, which is a pretty large drop. From all the above, and from these tests—and most of all because of the tide, which we experienced as being all the greater because it was the day of the full moon—we concluded, and became finally assured, that the river was no river but a lake, and I was confirmed in the conjecture that I had had earlier, that that lake was formed from the great tule swamps that exist in this vicinity and that it discharges through here into the sea, but not enough so as to count, since it has no current other than the ebb and flow of the tide.[234] And if after all—granting that it is fresh water—someone claims that it can be called a river just because it has some motion with the ebb and flow, then by the same reasoning we can call the sea a river.

Our commander still insisted on the decision that he had reached yesterday to go around the lake until he saw the end of it and proceed to the snowy range so as to follow along it, if the tule marshes would allow us to do so.[235] We set out, then, from the spot (where we felt only a little chilliness because of the wind) at a quarter past seven and traveled for a short way on an eastward course, intending to keep on along the water, either beside its edge or else in view of it. Immediately, however, the tule rush marsh and bogs that hindered us from reaching its shore yesterday lay in our way, making us alter our course and commencing to separate us from the water so that we had no further sight of it.[236] We took up an

---

[231] 3 varas equal 8¼ feet. So in the field text. In the final text: "some three varas." Anza's "three and a fourth varas" must rest on the same observation by Font of the tide marks.

[232] Not flowing, slack water.

[233] About 10⅓ inches.

[234] Replaced in the final text with: "... became finally assured that this gulf of water ought better to be called a freshwater sea than a river, as it does not have floods or a flow as a river does, and like the sea it has waters that are clear and bluish, and the tidal ebb and flow, with little waves upon the shore."

[235] Font introduces the paragraph in his final text with: "Although, because of all that is said before, we had become certain that there was no such great river hereabouts as had been said, nor even a small one, . . ." and he describes Anza's purpose as being "to follow the circuit of the water, cross the plain, and extend this exploration for some days' march toward the snowy range."

[236] The final text adds, "except from a distance and from the top of the range."

east-southeastward course and in that way traveled some three leagues, keeping to our right the wood of small live oaks which at about two leagues continued on as one of quite big tall white oaks at the foot of the southern mountain range. We followed it along to a distance of a bit over six or seven leagues, with the tule marsh on the left taking us farther and farther away from the water. Since we wanted to see if the tule marshes would allow us a way across, we turned east-northeastward with some veering to northeast and traveled in this way about a further league, but at once the tule marshes hindered us from following in that direction and although we tried to keep eastward, we commenced winding about, to the east-southeast, sometimes southeast, and also to the south, without being able to gain any distance toward the snowy range but rather getting farther out of the way.

We saw the many well-trodden trails[237] that are made by the great deer—whose hoof or track perfectly resembles that of cattle—as they go down to the water across that plain, and we followed some of them; always in vain, however, for we would come up immediately against a mire or an impassable ditch of water that made us turn back. Finally[238] we came across a little path with human tracks on it that we thought led toward a small village that we saw in the distance on a small elevation within the tule marsh.[239] Although we tried to follow it, we immediately found ourselves faced with a bog our animals were unable to get through and that even on foot could only be crossed with difficulty. Accordingly, two soldiers crossed through the first bad spot on foot and, with some trouble, their animals, and as we were so desirous of following this trail, our commander said that on foot or not, we would follow it until unable to go farther. He ordered a soldier to go out in front and inspect whether there would be any other bad spot ahead. When he had gone only a short way, we saw him and the mule he was riding not only stop but fall. By this we recognized the difficulty, and the fact that penetrating the tule swamp was impossible.

The soldiers then told us that going through the tule swamps is so risky that when they went to catch deserters in them, one of the deserters, seeing himself about to be captured, tried to get away by heedlessly throwing himself into one of these bogs, perhaps relying on the fact that he

---

[237] In the field text: "We kept finding countless tracks of great deer . . . and many of their trails." The field text places this description a little later, after the following mention of "rotten," ashy and dusty soil. Captain Rivera's account, written later in the same year, stresses the quantity of elk trails where he crossed the plain west of present Tracy, and likewise speculates that they have their "lair" or breeding-ground thereabouts—possibly a suggestion passed on by Moraga and others who had been with Anza.

[238] In the final text: "One time." The "finally" in the field text seems to place the event nearer the end of the "over four leagues" mentioned in the following paragraphs.

[239] A generation after Anza and Font, the missionary José Viader noted that "all these areas" along the Old River were submerged in the summer rising of the rivers, when "the heathens live on a few cramped small elevations [*unos pocos y reducidos altitos*]" (Viader 1810). For some locations of known native villages, see Bennyhoff 1977; Brown 1998: 25.

knew how to swim. However, he sank in it, unable to escape or receive help, and there he lay drowned and buried in the mud.

We went on in this way, eastward to southward, east-southeastward and southeastward, until over four leagues, making our way with some toil across the tule marshes, which were dry for a good stretch, and treading over[240] loose, rotten soil full of dry scum, and with such a biting dust raised by the wind from the ashes of burned tule rushes that it blackened us and burned harshly in our eyes, making us cry and hardly able to see, so that we had a very unpleasant day and departed from here with very red, inflamed eyes.

This occasioned our recognizing that the freshwater gulf that stretches through those tule swamps sometimes floods, and that when it rises it reaches much farther than the ground we were treading on, which was full of snail and turtle shells[241] and scum that had grown in the water when it reached up to here. There is no difficulty in believing that the water here rises, indeed it must naturally happen that way since with the snowy range being within view it is quite normal that there should be a number of rivers issuing from it and running out and ceasing upon the plains there, and that the freshwater sea—since it is fresh it may be allowed this exception to the rule[242] or, if not, it can be called a lake—should rise, either with the rains and flooding from the rivers in winter, or else in summer with the melting of the snows.

We headed to the south[243] and I said to our commander that if he thought it well, we would do better to return toward Monterey, in view of the fact that the tule marshes where we were are the same ones that run on until close to Mission San Luis and were taking us farther away from the range with every step, for it was already clear that what had been called a river had turned out to be a lake. But our commander, although already of the same opinion, had not yet entirely abandoned his determination to see whether we might approach the snowy range, and he chose to pursue the task a little farther just in case we might find higher ground farther down that would give us an easier way across. And so on going a short way we began heading eastward, and traveled for about three leagues, following a somewhat trodden trail for a good while.

It was already about two o'clock in the afternoon. Corporal Robles, who went out in front as a guide, halted as if he were thinking about where to go and in which direction to lead us. Our commander asked him, "What do you think? Is there any hope we can reach the mountain range today or tomorrow?" The corporal answered, "I don't know, Sir. What I can say is that once I came out past the point of that range there (the one that we saw looking southward from

---

[240] "Sinking into," in the field text.
[241] See the end of this entry for the field text's equivalent of this phrase.
[242] That is, "freshwater sea" may sound like a contradiction in terms, but Font thinks it can be a valid description.
[243] In place of this, the final text introduces the next passage with: "Already we had been realizing the impossibility of proposing to cross the plain and approach the snowy range."

the hill yesterday, and that runs southeast to northwest[244]) and I spent a day and a half trying to get around a tule swamp and saw that it still ran onward, and did so on the other side as well, but I did not get to the end of it nor did I see anything more, since I turned back from there."

Thereupon I said, "Sir, it is futile to involve ourselves in establishing a fact already known.[245] We are sure that the river we were looking for is a lake. The most we can learn is whether some rivers run into it from the snowy range, something that for our current purpose is not very important to learn and is likely enough to be true. It is also the fact that verifying this will require more days than what we suppose it will and that we can only accomplish this by rounding the whole tule marsh, which must occupy a district of about thirty leagues[246] on this plain. Meanwhile, the day is drawing to an end and if we go onward any farther our animals will spend a bad night. Unless we head to the mountains in time to look for a stopping place, we will spend the night here on these plains with no water, no firewood, and no grass: no grass and no firewood because there is none to be had, and no water because the bogs and extensive mires in the tule swamps keep us from reaching it. So, since there is nothing more to be seen here, it is better for us to return to Monterey."

Our commander, seeing all the difficulty that would be involved in approaching the snowy range as he had planned, then decided on our returning to Monterey. The soldiers, however, said that in order to do so it would be necessary to return to the place we had set out from. From there we would go the way we had come by, since they knew of no route hereabouts and no Spaniards had ever traveled in this area. This seemed hard to our commander and to me. I said that judging from the way that we had come, Monterey was to the south of us. If we could bring ourselves to cross the range in front of us, I dared to affirm that we would come out at the San Bernardino valley along this course, or at worst, at the Santa Delfina valley.

---

[244]In the field text, "the one we had had to the south, on our right." At the point they had reached, near and south of Byron Hot Springs, the peak of Mount Oso commences to stand out clearly from the main mountain range. Robles of course misidentified it with the peak a hundred miles further south. Anza's entry says that both soldiers, Robles and Soberanes, advised him that the tulares that started 20 or 30 leagues from San Luis Obispo and San Antonio were not fordable even in the dry season.

[245]In the final text, Font allowed himself to develop his report of this argument: "According to the reckoning, it is already clear that these tule marshes are the same as exist near San Luis mission and that they run on to there, and in order to get around them one has to go down to the neighborhood of that mission—which is what is necessary in order to get to the snowy range, the exploration of which can be carried out better by beginning the journey from there at that Mission San Luis. Besides which, Sir, we do not gain anything in terms of the purpose of our reconnaissance by involving ourselves in going to survey the snowy range; we are sure that the river that we had come to seek is a lake . . . [etc.]."

[246]78 miles.

Therefore, changing our course, we headed toward the range on a south-southwestward course. After going one league we came to very bare hill ranges which we called the *Lomas de las Tuzas*[247] because we saw a number of gophers in them and they were undermined with gopher holes. We went into them through a hollow made by hills from which we saw that there was a white oak grove upon the plain, about at the end of the tule marsh we had just left, and continuing very far onward. We traveled through the hills, going up and down over them, for a bit over two leagues on a south-southwestward course though veering to one side or the other because of the way the hills turned. And, having climbed to their top, we saw a spacious valley to our right that is formed between the hills we were crossing through and those others that we had kept upon our right while on the way to the mouth of the lake. It is the valley through which Captain Fages came out on his return after leaving the Arroyo de Santa Angela de Fulgino, and they called it Santa Coleta. Opposite us, far off, we made out the range of pines that runs toward the San Francisco harbor and ends at Punta de Almejas.[248] Then, having surveyed the country and seen we were on a right course, we went down from the top of the hills, kept on through them for about two leagues upon the same south-southwestward course, and proceeded straight toward hills that had trees upon them in hope of finding water there, which we did, although only a little. We reached them a bit after five o'clock in the afternoon and the pack train arrived at six o'clock. We had traveled some fifteen leagues in all, at a good pace, and we halted upon a small height next to a hollow in which a little water was found.

In the tule marshes we saw a great many dead snails and turtles, and a number of great deer in the woods, but we did not see a single Indian along the whole route today, and encountered only human footprints pressed into the dried mud. I thought it so poor a land as not to be easy for people to dwell in. I, at least, was left without any wish to travel back and see this piece of country again, for besides the burning in the eyes that I have brought away from there and my mouth inflammation that had already mended but which broke out again today, I have not seen an uglier country than this. For, although when seen from afar it strikes the eye as being something fine, so level and with a distant view stretching to so wide a horizon, in reality, however, it is an arid country, nitrous, all water and mires, not containing anything to please me or strike me as useful, except for the great deer that seemingly have their lair hereabouts.

---

[247] Gopher Hills.
[248] Font's viewpoint was from the ridge top some half a mile south of Patterson Pass, from which six or seven miles of the then strikingly tall redwood forest on top of the main ridge of the San Francisco peninsula in San Mateo County would have been visible. (Brown 1998: 31–33 and appendix 9).

[April] 5, Holy Friday.[249] Daybreak came with very bright, clear weather, no wind, and a small amount of heat that we felt during the course of the day. We set out from the hills at the beginning of the range at a little before seven o'clock in the morning, and at four o'clock in the afternoon halted in the *San Vicente* hollow (we named it thus because of its being the feast day of San Vicente) a little before it came to an end, having traveled some thirteen leagues on a poor, very rough and broken route and on a southward although changeable course, as I shall tell.

We commenced crossing the range upon whose skirts we were located and that we had kept upon our right while on the way up, and traveled for about three leagues on an east-southeastward course, with some veering off, in search of a hollow that we had thought we had opposite us.[250] It narrowed down so far as to keep us from continuing that way, for which reason we were required to climb to the summit of the range and we traveled about one short league—northward, eastward, southward, in every direction or no direction—until reaching the top. We stopped here for a bit in order to look for a way to get on, and from this height, and a great height it was,[251] we could clearly see the plains, water and tule swamps through which we had come yesterday, and were able to tell that they were continuing on downward toward Mission San Luis in a great level opening in which water could be seen in stretches, like a valley formed on this side by the range we were starting to cross and on the other side by the snowy range, which was in view very far off, and also, itself, continuing on down toward Mission San Gabriel.[252]

We came down from the top of the range and traveled up and down over a number of hills and ridges for about two leagues on a southeastward course because of the brokenness of the hills and slopes, until we came to a stream in a hollow. We continued through that narrow hollow on upward for about two leagues on a southeast and south-southeast course, and on reaching where it ended at the top of the pass that it made, we saw ourselves facing a great amount of very rough, broken mountains lying ahead and all of the country we had gone through—along with what was to be seen on all sides—very much grown over with white oaks, pines, and woodland. We kept on for about a league on the southeastward course with a great many turnings, sloping downward and

---

[249]The Friday of Holy Week is called "Holy Friday" (*Viernes Santo*) in Spanish, but it is normally called "Good Friday" in English.

[250]The wording only slightly disguises the fact that Font had hoped to find a valley route through the mountains. The final text: "that we saw."

[251]The final text adds, "marked by the letter **D** upon the map." The viewpoint was at 2,959 feet elevation on top of Crane Ridge.

[252]The final text adds, "Thus I felt confirmed in the judgment I had already made, which I recorded yesterday and day before yesterday."

a number of times upward as well, and then all at once the country[253] began opening out more, so that we came upon a rather wide, quite long hollow. And having traveled through it around about more than four leagues on a south-southwestward course, we halted a little before it came to an end, at the edge of a stream going through the midst of the hollow and having very little water, at a quarter after four in the afternoon, having traveled some thirteen leagues in all and over a poor route, very rough and broken.

At the beginning of this hollow where we halted, which the soldiers named San Vicente hollow,[254] we saw a high mountain, very red in color,[255] that drew everyone's attention by its configuration, whereas all the rest are very crowded with woods and trees, these heights have no trees on them, only some quite open-appearing scrub brush woodland. On the ridges and here and there, strips and patches of very white pebbles are revealed that the experts said were ore. Those mountains—which have a stream passing along their foot, not counting several other small streams in the hollow—are red in color, for which reason everyone said they held a great show of being ore. I myself thought they looked very much like the mountains at the Guanajuato mines.[256] They are situated in the center of the mountains there that we were crossing, which are very rough and broken.

Along the course of this hollow we saw some wretched little huts that were abandoned, but only a single Indian running along in the distance. As soon as he saw us he fled toward the mountain woods like a deer. All of this country which we are crossing is very rough and broken. It is the lair of many bears judging from the tracks that we saw today. Farther on, and although when viewed from the outside these mountains look bare and treeless on both sides, in the center they are very crowded and full of a great deal of woodland, pines, live oaks, white oaks, redwood[257] and many other kinds, among which is a tree like a fig tree, with smaller leaves and with its fruit resembling figs on the outside, while within they have a fruit to some extent resembling a chestnut, more so in the husk and the color than in the shape. It is eaten by the gentiles, to judge by the heaps of its rinds that we saw in the abandoned huts.

Without a doubt, these must be the chestnuts that at Monterey they told us were to be found on the way to San Francisco harbor. They formed this notion from having seen some of the rinds, but their opinion was a mistaken one because that sort of rinds are not those of chestnuts, for I investigated the matter thoroughly and there are no chestnuts anywhere that I saw. The soldiers said, also, that in going along the coast from Monterey to San Francisco, which is the route that

---

[253] "The mountains," in the field text.
[254] The final text adds, "marked on the map by the letter E."
[255] In the final text, "some mountains or hills."
[256] Guanajuato, in today's central Mexico, was in the eighteenth century one of the principal silver mining areas of the colony of New Spain.
[257] In the final text, "spruce" as usual (but in actuality there are no redwoods in the range).

was taken the first time by the expedition of Señor Portolá[258]—when they named Point Almejas because the soldiers stopped there to gather mussels in order to provision themselves with food since they had nothing left to eat—a great many hazelnuts are encountered before reaching the point. But if they do perhaps exist, I did not see any of them, since we did not travel that way.[259]

[April] 6, Holy Saturday. There was a good deal of chill last night and it froze a little, no doubt because we are in the center of mountains here. The weather at daybreak was very clear, with a bit of a chill that quickly ceased, and we felt a good deal of heat afterward during the course of the day. We set out from the San Vicente hollow at a quarter to seven in the morning and commenced traveling upon a southeastward course. After going a little way the San Vicente hollow came to an end and, shortly after setting out, we found ourselves amid rough broken mountains on all sides and with a very deep narrow canyon in front. We descended along it and at once came across a little water, the beginning of the Arroyo del Coyote, and followed it on a south-southeastward course for about three leagues with some short veering-off; however, we came to a bad spot and to get around it we spent over an hour getting to the top of a high hill. We kept on through the hollow for about two leagues farther; its stream, which is the El Coyote, changed direction toward the west and we commenced climbing through a range on a south-southeast course. On reaching the summit we went down to a hollow running in our direction which seemed to offer us a way out, and in doing this we must have traveled about two leagues. We then continued on through the canyon, the stream in which seems to be the El Coyote, the same one that we had left previously and had followed from its source;[260] and having traveled along it for about four leagues with great toil because of the rocks, bad spots and ups and downs that faced us, we stopped at four o'clock in the afternoon at a small, flat elevation next to the Arroyo del Coyote (where the stream's course is altering our direction to the westward), having traveled some ten leagues in all, on an even worse, more broken route than yesterday's. The main course that we followed was south-southeastward, with a bit southeastward; some veering also took place to eastward and westward because of the ins and outs of the hills.[261]

---

[258] The reference is to the first expedition of 1769.
[259] Thickets of edible "hazelnuts" (*avellanares*) were reported near Watsonville, Santa Cruz, and Pescadero by the first expedition in October 1769 (Brown 2001: 559–65, 580–81). As Font seems to want to hint, these probably were mostly California buckeyes (horse chestnuts), although it is possible that hazelnut bushes originally growing there were destroyed by subsequent livestock grazing.
[260] In the field text, which provides more details of this day's march than the other texts do, "the same one ... followed from its source" is added between lines.
[261] The name *Sierra del Chasco* first appears in the margin of Anza's record of the previous day's march as a laconic description of these hills. A *chasco* is a practical joke, a disappointment, or a deception. He and the soldiers were not holding the mountains themselves responsible for the prank played on them, but rather the mistaken geographic reckoning that had led Font to promise an easy way back to Monterey. See the introduction.

We did not see a single Indian the whole way, though we did come across some of their trails and here and there a few signs and traces of poor huts and abandoned small-sized villages. It is clear that they go into the mountains during some seasons and camp there, mainly during the harvest time for pine nuts and acorns. We were close to being able to leave the mountains here, but halted because the mule train was tiring out and so were we, what with so bad, rough and broken a route. Ever since we first set out for the mouth of the lake[262] there have been small, nearly black wood ticks sticking to us during the course of our travel—more of them today, however, than on any other day. We were covered with them and I plucked off fourteen from myself during one short period.

[April] 7, Easter Sunday. I said Mass. At daybreak the weather was clear, with no chill but instead considerable heat which we felt during the course of the day. We set out from the small elevation at a quarter past seven in the morning and traveled on a south-southeastward course with some veering to southward because of turnings in the hills, for about two leagues, descending through hills over which we came finally out of the mountains and down upon the flat ground of the San Bernardino valley, most of which consists of swamps and lakes but mostly was dry because it had not rained much this year, and we managed to cross it without trouble. Some ten or twelve Indians belonging to a village next to there at the edge of the lake came to meet and greet us as we finished our descent, and presented us with amole and with two matalote fish from the lake,
which is the sort of fish that I have spoken of a few times, the one that is found in the Gila River and the Colorado River. Judging from the shape, taste, and spines that it has, I think it is the same kind they call *saboga*[263] in Spain.
Our commander responded by giving them beads.

We then came into the San Bernardino valley, which we crossed upon a south-southwestward course, and having traveled a bit over three leagues through it, on coming into little low rolling hills and a little before reaching a small well of water in them near the El Pájaro River, we came upon the way which we had traveled before. Continuing over the hills for about a league, we crossed the Arroyo del Pájaro and traversed the San Pascual valley on a southwestward course with a bit of a southward slant. At two leagues we came to the stream and small hollow of San Benito. We went up the grade, southward, and upon coming down from it we continued westward for a little, then southwestward, and at about three leagues reached the place of La Natividad; and with four more leagues on a course south-southwestward at first and then southwest and finally

---

[262]After leaving the San Francisco peninsula. (In the final text: "for the mouth of the Freshwater harbor.")
[263]Said to be a synonym for *sábalo* (shad). But it was not shad. See the note under November 18, above.

Figure 35. Plaza del Presidio de Monte-Rey, 1791. By José Cardero.
Courtesy of The Bancroft Library, University of California, Berkeley.

with a slight westward slant, we crossed the Santa Delfina valley, which is very bare and has only grass and some lakes in it; and we forded the Monterey River with ease and halted at its edge at a quarter past five in the afternoon, having traveled a good sixteen leagues in all. The sound of the sea can be heard from this spot, from which I deduce that it is not far off. It is easily heard during the silence of the night as there is level land across as far as the shore, which I judge must lie some two leagues away from this place.

[April] 8, Monday. I said Mass. The weather at daybreak was clear, with a good deal of heat. We set out from the Monterey River a little after a quarter past seven in the morning, and, upon a southwestward course and at the end a bit south-southwestward, we passed over some hills and came to lakes and dunes which we crossed among on a westward course as far as the harbor. And then by heading almost eastward for a short stretch, at ten o'clock in the morning we came to Presidio of Monterey, where we stopped to dine. A number of people from the expedition at once came to greet us and were very pleased with the news we gave them concerning our journey, particularly the fine locale of San Francisco harbor that we had seen and that had been designated for the settlement and garrison. This gave them some encouragement, as they had been quite unhappy before, after they were told that the whole area of the harbor there was very poor country according to Señor Rivera's report.

Lieutenant Moraga stayed at the presidio and at a quarter past three in the afternoon we headed out for the mission, course southwest and a league's travel, along with the purveyor, who had come to receive us.[264] Before reaching the mission we came upon four Fathers who had come out to receive us, and we arrived at the mission together having traveled five leagues. There they received us with joy and many peals of the bells. Along the way we ate some strawberries, which were beginning to ripen and of which there are a great many there, where we were crossing the Sierra de Pinos.

---

[264] Anza's journal records that he went to the mission in order to get some treatment for his leg, which was still giving him considerable trouble—and also because the only lodging available to him at the presidio was his own command tent. The entries for April 13 and 14 mention the "good or bad treatment they tried upon me," from which his leg received very little benefit (understandably, since the trouble was a kidney stone).

CHAPTER 6

The Two Commanders

[April] 9, Tuesday. We stayed here at the mission, resting, and chatting about our journey with the Fathers, who were a good deal surprised by the news we gave them that there was no such great river of San Francisco as that which they had reported to exist. And since they were committed to their opinion, we had our friendly arguments on the matter.[1]

At one o'clock in the afternoon our commander went to walk by the shore with the Fathers, but I did not go along as I felt a bit ill with my mouth trouble, as the inflammation had been paining me and breaking out again ever since the tule marshes on Holy Thursday.

[April] 10, Wednesday. I occupied myself in producing a drawing of this journey that we had made from Monterey to the harbor and lake of San Francisco,[2] although I did not manage it very well. I was hardly up to the task and the conditions under which I was doing it were poor. There was a great stranding of small sardines at the shore today and they said there were so many of them that all the ground at the edge of the water was black with them. Our commander went to stroll there with the Fathers in the afternoon to see this wonder. I did not go along, still feeling ill with the mouth inflammation. During these days we have been eating plentifully of very large, tender, and fine heads of lettuce, with which I got a bit better.

[April] 11, Thursday. On waking, my mouth was a bit improved. We continued without incident here at the mission. Because of the drawing I produced yesterday, the Reverend Father President asked me to make another for him, and then Señor Anza asked me to draw another one for him, too. So I occupied myself with this all day today and finished the one that I made for the Father

---

[1] As Font makes clear earlier, the differences of opinion were quite severe in their consequences, especially for Juan Crespí's reputation. Crespí was conspicuously missing from among the group of friars who came over the hill from Carmel to say farewell to Font and Anza at Monterey on April 14.
[2] The final text has: "to San Francisco and Freshwater harbor."

President. Don Juan appointed a lad to serve me during the return journey in place of Silva, who said he would not serve me any more and wished to remain here, even though he was married in Sinaloa and his wife was there!

[April] 12, Friday. My improvement continued. I finished the map for Captain Anza before noon. It came out better than the two earlier ones, though not entirely perfectly because of the poor conditions under which I made it.

This drawing, which turned out most to my satisfaction, is the plan or map that I shall place here.[3] It depicts this whole journey that we made from Monterey to San Francisco, going and returning, with the route marked by dots.

It was decided that we would go to Monterey tomorrow and then return toward Sonora.

Señor Anza, seeing that Señor Rivera had not responded as requested to the communication that was dispatched to him on March 17, and that the period he had indicated to him for awaiting the reply had elapsed, decided to begin his return march. He no longer was thinking of taking the people to San Francisco, as he had promised to do had Señor Rivera agreed to that in a reply. Commander Anza dispatched Sergeant Góngora[4] from Monterey with a communication for Commander Rivera in which he advised him of his decision to return. That way, should he wish to meet with him he could come from San Diego to Mission San Gabriel, which was the agreement they last had made when we set out from San Diego.[5]

The Fathers here were so courteous that they prepared a great many vegetables for us for our journey—cabbages, lettuces and tender broad beans, and a great deal of dried salmon as well.

although I never got to taste the latter or saw any of it again, for Señor Anza kept it all so that he personally could give it out as presents.

---

[3]In the final text. Reproduced here, figure 20 in chapter 5.

[4]José María Góngora, the sergeant who lost his temper when Font was trying to pacify the colonists at Monterey on March 17.

[5]The equivalent passage in the field text, which is at the end of the next day's entry, adds: "and that he would be starting to travel today" (April 13, when they did start back). However, in the form in which it is preserved, Anza's letter of April 12 to Rivera implied the impending departure from Monterey without mentioning it specifically. The letter expressed hope that the two commanders would meet at San Gabriel later in the month, but, using the tone of a superior officer, Anza strongly demanded an answer to his letter, just in case the meeting might not come off. Anza went on to report the advantages of the San Francisco site at the mouth of the harbor. Clearly proposing to remove the decision from Rivera's hands, Anza wrote: "It is my conclusion that it [the site] shall instantly be occupied"; also, slightly less intrusively, "I now put forward my conclusion for you on the strength of what I have observed, as I am ordered to do by [his] Most Excellent Lordship [the Viceroy]." Anza went on to say that if the chosen site did not prove to have sufficient drinking water, the garrison could be placed one league or two leagues further inland, the farther location being the Los Dolores spring. The San Andrés hollow could support a mission with large irrigated and dry-farmed crops, serving as a way station between Monterey and San Francisco, or, alternatively, the second mission could be at the place called San Pedro Regalado, fifteen leagues south down the coast (present-day Pescadero). The letter closed with a repeated insistence upon a reply from Rivera.

Anza's journal entry gently summarizes this by stating that Rivera was sent the notification of the agreement that he and Anza had already made when they separated at San Diego, and as advised to be at San Gabriel on April 25 or 26 in order to arrange their mutual duties.

Five soldiers were sent carrying the message south.

[April] 13th, Saturday. I said Mass, and afterward, with much affection, we took leave of the Fathers there. We set out from Mission San Carlos del Río Carmelo at nine o'clock in the morning and at ten o'clock reached the Presidio of Monterey, having traveled one long league northeast by north. We stayed here today in order to allow our captain to finish arranging his affairs, both for our own return and with respect to handing over the management of the expedition, with Lieutenant Moraga taking charge of everything in the absence of Captain Rivera, who was at San Diego.

Even before beginning the journey, I had asked Señor Anza several times to tell me the precise number of people belonging to this expedition and the count of livestock, horses, and mules; but never could I get him to tell me, since he would make excuses by saying he didn't know because he had it all in note form, etc. I suspected that he did not want me to know so as not to risk having me say one thing and he another whenever he might need to change one or another entry in order to cover a shortfall while adjusting his accounts later on. At San Miguel, for this reason, at my urging he gave me a rough accounting of some entries, among which he told me there were twenty muleteers. But later on at Tubac, when the numbers should have been greater since that was where all the people had joined us, he told me there were fifteen. And I noted that in other accounts, such as the one of interpreters and servants, he counted one of them as two. And therefore, while I have set down entries for everything at the start of this journal and I think those are exact and, in the event that anything falls short or goes over, the error must be only a very small affair, still, I shall note that I set them down according to what I saw and learned along the way during the journey and not because they were told to me by Señor Anza, who was the precise, assured, and certain conduit through which I would have preferred to learn them.

Today once again I begged him to at least let me know the number of people who had come on the expedition and were remaining at Monterey for the new settlement and fort at San Francisco harbor. Even though it was mere curiosity on my part and truly there was no need for me to know it, I still wanted to know because I had come along with all of them. And I was allowed to see the list, which was incomplete. A few names were missing, such as the prisoners who were left at Mission San Gabriel. But I did learn from the list that one hundred ninety-three souls stayed behind at Monterey. Their names are included on the following list which I copied faithfully on the spot this day.

A Roster

Containing Officers, Sergeant, Soldiers and Settlers with their respective Families, prepared by order of the Most Excellent Lord Viceroy, by Lieutenant Colonel of Cavalry and Captain of the Royal Presidio of Tubac of the Province of Sonora don Juan Bautista de Anza to the Presidio of Monterey in Northern California, to be transferred to its Commander, don Fernando de Rivera y Moncada.[6]

---

[6] As Font indicates, this roster is based upon an official list, actually one signed by Anza at Tubac, October 20, 1775, "Noticia de la tropa reclutada . . . ," published for the first time by Garate 1995: facsimile 306–309; transcription/translation 159–65; a critical discussion including relationships between the document and Font's version 185–91. The list will be referred to in these notes as "Anza's list." (*continued, next page*)

	[Age according to Anza, October 1775]
PRESIDIO SOLDIERS	
1} Lieutenant don José Joaquín Moraga.	[34]
Came without his wife and family whom he left at Terrenate where they were living, his wife being ill.	
5} Sergeant Juan Pablo Grijalva	[33]
His wife María Dolores Valencia	[31]
Children:	
María Josefa	[6]
María del Carmen	[5]
Claudio[7]	[21]
6} Domingo Alviso[8]	[35]
His wife María Angela Chumacero[9]	[30]
Children:	
Francisco	[14]
Javier[10]	[12]
Juan Ignacio	[5 months]
María [de] Loreto	[8]

It includes, in addition to the categories of information used by Font, the dates when the soldiers and heads of families were recruited for the expedition, and also the ages of individuals. The order of families within the list's sections basically reflects the order in which they were originally recruited. Font did almost nothing to change this order, except in the list of non-military settlers, where his changes are of significance.

The individuals' age figures are added here in brackets following the individual names, for the sake of the extra information. Names without ages added are not found on Anza's list. "*De*" in family and personal names, from Anza's list, is also added within brackets because the differences might reflect some subtle social awareness on Font's part, since the use of *de* originally indicated a claim to higher social origins.

The notes are restricted to discrepancies with respect to other documents (especially Anza's list) that may reflect Font's individual knowledge of the expedition members, and to events immediately surrounding the time of the expedition. As elsewhere, the spelling of names is usually normalized.

A useful comparative table of material on the families and individuals, including information from two later censuses, is Christy 2003.

[7] From the placing of the name, it is clear that Font knew that "Claudio" was not a direct family member even though on Anza's list he was placed first among the Grijalva children in accordance with the normal format of having male children precede female ones. Later records and genealogical research by a descendant show that this was, in fact, Manuel Claudio Salvador Alvírez, recorded as an employee of Grijalva's in 1778 and forebear of a well-known San José Alvírez family. (Information from Pam Meeds, courtesy of Greg P. Smestad).

[8] The name is spelled (even in California) Albizu, Alvizu, Alviso, etc., elsewhere also Arbizu. Font uses "Alvisso, Alviso," Anza "Alvizo." See the subsequent note.

[9] Domingo Alviso's burial at San Francisco is recorded on March 11, 1777, at which time he was a corporal and husband of María Ángela Trejo (presumably for Chumacero de Trejo). In May 1777 his widow petitioned to be allowed to leave the country with her children, but in July 1777 she married the recently widowed Pedro Bojorques and the Alviso family name is still found in landmarks on the California map.

[10] "Francisco Javier" on Anza's list, separate from the preceding Francisco. In May 1777 the two children were referred to as José Francisco and Javier, no doubt correctly.

APRIL 13, 1776

8}	Valerio Mesa	[33]
	His wife María Leonor Borboa	[30]
	Children:	
	José Joaquín	[13]
	José Ignacio	[12]
	José Dolores	[9]
	José Antonio	[7]
	Juan	[5]
	María Manuela	[8]
4}	Ramón Bojorques	[32]
	His wife María Francisca Romero	[30]
	Children:	
	María Gertrudis[11]	[14]
	María Micaela[12]	[12]
2}	Carlos Gallegos	[34]
	His wife María Josefa Espinosa[13]	[17]
8}	Juan Antonio Amézquita[14]	[35]
	His wife Juana Gaona	[30]
	Children:	
	Salvador Manuel	[14]
	María Josefa	[12]
	María Dolores	[8]
	María Matilde	[4]
	María de los Reyes	[3]
	Rosalía Zamora, wife of Salvador Manuel[15]	[13]
6}	Ignacio Linares	[30]
	His wife Gertrudis Rivas	[22]

---

[11] At San Francisco in January 1777 she married José Francisco Sinova, a native of Mexico City and son of European Spanish parents (of Castilla la Vieja). As a boy, he had joined Visitador General Gálvez's military expedition to Sonora in 1767–1770 and had remained there. The Bojorques family was from the town of Sinaloa.

[12] She is clearly the Micaela whom Font married to the non-soldier settler Ignacio de Higuera at Mission San Xavier del Bac (see October 26 above, and Higuera's name in the list below).

[13] See Font's remark about these two persons, at the end of the list.

[14] Amézquita, born at the Sonora presidio of Terrenate, was already a widower in May 1777 when his very young daughter María Josefa married Hermenegildo Sal, a European Spaniard (from Valdemoro near Toledo in Castilla la Nueva) who had a long career ahead of him as an officer at San Francisco, where the wedding took place. The necessary affidavits as to his bachelor status were received from as far away as Sonora, from Antonio Castro, the mining executive with whom Font and Palma stayed in June 1776, at La Cieneguilla; Castro had known Sal both in Spain and in America, as had Pedro Garracino, a San Diego soldier.

[15] Manuela Rosalía Zamora, from Sinaloa, according to the Mission Dolores registers. She bore a child, José Gabriel Amézquita, at the new San Francisco settlement in 1776, and died there, extremely young, in March 1777.

Children:
- José Ramón [4]
- Salvador Ignacio[16]
- María Gertrudis [7]
- María Juliana [3]

4} Justo Roberto[17] [30]
His wife María [de] Loreto Delfín [27]
Children:
- José Antonio [7]
- José Matías [7 months][18]

6} Gabriel [de] Peralta [40]
His wife Francisca Manuela Valenzuela[19] [33]
Children:
- Juan José [18]
- Luis María [16]
- Pedro[20] [15]
- Gertrudis[21] [9]

RECRUIT SOLDIERS[22]

6} Juan Atanasio Vázquez [40]
His wife Gertrudis[23] Casteló [25]
Children:
- José Tiburcio [20]
- José Antonio [8]
- Pedro José [7]

---

[16]Born during the march on Christmas Eve, December 24, 1775, and hence Font added *Salvador*, "Savior" to his other names (see that entry). He is placed at the end of the family names in the field text. Unlike two other children born during the expedition, he survived, and the Linares family name became well known in California.

[17]Evidently, Justo Roberto Altamirano (cf. Eldredge 1910: 295). Font's and Anza's lists and Anza's correspondence (Garate 1995: 27) treat Roberto as the paternal family name and in the final text, Font gives "José Antonio Roberto" also for the first child but in California the man and his descendants were always Altamirano.

[18]In October 1775.

[19]In the Mission Dolores marriage register, entry no. 3, early 1777, her name is given as Francisca Javiera, not Manuela. Her husband was corporal in command of the mission guard, and her son Juan José was marrying Ana Isabel Berreyesa. Ana Isabel is apparently the "Ana María" of Anza's and Font's lists. See that entry below in the list.

[20]"Pedro Regalado," on Anza's list.

[21]"María Gertrudis," on Anza's list.

[22]Font's field text originally had this heading above the next entry, José Antonio García, making Juan Atanasio Vázquez a Sonora presidio soldier.

[23]In the field text, "María Gertrudis."

APRIL 13, 1776

María Antonia Bojorques, wife of José Tiburcio[24]

7} José Antonio García [42]
His wife Petronila Josefa[25] [28]
Children:
    José Vicente [12]
    José Francisco [9]
    Juan Guillermo [5]
    María Graciana [7]
    María Josefa [3]

8} Antonio Quiterio Aceves[26] [35]
His wife María Feliciana Cortés [30]
Children:
    José Cipriano [6]
    Juan Gregorio [4]
    Juan Pablo [10]
    José Antonio[27] [20]
    María Petra [12]
    María Gertrudis [3]

11} Felipe Santiago Tapia [39]
His wife Juana María Cárdenas [23]
Children:
    José Bartolomé [11]
    Juan José [9]
    José Cristóbal [8]
    José Francisco [7]
    José Víctor[28] [6 months]
    María Rosa [13]
    María Antonia[29] [12]

---

[24]She is not on Anza's list, but was married to Vázquez at San Xavier del Bac by Font on October 26, and therefore, she must have joined the expedition by that point, no doubt at Tubac. The two lists do not indicate whether she was a sister of one of the other October 26 brides, María Micaela Bojorques, daughter of the presidio soldier Ramón Bojorques. The husband's name is just "Tiburcio" in this entry in the field text, and Anza's list has "Juan Tiburcio," wrongly, since it was always "José" in later records.

[25]In Mission San Gabriel marriage register entry no. 54 (surviving only in the T. W. Temple II transcripts), April 7, 1776, she is Petronila Josefa Acuña; her husband is a native of Guanajuato (central Mexico) who had resided for four years at Culiacán. In the Mission Dolores (San Francisco) baptismal register, January 6, 1777, she is Josefa Tafoya; the infant (her sixth) is José de los Reyes García.

[26]On Anza's list, "*de* Aceves," is the form used for the family name of the first child.

[27]*Sic.* The entries are not in order by age.

[28]"Victorio," on Anza's list.

[29]Age 13 in April 1776 at Monterey, preparing to marry José Antonio Buelna, possibly against her family's tacit wishes. (Serra, *Affidavits*.) She was the daughter of Tapia's first wife, Juana María Hernández. The family was from Culiacán, Sinaloa.

María Manuela	[6]
María Isidora	[5]
5} Ignacio María Gutiérrez[30]	[30]
His wife Ana María [de] Osuna	[25]
Children:	
María de los Santos	[8]
María Petra	[7]
Diego Pascual[31]	
3} Agustín [de] Valenzuela[32]	[30]
His wife Petra Ignacia [de] Ochoa	[20]
Children:	
María Ceferina	[3]
4} Luis Joaquín Álvarez de Acevedo	[35]
His wife María Nicolasa Ortiz	[30]
Children:	
Juan Francisco[33]	[12]
María Francisca	[6]
4} Ignacio [de] Soto	[27]
His wife Bárbara [de] Espinosa[34]	[18]
Children:	
José Antonio[35]	[2]
María Francisca	[1]
6} Pablo Pinto	[43]
His wife Francisca Javiera Ruelas	[40]
Children:	
Juan María	[16]
José Marcelo	[14]

---

[30]A native of Los Alamos mining camp (Sonora), according to Garcés in Mission San Gabriel marriage entry no. 54.

[31]Born on November 19, 1775, during the expedition; see that entry.

[32]Like Gutiérrez just above, he was from Los Alamos, Sonora, according to a marriage affidavit recorded by Serra, May 1, 1776 (Serra, Affidavits). Anza's list includes in this family María Feliciana Arbayo (Arballo) and her two children. Font lists them separately, later. See the notes at the end of the list.

[33]"Juan José," on Anza's list.

[34]Espinosa was her paternal family name. The father, Joaquín Espinosa, had also been in California with the first expedition, 1769–1770. She is recorded as María Bárbara de Lugo (using the maternal family name) in the first entry in the Mission Dolores baptismal register, August 10, 1776, when her newborn son Francisco José was given emergency baptism and, when healthier, brought by Isabel Berreyesa to the missionaries. Her husband was serving in the mission guard at the time. He petitioned for retirement twenty years later, citing as his merits his coming with Anza in 1775 to be a *soldado fundador* of the harbor, "besides having contributed to its population with eighteen children." (Archivo General y Público de la Nación Mexicana 1940–: hoja 22).

[35]An elder child, Simón Antonio de Soto, age fourteen, is given just before here in Anza's list.

APRIL 13, 1776   339

	Juana Santos[36]	[16]
	Juana	[12]
3}	José Antonio Sotelo	[29]
	His wife Gertrudis Peralta	[25]
	Children:	
	Ramón[37]	[5]
3}	Pedro Bojorques[38]	[21]
	His wife María Francisca de Lara[39]	[18]
	Children:	
	María Agustina	[1]
8}	Santiago de la Cruz Pico	[38]
	His wife María Jacinta Bastida	[26]
	Children:	
	José María	[7]
	José Dolores	[6]
	José Patricio[40]	[3]
	Francisco Javier	[5]
	María Antonia Tomasa[41]	[2]
	María Josefa[42]	[15]
5}	José Manuel Valencia	[36]
	His wife María de la Luz Muñoz	[30]
	Children:	
	Francisco María	[5]
	Ignacio María	[2]
	María Gertrudis	[7]
5}	Sebastián Antonio López	[47]
	His wife Felipa Neri	[45]

---

[36]In Anza's list, Juana Santos Pinto, age sixteen, is entered with her husband, Casimiro Varela, below in the section for civilian settlers. Font has re-entered her here, but only in the final text. The reason is not clear, but may involve some confusion with the second Juana, who must be the Juana Francisca, daughter of Pablo Pinto and Francisca Javiera Ruelas, natives of the town of Sinaloa, who married the Monterey soldier Mariano Antonio Cordero in November 1776 in the first marriage that was recorded at San Francisco.

[37]A Juan Antonio, age twelve, is added in Anza's list after Ramón, not in order by age.

[39]She died in January 1777. See the note below on her husband's remarriage to the also recent widow of Domingo Alviso.

[40]A José Miguel, age four, is entered in Anza's list between Francisco Javier and José Patricio, who are thus in proper order for their recorded ages. Font's field text does not have José Miguel, but keeps the original order of the other two; however, the order is reversed in his final text. Likely he had some reason for doing this.

[41]"María Gertrudis Tomasa" in Anza's list.

[42]She is either age fifteen months, or else the entry is not in age order.

Children:
    Sebastián[43] [17]
    María Tomasa [20]
    María Justa [5]
9} Juan Francisco Bernal [38]
   His wife María[44] Soto [35]
   Children:
    José Dionisio [17]
    José Joaquín [15]
    José Apolinario [10]
    Juan Francisco[45] [14]
    Tomás Januario[46] [7]
    Ana María [5]
    María Teresa [2]
5} José Antonio Sánchez[47] [29]
   His wife María Dolores Morales [26]
   Children:
    José Antonio [2]
    María Josefa [3]
    Ignacio Cárdenas, his adopted son
11} Joaquín Isidro [de] Castro [43]
   His wife María Martina Botiller [40]
   Children:
    Ignacio Clemente [22]
    José Mariano [14]
    José Joaquín [7]
    Francisco[48] [5]
    Francisco Antonio [9]

---

[43]"Sebastián Antonio" in Anza's list.

[44]In Anza's list and the field text, "Ana María." In full, Ana María Josefa. In 1790, her husband is listed as a mestizo, from Sonora.

[45]These last two names are reversed from the order in Anza's list and in the field text, which keeps the order of the ages recorded by Anza.

[46]Spelled "Anuario" in Anza's list.

[47]Age thirty in mid-May 1776; he had lived in the town of Sinaloa from seven years earlier. (From marriage affidavits taken down by Serra, which like Anza's list add a "de" to the family name.) At the new San Francisco settlement as early as August 10, 1776, a newborn daughter was baptized when in danger of death.

[48]The confusion of Franciscos under the entry for this family is obvious, and highly understandable. Despite his age, Francisco Antonio appears at the end of the list of boys, because he must be identical with the Francisco María, Indian laborer age eight (!), in the 1777 San José record. He must have been originally a *níjora* slave (see what Font says on this topic in his December 7 entry). "Francisco," the actual child of the parents, must be the Francisco María or Francisco Manuel of later records.

APRIL 13, 1776

Carlos Antonio	[6 months]
Ana Josefa[49]	[18]
María Encarnación	[8]
María Martina	[4]
8} Vicente Féliz	[34]

Widower. His wife died on the journey on November 24 in the early dawn.[50]

Children:

José Francisco	[12]
José Doroteo	[10]
José de Jesús	[2]
José Antonio Capistrano[51]	
María [de] Loreto	[8]
María Antonia	[6]
María Manuela	[4]
7} Juan Salvio Pacheco[52]	[46]
His wife María Carmen del Valle	[40]

Children:

Miguel	[25]
Francisco	[15]
Bartolomé	[10]
María Gertrudis	[13]
Bárbara	[8]
4} Manuel Ramírez Arellano[53]	[33]
His wife María Agueda López de Haro	[17]

Children:

Mariano[54]	[1]
Matías Vega, his adopted son	[25]

---

[49]She was from the town of Sinaloa, whence her family set out with others in April 1775. She married the Monterey leather-jacket soldier José María Soberanes not long after her arrival (marriage affidavits recorded by Serra in May 1776).

[50]Manuela Piñuelas, age thirty-one in October 1775, according to Anza's list. María Ignacia Manuela, in full, in other records. See under October 23.

[51]In the field text he is listed at the end of the family, since born during the expedition (Font uses smaller script here). The infant died later in the year at San Gabriel.

[52]He died before May 1777, and his wife was among those who petitioned to be allowed to leave the San Francisco settlement and California. But the family remained and became successful, particularly a Salvio of the third generation.

[53]A native of Puebla, in eastern New Spain (Mexico), he had gone to Sonora with the unsuccessful military expedition mounted by Visitador General Gálvez in 1767 and following years.

[54]"Mariano Ramírez de Arellano," in Anza's list, presumably because of maternal family claims.

SETTLERS WHO ARE NOT SOLDIERS[55]

6} José Manuel González[56] [35]
His wife María Micaela Ruiz [28]
Children:
   Juan José [14]
   Ramón [6]
   Francisco [1]
   María Gregoria[57] [15]
3} Nicolás Galindo [33]
His wife Teresa[58] Pinto [18]
Children:
   Juan Venancio [5 months]
1} Casimiro Varela [27]
Husband of Juana Santos Pinto[59]
1} Ignacio Anastasio [de] Higuera [18]
Husband of Micaela Bojorques[60]
2} Cristóbal Sandoval[61]
His wife María Dolores Ontiveros
2} Nicolás Antonio Berreyesa [15]
María Isabel Berreyesa [18]
The two are brother and sister, unmarried.[62]

---

[55] "Residents or settlers," in Anza's list. Font has severely altered the order of the names in this section and has made important changes.

[56] Described in later California records as an Apache Indian. His wife María Micaela is also listed as Indian in 1777. In the field text, this family appears lower down, after Casimiro Varela.

[57] In the Anza list, María Ana, age eight, is added after this María Gregoria González, but she is not recorded by Font. The 1777 San José census gives the family, in addition to María Gregoria, a three-year-old daughter named Ana María, so that the source of the discrepancy may be an inaccuracy in Anza's list, detected but not fully corrected by Font.

[58] In the Anza list and field text, and in other records, María Teresa. The Galindos were from El Fuerte (Sinaloa).

[59] She, age sixteen, is placed here with her husband in Anza's list. Font's final text has her with the family of Pablo Pinto, above. Anza's list adds here Juan Antonio Varela, age five months. Is this child possibly the same as Juan Venancio Galindo, age five months, already listed just above with Teresa Pinto and her husband Nicolás Galindo?

[60] Presumably the María Micaela, age twelve, listed above in the family of the presidio soldier Ramón Bojorques. The relationship is not mentioned in Anza's list, where Higuera's is the last name. The family was from the town of Sinaloa.

[61] Font's evident mistake for Gregorio Antonio Sandoval, age thirty in Anza's list (second from its end and listed with no family). On October 26, 1775, getting the groom's name right on that occasion, Font himself had married Gregorio Sandoval to María Dolores Ontiveros at San Xavier del Bac (October 26 and fig. 9 in chapter 1).

[62] In the field text these two names appear at the top of the list of non-military settlers. "María Isabel" would appear to be the Ana Isabel Berreyesa, daughter of Luis Cayetano Berreyesa and the late María Micaela de Leiva of the town of Sinaloa, who married Juan José Peralta, son of the corporal of the Mission Dolores guard, at San Francisco early in 1777.

APRIL 13, 1776

3} Pedro Pérez de la Fuente[63] [28]
Marcos Villela
don Francisco Muñoz
The three are bachelors.[64]
3} Feliciana Arbayo. Widow.[65] [25]
María Tomasa Gutiérrez [4]
María Eustaquia [1 month]
The three have no husbands.
6} The four deserters and two servants stayed at San Gabriel and I do not know whether anyone else remained there.

This list indicates that one hundred ninety-three souls remained there. That is what I do not know, because I was unable to learn whether the list is complete or whether there is anything missing, and it was even suggested to me that I had been done a favor by being allowed to see the list that I copied.

And Señor Anza was still very annoyed at Caborca on May 25 because I once again asked him to tell me the number of people, animals, etc. This was the last time that I asked him, and I was left without learning it.[66] What I do know is that two persons should be taken off, namely Carlos Gallegos and his wife María Josefa Espinosa, who obtained permission to return to their country, Sonora, and came back along with us; and also I have added the four deserters and two servants[67] who remained at San Gabriel, and I believe that someone else remained there, because, out of the two hundred forty of us, subtracting one hundred ninety-one who remained at Monterey, nine who remained at the Colorado River and the twenty-nine of us who returned leaves eleven, and these are the four deserters, two servants, and some others who along with

---

[63]In May 1777 he was one of the petitioners asking for release from the San Francisco settlement on the grounds of loneliness and unemployment. He apparently succeeded, since his name disappears from California records afterward.

[64]In the field text, Pérez de la Fuente's name is separate from and earlier than the other two, which are not in Anza's list. Presumably the three shared a fire and food (formed a single "mess") during the march.

[65]The standard spelling is Arballo. In Anza's list, she and the two children are shown as being with, or as part of, the family of the soldier-settler Agustín Valenzuela. Presumably she decided to travel alone with her children after her experience at the December 17 camp. See her name in the list above, with note, and the introduction. Font's "the three have no husbands," applied to the children, might be an oversight or else some sort of oblique insult.

María Feliciana Arballo's age was given as twenty-four in April 1776 when she married an old California hand, Juan Francisco López (age forty) at San Gabriel. Francisco Garcés officiated, and the witnesses at her wedding were a noteworthy pair, Sergeant Grijalva of the expedition and Sebastián Taraval "an Indian of Californias," El Peregrino, Garcés's companion at the time. (Temple transcript of San Gabriel marriage register entry no. 54.)

[66]Anza refused to tell Font even after Caborca. These last two sentences are in the field text, and although they are not in the final text I have shown them as being written later, since this must have been done after Font left California. Examination of the manuscript shows cramped writing just before the beginning of the entry for the 13th, and an offset in the writing begins immediately after the comments at the end of the list, indicating that the whole list and the comments following it were entered into a blank area that must have been left for that purpose. See the introduction.

[67]One of them was José Miguel Silva, who went on to join the new San Francisco settlement (mentioned there in November 1776, in the first Mission Dolores marriage register entry).

these were not part of the roster that I saw. And thus by this account of mine it results that some two hundred souls of the people conducted by this expedition remained at Monterey.[68]

Today was cloudy, and damp at times.

[April] 14, Sunday. Daybreak came with a great deal of thick damp fog that lasted all day long. I said Mass for the people at the presidio and before doing so I learned and experienced how little they appreciate, if at all, the Mass and the Fathers at the presidio, and the disrespect that the latter suffer from the leaders there—just as I had heard them complain—by being given no quarters to stay at or food to eat when they go there to say Mass. What happened was that I asked for water to wash my hands before Mass. The quartermaster told me that unless my servants brought water for me, he had no idea how it could be managed as there was no one in the presidio who could bring me any, and with that he left me. So it was that the water I had asked for had to be brought by a servant of Señor Anza's. The crowd followed the example of their leaders[69] by paying no attention to the church bell and not coming to Mass even though the precept[70] calls for it, as I saw. And the Fathers are not able to take any action, since they do not have the right to correct any behavior among the troops.

After Mass, the Reverend Father President Junípero Serra came with other Fathers from Mission San Carlos del Río Carmelo, including Father Francisco Palóu, Father Pedro Cambón and Father Tomás Peña, and along with them Father Fray Miguel Pieras, Minister of Mission San Antonio, who had become much improved in health, in order to say farewell and embrace us for a final time; and then the four Fathers at once went back and the Father Minister of Mission San Antonio remained at Monterey in order to go to that mission in our company.

Señor Anza finished arranging the affairs of the transfer and the accounts of his expedition, and after dinner most of the people we had brought came to say farewell with many tears because of the fondness they had developed for us.[71] Before mounting on horseback, I decided to pay a visit to the room or rather

---

[68] As usual, "at Monterey" means at the Alta California settlements.

[69] The final text introduces this with "It all stems from Señor Rivera's dislike of the Fathers."

[70] One of the precepts of the Church was to attend Mass every Sunday.

[71] Anza's journal, unlike Font's, paints the scene with feeling. "This has been the most mournful day for this presidio ever since its existence, for at the point when I mounted on horseback in the midst of its plaza the people whom I have led from their homelands came recalling the good or ill treatment they have experienced from me while they were at my orders; most of them, especially the female sex, being dissolved in tears, and announcing that these were more because of my departure from them than over their own exile. I was laden with their sympathy, embraces and wishes for my good luck, along with praise I do not deserve: in gratitude for which and for the affection I had from all of them ever since the time I recruited them, and in honor of their loyalty—for until yet I have had no hint of a desertion in any of those whom I have brought to stay in this remoteness—I shall be allowed to make this record of persons who with time must become very useful to the monarchy for whose service they have willingly left their relatives and homeland—which is all that they possessed to abandon."

APRIL 14, 1776

pigsty they had lodged me in to see whether I had left anything in it, but the corporal had already locked it up. Seeing this, I opened the window and told a servant to go in. The corporal saw this and came quickly to see what it was all about, and I said to him, "What is it supposed to be about? You're getting rid of us in a hurry, locking the room before we leave." "Father," he answered, "I locked it because it has to be guarded since it belongs to my captain." I said to him, "What's there to guard in it? Chicken droppings!" and I left him there. Señor Rivera had behaved so discourteously that he had left his own room locked. It was the only one in the presidio fit for lodging us. It had an anteroom like a small living-room hall in which I was housed, which was full of lime and had been turned into a chicken coop. I have gathered that this was a tactic of his to keep from housing anyone. By his having the hall occupied in that way it served as a pretext that he had no other place to put people. To keep from having the naval officers come to lodge at the presidio whenever the ship arrives and to avoid paying his respects to them, he ordered a shelter built outside, at the edge of the sea on the harbor, to lodge them when they came ashore.

At last we took our leave of everyone except Lieutenant Moraga, who wished to accompany us to our stopping place. We set out from the Presidio of Monterey at two o'clock in the afternoon, and took an eastward course for awhile and then went east-southeast. We traveled until six o'clock and stopped at the edge of the Monterey River at the spot called Buenavista, having traveled some six leagues.[72] The pack train arrived a bit later.

There were twenty-nine of us returning[73]—not counting the lieutenant, who came with us this far, Father Pieras who stayed at San Antonio, and a servant[74] who remained at San Gabriel—; these are listed in the following entries.

---

[72] A marginal note to himself by Font in the field text reads: "Note: I shall estimate the travel during this return trip, with the pace that we took, as being three leagues per two hours, and shall also note down the courses, so that in case some discrepancy develops it will be reconciled later by paying chief heed to the observations in adjusting the map." This is also essentially repeated under April 29, below, in the field text. See the introduction.

[73] According to Anza's journal, they were: he himself; Father Fray Pedro Font; seven soldiers belonging to Anza's Tubac Presidio company (two others having been called away by Rivera, and another having been left at San Gabriel); the expedition's purveyor (Vidal); six expedition muleteers (the others who came had volunteered to stay); four deserters (those recaptured by Moraga) sentenced to labor on the fort at San Francisco until otherwise ordered by the viceroy; two cow herders out of an original three since one of them was also remaining; four employees of Anza's.—Only twenty-six total, but Anza has not included the two Gallegos, and Font has included among the returnees the third cowherd, who Anza says is staying.

Already at the start of the expedition, in a note placed at the end of his list of personnel, Anza had predicted that "besides those who are shown in this record, it is very likely that over a third of the muleteers and other employees and others associated with the expedition will remain"—that is, stay in the new settlements. According to Font, twenty muleteers had set out from Tubac, so that Anza's estimate of some of those who would stay in California was too small by a half!

[74] José Miguel Silva.

Lieutenant Colonel and Captain don Juan Bautista de Anza	1
Father Preacher Fray Pedro Font	1
Quartermaster don Mariano Vidal	1
Carlos Gallegos and his wife	2
Ten escort soldiers from the Presidio of Tubac	10
Muleteers, lads, and servants	11
The three cowhands	3
Sum total	29

The pack train consisted of nineteen pack mules, three of which were for Mission San Antonio, the remaining sixteen for the train of our own baggage.
And we were carrying four cats in a crate from Mission El Carmelo, two of them bound for San Diego and two for San Gabriel per request of the Fathers, who were very eager to have us take charge of them. The cats are valued very much there because there are so many mice in that country[75] and in its missions.

[April] 15, Monday. We set out from Buenavista at a quarter past six in the morning and stopped at a quarter to six in the evening at the spot that they call the San Bernabé hollow, having paused for about an hour to nap, and having traveled about a short eighteen leagues (we shortened the route a bit by cutting straight across without going by the spot called Los Ositos), eight of them to the east-southeast and the remainder southeast by south[76] and a bit southeastward at the end.

When we set out, Lieutenant Moraga took his leave of us with no small amount of feeling, and left for Monterey. Since I knew what was undoubtedly happening to him at this time, the last words I said to him were, "God grant you much strength and deliver you from vexations and annoyances with Captain Rivera." About two leagues after setting out from the spot,[77] we came upon Sergeant Góngora and the soldiers our commander had dispatched from Monterey with a communication for Captain Rivera on the 12th. They were now returning. They said that on the way they had come upon Captain Rivera, and that he was close behind. The sergeant said he had met his captain near Mission San Antonio and that he delivered to him the letter from Señor Anza that he was carrying. Rivera put it in his pocket without reading it, and then gave him papers and told him, "Go ahead of me and wherever you meet Captain Anza deliver this paper to him." The sergeant therefore delivered the papers to Señor Anza, but he was so upset that he said, "Sir, here comes my Captain Rivera, and he is so furious that I do not recognize him. I am sorry that I met you on the way, since my intention on reaching Monterey

---
[75]Alta California. This sentence, found in the final version, is written in Sonora.
[76]Evidently altered from "east-southeast."
[77]The field text has instead, "Having traveled for about a league this morning, we met [etc.]. . . ."

was to request a dismissal from my post and go with you."⁷⁸ Señor Anza answered him with whatever was appropriate to calm him, and we continued on our way, surprised that Señor Rivera was coming so unexpectedly and with such an anger that his greatest confidant and favorite, the sergeant, was insinuating that he was unable to put up with him. Señor Anza read the papers and saw that they were the reply to the letter he had written to Señor Rivera on March 17.

In it he exhibited himself as very resentful, calling Señor Anza inconsistent for having proposed to lead the people to San Francisco harbor on returning from his inspection of it, in the event that he had found a good location for establishing the settlement there—a matter that gave us a good deal to talk about and feel surprised at.⁷⁹ We thought that this behavior which we learned

---

⁷⁸From Anza's journal: The sergeant (Góngora) "asked me to hear him in private. When I had gone apart from the aforesaid group, he said to me, 'Señor, my captain is coming here, out of his senses or crazy, and the people with him say also that he has been excommunicated at San Diego presidio for having taken the Indian Carlos out of the church. I've had a thousand slights from him from the moment he saw me, even taking away my function as sergeant from me since he is acting as corporal for all nine men he has with him.'" (The sergeant was referring to Rivera's unorthodox style of command, no doubt.) When Góngora had met him on Saturday the 13th before coming to Mission San Antonio, Rivera asked him where he was going, and on being told it was to deliver the letters, said "Good, good, go to bed [*retírese Ud.*]," and did nothing else to call him all night long. As they were about to set out on Sunday, Rivera shouted "Bring up those letters of don Juan's!" Góngora did so, announcing they were from Anza and Moraga, to which Rivera said, "Good, good," thrust them into his pocket unopened and gave Góngora two other letters for Anza, which he ordered delivered to him wherever he should be found.

⁷⁹After receiving Sergeant Góngora's report, says Anza, he opened the letters, which were a mixture of official and personal communications (Anza deeply disapproved of mixing the two types), read them, and ordered the sergeant to proceed onward to Monterey.

In fact, in the form in which it is preserved, so far from being openly resentful, the main letter from Rivera dated April 2 at San Diego attempted to maintain a tone of friendship while stressing the writer's state of deep perplexity over the way in which Anza had suddenly preferred the settlement of San Francisco to the defense of San Diego: "Now, Señor don Juan, my fellow companion, . . . what is the cause for so different an opinion and change on your part, so few days after you departed from me?" Anza is reminded that he had agreed with Rivera to divide his own forces at San Gabriel, leaving the families there while sending Rivera further military reinforcements and going on by himself to San Francisco. Only when he learned that the colonists' discontent was growing dangerous did Anza very suddenly decide to take them north, a move to which Rivera, at San Diego, felt forced to agree. (In a communication to the viceroy cited in the note under May 3 below, the captain claimed that Anza had more than one motive in forcing this issue.) In the letter to Anza, Rivera brings out every indication of the dangers facing the California settlements, including Moraga's surprising report of finding hostile groups far in the back country who had been involved in the San Diego attack, as well as the problematic arrival of individuals including a Pima from across the desert in the wake of Anza's own expeditions and of the travels of Father Garcés—whose use of Indian guides Rivera disapproves of, and whose request for two or three soldier escorts and supplies he has refused because of scarcity of personnel and rations. "If I show concern about such small matters . . . , what stomach [i.e., enthusiasm] will I have for five or six hundred Yumas?" This is because Anza had offered to bring in hundreds of Quechán—Yuman—warriors to defend the settlements, if necessary. Rivera invites him to think seriously about the consequences of doing so. As for the missionaries, what they do is their own and their colegio's responsibility, but Rivera quotes a letter from Serra encouraging him to treat the reestablishment of San Diego as a priority. Anza is reminded, twice, of a promise he made to send Rivera some of the expedition's horses for San Diego's defense. The San Francisco settlers, in addition to realizing the military necessities, ought to understand that if they should find themselves in trouble in their new settlement, the longer established presidios will be their only defense. (*continued, next page*)

about here was quite absurd and very outrageous. What happened was that when Señor Rivera had written this reply and when the soldiers being sent to carry it were about to leave San Diego, he ordered them to wait and took back his reply. Then he left the presidio, feigning that he was setting out on a campaign against the rebellious Indians belonging to that mission. However, as soon as he was outside it, he changed his course and hastily took up this journey to Monterey. He became his own courier—he was so perturbed at Señor Anza's for having declared himself as being in favor of the Fathers and he very much disapproved of the founding of the Presidio of San Francisco.

We were convinced that the speed of his coming was so he could meet with Captain Anza before he[80] left the country and to discuss with him the matter of the expedition and its chief aim, which is the establishing of the fort and settlement at the San Francisco harbor. Those two captains had agreed to meet at San Gabriel upon our return, if it were not possible earlier, in order to discuss the subject. With this, we thought that it might perhaps be necessary to return to Monterey or at least to stop where we were. But we quickly saw that his coming caused us no delay, since on going a short way we met Captain Rivera. The two captains had greeted each other as though they were travelers in passing. Captain Rivera immediately continued on toward Monterey without pausing to speak about anything, and we pursued our own way toward Sonora.

They wasted very few words, and those spoken were curt. Then, leaving Señor Anza with words still in his mouth, Señor Rivera said to him, "Goodbye, goodbye," and spurring his mule he went on his way. He was so red in the face, angry, and upset with everyone that he did not say goodbye to me or to anyone else except to Señor Anza in the manner described.

This incident was even more absurd than his coming here, and even further from our imagining. Captain Rivera came wrapped in blue riding mantles and had a colorful cap pulled down over his head covering half of his face. All that was showing were his left eye and a bit of beard, which he wore quite long. We came face to face and the two captains greeted each other very superficially, because it was immediately clear that Señor Rivera was full of spite.[81] Don Juan asked how he was, and he answered that he was ill. Then turning to the soldiers he called out to one, "Alejandro, bring those letters." Taking them, he passed them to don Juan and said, "For you, these letters from San Gabriel; Father Garcés." Don Juan said to him, "I'm sorry that you're ill." He answered, "This pain in my thigh came on at San Gabriel" (pointing to his right leg). They stayed there for an instant, without talking. When don Juan was about to speak, Rivera did not give him a

---

Rivera's daybook also records his day of deep distress at having to balance the necessity of founding the San Francisco settlement with his own responsibility to pacify the situation at San Diego. (Burrus 1967 1: 246.)

Anza's journal entry summarizes Rivera's letter—"as witnessed by his communications and the replies to them"—as being a refusal to have the fort at San Francisco harbor founded even though Anza offered to achieve it with fewer forces than had arrived for the purpose

[80] Anza.

[81] "Because it was clear how full of spite señor Rivera was" is only in the final text.

chance. He reached his left hand partway across his right arm toward him, said, "Goodbye, don Juan," and went on his way. Don Juan replied, "Goodbye, don Fernando, from Monterey you will be able to send to Mexico City a reply to the letter that I wrote you which you have not yet answered." (This means the letter sent in the second mail,[82] since the one the sergeant delivered before was a reply to the first, sent in March, which Rivera himself had carried.) Rivera answered, "Very well." And don Juan, seeing himself so dismissed and even humiliated by Rivera's going on his way without saying a single word concerning the sole purpose of his coming,[83] said upon the spot, "Move on, everyone! Witness how Señor Rivera is going on his way without saying a word to me."[84]

Señor Anza asked me at once to give him a certified statement of the whole affair (and asked the same of Father Fray Miguel Pieras, who gave him one at

---

[82]The letter of April 12; see that entry and its note.

[83]To discuss affairs connected with "the matter of the expedition," the goal of founding San Francisco.

[84]It is worthwhile to quote both Rivera's account, which agrees reasonably closely with Font's, and the version in Anza's journal.

Rivera: "Even though I fell sick I did not cease to pursue my journey [to find Anza at Monterey] at speed; but I encountered him already traveling. We greeted each other, and, as well as I was able, I did so [also] to the Fathers accompanying him and don Mariano the purveyor. And, in view of the fact that I was not up to doing any more because of the pain in one thigh, tormented in my head or even fevered as I was . . . and that the Lieutenant Colonel [Anza] did not proffer anything upon his own behalf, we shook hands a second time in farewell, and departed. As we were beginning to ride off, he told me to direct to Mexico City my answer to his letter that he had recently received. 'All right! [¡Enhorabuena!]' was my answer." (Rivera, May 2, 1776, to the viceroy, Huntington Library.) Writing to Anza one last time, on May 3, 1776, Rivera said, "Coming together on the day of our encounter, we greeted each other. I, as best as I was able, greeted the two Fathers accompanying you and don Mariano the purveyor. And after I perceived that you did not offer anything more, we shook hands a second time and I halfway spurred off, being unfit for anything else on my own behalf. I say 'halfway' spurred, because I was not wearing a spur upon the side where I was in pain." (A poor attempt at a joke emphasizing Rivera's physical trouble.)

In Anza's journal entry: "Proceeding on my way in the aforesaid direction, and on going about a league, I encountered the aforesaid Commandant [Rivera]. I greeted him and courteously asked after his health, to which he answered 'I am ill in one leg.' I expressed regret for the illness, and at once, spurring his mount, he told me '¡Adiós!' and went onward. I answered accordingly and on his starting out said 'By the way, about the last letter I wrote you, will you send me an answer to Mexico City, or somewhere?' To which he answered, 'Very well [está bien].' Upon which reply and behavior, I said to the reverend Fathers who were accompanying me, and in a voice which he could easily overhear, 'Be pleased, Your Reverences, to witness this encounter and give me a certification of it.' . . . Other things that I might say to him did occur to me, but since during the little that I saw of this man I could not recognize any of the insanity that had been indicated by the aforesaid sergeant, but rather a great unwillingness to confer with me (as he had agreed to do in my earlier visit) over the topics he is entrusted with, I feared an encounter that might lead to the ruin of us both, and therefore, and because I had fulfilled on my part that which [the viceroy] commands of me, I dispensed with words and other measures." Here Anza seems to be defending himself against Rivera's later complaint that by not saying anything on his own side, Anza contributed to the difficulty of the situation.

Anza then adds a paragraph explaining that his letters to Rivera, copies of which he is going to present to the viceroy, are concerned only with the swift establishing of the settlement at San Francisco harbor, so that Rivera's only motive of resentment must be his opposition to the founding, which is known to the missionaries and other inhabitants, and this opposition is based only on his thinking that he has insufficient forces for the undertaking—whereas, says Anza, there are more than enough of them given the nature of the Indians who need to be dealt with hereabouts.

San Antonio)—to which I agreed without any repugnance as I thought it a very fair request. The certification that I gave to don Juan on this same day concerning this affair is of the following tenor:

I certify that Lieutenant Colonel of Cavalry and Captain of the Presidio of Tubac, don Juan Bautista de Anza, dispatched a second post to the Captain Commandant of Monterey don Fernando de Rivera y Moncada informing him that he had determined to undertake his return journey without any further pause since the period for replying to the first post had elapsed without a reply. During our journey, after we had traveled about two leagues[85] during the second day's march, we encountered the sergeant of Monterey who had been sent with the second set of papers. He delivered papers to Captain Anza sent from Captain Rivera (a reply to the first communication) and reported that Captain Rivera was closely approaching. We continued onward and after going a short way we came upon Captain Rivera. We all imagined that his coming would cause us to delay but we immediately saw the contrary for he wasted very few words. The two captains greeted each other and Señor Anza asked how he was feeling; to which Señor Rivera replied, "I am ill," and then, turning to the soldiers, he called out to one of them: "Alejandro, bring those letters." He took them and gave them to Señor Anza and said, "Those letters are for you from San Gabriel, Father Garcés." I said, "So Father Garcés is at San Gabriel?" And he replied, "He's there."[86] Señor Anza said, "I am sorry that you are ill." Señor Rivera replied, "The pain in this thigh came on at San Diego" (pointing to his right leg), and said no more. And then a little afterward, reaching out his left hand to don Juan, he spoke over his right arm and said, "Goodbye, don Juan," and spurred his mule. Don Juan, seeing that he had been dismissed, replied, "Goodbye, don Fernando; you will see fit to write to me in Mexico City from Monterey in reply to what I wrote to you, which you have not answered" (referring to the letter of the second post). Señor Rivera answered, "Very well," and continued on his way. Then don Juan said right there in front of everyone and in a loud voice, "Be witnesses for me of how don Fernando is continuing on his way without saying a word to me." Of all of which, at the instance of don Juan, I give this certification for this affair to be recorded wherever is proper, signing it on this same day of April 15, 1776. Fray Pedro Font (rubric).

This incident gave all of us no small subject for discussion, and I calculate that from this there will follow considerable unpleasantness and tribulations for the Fathers, and especially the Father President.[87]

The soldiers said that Captain Rivera had arrived from San Diego having been excommunicated. We do not know what have happened there or how true this news may be since Captain Rivera stopped for such a short time and the soldiers had no chance to talk with each other; so we will learn the facts later on.

What happened was that Captain Rivera remained at San Diego, as I said from February 3 to February 9, to catch the culprits and pacify that country, even though he himself did not catch anyone and all of the sallies and captures that were made were done by the sergeant there. Meanwhile, Señor Rivera stayed at the presidio eating what little the Fathers had and making them weary by his lack of respect in the way he treated them. So one day he decided to take to the field himself. This amounted to his arriving at a village. From the moment he saw that the Indians

---

[85]In the field text, altered from "about one league" (as earlier).

[86]Font's intrusion into the conversation, with Rivera's reply, is described only in this "certification," which was copied into both the field and the final texts.

[87]The final text adds: "as indeed happened." The Father President is of course Junípero Serra.

were taking up their weapons, he was trembling and fearful. He attempted to pacify them, telling them that they should be calm, that he was not coming after them but after a Christian Indian ringleader he had been told was there. And when they answered that he was not there, he went back to the presidio without doing any more. During the period of this sally, which took him three days going and coming, it so happened that the Indian Carlos escaped from his imprisonment and went and took refuge in the church. As soon as Señor Rivera came back and heard this news, he became highly resentful because the Fathers were sheltering him in the church. This only served to reinforce his opinion that his presence at the presidio was necessary since this had taken place once he had left it. And he immediately went into his little room without saying a word to the Fathers. He then addressed a note to them telling them to turn the offender over to him. As this note was not in any legal form and lacked the any acknowledgement of the formal legal restraints when immunity was involved,[88] the Fathers answered him with another note, refusing to hand the offender over and advising him at the same time that if he were going to try to take the offender out on his own authority—as in his own communication he had indicated that he would do if they did not give him up—he should understand that he would be excommunicated. With this reply, Señor Rivera turned spiteful. In the afternoon he assembled together all the soldiers and the lieutenant (whom he had relieved from duty and now restored him to command and authority for this occasion alone), and with them laid siege to the big jacal that was being used for a church. With his unsheathed sword in hand, he went in along with some other men to seize the offender on the basis that this place, which had earlier been a warehouse, was not a proper church and therefore not a sacred place. When the Fathers saw this they told him to watch what he was doing, that this affair would be very notorious and scandalous. However, he paid no attention to them. Father Fray Vicente Fuster, the minister there, seeing now that he was unable to restrain him, said to him in a loud voice, "Don Fernando, see here! If you remove the offender, you will be excommunicated, and I declare this to be so, henceforth." To this Señor Rivera, with his back turned so as to go into the church and waving him back with his hand, replied, "All right, Father Vicente, hurl your excommunications, hurl them, but that won't stop me from seizing this rogue." He entered and seized the offender. The Fathers were so distressed that they withdrew to their room and began to cry seeing themselves so scorned and disrespected. These are the dogmatic statements used by officers in far-away lands where they do not acknowledge a superior who can keep them in line and subject them to authority and where other alternatives are difficult. And such are the occasions of bitterness that face the ministers of missions.[89]

---

[88] Since the fifth century, the church had argued that those fleeing from justice or persecution could claim sanctuary within a church and thus possessed immunity from being seized while they were within the sacred precincts.

[89] The details of the event are recorded from Rivera's side in his daybook (Burrus 1967 1: 243–45; cf. also Montané 2000: 464–66). Rivera reported the affair to the viceroy as follows (letter of May 1, 1776): "One of these [captives] is Carlos, who functioned as a governor at the mission; he is mentioned in the proceedings [of the investigation into the revolt]. He took sanctuary, and after my asking for him and having him denied to me, they [the missionaries] referred me to the most honorable señor Bishop [of Durango, in Mexico], because of the nature of the culprit. Not having enough troops to hold him for the length of time necessary to send after and get a result, I decided to remove him. They proclaimed excommunication for me, as appears by their response, the proceedings of which I am remitting to Your Excellency. I have not regarded myself as being excommunicated, given the serious danger that if the culprit should escape he would cause renewed disturbances and harm, and the usual difficulty, greater or less upon occasion, that lies in [re]capturing such. I humbly beg Your Excellency for no delay in the return of the proceedings along with what has been decided, inasmuch as in order to avoid further scandal [i.e., being publicly turned away from the church service] the result is that I am unable to attend Mass or comply with the Church's precept [i. e., to attend Mass on Sunday and to receive communion at Easter]. It is a great burden to have one's recourse be so far away."

[April] 16, Tuesday. We set out from the San Bernabé hollow[90] at a quarter to seven in the morning and at a quarter past ten we reached Mission San Antonio, having traveled some five leagues on a varied course, first southward through the San Bernabé hollow and then continuing south-southwestward, then south-southeastward, and at the end a bit southwestward. This was because of the twists and turns that present themselves as one crosses the portion of the Santa Lucía mountains that runs by here and that extends from El Carmelo as far as San Luis, almost eastward and westward, and as wide as the distance between this mission here and the sea, which is one day's journey. The Fathers received us with great pleasure. They were surprised at our arrival and had not expected it because of Captain Rivera's passing through—but they were even more surprised afterward when they learned of the affair I told of yesterday. Father Dumetz said there were some grounds for the notification of excommunication on the basis of having interfered in a point of ecclesiastical jurisdiction. But he did not tell us anything more because he had no clear knowledge yet of the affair. He told us that perhaps we might find Father Garcés at San Luis, as he knew he had intended to go there; Father Dumetz wished to go there with us when we did.

[April] 17th, Wednesday. I said Mass. Father Fray Francisco Dumetz decided to go with us to San Luis since Father Fray Miguel Pieras, who came from Monterey with us, was in good health at San Antonio. And we proceeded to do so, after dinner. The Father set us a very full table, with blood sausage he had ordered made that very day and a roast pig to take on the road. We set out from Mission San Antonio at two o'clock in the afternoon and at a quarter past six halted in the same Los Robles hollow at the edge of the river after crossing it a single time, having traveled some seven short leagues. The course on setting out was east-southeastward with a little turning to southeastward and almost south; we turned back again to the east-southeast and after a bit over four leagues we deviated eastward and east by north and by south, up until the stopping point.

[April] 18, Thursday. We set out from the river's edge at a quarter past seven in the morning, and having traveled through the same places and countryside as on the way up, we stopped at a quarter past five in the afternoon at a small water source about three long leagues after crossing the Monterey River, having traveled some seventeen short leagues. At the start the course was eastward with an occasional quarter-point of deviation to south or to north, lasting about six leagues. We then traveled for about eight leagues as far as the Monterey River, slowly circling to the east-southeastward, southeastward, south-southeastward, southward, and south-southwestward, and the remainder, from the river

---

[90] "Alias El Roble Caído" (Anza).

onward, was a small way east-southeastward and the rest of it southeastward. The day was a bit cool, but fair. The Santa Lucía range runs from El Carmelo as far as San Luis and further on, becoming thicker until it gets to the sea. The Los Robles hollow through which we came out of the mountain range and crossed it is shaped by the range and one of its branches that runs northward, not a very long one. Issuing from the center of the range are the San Antonio, Nacimiento (which we crossed today), and Santa Margarita Rivers, which are small ones and all of which meet and swell the Monterey River, as I said on the way up.[91]

[April] 19. Friday. We set out from the small water source at a quarter past six in the morning and at a half past ten we reached Mission San Luis Obispo, having traveled for some six long leagues on a course: a little way southeastward at the start, then southward, until crossing the range, for about four leagues, and the remainder being about a league southwestward.[92] The range that is crossed here is a branch or skirt of the Santa Lucía range, which almost ends here, and which joins with the mountains running toward the San Bernardino valley and further onward. Father Garcés was not here as we had expected him to be. He had not come for the reason that I shall tell later. The Fathers received us with a great deal of pleasure, and no little surprise at our coming, having supposed we would be delayed by Rivera's[93] arrival, and they were much more greatly surprised by what had occurred concerning him on the way.

What with this set-to, and with reference to other affairs that had happened involving this captain, Father Mugártegui remarked, "Compared to Señor Rivera, Captain Fages was better, and we'd be happy to have him here now. However, since the Friars[94] requested the change, now we are paying for it." For in the end, the old woman's proverb is always true: May God deliver us from what is worse.

In the afternoon we went for a walk to the mission's wheat fields (which are close by, and very fine), and while there, we heard peals and musket fire as though there were someone arriving from Monterey. We began to wonder who might be arriving, and set off for the mission. Although most of us tended to think it was Señor Rivera, I could not convince myself of that, since I thought that going to Monterey and immediately returning would be a crazy thing for him to do. We reached the mission and found that Father Fray Pedro Cambón had arrived, coming as a courier sent by the Father President to give some papers

---

[91] On March 5; see that entry and footnote. In the final text, the list of rivers is introduced by: "On the way we crossed...."

[92] Anza's entry: "... two and a half leagues up the Santa Margarita hollow to its end at its village; turning southeastward, a not very high hill range upon which we made two and a half further leagues; and with the said hills continuing on southward, upon another league we came to Mission San Luis."

[93] From here onward, the field text frequently omits the respectful titles of "señor," "captain," and "commandant" that are still applied to Rivera's name in the final text.

[94] "we friars."

to Señor Anza for him to carry to Mexico City, in order to avoid trusting them to anyone else.[95]

They described the events that had happened at San Diego, which is why the Father President did not dare deliver them to the soldiers, so as not to expose himself to the risk of the soldiers losing them or of Señor Rivera holding them up: matters had become as delicate as all this. This suspicion was founded upon what had just occurred with Señor Rivera which was related to us by Father Cambón. What happened was that Señor Rivera arrived at Monterey early on the 15th, and in the afternoon the Father President immediately paid him a visit, with Father Fray Tomás Peña along. They spent a while with him but he did not provide them with many answers since the man was so beside himself that he was not up to responding to people. Seeing that he was not giving him any letter, the Father President said, "Well, since you are coming from San Diego, aren't you bringing some letter for me from the Fathers there?" As though he had forgotten it, Señor Rivera answered him, "Ah! Yes, Father. I have been ill and it slipped my mind. I think I have something in the pocket of that jacket." He began pawing through it as if he could not find anything. He finally pulled out some letters and gave them to the Father President. Among them was the letter Father Fray Vicente Fuster had written to him telling the story of Captain Rivera's excommunication. He also told of their sorrow regarding the Indian rebels who admitted their guilt and were willing to come and present themselves peacefully. However, the captain was so adamant that he refused to pardon anyone even if they humbled themselves. He had said, "Let them come, let them come, I'll receive them with a charge of shrapnel," etc. However, even though the letter had been given to him at San Diego sealed and in two envelopes, he gave it to the Father President opened and with the envelope torn along the sides. Therefore, the Father President concluded that Rivera had tried to hide it from him and had even read it, because when he handed the letter to him Rivera said, without being asked and without the Father President even having noticed the tears in the envelope, "This is the way it comes, but I would dare to swear that truthfully, I don't know, I don't know whether it was torn when I received it or if it got torn along the way."[96] He was quite disturbed as he said this. This is why the Father President wanted to take sworn testimony regarding how he had delivered that letter to him torn and open, whereas the other letters were intact. But Father Peña persuaded him to not pursue the matter alone since the man was so agitated that it seemed as if he were out of his mind.[97]

Hereupon the Father President decided to write at once to Mexico City and to have Señor

---

[95] The field text continues with the explanation in brief: "in view of the fact that Captain Rivera had given the Father President, opened, the letter that they had delivered to him at San Diego sealed and folded over twice, containing the accounts of Captain Rivera's excommunication; and how he had said that he would receive with a load of shrapnel the Indian culprits who had already confessed and were coming in to surrender peacefully, etc."

[96] Literally, "whether it's *pe* or *pa*" ("the beginning or the end"). In other words, Rivera simply said he did not know at what point on the journey from San Diego to Monterey the letter had gotten torn. I cannot account for the wording in the Bolton translation, according to which Rivera said, "The letter comes this way, but I would swear to you that it is the truth that I do not know a thing that is in it" (Bolton 1930 vol. 3, 1931: 446). The original text is, "'Ésta viene así, pero me atreviera a jurar que en verdad, no sé, no sé, si es pé o si es pá'; y esto bien perturbado."

[97] Font's account, which he reports as coming from Serra, is somewhat at variance with the latter's letter to his colegio of April 17, 1776, according to which Rivera swore to Serra on his oath that the letter had been damaged, which is consistent with the version Font gives, and that he did not know what it said, which goes beyond what Font reported. After a day, the missionary Tomás de la Peña officially informed Rivera of Serra's decision to sustain the excommunication. (Tibesar 1956 3: 2–4).

Anza carry the letter. So on the following day, the 16th, he asked Señor Rivera for four soldiers to go and catch up with Señor Anza and deliver the letter to him. The soldiers were granted to him. As Father Cambón was about to leave Monterey, Father Tomás Peña told Captain Rivera on behalf of the Father President that the latter was intending to go to San Diego[98] to see whether he might settle the affairs that had happened there, which is why he asked him to give him an escort. To which Señor Rivera answered that he himself was about to return there and would be going on the 19th, which is today, or Saturday. If he cared to accompany him, the two of them could go together. The Father President accepted the proposal, and thereupon decided that, for the sake of the letter's safety, Father Cambón should go with the four soldiers so he could carry it. He ordered him to wait for him at San Antonio or San Luis, wherever he met up with Señor Anza, so that he might continue on afterwards with him to San Diego as his companion. Therefore, Father Cambón set out from Monterey on Wednesday afternoon the 17th and arrived today, this afternoon, here at Mission San Luis. He told us about this whole matter, and how Señor Rivera and the Father President were on their way; even though, afterwards, that did not happen, as I shall tell.

Father Cambón also said that because of his unheard of and even scandalous actions, Captain Rivera was being talked about openly at the presidio[99] and that he already had had a clash with Moraga, the lieutenant of the expedition. For, when he[100] asked him whether any of the new soldiers had gone with us to survey San Francisco harbor, Moraga answered that they had not. And then Rivera said to him, "It would have been good for some of them to have gone along in order to see whether that place is as good as you people say." To which the lieutenant answered that he had seen it himself and could assure him that it was a good place for the settlement. And on Rivera's retorting that it would have been better for the soldiers to have seen it in order to have that fact ascertained and to have them see whether it suited them, the angry lieutenant answered, "I saw it myself, and my saying that it is good is all that is needed for people to believe it." And slapping his hand on the table, he continued, "My word is valued more than the entire company's. It makes no difference if it suits the soldiers or not because the soldiers will go where they are ordered to go. That is what the king pays them for." This reply left Rivera dumfounded, and he said nothing further to him. He had now declared him his enemy because anyone who spoke in favor of this founding and establishment was an enemy of his.[101]

Father Cambón set out from Monterey on Wednesday afternoon because Rivera did not give him an escort before that. He said that Captain Rivera was

---

[98]This beginning of the sentence is taken from the field text's account, which appears in the following entry.

[99]In the final text: "that there was much gossip and talk at the presidio about the captain and his so untimely arrival, and that the people were very dissatisfied there."

[100]Rivera.

[101]According to Anza's entry for April 19, Cambón also brought a letter to Anza from Lieutenant Moraga expressing his judgment that the Monterey commandant (Rivera) was demented.

to leave today or tomorrow and that the Father President would also be coming and he would wait for him here in order to accompany him, as he intended to go to San Diego to settle the affairs that had happened there.[102]

[April] 20, Saturday. I said Mass. It was decided to delay for a little here at the mission because its minister, Father Cavaller, wanted us to stay a few days. Since he is my fellow countryman I asked Señor Anza if we might stay at least three days.[103] What with all of the happenings we had plenty to talk about. We spent a very pleasant day because the six Fathers who gathered here have a good sense of humor.

[April] 21, Sunday. I said the last Mass, and afterward solemnly baptized five adult gentiles, two men and three women, all of whom had Captain Anza as their godfather. Right after baptizing them I married the two men, one of them with an Indian woman previously baptized and the other with an Indian woman who had just been baptized then and there, so that of the two men and three women whom I baptized, I married one of the women and the two men.

Four soldiers arrived at mid-afternoon and all they did was greet and give reports to Captain Anza, but they did not bring a single letter. All they said was that Rivera had been coming from Monterey and had remained at the gap a little over a league away from the mission, since he said he was fatigued and the weather was not very good.

This was a frivolous excuse, and the reality was that he avoided the mission so he would not have to meet with Captain Anza. The soldiers gave a message to Señor Anza on behalf of Señor Rivera, saying he was sending them to greet him and tell him that he was not coming to the mission, for the reason that he was fatigued. But afterwards we learned that this was a lie made up by the soldiers (lying was a common habit of theirs), for Señor Rivera did not give them a letter or any such message nor did he send them for that purpose. Instead, when they saw that their captain was stopping along the way, they asked him for permission to go on to the mission on the pretense of furnishing themselves with something or other, so that they could visit their friends. We asked them whether the Father President was coming as well and they answered that he was not. Although the two of them had agreed to come on the 19th, as I said yesterday, Señor Rivera quickly changed his mind. On Thursday afternoon, the 18th, he ordered mounts brought in very quickly and arranged for his march, taking Sergeant Góngora and a small number of soldiers along with him. While on horseback, he sent a message to the Father President telling him he was not waiting for him because he had decided to set out quickly so that he could catch up with Captain Anza and meet with him before he left. And this was not the reason; instead he wanted

---

[102]Anza in his account of Cambón's mission states that Serra's journey to San Diego is planned in order to settle and accord the clashes between Rivera and the San Diego missionary, Fuster, and to intercede for the rebel Indians, who are offering to turn themselves in peacefully. Anza repeats Fuster's statement that Rivera had said that if they did so, he would receive them with a load of shrapnel.

[103]However, according to Anza's entry, the layover was because Serra's letter, brought by Cambón, had asked Anza to wait for him so that they could keep company together to San Gabriel. The suggestion may be that Serra wished to avoid traveling all the way alone with Rivera, whom initially he was supposed to accompany.

to prevent the Father President from going to San Diego, and it even seems, or so we heard, that he left orders for Lieutenant Moraga (to whom he entrusted the care of the presidio) not to provide the Father President with any escort if he should happen to ask for one.

For this reason, Father Cambón pressed Señor Anza to read a letter that he had brought from Señor Rivera and which he had refused to look at or to receive.[104] He acquiesced, read it, and immediately replied to Señor Rivera by sending him a communication. He told him that he had decided to pursue his journey tomorrow. However, in view of the fact that he[105] had arrived, should he wish to discuss the pending affairs of the expedition, he would not refuse to do so, and would delay for whatever time was needed, judging that by this he would be serving God and the king. And if he wanted to meet at San Gabriel, as they at first had agreed to do, he would not refuse this either. And so, he should decide what he preferred to do. However, he should be warned that since he had gone out of his way on the route to avoid speaking with him as a means of avoiding a conflict, he[106] therefore was unwilling to waste words and should only speak to him officially in writing. He would answer him in kind. And he instructed the soldier who was the courier, who was one of his own men, that if Rivera wished to reply, he should wait for the answer and bring it, and if not, he should return at once.[107]

---

[104] Anza's journal does not mention his initial refusal to read the letter. Rivera's letter, which was written at Monterey on April 17 two days after the disastrous passage on the trail, is not compatible with the way in which Font describes the captain's attitude. Rivera began by very much expressing his regret. His excuse was his health: a crippling pain in the leg, "and now, I think that besides the thigh pain I had also a deal of fever. Otherwise, I doubt which I would have done, whether to have come on here or to have gone on with you to San Gabriel." He was now better and was ready to take the chance that the pain would subside when he set out traveling on the 19th, "following your own tracks. I hope that, since we are dealing with matters so weighty and so much a part of our duty, I may obtain your taking just a bit of time in order to wait for me if I do not chance to overtake you by riding. You may be sure that I shall not trouble you very much," since in case he became disabled by pain he would inform Anza by courier to San Gabriel, "which is where I beg you will be pleased for us to meet if possible." (Cf. Garate 2006: 228–29; 46–47.)

[105] Rivera.

[106] Anza.

[107] Anza's communication to Rivera was considerably sterner in its tone than Font suggests. "In reply to yours of the 17th, I shall say that although I count myself freed from any requirement to answer you, because of the incident that occurred on the day of our encounter, I shall nonetheless make the sacrifice of doing so in deference to the king's service; and in view of the fact of my acquiescence I shall consent to answer you only in writing, [and] solely in regard to matters connected with the founding at San Francisco harbor. I depart tomorrow morning for Mission San Gabriel, where my offer to you will be carried out; but should [there be any matter] favoring the king's service you will inform me so that I may delay [here]. I have answered your letters of March 28 and April 2 this year, [answers] which I shall give you at a proper time and occasion so that the king's service, and the [official] correspondence that I am agreeing to in deference to it, shall not be interrupted by their subject matter." The last sentence is meant as a clear indication for Rivera that Anza is reserving reproaches that will make any peaceful relations between them impossible. Although the brief summary of the letter in Anza's journal is more accurate than Font's representation, nonetheless, as Guerrero (2006: 208) points out, it vastly misrepresents Anza's own effective denial of an immediate meeting: "In substance, he [Rivera] tells me he regards Mission San Gabriel as the place better suited for discussing these matters . . . it is all just to delay the San Francisco founding to which he is opposed."

The day was very foggy, with fine rain, and a bit of a chill.

This evening we had a bit of entertainment using the musical instrument. The unmarried converted Indian girls, whom they call "nuns," were given permission to come out of their seclusion and spend some time with us, which pleased them very much. Father Caballer made me laugh a great deal by his saying he had a father who was an ox, etc.[108]

[April] 22, Monday. As I was on my way to say Mass, Father Caballer came over, all excited, demanding that I should place a veil on the Indians whom I married yesterday. When I answered that I would, he fooled me by saying they were not here.[109] I said Mass.

Since Rivera had said that he was setting out from Monterey so quickly in order to meet up with Señor Anza wherever he found him, it naturally seemed— we all thought this—that he would decide to meet with Señor Anza here, since this was where he caught up with him. But we soon realized that his intentions were different. As we were sitting down to dine at noon today, the soldier who had been sent as a courier yesterday came with a letter from Rivera for Señor Anza in which, without broaching the matter of their meeting here, he seems to blame Señor Anza for their not speaking to each other on the road, citing his frivolous excuses concerning his illness, which he pretended had made him unable to stop, etc.[110] After keeping the soldier who had gone as courier for such a long time, even though he was so close, he finally came up with this reply!

About an hour afterward, a little after noon, as we finished our dinner and were about to retire to take a nap, Captain Rivera arrived at the mission. He stayed a very short time and at that same hour left for San Gabriel without meeting with Señor Anza. As soon as he arrived the Fathers went out to receive him, but because he had not chosen to speak to us along the way, Señor Anza and I refused to go out. We stayed in our rooms instead as though we had retired for our nap.

He said he wished to speak to Señor Anza. The purveyor went in to carry this message on his behalf, and Señor Anza replied, through the same purveyor, that at that hour he had withdrawn to take a nap. If he would like to speak with him afterwards, he would not refuse, but since the only business that they would have to discuss would be concerning the expedition and his survey of San Francisco harbor, he should communicate with him in writing about this as he had already instructed him to do. He would respond in the same manner to avoid argument.

Señor Rivera, then, waited for about an hour. Afterward, without meeting with Señor Anza (though he greeted me in passing because at that time I needed to leave my room to go to the latrine and so he saw me by chance), and without making the slightest display of any intention to make amends for the slight he

---

[108] The context of the joke is not made clear.
[109] Evidently this was another fraternal and fellow-countryman jest.
[110] See the next note.

had given him while on the way in order to allay his anger (for if Señor Anza was angered with Señor Rivera now, Señor Rivera had previously been even more so with Señor Anza), at that same hour he decided to go on ahead and wait for Captain Anza at San Gabriel. He then headed out and left us hanging. Today's march was ruined because of him.[111]

Added to this is the fact that he left Padre Fray Pedro Cambón with no possibility of returning, since the four soldiers who came as his escort were ordered by Rivera to go on with him to San Gabriel. Therefore, by this new order, Father Cambón was left without any escort for going farther or returning, whenever he should think of returning to Monterey on the presumption that the Father President, whom he was to have waited for here, would not be coming as had been supposed. And besides this, he[112] took as many animals as he could from the mission and left its guard almost without horses and on foot, thus preventing the soldiers here from escorting Father Cambón should he wish to go back. All of which led us to suppose—what we had already thought when we saw his ill-timed arrival—that he plans to leave Monterey with few soldiers, using the excuse of San Diego so that the establishment of the fort at San Francisco harbor, to which he is utterly opposed, shall not go forward, and so that the Father President shall not go to San Diego. We did not find out if he went afterwards or not, and because we left for Sonora, I know nothing more concerning the Fathers there nor how these events may have ended.[113]

Here there are girls who already know how to sew as well as any Spanish woman. On the spot they stitched up a little piece of work that I ordered from them. They also know how to make baskets and other things very finely. In sum, they are Indian men and women who are as neat and clean as is attainable for such folk.[114] It was decided that six Indians belonging to this mission should come with us as far as the channel in order to buy two[115] boats to be used for

---

[111] Rivera in his May 2 letter to the viceroy agrees that he sent a message in to Anza, who did not come out. (Huntington Library.) Otherwise, Font's account is seriously skewed. Rivera's decision to postpone the meeting until San Gabriel had been announced in the communication that Font says was received at the beginning of the noon meal. In this letter, which was very conciliatory in tone, Rivera offered to have the four soldiers accompany Anza's party south if desired: "*dispóngalo y déles la orden*," "just give them the order." (The soldiers did go with Anza, although in his April 28 entry Font says it was at Rivera's orders.) Rivera's need to be nearer to events at San Diego was his claimed reason for waiting until San Gabriel. In his own journal entry, Anza's interpretation of this was that "maybe from there he will put it off to somewhere else," Rivera's only interest being in delay.

[112] Rivera.

[113] Serra boarded the supply ship *El Príncipe* when it left Monterey at the end of June 1776, and reached San Diego on July 11 or 12 (Geiger 1955: 434). He remained in southern California five months, rebuilding the mission, supposedly against Rivera's opposition, and re-founding Mission San Juan Capistrano.

[114] This sentence is part of a paragraph that mostly repeats a description already given under March 3 in the field text (March 2 in the final text).

[115] In the field text, altered from "three."

Figure 36. A California mission boy with a basketry hat surrounded by mules, 1816. By Louis Choris. *Courtesy of The Bancroft Library, University of California, Berkeley.*

fishing—as in fact they did. Señor Anza gave them beads for the purchase. Afterward they returned by sea in the boats. In addition to this, Señor Anza offered to take along with him to Mexico City (and indeed did so) a very bright Indian about ten years old, named Pedro. He is a son of the famous chief Buchón and an Indian concubine of his who is now a Christian and is married to a soldier here. Anza promised to take great care of him while along the way and said that he himself would bring him back within two years. (I do not know what this promise was based on.) The Fathers agreed to this, depriving themselves of this boy who was the best interpreter they had, so that the viceroy could see a Christian belonging to this mission and know that he is already a fine Spanish speaker and knows how to read. And the boy was very pleased to be able to go; so after I said Mass he took his leave of the people and his relatives in the church with a great deal of poise and grace, at Father Cavaller's urging.[116]

In the evening we enjoyed ourselves for a while.

[April] 23, Tuesday.

Father Cavaller had offered me baskets but as I had nothing to carry them in or with, I answered him that he should try to get on Señor Anza's good side, since he himself was always on mine, and I knew that he[117] wanted very much to take these kinds of things to give as presents in Mexico City. Also, I hoped some of them would fall to my lot, since, as I said on February 25, he had told me that when we reached San Miguel on return from our journey, he would give me the choice of whatever I pleased. Thereupon Father Cavaller gave Señor Anza a great many baskets, some bear skins (I think there were eight of them), and thirty-some otter skins and other things. This morning he also gave me, separately, two choice otter skins, saying in front of everyone there that he had kept them to give to me. With this in mind and knowing what was about to happen to me, and so that Señor Anza would understand that it was through my suggestion that Father Cavaller had given him everything, I said to Señor Anza, "Look how this Father Cavaller

---

[116] Research by Joseph A. Carotenuti indicates that he must have been the eighth person baptized at San Luis Obispo, recorded in the mission register on May 13, 1773, as a boy about six years of age, child of gentile parents, who was voluntarily offered to the Holy Church. He was christened Pedro Regalado, and his godfather, perhaps his stepfather, was Gerónimo Bullferich (spelled Bulfarique in the register) of the Catalonian Volunteers. The mission's register of marriages, which would have helped to establish family relationships, was destroyed in a native attack late in 1776.

John Johnson of the Santa Barbara Museum of Natural History has generously provided additional information. He informs me that the mother of Pedro Regalado was baptized on September 30, 1774 (SLO Baptism 83), when she was approximately twenty years old. She was one of the wives of the late Chief Buchón and was given the name María de los Dolores. She married soldier Francisco Cayuelas. Unfortunately, no ranchería of origin was given for either María or her son Pedro. After his time with Anza, Pedro Regalado returned to San Luis Obispo. He was married to the *neófita* Seculina on January 3, 1785 (SLO Marriage 147). It appears that Pedro was deemed to be hispanicized enough to live apart from the mission. Pedro Caguelas and his wife Secundina were listed at the pueblo of San José in the 1790 census, and his occupation was given as vaquero (Mason 1998: 100). Seculina died and was buried at the Presidio Chapel in Monterey on May 27, 1792 (San Carlos Burial 908). Pedro's mother, María Dolores, died at Mission San Luis Obispo on April 18, 1820, and her husband, the retired soldier Francisco Cayuelas died there on April 15, 1830 (SLO Burials 1851 and 2182). At the present time, it is not known what happened to Pedro after his wife's death.

[117] Anza.

manages his affairs! I told him to get on your good side and give you everything he was intending to give to me, since you told me that you would give me something later. Now he has taken it into his head to have me take these two skins." Señor Anza answered, "Then take them, Your Reverence." And that is what I took away. Later, he did not even give me a mediocre basket. Despite the fact that he distributed a great many of them at San Miguel, which meant that there were enough of them for many people, he did not even have the courtesy to ask if I wanted anything from all that he had brought.

We set out from Mission San Luis Obispo along with sixteen pack mules at seven o'clock in the morning. With special displays of feeling and affection, we bid farewell to the Fathers, three of whom accompanied us for a distance. At a half past six in the evening we stopped at the Laguna Graciosa, having traveled some seventeen leagues on the same route as the way up. The course was a very varied one: we set out east-southeastward, which immediately began turning southeastward, and south-southeastward at four leagues, then a little southward until the sea. We followed the shore south-southeastward about two leagues. On leaving the shore and entering to the southeastward into the dunes, we happened to lose our way for a bit, as there is no evidence that there has ever been a road there. And, we missed the sign, which were some whale bones that were supposed to show us which way to go. We mistook some other bones that we came upon first for the whale bones. After one league we continued on for two more, southeastward, and two south-southeastward, until reaching the *Laguna Larga, o Grande*.[118] We then headed two leagues southward as far as the village and the foot of the grade, then up the grade one league south-southwestward, passing some hills, and the remainder until halting was southwestward through dunes and with some veering westward. Since it was his first day of travel, the little Indian was a bit tired but kept on with good humor and he was not particularly sad. We collected some unusual shells today, but only a few of them because they are very scarce along the whole coast there and only an occasional one is to be found.[119]

[April] 24, Wednesday. We set out from the Laguna Graciosa at a half past six in the morning, and at a quarter to five in the afternoon we stopped at a small stream on the channel at the edge of the sea near the El Cojo village, the same spot where we camped on February 27 on the way coming, having traveled some fifteen leagues. The course was a varied one. On setting out we traveled to the south, with some slight veering, as far as the Santa Rosa River, which we forded with no delay as the tide was low at the time. We then continued southeastward,

---

[118] Long or Large Lake

[119] Anza's entry adds the fascinating story which the missionary Juan Figuer had just received from the Indians, concerning the wreck of a boat containing Europeans on rocks some distance off the shore (Morro Rock, presumably), twenty-three winters (years) earlier. "What folk would these have been? It remains to be discussed by someone more learned than I."

south-southeastward, and finally southward for about five leagues until rounding Punta de la Concepción, where (with that whole country being very full of flowers) I saw a great deal of flowering larkspur and some very pretty small pink carnations and other flowers. We then continued eastward as far as the *Los Pedernales* village, then southeastward to the *La Espada* village, and then southward as far as another point that some would hold to be Punta de la Concepción since it juts out quite far and the two points together make a **C**. I, however, hold that Punta de la Concepción is the first and more northerly of them because the coast trends more to the northward beyond there than it does up to here and the route that we always took at the edge of the sea or in view of it nearby, indicates the fact.[120] We then traveled southeastward about a further league in order to camp.

[April] 25, Thursday. I said Mass. We set out from near the El Cojo village at a half past six in the morning and at half past five in the afternoon we halted at Mescaltitán, very near the village, before coming to it, having traveled some sixteen long leagues, most of the way or almost the whole of it along the shore, a better, more unbroken route because the footing is level and solid. We went past eight villages and two abandoned ones, the same as on the way coming between El Cojo and here. For about three leagues the course was east-northeastward; then the remainder continued eastward up until the last, about two leagues from the San Pedro y San Pablo village, where since the route goes away from the shore because of the Mescaltitán inlets we went almost east-northeastward. In essence, the route was eastward with some veering northward because of some small bends in the coast.

At the villages there was nothing particular in the way of baskets and other items that could be obtained, because, as it appears, when the expedition came here[121] the Indians were left with no baskets because they sold all of them at that time. Some Indians belonging to the Mescaltitán village came to our camp and at once gave proof of their skill at stealing. In plain sight and without anyone's noticing it, they made off with the iron ladle from the kitchen, which was not missed until after they left. Even though an attempt to recover it was made the following morning, it could not be gotten back since they said it had been taken away by the Indians from the other village on the other side of the inlet.

The Indians were very cheerful tonight, singing until very late. Perhaps they were having a party to celebrate the stealing of the ladle.

[April] 26, Friday. We set out from close to the Mescaltitán villages at a quarter past six in the morning, and at close to five o'clock in the afternoon we halted

---

[120]However, Font's "La Concepción" is now Point Argüello, and the southern point is Point Concepción.
[121]Late in the preceding February, as described earlier.

right next to the La Asumpta River[122] before crossing it, having traveled some sixteen long leagues, going most of the way along the shore and passing by the same villages as on the way coming. And the course was, on setting out, northeastward for about a league; then eastward and southeastward, going around for about two leagues as far as the La Laguna village; then we continued eastward along the shore with a few slight veerings northward and many southward. There were points of land at stretches of two or three leagues or a single league so that people traveling eastward go turning east-southeastward to cut across them, chiefly beyond the first village while going, San Buenaventura. The course lies east-southeastward with veerings eastward at the bends on the sea at the La Rinconada village, Los Pitos village and the other points of land.

In one of the villages I saw the Indians were barbecuing a good number of lobsters along with some big crabs they had caught among large rocks on the shore, and they gave me one. I gave it to the cook so he could prepare it. Although Señor Anza had told me along the way that it was a very delicious dish and he liked it a great deal, he later refused to eat any of it or even taste it no matter how much I urged him to. He said that he did not want any because it was a food he had no stomach for and he feared it would do him harm. But this was not the case. He refused to taste it because I was the one they had given it to. It was his habit to despise and reject anything that belonged to me or had been given to me. He would rather let it spoil than eat it. This happened with a bag of mincemeat I was carrying and made no use of because of him, with a quail and a duck that the soldiers gave me, with a piece of the *tollo* fish they gave me at the Freshwater Harbor, and with cheeses that they gave me at San Gabriel.

Yesterday was clear during the day, but with such thick haze that we were scarcely able to pick out the islands, or large island, called La Santa Cruz. Today the fog was so thick we could see nothing during the morning. The fog lifted at noon but the air remained hazy until nearly sundown. Then, from the spot where we had halted—with respect to which the large island bears southwestward and the others south-southwestward—we were able to catch a glimpse of the Channel Islands, which we had not been able to see clearly up until now, neither on the way up nor on the return, but instead only very hazily and slightly, because of the fog that is so prevalent on the sea here. I took this opportunity to sketch the islands according to the outline they present as seen from this spot of La Asumpta, which is what I shall place here:

FIGURE 37. Santa Cruz Island. *Pedro Font sketch.*

---

[122] The field text again refers to this incorrectly as "the stream belonging to the La Carpintería village." Anza's journal calls it the river of San Buenaventura (its later name also).

I noted that when looking southward from that spot the large island, the one of La Santa Cruz, bore southwestward and the others came after it following around to the south; and I shall note that all of these islands lie some six or eight leagues out at sea and are the ones forming the channel. Others lie still farther out, the smallest ones the farthest, and I do not know what they are called. On farther ahead, as seen from the Santa Ana River beyond the San Pedro bight, is the island called *Santa Catarina*, which is some six leagues from land, and beyond that, it can be seen from San Diego. About fifteen leagues out at sea is the island of *San Clemente* and seen from opposite the mouth of San Diego harbor are the small islands called *Los Cuatro Coronados*.

[April] 27, Saturday. We set from the La Asumpta River after a quarter past six in the morning and at a half past five in the afternoon stopped at the spot called El Agua Escondida, where we camped on February 22 during the way up—having traveled a long seventeen leagues, which can almost be reckoned as eighteen. The course was a varied one. On setting out, we followed the shore for about a league, course eastward. Then, with the shore continuing on about southeastward toward San Diego, we departed from the sea and entered upon level land on the same eastward course with very slight veering toward one side or the other, and crossed the river and went on across the plain to the foot of the grade, about some seven leagues. Before leaving the sea, we passed by the village called La Carpintería next to the spot we set out from. On crossing the river we stopped by the village there.[123] Before going up the grade, we paused a little while at the small spring of water at its foot, close to the village there, and in the midst of the plain we saw a small village that had not been there on our way up. Close to the spring, at a distance of ten to twelve varas,[124] is quite a large spring of tar (as I said on February 23) that overflows higher than the ground level. We climbed the grade at noon and traveled a short way southward, and then began to head eastward for some leagues, winding about now east-northeastward, now east-southeastward. (In the mountains, we found that the three villages that we saw on the way up were abandoned. Their Indians had moved because their watering places had dried up because it rained so little this year. The ground was already very dry and cracked. We did not find water except at the spot called Los Conejos about two leagues this way from the grade, and a very little here at El Agua Escondida.) Then, beyond the spot of El Triunfo, where we came into more broken land than before, we altered course to northeastward and a bit northward, and finally, before stopping, east-northeastward.

---

[123]Anza's journal distinguishes correctly between the San Buenaventura and Santa Clara rivers. Font seems to collapse them into a single one; his "La Asumpta" is mostly the San Buenaventura.
[124]27 or 33 feet.

Ever since we came into this country we have been bothered by fleas, but the last few days have been excessive in this respect, so that wherever one camps, everything is teeming with fleas, very hungry ones. There is no land that does not have its own plague, and the one this land has is fleas. The smaller islands of the channel follow the same direction as the shore, at a moderate distance, so that today we saw the small ones lying closer than they did yesterday.

[April] 28, Sunday. I said Mass. We set out from El Agua Escondida at seven o'clock in the morning and traveled northeastward through hills for about a league. We then went down the grade and, by it and the hollow, traveled about a league east-northeastward and came out upon the Santa Isabel plain and traveled eastward over it for some eight long leagues. Then we went into the gap and continued through hills, course east-southeastward with some veering east and east-northeastward, as far as the Porciúncula River, and halted there at a bit before five o'clock in the afternoon, having traveled some fourteen leagues. The dryness continued hereabouts and as far as the snowy range which had almost no snow because there had not been any rain and there was heat here.

As soon as we halted, Señor Anza ordered the four soldiers who had come from Monterey with Father Cambón and then, because they were so ordered by Señor Rivera,[125] continued on with us to San Gabriel to greet Señor Rivera on his behalf (Rivera had reached that mission the day before, Saturday at noon), and to give him a courteous message telling him that he would be arriving there tomorrow. Afterward, Señor Anza told me that his plan was to camp outside the mission in his tent, since he was unwilling to put himself in the position of being slighted again by Señor Rivera, who was being lodged there. He said he was not doing it for the Fathers' sake but rather to avoid any incident, perhaps a public one that might arise if he met Señor Rivera there. And even though I attempted to dissuade him from doing this because of the notoriety that it might cause, I could not persuade him to change his mind. Afterward, however, I recognized that he had been right. It was better for him to behave in this way since something undoubtedly would have happened that might have been worse—

And, it might even be that they would have come to blows because of the hostility existing between the two of them, based on what we saw later and what was to happen, as I shall tell tomorrow.[126]

[April] 29, Monday. We set out from the Porciúncula River at a quarter past six in the morning and at eight o'clock reached Mission San Gabriel, having

---

[125]This is probably inaccurate, since at San Luis Obispo Rivera had written Anza that he could take them under his own orders if he wanted (note to April 22 above).

[126]In the field text, this whole discussion is in the next entry, introduced with "Yesterday señor Anza told me. . . ."

traveled two leagues on a course east-southeastward for a very little way, eastward a little and the remainder east-northeastward for a bit over one league.[127]

Commander Rivera was here at this mission but he neither came to greet us when we arrived nor did he meet with Commander Anza during the days that we remained here. While on the way, I had begun persuading Señor Anza to go and camp at the mission or at least to go and dismount there. We finally agreed he would dismount at the mission and that if Señor Rivera came out to receive us and showed some sign of meekness and kindness, he would forget all that was past and would lodge at the mission and would also speak with Señor Rivera. But if Señor Anza is stubborn, then at this juncture Señor Rivera showed himself to be more stubborn. We arrived at the mission and dismounted there. Although Señor Rivera ordered the soldiers to line up and fire their muskets upon our arrival as is the custom there, he stayed inside his room, listening to the shots and the peals, and refused to come out. Notwithstanding, Señor Anza stayed at the mission for about half an hour, giving Señor Rivera an opportunity to make an appearance but, seeing that he would not come out of his room or show himself, he said to me, "Father, I am going to do what I told you I would do, since Your Reverence can see how this man is behaving and what I will be exposed to if I remain here." I told him he was quite right and that now I agreed with his opinion. He immediately ordered that his tent be set up a bit away from the mission and then went to lodge in it. After he had left, we clearly recognized that Señor Anza's decision was very well taken, thus avoiding some greater scandal that might have occurred.[128]

For, after arriving, I learned for certain—although Father Paterna, (being who he is, attached to Rivera) had tried to make the matter look favorable by saying that Señor Rivera was very busy writing, and attempted to hide from me what his outspoken intention and purpose had been—that Rivera had said that at Anza's arrival at the mission he would not leave his room not even to eat, so as to avoid meeting him. And this is very believable (and so I did believe it), from the evidence he gave of his intentions. For, when Father Cruzado told him that we were arriving, as a means of having him come out, he did not say a word nor did he move. Consequently, he did not go come out to meet us when we arrived. Since I stayed in the mission, I did not see his face earlier than noontime when we sat down to table. He then greeted me very superficially, saying nothing more than "God keep you." We wasted no further words on each other. The anger in his heart was very plain to see from how silent and flushed he was.

And I shall note that when they went to tell him to come to dinner he asked if Captain Anza was there. When he was told that he was not there and had gone off to his tent, he then came out of his room and went to dine, very pleased with his own behavior.

---

[127] Here in the draft Font repeats his note to himself before leaving Monterey (April 14): "Note that the courses and leagues that I recorded on the way up between here and Monterey are to be corrected by the leagues and distances I have been noting down now on the return, as I am better satisfied with the latter than with the former; and I have estimated the leagues (being Mexican leagues) on the return, which we took at a steady pace, as three leagues per two hours of travel [i.e., roughly 3.9 miles per hour], although the dividers will determine this when the map is drawn up."

[128] Rivera, in his letter to the viceroy of May 27, gives exactly the same reason for refusing to meet as Anza did: "so as not to exacerbate the situation."

[April] 30, Tuesday. We remained here at the mission and the two commanders communicated with each other in writing, handling their affairs through official communications and expending paper, one of them from out of his room and the other from out of his tent. Each man relayed his message by means of his own soldier. That way they did not have to see each other's faces. Señor Rivera was very pleased with himself and he acted so haughty with me. This morning, when I passed in front of the door of his room and greeted him, he let me walk by without answering me or looking at me.

May 1, Wednesday. I said Mass. As Silva had insisted on staying with Rivera, the latter agreed he should do so on the condition that Captain Anza also agreed. Anza said that he could agree to his staying, only if a certain Father were of the same opinion. But the Fathers did not agree that he should stay and Silva spread the malicious rumor that he was unable to stay because I refused. That is how that ungrateful lazybones is! Señor Rivera and Señor Anza continued, as they did yesterday, with their writing and sending one another official letters.[129] In the evening I started a conversation with Señor Rivera, who still was obstinate and would not speak to me about his having refused to grant Father Garcés what he had asked for.

It happened like this. When Father Garcés arrived at this mission, San Gabriel, in company with two Jamajaba[130] Indians, he planned on going to San Luis and then upcountry but was unable to do so because Señor Rivera denied him everything he asked for, as Father Garcés relates in his journal on March 24 where this affair appears at length.[131]

We had lettuces at the start of the meal. Father Paterna[132] told me that I would remember San Gabriel because of its good lettuces that I was eating. To which I answered, "I certainly will, in days to come at the Colorado River." Father Sánchez said, "What? Won't Father Tomás have lettuces there?" I answered, "Where would he get them from?" He replied, "Well, didn't they carry seeds?" I answered that they didn't. Then Father Paterna said, "Perhaps Father Garcés will be there when you people reach it." I said I didn't know, and don Fernando followed up with "That Father must have had some real hardships along the route that he took." I then said, "Undoubtedly. And, don Fernando, since you are bringing up this topic in our conversation, I beg you to please tell me what your reason was for denying Father Garcés what he asked for." Father Paterna,

---

[129] According to his journal, Anza started the day's exchange of paper at dawn by notifying Rivera that he was leaving the same day. This was because on arrival, he had allowed the commandant three days to prepare dispatches for Anza to carry to Mexico City. Rivera replied that he would send his reports out to catch Anza on the road that night. (These two actual memos do not seem to have been preserved.)

[130] Mojave.

[131] Garcés's journal, under March 24, 1776, gives a detailed account of the affair, followed by an essay (composed after his return to Sonora) that politely but thoroughly disagrees with Rivera's dislike for dealings with the Indians of the interior (Galvin 1967: 39–41).

[132] Antonio Paterna, who had told Font that California was "a Promised Land" (January 5).

as attached as he is to Rivera, immediately became upset (no matter what the incident or the topic, contrary opinions are never lacking since everyone has his own way of thinking). Don Fernando said, "Father, Father Garcés asked for animals,[133] one or two soldiers to escort him, and provisions, and I refused them because I have no order from the viceroy to give him that, which is what I communicated to Señor Anza." I replied that I think no order from the viceroy is needed for these details, and that he who is in command when it comes to major matters is also in command with regard to incidental affairs. Therefore, the viceroy should not have to concern himself with ordering this and that, especially something like "that," which consists of affairs of small importance that are linked with his general orders and are understood to be part of his overall orders which the officers can decide upon. To this he said, "I had no animals; the ones belonging to the expedition were not in my charge and thus they were not at my disposal; and besides, will Your Reverence be able to dispose of what belongs to this mission, that which is not in your charge, however you see fit?"[134] I answered, "All right then, let us drop the topic of the animals, but you at least could have granted him the rest of what he asked for." He answered me, "The Father asked me for one or two soldiers to escort him, and that was insufficient. I was unable to give him more soldiers because I do not have them. Your Reverence is aware that four or five soldiers are sent just to carry mail. Had something happened to the Father with such a small escort, I would have been responsible." I replied that he would not have been responsible, since he is not responsible now that the Father has gone on his apostolic excursions with no escort at all, "since," I said to him, "Father Garcés's spirit is not unknown to you." Father Paterna said, "Certainly it is unknown. Don Fernando does not know Father Garcés's spirit." I replied, "Certainly he does, and very well, too." To which don Fernando said that it was true that he had heard of his courage and spirit. And he continued by saying, "I told the Father: 'Father, Your Reverence, wait for Captain Anza, he will not be late in coming, and seek his advice, Your Reverence, for he can decide in these matters.'" I answered, "Then Father Garcés would not have gained anything, for if he had waited for us he would either have had to leave the country with us, or we would have had to leave him here." Father Paterna answered, "Don Fernando did well not to give him what he was asking for, since the viceroy does not order Father Garcés to go about these upcountry lands." I said, "The viceroy's order is that if the Father emboldened himself to do so, he might remain at the Colorado River to survey the tribes living up and down the river. The Father's coming here was due to the fact that the gentile Indians

---

[133]Horses and/or mules.
[134]According to Garcés's record, Rivera did let him take one of the expedition's horses.

did not dare to accompany him upriver without making a detour because there was a tribe in between that was their enemy. And when the Father wished to travel westward to see whether he might discover a way to Monterey from there, as planned, the Indians offered to accompany him to another tribe above the Jamajá.[135] Since the Father travels at the will of the Indians who guide him, they brought him here, as you saw. But even if this were not the case, I think neither the viceroy nor the king is so mean and stingy as to refuse him a few provisions, which he was requesting for two gentile Indians who were going with him." He[136] answered me that he had had very little left, and that it was not his to dispose of. I replied that provisions for two Indians, which might amount to a fanega of maize[137] was no great matter, "since you are aware that Father Garcés is content with very little and knows how to live on grass of the fields." He said to me, "Father, that is why I told him to ask Father Paterna for whatever he required. The king would pay him for it later." Father Paterna then said, "It isn't necessary; and why bring this up now? Wasn't Father Garcés given what he needed? If don Fernando didn't give him provisions it was so he would not be responsible for the outcome if anything happened to Father Garcés during this journey, and he did well to refuse what he asked for, so as not to contribute to the harm that might follow." "Then, if that is so," I replied, "Your Reverence is responsible for harm to Father Garcés." "And why?" he said. I answered him, "Because if don Fernando, in order not to be responsible, did well to refuse him provisions, then Your Reverence is responsible because you gave him provisions. Therefore, you contributed to his journey by giving the provisions to him." Then, Father Paterna, who was quite upset, said, "Oh, come on, let's leave this." And getting up from the table he asked don Fernando if he would like to go to his room, but the latter did not move (the opposite of the other times when after dinner or supper he got up at once and left), but kept on for over half an hour mounting a discussion of how few supplies he had and the hardships that there would be at San Diego if the ship did not come soon, etc.

In order not to aggravate the matter I did not want to touch upon the other notion that Señor Rivera admitted in the letter he wrote to Señor Anza, and that Father Paterna regarded as being very bad, as he told me when he narrated it to me. And that was his having ordered some gentile

---

[135]Mojaves. Font was obviously reporting Garcés's travels to this point on the basis of what the San Gabriel missionaries had been able to tell him. It is far from clear that Garcés had been authorized, or encouraged, to attempt to discover a shorter route to Monterey. He had in fact been ordered by the viceroy, under date of January 2, 1775, to "go only to the Colorado and Gila Rivers," and await Anza's return. Later, this was expanded to his going down and up the Colorado. Elsewhere, Font argues (December 1, above) that a wider commission was implied by the viceroy's sending Garcés a copy of the New Mexico missionary Escalante's letter (the one which is quoted by Font, above, at the end of the April 3 entry).

[136]Rivera.

[137]Perhaps 1½ to 2 bushels.

MAY 2, 1776

Indians who had gone from the Colorado River to that mission[138] to be seized and expelled—as is also narrated by Father Garcés in his journal on March 24[139]—an order that was not carried out because it was God's will that the Indians had already left when the order was supposed to be carried out. For it was clear to me that I would not improve or achieve anything by touching on that subject and would likely speak in a rather direct manor to him and nothing would be gained since he was so pleased with himself and with his own behavior, by which, he said, his credibility was thoroughly established at Mexico City. All the more so[140] on this occasion, during which Father Paterna was so outspokenly in favor of him and the other two Fathers did not say a word because of their respect for him. But I have set down this whole discourse here to show how people reason when they wish to support any matter, for there is never any lack of reasons, either solid ones or false, for any purpose, and the certainty is that on any topic, partisans and enthusiasts are never wanting, because "There are as many opinions as there are people," *Quot homines tot sententiæ*.[141]

[May] 2, Thursday. I said Mass.

After we arrived at the mission here, Señor Rivera passed an official communication to Señor Anza asking him how long he would be remaining here, for his own information, since he was writing to Mexico City. Señor Anza answered that he would be staying three days, which ended today in the afternoon. Señor Rivera said that he thought that would be enough time to finish what he was writing to the viceroy. However, the hour for our setting out today arrived and he sent an official letter to Señor Anza telling him he had not yet finished, but that he should not delay for that reason.. He could easily leave, since tonight or tomorrow he would send him the letters by means of soldiers who would catch up with him on the way.[142] This is why Señor Anza decided to march without waiting any further. Therefore, we took our leave of the Fathers, but not of Captain Rivera because he did not come out of his room to say goodbye nor did he show himself. He stayed in his room writing, without having dispatched the letters that Señor Anza is to carry to Mexico City.[143]

We set out from Mission San Gabriel at four o'clock in the afternoon, and at a half past five halted at the edge of the stream that turns into the San Gabriel River, where we stopped on January 3, having traveled two leagues course eastward, a little way east by north, and the remainder east by south. The party consisted of the same ones I spoke of on April 14. Including the boy Pedro from

---

[138] San Gabriel.

[139] They were to be escorted several days into the desert and told not to return.

[140] Avoiding the subject was even more of a good idea. . . .

[141] Meaning, there are as many opinions as there are people to hold them. This is a well-known quotation from the Roman playwright Terence.

[142] Among the last-minute flurry of notes between the two commanders, three communications from each are dated April 29 at San Gabriel. Rivera's shortest note began: "You have shown me that you are offended. I am sorry that you are departing in the same state. If any satisfaction exists and can cure [the offense], be pleased to tell me what I ought to do. The sergeant has come with this to await your letter. I have a number of topics to write about in making a report to His Most Excellent Lordship. Without vexing yourself over the matter, will you please tell me whether I will have the time, or else what day you are setting out, so that I may restrict myself to what is most needed." Anza's reply to the request: "I . . . shall wait tomorrow and the day after tomorrow for whatever occurs to you to write to His Excellency, which is the most that I can bring myself to do solely for that purpose. [This] will serve you for [your] guidance, to the same purpose." (Cf. Garate 2006: 84, 86, 236, 189.)

[143] The final text, based on Font's later conclusions, adds "(or so he said, but it was not true)."

San Luis we amounted to thirty persons in all.[144] The baggage was twenty mule loads; and the mounts, between mules and horses, totaled eighty-six animals.

[May] 3, Friday. I said Mass. We set out from the Arroyo de San Gabriel at a little after half past six in the morning and at half past eleven we came to the Arroyo de los Alisos, where we napped until half past two in the afternoon. At a quarter to six in the evening we halted at a plain before reaching the Santa Ana River, having traveled some ten leagues. The course was eastward for about four leagues with some deviation northward and the remainder east-southeastward (inexact). Because the soldiers that Señor Rivera had said he would send with letters did not catch up with us last night nor this morning either, along the way I said to Señor Anza, "Don't expect any such letters, because I have heard that he intends to send them by way of California[145] and does not want you to carry them. I also learned that he said, 'That was what Captain Anza wanted, to carry my letter for the viceroy. So, he won't get it.'"

As soon as we halted, Señor Anza and I started talking about the incidents with Señor Rivera, and I told him, "If, as I suspect, the courier does not arrive, or, as I presume, does not bring letters for the viceroy because he supposes that he would be doing you a great favor and he is not in the mood to do you favors, then my suspicion will be confirmed, which is that along the way, Rivera opened Father Vicente's letter to the Father President and gave it to him with the envelope torn. For, just as the thief thinks that everyone is of the same ilk, Rivera will assume that you will do the same with letters that he gives you, since his opinion of you is as low as his own deeds have been. And I say this on the grounds that I have learned a piece of information I now wish to share this with you, as a friend. Señor Rivera is writing against you to the viceroy which is why he cannot entrust the letters to you; so beware of what he can accuse you of concerning the past incidents," etc.[146] He answered me that he was keeping all of his letters, papers, and communications for this purpose and intended to present them to His Excellency. Indeed, he did make up a sort of docket of those papers,

---

[144]The field text: "We set out with twenty-nine persons"—Font evidently failing at first to remember the San Luis Obispo boy. Anza states they were himself, his ten Sonora presidio soldiers, Font, the purveyor, eight muleteers from the expedition, and his own employees from the start of the expedition (apparently still four). But again the Gallegos husband and wife are not mentioned, nor is Pedrito from San Luis, so twenty-eight seem to be accounted for. Then, the commander's four employees and the eight muleteers, deducted from the total fourteen "muleteers, lads and servants" and "cowhands" mentioned by Font on April 14, seem to leave two lads or cowhands over, so that thirty is correct.

[145]Baja California.

[146]Such a letter of complaint does exist, dated May 2 at San Gabriel and backed by transcripts of documents. On the other hand, the letter that Rivera actually intended to have Anza carry was probably the one which he began writing at the end of April but finished and dated on May 1 (Garate 2006: 158–60, 100–103, from Rivera y Moncada Papers C-A 368: 16A). The letter summarizes events at San Diego and elsewhere and does in fact mention that Rivera is remitting, along with it, the account of the Carlos affair. The one item derogatory of Anza is the statement that Anza had not informed Rivera in advance that he would be moving the colonists from San Gabriel to Monterey, "and I recognized that he was acting with a double motive."

which he placed in order along with the answers to them. This was not going to be very beneficial for Señor Rivera.[147]

We were in the midst of this conversation when the courier from Señor Rivera came up to us with two letters, one for the Father Guardian of the Colegio de San Fernando and another for Señor Anza, but none for the viceroy. And with this classic nonsense Señor Rivera crowned the work of the expedition and his own very strange behaviors.

And he told Señor Anza that he was not sending letters for the viceroy because as he was about to seal them, he discovered that a paper he had mentioned in the letters was missing. This paper dealt with the events at San Diego concerning the captivity of the Indian Carlos. The letters could not be sent without this paper. He surmised that he must have left it at San Diego since he could not find it no matter how much he searched. So he decided to leave at once for San Diego and would send his letters to the viceroy from there, through California. In a postscript after the signature he asked him to give his regard to the viceroy and tell him on his behalf that he was a bit ill.[148]—Everything was said and done just as I had warned Señor Anza it would be!

Thus, the lost paper was only a pretense. For, at this point in time, learning of his excommunication would be of little or no importance to the viceroy. The main concern was to know that he had received the people belonging to the expedition with all of its associated mounts, livestock, etc., and the decision he had taken with regard to the establishment at San Francisco harbor, a decision they were anxiously awaiting in Mexico City and even more so in Madrid.[149] However, who knows what he may have written since he was opposed to this; all the more so since Señor Anza had stated that he was against his position on this matter. Because of this and the set-tos that had taken place, I always supposed that he was not going to give his letters to the latter to carry since he did not trust him; and all the more so because of what I learned at San Gabriel and have told above.

[May] 4, Saturday. Very early in the morning Señor Anza dispatched the soldiers who had come as couriers, writing a letter to Señor Rivera that corresponded in kind to Rivera's letter and served as a finishing touch to this affair.[150]

---

[147]This "docket" of Anza's letters to Rivera (omitting two of them) appears to be the one preserved as Rivera y Moncada Papers C–A 368: 17. Rivera's corresponding compilation of both sides of the correspondence is Rivera y Moncada Papers C–A 368: 19. (Cf. Garate 2006: ix.)

[148]Despite what Font says, the postscript with Rivera's request for a verbal message to be carried to the viceroy seems to refer to the misfortune of the lost paper, not to Rivera's illness ("suplico se sirva Ud. noticiar al señor excelentísimo de ésta mi desgracia para que no extrañe su excelencia la falta de mi carta"). The letter also included Rivera's recollection of the trailside encounter (see note to April 15) along with mild remonstrances against Anza's written reproaches.

In his journal and in a reply to Rivera, Anza savagely criticized both the letter and the request.

[149]Font's reasoning here led him to false conclusions. In fact, as can be seen in the notes to April 15 and May 3 above, the letter (of May 1) to the viceroy did exist and it contained Rivera's plea for assistance in resolving his excommunicated status. Also, in the same May 1 letter, Rivera announced to the viceroy that he was about to issue the detailed dispositions for the founding of the San Francisco settlement, although delaying that of the two missions—which Anza (perhaps with ulterior motives) had agreed might be done, in a letter to Rivera of April 29.

[150]Refers to Rivera's supposedly improper request that Anza carry his excuses for not writing to the viceroy. These replies to Rivera's requests were among the amazingly insulting contents of Anza's two letters dated May 3.

At the same time he sent him back the letter for the Father Guardian of San Fernando, telling him that since he had no letter to carry from him for the viceroy he did not wish to carry a letter for any private person.[151] He wrote another letter to Lieutenant Moraga informing him of what had happened,
and forewarning him of whatever would be appropriate in the event that Señor Rivera should be declared insane, judging by the signs of madness he had been exhibiting in his wholly imprudent behavior.

I wrote a letter, also, to the Father President, informing him of this and of everything that had happened since we set out from Monterey, and another one to Father Paterna in which I sent him ground-plan for a church and building that he wished to build, which is something that he had asked me to make for him. And with this, we ended our departure from Monterey and tossed away the key of the expedition's whole history of encounters with Señor Rivera.[152]

At daybreak the weather was very overcast, damp, and raining a few small drops before we set out. It cleared later, and a little before we left three or four not very loud thunderclaps were heard, an unusual event since they are not heard in these lands very often. We set out from the plain a little before seven o'clock in the morning, and at a quarter past eight came to the Santa Ana River, where we napped until two o'clock in the afternoon, having traveled some two leagues on a course east-southeastward (inexact). We set out from here a little after two o'clock in the afternoon, passing through the Santa Ana valley, a hollow and hills, and this valley that ends here, and at a quarter past six in the evening we halted at the foot of some hills forming a gap that issues onto the San José valley, a little way before arriving opposite the spot where we camped on December 30, having traveled some seven leagues course eastward or almost east-southeastward, with a very little veering one way or the other, in the hollow. We found all of the ground here to be dry, with very little grass and no water or firewood. We began taking a straighter course[153] in order to come out more directly upon the San José River tomorrow. The sky cleared before noon, though with some continuing cloudiness. The snowy range had no snow on it now. It had melted in the hot weather except for a very little, seen in crannies.

---

[151]"Advising him that I would not carry it as I did not hold it to be duly respectful to His Excellency—to whom he was not writing—and neither to myself." (Anza.)

[152]The field text puts its equivalent passage at the end of the preceding entry: "And with this, the expedition has concluded, with Rivera deeply entangled and providing much matter for talk."

[153]A shortcut avoiding part of the earlier route.

CHAPTER 7

The Return to Sonora

[May] 5, Sunday. I said Mass. We set out from the foot of the gap at six o'clock in the morning, course east by south and a bit east-southeastward, passing the gap and crossing the San José valley. At ten o'clock we came to the San José stream,[1] where we napped until half past two in the afternoon. We traveled six leagues. This spot seems to me a very fine one for a mission. And in this stretch, at the foot of some small rocky hills next to the route, we saw a good-sized village that we had not seen when we had come on the way. Despite being armed, the village Indians, whom we called Dancers because of the absurd wiggling they make while speaking forcefully,[2] went scrambling up amid the rocks there. At seven o'clock in the evening we halted at the San Patricio hollow close to the source of its stream and a little bit before the spot where we had camped during the way up on December 27, having traveled some seven leagues (making thirteen in all) course southeastward (inexact), with some veering because of the ravine's or hollow's turnings as it continues upstream, quite narrow in places (although broadening at the end). We found the route in this hollow with more brush and stones than on coming. In two spots there was a quantity of rocks that seem to have been brought down from the heights by the rains, and only a few more would have stopped our way. From this I infer that the route through the San Patricio hollow here may become closed off by the rains and not be a year-round one. It was cloudy most of the day today and we have felt a good deal of chill yesterday and more so today, at this spot.

[May] 6, Monday. We set out from the San Patricio hollow at a quarter to seven in the morning. The day was overcast and drizzling. We finished passing through the San Patricio hollow, crossed the El Príncipe valley, and went through the Puerto de San Carlos, which is formed by mountains of many large rocks. The fine rain kept up at intervals until after midday with such a cold

---

[1] San José River, in the field text.
[2] See the December 24 entry and note.

northwest wind that we felt more of a chill now than when we were on the way up.[3] So, when we reached the spring we had camped at on the way up, at a half past eleven we paused at the low spot next to the Puerto de San Carlos to eat a bite and light a fire to warm ourselves. We had become so frozen. This chill kept upon us until afternoon. But on the other side of the main California range there is already a different climate, so that this main range here shares both of the land's climates. However, the strong wind lasted all night, and thus the land of Monterey sent us off with the wind that prevails there.

We then passed the grade and continued through the hollow in which we had spent Christmas Eve. Finally, following the course of the stream and the hollow, which is formed by mountains of piled-up rocks, crags, and sandy soil, all of it unproductive and grassless, we came to the stopping place and the shade of the willow tree. The course as far as the Puerto de San Carlos was southeastward (inexact), and the remainder east-southeastward with considerable veering because of the turns on the grade. At a quarter to four in the afternoon we stopped at *El Pie del Sauce*[4] on the Arroyo de Santa Catarina, where we camped on December 23 having traveled some thirteen leagues.

Among the crags forming the Puerto de San Carlos we saw a great many Indians who had scrambled up among the rocks, and although we called to them none of them would come down. There were also a good many Indians, laden with their children and their possessions, at the stopping place. They scrambled up through the rocks as soon as they saw us. These are those same unfortunate sooty people who dwell in these mountains, the ones whom I spoke of on the way up: children of fear and of night.

[May] 7, Tuesday. At daybreak the wind continued still furious, which along with the dust caused us a great deal of trouble, mainly when we set out from the hollow at the start of the morning. It kept up in that manner during the entire day, which was favorable only in being cool so that we felt no heat. This is a west wind, the same one which bothered us while on the way from Santa Rosa—a wind which seems to prevail very much hereabouts. The Indians have not appeared, except for when they were walking around on the mountain at night, which is what the soldiers guarding the mounts said. Perhaps they were looking to see if they might steal or do some harm, as they are very bad people. They have the same *miau* as at San Diego, the Indians say *miau*, like cats, which means "yes."

We set out from El Pie del Sauce at five o'clock in the morning. The course lay east by south for five leagues until reaching the place called San Gregorio, where

---

[3] In January.
[4] The Foot of the Willow.

we napped until two o'clock in the afternoon. We found so little water there that not all of the animals could drink. Then came five leagues east-southeastward (inexact), and four eastward. At a quarter past seven in the evening we came to the place called San Sebastián, where we halted on December 13, having traveled some fourteen leagues. On all sides, sterile land, no grass, and nothing good about it: in the end, everything is dunes, sand, and rocks on the mountains, as I said on the way up.

[May] 8, Wednesday. The wind ceased last night. Here we continued killing the fleas that we brought from Monterey and San Gabriel. I said Mass to our patron San Miguel Arcángel that he might bring us safely out of the dunes that follow beyond here and that we must cross. The reason that we did not set out from here in the morning, and why I said Mass, was that Señor Anza decided to cross these plains and dunes in a straight line and see whether, between today and tomorrow, we might arrive at the height of San Pablo, or its immediate area, with a single pause and a night without water, using these two days' marches to replace the seven marches that we made between December 5 and 13 inclusive —although I told him this would not be possible because it was a very far way to go, and we would be putting ourselves at risk of difficulties, and I even showed him the distance by using the dividers. He still could not be dissuaded from asserting that it could not be over twenty or twenty-five leagues at the most. Then, just before we set out, the experienced soldier who was to serve as our guide said he would not dare lead us to the height because it was very far off and in such bad country, with no grass or water. Things would be bound to go badly for us, so that we might suffer harm. It would be best to go so we could arrive at the brackish El Carrizal well, where indeed he would be willing to guide us. We could arrive there tomorrow.

At that point it was decided to cross the plains and dunes lying beyond in as straight a line as possible and arrive at the brackish El Carrizal well, known as *La Alegría*,[5] without going as far down as the Santa Rosa wells, in order to save some distance. Therefore, we set out from San Sebastián at a little after midday, and at not quite a quarter to eleven at night we halted in the midst of the dry plain, with no water or grass, having traveled some fourteen leagues, course almost eastward for the first three of them and the remaining eleven being to the east-southeastward, and a bit nearly southeastward.

The day broke windless and very warm, as we might expect and as one experiences in this country. The Indians belonging to San Sebastián were friendly and pleased to see us, although they are not of very good character (not so much as those of the Colorado River), and three of them went along with us today,

---

[5]On February 15, 1774, during Anza's first expedition, a well was dubbed "Distress" (Las Angustias) because the horses and mules were unable to get beyond it. "Happiness" (La Alegría) was so named with deliberate frontier irony on February 17 since it was a waterhole that earlier had seemed less good than Las Angustias, but now "the soldiers were happy [to reach there] even walking on foot" (Garcés's journal). See also under December 10 above.

although two of them turned back and only one reached the Puerto de la Concepción with us. At about two leagues along the way we found a well of water that had some tule rush and cane grass on it, fresh water but tasting of swamp a great deal. One league farther on, we found a little well of cold water. However, we could not drink it because it causes the mouth to pucker as though it had a great deal of bitterness it. Near this we found another well of water that was boiling with great force. The well was so deep that the bottom could not be reached using a lance; it could not, however, be drunk because the water was hot and very salty. And this is all the water that we found in that whole stretch.

My mouth inflammation has been breaking out again ever since April 27, and worse every day, so that I have felt greatly distressed during the last few days and today. The dog seems to have gone missing. We have not seen him following us since it got dark.[6] The route has been free of dunes but we passed over patches[7] of irregular ground that we called *almondigones*.[8] The land is extremely poor and sterile everywhere. Tonight the animals are dining on sticks and there are not many of them.

[May] 9, Thursday. We set out from the dry plain at a quarter to five in the morning, and at a quarter to one at night we reached the Santa Olalla Lake, having traveled some twenty leagues. On setting out, the course was east-southeastward for about a league; then we continued for about three leagues southeastward and came across the track left by Lieutenant Moraga when he caught the deserters. We followed it east-southeastward for about two leagues until the scouts lost it. We then headed southeastward with a good many deviations eastward and southward, winding about, and went on so for about four leagues, and came upon the trail taken by the livestock when we were coming. We followed it east-southeastward for about a league, until at last we joined the route we had taken for Santa Rosa, and at about two leagues came, at a quarter to one, to the El Carrizal well, called La Alegría. We found the water as red as though it had vermilion in it, very salty, and worse than on the way coming. Even after the wells were cleaned out the animals had great difficulty drinking and some of them immediately suffered belly aches, with no cane grass for them to eat because it had been used up during the way coming. It was decided to go onward as far as Santa Olalla Lake to avoid spending the night here. We delayed only until a half past five in the afternoon so we could rest a bit and wait for the strength of the sun to pass.

We set out from the wells at a half past five in the afternoon, traveling seven

---

[6]This is the only mention of a dog apparently having followed them from the California missions.
[7]In the final text, "a piece."
[8]*Albondigones*, meatballs, as in the December 11 entry.

leagues upon a course eastward and east-southeastward, and at ten o'clock at night we arrived close to the lake. However, in this area there are trees, grass, and hard soil which does not take tracks. So, the guides lost the trail because it was dark and we went wandering off for a long while without being able to come upon the lake. We finally paused and the soldier Juan Angel[9] went with some others to search for it and after a while found it. They guided us to the lake and we were able to drink its fine water and rest on its shore. Only one Indian out of those who followed us from San Sebastián yesterday stayed with us today, and we had to encourage him to do so because he was scared to death finding himself among all these Yumas, who used to be his enemies. The lake had little water in it.

[May] 10, Friday. At the stopping place, which was the same one where we had halted on December 6, a great many very obliging Cajuenche Indians came to the camp to see us. They brought maize, beans, and gourds that were dried into what they call *bichicoré* in Sinaloa. They also brought ground-up péchita and screwbean made into loaves. We set out from Santa Olalla Lake at a quarter to four in the afternoon, and at a quarter past six we halted at the villages of El Cojat where we had stopped on December 5, having traveled some five leagues. The course was mostly northeastward and north-northeastward, but winding about with veerings eastward and, more, northward. As soon as we halted, Palma's relative, the Indian who came to meet us at the Gila River, came to visit us. He was very pleased to see us. Several Indians came with him.

[May] 11, Saturday. We set out from the El Cojat villages at a quarter to five in the morning and before nine o'clock came to the small mount of San Pablo, along the foot of which the river goes. At a quarter to eleven we finally reached the Puerto de la Concepción on the Colorado River, where we found Father Tomás alone. We had traveled some eight leagues which the turnings made into nine. The route was quite winding and a bit different from the one on going up, as the river had risen greatly and a great deal of land in the river bottom was already flooded. At the start the course was north-northeastward, and at once we came upon water that was already extending over the plains. It was therefore necessary to travel northward; and we continued winding about, all during our route, in every direction between northward and eastward. Indian men and women at all the villages came out to greet us with a great deal of pleasure and joy at seeing us, and some of them went with us the whole way. One of them persisted in giving fodder to my mule, taking grass and putting it into the mule's mouth, and in

---

[9]Juan Angel Amarillas, a California soldier who had been with Portolá in 1769 and now returning with Anza to Sonora. He was killed in 1781 in the Yuma uprising. Could he have been acting as a guide here? He had been in the area before and was involved in the desertion episode involving the muleteer with the same family name.

order to indulge him I found it necessary to halt. At other times, so as not to delay me, he went in front very close to the mule facing backward with a clump of grass in his hand. Another one, doing the same thing, was feeding it screwbeans. Others went ahead of us, playing and running with their long sticks and hoops.

Both mutual and great was the joy felt at finding Father Fray Tomás Eixarch so happy and safe at this place, living so contentedly among so many gentiles who are very attached to Spaniards and deserving of esteem and appreciation, with Chief Palma in first place. These Yumas are very tall people and they have fine bodies, both men and women, since they have a great deal to eat. We measured one Indian and he was nine and three-eighths cuartas tall; many are nine cuartas tall and they commonly are over eight.[10]

The Puerto de la Concepción here, which is located a little below the junction of the Gila and Colorado Rivers, is a spot consisting of some heights of middling elevation that form a small pass through which the Colorado River (which is so spread out as it passes over those plains that when it rises it is leagues in extent) runs much constricted and then it widens once more on coming out of it. Thus, this locale is a most pleasing prospect and the best site I have seen on this river for a settlement, since it is next to the river and safe from its flooding no matter how it rises. Although it is so small that on the little somewhat uneven tableland formed by it there is only enough room for a church and a few buildings, at the foot of the tableland there is a large plain, also safe from river floods, where a big settlement would fit.

Here we encountered Father Fray Tomás Eixarch. He had come to live with Chief Palma at this spot, since it is a better one than where we left him on the way up. It lies a league upriver from the pass here and he could not remain there with the river rising. We had expected to find Father Fray Francisco Garcés here, but he was not present nor did his companion Father Fray Tomás have further news of him from the time he left for the Jalchedunes, upriver. The last notice that we had of Father Garcés was on April 15 through a letter that the Father had written at the beginning of April to Commander Anza from Mission San Gabriel, where he had been during Holy Week. He had arrived there (so I understood) because when he went above the Jalchedunes and encountered the Jamajá tribe they received him peaceably and offered to go with him to another tribe. However, since there was a tribe that was their enemy in between, it was necessary to go in a circuitous fashion in order to reach the other tribe, and the route was so great that he arrived at Mission San Gabriel, accompanied by two gentile Indians from the Jamajá tribe.[11] He said in his letter that he was returning to the Jamajá tribe because he had to, and that if he learned that he might find something worthwhile beyond there he would go onward; if not, he would return to the Colorado River where he would wait for us so that we might return together. We came to Mission San Gabriel and the Fathers there told us that when Father Garcés left he had said,

---

[10]The man was about 6 feet 4½ inches. For the other measurements, see the similar passage under December 6, 1775, above. Anza's party in 1774 measured one man, very possibly the same man, as 9 palmos 3 dedos, approximately 6 feet 4⅓ inches.

[11]According to the Garcés journal (Galvin 1967: 34; February 29, 1776), Garcés "laid before them [the Jamajab (Mojaves)] my desires to visit the Fathers living near the sea; they gave assent and offered to accompany me, for they had heard of them and knew the way." Font's "understanding" therefore may be wrong, or perhaps he wished to avoid the charge of deliberate irresponsibility that Rivera and no doubt others had raised against Garcés's explorations.

speaking of his journey, that if he encountered Indians who were willing to accompany him—and he did not foresee much difficulty in his project—his plan was to proceed upcountry and discover a route to New Mexico. We came to the Puerto de la Concepción and here we obtained some rather confusing news to the effect that Father Garcés was at the Jalchedunes. Our commander immediately sent an Indian interpreter there with a letter advising him of our coming, and that we would be continuing on our journey within three days, which was enough time for the Father to come here if he was there. But neither Father Garcés nor the messenger came during the three days, and we have not obtained any more news of him during these intervening three months. From this I infer that either Father Garcés has found a route and easy access for reaching New Mexico, or else he has suffered some great setback in his apostolic pilgrimage since he had been rather ill already. Perhaps he has died or been killed by Indians.[12]

I shall note that when Señor Anza dispatched the interpreter with the letter, he ordered him that if he should not find Father Garcés and did find his animals he should bring them back to him. The man in fact did this, not considering that Father Garcés might be somewhere thereabouts or farther up and when he came back would certainly miss having them, as in fact did happen. So far do Señor Anza's favors extend; and such are the benefits that he says he is always doing for the Fathers! And I learned this for a fact because when the interpreter came back he told me, when I asked him why he had brought the animals, leaving the Father without any. He responded that he was unable to do anything else because he was a person under orders and his master Señor Anza had thus commanded him. He said this to me in front of Señor Anza who did not contradict him.

Father Tomás told us that Chief Palma had decided to go to Mexico City with us and that he had been wishing for this since the Father had told him of the festival held in Mexico City for the Most Holy Virgin of Guadalupe, which the Father himself says in his journal on December 12.[13] Before that, he had not thought of doing such a thing, and had not even spoken to Captain Anza or anyone else about this topic. We disputed whether or not it would be proper to take him and whether with his absence any problems would arise among the Yuma tribe and along the river. At first Señor Anza showed some reluctance to taking him. However, after we had discussed this matter among ourselves, he agreed that he would do so, first laying out for Palma what he thought proper to say concerning so long a travel, so that he would not be ignorant of anything and would not imagine that he had been deceived when taken along. This was done, as I shall relate during the next day's entry.[14]

---

[12] Font's letter of July 18 adds that the messenger traveled eight days without finding Garcés, only some animals that the missionary had abandoned along the trail. By September 17 Garcés had reached the Hopi pueblos, had been turned away from them, and had made his return journey all the way to his mission near Tucson, from which the news of his return spread quickly. Font's comment here seems to indicate that the final text was nearly complete at that early a date, despite the colophon dated 1777. However, he may have left the mystery open in order to increase the dramatic effect.

[13] Eixarch stressed not only the glories of the religious feast and of Mexico City but also the viceroy's power and his desire to meet Palma and give him gifts. Likewise he dwelled on the size of his own mother Colegio de la Santa Cruz at Querétaro and the number of its missionaries. (Montané 2000: 365. Cf. Bolton 1930 3: 319.)

[14] Father Eixarch's journal kept at Yuma is inserted after this point in the final text, occupying pages 271 through 310 of the manuscript, with the following introductory note by Font: "He also informed us of how he had gotten along at the Colorado River during the whole period of our absence, and what he had noted there. And since the Father kept up his journal there, in order that nothing shall escape me I shall place a copy of it here, containing between December 4 and the present May 11 inclusive, which letter by letter is as follows." Eixarch's journal as presented by Font is printed in Montané 2000; translated in Bolton 1930 vol. 2.

Señor Anza, then, wrote the letter to Father Garcés that he intended to send him[15] and very thoughtfully read it to us in a friendly fashion (although he said nothing to us concerning the notion that he had of ordering the animals brought in if the Father was not there). Ever since the squabbles with Señor Rivera he maintained a great deal of friendliness with me to the extent that, while at San Gabriel, he did me the honor of sharing with me all of Señor Rivera's writings and communications and all of the responses and letters that he wrote back to him. Perhaps he did this simply because he had no one else there with whom he could discuss these matters and saw that I was on his side, for indeed I found such low doings offensive. But later this friendliness stopped, and all the consideration he had been showing me came to nothing, and I ended out of favor with him, as I shall tell.

[May] 12, Sunday. I said Mass. The letter for Father Garcés that I spoke of yesterday, telling him we wished him to come at once, as the river was rising a great deal and we could not delay, was sent off with an interpreter and preparations were begun for crossing the river, which had risen a great deal although its current was flowing very smoothly. During the days we spent here, I noticed that the river rose three or four dedos each day, but did so deceptively,[16] inasmuch as its flow derives from melting snow; and that it was carrying a good deal of timber and its water was very cloudy.

Chief Palma (as I recorded yesterday) said he wanted to come with us to go on to Mexico City to greet the viceroy and tell him that he and his Yumas wished greatly, and would be very pleased if Spaniards and Fathers would come to their country to live together with them. And in order to handle this matter in a proper fashion, at nightfall Señor Anza, Father Fray Tomás, and I went inside the house with Palma and three or four old men whom we allowed into the conversation to hear what was being said, and we spoke together upon it at great length. Our commander described for him the length of the journey and the delays that would be faced, which meant that he would not be able to return to his country for a long time. And Palma responded by asking how many years it might take for him to return. Our commander told him, a year at most, and also added that perhaps he himself would come with him next time and stay once and for all in his country. (I do not know what grounds he had for making this offer. All that I do know is that I heard him say several times that he would be glad to go and live at the Colorado River because he liked the Indians there.) Then Palma said that that was good, and since he was persisting in his wish, our commander accepted him into his company to be taken to Mexico City. But he was not to go alone but rather with a few others who might wish to accompany him voluntarily. That way he would be happier and they could help in case of any accident. Out of a great many persons who offered to do so, Palma chose two companions, a brother of his and a son of Chief Pablo; they were joined by a young Cajuenche who, ever since Father Garcés visited his tribe, had also made up his mind to go to Mexico City.[17] (And the three of them, with Chief Palma, came

---

[15] Anza's journal reports that the letter appointed May 14 (two days later) for Garcés to join Anza's return journey if he wished. If he did not appear, Anza would leave for him some articles that Garcés had requested in a letter, for his maintenance. Garcés did receive the letter, along with one from Eixarch, but only on his return from California three weeks later, and among the Mojaves far up-river. After a further delay there, he set out for New Mexico instead of returning to Yuma.

[16] Almost invisibly. 3 dedos is just over 2 inches; 4 dedos is 2⅘ inches.

[17] As Anza describes it, he told the chief he must take at least three companions as witnesses to the treatment he would receive. "Around two hundred males" at first offered to go on the journey.

with us as far as the Presidio of San Miguel, where I left them with Captain Anza, with whom they later went on to Mexico City.) To seal this decision, Palma was told to go to his house and explain to the Indians how he was going away so that everyone would know about it and there would be no disturbance because of his absence. And Palma indicated on the spot his choice of an old Indian man, to whom he said that he was bestowing the quiver for him to defend the country from its enemies and to symbolize that he was in command at the river. Then he went to his house where, calling his Indians together, he entrusted them with his sowing grounds and told them to plant a great amount and live together in peace, and so forth.

[May] 13, Monday. I said Mass. The river rose around three dedos farther above what it was yesterday here at Puerto de la Concepción. Our effects, along with some boys, started to be taken across the river on a very large raft consisting of a great many poles that was built by the Indians this morning. The operation was attended to by Chief Pablo, who did not stop for an instant and worked harder than anyone (Chief Palma had gone to call in people and horses). And before noon, during the morning, the raft made a trip in which they very easily carried across packs and two muleteers. Another raft load crossed in the afternoon with some people, and the Indians labored hard during the crossing since the river had risen around three dedos farther and there were big swirls. Due to the swirls here in the narrows of this pass, the raft was so battered by the force of the water that it had to be taken apart with its grass ropes, poles, and so forth and brought back across to this side, to build it anew.

I observed the latitude of the pass here and found it, by the tables of Jorge, in 32° 39½'[18] with no correction, and in 32° 47', with correction.[19] And thus I say: at the Puerto de la Concepción on the Colorado River, May 13, 1776: meridian altitude of the sun's lower limb: 75° 38'. I took great pains, but was unsuccessful, in measuring the river's width here at the narrows made by the pass. I used a cable that I had put together some one hundred twenty-five varas long,[20] and had an Indian man and three women who had offered to swim across the river at the narrowest spot, stretch the cable across to the other side. But, before they got halfway on the water, the river pulled them down stream and the cable got caught upon one of the many pieces of timber carried by the river and it broke. Some of the cable pieces were lost. Had the Indians not been such skilled swimmers there might have been an accident, therefore, I ended my attempt. In the end, I estimated a hundred varas,[21] more or less, as being the river's width at this spot. What I do know is that from the top of the mount, an Indian shot an arrow and it fell on the opposite bank very close to the water's edge. Therefore, the width at the narrowest point of the river must be an arrow flight.

---

[18] The figure has been altered from some other value, as have the results from the use of Gasco's antiquated tables (as usual, not given in this translation).
[19] About 32° 43.5', in actuality.
[20] Almost 344 feet.
[21] About 275 feet.

[May] 14, Tuesday. Measures were taken to have the Indian women swim across carrying some items in their baskets and boxes while the raft was being built. This was done, and the women spent the entire day making trips in this way.

At noon the raft was finished and five soldiers, some boys, and as much load as possible were taken across. They took the raft apart again, brought back the poles, and made two rafts that were finished at about six o'clock in the evening, whereupon our commander determined that we should cross the river. One of the rafts was loaded with our effects with one man on it, and some four mule loads were put onto the other raft. Our commander, Father Fray Tomás, I, and others, thirteen in all, ten men and three boys also embarked on that raft. But as soon as we got onto the river the raft began to take on water, and this, together with a swirl that came by just then, placed us in danger. A soldier named Angelo[22] instantly jumped ashore with a single leap, out of fear, and following his example the little Indian Pedro from San Luis threw himself into the water like lightning. I was unable to restrain him even though I had him by my side. They remained ashore along with others in the hope that they would be able to cross tomorrow. The eleven of us who were left found ourselves in no small danger because, in addition to the raft not steering easily because of its heavy load, and sinking a great deal, at the moment it left land there came a strong swirl that submerged it.

Thereupon the Indians were of the opinion that we should go back ashore, but Chief Pablo, who was up at the head steering this raft, and doing so with great verve, disagreed. He regarded returning as an insult. To judge from his expressions, it looked as though he alone was going to carry us in his arms to the other side. This view finally prevailed and they moved the raft from the shore and began to put us out into the river, down deep into the water as we were. Even though I was seated on top of a chest I got wet up to my calf. It is to be noted that the raft must have been a bit over a vara and a half tall.[23] A great many Indians standing on the shore and seeing what was happening threw themselves at once into the water. About forty of them surrounded the raft and brought us across to the other shore in a dozen minutes with great shouting and hubbub, especially when we were in the middle of the river and a soldier shot off his musket (something that pleases them very much). All this happened without any greater misfortune than getting most of the load and our feet wet. We reached the other side lower down than the other raft loads did, which were not as heavy as this one.

At about half past six in the evening we were over our scare. Certainly these Indians are great swimmers, great friends of Spaniards, and extremely worthy

---

[22]Juan Angel Amarillas?
[23]Thus, "a bit over" 4⅛ feet.

FIGURE 38. A raft crossing the Colorado River near the Mojave villages, 1854. By Albert H. Campbell and John James Young. *From Whipple 1855–1856: frontispiece.*

of esteem for their affection and loyalty, since our lives and possessions were at their mercy.

From the river, while crossing it, I took care to observe how narrow it is between the two heights of the Puerto de la Concepción where the river goes through, and estimated the width at one hundred varas. During all of the trips made by the Indian women, the only thing lost was the mules' shoeing materials which a woman was taking across in a basket. It began to take on water because of the weight and sank to the bottom. The woman was unable to save the basket much less the irons.

[May] 15, Wednesday. I said Mass. In the morning the Indian women finished bringing some effects across in their baskets, and on a raft they built today the men brought across the few people and the boy Pedrito who had remained on the other side yesterday. Everything was gotten across in six raft loads and the trips made by the Indian women, and we had crossed the river. The mounts swam over yesterday at noon, a good distance above the pass. Our commander dealt out beads to everyone in payment of their hard work and dismissed them. They took their leave with a good deal of tenderness for us, wanting to know when we would come back, but such is the affection shown by these Yumas that many of them would not depart until we ourselves did. Chief Pablo, among them, stayed and even though, as Father Tomás says in his journal,[24] he is sick, he distinguished himself in all ways on this occasion. He was constant and assiduous in the building of the rafts, in bringing the effects over, in ordering people to help and working right in front himself, and doing more than anyone. All of this made him much prized.

I am not sure whether Pablo may not be like all other Indians, insofar as stealing is concerned. It is certain that Señor Anza, before we set out, found his pocket knife missing and when he asked the Indians there for it, no one knew anything about it. We were just about to mount up on horseback, and Chief Pablo went directly to one corner of the little ramada that had been put up there to shelter us from the sun, and while acting as though searching for something, he got the knife out of the ground in an instant and gave it to Señor Anza. From this we deduced that if he did not hide it himself, he had seen who did it, for the Yumas are very skillful at this, and in the end, even though they are good Indians, they do not lack the Indian characteristic of stealing. Thank God that they did not steal a great amount, as they might have done, for even though some things were found missing—the cloak belonging to our purveyor among them—this was nothing considering the disorder involved in crossing the river, when our effects were passed to them in a very scattered fashion and in small lots.

To finish what I have said concerning Chief Pablo, I wish to narrate here what Señor Anza told me about him and what happened the time before, during his first expedition. Under November 27, I have already told how this chief at that time intended to stop him from crossing the river and to kill him and his soldiers in order to keep what they were carrying. Then later he acted very much the opposite. What happened was that at that time, when Señor Anza came back from Monterey and was about to set out from the river, he found two mules missing and complained to the Indians of their having been stolen from him. Chief Pablo heard this and, saying nothing, went in search of the robber and caught the Indian—who had taken them to his house—redhanded; that is, with the two mules, one of which he had there alive and tied up, and the other one dead, which he was butchering. Pablo then, very angry, tried to kill the criminal for having done this, but the Indian fled, and since he could not kill him, he killed his wife with an arrow shot. Then, he pulled out the arrow that he had used to shoot through the heart, took the live mule, and went off to Señor Anza and presented it to him. He told him that he was bringing back only one mule because the thief had slain the other one already, but that he had already avenged this wrong and that he was presenting him right then and there with the arrow with which he had slain the thief's wife since he had not been able to kill the thief himself. Señor Anza condemned the act very much, telling him he was not pleased with that. He would rather have given up his two mules for lost than for him to have done such a thing—killing someone. Pablo nonetheless pressed him to accept the arrow he was presenting to him, but Señor Anza refused to accept it, showing that he was very much displeased at his having killed the woman.

---

[24]Eixarch's journal, which Font copied into his final text.

When Pablo saw that he was being scorned, then became offended and asked what was the issue in having killed a woman, and why did that matter so much that the Spanish captain would not take the arrow by which he had avenged the offense? I cannot tell whether this case proves that Chief Pablo is loyal or bloodthirsty, since he shows traces of both one and the other.[25]

A grown-up daughter of Chief Palma, whom we called Francisca, was one of the Indian women who made their trips yesterday. She is a great swimmer and she went at the head of the others although, as is their custom, she was painted with red ochre applied in such a way that it does not come off even though they spend the entire day in the water, as they did yesterday. Already earlier I had said to her and to others that it was not good for them to paint themselves, because Spaniards and Christians do not do this. Today on saying farewell I told her the same thing and suggested that she wash herself using some water I had there and it would be better that way, or that if she wished I would wash her myself. She agreed to have me wash her,[26] and to her delight and that of those present I gave her a good soaping on face, arms and body as far as the waist,[27] by which I managed to remove the paint and immediately gave her a mirror so she could see herself and how good she would look that way. And, upon seeing herself, she broke out giggling a great deal and saying "*Ajót, ajót*," meaning "Good, good."
I am recounting this as being an unusual case, since the Indians there are such lovers of body painting that it will be an affair of great difficulty to have the women give it up, and much harder than that to remove it from the men, with whom I did not have another such success. They regard going painted up and sooty as devils as being finely dressed.

As we were starting dinner, the Indians said that there were Spaniards on the other side of the river, and some said that it was Father Garcés, but immediately they said "*Assende jecó*," meaning "one Spaniard," and that he was coming from the Cajuenche mountains.[28] The Father would not have been coming alone. Our commander suspected it must be some deserter from the Presidio of Monterey, which was the case. He ordered the Indians to carry him, whoever he was, across the river and bring him to him at once. And at the end of dinner, the Indians came with the jecó, bringing him in their midst like a prisoner. We saw that indeed it was a deserter, one of the three deserters from our expedition that Captain Rivera had been holding, unsecured, at San Diego. He had escaped from that presidio on Sunday, May 5, and had come this far with great hardship. And Señor Anza accepted him and put him with the muleteers.

---

[25] Garcés in his 1774 journal expressed skepticism about the chief's whole story: "I thought it a fiction, all the more so because he was wearing the horseshoes hanging and would not let go of them." In other words, if the tale was a made-up one to impress the Spanish commander or avoid blame for the mule, it backfired.

[26] The final text has it differently: ". . . with water that I had there. She answered me that she did not know how to wash herself and so I myself should wash her, and. . . ."

[27] The details here are only in the field text.

[28] In the final text, "from the Cajuenches."

We asked him about the route he had taken and he told us that he had had a good and not a very long one in the mountains until he arrived at the Santa Rosa wells. His greatest hardship had only been in the dunes because of his complete lack of provisions, as he had taken from San Diego no more than four or six tortillas for the road. Therefore, I felt reaffirmed in my previous conclusion that San Diego harbor does not lie very far from the Colorado River and that the only obstacle to connecting them is the bad way through the dunes. If these can be gotten around, the connection will be an easy one.[29]

At last, with a good deal of fondness because of the faithfulness and affection they had shown us, we took our leave of the Yumas. They still wanted to know when we would return. So we went on our way with Father Fray Tomás, no longer waiting for Father Garcés, and with our number increased by Chief Palma and his companions. The party consisted of the thirty people already mentioned; Palma with three companions; Father Tomás with two interpreters, one employee, and his boy; these along with the deserter made up our full company of forty. We set out from the edge of the Colorado River at a little before five o'clock in the afternoon, and at about nine o'clock at night, having traveled some six leagues, on a southeastward and east-southeastward course for the first two, and the remainder by taking up our route on the same course as on coming up. Our captain along with the mule train reached the pass and banks of the Gila at the point of the mountain range where on November 27 Chief Palma had come to meet us on our way up. It happened that Señor Anza went ahead with some soldiers to look for grass, and he strayed some way off the road. I and the rest of the people were guided by Chief Palma along the route. Since it was nighttime and we were not able to see, we went on ahead. When I realized that it must be past ten o'clock at night and the stopping place could not be all that far away, I stopped, struck a light, and had them inspect the way. When I saw that there were no fresh tracks upon it, I realized that we had left Señor Anza behind. For this reason I decided that we should stop there and spend the night until we could rejoin each other at daylight; and so we stayed there, close to a little bit of grass for our animals. We spent the night separated in this way, without any provisions.

[May] 16, Thursday. We saddled up at daybreak at a half past five in the morning and I told two men to go back and see where Señor Anza was. He arrived at our stopping place at a quarter past six, and we continued onward, rejoicing a great deal because we had rejoined. During the morning we traveled a bit over two leagues eastward by north and east-northeastward, with, as yesterday, some veering as we wound to one side or the other. The river was quite high and the land was as sterile as when we were coming. Now we felt hot weather that was as

---

[29]Font's following entry for May 16 reports more briefly on a second examination of the deserter, with similar results.

heavy proportionately as the cold we had endured here at that time. At a quarter past seven, we stopped at the edge of the Gila River where we had halted on November 26, having traveled some two leagues. We built a ramada, the mule train came up, and at nine o'clock I said Mass, since it was Ascension Day.

Some Indians had followed us on foot up to here, and although they were persuaded to turn back, they had been so determined to follow Palma that it was necessary to belabor the point. Despite their attempt to persist in continuing with us, we finally sent them off. Only a Cajuenche boy remained. He said that just for today he wanted to come along and spend the night with us and would go back the next day. But by what happened afterwards, he wanted to see whether he could filch something.

What happened, then, was that in the afternoon before we loaded up, the machete belonging to the head muleteer was found missing, and Palma was told that some Indian had taken it. Palma grew heated and gave his companions a reprimand. Immediately, his comrade the Cajuenche said that the Indian who had remained and not wanted to go back had hidden it. The latter denied it and Señor Anza threatened him, saying that if he did not return the machete he would order him tied up and whipped until he handed it over. The Indian became afraid and began to look over the ground as though searching for something. From the way he was looking, Palma's brother figured out the spot where he had buried it. When he dug there he immediately found it and pulled it out. At that point I caught the Indian thief by the arm, and, calling to Palma, handed him over to him, gave him my quirt, and told him to give him some lashes with it, to test how he would do it. Palma thereupon, very angry, gave him three lashes using his left arm (he is left-handed) with such determination that I at once restrained him and would not have him continue, since to judge by the heat with which he began, he would have flayed him.

We set out from here at a quarter to four in the afternoon and at a half past six we halted at the brackish lake, the same spot where we stopped on November 25, having traveled four leagues, making six together with the two leagues in the morning. The course was eastward with some veering northeastward and a great deal more southeastward, winding about. At nightfall, the three boys who remained at the Colorado yesterday came bringing the horses that were left there. It was decided from here onwards to leave our route of the way up and, crossing through the Papaguería, to arrive at Caborca mission, since this was a straighter way to reach San Miguel de Horcasitas.

Señor Anza examined the deserter at length. The route he had taken had him setting out from the Santa Rosa wells. From what he said, I reaffirmed my judgment that San Diego harbor was some fifty leagues from the Puerto de la

Concepción.[30] The climate that we experienced at the Colorado River and on the Gila River is a very cold one in winter, and very hot in summer.

[May] 17, Friday. I said Mass. We delayed here until evening in order to take the route from this river toward Caborca. What with the heat that we felt here, my mouth inflammation worsened today, and what with the brackish water, our animals fell ill (for the Indians may well call this the Salt River). Two mules and a horse gave out on the way today and were lost. We set out from the brackish lake at a quarter past four in the afternoon, and at a quarter to twelve at night we halted at a patch of the tough grass the soldiers call galleta,[31] one league after crossing the stream full of sand that they call *Los Pozos de Enmedio*,[32] having traveled a long eleven leagues on a course about three leagues south-southeastward as far as some small heights, then southeastward for some six leagues. Here we hit upon the route taken by Señor Anza the first time and which Father Díaz records in his journal[33] and afterward we went about two leagues east-southeastward. The entire way was a level one over sandy, dry, horrible soil without any more trees than wretched little mesquites at the edge of Los Pozos de Enmedio, a good deal of creosote bush and a bit of the galleta hay.

[May] 18, Saturday. We set out from the patch of tough grass and the plain at five o'clock in the morning, and at a quarter of two at night halted near the *Llano del Tuzal*,[34] before the *Puerto Blanco*,[35] having traveled eighteen leagues on a very varied course. The three first leagues were mainly eastward, over level land, then about two leagues winding about east-southeastward and, more, east-northeastward and a bit northeastward in among mountain ranges, and the remainder, one league, east-southeastward. Having traveled six leagues, we came to the tanks of *La Candelaria*, where we paused to nap between nine in the morning and a quarter to six in the evening. This spot consists of mountains or very steep, fierce, and bare rocks, in which there are some cavities they call *Las Tinajas*[36] and usually there is water in them. There are nine tanks formed in the rocks at this spot, each over the other, or higher than the other, and water is obtained by using baskets to empty the upper ones. Our animals, amounting to over one hundred in number, were watered twice, and most of our time was spent in this operation.

Then, with the purpose of heading directly to El Carrizal in one day's march without touching at the *Aguaje Empinado*[37] which we left upon our right since it

---

[30] This repeats some of the material already given in the preceding entry.
[31] Galleta means biscuit or crackers and refers to the course quality of the grass. The short text adds and then strikes out the phrase "on a plain."
[32] The Well In-between.
[33] Of Anza's first march through here in 1774.
[34] Gopher Plain.
[35] White Pass.
[36] The Tanks.
[37] Steep Water.

is not possible to water our animals there. We headed straight across the plain and traveled until a little after a half past one in the morning: about three leagues east-northeastward and northeastward with some variance, through rocky badlands; then a bit over six leagues southeastward deflecting a bit eastward, until hitting upon the route; and the remaining three east-southeastward along the road. And on coming into the Llano del Tuzal we dismounted so we could rest and lie down a bit without freeing the reins from our animals, while the pack train was on the way to reaching here.

[May] 19, Sunday. We slept for a little. The pack train arrived at four o'clock in the morning and went on ahead without stopping. We ate breakfast and some of us changed our mounts in order to undertake the day's march. We set out from the beginning of the Llano del Tuzal at five o'clock in the morning, and at a half past eleven came to the Arroyo del Carrizal, having traveled some ten good leagues, upon a course east-southeastward for a little more than three leagues as far as the Puerto Blanco, and the remainder southeastward (inexact) or southeast by south. A level route almost the whole way, all of it sandy, bad soil with no more grass than a little galleta. Today three horses and a mule were left worn out and lost. The pack train traveled for over nineteen hours without halting and arrived at one o'clock in the morning. The heat left us exhausted, although it cooled off so much after nightfall that a blanket and my cloak folded double were not enough to hold off the chill. There is usually water at this spot almost all year long; it is a bit brackish but not very bad, and there is some grass. The stream here comes from the east and from not very far away, rising from a number of indentations in the mountain range next to here and going southward and westward to the sea. They say that it has a little water in small pools all along its course. There is a bit of a flow here at this spot.

[May] 20, Monday. We set out from the Arroyo del Carrizal at a quarter to six in the morning and came to the pueblo of San Marcelo de Sonoitac at a half past eleven, and the pack train at one o'clock in the afternoon, where we stayed on to nap until half past five in the evening, having traveled nine leagues, six of them eastward and the last three east-southeastward, inexact at times. The whole way is rather uneven, with a good amount of bush and not such savage country as that before, with some mesquites and saguaros and a great deal of brush and creosote bush. The mountains, although arid, are not quite so arid and are not just sheer rocks like those at La Candelaria. About three leagues along the way, we were met by an Indian from Sonoitac who was going as a courier to the Colorado River with letters for Señor Anza, and one from the viceroy for Father Garcés that was opened by his companion Father Tomás to see if it contained some government order, and we saw that it was the one that I mention under December 1, by which His Excellency was sending on the information furnished to Mexico City by Father Fray Silvestre Vélez de Escalante in case it might serve to shed some light for his travels. However, it lacked that report or copy because it had been misfiled in the secretariat, as I told on April 3,

and by this we learned here of the handing over of the Pimería Baja missions, etc.[38]

Near El Carrizal we saw an Indian with his family. We passed by some deserted little huts about three leagues before Sonoitac. Here at Sonoitac we saw about twenty Indians, or families,[39] with their governor. Sonoitac was once a mission, although a small one. It has water, year round, in a small stream, sufficient for a small settlement and some small-sized plantings, but this is a dreadful spot in which to put up buildings since the only wood it has are a few very wretched willows near the water and some scrubby mesquites.

We left Sonoitac at a half past five in the afternoon; then during the evening we traveled some four leagues, two leagues south-southeastward and two southeastward winding about a bit, and at a half past eight we came to stop at the foot of steep heights that we had been following to our right hand, a spot with a bit of grass, no water. The route is a bit steep but not very rough, with considerable bush and a great deal of jojoba, green and plentiful to our view, and which continues for a good stretch today and tomorrow. This district seems to have a show of gold ore. Those who are expert say that the best showings are about two leagues from Sonoitac. Some of the men gathered soil from the surface to wash it. They got no gold but did find some[40] copper ore. Setting out from Sonoitac, we passed by the spot and small height where the Indians killed their Jesuit Father minister at the foot of a saguaro on which he had hung his crucifix. There is a cross set up there.[41]

[May] 21, Tuesday. At a half past four in the morning we set out from the foot of the heights and—having traveled some eight short leagues, on a course, for the first two, southeastward and a bit south-southeastward, then continuing southward for about five leagues with some veering south-southeastward, and finally, for about a league, turning about as far as southwestward in order to come at the stopping place—at a half past nine we came to the pueblo of Quitobác, a former station belonging to the mission of Sonoitac and called San Luis de Bacapa by the Jesuits, where we paused to nap until five o'clock in the afternoon. The route, fairly level and with a bit of bush, lay alongside the steep mountain range to the right that we began following yesterday evening. A mule

---

[38] Font's superiors at Querétaro had handed over that mission field, including Font's own mission of San José de Pimas, to the clergy belonging to the Franciscan colegio of Zacatecas.
[39] "Or families," only in the final text, is apparently intended as a correction.
[40] The field text: "but there is a great deal of."
[41] The missionary Heinrich Ruhen was slain in 1751.

was left worn out and lost along the way. The day was cool from the air flowing steadily since last night. The Indians of this place, Quitobac, otherwise called Bacapa, of whom we saw many more than at Sonoitac, were very attentive to us; their governor came out on horseback to meet us, and they at once formed a good-sized shelter to shade us, employing large, well-made mats of small cane grass that they brought up. This spot has some small springs of year-round water, though it is all a very small affair for a settlement and plantings, and not very good for that. Since there was no grass, our animals left here hungry.

We set out from Quitobac at five o'clock with our mules hungry from lack of grass. Then in the evening we traveled about a league east-southeastward, then about two leagues southeastward, and continued on for a little along a dry sandy stream at the foot of a hill or height that is crossed by a kind of a pass, south-southeastward and almost southward, for a bit over a league. Then we went turning to southeastward about three leagues, and ended with one to the east-southeastward, until we halted along the way at eleven o'clock at night at a grass patch that we found. The route here is level and the country has a bit of bush. Alongside us to our left and at some distance away there are some mountains running toward Sonoitac in which they say there is a mount of salt near Sonoitac.[42] The night was cool.

[May] 22, Wednesday. Yesterday was a cool day, and today continued in the same fashion, something we had not expected here in the Papaguería, which is so dry, inhabitable and hot. We set out from the grass patch at a quarter to six in the morning and at a little after eleven o'clock, having traveled some eight leagues—course east-southeast for about two leagues, then southeast by east for a bit over five leagues, and the remainder almost south-southeastward, winding about so variably because of a low range that one commences to leave upon the right beginning from two leagues before Quitobac—we came to *San Eduardo de La Aribaypia*, which is a stream full of sand. We delayed there, in order to nap, until a half past five in the afternoon. The route is an entirely level one, somewhat wooded with mesquites, palo verde, and a great deal of brush and creosote bush. Aribaycpia is a place with a very sandy stream that always has water, but it is necessary to dig a yard or more deep in the sand in order to find it. There is some grass to be found here and along the way.

Then, in the afternoon, we set out from the spot at a half past five and traveled the first three leagues southward until we came across the route that goes toward the pueblo of Bisanig,[43] which we left behind. We traveled three more leagues

---

[42]Díaz's journal (used by Font), January 29, 1774: "a range in the midst of which is the Cerro de la Sal, so called because of the many veins of rock salt existing among its rocks, with which the natives supply themselves plentifully, getting it with very little labor during the rainy season."

[43]Originally written "Bisanic" in the field text.

south-southeastward and southeastward over a stony route rather close up to a mountain range, and about one league southwestward until we struck upon the better route where there is grass. And having traveled some seven leagues we halted at a little after half past ten at night near the spot they called San Ildefonso the other time, during the first expedition.

   Aribaycpia means "Wells of water in the sand."

[May] 23, Thursday. We set out from the spot of San Ildefonso at a half past five in the morning and shortly after twelve noon reached Caborca mission, having traveled some eight leagues on a course three southward and deviating a bit eastward, then southeastward for a little, and the remainder east-southeastward. The whole route through the Papaguería is very twisting and winding because of the great scarcity of grass along it, and even greater scarcity of watering places, which are very few and have to be searched for, which makes this route so difficult to travel.

We were received by this mission's Father minister, Fray Ambrosio Calzada, with brotherly affection and joy, and in the afternoon, his companion, Fray Matías Moreno,[44] came over from El Pitic, a station belonging to this mission two leagues away, where he had been. We requested animals from the Presidio of El Altar eight leagues to the east from this mission to relieve our beasts that had become worn out by the bad road through the Papaguería. In the afternoon our commander sent two soldiers there with orders to return tomorrow.

[May] 24, Friday. I said Mass. We delayed at the mission.[45] I observed the latitude of the mission here, and found it, by the tables of Jorge Juan, with no correction, in 30° 38½′, and with correction, in 30° 44′.[46] And thus I say: at Caborca mission, May 24, 1776: meridian altitude of the sun's lower limb: 80°. At nightfall the soldiers who went to the Presidio of El Altar yesterday returned from there with twelve animals. The alférez of Tubac, don Felipe Velderrain, arrived from the Presidio of El Altar bringing the news that at Mission Tumacácori nothing was left, that the Apaches had carried off everything, were not departing from thereabouts, and were inflicting all sorts of damage. And he related these events and affairs with an impertinence that was very foreign to his duty and that disgusted me to hear it.

[May] 25, Saturday. I said Mass.
Before I went to Mass, the Tubac alférez came in, and without greeting me began talking to the purveyor and others there, and because of his great impertinence in telling of the incidents caused by the Apaches and of that district's misery, as though he were making merry about

---

[44]José Matías Moreno, a Spaniard. A few years afterward, Font was to join him at El Pitic (now Pitiquito), where they built the still existing church. Moreno then went to the Yuma missions, and perished in the massacre.

[45]The soldiers who were sent for mounts, ordered to come back by noon, did not return by nightfall.

[46]Font's latitude is seven minutes too high.

them—saying that all that was needed now was for them to come with their women and load up, and similar things—I was unable to restrain myself and told him that it was shameful to see the laughter and the manner with which he related such unhappiness, etc. When he tried to justify himself by saying to me, "So, Father, am I supposed to be weeping?" I answered, "Yes sir, you ought to be weeping, because I, who am not from this country, am very sorry over its misfortune, and you people whose duty it is to attempt to remedy this by restraining the enemy don't have any interest in doing so. Your only interest is in playing cards, dancing, etc., and wearing a lot of braid on your hats" (he was wearing two pieces of braid on his hat).[47] With no expression on his face he told me to go and try my hand at commanding the military command. Then it would be seen what my ability was and what I was good for. After he had said this to me twice, I replied that military command was not my business, and I concluded, finally, by telling him that I refused to have any more discussion with him as he was a man who had no manners, etc., and I went off to say Mass. Undoubtedly, the alférez, who was Señor Anza's godson, conveyed to him what I had said, because he was grouchy the entire morning, with a book in his hand. Later this alférez was demoted in rank for poor conduct, and that is why a certain don Diego Oya was sent as his successor. But because Señor Anza, was his compadre,[48] he arranged at that time with the governor at San Miguel not to admit him[49] as such, characterizing him as worthless as a soldier, whereupon he was forced to leave the country again. Later, however, the higher command ordered him brought back from Durango and he went to take his post, leaving Alférez Velderrain reduced to the ranks, with his compadre Señor Anza unable to interfere.[50]

Father Tomás decided to leave for Tubac with the alférez and people who were going there.

Before rising from the table at noon, Father Tomás told Señor Anza that he needed animals in order to go to Tumacácori. What had happened was that Señor Anza, while on the way, had told him that he would be very pleased if he would proceed on to San Miguel in his company. However—inasmuch as this must have been only a superficial politeness on his part—now, in order to rid himself of the Father, he told him it would be better if he left for his mission along

---

[47]According to Father Barbastro, a common soldier—not an officer like Velderrain—would aspire to owning a plain hat with two or three yards (varas) of ribbon around it, amounting, at four reales the vara, to a peso or 1½ pesos' worth; the ideal would also include underclothing of imported linen cloth and a velveteen shirt and breeches, but the soldier's pay would not be sufficient for all of this. (Gómez 1771: 81.)

[48]Compadre is the godfather seen from the point of view of the child's godmother or parent. For example, if I am the child's godmother, my compadre is my fellow godparent and if I am the child's parent, my compadre is my child's godfather.

[49]Oya.

[50]At the time when he and Font were here at Caborca, Velderrain had already survived an attempt by Commandant Inspector O'Conor to cashier him for taking a dishonest profit from the pay of the soldiers of his company.

It has been argued that the alférez was merely playing a trick on Font by telling him that a mission had been destroyed, and that Font was fooled by this misinformation. The argument is that there is no evidence that such a thing happened at Tumacácori at that time, and Font himself in a later letter describing Apache attacks fails to mention the supposed event. (Kessel 1976: 120.) The alférez, however, may merely have been exaggerating, since there were many raids short of complete destruction of settlements. Font's letter (Brown 2005: 24) does speak of Tumacácori as having been threatened with destruction during the attacks of December 1776—and therefore not yet destroyed—but there he is only attempting to describe what happened during that month, as a sample of the terrible situation in Sonora. Describing any earlier assaults, which may well have taken place, would be against his purpose. If Font had been the victim of a practical joke by Velderrain, he would have learned the truth about Tumacácori long before finishing his journal's final text, and surely he would not have included the incident with the alférez as it is described.

with the alférez, who was going in that direction. Thus he answered that he would give him the animals. The Father then asked him to give something to the employee who had accidentally remained at the Colorado River[51] and had served him there as cook and in other capacities, since he had served him well. Señor Anza answered that he had no obligation to give him anything, since he was not in charge of this employee. He had not included him in his accounts, and if he were to give him anything it would have to be out of his own pocket. Thereupon I said, "But sir, in your journal did you not say: 'Three employees for the three Fathers?' Where are these employees?" He answered me, already perturbed, "But wasn't Your Reverence given your own employee?" I answered him, "Yes sir, after I had asked for one a few times, but that falls two short of making three, since you also said that you were not in charge of the man Father Garcés took along and who came back from the Colorado River, and he was given nothing; that is, unless you count as his employee Sebastián, whom you have counted as a muleteer, a cook, an interpreter, and at first as my employee. Neither is the boy who was taken along by Father Tomás counted as an employee. So that if this boy whom the Father is asking for is not an employee at your expense, I cannot find the three employees you mention." It had happened, even before dinner, that I had asked him to tell me how what he said in his journal was to be understood—that is, the "five interpreters of five tribes," since I was unable to find more than three, or four at the most by counting a servant of his as an interpreter of the Pima tribe. His response to this was as if he were dismissing me from his presence, "Your Reverence, leave that until San Miguel. When we reach there we will take a look at it and you will hear."

The fact was, that in order to exaggerate the number of positions, he had set down "an interpreter of the Níjora tribe," and there is no such tribe, since in the Pimería "Níjoras" is the name given to Indians whom the upcountry tribes take as captives in their wars with each other, and afterward the Yumas and Pápagos bring them to El Altar and elsewhere in order to sell them as captives or slaves, whatever tribe they belong to. And, since Señor Anza was not willing to allow me to learn of these matters, he therefore was never willing to go over the expedition's rosters with me even though I asked him to a number of times. He would even act resentful when asked. This was the last time that I asked him about it. Because of this, Señor Anza then developed a great deal of resentment, saying that I kept dropping these hints that offended him a great deal. I answered him, "Sir, they are not hints, they are quite clear, unless you are so sensitive that you are upset when anything you dislike is mentioned." This was how the conversation finally ended, just as it was beginning to get heated, since the Fathers stepped in to stop it; and Señor Anza stayed very angry this whole day. The friendliness that up until now he had shown me was over, from now on I was in his disfavor.

I have come out the loser in discussions with him more than twice, not because of anything that had to do with me personally but rather with two of the Fathers. In the end, I have been blamed because the habit of speaking plainly does not sit well with them. The proverb that says: "Speaking truths spoils friendships" usually rings true.

In the afternoon, Father Fray Tomás Eixarch set out for El Altar to go to his mission, Tumacácori, with the alférez. We set out from Mission Caborca at a quarter past four in the evening, traveled until half past eleven at night, and halted at the low spot belonging to the place called El Bámuri, having traveled

---

[51]According to Eixarch, the servant had had some disagreement with the family he was traveling with. See also under December 1, 1775.

some ten long leagues on a course southward for about two leagues and the rest south-southeastward and southeastward. This whole way is level ground.

[May] 26, Pentecost. We set out from El Bámuri at a quarter past five in the morning, and at a quarter after eight we reached the mining camp of La Cieneguilla, having traveled some five leagues course southeastward. As soon as we arrived Lieutenant don Pedro Tueros[52]—who assigned us a building in which to lodge—and the other gentleman merchants of this camp, came to welcome us. After the necessary exchange of pleasantries, I went to say Mass. I went in the afternoon to see the placer mines at the invitation of don Francisco de Guizarnótegui, who went with me, and I saw how the Indians take out the gold. They are a league away from the camp, and we returned at nightfall.[53]

[May] 27, Monday. I awoke completely relieved from my mouth sickness and my ailments,
in such a way that the diarrhea and stomach upset that had accompanied me for the whole way and from which I was only occasionally relieved for a short time was totally alleviated from today on and I felt it no more. And the mouth inflammation began lessening and improving every day until it left me entirely at Ures, a few days after arriving there.

We delayed this day. At the request of the parish priest of the camp, don José Nicolás de Mesa, I sang Mass at the altar. I observed the latitude of the camp there, and by the tables of Jorge Juan I found it, with no correction, in 30° 9½', and with correction, in 30° 14½'.[54] And thus I say: at La Cieneguilla camp, May 27, 1776: meridian altitude of the sun's lower limb: 81°. I dined at don Francisco de Guizarnótegui's. He invited me to his house and that evening we enjoyed ourselves for a while there in his house.[55]

[May] 28, Tuesday. I said Mass, and afterward in the choir, using the instrument,[56] I accompanied the Mass which the parish priest sang at the altar. Although our captain had decided we should depart today, later he decided to leave tomorrow, in order to oblige a request made by doña Ignacia, don Antonio Castro's wife[57] and to take the opportunity that was offered of traveling together in convoy with other people who are leaving tomorrow. For the road we still had

---

[52] The royal official administering the mining camp. In 1778 he succeeded Anza as military commandant of the province.

[53] When Cieneguilla declined in the following decade, Francisco Guizarnótegui, one of the most successful of the Basque merchants on the frontier, moved his operations over the mountains to Chihuahua (Moorhead 1975: 215–18).

[54] Font's latitude is a few minutes higher than that of the modern mining district.

[55] The day's delay at the camp was because news had arrived from the settlements further in that a mounted group of over one hundred Apaches were on the roads nearby.

[56] Font's psaltery.

[57] Antonio Enríquez (de) Castro, a European Spaniard, was the financial agent for the Sonora missions as well as being chief investor and exploiter of these important mines. See also the note on the family of Juan Antonio Amézquita, in the roster under April 13. His wife was Ignacia Valdés.

to travel is a very dangerous one because of the enemy Apaches who have committed a number of attacks and killings along it in recent time. And, even more than Apaches, the Seris and renegade Pimas or Piatos, more bloodthirsty still, have committed dreadful acts of enmity, destruction, robberies, and murders.[58]

Thereupon we went in the evening to sing vespers, as the most holy Sacrament was displayed during these three days, and at night we went to enjoy ourselves for a while at don Antonio de Castro's, yielding to the insistence and plea made to us by Castro and his wife. They are persons worthy of being indulged for the kindness of their affection, and all the more so at the present juncture when with great fondness they lodged Chief Palma and his companions within their home.

[May] 29, Wednesday. I said Mass. I turned over to Lieutenant don Pedro Tueros the vestments from San Ignacio that Father Fray Francisco Zúñiga loaned me for the purpose of saying Mass along the way, as I say under October 10. He took it upon himself to return them to that mission. We bid farewell to the Lieutenant, Father Mesa the parish priest, the Señores Mugarrieta and Castro, and so forth. All of them had been very demonstrative, courteous, and thoughtful in every way. We set out from La Cieneguilla camp at a quarter past five in the afternoon, and at ten o'clock at night halted on a plain with a good deal of grass, at the spot called Los Cerritos, having traveled some seven leagues, on a course southeastward with some slight variation for the first two, and the remaining five to the east-southeastward, winding about, mostly a quarter-point more to eastward and a quarter-point to southward, and with many portions to southeastward and even further toward eastward.

Our number was swelled by a pack train going toward Guasabas[59] with its escort of Ópata Indians and others who joined us, so that we were more than sixty souls in all. People do not set out to travel from La Cieneguilla unless in convoy with others since this route is so risky and dangerous because of enemy Apaches, as I said yesterday. Señor Guizarnótegui came out to keep us company a little way.

[May] 30, Thursday. We set out from Los Cerritos at a quarter to five in the morning and at ten came to the watering place of El Tecolote, having traveled for some seven leagues on a course east-southeastward and winding about a bit, now eastward, now southeastward. We paused to nap between ten o'clock in the morning until four o'clock in the afternoon at this spot, which is a narrow, rather long canyon where the Indians killed one of the governor's soldiers.[60] The whole route is a level one except for about a league that lies a bit before and beyond the heights at El Tecolote and it is rather broken and in a canyon, and therefore

---

[58] The latter parts of several paragraphs from this point onward are found only in the final text.
[59] A mission far to the east, in Ópa country.
[60] In the final text, "the enemies have committed some ravages."

more dangerous. Halfway along the way, at a half past seven, we passed by the watering place of El Carrizal,[61] where there are a number of crosses because of the slayings committed there by the enemy Piatos,[62] who killed Señor Michelena and his companions there.

We set out from El Tecolote at four o'clock in the afternoon, and at a quarter past nine halted along the way on a level place about a league after the meeting of the roads where the route going to the watering place called La Tortuga comes in, having traveled a long seven leagues on a course east-southeastward for the first league; two leagues eastward as far as the spot called Las Milpas where the La Tortuga road goes off (up to here it is a rather rough, broken route down inside a hollow that continues still farther on); and the remainder east-southeastward, varying, while winding about, to southeastward and further eastward until coming out from among heights.

The night and the day were quite cool.

[May] 31, Friday. We set out from the plain at a little before five o'clock in the morning and stopped at a little after half past eight, at the spot called *El Pozo de Crisanto*[63] where we paused to nap from a little after half past eight until half past three in the afternoon, having traveled five leagues east-southeastward, with a quarter point's variation to one side or the other at times. The route is a level one for almost the whole way. This spot, in a hollow, is an open well and rather a deep one so that it is necessary to water the animals by hand. It is so named because Crisanto, the governor of the Seris, discovered it at the time of the expedition[64] when those Indians were in rebellion and this was one of their retreats. Since the time we set out, we have already had the Cerro de Nacameri in view—known territory!

We set out from the spot at a half past three in the afternoon, and at a quarter past ten halted along the way about two leagues beyond El Zanjón,[65] as they call it, on a plain of very good grass, and quite open, having traveled some ten long leagues on an east-southeastward course though with portions varying southeastward and many of them more to eastward. At halting, the people in the rearguard reported that they had come upon footprints that they judged belonged to Apaches.[66] The fact is that this road from La Cieneguilla is strewn with crosses from the killings committed along it by the enemies, Seris, Piatos, and Apaches.[67]

---

[61]In the field text, El Carrizito (Carricito).
[62]Rebel O'odham (Pimas).
[63]Crisanto's Well.
[64]The Sonora expedition (1767–1770) planned and administered by Visitador General Gálvez. Chieftain Crisanto of the Seris was still alive at the time Font wrote this. The place is still called Pozo de Crisanto.
[65]"The Slough," the long drainage swale leading down toward modern Hermosillo.
[66]Anza tells much more of this incident, details of which possibly were withheld from Font.
[67]The field text mentions only Apaches.

Figure 39. San Miguel de Horcasitas, 1767. By José de Urrutia. (Detail.) Side profile of the presidio compound, and plan showing buildings including the governor's house and church. *Courtesy of the British Library, London, © British Library Board. All Rights Reserved.* MS *Additional 17662d.*

June 1, Saturday. We set out from the plain at five o'clock in the morning, and a little before eight reached the Presidio of San Miguel de Horcasitas, having traveled some four leagues course east-southeastward and with some veering and deviations even almost eastward. At the river ford we joined the route that we had taken on going. While setting out from the spot, we saw a cloud of dust on the road near the pass they call El Voladero, and given last night's news about the track of Apaches, we assumed it was from enemies waiting for us at the pass. And therefore, leaving the pack trains in the rear and putting the people in formation, our commander and some soldiers went in that direction with weapons in hand. At first we were scared, but as God willed, it was nothing, for they encountered some pack trains going toward La Cieneguilla.

Upon our arrival we were visited by the governor, don Francisco Antonio Crespo,[68] the parish priest, and the other gentlemen of San Miguel, and the governor took me and Captain don Juan to dine at his house.

Shortly before we entered San Miguel, Señor Anza told me to dismount at his house while he went to greet the governor, which I indeed did, but realized at once how little I was respected by Señor Anza's household. After the first pleasantries they lodged me with the purveyor don Mariano in a small room that had no window and was full of junk, since the house was very restricted in size. Considering the discomfort of the place, I told Señor Anza after the afternoon nap that if he approved I would go to the Monteagudo house, since his wife doña Catarina[69] had offered me the room that I stayed in the other time and had been lodged in during the days I spent here before beginning our journey. But that was not the reason why I was leaving his house. I would go there to dine and would remain at the presidio for as long as he liked. Since I was not required to go directly to my mission, I would stay there at his disposal as long as it pleased him. I was only planning on going to Ures whenever he decided I should, since I did not want to be a further burden upon him. Señor Anza agreed with everything. He did not even ask me out of politeness to remain for a few days so I could rest. Instead, he told me that there was no difficulty in connection with my wanting to go to Ures. I should leave whenever I wished and he would make sure that I was provided with animals. With that said, I decided to leave for Ures as soon as possible, and did so in the afternoon of the 5th and reached that mission at ten o'clock at night.

Also I proposed to him that Mass be sung tomorrow[70] to the Most Holy Trinity, in thanksgiving for our reaching here and having successfully concluded our journey. However, no one paid attention to me, on the grounds that the church is being repaired and Mass was being said in the ramada at the governor's house, which had been selected as a temporary church; and mainly because Señor Anza did not like the idea. My proposal was not accepted, it being claimed that it might annoy the governor—just as though it had not been sung at our going, etc., etc., and it was even said that I was trying to profit from Masses, etc.[71]

[June] 2, Sunday, The Most Holy Trinity.

At the appropriate hour, I went to Señor Anza's to greet him and to ask whether he had come to a decision regarding my suggestion from yesterday about singing Mass. He answered me that I could certainly go say Mass if I wished; that he himself was going later to hear the parish priest's Mass. Whereupon, I went off to say low Mass to the Most Holy Trinity—doing, for my own part, everything that I was able to do.

I remained at the presidio. At noon, I observed the latitude of this presidio here and found it very far from the observation I had made on September 21 of last year, when I found it, at that time, in latitude 29° 45', and continued to do so on the following days with a very slight difference in the result; so that I do not understand how there can be such a difference. I am somewhat satisfied with

---

[68]Civil-military governor of Sonora and Sinaloa.
[69]Wife of Manuel Bernardo de Monteagudo, a business agent for the missions (Kessel 1976: 74). See also under February 6 above.
[70]Sunday, June 2.
[71]The same accusation that infuriated Font just before the expedition.

the present observation, which is, by the tables of Jorge Juan, with no correction, 29° 28', and with correction, 29° 30'.[72] And thus I say: at the presidio and pueblo of San Miguel de Horcasitas, June 2, 1776: meridian altitude of the sun's lower limb: 82° 34'.

Immediately after I finished observing, I handed over to Señor Anza the key of the instrument that he had handed to me at Mission San Gabriel, as I said on January 6. When I gave him the key he said that if I wished to take the instrument with me to Ures in order to make observations there or elsewhere I could keep it. I answered him that, my primary responsibility during the expedition was to make observations but since he had not handed the instrument over to me from the start and that our journey was now over and I had completed my responsibilities, I did not want to take responsibility for the instrument now since he was not ceding it to me but only loaning it to me. So he kept the instrument and the key. The truth is that the viceroy ordered that the astronomical quadrant be delivered to me for my use in observing along the way. But Señor Anza wanted to appear as the originator of the observations, so he immediately made himself its owner and would not deliver it to me.

I realized this from the first time we met and talked, which was May 23 last year when he came to my mission. Since I knew that he was bringing this instrument to deliver it to me, I was hoping to see it as soon as he arrived. But seeing that the day was passing by without his broaching the subject, I asked him about the instrument and he replied that it was coming later with the pack mules. Thereupon I said to him, "But sir, I wanted to see it in order to be better informed as to what I am being charged to do by my Father Guardian in the viceroy's name, with regard to making observations during the journey." He answered me, "But you shall see it, Your Reverence, and see something indeed, for it is the best instrument that was to be found in Mexico City; it belonged to Count Thus-and-so,[73] who was so enamored of his quadrant that he would not give it up, and when the viceroy ordered him to do so the Count turned it over but said that he would not sell it, he was only giving it up on the condition that His Excellency should order a similar one to be brought from Paris or London." Thereupon he brought out an instruction booklet he was carrying for his own comprehension, and told me to keep it. He immediately summoned his purveyor and ordered him to have them show me the quadrant as soon as the pack beasts arrived, and said to him, "The Father wishes to see it, as he seems to know something about it and perhaps will help us observe upon the way."

The pack beasts did come up, along with the people of the expedition, on May 26. I saw the quadrant, and on the following day they took it away with the pack mules to San Miguel, where Señor Anza already was, but I still had the instruction booklet. However, within a few days he sent a request asking me for the booklet. He said that I should send it to him because he needed it to inform himself, so he ended up with that as well. Later I went to the Presidio of San Miguel to join Señor Anza and the people. On September 17 I told him that I wished to observe. He agreed, brought out the quadrant, and invited the parish priest and other gentlemen to watch to see how it was done. The observation, indeed, was taken, but was worth nothing since it was only a

---

[72] Very close this time, since the small town of San Miguel de Horcasitas is in 29° 29.4'. The earlier observation Font refers to here is recorded under September 29, above, as 29° 40', not 45'. In the final text, he reports that the two sets of observations were "the same... with a few minutes' difference," which seems overly favorable to him.

[73] So called because Font, at the time of writing, does not remember the name (see below). "*El Conde de Tales*" is similar to the phrase *fulano de tal*, a legal term for an unknown name, equivalent to "John Doe" in English.

matter of viewing the sun through the eyepiece and seeing what its color was, each of the invited gentlemen stepping up to take his turn making this inspection. And Señor Anza said, during the conversation, that he had been observing along the way up from Sinaloa, Culiacán, and other points. When I asked him what were the latitudes he had found these spots in, he answered that he did not have them at hand because he had recorded those observations. And it is to be noted that he neither had tables with him nor knew how to do the calculation! They asked him how much the quadrant must have cost and where he had gotten it. Señor Anza answered that it had cost nothing, that the quadrant belonged to the viceroy's secretary don Melchor Peremás[74] who, in order to see whether he might avoid surrendering it, had employed the stratagem that it did not belong to him but to Count Thus-and-so (or someone, I do not remember whom) who had loaned it to him, but that His Excellency ordered him to hand it over, whomever it belonged to. The subject of the quadrant came up at the pueblo of Santa Ana on the occasion of the observation I made there on October 7, and Señor Anza told his father-in-law don Francisco Serrano that the quadrant belonged to him, that he had bought it in Mexico City with his own money, and that it had cost him I don't know how much.

At Mission San Gabriel, because of my complaint to him that I recorded on January 6, when he handed me the quadrant's key he told me that the reason he had not given it to me at the start was that when they gave him the quadrant in Mexico City they ordered him to provide a receipt that it was handed over. Therefore, he was legally bound to answer to Mexico City for the instrument and return it when he came back. He said that I should give him a receipt if I wanted to take charge of it. He would hand it over to me if I took responsibility for its restitution and if I would account for it whenever it should be required of me. I refused to agree to this.

At San Diego, because of the observation I made there on February 2, the subject of the quadrant came up and at that time one of the Fathers there asked whether it was mine. I answered no, that Señor Anza had brought it from Mexico City. They kept on talking about how finely made it was and about its value, and one said it must be worth fifty pesos. Señor Anza replied, "I am a poor man, nevertheless I would very gladly give five hundred pesos for it if they would sell it to me." I understood this remark to mean that it would be hard to have it given or granted to me, as though to make me understand that the viceroy was not about to order that I be given such a valuable treasure. And henceforth he called it The Expedition's Quadrant.

Finally, at the end of the journey, he had the quadrant, and I understood that he wanted it in order to return it to Mexico City. Under this supposition, when later he went to Mexico City and passed through my mission of San José de Pimas, August 20 of this[75] year 1776, I asked him for the quadrant because I wished to observe the latitude of this mission that I am in charge of. Señor Anza answered that he did not have it with him. I then said to him that I found it strange that he did not have it. Given the fact that he was on his way to Mexico City, I had assumed that he was taking it back to return it, because of what he had told me at San Gabriel, which was that when they handed it over to him they ordered him to provide a receipt. He said that was true, but he did not have it along because he did not know to whom he was to hand it over. I then said

---

[74]*Sic*; Peramás, the head of the viceregal secretariat.

[75]"This year of 1776" is an indication that the author finished writing most of the final text long before signing it on May 11, 1777. In the field text, "today August 20" is mentioned in a marginal note containing references for treating this topic in the final version: "As soon as I finished observing I handed over the key to Señor Anza, etc. *Vide* [see], concerning the instrument and *de quoenera*, under December 1 of the general journal; and February 2, and what [happened] today August 20." In *de quoenera*, "de quo" might be Latin, "concerning what . . . ," but the phrase seems to contain at least a few letters in a private cipher.

to him, "You aren't unaware that you were to have handed it over to me, for you very well knew what my duty was when I went upon the expedition. I am not saying this, however, in order to have you surrender it to me, since the time for that has passed and I would not accept it now even if you did give it to me. But inasmuch as you did not hand it over to me, you obviously should know who its owner in Mexico City is who loaned it, so that you can return it to him." To this he responded that he had left it at San Miguel, because once the viceroy had appointed its use for this expedition, he realized that the instrument might perhaps serve His Majesty here in these lands better than in Mexico City, where there are other ones. In case there should be another expedition, its leader would find the quadrant there at that presidio without it being necessary to bring it from Mexico City, and without incurring a new expense for the king. He added that, as far as not having handed it over to me was concerned, he had acted according to what he had seen the Marqués de Rubí do. When he came surveying all the frontier presidios, the marqués had all of the instruments for observing in his charge—in this he spoke wrongly, for he did not have them in his charge but rather possessed them as his own—and only gave them to the specialists for them to use. I said to him, "Very well, sir, but with me you did not even do that, since you did not allow me the instrument so that I might make use of it and fulfill my duty."

Finally, Señor Anza departed for Mexico City. Because I had spoken the truth, I was not left in his good graces. I recently learned that Señor Anza left the quadrant at Monteagudo's intending to see whether he might keep it. If they did not ask him for it in Mexico City, he would take it as a sign that it had been given to him. He said that if they did ask him for it, he would answer with the excuse that he had no way of carrying it or that he had forgotten it, all in order to see whether this was the way he might devise keeping this treasure. I learned this, in so many words, from the mouth of Governor don Francisco Antonio Crespo.

I have recorded all of this here in order to keep in mind the inconsistency practiced by a person who prizes himself on being a man of honor and yet acts so basely over a bagatelle.[76]

That night there was entertainment at Señor Anza's,
with a dance that was organized to celebrate the joy at his arriving successfully. I was at the Monteagudo's when a message came for the family to leave for there. But since the message did not come for me nor had I been informed of any such thing, I refused to go even though Señor Monteagudo urged me to, and I stayed. Shortly thereafter the purveyor came looking for me, telling me I should go there, that Señor Anza would very much like me to go and attend the party, etc. I made up a few excuses for not going and even said that I did not really think that Señor Anza would be pleased if I attended. And finally, after all of his pleas, I said, "I would go, and would have attended the dance without the slightest hesitation, since those gathering there are all respectable people, because I too am happy that we have completed our journey so successfully. But considering that my proposal to sing Mass this morning was met with disdain, when I wished to say four words to the public in gratitude to God and the Most Holy Virgin for our successful travel to make clear to everyone the reason for our happiness, it does not seem right to me nor do I wish now to attend that pastime where the everyone is happy without first having publicly given thanks to God." With this the purveyor left and I remained alone at the Monteagudo home.

In order to avoid approving, by my presence, this society party, I did not see fit to attend the dance, since Señor Anza did not approve the church festival

---

[76]The quadrant apparently remained in Sonora, but designated for the use of missionaries, not soldiers, in possible further explorations. See the introduction.

that should have come first and that I had proposed to him, with a sung Mass to the Most Holy Trinity in thanksgiving for our successful arrival, such as I had wished for, in which I had thought to say something in order to publicly recognize the favors so clearly granted to us by God during so long a journey, through our chief patroness La Santísima Virgen María de Guadalupe. To her glory I had thought to combine the three Gospels, the one from yesterday and the two belonging to today, taking these three themes: the one from yesterday when we arrived, "Jesus, arising from the synagogue, entered into the house of Simon," *Surgens Jesus de synagoga introivit in domum Simonis* (Luke 4:38); the one from today's feast-day, "All power has been given to me in heaven and in earth," *Data est mihi omnis potestas in cælo et in terra* (Matthew 28:18); the one belonging to the present Sunday, "Be ye therefore merciful, even as your Father is merciful," *Estote ergo misericordes sicut et Pater vester misericors est* (Luke 6:36); and to say whatever God had given me to say concerning them.

And after succinctly recounting the journey, the incidents, and fortunate outcomes that took place during it, I meant to summarize it all by ending the discourse with a consideration in which I would reflect upon the time which we spent in the expedition, between September 29 and today June 2, inclusive, which amounted to 248 days, numbers of geometric progression through which Divine Grace revealed to us the benefits bestowed upon us during this period, multiplying them apace with the days and the marches. Of the latter there were 145, a figure in which are expressed our three patrons who favored us during them: with the number one representing for us our chief patroness, unique among all created beings, La Santísima Virgen María de Guadalupe; the number four, the prince San Miguel whom the Church calls Signifer or leader of souls,[77] which he guides with the banner of the Cross, which has four points just as his care stretches to the four corners of the earth because the redemption performed upon the Cross extends to everyone; and the number five, Our Father San Francisco on the strength of his five marvelous wounds.

And, finally, the whole amount of time consisted of eight months, three days, exceedingly mysterious numbers that conceal a riddle in them, namely that the Most Holy Trinity, signified by the number three, granted us our successful return upon its own festival day through the means of our Patroness the Virgin of Guadalupe, signified in the eight, which alludes to the number eight that was discovered among the figures and flowers of her clothing by the acuteness of the famous and notable painter Cabrera at Mexico City not many years ago. Several people have held several opinions about this, but I for the purpose of the present

---

[77]One of the traditional titles of San Miguel was "signifer," or "standard bearer," the one who leads the army and carries God's banner into battle with the devil.

argument wished to call her the Virgin of the Eight, for the eight months during which she so clearly showed us her favor as our chief Patroness.[78]

But since I was not able to say this in public, I record it here so that I will not forget it and may always be grateful to so merciful a Mother, the universal Patroness of America and, because she deigned to appear with the features and color of an Indian woman, even more our chief patroness for the advancement of spiritual conquests. And herewith I now set an end to this journal, at the end of this second day of June 1776.[79]

Our journey, going and returning, ended here at the Presidio of San Miguel de Horcasitas, from which the expedition had set out, and on June 5 I went on to the mission of Ures, where I drew up the journal that I sent to the Holy Colegio,[80] consisting of nine folders and containing the main parts of this journal, and also produced the map which accompanies it and which I sent; all of which I completed on June 23, 1776.[81]

Afterward I went to my own mission of San José de Pimas, reaching there July 24 of the same year. This mission was turned over to the Observant Fathers[82] of the Province of Jalisco on the following September 10, and I went to Ures, where I joined other Religious who were going to the Pimería Alta, and we reached Mission San Ignacio on the following October 14. Here it was decided that I should stay at the pueblo of Santa María Magdalena, a station belonging to this mission, to which I went on October 29. Here on the following November 16, renegade enemies, Piatos and Seris joined with some Apaches, attacked, destroyed, and burned that pueblo and I felt that I would die at their hands. But I escaped alive, and God delivered me by His infinite mercy from their ferocity. For that reason I withdrew to San Ignacio and to Imuris and finally to here, at Mission Tubutama where I arrived last December 31 in the early dawn before daylight. I have remained at this mission ever since, and, finding myself here without any particular duty or assignment, I have dedicated myself to fair-copying this journal, which is precisely the same journal, or draft, that I kept up along the way, different only in that that one consisted of only twenty folders while this one is larger because some of what is recorded there is set down here with greater length and clarity. As a conclusion to this journal, I declare and affirm that in everything I say herein I have attempted to tell the truth insofar as it lies within human trustworthiness and my own limited knowledge. I caution, also, that in relating affairs and incidents in which I name persons I do not do this to bring disrepute upon anyone nor to provide any basis for discontent. Rather, I have written them down solely for what light they may shed in similar circumstances either for myself or for anyone else who may come to read this journal, and so that we may understand that *nihil sub sole novum*, there is nothing new under the sun.[83] And with this caution, I end this journal here at Mission Tubutama, today, May 11, 1777.

---

[78] Miguel Cabrera (1695–1768), the "American Michelangelo" (Anonymous 2005: 93), is now perhaps best known for his portraits, including that of Sor Juana Inés de la Cruz. According to Cabrera himself, the possible significances of the figure eight that he detected in the traceries on the Virgin's tunic in the famous *lienzo* of Guadalupe were (1) that the picture first appeared during the octave (eight days) of the Most Pure Conception; (2) or else that it is the Eighth Wonder of the World (Cabrera 1756: 25).
[79] Signed here in the field text, "Fr. Pedro Font," with rubric.
[80] This refers to Font's short text, which of course reads "this journal" for "the journal." For the pertinent passage in Font's July 18, 1776, letter which accompanied the text, see Brown 2006: 94.
[81] Signed "Fr. Pedro Font," with rubric, in the short text, which ends here.
[82] Also Franciscans.
[83] Ecclesiastes 1:9.

APPENDIX

The Days' Marches
Distances and Bearings in the Three Texts and in Anza's Journal

This table provides a comparison of the variant courses which are given for each day's march in the descriptive entries of Font's texts and Commander Anza's journal. In the table's first column, the date and Font's serial number for the march are given (compare his general map, figs. 6–11), along with a modern identification for the approximate location of the place where the expedition stopped at the end of that march. In the other columns, the symbol ">" indicates that a distance or directional value was altered in the particular manuscript text, as shown. All numerical figures refer to distances in Mexican leagues, approximately 2.6 miles, 4.18 kilometers. Abbreviations for bearings refer to Font's 32-point compass. For instance, going clockwise, N=north, NbE=north by east (11¼°), NNE=north-northeast (22½°), NEbN=northeast by north (33¾°), NE=northeast (45°), NEbE=northeast by east (56¼°), ENE=east-northeast (67½°), EbN=east by north (78¾°), E=east (90°), and so on around. Distance figures in parentheses are those that are found only in the margins of the original texts.

Dates, 1775-1776	Field Text	Intermediate and Canceled Figures in the Draft of the Shortened Text	Final Text	Anza's Journal
29 Sept., march 1 Río San Miguel de Horcasitas	1 short	1 short NWv	1 short	—
30 Sept., march 2 Chupisonora	3>4 NW	some 4 NNW>NW	some 4 NNW	—
2 Oct., march 3 El Palmarito	4>5 NW	5 NNW>NbW	5 NNW	—
3 Oct., march 4 (?)	5>6 NW	6 NNW>NWbN> NbW >NNW	6 NNW	—
4 Oct., march 5 Cerros los Puertos	6 NW	some 6 long NNW> NWbN>NbW> NW> NNW	some 6 long NNW	—
5 Oct., march 6 Estación Llano	6>7 NW	some 7 long NNW	[same]	—
6 Oct., march 7 Santa Ana Viejo	4>5 NNW	5 long N>NNW	5 NNW	—
8 Oct., march 8 Magdalena de Kino	4>6 NNE	some 4 NEbE	some 6 NEbE	—
9 Oct., march 9 San Ignacio	2 NNE	2 NEbE	[same]	—
11 Oct., march 10 Imuris	3>4 NNE	3 NNE	4 NNE	—

APPENDIX 409

12 Oct., march 11 Arroyo Bambuto	4 N	4 NNW	[same]	—
13 Oct., march 12 Cibuta	4 N	[same]	[same]	—
14 Oct., march 13 Nogales, Ariz.	8 N with some veering NW	9 N, some veering NW [stricken]	8 long, about 4 NW and 4 NNW	—
15 Oct., march 14 Tumacácori	7 N	some 7 N	some 8 N	—
16 Oct.	2 [going to and returning from Tubac]	—	—	—
23 Oct., march 15 S end Canoa Ranch/near Arivaca Junction	5 NNE	some 5 NNE	5 NNW	4 N with slight deviations NE
24 Oct., march 16 Green Valley/ Sahuarita	3 NNE	[same]	3 NNW	about 4, generally N
25 Oct., march 17 San Xavier del Bac	6 NNE>NEbN	6 long, NbE	6 long, NbW	about 5, N except 1 NNW [at end]
26 Oct., march 18 N side Tucson	4 N	4 very long; almost N	[same]	5; 4 NNW, 1 [...]
27 Oct., march 19 Rillito	5 NNW then NW	5: about 2 NNW then NW	[same]	5 NNW and some deviations NW
28 Oct., march 20 north Avra Valley (Pinal Airpark)	6 WNW with some veering W	6 long, WNW with some deflection W	6 long, WNW, at times almost W	[...]: WNW 3 to lakes; NW to others

410 WITH ANZA TO CALIFORNIA, 1775–1776

Dates, 1775–1776	Field Text	Intermediate and Canceled Figures in the Draft of the Shortened Text	Final Text	Anza's Journal
29 Oct., march 21 Picacho Peak	5 NW and afterward NNW	some 5, about 2 NW, the rest NNW	[same]	5, mostly NW with only small deviations NNW
30 Oct., march 22 NE of Sacaton Mountains	12: NW then NNW, finally N	some 12: about 6 NW, 3 NE [sic], some 3 almost N	some 12: about 6 NW, 3 NNW, some 3 almost N	2 NW then 3 N to Gila
31 Oct. to Casa Grande and return	6 [going to Moctezuma's Big House and returning]	—	—	going 3 to a building of the ancient Indians, [and back]
1 Nov., march 23 West of Sacaton/Sweetwater	4 ENE(?) > WNW	[same]	[same]	4 generally WNW
2 Nov., march 24 North of Sacaton Butte	(3>4): 3 WNW with some veerings E	some 4 WNW	some 4 WbN	2 generally WNW and some small bendings W
3 Nov., march 25 Pima Butte	2 WNW	2 long, almost NW	2, almost NW	about 2, WNW
7 Nov., march 26 Mobile	6: a bit over 1 SW, about 2 WSW, the remainder W	some 6: about 2 SW, 1 W, the rest W	some 6: about 1 SW, 2 WSW, the rest W	7: 2 SW, 5 W and WSW
8 Nov., march 27 Sil Murk (Tesota)	8(?)>9: about 2 WSW; about 1 W in a pass; WSW	some 9: 2 WSW; 1 W; WSW with some deflection W	[same]	7: about 2 WSW; about 1 across pass; 4 WSW

APPENDIX   411

11 Nov., march 28 Gila Bend Indian Reservation	2: 1½ W	some 2 short W	[same]	1½ WSW
12 Nov., march 29 Painted Rock Dam	5 WNW	5 WbN	[same]	4 WSW to hills
13 Nov., march 30 Across from Oatman Flat	4 W	some 4 WbS	[same]	4: 1 SW; down to a hollow; 3 turning W and also SW
14 Nov., march 31 Agua Caliente	4 WSW	[same]	[same]	4: about 1 SW; 3 SW with few changes, and W
16 Nov., march 32 Near Kofa siding	9 WSW with some veerings W	9 WSW	[same]	7 SW and some veerings W
17 Nov., march 33 Texas Hill	about 2 WSW	some 2 WSW	[same]	about 1½ SW
18 Nov., march 34 Sears Point (N end Mohawk Mountains)	4 SW with a few veerings either way	some 4 SW	[same]	3: 1½ SW, recrossing the Gila; 1½ WSW
22 Nov., march 35 Antelope Hill	6 WSW with a few veerings SW	some 6 long SW> WSW, with some deviations S	some 6 long SW	5 WSW
25 Nov., march 36 W of Wellton	(4>5): 4 WSW> SWbW	4 long WbS>WbN	some 5 WbN	4 WSW to the Salt lake
26 Nov., march 37 Dome Valley	4 W with a bit of, or else mostly, veering WNW	some 4 WNW	some 4 NW	about 4 WSW and some bendings W, to El Cajón hills

Dates, 1775–1776	Field Text	Intermediate and Canceled Figures in the Draft of the Shortened Text	Final Text	Anza's Journal
27 Nov., march 38 between the Gila and Laguna Mountains	2 W>NW	some 2 NW	some 2 WNW	3 W with some bendings WNW
28 Nov., march 39 Colorado River	5 WSW with some turns	some 5 WbS	[same]	4 WSW, across the confluence of the rivers
30 Nov., march 40 The Island	1 [across river]	about 1 short N	[same]	about ¼ up the river, then across
3 Dec., march 41 Yuma	1 short, downriver	around about 1 N or [NE? illegible: . . . E]	around about 1 WbS	a little under ½ along the river
4 Dec., march 42 Cuervos (Ciudad Morelos) BC (?)	5 WSW	some 5 WbS with a number of twists and turns	some 5 WbS	4½ W with a good many deviations
5 Dec., march 43 Tabasco (?)	some 4 SW with turns WSW, S, SSE andc.	some 4 SW with no few twistings about	some 4 SW with many twistings about	3 in all directions between W and S, down the river
6 Dec., march 44 Jiquilpan (?)	about 5, mostly SW and SSW turning often between S and W	some 5 SW but twisting about almost anywhere between S and W	[same]	4 in directions between W and S along the river plain
9 Dec., march 45 Guanajuato/ Cuernavaca (?)	7 W>WNW	some 7 WNW	[same]	5 W

10 Dec., march 46 Progreso (?) Estrella/Santa Isabel (?)	7 WNW	some 7 WNW	[same]	about 5 W and some slight bends WNW
11 Dec., march 47 Yuha Well (CA)	13>(14)>15 WNW, deviating as far as WSW a little before stopping	some 14: about 10 WNW; the rest a little W and mostly WSW	[same]	10 W and some bends WNW
12 Dec., march 48 Coyote Wash	3 N with an occasional quarter-point bend to one side or the other	3 N	[same]	about 4 NNW with some bendings N
13 Dec., march 49 Harper's Well, San Felipe/ Carrizo Creeks	7 NNW and mostly almost N	some 7 long NNW with some deviation N	[same]	about 5½ NNW; then 1½ N
18 Dec., march 50 Ocotillo Wells	4 WbN	[same]	[same]	3½ W with some bends WNW
19 Dec., march 51 Borrego Spring	5 short WNW	some 5 WbN	[same]	4 W with repeated bends WNW
20 Dec., march 52 Coyote Creek, Borrego Valley	4 NW	some 4 NW	some 4 NWbW	4 WNW: 3 of them with some dune
23 Dec., march 53 Lower Willows, Collins Valley	a bit over 1 NW with occasional turning	1 long NWbW	[same]	1½ NW and WNW
24 Dec., march 54 Fig Tree Spring, Coyote Canyon	a bit over 3> about some 4 WNW	some 4 short WNW	[same]	3 NW with some bendings WNW in the rockiest part

Dates, 1775–1776	Field Text	Intermediate and Canceled Figures in the Draft of the Shortened Text	Final Text	Anza's Journal
26 Dec., march 55 E end of Terwilliger Valley	about 3 or a bit more NW then changing between N and W. [Again:] NW; WNW at a little over a league; W, turning until N and then NNW from the summit; NW	some 3 long NW deviating almost to N, twisting about on the grade	some 3 long NNW, twisting about on the grade until topping the mountain, a stretch that must be about a league	about 2½: about ¾ WNW through hollow; leaving it where it narrowed and up a little grade followed by 2 smaller ones to the puerto o abra of San Carlos
27 Dec., march 56 head of Bautista Creek Canyon	(6): 5>6 NW changing to WNW after 3 leagues	some 6: about 3 NW, the remainder WNW	[same]	(5): 2½ WNW, up at once through a narrow clump of rocks and out to level land, till passing Laguna del Príncipe; 2½ more
29 Dec., march 57 San Jacinto	a good 7 WNW with some veerings to NW	a long 7 NWbW with some veering to N twisting about	[same]	6, most often W to WNW, down to Río San José
30 Dec., march 58 San Jacinto Valley by Mount Rudolph	a long 5 WNW	a long 5 WNW	5 WNW	a little over 4 WNW
31 Dec., march 59 Riverside	8 W with an occasional veer to WNW	some 8 WNW, occasional short veer to W	[same]	(7): 1 W going left around heights; 6 WNW
1 Jan. Pedley	[forded the Río Santa Ana]	[same]	[same]	[same]
2 Jan., march 60 San Antonio Canyon Creek	a long 6 W	6 WNW with an occasional short veer to W	6 WNW	6 WNW across flat land with a great deal of grass

APPENDIX 415

3 Jan., march 61 Baldwin Park/ Irwindale	6 W	some 6: WNW about 2 leagues, the rest W with an occasional short deviation S	some 6 WNW	5 W with some bendings WSW, to across the San Gabriel Mission river
4 Jan., march 62 San Gabriel	2 W	some 2 W trending a bit NW	some 2 WSW trending a bit W	2 W
7 Jan., march 63 Anaheim, S side	(12>10): 12 SE with some variation. [Respecified under 8 Jan.:] 6 SE; about 4 ESE; 1 E; 1 ENE to seek the river ford	some 10 long: 8 SE deviating at times S and SSE; the last 2 E a bit and mostly almost N to river ford and across	some 10 to long: 5 SE; 3 ESE; the last 2 almost E with an occasional veer NE	6 starting toward San Diego, estimated as lying SE to ESE 40 leagues from San Gabriel
8 Jan., march 64 San Juan River/ Cañada Gobernadora	(15>14); about 15 ESE with some variation: at about 7, Los Ojitos; 4 to Arroyo el Trabuco. [Again:] ESE to about halfway of the march; E to Arroyo el Trabuco; SE	some 15 long: about 5 ESE; about 4 SE (inexact) to Arroyo el Trabuco; the remaining 5 [sic] SE with an occasional short veer S	some 14; about 5 ESE to Los Ojitos; 4 SE to El Trabuco; the rest SEbS	11
9 Jan., march 65 San Luis Rey	(15>14); 15 ESE varying at times anywhere between E and S: 8 to Las Flores, 11>9 to Río San Juan Capistrano	some 14 long; about 3 ESE; 3 EbS as well as SE; 2 SbE; the remaining 4 [sic] SE	some 14, very changeable, amounting I think to half ESE and half SE: 7 to Las Flores, 2; then to Río San Juan Capistrano	11 to Arroyo San Juan Capistrano
10 Jan., march 66 Sorrento	some 14 SE with a number of veers to ESE and much more to S: at about 8>6 Los Batequitos; at 2 more San Alejos	some 12 long; about 3 SE and with some trend E; about 2 SSE; about 4 S (inexact); the remaining 3 SSE and almost SE	some 12 on a varied course: about 3 SE; some 2 SSE; about 4 S (inexact); the rest SSE and at the end almost SE	9

Dates, 1775–1776	Field Text	Intermediate and Canceled Figures in the Draft of the Shortened Text	Final Text	Anza's Journal
11 Jan., march 67 San Diego Old Town	4 SE	4: 2 almost SSE deviating S; 2 SE, mostly along the Puerto Anegado	4 long: 2 almost SSE deviating S; 2 SE and SSE mostly along the Puerto Anegado	3
9 Feb., march 68 Agua Hedionda Creek	(14 >13): about 14, W> N "and NNE"> NW varying to NNE	some 13 by the same route and courses as on coming, mainly NW	[same]	to Agua Hedionda
10 Feb., march 69 Cristianitos Canyon	18 NW with a number of veers to W and other directions	some 16, main course NW with variations as on coming	[same; "variations as on coming"]	to La Quema
11 Feb., march 70 Anaheim, S side	16 NW with a number of turns	some 15, course varying as on coming, mainly NW	[same]	to Río Santa Ana
12 Feb., march 71 San Gabriel	12 NW with veers WNW etc.	some 10, courses as on coming and following the same route, the main course being NW	[same; "and following the main NW course"]	to San Gabriel mission
21 Feb., march 72 Hollywood, at the S end of Cahuenga Pass	5 WNW with a few veers to one side or another	some 6: the first 2 W with veers to one side or another, and the remaining 4 WNW	6: 2 W with an occasional veer to one side or another, and the rest WNW	a little over 1 SW; 1 SW crossing Río Porciúncula; then 3
22 Feb., march 73 Liberty Canyon	9 (>10) W with a few veers. In the range [at end of march], course veers as far as to SW	some 10: about 7 W, the remaining 3 ["3" stricken] WSW, and a bit SW, inexact	some 10: about 7 WbN ["bN" added], and the remainder WSW	7 usually W

APPENDIX 417

23 Feb, march 74 El Río, W side	14 (>15) W with a good many veers S and as far [around] as NNW. At a little over 1, El Triunfo; at a little over 8, the steep grade	some 15 long; at outset WSW, a bit S and SW for about 3, then W with a few veers to one side or the other for some 5; about ½ NE>almost N to the steep grade; after the grade some 6 W	some 15; 3 WSW, 5 W, 1 NW to the steep grade; finally, after the grade some 6 W to the river	[9]: 1 SW; then, rising gradually for three hours, to a dangerous descent; 5 NW
24 Feb, march 75 El Rincón	7 (>9) W	some 8 long; 3 W to seashore . . . , the remaining 5>6>5 WNW>WbN with some slight deviation W at the three points along the coast	some 9; 3 W to seashore . . . , the remainder WbN with some slight deviation W at the points along the coast, of which there are several	[6]: 2 W to the first village of Channel; 4 W save for slight bends it makes N
25 Feb, march 76 Goleta	(7>10>9) 7 W with very slight veering N: at a little over 1, San Buenaventura . . . ; at 2 more, a village, and at 1 further, La Laguna	some 9: the first 6 W with some small deviation SW on getting around three points, and a much greater one NW, which may be called WbN; 3 mostly a bit W; about 1 short SW	some 9: about 6 WbN, 2 NW, and at the last 1 short SW to get around some inlets near there. At 2, San Buenaventura; at another 1, a village, and at 1 more, La Laguna	7 W
26 Feb, march 77 Refugio Beach State Park, W side	(7>9>10): a bit over 7: about 1 S to Mescaltitán . . . ; 3 more W to San Pedro y San Pablo; a little over 2 to the Ranchería Nueva . . . ; stopped shortly afterward	some 10 short along the shore: about 1 SW, 2 WSW around Mescaltitán inlets, the remaining 7 WbN>WNW with a little deviation W>WbN	some 10 [figure altered] mostly along the shore: about 1 SW, 2 WSW around the Mescaltitán inlets [= 2 W to San Pedro y San Pablo]; WNW, inexact, or with a little deviation W	around 1½ WSW down to and past Mexcaltitán villages; 6½ mostly W
27 Feb, march 78 Cañada del Cojo (El Cojo Viejo)	8 W with a little veering WSW	some 10 WbN and with a little deviation and veerings WSW getting around the points	some 10 [altered from another figure] WNW, inexact or with deviation W	8 W

Dates, 1775–1776	Field Text	Intermediate and Canceled Figures in the Draft of the Shortened Text	Final Text	Anza's Journal
28 Feb, march 79 Santa Ynez River, S side	(10>12): 6 NW altering to WNW and finally W until rounding Point or Cape La Concepción; N 4; a bit over 3; 2	some 12 short: about 1 NW, about 2 N and a bit NNE, about 2 NW and about a bit over 1 W; some 2 N; 2 (N?>); 2 (?>) 2 NW	some 12: about 1 NW, 2 NNW, 2 NW and 2 WNW until rounding Punta Concepción; about 1 N; 2 NNW; 2 NW; 3; 2	[9]: 4½ W with short bends WNW to last village, called Los Pedernales and end of the Channel; 5 NW
29 Feb, march 80 Bass Lake, N side San Antonio Creek, Vandenberg Air Force Base	(3>4): only a little over 3 N with a little veering NE	some 4 short, N and a very slight deflection NE	some 4, N and with a little deflection NE	about 3 NW
1 Mar, march 81 Price Canyon/ Harris (Cuevitas) Creek, N of Pismo Beach	(10>11>13). 10, varying from NE to W: some 3; N a bit over 1; some 3 NW; about 1 W; some 2	some 13 long; about 3 NE, 1 NNE, 2 N, 2 NNW, 2 NW along the shore, and 2 NNW	some 13: about 3 NE, 1 NNE, 2 N, 2 NNW, 3 NW along the shore, and 2 NNW	about 3 NE and some bendings N to Laguna Larga; 2 N; about 2½ NW, WNW and W to seashore; about 1½ N
2 Mar, march 82 San Luis Obispo	(3>4). 3: 1 N and 2 NW	some 4: about 1 N and 3 NE, deviating a little W a little before arriving	some 4: about 1 N; NNW and NW, deviating a bit W a little before arriving	[3]: 1 NE; 1 N; 1 slowly around to NW
4 Mar, march 83 Atascadero (Asunción stop on the railroad)	10, beginning NE ending WNW: about 1 NE; N about 5, then around slowly to WNW	10: 1 long NE; some 4 N; 1 NNW; 2 NW; 2 W	some 10: about 1 NE; 4 N; 1 NNW; 2 NW; 2 WNW	[7]: about 1½ NE; 1½ or a bit more N to cross Río Santa Margarita; down it NW to WNW, to La Asunción

APPENDIX 419

5 Mar., march 84 San Antonio Reservoir	10: 3 N; about 5 NW with some turns WNW; 2 WNW	some 10: 3 almost N; 5 NW; 2 WNW	some 10: about 3 almost N; 5 NW; 2 WNW	8: 3 N with some bendings NW; 4 NW and WNW; 1 W
6 Mar., march 85 Mission San Antonio	10 long, WNW with variation: a very short way S; W about 4; WNW	10 long: 4 W; 2 NW; 2 almost N; 2 NW and a bit WNW	10 long: some 4 W and WNW; 2 NW; 2 almost N; 2 NW and a bit WNW	8: about ½ WSW, up river flat slowly turning from WSW to NW
8 Mar., march 86 SE of Greenfield	some 7>some 9: about 2 NE, then N and on about 3; NW	some 9: about 2 NE; 3 N and a bit NNW; 4 NW	some 9: about 2 NE; 3 N and a bit NNW; the rest NW	[7]: 3 NE and also N to El Roble Caído; 4 NW
9 Mar., march 87 W side of the Salinas by Mount Toro	10 WNW	10: about 6 NWbW; 4 WNW	10: about 6 NWbW; WNW	about 8 WNW
10 Mar., march 88 Monterey	10: 4 WNW, the rest W	some 10: 8 WNW; 2 W (inexact)	[same]	7: 3 WNW along river; then W and SW
11 Mar., march 89 Mission San Carlos Borromeo (Carmel)	1	1 long SWbS	[same]	[1, to the mission]
22 Mar., march 90 Monterey	2, including going about ½ beyond harbor and returning	1 NW [sic]	1 NEbN: 2 leagues in all, ½ beyond harbor and returning	[to the presidio]
23 Mar., march 91 Gavilán Creek at the foot of the Sugarloaf, near Lagunita School	8 long: NE and a bit NNE; at about 4 across river, course varying a quarter-point N; NE with a short veer	some 8 long; a bit over 1 E; 3 NE with a bit of deviation N; about 3 NE and 1 NNE	[same]	7: about ½ E; 4 ENE to Río de Monterrey crossing; about 3 NE and NNE

Dates, 1775–1776	Field Text	Intermediate and Canceled Figures in the Draft of the Shortened Text	Final Text	Anza's Journal
24 Mar., march 92 Llagas Creek a half mile W of the El Camino Real	some 12, a very varied course: uphill at 1, E; about 1 N; NE and NNE into Valle San Pascual and across Río Pájaro; a short way to Valle San Bernardino; about 3 NNW; 2 NW; 2	some 12: 2 NE and a bit E on topping the range; 1 N; 2 NE with a little trending N; 1 NNW; 1 almost NW; 3 NNW; 3 NW with some slight deflection W before stopping	some 12: 2 NE and a bit E on topping the range; 1 N; 2 NE with a little trending N across Valle San Pascual and Río Pájaro; 1 almost N; 3 NNW through Valle San Bernardino; 3 NW	8: NE up hollow and ravines, ending in a precipitous descent to Arroyo San Benito; at 2 leagues turned NNW with sizeable bendings to NW until 6 further, to San Bernardino alias Las Llagas
25 Mar., march 93 Los Altos Hills, W side of Stevens Creek Blvd., due W of Cupertino	some 12: about 2 NW, then over small hills; about 1 NW with some deviation W and over more small hills, meeting Indians; probably a bit over 2 WNW and over a gap; a bit over 4 WNW; about 2 W	some 12: 3 NW; 2 NWbW; 5 WNW; 2 W (inexact) with a little deflection NW	some 12: 3 NW; 2 NWbW; 5 WNW; 2 WbN	8: NW a little over 3 at edge of low hills on left, then onto white- and live-oak plain and after a short distance [under 1½] met Indians; 3½ WNW, then W, drawing close to hills on left, to Arroyo San José Cupertino
26 Mar., march 94 Ralston Creek/ Burlingame Creek, Burlingame	12: a bit over 1 NW with occasional veer NNW; then NW; about 3 WNW to Arroyo San Francisco; about 3 NW; some 5 WNW to Arroyo San Mateo; on to stop.	some 12 long; 1 N; 1 NNW; 3 WNW till crossing Arroyo San Francisco; 3 NW; 3 WNW [apparently 1 short is to be added after crossing Arroyo San Mateo]	some 12: 1 NW; 1 NNW; some 4 WNW till across Arroyo San Francisco; 3 NWbW; 3 WNW [apparently then 1 short after crossing Arroyo San Mateo]	8: a little under 4 NW to Arroyo San Francisco, then generally WNW with only small veerings NW to about ½ beyond Arroyo San Mateo

APPENDIX 421

27 Mar., march 95 Mountain Lake, Presidio of San Francisco	some 6: 3 NW; 3 N; some 3 long exploring around harbor mouth	some 6: 3 NW; 3 NNW and even almost N	[same]; exploring around harbor mouth, some 3	4, most commonly NW; then exploring W and S around harbor mouth
28 Mar., beyond the Marina and return to camp	some 2 long with the scouting party		some 2	
29 Mar., march 96 San Mateo	about 15: E a bit over 1; a bit over 1 SE; onward a short way; about 3 more, around to almost WNW; SE; turned off SW, about 1 with a change of course; SE evidently a bit over 3 and met a bear; about 1 to stream; over 2 ESE; N about 2	some 14: About 1 E, 1 ESE and 1 SE; on a little; about 3 further, S, SW and WNW; a little way SE; about 1 short, SW and a bit S; [deleted: at about 4 is Arroyo San Mateo] some 4 short through hollow; about 1 before Arroyo San Mateo, met a bear; some 2 ESE; some 2 N	some 15 (a straight route from the harbor must only be 6): about 1 E; 1 ESE; 1 SE; onward a little; about 3 S, SW and W at the end; a little way SE; about 1 short SW and a bit S; some 4 short and crossed Arroyo San Mateo (about 1 before it, met a bear); 2 ESE; some 2 nearly N	[exploring to the southeast and south, ending at Arroyo de San Mateo]
30 Mar., march 97 E side of the Guadalupe River, just S of the Milpitas-Alviso Road/North First Street intersection	(10-12): some 10, actually a bit over 11 with turns to ford the river (courses inexact). About 3 ESE; about 2 slanting SE a bit; a bit over 2 E; onward a bit over 2 NE and then NNE to river; about ½ almost W searching for a ford; back E; about ¼ NE with small difference	some 12, a varying course: some 3 ESE and 3 more SE; some 3 E; 1 NE; 1 NNE; 1 NE beginning to go around the head of the harbor, finally winding about E to W to ford the Río Guadalupe and to camp	some 12, a varying course: 6 on the former route; departing from the route, some 3 E; 3 NE beginning to go around the head of the harbor . . . [the rest the same]	about 6½: about 3½ ESE; about 1 ENE, leaving the [old] route for a new way and finding three abundant springs flowing into the inlet; at ½ more, another spring with about 100 heathens dwelling there; at about another 1½ a large stream or moderate river, christened Guadalupe, with a hard to locate ford

Dates, 1775–1776	Field Text	Intermediate and Canceled Figures in the Draft of the Shortened Text	Final Text	Anza's Journal
31 Mar., march 98 San Lorenzo	(14>10): about 1 N and soon NNW, turning back; over a league in all directions, an estimated 3, E, NE and a bit N; about 2 NNW; NW until halt. At about 6, a stream and Indians; a bit over 2 NNW; then about 1 NW	some 12, a varied course: about 1 short NNW; 1 E, 1 NE, 1 almost N, twisting about; 2 NNW and [some 6>] another 2 NW	some 10 to long, a varied course: about 1 short NNW; about 3 varying ENE and NE, twisting about; some 3 NNW and 3 more NW. About halfway, a stream and Indians; a bit over 2, then 1	about 7: about 1 NNW; back 1 to mouth of a stream the soldiers believe is the Coyote; N about 2 to previously traveled route, the first hollow on it having a good many trees and plenty of water; NW past 4 streams
1 Apr., march 99 Rodeo	about 15; about 2 NW; about 2 WNW to opposite a wood of white and live oaks; about 2 (NE>)NW and WNW; around 1 NW; then to some hills and on about 2, and a little further to a stream and village; about 3, NW for a little and then NNW to a village; about 3, N though occasionally NE, and a bit E	some 15; (2 almost NW, 2 WNW with a bit of veering NW to a hill opposite a rather large grove of white oaks....)>about 9 almost WNW; 1 NW and 1 WNW; some 3 WbN; some 3 WNW> NWbW across two streams; some 2, mostly a little N; (a good distance)> 1 ENE>NE and a bit E	some 14: about 9 WNW, then some 3 NW and NWbW through hills... and the remainder NW and NNW and a bit N, twisting about through the same hills	about 10: about 2½ NW to opposite large patch of redwoods; about ½ to opposite the harbor mouth; about ½ NNE; 2 leagues of plains; then hills and a deep-down stream with a village; N, NE etc. to another village; 1 along hills and coast to camp at a hollow with standing water and very little wood

APPENDIX

2 Apr., march 100 on Walnut Creek near Concord (Pacheco)	about some 7 long: a little N and then NE, to village…; about 1 long to mouth. Later, a bit over 1 upriver, then ESE about 1. A very little NE, then E onto plain and soon ESE and finally S: it must have been 3, mostly ESE	some 7 ["long" stricken and reentered]: a short way, to a village…, about 1 long N and NE to water… Later, 6: 1 ESE on hills and 1 ESE in hollow…, about ½ NE, some 3 ESE	some 7 long: a short way, to a village…, about 1 long N and NE to water. Later, 6: 2 E on hills, 1 ESE up through hollow…; about ½ NE, some 3 ESE	5: less than ¼ E over hills to village; on through higher, heaped-up hills to end of 1 and to meeting of river and Inlet; about 1 E and ENE, and 1 ESE and SE, all over high hills; at [a total of] 2 along the river, about 2 SE with some deviations S, to avoid marshes
3 Apr., march 101 San Joaquín River W of the south approach to Antioch Bridge	about 10: 3 ENE; about 1 NE through hollow to hilltop…, a total of some 4; then toward a low range, about 4 EbN to a village…; ESE a bit over 1 to a very bare hill…; about 1 NE; W about ¼	some 10 long: some 3 ENE, about 1 NE through hollow to a hilltop…; then toward a low range, some 4 EbN to a village…; ESE about 1 long to a bare hill…; about 1 NE; W about ¼	some 10 long: some 3 NE…, [the rest the same]	about 6: about 1 across grassy plain; ½ NE over hills; (marshes blocked the way over to the river); 2½ ENE with some slight bendings E; about 1 ENE over the plain to a high hill at its end…; ½ NE

Dates, 1775–1776	Field Text	Intermediate and Canceled Figures in the Draft of the Shortened Text	Final Text	Anza's Journal
4 Apr, march 102 E of Livermore, S of Tesla Road, at S end of Greenville Road	some 17>15: E . . . ; some 3 ESE, after 2 the wood of small oaks on right continuing on as white oaks; about 1 ENE with a bit of veering NE; ESE, sometimes SE and also S, on to over 4, E to S, ESE and SE; S, and then shortly about 3 E.; 1 SSW, 1 to hills; a bit over 2 SSW with some veers to one side or the other; still SSW to hills with wood by a hollow with water	some 17, so varied that it went against our first purpose: a little E; some 2 ESE with an oak grove on right that keeps on as white oaks on about six leagues; about 1 NE, then twisting S, SE and ESE, SSE, S; onward some 4, 3 roughly SSE; some 3 further, 1 S, the other 3 almost E; about 1 S to hills, then to summit and about 2 SW; some 2 SSW through other hills	some 15 long, so varied that it went against our first purpose: a little E; some 3 ESE with an oak grove on right that keeps on about six leagues; about 1 NE, then twisting SE, ESE, S, SSE. Went thus for over 3, roughly SE; some 3 further, a little S and most of it nearly E, and ESE. [The rest the same as the short version]	12½: about 5 while being driven to E and SE by water and bogs; turned to go about 1½ straight SSW across a barren plain; another 1½ over a hill range . . . and down to other hills whence the Santa Angela de Fulgino hollow rises; then another 1½, following along those [hills] to spend the night at the first water and wood found upon them
5 Apr, march 103 S end of the San Antonio Valley	(13>15 [or] 15>13), some 14>13; about 3 ESE with a bit of veering; about 1 short, in no direction or all; about 2 SE; about 2 up narrow hollow SE and SSE to top; about 1 SE down with a number of turnings and climbs; more than [sic] 4 SSW	some 14, although very varying: some 3 SE; about 1 N, E, S, in all directions or none, to top of mountain; about 2 S and with a good many veers SE; about 2 SSE to top of gap; about 1 S down with many turnings; some 5 almost SSW and mostly SbW	some 13, S, although varying; some 3 SE; about 1 N, E, S, in all directions or none; about 2 S and with a good many veers SE; about 2 SSE to top of gap; about 1 S down with many turnings; some 4 S, and SSW a little before halting	7: started out over hills and began crossing the range, climbing, 2 E; 1 ESE and also SE; down to a hollow running SE, 1½ till it narrowed; 1 SE up wooded hills; down to small flats about 12 [sic; although the same figure "12" is in both copies, it must be a miscopying of either "2" or "4"] leagues long and having ponded water at their end.

APPENDIX 425

6 Apr., march 104 Coyote Creek, Henry W. Coe State Park, intersection of Cañada and Gilroy Hot Springs roads,	some 12>10, mainly SSE with a bit SE, and some veering E and W: SE a little; about 3 SSE down canyon with some slight veers; 3>2 on down the canyon; about 2 SSE over to a canyon (apparently the same); in it about 4	some 10, mainly S though varying a bit: about 3 SSW [sic] >SSE into a narrow very deep hollow; some 2 SSW; 2 SSW [sic] >SSE, twisting about to climb hills and down again to the hollow; some 3 SSW [sic]> SSE up and down	7: about 2 SSE over hills into hollow, stopped by a waterfall; about 1 to get out; about 1 in the hollow again; 3 SSE, very difficult terrain and out to another hollow
7 Apr., march 105 Marina, W side of the Salinas at the Blanco Road	(16>15). A good 16. About 2 SSE with a little veering S; a bit over 3 SSE; about 1 S across the Arroyo Pájaro and SW across valle San Pascual with some S trend at its end; at 2, Arroyo San Benito; S up and then a little W down; SW, La Natividad at about 3; 4 mainly SSW and then SW and across river	some 15. The first 2 S, and out of the mountains; across valley some 2 long, SSW, into low hills close to the Río Pájaro and thence on route followed on way up, on the corresponding courses	12: 1½ SSE in hollow to low hills; ½ to San Pascual valley; S 2½ across it, to route that was followed on coming; S 1½ on it till fording the Río Pájaro; 1 SW till crossing Arroyo San Benito; 1 up its high grade; apparently 2 SW past ravines and a hollow; 3 WSW and SW over Río Monterrey plain and across river
8 Apr., march 106 Mission San Carlos Borromeo (Carmel)	5, SW and a bit SSW at the end, then W to harbor and a short stretch E to presidio; 1 SW	5, on same courses as on going; 4 to presidio and 1 to mission	4: 3½ WSW on former route; ½ W, to Monterrey presidio
13 Apr., march 107 Monterey	1 long, NWbN	1 to the presidio	[same]	[to the presidio]

Dates, 1775–1776	Field Text	Intermediate and Canceled Figures in the Draft of the Shortened Text	Final Text	Anza's Journal
14 Apr., march 108 Salinas River near Spreckels	some 6, E a little and then ESE	some 6. Courses during the whole return correspond to those in coming	[same]	4 ESE mostly through hills, to Río Monterrey and to Buenavista
15 Apr., march 109 W side of the Salinas just S of King City	some 17 long>some 18 short: 8 ESE and the remainder ESE>SEbS and finally a bit SE	some 18 short	[same]	16: at about 2 SE, met Sergeant Góngora; at about 1 SE, met Captain Rivera; SE to San Bernabé
16 Apr., march 110 Mission San Antonio	some 5, first S through the San Bernabé hollow, then now SSW, now SSE, and finally a bit SW	some 5	[same]	5; 2½ most often S up cañada San Bernabé; 1½ S through hills; down to Mission San Antonio
17 Apr., march 111 between Lockwood and San Antonio Reservoir	some 7 short: ESE with some turnings SE and nearly S, then back ESE and, at a bit over 4, deviating E and EbN and EbS	some 7	[same]	about 5, most often SSE to E, down along the San Antonio hollow or river
18 Apr., march 112 S side of Atascadero, near State Hospital	some 17 short: about 6, E with a few ¼-point variations to S and N; about (an altered number)>8 to Río Monterrey, circling slowly ESE, SE, SSE, S and SSW; a small way ESE and the remainder SE	some 17	some 16	14: about 5 most often ESE, along the river; about 1 till crossing Río Nacimiento; 2 SSE and SE and down to Río Monterrey; 4 ESE along and across the river; 2 ESE up the Santa Margarita hollow

19 Apr., march 113 Mission San Luis Obispo	some 6 long: SE a little way; about 4 S across range; about 1 SW	some 6	some 7	6: 2½ ESE up the hollow; 2½ SE over a not very high hill range; 1
23 Apr., march 114 Bass Lake just N of San Antonio Creek, Vandenberg Air Force Base	some 17, much varied: ESE, at once turning SE, and SSE at 4; S a little to sea; about 2 SSE on shore; SE into dunes; after 1, 2 SE and 2 SSE to Long lake; 2 S; 1 SSW over the grade; SW with a bit of veering W	some 17	[same]	13: 1 SE on the highway; 1 SW; 1 S past El Buchón village and tar springs, down to shore; about 2 S along it; about 5, E over middling sand dunes then S and SSE across plain to Laguna Larga village; 3 S and SSE over hills to Laguna Graciosa
24 Apr., march 115 the Cojo Viejo	(15>16). Some 15, varied: S with some slight veering; about 5 SE, SSE and last S rounding punta La Concepción; E to Los Pedernales; SE to La Espada; S to a point possibly La Concepción; about 1 SE	some 16	[same]	12: 3 most often SSE to Río Santa Rosa; 1 SSE; 2 slowly around to E to easternmost Channel village; 5 E on shore past another village to next to ranchería El Cojo
25 Apr., march 116 Goleta	(16>18). Some 16 long, essentially E with a bit of veering N: about 3 ENE; E; about 2 ENE because of Mescaltitán inlets	some 18	[same]	about 14 E, past eight Channel villages to next to Mexcaltitán

428　　　　　　　WITH ANZA TO CALIFORNIA, 1775–1776

Dates, 1775–1776	Field Text	Intermediate and Canceled Figures in the Draft of the Shortened Text	Final Text	Anza's Journal
26 Apr., march 117 Ventura, NW side	(16>17). Some 16 long; about 1 NE; about 2 E and SE; E along shore with a few slight veerings N and many S because of cutting ESE or E across points and bends	some 17	[same]	12: E past the three large Mexcaltitán villages and La Laguna village and, beyond, the four villages next to the Río San Buenaventura and the last one, La Carpintería
27 Apr., march 118 Liberty Canyon	(17>18). A long 17, which can almost be reckoned as 18: about 1 E; about some 7 E with very slight veering to one side or the other; up the grade and S a little way; E a few leagues, twisting now ENE now ESE; beyond El Triunfo, NE and a bit N; ENE	some 18	[same]	10: 2 E leaving the Channel and fording Río Santa Clara; 4 ESE and up a high grade; 3 N through a small range; 1 NE
28 Apr., march 119 downtown Los Angeles, on Los Angeles River	some 14: about 1 NE; about 1 ENE down the grade and through the hollow; some 8 long E, then through the Gap and ESE through hills to river with some veering E and ENE	some 14	[same]	a little over 8: more than 1 EBNE descending from range; about 4 E across a plain; 3 E in broken land, to Río Porciúncula

APPENDIX 429

29 Apr., march 120 Mission San Gabriel	2: a little ESE; a little E; about 1 a bit more ENE	2	[same]	1 ENE; 1 NE
2 May, march 121 Baldwin Park/ Irwindale	2, E: a little EbN and the rest EbS	2	[same]	2 ENE across river of the former mission
3 May, march 122 Mira Loma (?)	some 10: about 4 E with some deflection N; ESE, inexact	10, (to a little short of) > to about 1 short of reaching Río Santa Ana	some 10, to about 2 short of reaching Río Santa Ana	9½: 5 ENE to Arroyo Alisos or Ososos; then about 4½ ESE
4 May, march 123 NW foot of Lakeview Mountains	9: some 2 ESE (inexact); some 7 E or almost ESE with very little veering. Began a shorter route	9	some 9	1½ ESE to Río Santa Ana; about 3 ESE to end of low hills; 3 SE
5 May, march 124 just short of head of Bautista Creek Canyon	13: 6 EbS and a bit ESE to Río San José; some 7 SE (inexact) with occasional veering, up hollow	13	some 13	12: 2½ E to beginning of valle San José; 3 ESE through it to its river at mouth of cañada San Patricio; 6 E and ESE up it almost to its end
6 May, march 125 Lower Willows, Collins Valley	some 13: SE (inexact) as far as Puerto San Carlos, and the rest ESE with considerable veering because of the turns on the grade	13	some 13	10: 2½ ESE up the ravines of cañada San Patricio; 2½ down to and across Valle El Príncipe to San Carlos Pass; down it and down through its main hollow generally SE with some bendings ESE

Dates, 1775–1776	Field Text	Intermediate and Canceled Figures in the Draft of the Shortened Text	Final Text	Anza's Journal
7 May, march 126 Harper's Well, San Felipe/Carrizo Creeks	some 15>14: 5 ESE>EbS; 5 ESE (inexact) and 4 E	14	some 14	13½: 6 ESE down the hollow; 4 ESE; 3½ E
8 May, march 127 NW of Imperial (?)	some 14, taking a straight route toward El Carrizal: some (3>4>)3 E; ESE	14: 3 E; 11 ESE	14: 3 almost E; 11 ESE and a bit nearly SE	12: about 1½ E to a fair-sized spring of thick water; about 10½ ESE
9 May, march 128 Jiquilpan (?)	some 20: about 1 ESE; about 3 SE; about 2 ESE on Moraga's old track; about 4 SE with a good many deviations E and S; about 1 ESE along old stock trail; round about 2 on our old Santa Rosa track . . . ; 7 E and SE	20: 1 ESE, 10 SEbS with some veers S and E, and finally, striking our route coming up, 2 ESE: [total of] 13 to El Carrizal at midday . . . [nothing on the rest of the march]	20: 1 ESE, 10 SE a bit SSE, with some veers S and E, and finally, striking our route coming up, 2 ESE: [total of] 13 to El Carrizal at one o'clock . . . [nothing on the rest of the march]	about 8 ESE past some points of sand dune to El Carrizal wells alias Alegría; 5 to the spot at Laguna Santa Olaya
10 May, march 129 Tabasco (?)	5: mostly NE and NNE but winding about, with veerings E and, more, to N	some 5	[same]	4: E to S following up the bends of the Río Colorado by several villages of the Cahuen tribe
11 May, march 130 Yuma	8, actually 9 because of the turnings: NNE till water; N and winding in all directions between N and E	8	some 8	7½, along the river

15 May, march 131 between the Gila and Laguna Mountains	some 6, ENE	6, same course as on coming, striking our route at around about a league	7: 2 SE and ESE; the rest on the same course as on coming	about 5 E and ESE up the Río Gila
16 May, march 132 W of Wellton	6: a bit over 2 EbN and ENE with some veering, twisting one way or another, to Gila camp of 26 November; 4 E with an occasional veer NE and much more SE, winding about.	6	6: 2 to Gila camp of 26 November; to 25 November camp	7: 3 ENE along river; 4 to the Laguna Salada on the same river
17 May, march 133 Lechuguilla Desert, Coyote Wash	a long 11: about 3 SSE; some 6 SE, striking the route described by Díaz; about 2 ESE	some 11: the first 3 S; 6 SSE; 2 SE	11: 3 S; 6 SSE striking Anza's route used the first time [1774]; 2 SE	8: about 2 cutting directly SE over good ground; 6 ESE over the same
18 May, march 134 near S end of Sierra Pinta, lava plain of El Tuzeral (?)	18: 6 to La Candelaria: 3 E or nearly so; about 2, winding about ESE and more ENE and a bit NE, and the rest ESE. Then 12: 3 ENE and NE with some variance; a bit over 6 SE, deflecting a bit E till striking the old (1774) route and the rest ESE along the route	18, a very varied course: 3 EbN, 2 NE, 1 ESE, to La Candelaria; 3 NE over mal país, 6 SE and 3 ESE	[same]	17: 5 ESE to tinajas La Candelaria; ESE 3 along the usual route opened in our first journey and across heights; leaving these and the route, about 9 heading straight E, to Puerto Blanco;

Dates, 1775–1776	Field Text	Intermediate and Canceled Figures in the Draft of the Shortened Text	Final Text	Anza's Journal
19 May, march 135 Río de Sonoita, Agua Dulce near Cerro Blanco	a good 10: a bit over 3 ESE to Puerto Blanco; remainder SE (inexact) or SEbE	10: 3 ESE, the rest SE with some deflection S	10: 3 ESE, the rest SEbS	(18 total for the uninterrupted march of eighteen and a half hours;) 3 SE; 3 ESE. . . .
20 May, march 136 Piedra Parada, Sierra Cubabi	13: 9 to Sonoitac: 6 E; 3 ESE (inexact at times). Then some 4: 2 SSE; SE, winding about a bit	13: 6 E and 3 ESE to Sonoitac; 2 SSE and 2 SE	[same]	11: 8 E to Sonoitac; 3 SE and SSE along skirt of heights
21 May, march 137 Costa Rica or Cozón	17: Some 8 short to Quitobac: 2 SE and a bit SSE; about 5 S with an occasional veer SSE; about 1, turning as far as SW. Then some 9: about 1 ESE; about 2 SE; a bit over 1 SSE and almost S; about 3 turning SE and finishing ESE	17: 2 SSE, 2 SSW, 2 SW and 2 WSW to Quitobac. About 1 ESE, 2 SE, 1 SSE and 1 S, 3 SE and 1 ESE	[same]	14: 5 mostly S because of the heights, to Quitobac village. 2½ ESE on skirts of small heights to right; 1½ SW; 2 S and SE leaving the heights and across a waterless valley with some grass; about 3½ SE to bajío San Juan Mata, with grass
22 May, march 138 Ejido Tajitos (?)	15; some 8 to Aribaicpia: about 2 ESE; a bit over 5 SEbE, almost SSE. Some 7 S; 3 SSE and SE; about 1 SW	15: 2 ESE; 5 SE and 1 S to La Aribaicpia. 3 SSE; 2 SE; 2 SSW to San Ildefonso	15: 2 ESE; 5 SE; 1 S to La Aribaicpia; 3 SSE till a route to Bisanig which we left behind us; 2 SE; 2 SSW	11½: 3½ SE to San Eduardo de La Arivaypia; 6 on the traveled route to bajío San Ildefonso
23 May, march 139 Caborca	(8>9): Some 8: 3 S deviating a bit E; SE a little; ESE	8 [sic]: 3 S; 3 SE; 3 ESE	9: 3 S; 3 SE; 3 ESE	6 SE and some brief bendings ESE

25 May, march 140 Laguna El Bamuri	some 10 long; about 2 S; SSE and SE	10, SSE	[same]	8 ESE on highway to La Cieneguilla
26 May, march 141 La Ciénega	7. Some 5 SE to La Cieneguilla. To the mines: 1 going and 1 coming back	5, SSE	[same]	about 6 on same, [ESE], good ground, to La Cieneguilla
29 May, march 142 near Cerro Colorado	some 7: 2 SE with some slight variation; ESE, mostly turning a quarter-point to E or S, in many parts SE and even further E	7: 2 SE; 5 SEbE	7: 2 SE; 5 ESE	about 7 [ESE]
30 May, march 143 vicinity of Los Nidos or San Francisco	14: some 7 ESE and winding a bit now E now SE, to El Tecolote; a long 7, 1 ESE, 2 E, the remainder ESE with variation, winding about SE and further E	14: 7 SEbE to El Tecolote; 7 ESE	14: 7 SE to El Tecolote; 7 SEbE but twisting about a bit	10 to vicinity of La Tortuga
31 May, march 144 upland S of El Tesotal	15: 5 ESE with ¼-point's variation to one side or the other at times; some 10 long ESE though with portions varying SE and many more E	15: 5 SE to Pozo Crisanto; [the rest the same]	15: 5 SE and SSE to Pozo Crisanto; 10 ESE with some variation	5 [ESE] to Pozo Crisanto; 5 to La Mesa
1 June, march 145 San Miguel de Horcasitas	Some 4 ESE with some veers and deviations E	4 ESE and even almost E	[the same]	2 to presidio San Miguel de Horcasitas

Bibliography

Manuscripts and Archival Sources

Archivo General de la Nación, Mexico City

Anza, Juan Bautista de. "Diario de la ruta y operaciones." Historia, Tomo 396, Folio 148 ff. A contemporary copy is in Provincias Internas, Tomo 169, Expediente 7. Consulted through microfilm held by The Bancroft Library, University of California, Berkeley and the transcription of Don L. Garate at http://anza.uoregon.edu/anza76hsp.html. Accessed December 2006 through August 2007. I have not seen the reported edition by Julio César Montané Martí.

Carrillo, Mariano. "Noticias de algunas cosas que han pasado en la nueva conquista de Monte Rey." Californias, Tomo 66, Fojas 33–37.

Moraga, José Joaquín. "Carta del theniente don Josef [Joaquín] de Moraga en que da qüenta [de la] ocupación del puerto de San Francisco, erección de una misión, terreno reconocido, y demás progresos." Californias, Tomo 66, Folios 428r–438v. Translated in Bolton 1930 3: 395–99.

The Bancroft Library, University of California, Berkeley

Archive of California. C-A 1-63.

Archivo General de Indias, Sevilla. Audiencia de Guadalajara, and Estado. Consulted through films and transcripts.

Bowman, Jacob N. "The Roads of Provincial California." 1946. mF870.H4B5.

Donohue, John Augustine. "Jesuit Mission in Northwestern New Spain, 1711–1767." Ph.D. diss., University of California, Berkeley, 1957.

Fages, Pedro. "Informes particulares al gobernador Romeu, 1791."

Font, Pedro. "Diario que forma el Padre Fray Pedro Font, predicador apostólico del Colegio de la Santa Cruz de Querétaro, sacado del borrador que escribió en el camino del viage que hizo a Monter[r]ey y puerto de San Francisco." ms. M–M 1724. (The shortened text.) ms. M–M 1725 is a contemporary calligraphic copy made at Querétaro with Font's original maps inserted.

Rivera y Moncada Papers. ms. C–A 368.

John Carter Brown Library, Providence, Rhode Island

Font, Pedro. "Diario que formó el Padre predicador apostólico Fray Pedro Font, misionero apostólico del Colegio de la Santa Cruz de Querétaro, en el viage que hizo a Monte[r]rey." (The final text.)

Chancery Archives, Archdiocese of San Francisco, Menlo Park, California
Serra, Junípero. Affidavits concerning marriage applications. Taylor Collection, vol. 1.

Franciscan Historical Archive, Curia Generalizia dei Frati Minori, Rome
Barbastro, Francisco Antonio. "Compendio de lo más notable que han trabajado en Sonora." Marcellino da Civezza Collection, 202/35.
Díaz, Juan Marcelo. "Diario formado por el Padre Fray Juan Díaz del Colegio de la Santa Cruz de Querétaro, en el viage que hizo desde el presidio de El Tubac en compañía del Reverendo Padre Fray Francisco Garzés y del Capitán don Juan Baptista de Anza." Marcellino da Civezza collection 201.1 (holograph). Published in Soto Pérez 1998 1: 702–30.
Font, Pedro. "Diario que forma el Padre Predicador Fray Pedro Font, misionero apostólico del Colegio de la Santa Cruz de Querétaro, en el viage que hace a Monter[r]ey en compañía del señor teniente coronel y capitán del presidio de Tubac don Juan Bautista de Anza." M/62 (Mexici missiones, 2), Folios 177r–257r. (The field text.)
Garcés, Francisco Tomás Hermenegildo. "Cartas del V. P. Fray Francisco Garcés desde el año de 68 hasta el de 81 en que fue sacrificado." Marcellino da Civezza Collection, 201/16–201/25.
Marcellino da Civezza Collection.

The Huntington Library, San Marino, California
Fort Sutter Collection, vol. 32: "Early Expeditions and Studies among the Indians of the Southwest carried on by Edward and Richard Kern . . . , Sante [sic] Fe and Washington 1849:1850:1851:1852."
Rivera y Moncada, Fernando de. "Letter to Viceroy Bucareli, 2 May 1776." MS. HM 37547.

Mission Repositories
Mission San Francisco, registers of baptisms, marriages, and deaths (1776–). Originally consulted at the Chancery Office of the Archdiocese of San Francisco; later on microfilm, Moraga Historical Society, Moraga, Calif.
Mission San Luis Obispo, register of baptisms (1772–1797). "Libro primero en que se asientan las partidas de los bautismos de la gentilidad que se christiana en esta nueva misión de San Luis Obispo de Tolosa." Originally consulted at the Mission; subsequent assistance from Joseph A. Carotenuti is gratefully acknowledged.

Newberry Library, Chicago
Garcés, Francisco Tomás Hermenegildo. "Relación para el guardián Jiménez. October, November or December 1776." Ayer MS 1092. A contemporary calligraphed copy.
Reyes, Antonio María de los. "Breve descripción y relación de la parte . . . más útil y digna de atención . . . 2 April 1772." Ayer MS 1122.

Santa Bárbara Mission Archive-Library, Santa Barbara, California

Viader, José. "Journal of an expedition to the San Joaquín, 1810." Holograph manuscript, 537. Translated in Cook 1960 from a manuscript copy in The Bancroft Library, University of California Berkeley, "Documentos para la historia de California, Tomo IV, Parte 1a."

University of California, Los Angeles

Anonymous. "Convite evangélico a compasión y socorro de la viña del Señor." Manuscript Collection. Image on University of Arizona Library, Film 71.

Temple, T. W. "Transcripts of mission records." Courtesy of the late Thomas Workman Temple II and Greg P. Smestad.

Published Primary Sources

Anonymous. *Apostólicos afanes de la compañía de Jesús, escritos por un Padre de la misma sagrada religión de su provincia de México*. Barcelona: P. Nadal, 1754.

———. *Carta geográphica de la costa y parte de la península de la California[,] naciones que comprehende hasta el Nuevo México, y viage que hizieron fr. Francisco Garcés, y fr. Pedro Font al río Colorado[,] San Gabriel, y Moqui el año de 1777*. Mexico City: Manuel Villavicencio, 1781.

———. *Breve explicación de los bienes que gozan los que hacen la donación de sus obras satisfactorias, con voto, en manos de María Santísima a favor de las ánimas del purgatorio. Sacada de los Diálogos del Purgatorio, del Padre Oliden, C. R. teatino. Por un sacerdote de este Arzobispado. Va añadida la canción de la Santísima Virgen a devoción de J. de V.* Mexico City: María Fernández de Jáuregui, 1806. The original approbations are dated 1760.

Archivo y Biblioteca de la Secretaría de Hacienda, Mexico. *Las misiones de la Alta California*. Mexico City: Secretaría de Hacienda, 1914.

Arricivita, Juan Domingo de. *Crónica seráfica y apostólica del colegio de propaganda fide de la Santa Cruz de Querétaro*. Mexico City: Viuda de don J. B. de Hogal, 1792.

Bartlett, John Russell. *Personal Narrative of Explorations and Incidents in Texas, New Mexico, California, Sonora, and Chihuahua, connected with the United States and Mexican Boundary Commission, during the years 1850, '51, '52, and '53*. 2 volumes. New York: D. Appleton and Company, 1854.

Beaglehole, J. C. *The Journals of Captain James Cook on his Voyages of Discovery: The Voyage of the Endeavour 1768–1771*. Cambridge: Hakluyt Society and Cambridge University Press, 1955.

Beebe, Rose Marie, and Robert M. Senkewicz, trans. and eds. *Testimonios: Early California Through the Eyes of Women, 1815–1848*. Berkeley: Heyday Books, 2006.

Bolton, Herbert Eugene. *Anza's California Expeditions*. 5 vols. Berkeley: University of California Press, 1930; reproduced, New York: Russell and Russell, 1966.

Bolton, Herbert E. *Fray Juan Crespí: Missionary Explorer on the Pacific Coast, 1769-1774*. Berkeley: University of California Press, 1927.

———. *Outpost of Empire: The Story of the Founding of San Francisco*. New York: Alfred A. Knopf, 1931.

Brown, Alan K. *A Description of Distant Roads: Original Journals of the First Expedition into California, 1769–1770, by Juan Crespí*. San Diego: San Diego State University Press, 2001.

———. "Three Letters from the Pen of Fray Pedro Font." *Boletín: The Journal of the California Mission Studies Association* 23.1 (2006): 85–118.

Browning, Peter. *The Discovery of San Francisco Bay: The Portolá Expedition of 1769–1779: The Diary of Miguel Costansó in Spanish and English*. Lafayette, Calif.: Great West Books, 1992.

Burrus, Ernest J., ed. *Diario del capitán comandante Fernando de Rivera y Moncada*. 2 vols. Madrid: José Porrúa Turanzas, 1967.

Cabrera, Miguel. *Maravilla americana, y conjunto de raras maravillas observadas con la dirección de las reglas de el arte de la pintura en la prodigiosa imagen de Nuestra Señora de Guadalupe de México*. Mexico City: Colegio de San Ildefonso, 1756.

Cerruti, Henry. *Ramblings in California, the Adventures of Henry Cerruti*. Edited by Margaret Mollins and Virginia E. Thickens. Berkeley: Friends of The Bancroft Library, 1954.

Colegio Apostólico de San Fernando de México. *Informe de el Appostólico Colegio de San Fernando de México, sobre los descubrimientos entre los 30 y 60 grados de latitud*. Mexico City: Vargas Rea, 1948.

Costansó, Miguel. *Noticias of the Port of San Francisco in letters of Miguel Costansó, Fray Juan Crespí, and Fray Francisco Palóu in the year 1772*. San Francisco: Windsor Press, 1940.

Coues, Elliott. *On the Trail of a Spanish Pioneer, the Diary and Itinerary of Francisco Garcés (Missionary Priest) in his Travels through Sonora, Arizona, and California, 1775–1776*. 2 vols. New York: Francis P. Harper, 1900.

Crespí, Juan. *Mapa de lo substancial del famoso Puerto y Río de San Francisco explorado por tierra en el mes de marzo del presente año de 1772, sacado por el diario y observaciones del R. P. Fr. Juan Crespí*. San Francisco: Book Club of California, 1950.

Freeland, Jane Patricia, and Agnes Josephine Conway. *St. Leo the Great: Sermons*. Washington, D.C.: Catholic University of America Press, 1996.

Galvin, John. *A Record of Travels in Arizona and California, 1775–1776: Fr. Francisco Garcés: a New Translation*. San Francisco: John Howell Books, 1967.

———. *The First Spanish Entry into San Francisco Bay, 1775: The Original Narrative, Hitherto Unpublished, by Fr. Vicente Santa María*. San Francisco: John Howell Books, 1971.

Garate, Don L. *Captain Juan Bautista de Anza: Correspondence on Various Subjects, 1775; Archivo General de la Nación, Provincias Internas 237, Section 3*. Antepasados 8. San Leandro: Los Californianos, 1995.

———. *The Juan Bautista de Anza–Fernando de Rivera y Moncada Letters of 1775–1776: Personalities in Conflict*. Antepasados 12. San Diego: Los Californianos, 2006.

Garcés, Francisco Tomás Hermenegildo. *Diario de exploraciones en Arizona y California en los años de 1775 y 1776*. Edited by John Galvin. Instituto de Investigaciones Históricas, Cuadernos, Serie documental 6. Mexico City: Universidad Nacional Autónoma de México, 1968.

Gómez Canedo, Lino. *Sonora hacia fines del siglo XVIII: un informe del misionero franciscano fray Francisco Antonio Barbastro, con otros documentos complementarios*. Documentación Historica Mexicana, no. 3. Guadalajara (Jalisco): Librería Font, 1971.

Harlow, Neal. *Maps of San Francisco Bay from the Spanish Discovery in 1769 to the American Occupation*. San Francisco: Book Club of California, 1950.

Humboldt, Alexandre de (Alexander von). *Essai politique sur le royaume de la Nouvelle-Espagne; Voyage de Humboldt & Bonpland: Voyage aux régions équinoxiales du nouveau continent, troisième série. Facsimilé intégral de l'édition Paris 1805–1834*, Tome 1. Amsterdam and New York: Da Capo Press, 1971.

Ives, J. C. *Report upon the Colorado River of the West Explored in 1857 and 1858*. 36th Congress, 1st Session, 1861. House Executive Document 90.

Lorenzana, Antonio. *Concilios provinciales primero y segundo*. Mexico City: Imprenta del Superior Gobierno, del bachiller don J. A. de Hogal, 1769.

Matson, Daniel S. "Letters of Friar Pedro Font, 1776–1777." *Ethnohistory* 22.3 (1975): 262–93.

——— and Bernard L. Fontana. *Friar Bringas Reports to the King*. Tucson: University of Arizona Press, 1977.

Möllhausen, Baldwin [Heinrich Balduin Möllhausen]. *Diary of a Journey from the Mississippi to the Coasts of the Pacific*. New York: Johnson Reprint, 1969.

Montané Martí, Julio César. *Juan Bautista de Anza, diario del primer viaje a La California*. Hermosillo: Sociedad Sonorense de Historia en coedición con Reprográfica, S. A., 1989.

———. *Fray Pedro Font, diario íntimo, y diario de fray Tomás Eixarch*. Hermosillo: Universidad de Sonora; Mexico City: Plaza y Valdés, 2000.

Sales, Luis. *Noticias de la provincia de Californias 1794*. Colección Chimalistac 6. Madrid: José Porrúa Turanzas, 1960.

Servicio Geográfico del Ejército Spain. *Cartografía del Ultramar*. Madrid: Servicio Histórico Militar, 1949–1957.

Solórzano Pereira, Juan de. *Política indiana*. Madrid: Diego Díaz de la Carrera, 1647–1648.

Soto Pérez, José Luis. *Fr. Francisco Palóu, O.F.M. Recopilación de noticias de la Antigua y Nueva California (1767–1783)*. 2 vols. Mexico City: Editorial Porrúa, 1998.

Stanger, Frank M., and Alan K. Brown. *Who Discovered the Golden Gate? The Explorers' own Accounts: How they Discovered a Hidden Harbor and at Last Found its Entrance*. San Mateo, Calif.: San Mateo County Historical Association, 1969.

Teggart, Frederick J., ed. *The Anza Expedition of 1775–1776: Diary of Pedro Font*. Publications of the Academy of Pacific Coast History 3(1). Berkeley: University of California Press, 1913.

——— and Manuel Carpio, eds. *The Portolá Expedition of 1769–1770: Diary of Miguel Costansó*. Publications of the Academy of Pacific Coast History 2(4). Berkeley: University of California Press, 1911.

Tibesar, Antonine. *Writings of Junípero Serra*. 4 vols. Washington, D.C.: Academy of American Franciscan History, 1956.

Tosca, Tomás Vicente. *Compendio matemático en que se contienen todas las materias más principales de las ciencias que tratan de la cantidad*. 9 vols. Valencia, Spain: J. García, 1757.

Wagner, Henry R. *The Cartography of the Northwest Coast of America to the Year 1800*. Mansfield Centre, Conn.: Martino Publishing, 1999.

Weber, David J. *Richard H. Kern: Expeditionary Artist in the Far Southwest, 1848–1853*. Albuquerque: University of New Mexico Press for Amon Carter Museum, 1985.

Whipple, A. W., Thomas Ewbank, and William M. Turner. *Reports of Explorations and Surveys, to Ascertain the Most Practical and Economical Route for a Railroad from the Mississippi River to the Pacific Ocean* ["Pacific Railroad Reports"], Volume 3. Part 3, *Report upon the Indian Tribes*. 33rd Congress 2nd Session, Senate Executive Document 78 (serial 760). Washington, D.C.: Beverley Tucker, 1855–1856.

Williamson, R. S. *Explorations and Surveys for a Railroad Route from the Mississippi River to the Pacific Ocean* ["Pacific Railroad Reports"], Volume 5. *Routes in California to Connect with the Routes near the Thirty-fifth and Thirty-second Parallels*. 33rd Congress 2nd Session, Senate Executive Document 78 (serial 762). Washington, D.C.: U.S. Government Printing Office, 1856.

Books and Articles

Archivo General y Público de la Nación Mexicana. *Guía del Archivo Histórico de Hacienda*. Mexico City. Mexico: Secretaría de Hacienda y Crédito Público, 1940.

Bahr, Donald, Juan Smith, William Smith Allison, and Julian Hayden. *The Short Swift Time of Gods on Earth: The Hohokam Chronicles*. Berkeley: University of California Press, 1994.

Bancroft, Hubert Howe. *History of California*. Vol. 1: 1542–1800. Santa Barbara: Wallace Hebberd, 1963.

Bennyhoff, James A. *Ethnogeography of the Plains Miwok*. Center for Archaeological Research at Davis, Publication Number 5. Davis: University of California, 1977.

Bolton, Herbert Eugene. *Guide to Materials for the History of the United States in the Principal Archives of Mexico*. Washington, D.C.: Carnegie Institution of Washington, 1913.

Boneu Companys, Fernando. *Gaspar de Portolá, Explorer and Founder of California*. Translated and revised by Alan K. Brown. Lérida, Spain: Instituto de Estudios Ilerdenses, 1983.

Borges Morán, Pedro. "Expediciones misioneras al colegio de Querétaro (Méjico), 1683–1822." *Archivo Ibero-Americano*, 2nd series, 42 (1982): 809–58.

Bowditch, Nathaniel. *American Practical Navigator: an Epitome of Navigation*. Published by the Defense Mapping Agency Hydrographic Center. Washington, D.C.: United States Government Printing Office, 1975.

Bowman, J. N. "Weights and Measures of Provincial California." *California Historical Society Quarterly* 30.4 (1951): 315–38.

Brown, Alan K. "Anza and Font in the San Francisco Reconnaissance." In *Mission San Francisco de Asís in the Ohlone Village of Chutchui. Proceedings of the 24th Annual Conference of the California Mission Studies Association*, edited by Rose Marie Beebe and Robert M. Senkewicz, 169–78. Santa Clara: California Mission Studies Association, 2007.

———. "The Anza Expedition in Eastern Contra Costa and Eastern Alameda Counties, California: A Report for the Anza Trail Team, Western Region, National Park Service," April, 1998.

———. "The English Compass Points. *Medium Ævum* 47.2 (1978): 221–46.

———. "The European Contact of 1772 and Some Later Documentation." In *The Ohlone Past and Present: Native Americans of the San Francisco Bay Region*, edited by Lowell John Bean, 1–39. Menlo Park, Calif.: Ballena Press, 1994.

———. *Indians of San Mateo County*. San Mateo, Calif.: San Mateo County Historical Association, 1973.

———. "The Men of the 'First Expedition.'" *La Península: Journal of the San Mateo County Historical Association* 15.1 (1969): 3–9.

———. *Place Names of San Mateo County*. San Mateo: San Mateo County Historical Association, 1975.

———. *Reconstructing Early Historical Landscapes in the Northern Santa Clara Valley*. Research Manuscript Series 11, Santa Clara University Department of Anthropology and Sociology, Santa Clara, Calif.: Santa Clara University, 2005.

———. "Rivera at San Francisco: A Journal of Exploration, 1774." *California Historical Society Quarterly* 41.4 (1962): 325–41.

———. "The Various Journals of Juan Crespí." *The Americas* 21.4 (1965): 375–98.

Chapman, Charles Edward. *The Founding of Spanish California: The Northwestward Expansion of New Spain, 1687–1783*. New York: The Macmillan Company, 1916.

BIBLIOGRAPHY

Christy, Julia. 2003. Directory de Anza. California Spanish Genealogy by sfgenealogy.com. www.sfgenealogy.com/spanish/anzadir.htm. Accessed July 2007.

Cook, Sherburne F. *The Aboriginal Population of Alameda and Contra Costa Counties, California*. Anthropological Records 16.4. Berkeley: University of California Publications, 1957.

———. *Colonial Expeditions to the Interior of California's Central Valley, 1800–1820*. Anthropological Records 16.6. Berkeley: University of California Publications, 1960.

Crosby, Harry W. *Antigua California: Mission and Colony on the Peninsular Frontier 1697–1768*. Albuquerque: University of New Mexico Press, 1994.

———. *Gateway to Alta California: The Expedition to San Diego, 1769*. San Diego: Sunbelt, 2003.

Cuadriello, Jaime, Iván Martínez, Martha Reta, and Lenize Rivera. *Zodíaco Mariano: 250 años de la declaración pontificia de María de Guadalupe como patrona de México*. Villa de Guadalupe: Museo de la Basílica de Guadalupe/Museo Soumaya, 2005.

Davidson, George. *The Discovery of San Francisco Bay. The Rediscovery of the Port of Monterey, the Establishment of the Presidio, and the Founding of the Mission of San Francisco*. San Francisco: F. F. Partridge, 1907.

Diez, Stephen A. et al. "Report of archaeological investigations at Sánchez Adobe Park Historic District for County of San Mateo," August 1979.

Eldredge, Zoeth Skinner. *The Beginnings of San Francisco from the Expedition of Anza, 1774 to the City Charter of April 15, 1850*. 2 vols. San Francisco: Zoeth S. Eldredge, 1912.

Engelhardt, Zephyrin. *San Juan Capistrano Mission*. Los Angeles: Standard Printing Co., 1922.

Fenaroli, Luigi, and Umberto Tosco. *Flora mediterranea: vegetazione e flora dei litorali italici e mediterranei*. 2 vols. Milan: Aldo Martello, 1964.

Flórez, Enrique. *España sagrada: theatro geográphico-histórico de la iglesia de España*. Vol. 1, *Clave geográphica y geographía de los patriarcados*. Madrid: M. F. Rodríguez, 1747.

Forbes, Jack D. *Warriors of the Colorado, the Yumas of the Quechán Nation and Their Neighbors*. Norman: University of Oklahoma Press, 1965.

Fritts, Harold C., and Geoffrey A. Gordon. *Annual Precipitation for California since 1600 Reconstructed from Western North American Tree Rings*. Sacramento: California Department of Water Resources, 1980.

Garate, Don L. Mission 2000 Database. http://home.nps.gov/applications/tuma. Accessed August and September 2006.

Geiger, Maynard. *The Life and Times of Fray Junípero Serra, O.F.M.: or, The Man Who Never Turned Back, 1713-1784, a Biography*. 2 vols. Washington, D.C.: Academy of American Franciscan History, 1959.

Giffords, Gloria Fraser. *Sanctuaries of Earth, Stone, and Light: The Churches of Northern New Spain, 1530–1821*. Tucson: University of Arizona Press, 2007.

Gómez Canedo, Lino. *Archivos franciscanos de México*. Mexico City: Universidad Nacional Autónoma de México and Instituto de Estudios y Documentos Históricos, A. C., 1982

Gudde, Erwin G. *California Place Names: The Origin and Etymology of Current Geographical Names*. Berkeley: University of California Press, 1969.

Guerrero, Vladimir. *The Anza Trail and the Settling of California*. Santa Clara, Calif.: Santa Clara University; Berkeley: Heyday Books, 2006.

Hayes, Derek. *Historical Atlas of California*. Berkeley: University of California Press, 2007.

Hoover, Margaret, Ethel G. Rensch, Hero Rensch, and William N. Abeloe. *Historic Spots in California*. Third edition. Stanford, Calif.: Stanford University Press, 1966.

Hoover, Mildred Brooke, and Douglas E. Kyle. *Historic Spots in California*. Fifth edition. Stanford, Calif.: Stanford University Press, 2002.

James, Montague Rhodes. *The Apocryphal New Testament*. Oxford: Clarendon Press, 1924.

Kessell, John L. *Friars, Soldiers, and Reformers: Hispanic Arizona and the Sonora Mission Frontier 1767–1856*. Tucson: University of Arizona Press, 1976.

———. "The Making of a Martyr: The Young Francisco Garcés." *New Mexico Historical Review* 45.3 (1970): 180–96.

Kingsborough, Edward King. *Antiquities of Mexico*. London: A. Aglio, 1830–1848.

Kowalczyk, Zygmunt. *Geodesy*. 2 vols. Warsaw: Published for the U.S. Dept. of Commerce and the National Science Foundation by the Scientific Publication Foreign Cooperation Center of the Central Institute for Scientific, Technical and Economic Information, 1968.

McCarty, Kieran. *A Spanish Frontier in the Enlightened Age: Franciscan Beginnings in Sonora and Arizona, 1767–1770*. Washington, D.C.: Academy of American Franciscan History, 1981.

Meadows, Don. "First European Contacts with the Indians of Orange County." *Pacific Coast Archaeological Society Quarterly* 1.3 (1965): 15–25.

Milliken, Randall. *A Time of Little Choice: The Disintegration of Tribal Culture in the San Francisco Bay Area, 1769–1810*. Menlo Park, Calif.: Ballena Press, 1995.

Moorhead, Max L. *The Presidio: Bastion of the Spanish Borderlands*. Norman: University of Oklahoma Press, 1975.

Officer, James E., Mardith Schuetz-Miller, and Bernard L. Fontana. *The Pimería Alta: Missions and More*. Tucson: Southwestern Mission Research Center, 1996.

Olvera H., Jorge. *Finding Father Kino: The Discovery of the Remains of Father Francisco Eusebio Kino, S.J., 1965–1966*. Foreword and afterword by Bernard L. Fontana. Tucson: Southwestern Museum Research Center, 1998.

Perry, Richard D. *The Devil, the Skeleton and the Angels: The Frescoes at Pitiquito*. Exploring Colonial Mexico, the Espadaña Press web site, 2004. http://www.colonial-mexico.com. Accessed December 2007 to January 2008.

Real Academia Española. *Diccionario de la lengua española*. Madrid: Real Academia Española, 1994.

Redlands Institute, University of Redlands. *Salton Sea Atlas*. Redlands: ESRI Press, 2002.

Santamaría, Francisco J. *Diccionario de mejicanismos*. Mexico City: Editorial Porrúa, 1974.

Saxton, Dean, and Lucille Saxton. *O'othham hoho'ok A'agitha: Legends and Lore of the Papago and Pima Indians*. Tucson: University of Arizona Press, 1973.

Schuetz-Miller, Mardith K. "Survival of Early Christian Symbolism in Monastic Churches of New Spain and Visions of the Millennial Kingdom." *Journal of the Southwest* 42.4 (2000): 765–97.

Schwartz, Stuart B. *All Can Be Saved: Religious Tolerance and Salvation in the Iberian Atlantic World*. New Haven, Conn.: Yale University Press, 2008.

Smestad, Greg. *A Guide to the Juan Bautista de Anza National Historic Trail*. Antepasados 11. San Diego: Los Californianos, 2005. Also at http://www.nps.gov/juba/. Accessed 2005 through 2007.

Smith, Clifton F. *A Flora of the Santa Barbara Region, California: An Annotated Catalogue of the Native and Naturalized Vascular Plants of the Santa Barbara County Mainland and Nearby Channel Islands*. Santa Barbara: Santa Barbara Museum of Natural History, 1976.

Smith, Helen C. "The Portolá Camps Revisited." *Pacific Coast Archaeological Society Quarterly* 1.4 (1965): 28–32.

Sphar, Ginny. Summary Biographies of Sonora-Arizona Missionaries. Accessed from August to October 2007 at www.nps.gov/tuma/historyculture/.

Stephenson, Terry E. *Caminos Viejos: Tales Found in the History of California*. Santa Ana: Press of the Santa Ana High School and Junior College, 1930.

Sykes, Godfrey. *The Colorado Delta*. Washington, D.C.: Carnegie Institute; New York: Geographical Society of America, 1937.

Treutlein, Theodore E. *San Francisco Bay, Discovery and Colonization, 1769–1776*. San Francisco: California Historical Society, 1968.

———. "Fages as Explorer, 1769–1772." *California Historical Quarterly* 51.4 (1972): 338–56.

Valenzuela Morales, Felipe de Jesús. Buscando la tumba de Kino. Instituto Sonorense de Cultura, Festival del mes, May 24, 2007. http://www.isc.gob.mx/contenido/festivales/.

Web de Anza. http://anza.uoregon.edu/. Accessed 2002 through September 2006.

Index

Aceves, Antonio Quiterio, 337
Aceves, José Antonio, 337
Aceves, José Cipriano, 337
Aceves, Juan Gregorio, 337
Aceves, Juan Pablo, 337
Aceves, María Gertrudis, 337
Aceves, María Petra, 337
Acuña, Petronila Josefa, 337
Agua Caliente (Ariz.), 98, 102n111, 111, 114
Agua Caliente, San Bernardino del (Cocomaricopa village), 108–109, 112
Aguaje Empinado (Ariz.), 390
Aguirre, Juan de, 290n124
Akimel O'odham. *See* Gila Pima Indians
Altamirano, Justo Roberto. *See* Roberto, Justo
Altar, Presidio of, 103, 394, 396
Álvarez de Acevedo, Juan Francisco, 338
Álvarez de Acevedo, Luis Joaquín, 338
Álvarez de Acevedo, María Francisca, 338
Alviso, Domingo, 334, 334n9, 339n39
Alviso, Francisco, 334
Alviso, Javier, 334
Alviso, Juan Ignacio, 334
Alviso, María de Loreto, 334
Amarillas, José Ignacio, 211, 239–40, 239n83, 240n87
Amarillas, Juan Angel, 384
Amézquita, Juan Antonio, 335
Amézquita, María de los Reyes, 335
Amézquita, María Dolores, 335
Amézquita, María Josefa, 335, 335n14
Amézquita, María Matilde, 335
Amézquita, Salvador Manuel, 335

Amurrió, Fray Gregorio, 188, 190–91, 193, 197, 198, 200, 203, 205, 209
Angel, Juan, 379
Anza, Carlos Antonio de, 234
Anza, Juan Bautista, 36, 40, 176, 187, 198, 237, 344; 1774 expedition of, 22, 24, 25, 32, 92n73, 158n145, 315; ambitions of, 56–57; arrival of at Monterey, 242; attitude of toward Font, 19, 31n55, 32, 38, 39, 80, 80n27, 81, 82, 109, 110, 122–23, 124, 125, 154, 165, 172, 182, 200, 203–205, 210, 212, 214, 223, 260, 277, 333, 343, 361, 362, 364, 368, 382, 395–96, 401, 404; attitude of toward Indian tales, 122n20; attitude of toward priests, 123–24; and California–New Mexico route, 23; campaign of against Apaches and Seris, 59; and choosing site for San Francisco settlement, 279–81; as commander of expedition, 21, 31, 84, 86, 146, 151, 154, 178n32, 206, 247, 259, 333; conflict with Font over distribution of liquor, 131; conflict with Font over quadrant, 32, 33, 35, 122, 182, 402–404; and crossing of Colorado River, 119, 385; and danger of hostile Indians, 51; departure from Monterey by, 42, 344; departure from Yuma by, 388; and desertion of mission soldier and muleteers, 211n144, 239n83, 240n86, 240n87, 241, 387; and discontent of expedition soldiers, 212; and dispute with Rivera y Moncada, 167, 178n32, 197n102, 200, 202, 206, 207, 209, 251, 252–53, 332, 346–50, 354–55, 356–57, 358–59, 366–68, 370–73, 382; and erecting

Anza, Juan Bautista (*continued*)
a cross at San Francisco Bay, 272, 274, 277, 279; and expedition members, 39, 84n45, 113; and exploration for San Francisco River, 26, 167n1; Font's maps of routes of, 62, 331–32; on Font's sermon at Monterey, 247n116; and Garcés explorations, 382n15; and Garcés's explorations, 90, 380, 381, 382; on geographical landmarks, 90n68, 129n49, 147, 147n116, 149n119; as governor of New Mexico, 60; as honorary lay brother of Colegio de la Santa Cruz, 73; illness of, 213, 214, 250–51, 250n130, 252, 253, 255, 257, 263; on Indians near San Francisco Bay, 298n151; interaction with Indians by, 23, 45, 50, 60, 100, 108, 129, 159–60, 172, 221–22, 228, 233, 234, 234n57, 268, 274, 291–92, 293, 296, 300, 302–303, 305–306, 310; interaction with Quechán Indians by, 23; journey to San Diego by, 183–87; lack of communication with Font by, 163, 103, 131, 161, 162; and locating sites for San Francisco settlements, 250, 254; and loss of expedition livestock, 157; in Mexico City, 59; at Mission San Carlos, 331; at Mission San Gabriel, 209; at Monterey, 243, 257; and Pablo Feo, 116, 386; and Pedro Regaldo, 361; and priests at Yuma, 121; and provisions for expedition, 154, 154n134, 167n1, 213–14, 227; and provisions for priests at Yuma, 123–24, 127; and punishment of Indians, 117n12, 152, 389; purpose of expeditions of, 22, 23, 24; reconnaissance of San Francisco Bay area, 208, 209, 282, 284, 285, 294; reconnaissance of San Francisco Bay area by, 37, 45–46, 254, 327n261; relationship of with Quechán Indians, 117; relationship of with Rivera, 49, 50, 51, 51n101, 52–57; relationship of with Salvador Palma, 102n112, 125, 133; reprimanding of, 60; and return journey to Sonora, 346, 377, 400, 401; and role of Sebastián Taraval in expedition of, 44n81; route of return journey to Sonora, 390; and Salvador Palma, 115, 122; in San Diego, 181, 188, 203; and San Diego uprising, 175n17, 178, 187n67, 190, 195; and San Francisco missionaries, 250n130; scientific devices used by, 32–34, 33, 35; and search for San Francisco River, 47–48, 208, 300–301, 308, 309, 314, 316, 317, 319–23; and taking Salvador Palma to Mexico City, 381, 382–83; and treatment of local Indian tribes, 157; view of Jesuits missionaries by, 128

Anza, Juan Bautista (father), 21
Apache Indians, 96, 107, 406; Anza campaign against, 59; attacks of, 76, 78, 154; as colonist, 40, 42, 342n56; crops of, 133; and destruction of Mission Tumacácori, 394, 395n50; as enemy of Pima and Maricopa Indians, 92, 98, 101, 105; impact of attacks of, 24, 82, 87, 90; Magdalena de Kino attack by, 15; threat from, 60, 80, 81, 89, 191, 245, 398, 399, 400; weapons of, 221. *See also* Havasupai; Navajo Indians
Aquituni (Pima village), 91
Arballo, María Feliciana, 39, 41–42, 154, 338n32, 343
Arellano, Manuel Ramírez, 341
Arellano, Mariano, 341
Aritoac (Gila River ford), 107–108
Arrequíbar, Fray Pedro, 82–83
Atizón (Pima village), 101
Ayala, Bruno de. *See* Eceta, Bruno de
Ayala, Juan Manuel, 31n54, 207
Azul River (Ariz.), 107–108. *See also* La Asunción River (Ariz.); Verde River (Ariz.)

Baja California, 24, 50, 84n43, 130, 145, 147, 168n3, 188, 203, 211n144; on Font's maps, 37; foreign scientists in, 33; governor of, 178n32; missions system of, 190, 194n90; Neve as governor of, 51; Rivera y Moncada in, 54, 60, 255, 255n140
Barbastro, Francisco Antonio, 21, 35, 63
Barragán, Manuel, 128
Bastida, María Jacinta, 339
Beñemé Indians, 179, 219
Bernal, Ana María, 340
Bernal, José Apolinario, 340
Bernal, José Dionisio, 340
Bernal, José Joaquín, 340

Bernal, Juan Francisco, 340
Bernal, María Teresa, 340
Bernal, Tomás Januario, 340
Berreyesa, Ana Isabel, 336n19, 342n62
Berreyesa, Luis Cayetano, 342n62
Berreyesa, María Isabel, 342
Berreyesa, Nicolás Antonio, 342
Bodega Bay (Calif.), 208, 255–56, 275, 298, 313
Bodega y Cuadra, Juan Francisco de la, 208n132, 275, 298, 313
Bojorques, María Agustina, 339
Bojorques, María Antonia, 87n59, 337, 337n24
Bojorques, María Gertrudis, 335
Bojorques, María Micaela, 87n59, 335, 342
Bojorques, Pedro, 334n9, 339
Bojorques, Ramón, 335, 337n24, 342n60
Borboa, María Leonor, 335
Bosque Espinoso (Calif.), 266
Botiller, María Dolores, 398
Botiller, María Martina, 340
Bucareli, Antonio de, 24, 82, 122, 222, 315, 372; Alta California place named for, 25; and California–New Mexico route, 23, 317; correspondence from, 373; and founding of San Francisco, 251n132, 253; and founding of San Juan Capistrano, 254–55; and Garcés at Colorado River, 123; and meeting with Salvador Palma, 59, 133, 381n13, 382; and orders for Anza's expedition, 28, 31, 32, 38, 52–53, 167n1, 208, 402; and orders for Garcés, 369, 370, 391–92; Rivera y Moncada's reports to, 55, 372; and survey of San Francisco Bay, 206
Buchón (Cuabajay chief), 230, 361
Buelna, José Antonio, 337n29
Buenavista (Calif.), 243, 313, 345, 346

Caballer, Fray, 39, 358
Cabo de la Concepción (Calif.), 231. *See also* Punta de la Concepción (Calif.)
Cabo de la Galera. *See* Punta de la Concepción (Calif.)
Caborca, La Purisima Concepción (mission), 122, 125, 343, 389, 390; Anza and Font at, 394, 396
Cahuilla Indians. *See* Jecuiche Indians

Cajuenche Indians, 144, 382, 389; culture of, described, 132n56, 134; expedition at village of, 131, 141, 149; expedition interpreter for, 84; lands of, 132; language of, 138, 150, 160; naming of, 149n119; relations of with Quechán Indians, 133; visit to expedition camps by, 379; wars conducted by, 138n72. *See also* Jecuiche Indians; Kohuana Indians
Cajuenche Mountains (Calif.), 387
Calabazas, San Cayetano de (pueblo), 82
California, 19, 23, 49, 66, 68, 122; Anza's 1774 expedition to, 25, 32, 92n73, 338n34; Anza's 1775–76 expedition to, 20, 31, 50; Anza's and Font's departure from, 41, 57; colonists of, 40–41, 84; Costansó expedition to, 32; exploration of, 27–28; foreign scientists in, 33; Garcés explorations of, 382n15; Indians of, 43, 169, 172, 186, 194; landscape of, 35; leading families of, 154n135; maps of, 63; mission system of, 24, 24n31, 39, 44, 50, 52, 61, 70, 122n20, 154n134; mountains of, 130, 145, 148, 149, 151, 152, 155, 156, 158, 164, 168, 177, 188, 201, 245, 312, 376; Neve as governor of, 51; Pedro Cayuelas return to, 59; Portolá's expedition to, 174; role of colonists' descendants in, 42; routes to, 23, 24, 60, 153n131, 201. *See also* Alta California; Baja California
Calzada, Fray Ambrosio, 394
Camacho (Spanish soldier), 44, 56, 220
Cambón, Fray Pedro, 244, 256, 257, 344; as priest for San Francisco missions, 250, 254; and Serra's dispute with Rivera y Moncada, 353, 354–55, 356n102, 357, 359, 366
Cañizares, José de, 31, 46, 47, 201, 207–208, 238
Cárdenas, Ignacio, 340
Cárdenas, Juana María, 337
Carlos (Cocomaricopa governor), 108, 117, 119
Carlos (San Diego Indian conspirator), 53, 199, 347n78, 351, 373
Carlos, Ana Josefa de, 341
Carlos III (Spain), 25, 27, 92, 102, 168n3
Carmel Mission. *See* San Carlos Borroméo de Carmelo (mission)

Carpintería Valley. *See* San Buenaventura Valley
Carrasco, Fray Manuel, 80, 81n29
Carrillo, Guillermo, 174, 175n17, 199n110, 203n119, 240n87, 240n88, 241n91
Carrillo, María Antonia Victoria, 203
Carrillo, Mariano, 30, 203n119, 208, 241n91
Casa Grande de Moctezuma (Ariz.), 94n80; Font's and Anza's trip to, 35, 92; Font's description of, 42, 65, 66, 94–96; Font's drawing of, 103; Font's latitude calculation of, 93; Piman legends about, 98
Castaño, Father Bartolomé, 180
Casteló, Gertrudis, 336
Castro, Antonio Enríquez de, 335n14, 397, 398
Castro, Carlos Antonio de, 341
Castro, Francisco Antonio, 340, 340n48
Castro, Francisco María, 340n48
Castro, Ignacio Clemente de, 340
Castro, Joaquín Isidro de, 259n3, 340
Castro, José Joaquín de, 340
Castro, José Mariano de, 340
Castro, María Encarnación de, 341
Castro, María Martina, 341
Catalonia, Spain, 16, 17, 17n11, 211, 266
Cavaller, Fray José, 232, 234, 315, 356, 361
Cayuelas, Pedro Regalado, 59
Cerro del Imposible Mountain (Calif.), 147
Cerro del Metate hill (Ariz.), 113
Cerro de Nacameri (Sonora), 399
Chiruma Indians. *See* Halchidhoma Indians
Chuchumaopa Indians, 102. *See also* Maricopa Indians
Chumacero, María Angela, 334
Chumash Indians, 219n15. *See also* Cuabajay Indians
Chupisonora (Sonora), 76, 78
Cieneguilla, Sonora, 60
Cocomaricopa Indians, 102, 108; Anza's interaction with, 109, 111; description of, 111; language of, 108; missions for, 112; Quechán Indians peace with, 111, 117, 119; trade by with other tribes, 135. *See also* Maricopa Indians
Cojat (Pápago village), 100
Cojat Indians, 128, 129, 132. *See also* Kohuana Indians
Colegio de la Santa Cruz (Querétaro), 17, 24, 189, 381n13, 392n38, 406; Anza as honorary lay brother of, 73; and Colorado River missions, 58; commissioning of Font-Garcés map by, 63; Font member of, 19, 20, 84; and Font's assignment, 31–32, 36; Font's reports to, 49, 57, 68, 200; residents of, 74n3, 76n13; and San Francisco missions, 250
Colegio de Nuestra Señora de Guadalupe de Zacatecas, 392n38
Colegio de San Fernando de México, 17, 26, 26n36, 27, 314, 315, 373; California missions of, 185
Colorado River, 17, 35n63, 51, 94n80, 109, 124, 163, 177, 318n225, 328, 343, 368, 389; Anza and Font at, 379, 388, 391; Anza influence at, 57; Anza's 1774 expedition crossing of, 116; Anza's and Font's crossing of, 382–85; Anza's expedition at, 116, 124, 245; Anza's expedition to, 22, 23, 24, 25, 50, 92n73; climate on, 390; confluence of with Gila River, 32, 114, 116, 133; course and terrain of, 128, 145, 318; description of, 132, 133; deserting soldier and muleteers headed to, 239n82, 240n88, 241; destruction of missions at, 60, 63, 259n3; distance to from San Diego, 37; expedition's crossing of, 83, 118, 119, 121, 126; flooding of, 118; Garcés and Eixarch at, 82, 84, 121, 123, 369, 381n14, 396; Garcés's exploration of, 22, 57, 58, 101, 130, 158n145; Indian tribes along, 25, 42, 43, 84, 111, 138, 138n72, 143–44, 152, 219, 298n151, 371, 377; missions at, 21, 44, 57, 58, 128, 200n112; at Puerto de la Concepción, 380; Quechán Indians on, 23, 132; and reaching the Pacific Ocean, 27, 147n116; routes to, 24, 30, 37, 58, 84n43, 201, 314, 315, 319. *See also* Río de los Misterios
Comar Mountains (Ariz.), 102, 105
Comari (Ariz.), 92
Consag, Father Fernando, 201
Constanzó, Miguel. *See* Costansó, Miguel
Cordero, Mariano Antonio, 339n36
Cortés, María Feliciana, 337

Cosnina Indians, 317–19
Costansó, Miguel, 28, 32, 46, 63, 75n9, 187, 188n71, 212, 218n12
Coyote Hills (Calif.), 276n82, 288–89
Crespí, Fray Juan, 31, 244; on expedition camp sites, 184n52; exploration of San Francisco Bay by, 205, 254, 277, 291, 292, 295, 296, 298n151, 306, 307, 308; Font's rivalry with over recording Pacific Coast geographical discoveries, 47–48; journal of, 26, 27; latitude measurements by, 253, 256, 257; maps of, 17n8, 46, 254n138; on San Francisco Bay Indians, 282; on San Francisco River, 208; and search for route to San Francisco, 29–30; and search for San Francisco River, 331
Crespo, Francisco Antonio, 63, 92, 92n74, 317, 401, 404
Croix, Teodoro de (Caballero de), 35, 44, 63
Cruzado, Fray Antonio, 178, 368
Cuabajay Indians, 219–24, 227–28, 363, 364
Cuadra, Juan de la. *See* Bodega y Cuadra, Juan de la
Cuitoa (Pima village), 90
Cupeño Indians. *See* Jecuiche Indians
Cuytoa (Pima village), 91–92

Davidson, George, 69
Delfín, María de Loreto, 336
Díaz, Fray Juan: with Anza's 1774 expedition, 32, 59, 390; death of, 62; Font's correspondence to, 200; Indian attacks on, 158n145; on Jesuit geographical observations, 32n57; language skills of, 21; on Mission San Gabriel's location, 212; on Santa Olalla Lake, 129n49
Dumetz, Father Francisco, 237, 238, 244, 352

Eceta, Bruno de, 262, 272n55, 284n103
Eixarch, Fray Tomás, 17, 17n11, 72, 82, 102, 391; assignment of at Colorado River, 84, 125, 368, 379, 380; on Chief Pablo Feo, 386; and crossing of Colorado River, 384; dealings with tribes by, 138; departure from Yuma by, 388; fish caught by, 111, 114; illness of, 109, 110; journal of, 381n14; and peace between Quecháns and Cocomaricopas, 117; and Quechán Indians, 121, 123, 126, 137n71, 143; religious duties of, 87, 102, 124; and Salvador Palma, 381, 381n13, 382; servants of, 124; to Tumacácori, 395–96; at Uturitúc, 99
El Agua Escondido (Calif.), 215, 216, 365, 366
El Agua Hedionda (Calif.), 210
El Agua Zarca (Sonora), 81
El Bámuri (Sonora), 396–97
El Bauquíburi (mountain), 108, 126, 130, 147
El Bosque, Arroyo de (Calif.), 295
El Buchón (Cuabajay village), 230, 231
El Bulillo (Cuabajay village), 227
El Cajón Valley (Calif.), 263
El Capitán Feo. *See* Pablo Feo, Capitán
El Carmelo Bay (Calif.). *See* Monterey Bay (Calif.)
El Carrizal (Sonora), 399
El Carrizal, Arroyo de (Ariz.), 390, 391, 392
El Carrizal (well) (Calif.), 144, 146, 148, 150, 153, 172, 239, 377, 378
El Charco de Gauna (Sonora), 79
El Charco del Canelo (Sonora), 78
El Cojat (Quechán village), 379
El Cojo (Cuabajay village), 227, 228, 362, 363
El Coyote, Arroyo de (Calif.), 327
Eldredge, Zoeth, 69
El Encino Spring (Calif.), 216
El Fuerte, Sinaloa, 342n58
El Gigante (peak), 126
El Guambút (Sonora), 81
El Incendio (Calif.), 184n52
El Pájaro River (Calif.), 328
"El Peregrino." *See* Taraval, Sebastián
El Pie del Sauce (Calif.), 158n145, 159, 376
El Pitic, Sonora. *See* Pitiquito, Sonora
El Pitiqui, Sonora. *See* Pitiquito, Sonora
El Pitiquito, Sonora, 394
El Portezuelo (Calif.), 215
El Pozo de Cristano (Sonora), 399
El Príncipe Valley (Calif.), 162, 168, 168n3, 168n5, 210, 375
El Puerto, Arroyo de (Calif.), 275, 282
El Puerto del Azotado (Ariz.), 89, 90
El Puerto de los Conejos (Sonora), 78, 79
El Puerto de los Osos (Calif.), 176
El Rincón (Indian village), 189
El Rosario (well), 145

El Síbuta (Sonora), 81
El Tecolote (Sonora), 398
El Templo. *See* Colegio de la Santa Cruz (Querétaro)
El Toro Rabón (Calif.), 243
El Trabuco Stream (Calif.), 184, 185
El Triunfo (Calif.), 215, 216, 365
El Tuquisón. *See* Tucson (pueblo)
El Voladero Pass (Sonora), 400
El Zanjón (Sonora), 399
Escalante, Fray Silvestre Vélez de, 36, 123, 317–18, 319, 392
Espinosa, Bárbara de, 338
Espinosa, Joaquín, 338n34
Espinosa, María Josefa, 335, 343
Esténaga, Tomás, 46mn85
Eustaquia, María, 343
Expedition, 183; camps of, 86, 108, 110, 112, 122–23; crossing of Colorado River by, 118–19, 121, 126, 245; deaths during, 86; desertion of muleteers of, 211, 213, 239, 240, 387; equipment and livestock of, 79, 83, 85–86, 92, 104, 110, 112, 156, 157–58, 160, 167n1; Font as chaplain of, 31–32, 40n71; fording of Gila River by, 107–108, 111, 116; fording of other rivers by, 174, 175, 229, 235, 236; founding of San Francisco settlements by, 205–207, 247, 251, 251n132, 253, 332; illness among members, 103, 106, 112–13; impact of weather on, 151, 153; Indians steal from, 152, 228; Indians trade with, 129, 131, 138, 142; Indians visit camps of, 100–101, 115, 141, 222; marches of, described, 78, 86, 142, 151, 155, 164; at Mission San Antonio de Padua de los Robles, 237, 239; at Mission San Luis Obispo, 232, 234; at Presidio of Monterey, 242–48, 251–52; provisions for, 167n1, 174, 201–202, 213–14, 227; roster of members of, 84; water supply for, 25, 76, 78–79, 81–82, 87, 90–91, 103–104, 108–11, 128, 142, 145–47, 149–51, 153–56, 173, 216, 223, 230, 243

Fages, Pedro, 30, 188; behavior of soldiers of, with Indians, 233; conflicts with missionaries by, 223n25, 315, 353; exploration of San Francisco region by, 28, 254, 259, 292–93, 305–11, 324; exploration of San Francisco regions by, 205; as military governor of California, 255; and search for route to San Francisco, 28n47, 29–30; and search for San Francisco River, 208
Farallones (Calif.), 270
Féliz, José Antonio Capistrano, 86n55, 341
Féliz, José de Jesús, 341
Féliz, José Doroteo, 341
Féliz, José Francisco, 341
Féliz, María Antonia, 341
Féliz, María de Loreto, 341
Féliz, María Manuela, 341
Féliz, Vicente, 86n55, 341
Figuer, Fray Juan, 232, 362n119
Flórez, Fray Enrique, 75, 75n11
Font, Fray Pablo, 254
Font, Fray Pedro: on ancient sea bed, 130, 145–46, 147, 162; Anza's attitude toward, 38, 39, 57, 80, 80n27, 122–25, 182, 200, 203–205, 210, 212, 214, 223, 260, 277, 333, 343, 361, 362, 364, 368, 382, 395, 396, 401, 404; on Anza's interactions with Indians, 56, 122; on Apache threat, 398, 399, 400; on attitude of presidial soldiers, 394–95; on attitudes toward priests by colonists, 344; background of, 16, 17, 19–20, 21, 60; on Cajuenche Indians, 379; on California flora, 175; on California Indians, 169, 172, 216–17, 262, 264–65; on campaign against rebellious Indians, 198–99; on Chief Pablo Feo, 386, 387; on Cocomaricopas, 109; on Cojat Indians, 129; conflicts with Anza by, 103, 154, 161, 162, 163, 165, 172; on conflict between Rivera y Moncada and Serra, 254–55; conflict with Anza over quadrant, 131, 402–404; criticism of Anza by, 154; criticism of presidial soldiers by, 44; criticism of Rivera y Moncada by, 241, 345; criticisms of Rivera y Moncada by, 54, 56; on crossing Colorado River, 383–85; on crossing of Colorado River, 119, 121; on Cuabajay Indians, 219–22, 224, 227, 364, 365; on danger of hostile Indians, 51; death of, 62, 63; definition of league by, 75; departure from Horcasitas by, 41; description and drawing of

Casa Grande by, 94–95; description of Colorado River by, 132–33; description of El Príncipe Valley by, 168; on desertion of mission soldier and muleteers, 211, 239–41; on discontent of expedition members, 212, 252; discussion on the salvation of Indians' souls by, 139–42; on dispute between Anza and Rivera y Moncada, 49, 206, 209, 251, 252–53, 346–50, 353, 356–57, 358–59, 366–67, 371–73; drawing of maps by, 254, 255, 331, 332; and encounter with Palma's daughter, 387; on erecting cross at San Francisco Bay, 279; and Escalante's expedition, 317–18, 319; on excommunication of Rivera y Moncada, 351; on expedition operations, 157; as expedition's chaplain, 31–32, 84; and Father Crespí, 47–48; on Father Paterna's refusal to provision Garcés, 369–70; field text of, 65, 66; final text of, discussion of, 69–71; on flora and fauna of California, 169, 173, 176–77, 184–85, 186, 211, 229, 234–35, 235n62, 236, 242, 261, 262, 264, 265, 266, 282, 284, 309, 324, 327n259; on fording of rivers, 174, 175, 288–89; on founding missions, 196; on Francisco Garcés, 144; on Garcés's explorations, 22, 58, 143; on Gila Pimas, 99, 100; on goal of expedition, 250; ground plan for Mission San Gabriel church by, 374; humor of, 39; illnesses of, 82, 103, 105, 106, 107, 108, 111, 112, 113, 124, 130, 155, 157, 173, 195, 198, 199, 203, 251, 252, 331, 378, 397; and Indian attack on Magdalena de Kino, 15–16, 59, 406; on Indian culture, 263; on Indian languages, 90n68, 96, 105, 108, 128, 138, 238; on Indians near San Francisco Bay, 268, 269, 282, 283, 285, 286, 287, 290, 291–93, 295–302, 305–306, 307, 310, 311, 326; on Indians of Mission San Antonio, 237–38; on Indians stealing, 389; on islands in San Francisco Bay, 294; on Jecuiche Indians, 150, 156–62, 375, 376; on journey along Gila River, 109–10; on journey to Monterey, 200, 215; on journey to San Diego, 183–87; latitude calculations of, 36–37, 72, 74, 75, 79, 80, 82, 83, 89, 93, 103, 109, 112, 113, 131, 153, 169, 189, 201, 212, 213, 214, 234, 239, 247, 252, 253, 256, 257, 281, 304, 383, 394, 397, 401–402; on local cuisine, 187; luggage of, 76; maps of, 19, 35, 57, 62–63; on Maricopa Indians, 105–106; measuring of large redwood by, 286–87; and mines of La Cieneguilla, 397; on Mission San Antonio de los Robles, 236–37; at Mission San Carlos, 244, 248, 249; on Mission San Diego, 201; at Mission San Gabriel, 363; on Mission San Gabriel, 178, 179, 180, 209, 212; Mission San Gabriel building designs by, 61; at Mission San José de Pimas, 392n38; and Mission San Luis de Obispo, 234; and Mission San Luis Obispo, 232; on Monterey Bay, 250, 253; musical ability of, 19, 213; and naming of geographical features by, 30; and naming of geographical landmarks, 41; on Nochi Indians, 232–33; opposition of to Colorado River missions, 58–59; Palma's meetings with, 118, 125; on peace between Quecháns and Cocomaricopas, 117; on Pedro Regaldo, 361; on Pima Indians, 103–104; on potential mission sites, 104, 106, 109, 111–12, 222, 224, 267, 282; on potential site for San Francisco settlement, 272, 274; on preaching to Indians, 143; and Presidio of Monterey, 243; on Presidio of San Diego, 188; on Puerto de la Concepción (Colorado River), 384; on Quechán Indians, 23, 132, 134–38; on Quemeya Indians, 189; and reconnaissance for San Francisco settlement sites, 45–46, 250, 279–81; and reconnaissance of San Francisco Bay, 207, 208–209, 268–69, 283–84; and reconnaissance of San Francisco Harbor, 205; religious duties of, 40–41, 81–82, 87, 101, 102, 111, 161; and return journey to Sonora, 346, 377; return to Horcasitas by, 400, 401; and route from Gila River to Caborca, 390–94; on route from Gila River to Caborca, 389; and route from San Francisco Bay to Monterey, 326–27, 326–29; and Salvador Palma, 122; on Salvador Palma, 133, 381, 382–83; and San Diego, 51, 188–89; at San Diego, 182; and

Font, Fray Pedro (*continued*)
San Diego harbor (Mission Bay), 188–90; on San Diego Indian uprising, 43–44, 177–78, 190–94; on San Diego Indians, 200; and San Francisco Bay, described, 274–76; at San José de Pimas, 20, 406; and San José Valley, described, 169–70, 171–72; and search for San Francisco River, 26, 31, 47–48, 49, 207–208, 287, 300–301, 303–304, 308, 309, 311–17, 319–23; and Sebastián Taraval, 44n81; sermons of, 40–41, 73, 83, 89, 90, 114, 154, 162–63, 213, 215, 233, 244–47, 252; and Serra's conflicts with Rivera y Moncada, 354–55; Serra's meetings with, 52; servants of, 78, 80, 80n27; on settlers for San Francisco, 334–43; shortened text of, discussed, 66–69; on soldiers killing bear, 285; story of "The Prince" by, 128–29; on tar pits, 217; on terrain near San Francisco Bay, 284, 288, 294, 296, 297, 298, 312, 313; at Uturitúc, 99; on visits of Indians with expedition, 228; on whales, 198, 224; at Yuma Crossing, 380, 388

Font, Pablo, 17, 26, 26n36, 46

Francisca (Quechán, Palma's daughter), 387

Freshwater Harbor (Calif.), 276, 277, 294, 297n150, 300n159, 301, 306, 307, 308, 314, 331n1

Fuster, Fray Vicente, 53, 188, 190, 191, 193, 197, 198, 200, 203, 205, 209, 356n102, 372; and excommunication of Rivera y Moncada, 351, 354

Galindo, Juan Venancio, 342, 342n59
Galindo, Nicolás, 342, 342n59
Gallegos, Carlos, 335, 343, 346, 372n144
Gálvez, José de, 26, 244, 335n11, 341n53, 399n64; and Anza expedition, 26; Font's correspondence to, 59, 63; places named after, 25
Gamarra, Fray Félix, 82
Gaona, Juana, 335
Garcés, Fray Francisco, 24, 44n80, 83, 129n49, 348; Anza's opinion of, 38; Anza's refusal to provision, 368; arrival of, in Mexico, 16–17; assignment of at Colorado River, 84; in California, 177, 233n55, 292n130, 312, 312n204, 314, 317; California explorations of, 369–70; cause of Anza's delay at Yuma, 381–82, 382n15, 387–88; as co-leader of Anza's 1774 expedition, 22, 24, 32; on Colorado River, 130, 380; with Colorado River Indians, 132n56; and Colorado River missions, 58; on danger of native tribes, 51; death of, 60, 62; on Escalante's expedition, 318n225; explorations of, 19, 21, 23, 25, 27, 36, 57–58, 123, 127, 318n226, 319n229, 381n12; Font's maps of explorations of, 62–63; Indian attack on, 158; interaction of with Indians, 122n20, 144, 160n151; interaction with Indians by, 102, 104, 105, 138n72, 143–44, 145, 149n119, 150, 382; journal of explorations of, 57; language skills of, 21; as member of expedition, 82; at Mission San Luis Obispo, 352, 353; and naming of landmarks by, 145; and peace between Quecháns and Cocomaricopas, 117; preaching to Indians by, 142–43; provisions for to stay with Quechán Indians, 123–24, 125, 127; relationship of, with Anza, 90, 124, 381, 382; with Quechán Indians, 115, 121, 126, 136n67; with Rivera y Moncada, 50, 371; religious duties of, 100–101, 102, 118, 154n135, 343n65; and river to Pacific Coast, 147n116; and routes to California, 153n131; for route to New Mexico, 23, 381; at San Xavier del Bac, 86, 87; scientific tools used by, 35; servants of, 124, 396; at Uturitúc, 99–100; view of scientific subjects by, 32

Garcés, Fray Julián, 238
García, José Antonio, 337
García, José Francisco, 337
García, José Vicente, 337
García, Juan Guillermo, 337
García, María Graciana, 337
García, María Josefa, 337
Gila Pima Indians, 102; Anza's interaction with, 100–102; attending of Mass by, 99, 101; Casa Grande legends of, 92, 94–96; description of, 91–92, 100, 101, 103–104, 105–106, 143, 219; Font's suggestion for missions for, 112; irrigation system of, 102;

lands of, 111; myths of, 96, 98–99; trade with other Indians by, 103, 222; villages of, 99, 101; war with Apaches by, 92, 101. *See* River O'odhams

Gila River, 101, 103, 148, 177, 262; 1774 Anza expedition on, 25; Casa Grande de Moctezuma near, 92–93, 94; climate on, 390; confluence of with La Asunción River, 102, 104; confluence of with Colorado River, 32, 114, 116, 121, 126, 380; description of, 106–107, 132; expedition's travel along, 23, 38, 92n73, 116, 245, 388–89; fish of, 328; flooding of, 118; Garcés exploration of, 22; Indian tribes along, 42; Indian use of, for irrigation, 100, 101, 105; Indian villages along, 92, 107, 109; missionaries at, 21, 22; missionaries on, 200n112; mountains near, 81; Pima Indians on, 90; Pima villages on, 91, 93, 99, 101, 102; Quechán Indians on, 23, 133; route to, 91; terrain of, 105, 110, 111, 113, 114, 115; watershed of, 87

Góngora, José María, 252–53, 332, 332n4, 346–47, 356

González, Ana María, 342n57

González, Francisco, 342

González, José Manuel, 342

González, Juan José, 342

González, María Gregoria, 342

González, Ramón, 342

Grand Canyon (Ariz.), 36, 58, 318n225

Grijalva, Claudio, 334

Grijalva, Juan Pablo, 84, 110, 334, 343n65

Grijalva, María del Carmen, 334

Grijalva, María Josefa, 334

Guadalupe River (Calif.), 286, 288, 289, 290

Guasabas, mission, 398

Guillén, Fray Felipe, 80, 81n29

Guizarnótegui, Francisco de, 397–98

Gutiérrez, Diego Pascual, 338

Gutiérrez, Ignacio, 338

Gutiérrez, María de los Santos, 338

Gutiérrez, María Petra, 338

Gutiérrez, María Tomasa, 343

Guzmán, Nuño de, 40

Halchidhoma Indians, 318; presents given to, 66. *See also* Jalchedun Indians

Havasupai Indians, 58

Higuera, Ignacio Anastasio de, 342

Honker Bay (Calif.), 31, 207n131

Hopi Indians, 27, 381n12. *See also* Moqui Indians

Horcasitas. *See* San Miguel de Horcasitas, Presidio of

Hospital Lake. *See* La Laguna del Hospital (lake)

Huevavi, Mission. *See* Guevavi, Los Santos Ángeles de

Imuris, San José de (mission), 16, 57

Imuris, Sonora (pueblo), 80

Indians, 50, 239; of California, 216–17, 315; Font's writings on, 42; at Mission San Antonio, 239, 249; at Mission San Carlos, 249; at Mission San Diego, 249; at Mission San Luis Obispo, 232; and San Diego uprising, 240; near San Francisco Bay, 263, 267, 279, 281, 282, 283, 285, 286, 287, 289, 290, 291–93, 295, 296, 297–98, 301–303, 305–306, 307, 310–11, 324, 326, 328; of Santa Bárbara Channel, 224, 227–28; threat of to Anza's expedition, 51–52; trade among, 222; visits by to expedition, 235, 242, 260, 262, 264–65, 268, 269, 274, 299–300. *See also names of individual tribes*

Isla de Santa Catarina, 185

Isla de Santa Cruz (Calif.), 222, 233

Isla de Santo Tomás, 185

Isla del Angel (Calif.), 276

Jaime, Fray Luis, 178, 190, 191, 192

Jalchedun Indians, 114, 122n20, 380, 381; Anza's meetings with, 119, 122; expedition interpreter for, 84; Garcés's visit with, 143; lands of, 111; language of, 138; relations of with Quechán Indians, 133; and trade with other tribes, 117, 135, 138

Jallicaumai Indians. *See* Quíquima Indians

Jamajá Indians, 219, 368, 370, 380, 382n15

Jecuiche Indians, 189, 376, 377–78, 379; and dealings with expedition, 149, 156–62; description of, 150; and San Diego uprising, 190, 239. *See also* Cajuenche Indians; Quemeya Indians

Jenigüechi Indians, 149n119, 159, 179

Jesuits: geographical observations of, 32n57; on geography of Colorado River and Gila River confluence, 32; missionary work of, 19, 20, 21, 24, 50, 54, 68n148, 128, 194n90, 392
Jiménez, Fray Diego, 57, 200, 373, 374, 402
Josefa, Petronila. *See* Acuña, Petronila Josefa
Juan y Santacilia, Jorge, 36, 74, 75, 79, 83, 89, 93, 103, 109, 112, 113, 131, 153, 169, 189, 201, 213, 234, 247, 252, 256, 281, 304, 383, 394, 397, 402
Juncosa, Fray Domingo, 314

Kohuana Indians, 42, 44, 67
Kumeyaay Indians, 45, 117n12

La Alegría (well). *See* El Carrizal (well)
La Aribaca (Ariz.), 81
La Asumpta (Cuabajay village), 221, 364
La Asumpta River (Calif.), 217, 364, 365
La Asunción (Calif.), 234, 235
La Asunción River (Ariz.), 102, 104, 105, 106–107, 132. *See also* Azul River
La Asunción River (Calif.), 217
La Barajita (Sonora), 79
La Bocana, Arroyo de (Calif.), 296
La Cabeza del Gigante (mountain), 108
La Campana Mountains, 126, 130, 145
La Cañada de los Robles (Calif.), 236
La Cañada del Paraíso (Calif.). *See* San José stream (Calif.)
La Candelaria Tanks (Ariz.), 390, 391
La Canoa (Ariz.), 86
La Carpintería (Cuabajay village), 217, 221n22, 365. *See also* La Asumpta (Cuabajay village)
La Cieneguilla, Sonora, 240, 335n14, 397, 398, 399, 400
La Encarnación Stream (Calif.), 291
La Encarnación de Sutaquison (Pima village), 91. *See* Sutaquison (Pima village)
La Espada (Cuabajay village), 228, 363
La Frente Negra Mountains (Ariz.), 89
La Gaviota (Cuabajay village), 227
La Graciosa Lake (Calif.), 229–30
Laguna Graciosa (Calif.), 362
Laguna Grande (Cuabajay village), 230
Laguna Grande (lake), 362

Laguna Larga (lake), 362
Laguna Seca (drainage), 27, 147n116
La Harina, Arroyo de (Calif.), 293, 294
La Isla de la Trinidad, 116
La Isla del Angel, 207
Lake Merced (Calif.), 46, 46n85
La Laguna (Cuabajay village), 223, 364
La Laguna del Hospital (lake), 41, 102n114, 104, 105, 106
La Merced Lake (Calif.), 269, 284
La Natividad (Calif.), 260, 261, 328
La Oreja del Oso (hill), 41
La Palma (Sonora), 78
La Piriguita (Sonora), 79
La Puerta de la Concepción, 126, 133
La Punta de las Almejas (Calif.), 206
La Punta de los Llanos (Ariz.), 86, 87
La Quema (Calif.), 184, 185, 188, 190, 210
Lara, María Francisca de, 339
La Rinconada (Indian village), 188, 189, 217, 222–23, 364
Las Almejas (Calif.), 263
Las Angustias (well), 146
La Santísima Virgen de Guadalupe, 73, 76, 83, 89, 118, 121, 147, 245, 246, 381, 405
Las Bolas (Ariz.), 81
Las Flores Lake, 185
Las Lagunas (Sonora), 81, 82
Las Llagas, Arroyo de (Calif.), 262, 263, 268, 277, 281, 288, 289
Las Llagas, San Francisco de (Calif.), 73n2, 132n56
Lasuén, Fray Fermín, 188, 190, 191, 193, 194, 197, 198, 200, 203, 205, 209
La Soledad (Calif.), 186, 187, 199, 242
La Soledad (San Diego village), 51
La Tortuga (Sonora), 399

Leiva, María Micaela de, 342n62
León, Nicolás, 70
Linares, Gertrudis, 41. *See* Rivas, Gertrudis
Linares, Ignacio, 113, 335
Linares, José Ramó, 336
Linares, María Gertrudis, 336
Linares, Salvador Ignacio, 161, 336
Llamshin Indians. *See* Los Gritone Indians
Lomas de la Tuzas (Calif.), 324
Lomas de las Lágrimas (hills), 41

Lomita de la Linares (hill), 41
Llano de los Robles (Calif.), 264, 281, 283, 313
Llano del Tuzal (Ariz.), 390, 391
Llano de Santa Angela (Calif.), 310
López, Fray Francisco Antonio, 76, 76n13
López, Juan Francisco, 154n135, 343n65
López, María Justa, 340
López, María Tomasa, 340
López, Sebastián (son), 340
López, Sebastián Antonio, 339
López de Haro, María Agueda, 341
Lorenzana, Archbishop Francisco Antonio, 181n40
Loreto, Baja California, 60, 178n32, 203, 255n140
Los Alisos (Sonora), 81
Los Alisos, Arroyo de (Calif.), 175, 176, 372
Los Batequitos (Calif.), 186
Los Cerritos (Sonora), 398
Los Conejos (Calif.), 216, 365
Los Correos (Calif.), 242
Los Cuatro Coronado (islets), 189, 190, 365
Los Dolores (Calif.), 46
Los Dolores, Arroyo de (Calif.), 282, 283
Los Dolores Spring (Calif.), 332n5
Los Gritone Indians, 268
Los Laureles, Arroyo de (Calif.), 266
Los Llanos de la Virgen (Sonora), 78
Los Mártires (islet), 189
Los Nogales Spring (Calif.), 216
Los Ojitos (Calif.), 184
Los Ositos (Calif.), 241, 242, 346
Los Pedernales (Cuabajay village), 228, 363
Los Pitos (California Indian village), 217, 364
Los Pozos de Enmedio (Ariz.), 390
Los Robles Valley (Calif.), 241, 242, 352–53
Lugo, María Bárbara de. *See* Espinosa, Bárbara de

Madrid, Spain, 23, 26, 33, 45, 53, 59, 181n41, 205, 373
Margil de Jesús, Fray Antonio, 124
Maricopa Indians, 23, 108; Anza's interactions with, 105–106; description of, 102, 105–106; as friends of Pima Indians, 98; missions for, 109; at peace with Quechán Indians, 101, 117; preaching to, 143; tribes of, 102n111; villages of, 105, 107

Mascaró, Manuel, 63
Mesa, Father José Nicolás, 397–98
Mesa, José Joaquín, 335
Mesa, Valerio, 335
Mescaltitán (Cuabajay villages), 223, 224, 363
Mexico City, 17, 23, 24, 26, 31, 33, 40, 45, 47n87, 53, 55, 62, 63, 74, 123, 154, 181n 40, 194n90, 205n123, 206, 246, 249, 255, 315, 317, 349, 354, 371, 381n13, 392, 403, 404; Anza in, 47, 213, 251n132, 361, 402; correspondence dispatched to, 201; engraving of Font map at, 63; Palma visit to, 382; Rivera y Moncada in, 255
Mission Bay (Calif.), 27, 175, 178n32, 188–90, 389
Moctezuma's Palace. *See* Casa Grande (Ariz.); Casa Grande de Moctezuma (Ariz.)
Mojave Indians, 51, 318n226. *See also* Jamajá Indians; Tomascaba Indians
Mojave River (Calif.), 58
Monteagudo, Catarina, 401
Monteagudo, Manuel, 204, 404
Monteagudo, Manuel Bernardo de, 401
Monterey, Presidio San Carlos de, 53, 65, 82, 194n90, 205, 235, 272n55, 281, 313, 326, 332, 353; Anza's 1774 expedition to, 386; Anza's 1775–76 expedition to, 31, 37, 73; Anza and Font depart from, 259, 332, 345, 374; Anza and Font return to, 322, 323, 327n261, 329, 332; Anza at, 23, 42, 52, 62, 240n87, 257, 314; Cañizares at, 208; defenses of, 51; deserters from, 315, 387; expedition at, 40, 50, 178n32, 202n118, 242–48, 251, 252, 333, 343, 344, 346; expedition to, 26, 83, 154, 167, 197n102, 200, 202, 205, 207, 207n127, 211, 214; Fages as commandant of, 28; Font's latitude calculations of, 247; harbor of, 27, 28, 253; missions near, 231n47, 249; Rivera y Moncada at, 30, 49, 54, 59, 177, 178, 206, 348–49, 354, 355, 356, 357n104, 359; routes to, 36, 58, 319, 369; route to San Francisco from, 332; soldiers of, 84, 184, 259, 339n36, 341n49; terrain near, 235
Monterey Bay (Calif.), 243, 249, 253, 255, 257, 261
Monterey River (Calif.), 234, 236, 241, 242, 243, 249, 260, 313, 329, 345, 352

Moqui Indians, 105, 317, 318; Garcés's encounter with, 58, 127; and trade with other tribes, 117, 131, 135, 138
Moraga, Gabriel, 49
Moraga, José Joaquín, 53, 76n16, 84, 334; capture of deserted soldier by, 211, 213, 214, 239, 239n83, 240, 240n87, 241, 241n91, 253n137, 378; clashes with Rivera y Moncada by, 355, 357; criticisms of Rivera y Moncada by, 54; encounter with Indians by, 51, 239n84; as leader of colonists to San Francisco, 59, 167n1, 201, 251n132, 280n88, 333, 345, 346; as leader of expedition section, 152, 153; at Mission San Carlos, 257; at Presidio of Monterey, 248, 249; on San Francisco Bay reconnaissance, 45–46, 202n118, 259, 299n156, 330; and search for San Francisco River, 48–49, 317; at Yuma, 124
Morales, María Dolores, 340
Moreno, Fray José Matías, 62, 394
Morgan Hill (Calif.), 41
Mortar Hill (Ariz.), 113
Mount Davidson (Calif.), 30, 206n 124
Mount Hamilton (Calif.), 37
Mount Oso (Calif.), 323n244
Mount Tabor (Israel), 233
Mourelle, Francisco, 56
Mugarrieta, Señora, 398
Mugártegui, Fray Pablo, 232, 250, 353
Muñoz, Francisco, 343
Muñoz, María de la Luz, 339
Murguía, Fray José, 244, 248, 254, 257
Mussel Point. *See* La Punta de las Almejas (Calif.)

Nabcúb, San Serafino de (Pima village), 102, 104
Nacameri, Sonora, 79
Nacimiento River (Calif.), 235, 353
Nanaxi Indians, 105
Navajo Indians, 58
Neri, Felipa, 339
Neve, Felipe de, 51, 56
New Mexico, 58, 123, 309, 317; Anza as governor of, 60; Garcés journey to, 382n15; route to California from, 23, 27, 36, 317, 319, 381; route to Monterey from, 58

Nijora Indian, 84n45, 396
Nochi Indians, 232–33

Ochoa, Petra Ignacia de, 338
Ontiveros, María Dolores, 87n59, 342, 342n61
O'odham Indians, 87n58, 94n80; and attack on Magdalena, Sonora, 15; Font as priest for, 60; missionaries to, 21. *See also* Desert O'odhams; Pápago Indians; Pima Indians; River O'odhams
Opa Indians. *See* Maricopa Indians
Ópata Indians, 398
Ortega, Antonio Francisco. *See* Ortega, José Francisco
Ortega, José Francisco, 49, 183n49, 193, 194, 197, 203n119, 241n91; exploration of San Francisco Bay by, 288n114; Rivera y Moncada's attitude toward, 209, 255, 255n140; and San Diego uprising, 178n32, 187n67, 196
Ortiz, Catalina, 204–205
Ortiz, María Nicolasa, 338
Oryabe (Moqui village), 317
Osuna, Ana María de, 338
Oya, Diego, 395
Oytaparts lakes (Ariz.), 90

Pablo (San Diego uprising leader), 195
Pablo Feo, Capitán, 23, 117, 144, 382; body decorations of, 137; character of, 386–87; description of, 116; Font's meetings with, 118, 125; Font's opinion of, 133; overseeing of Anza's and Font's river crossing by, 383–84; relationship of with Spanish, 116; village of, 115, 126, 128
Pacheco, Bárbara, 341
Pacheco, Bartolomé, 341
Pacheco, Francisco, 341
Pacheco, Juan Salvio, 341
Pacheco, María Gertrudis, 341
Pacheco, Miguel, 341
Pájaro River (Calif.), 261
Palma, Salvador (Quechán chief), 17, 119, 335n14; Anza's interactions with, 50, 121; background of, 128; body decorations of, 137; daughter of, 387; Eixarch living with, 380; Font's description of, 23, 115; Font's meetings with, 118, 125; greeting

of expedition by, 114, 115; journey to
   Horcasitas by, 398; meeting by with
   Cocomaricopa governor Carlos, 117;
   to Mexico City, 381, 382–83, 388; and
   punishment of Indians, 389; as Quechán
   chief, 133–34; relationship of with Spanish,
   59, 122, 133; and relations with lower
   Colorado River tribes, 144; social behavior
   of, 135; villages of, 116, 122, 124, 126, 133,
   203; war conducted by, 133, 138, 138n72
Palóu, Fray Francisco, 192, 242n97; at
   Anza's and Font's departure, 344;
   exploration of San Francisco Harbor by,
   30, 47n87, 48, 206, 262, 268–69, 272n55,
   277, 284; with Indians, 263; measurements
   by, 253, 256, 257; at Mission San Carlos,
   249; and San Francisco missions, 244,
   250, 254; scientific equipment of, 37
Pápago Indians, 391, 392, 393; land of, 145;
   myths of, 134; trade with Pima Indians
   by, 103; villages of, 90, 100; water holes
   of, 91. *See also* Desert O'odhams; Piato
   Indians
Pápago Pima Indians, 90. *See also* Papago
   Indians; Pima Indians
Papaguería, 87, 90, 91, 102, 105, 110, 114,
   389; 1774 Anza expedition through, 24;
   Garcés's exploration of, 22; return route
   through, 393, 394
Pascual, Diego, 111
Paterna, Fray Antonio, 83n39, 178, 178n31,
   179, 181, 213, 368, 374; conflicts with Fages
   by, 315; and provisions for expedition,
   201, 212; and refusal to provision Garcés,
   369–70; support of Rivera y Moncada by,
   367, 371
Patterson Pass (Calif.), 324n248
Paul III (pope), 238
Pedro Regaldo (Cuabajay Indian), 361, 362,
   371, 372n144, 384; at Yuma Crossing, 385
Pedro y Gil, Rafael, 198
Peña, Fray Tomás, 55, 244, 250, 254, 256, 257,
   344, 354
Peralta, Gabriel de, 336
Peralta, Gertrude (wife of José Sotelo), 339
Peralta, Gertrudis de, 336
Peralta, Juan José de, 336, 342n62
Peralta, Luis María de, 336

Peralta, Pedro de, 336
Peremás, Melchor, 317, 403
Pérez de la Fuente, Pedro, 343
Piato Indians, 81, 399, 406. *See also* Papago
   Indians, Pima Indians
Picacho de Tacca (Ariz.), 90–91
Pico, Francisco Javier, 339
Pico, José Dolores, 339
Pico, José María, 339
Pico, José Miguel, 339n40
Pico, José Patricio, 339
Pico, María Antonia Tomasa, 339
Pico, María Josefa, 339
Pico, Santiago de la Cruz, 339
Pieras, Fray Miguel, 237, 238, 244, 256, 257,
   344, 345, 349, 352
Pima Indians, 87, 90, 90n68, 105, 128, 130,
   237, 396, 406; as friend of Maricopa
   Indians, 105; of Gila River, 90, 91, 93;
   language of, 90n68, 96, 105, 128, 138;
   legends of, 94, 98, 134; stealing of livestock
   by, 78; weapons of, 221. *See also* Gila Pima
   Indians; Piato Indians; River O'odhams
Pimería Alta, 21, 27, 57, 92, 99, 145
Pimería Baja, 20, 57, 392
Pino, Miguel del, 220n18
Pinto, José Marcelo, 338
Pinto, Juana, 339
Pinto, Juana Santos, 339, 342
Pinto, Juan María, 338
Pinto, María Petra de, 259n3
Pinto, Pablo, 113, 338, 339n36, 342n59
Pinto, Teresa, 342, 342n59
Pipatsje Indians. *See* Maricopa Indians
Pitiquito, Sonora, 60–62, 394n44
Porciúncula River (Calif.), 215, 366
Portolá, Gaspar de, 24, 174, 183, 184, 185,
   186n62, 186n63, 187, 189, 215n2, 218, 219n15,
   224n31, 230, 242, 327
"Prince, The" (Pima/Quechán Indian),
   128–29, 130, 133
Puerto Anegado (Calif.), 187, 188, 195
Puerto Blanco (Ariz.), 390, 391
Puerto de la Concepción (Colorado River),
   378, 379, 381, 383, 389–90; description of,
   380, 384; latitude calculations of, 383
Puerto de la Concepción (Pacific Coast),
   122, 318

Puerto del Azotado (pass), 41
Puerto de San Carlos (Alta California), 25, 152, 163, 172, 175, 177, 186, 204, 210, 312, 375, 376; expedition crossing of, 164, 167, 168, 170; Indian tribe at, 150; naming of, 168n3
Punta de Almejas (Calif.), 270, 275, 281, 284, 324, 327
Punta de Año Nuevo (Calif.), 243, 253, 257, 260, 261
Punta de Arena (Calif.), 275
Punta de Cipreses (Calif.), 248–49
Punta de Guijarros (Calif.), 188
Punta de la Concepción (Calif.), 228, 229, 231
Punta de la Concepción (Calif. coast), 363
Punta del Cordón (Calif.), 275
Punta de los Reyes (Calif.), 270, 275, 276n77, 281
Punta del Pájaro (Calif.), 261
Punta de Pinos (Calif.), 243, 248, 252, 253
Punta Murguía (Calif.), 275

Quadrant: Anza and Font's conflict over, 402–404; Anza gives to Font, 182; Anza's and Font's use of, 32, 35, 37; Font's latitude calculations with, 74, 79, 80, 82, 131
Quechán Indians, 17, 240; affection for Spaniards by, 386; agriculture of, 133; and Anza's and Font's river crossing, 383–85; and arrival of Font and Anza, 379; chiefs of, 128–29; clothing of, 106; Cocomaricopas' peace with, 111; as compared to Cajuenche Indians, 131; culture of, 123; and death of Rivera y Moncada, 54; and departure of Anza and Font, 388–89; description lifestyle of, 114, 387; description of preaching to, 143; desire for missions, 382; expedition interpreter for, 84; and expedition's crossing of Colorado River, 121; Font's description of, 66, 71, 134, 142, 380; Font's ethnographic writings on, 42, 45, 67; friendliness of toward Spanish, 119; friendly relations of with Spanish, 51; as good swimmers, 318–19; and greeting of expedition, 114; greeting of expedition by, 115; Jecuiche Indians as enemies of, 379; lands of, described, 132, 133; language of, 138, 150; Maricopa Indian's peace with, 98; and missionaries, 44; names of neighboring tribes of, 149n119; and Palma's visit to Mexico City, 383; and peace with Cocomaricopas, 117; peace with Cocomaricopas by, 119; and peace with lower Colorado River tribes, 143; people and culture of, described, 134–38; playing music for, 80; possible mission among, 118; presents for from Anza, 119, 122, 124; rebellion of, 60, 62, 136n67; as Spanish allies, 59; Spanish relations with, 23; Spanish relationship with, 116–17; trade with other Indian tribes by, 117; visit to expedition camps by, 144; wars of, 138n72. *See also* Cojat Indians
"Queen, The" (Pima Indian), 128–29
Quemeyá Indians, 117n12, 150, 198; at Mission San Diego, 189; and San Diego uprising, 190, 193, 245
Querétaro, 59; Colegio de la Santa Cruz in, 17, 24, 31, 36, 49, 57, 58, 68, 74n3, 76n13; Font in, 60; Franciscan missionaries from, 19; missionaries of, 61–62, 63
Quitobác, Sonora, 392–93

Ranchería Nueva (Cuabajay village), 224, 227
Río Carmelo (Calif.), 248, 249, 256, 272n55, 306
Río de la Bocana. *See* Bocana, Arroyo de la
Río de la Virgen de Guadalupe. *See* Guadalupe River
Río de los Alisos (Calif.), 175
Río de los Misterios, 317, 318, 318n225, 319
Rivas, Gertrudis, 113, 335
Rivera y Moncada, Fernando, 28, 242, 371; Anza's correspondence with, 167, 175n17, 250; attitude of toward José Ortega, 255, 255n140; attitude of toward priests, 193; background of, 50, 54; and campaign against rebellious Indians, 194–95, 197n102, 198, 200, 202, 214; clash with José Moraga by, 355; as commandant of Presidio of Monterey, 30, 49; as commander of Los Angeles colonists, 60, 333; as commander of San Francisco colonists, 59, 178n32, 280n88; and conflict with Junípero Serra, 54; conflict with Junípero Serra by, 354, 356;

conflict with San Diego missionaries by, 356n102; conflicts with Junípero Serra by, 359; criticism of command of, 44, 52, 54–55, 56, 345; criticisms of, 71; death of, 60; and discipline of soldiers, 192, 240n87; and dispute with Anza, 178n32, 197n102, 202, 207n127, 209, 251, 252, 253, 332, 346–50, 352, 353, 358, 366–68, 371–73, 382; excommunication of, 53, 55, 347n78, 351, 352; and expedition deserters, 387; exploration of San Francisco Bay by, 28, 30, 45, 259, 268–69, 269, 274, 284, 288n114, 310n191, 321, 329; and founding of missions, 254–55; lack of discipline of soldiers of, 196–97, 217n10, 241; as member of Portolá's expedition, 218; as military governor of California, 255; at Mission San Gabriel, 177; opposition to San Francisco settlements by, 46, 50–51, 205–206, 250, 254, 277, 346; over missions, 254–55; and refusal to give provisions to Garcés, 370; relationship of with Anza, 39, 45, 49, 50, 51, 51n101, 52–57; relationship with Font, 32; and route to Colorado River, 30; at San Diego, 181, 183, 188, 333; and San Diego uprising, 178, 187n66, 190, 194, 195, 201; and search for San Francisco River, 47, 49, 178n32, 207, 238; warnings of danger of hostile Indians by, 50–51, 51n99

River O'odham Indians, 21–22, 42. *See also* Gila Pima Indians

Roberto, José Antonio, 336
Roberto, José Matías, 336
Roberto, Justo, 336
Robles, Juan José, 46, 259, 268, 280n88, 282, 285, 322–23, 323n244
Rocha, Jerónimo de la, 63
Romero, María Francisca, 335
Rubí, Marqués de, 404
Ruelas, Francisca, 113, 157, 338, 339n36
Ruia, María Micaela, 342

Sacramento River (Calif.), 31, 48, 207n131
Sacramento Valley (Calif.), 49
Sal, Hermenegildo, 335n14
Salado River (Ariz.), 104, 106. *See also* La Asunción River (Ariz.)

Sales, Luis, 70
Salton Basin (Calif.), 23, 27, 35
Salt River (Ariz.), 390. *See also* La Asunción River (Ariz.); Salado River (Ariz.)
San Alejos (Calif.), 186
San Andreas Lake (Calif.)., 206n 124, 269
San Andrés (Pima village), 92, 101
San Andres Valley (Calif.), 281
San Andrés Valley (Calif.), 263, 284, 285, 332n5
San Antonio de Padua de los Robles (mission), 23, 65, 180, 236–37, 241, 244, 313, 315, 323n244, 344, 345, 347n78, 350, 355; Anza and Font at, 352; Font's latitude calculations of, 239; Indians of, 237–38, 249; supplies for, 346
San Antonio River (Calif.), 235, 241n93, 242, 353
San Benito, Arroyo de (Calif.), 260
San Benito, Fray José de, 140
San Benito Valley (Calif.), 328
San Bernabé Canyon (Calif.), 241, 346, 352
San Bernardino (Ariz.), 109
San Bernardino del Agua Caliente (Cocomaricopa village). *See* Agua Caliente, San Bernardino del (Cocomaricopa village)
San Bernardino Valley (Calif.), 261, 265, 266, 291, 313, 323, 328, 353
San Bruno, Arroyo de (Calif.), 284
San Bruno Mountain (Calif.), 28, 30, 206n 124, 279n88
San Buenaventura (Calif.), 364
San Buenaventura (mission), 223, 233n56
San Buenaventura Valley, 223
San Carlos (frigate), 207, 270, 272, 272n55, 276
San Carlos Bay, 201
San Carlos de Borroméo de Carmelo (mission), 19, 30, 37, 47n87, 68n148, 193, 206, 231n47, 235, 236, 237, 244, 268n44, 286, 293, 306, 315, 344, 346, 352, 353, 359, 377; agriculture at, 249; Anza and Font at, 247, 257, 333; Cañizares at, 208; description of, 248–49; Font's latitude calculations of, 252, 253, 256, 257; priests of, 244, 247
San Carlos Pass. *See* Puerto de San Carlos (Alta California)

Sánchez, José Antonio, 340
Sánchez, José Antonio (son), 340
Sánchez, Fray Miguel, 178, 179
Sánchez, María Josefa, 340
Sánchez, Nellie Van de Grift, 71
San Clemente (island), 190
San Diego (Maricopa village), 107
San Diego (mission), 19, 32, 38, 168, 168n4, 172, 254, 311; Anza and Font travel to, 182, 183; condition of, 181; distance to Colorado River from, 37; and excommunication of Rivera, 55, 351; Font's latitude calculations of, 189; Indian uprising at, 43, 49, 50, 51, 51n99, 53, 152, 174–75, 175n17, 177–78, 181, 185, 187, 188, 190–95, 199, 206, 239, 239n84, 240, 245, 373; Indian villages attached to, 187; Indians of, 249, 376; lack of supplies at, 370; road to San Gabriel from, 174, 187, 239n83; Serra to travel to, 355; taking cats to, 346; terrain near, 174
San Diego, Calif., 183, 389; coastline of, 365; harbor of, 27, 175, 178n32, 188–89
San Diego, Presidio of, 44, 45, 56, 168, 168n4, 172, 255, 315, 335n14, 365; Anza and Font at, 47, 182, 187, 200, 204, 209, 210; Anza's 1774 expedition to, 185; Anza's departure from, 51, 52; and campaign against Indians, 197n102, 198–99, 202, 347n78, 347n79, 351; and conflict with mission, 53; description of, 188, 198; and excommunication of Rivera y Moncada, 354; expedition deserters held at, 241, 387, 388; expedition provisions from, 210, 214; expedition soldiers at, 202n118, 214; Font's latitude calculations of, 189, 201; Indian uprising at, 175, 175n17, 190–95, 206, 239, 373; lack of soldier discipline at, 196–97; Rivera y Moncada at, 54, 332, 348
San Diego Indians, 188; uprising of, 175, 177–78. *See also* Quemeyá Indians
San Dieguillo (Calif.), 187, 210
San Dionisio (Calif.), 189
Sandoval, Cristóbal, 342
San Eduardo de La Arivaypia (Sonora), 393
San Felipe River (Calif.), 314
San Fernando de Velicatá (Baja California), 194n90
San Francisco (Cojat village), 132n56
San Francisco (mission), 45–46
San Francisco (saint), 245, 246
San Francisco, Arroyo de (Calif.), 267, 281, 283, 285, 286
San Francisco Bay, 24, 26, 65, 138, 175, 300, 326; Anza's and Font's exploration of, 197n102, 257, 266; Anza's reconnaissance of, 45–46, 62, 254, 268, 355; crosses erected at, 267, 270, 274, 277, 279; defenses of, 25, 45–46; description of, 46, 67, 274–77; expedition to, 250, 251; explorations of, 28, 178n32, 262, 268, 272n55, 307; Font's latitude calculations of, 281; founding of missions at, 27, 244, 254, 259, 314; founding of settlements at, 241, 250, 253, 329, 333, 347, 348, 373; Indian groups around, 44; islands of, 272, 274, 276–77, 279, 294, 298, 298n154, 308; maps of, 17n8, 65, 254, 332; planting of cross at mouth of, 272–73; reconnaissance of, 202n118, 207, 207n131; Rivera y Moncada exploration of, 30, 208; Rivera y Moncada's opposition to project of, 205; routes to, 315; terrain around, 234, 241, 313, 324
San Francisco, Calif., 202n118; Anza and Rivera y Moncada dispute over settling of, 197n102, 332, 346–49; Anza's 1775–76 expedition's arrival at, 41; expeditions to, 26; founding of settlements at, 52, 53, 59, 60, 83, 205, 251n132, 259, 314, 332n5; missions at, 85, 263; reconnaissance for site of, 23, 28, 45–46; Rivera y Moncada's visit to, 49; search for route to, 29–30; settlers of, 48, 334–43, 334n9, 335n14, 340n47
San Francisco, Presidio of, 46, 205
San Francisco River, 26, 30, 241, 244; maps of, 17n8, 254; reports of, 25, 205; search for, 26, 27, 31, 47–49, 167n1, 178n32, 197n102, 207–208, 238, 239, 239n81, 276, 287, 294, 297, 300–301, 303–304, 307–17, 319, 320, 331. *See also* San Joaquín River
San Gabriel (mission), 50, 168n3, 172, 185, 217, 254, 325, 337n25, 341n51, 343n65, 345, 377; agriculture at, 179; Anza and Font at, 175n17, 183, 356n103, 371, 402, 403; Anza and Rivera y Moncada to meet at, 332,

348; Anza correspondence with, 163, 174; Anza's correspondence with, 165, 167; Anza's meetings with Rivera y Moncada at, 356–57, 358–59, 366–68; Anza's soldiers at, 347n79; Colorado River Indians at, 371; description of life at, 180, 212; desertion of soldier from, 211, 239, 239n83, 240, 241, 343; expedition at, 33, 177, 178n32, 182, 197n102, 200, 202n118, 206, 207, 215, 245, 333; expedition provisions from, 167n1, 201–202, 212; Font designs church for, 61; Font's latitude calculations of, 212, 213, 214; founding of, 194n90; Garcés at, 32, 127, 312n204, 380; Indians of, 193; location of, 177, 188n71, 312, 315; military garrison of, 167n1; Rivera y Moncada at, 178n31; road to San Diego from, 174, 187; taking cats to, 346; Taraval at, 25; troubles at, 223n27, 311; water supply of, 282
San Gabriel River (Calif.), 176–77, 183, 371, 372
San Gerónimo Mountains (Calif.), 145, 147
San Gregorio (well), 155, 156, 193, 239, 376
San Gregorio Mountains (Calif.), 151. *See also* San Sebastián Mountains (Calif.)
San Gregorio Pass (Calif.), 155
San Ignacio (mission), 76n13, 86n5, 87, 398, 406; description of, 80; expedition arrives at, 79, 80; Font's arrival at, 57; visitas of, 80
San Ildefonso (Sonora), 394
San Jácome Hill (Calif.), 145
San Jácomo (Indian village), 132n56
San Joaquín River (Calif.), 31, 48, 207n131. *See also* San Francisco River
San Joaquín Valley (Calif.), 23, 37, 49, 59, 233n55, 292n130, 312n204, 313n207
San José Cupertino, Arroyo de (Calif.), 266, 281
San José de Pimas (mission), 20, 57, 123, 392n38, 401, 403, 406
San José Lake (Calif.), 186
San José River (Calif.), 169–70, 171, 172, 174n15, 374, 375
San José Valley (Calif.), 152, 169–70, 171, 173, 176, 374, 375
San Juan Capistrano (mission), 50, 185, 188, 190, 193, 195–96, 254

San Juan Capistrano de Uturitúc (village). *See* Uturitúc (village)
San Juan Capistrano River (Calif.), 185, 186, 210
San Luis (Quemeyá village), 194, 198
San Luis de Bacapa (Sonora), 392–93
San Luis Obispo (mission), 23, 59, 122, 181, 202n118, 230, 231, 236, 241, 259, 313, 314, 315, 319, 322, 323n244, 323n245, 325, 352, 355; Anza and Font at, 56, 353, 356, 362; description of, 232; Font's latitude calculations of, 234; Garcés at, 352, 368; Indians of, 233n55, 359, 361; Pedro Regaldo from, 361, 372, 372n144, 384; soldiers near, 255
San Luis Valley (Calif.), 232
San Marcial (camp), 145
San Marcos Mountains (Calif.), 312
San Mateo, Arroyo de (Calif.), 268, 282, 283n100, 284, 285, 286, 293
San Miguel Arcángel (saint), 73, 204, 245, 246, 377, 405
San Miguel de Horcasitas (town), 76, 157, 245, 317, 389
San Miguel de Horcasitas, Presidio of, 76, 154, 173, 182, 205n123, 362, 395, 396, 401, 406; Anza and Font's return to, 74n3, 400, 404; Anza expedition at, 35, 38; Anza socializes at, 33; expedition departure from, 73, 204; Font at, 39, 401; Font's calculations of latitude of, 74, 402
San Miguel River (Sonora), 73, 76
San Onofre Mountain (Calif.), 186n62
San Pablo (Cuabajay village), 224, 363
San Pablo Bay (Calif.), 298n154
San Pablo height (Calif.), 126, 128, 130, 377, 379
San Pascual Hill (Ariz.), 110, 111, 112, 113
San Pascual Valley (Calif.), 261, 328
San Patricio Hollow (Calif.), 160n151, 168, 169, 172, 173, 375
San Pedro (Cuabajay village), 224, 363
San Pedro de Yumas, 138n72
San Pedro Bay (Calif.), 185, 215, 365
San Pedro River (Ariz.), 87
San Roque River. *See* Sacramento River (Calif.)
San Salvador, Arroyo de (Calif.), 293

San Salvador stream (Calif.), 292
San Sebastián (Jecuiche village), 149, 153, 155, 159, 239, 245, 377, 379
San Sebastián (well), 193
San Sebastián Mountains (Calif.), 130, 142, 145, 152, 156, 158. *See also* San Gregorio Mountains (Calif.)
San Serafino (Pima Village). *See* Nabcúb, San Serafino de (Pima village)
San Simón y Judas de Uparsoytac (Maricopa village). *See* Uparsoytac, San Simón y Judas de
Santa Ana, Sonora, 76, 78–79
Santa Ana River (Calif.), 173–76, 183, 184, 203, 210, 211, 365, 372, 374
Santa Angela de Fulgino (stream), 305–307, 324
Santa Bárbara Channel, 228; description of, 218; Indian settlements on, 44, 217, 217n10, 219–21, 230, 233, 298n151; Indian trade route through, 58; Indians of, 54n104, 202n118, 233n55, 233n56; islands of, 37, 216, 364, 365, 366
Santa Catalina Mountains (Ariz.). *See* Santa Catarina Mountains (Ariz.)
Santa Catarina (Calif.), 156, 158
Santa Catarina, Arroyo de (Calif.), 376
Santa Catarina Island (Calif.), 365
Santa Catarina Mountains (Ariz.), 87
Santa Catarina stream (Calif.), 158–59
Santa Cecilia del Metate hill (Ariz.), 113, 114
Santa Clara (mission), 49, 59
Santa Clara River (Calif.), 216, 217
Santa Coleta Valley (Calif.), 306, 324
Santa Cruz Island (Calif.), 364, 365. *See also* Isla de Santa Cruz (Calif.)
Santa Cruz River (Ariz.), 91
Santa Delfina Valley (Calif.), 260, 313, 323, 329
Santa Eulalia Lake. *See* Santa Olalla Lake (Calif.)
Santa Isabel Valley (Calif.), 216
Santa Lucía Mountains (Calif.), 231, 232, 234–37, 241, 241n93, 242, 248, 260, 352, 353
Santa Margarita River (Calif.), 185, 234, 353
Santa Margarita Valley (Calif.), 234
Santa María Magdalena, Sonora (pueblo), 79, 80; Indian attack on, 406; priests of, 81n29; terrain at, 81

Santa María Magdalena de Kino (mission): Font at, 57; Indian attack on, 15–16, 69
Santa María Magdalena River (Calif.), 184
Santa Olalla Lake (Calif.), 128, 129, 132n56, 144, 146, 150, 153, 239, 378, 379; description of, 130; deserting soldier and muleteers headed to, 239n82, 240n88; Font's latitude of, 131
Santa Rosa (Quíquima Indian village), 132n56, 245, 376
Santa Rosa de las Lajas (wells), 132n56, 146, 148, 149, 151, 153, 377, 378, 388, 389
Santa Rosa River (Calif.), 228, 229, 362
San Vicente (saint), 325
San Vicente Valley (Calif.), 325, 326, 327
San Xavier del Bac (mission), 22, 62, 337n24, 342n61, 381n12; expedition at, 87; Font borrows compass from, 75; Font's religious supplies from, 80; Garcés at, 86; priests of, 82; river at, 91; Tucson as visita of, 89
Seri Indians, 15, 59, 78, 81n29, 399, 406
Serra, Fray Junípero, 25, 26, 32, 47n87, 331; and Anza expedition, 24; at Anza's and Font's departure, 344; conflicts with Rivera y Moncada, 193, 206n126, 254–55, 354–56, 356–57, 359, 372; criticism of Rivera y Moncada by, 52, 54, 55, 56; expedition greeted by, 244; Font's map left with, 68n148; and founding of San Francisco mission, 29; meetings with Font and Anza by, 247, 254; at Mission San Carlos, 248, 257; at Monterey, 242; as president of Alta California missions, 24n31; support of San Francisco settlements by, 24, 45
Serrano, Ana Regina, 204
Serrano, Francisco, 403
Serrano Indians. *See* Cuabajay Indians
Shouter Indians, 268n44
Sierra del Chasco, 37, 327n261
Sierra del Trabuco (Calif.), 172, 174
Sierra de Pinos (Calif.), 243, 330
Sierra de San Marcos (Calif.), 176
Sierra Nevada, 23, 57, 58, 312n204
Silva, José Miguel, 80n27, 82n35, 87, 319, 332, 343n67, 345n73, 368
Sinaloa, New Spain, 26n38, 40, 60, 82n35, 92n74, 247, 259n3, 332, 335n11, 339n36, 340n47, 341n49, 342n60, 342n62, 403

Sinova, José Francisco, 335n11
Sitjar, Fray Buenaventura, 180, 237, 238
Sobaipuri Indians, 87, 89. *See also* Pima Indians
Soberanes, Ignacio, 259n3, 293, 308, 311, 323n244
Soberanes, José María, 259n3, 341n49
Solórzano Pereira, Juan de, 181
Somera, Fray José Ángel Fernández, 194
Sonoitac, San Marcelo de (Papago pueblo), 391–92
Sonora, New Spain, 56, 58, 92n74, 122, 124, 314, 333, 343; 1774 Anza expedition at, 25; Anza and Font return to, 49, 315, 332; Anza's influence in, 57; Apache attacks in, 15, 191; capital of, 38; deserters head for, 240, 240n87; expeditions from, 40, 167; Font in, 36, 39, 44, 59, 66, 200n112, 276n79; Font's maps of, 63; Franciscan missionaries in, 19–20; Garcés's return to, 57, 58; governor of, 317; Los Angeles settlers from, 60; missions of, 21, 24, 397; presidios of, 84; route to California from, 27, 30, 202n118; routes to California from, 24; Taraval arrives in, 24, 25
Sotelo, José Antonio, 339
Sotelo, Ramón, 339
Soto, Ignacio de, 338
Soto, José Antonio, 338, 338n34
Soto, María (wife of Juan Bernal), 340
Soto, María Francisca, 338
Soto Pérez, José Luis, 66, 69
St. Anthony of Padua (saint), 238, 239
St. Paul (saint), 139–41
Suisin Bay (Calif.), 31, 207n131
Sutaquison (Pima village), 91, 101, 102, 103, 106, 112

Tafoya, Juana. *See* Acuña, Petronila Josefa
Tapia, Felipe Santiago, 337
Tapia, José Bartolomé, 337
Tapia, José Cristóbal, 337
Tapia, José Francisco, 337
Tapia, José Victor, 337
Tapia, Juan José, 337
Tapia, María Antonia, 337
Tapia, María Isidora, 338
Tapia, María Manuela, 338
Tapia, María Rosa, 337

Taraval, Sebastián ("El Peregrino"), 44n81, 122, 343n65; background of, 24–25; death of, 62; death of family of, 37; with Garcés, 123; as guide for 1774 Anza expedition, 25, 168n3; as muleteer for expedition, 84n43; spring named after, 149n119
Teggart, Frederick, 68–69
Tejua Yabipay Indians, 105
Ternaux-Compans, 65
Terrenate, Presidio of, 334, 335n14
Tomascaba Indians, 318
Tomiár Indians, 159
Tosca, Tomás Vicente, 74n3, 75
Trejo, María Angela. *See* Chumacero, María Angela
Tubac, Presidio of, 205n123; Anza as commander of, 333; Apache attack on, 154; expedition at, 78, 82, 83, 86, 87, 245, 337n24; expedition soldiers from, 84, 85n51; Font's latitude calculations of, 83; Pima Indians trade with, 103; soldiers of, 237, 259, 345n73, 346, 372n144, 394; transfer of to Tucson, 89
Tubutama, San Pedro y San Pablo de (mission), 57, 69, 406
Tucson (pueblo), 89, 90, 91, 381n12; expedition at, 87; Font's latitude calculations of, 89; Indian residents of, 89; river at, 91
Tucson, Presidio San Agustín del, 89
Tueros, Pedro, 397, 398
Tumacácori, San José de (mission), 80, 82, 394, 395–96, 395n50
Tuquisón, Arizona. *See* Tucson (pueblo)
Uparsoytac, San Simón y Judas de (Maricopa village), 105, 107, 112
Ures, San Miguel (mission), 57, 62, 67, 401, 402
Urrea, Bernardo de, 115, 124n26, 133
Uturitúc, San Juan Capistrano de (Pima village), 91, 92, 96; expedition at, 99–100, 101; Font recommend mission at, 112

Valencia, Francisco mar, 339
Valencia, Ignacio María, 339
Valencia, José Manuel, 339
Valencia, María Dolores, 334
Valencia, María Gertrudis, 339
Valenzuela, Agustín, 154, 343n65

Valenzuela, Agustín de, 338
Valenzuela, Francisca Manuela, 336
Valenzuela, Juan José, 336n19
Valenzuela, María Ceferina de, 338
Valerio, José Antonio, 335
Valerio, José Dolores, 335
Valerio, José Ignacio, 335
Valerio, Juan, 335
Valerio, María Manuela, 335
Valle, María Carmen del, 341
Valle de los Robles (Calif.), 265
Vancouver, George, 233n56
Varela, Juan Antonio, 342n59
Vásquez, José Antonio, 336
Vásquez, José Tiburcio, 336, 337
Vásquez, Juan Atanasio, 336
Vásquez, Pedro José, 336
Vásquez, Tiburcio, 87n59
Vega, Matías, 341
Velderrain, Felipe, 394–95, 395n50, 396
Velderrain, Juan Bautista de, 20
Verde River (Ariz.), 104. *See also* Azul River (Ariz.); La Asunción River (Ariz.); Salado River
Viadar, Father José, 321n239

Vidal, Mariano, 84, 102, 163, 165, 182, 206–207, 211n144, 257, 299n156, 345n73, 346, 349n84, 372n144, 394, 401
Vieyra, Father Antonio, 238n79
Villela, Marcos, 343
Vizcaíno, Fray Juan, 189
Vizcaíno, Sebastián, 185n57, 189, 244, 248, 249, 250, 253

Wagner, Henry, 63

Yaqui Indians, 60, 318
Yaqui River, 133, 145
Yépiz, José Mariano, 211, 239–41, 239n83, 241, 241n91
Yuma, Ariz.: Anza at, 56; Garcés at, 382n15; missions at, 60, 72; Rivera y Moncada's death at, 54. *See also* Puerto de la Concepción (Colorado River)
Yuma Indians. *See* Quechán Indians; individual tribes

Zamora, Manuela Rosalía, 335
Zuñiga, Fray Francisco, 80, 398
Zuñi Indians, 317

www.ingramcontent.com/pod-product-compliance
Lightning Source LLC
Chambersburg PA
CBHW080833230426
43665CB00021B/2826